THE
DOLPHIN
READER

THE
DOLPHIN
READER

SIXTH EDITION

DOUGLAS HUNT

University of Missouri

WADSWORTH
CENGAGE Learning™

Australia • Brazil • Japan • Korea • Mexico • Singapore • Spain
United Kingdom • United States

WADSWORTH
CENGAGE Learning

**The Dolphin Reader,
Sixth Edition**
Douglas Hunt

Senior Sponsoring Editor:
  Suzanne Phelps Weir

Development Editor:
  Janet Young

Senior Project Editor:
  Rosemary R. Jaffe

Associate Production/
  Design Coordinator:
  Christine Gervais

Manufacturing Manager:
  Florence Cadran

Marketing Manager:
  Cindy Graff Cohen

COVER ILLUSTRATION ©
James Kraus/ArtGuy.

*Text Acknowledgments follow the
Author/Title Index.*

For product information and technology assistance, contact us at **Cengage Learning Customer & Sales Support, 1-800-354-9706**

For permission to use material from this text or product, submit all requests online at **www.cengage.com/permissions**
Further permissions questions can be e-mailed to **permissionrequest@cengage.com**

Library of Congress Control Number: 2001133276

ISBN-13: 978-0-618-21846-2

ISBN-10: 0-618-21846-7

Wadsworth
20 Channel Center Street
Boston, MA 02210
USA

Cengage Learning is a leading provider of customized learning solutions with office locations around the globe, including Singapore, the United Kingdom, Australia, Mexico, Brazil, and Japan. Locate your local office at **www.cengage.com/global**

Cengage Learning products are represented in Canada by Nelson Education, Ltd.

To learn more about Wadsworth, visit **www.cengage.com/wadsworth**

Purchase any of our products at your local college store or at our preferred online store **www.CengageBrain.com**

Printed in the United States of America
4 5 6 13 12 11 10

Brief Contents

Annotated Contents

and more like the bond between any two Red Sox fans (or
perhaps any two devoted Honda owners): they root for the
same team and they share some of the same interests, but they
are unaware of each other's existence.

    . . . despite Putnam's title, they don't bowl alone. They bowl
    with friends, on dates, with their kids, with other families.
    The bowling story could be told as one of happy progress:
    from a drink-sodden night of spouse avoidance with the same
    old faces from work to temperate and spontaneous fun with
    one's intimate friends and relations.

    The Greeks thought of the polis as an active, formative thing,
    training the minds and characters of the citizens; we think of
    it as a piece of machinery for the production of safety and
    convenience. The training in virtue, which the medieval state
    left to the Church, and the polis made its own concern, the
    modern state leaves to God knows what.

    They work in the white man's world all day and come home
    in the evening to this fetid block. They struggle to instill in
    their children some private sense of honor or dignity which
    will help the child survive. This means, of course, that they
    must struggle, stolidly, incessantly, to keep this sense alive in
    themselves . . .

    When Jimmy Rogan fell through a plate-glass window (he was
    separating some scuffling friends) and almost lost his arm, a
    stranger in an old T shirt emerged from the Ideal bar, swiftly
    applied an expert tourniquet and, according to the hospital's
    emergency staff, saved Jimmy's life. Nobody remembered
    seeing the man before and no one has seen him since.

    I might have known she needed help! I know how things can
    be—for women. I tell you, it's queer, Mrs. Peters. We live
    close together and we live far apart. We all go through the
    same things—it's all just a different kind of the same thing.

It was a country in which families routinely disappeared, trailing bad checks and repossession papers. Adolescents drifted from city to torn city, sloughing off both the past and the future as snakes shed their skins, children who were never taught and would never now learn the games that had held the society together. People were missing. Children were missing. Parents were missing. Those left behind filed desultory missing-persons reports, then moved on themselves.

There were more letters back and forth. It meant a lot to me to hear from someone—from two people, really—who could tell me what baseball was like far from the crowds and the noise and the fame and the big money that I had been writing about for many summers. And by this time, of course, I cared about Ron and Linda, and worried about what would happen to them.

When her police shift ends, at 4 A.M., she sleeps for two hours, wakes her children for three different schools, sees one to the bus and drives the two others, along with four neighborhood kids who depend on her, to their schools. Then she heads downtown to her part-time job as a private security guard. When she finishes, at 5 P.M., she fetches her children and the four others from their schools, drops them all at their doors, and goes to the police station to start her shift. On days off, she sleeps.

PREFACE

The best way to explain the nature of the sixth edition of *The Dolphin Reader* is to explain my day job during the two decades since the publication of the first edition. Besides teaching, I have been directing a writing-across-the-curriculum program and directing a freshman composition program, in both capacities working with teachers on the development of writing assignments and the readings that accompany them. Excepting the irritations that come with every administrative job, this has been interesting work. It has kept me reading and thinking not only about English, but also about sociology, biology, history, and many other disciplines. More pertinently, it kept me thinking about undergraduate writers and how the composition course can help them succeed in other disciplines.

I've learned two broad lessons from this work. One is to focus reading and writing on large, central questions that students will think about in many classes and for the rest of their lives: *What glue holds a community together?* and *In what ways are the actions of even strong individuals determined by history and culture?* and (above all) *How do we know?* The undergraduate who stays engaged with central questions like these will produce good papers in any discipline. The second lesson serves as a check on the first. It is that even a central question can produce lifeless papers if it is discussed from a single perspective. Pluralism is the most invigorating force on our college and university campuses. "Even the questions," one student said to me recently, in a voice that seemed to combine shock and delight. "The professors can't agree even on the questions!" Many undergraduates come to campus primed for a period of tremendous intellectual growth as they are exposed to multiple and contradictory views on everything under the sun and above it.

On the one hand, then, a centripetal force drove me as I worked on *The Dolphin Reader:* "Get to the central issues; don't lose focus." On the other hand, there was the centrifugal force of pluralism: "Be sure that lots of perspectives are represented, lots of different types of evidence, lots of different ways of writing, based on lots of different experiences with life." These opposing impulses cannot be averaged or reconciled, even to my own satisfaction, let alone to the satisfaction of every reader of the book. They can only be borne in mind, in editing as in life, with as much intelligence and grace as possible.

In the case of this edition of *The Dolphin Reader*, the result has a shape I can best describe by analogy. Imagine the book laid out, not as a set of pages, but as a large room. In the room are nine tables around which our various writers are gathered. At one table a sociologist, an essayist, a journalist, a self-educated expert on city life, a professor of classics, and a playwright are talking about what holds communities together and what happens when they fall apart. At other tables equally diverse sets of writers (some living and some dead) are talking about religion, technology, sex, working life, social upheaval, poverty, and the way an individual life fits into its times. A good portion of what people talk about, anywhere, is being talked about in this room.

My role as editor and host is to invite guests who will talk well together, and to seat them in a pattern that will help the conversation get started. The student's role, like the role of any guest among strangers, is first to listen, then to speak. Some students will hear what every one of the writers has to say; others will limit themselves to three or four tables, hearing only snippets of the other conversations in the room. Every student, I hope, will realize at times that the conversations overlap, that a writer from the religion table, for instance, has something valuable to contribute to the discussion at the poverty table.

Having ridden this analogy a bit farther than I intended, I will dismount. *The Dolphin Reader* isn't a dinner party, but a textbook. Once I let it go, it will become whatever teachers and, especially, students make of it. My advice to students would be to read the pieces the teacher assigns, of course, but also to "read around" a bit in the unassigned readings. I've done my best to put together a book that rewards this kind of browsing, one where any piece could cast a serendipitous light on any other piece. My advice to my fellow teachers I will reserve for the *Instructor's Resource Manual*, where I can offer it unstintingly and they can ignore it if they wish. There instructors will find overviews and lesson plans for each unit and for each separate essay, along with dozens of questions for writing and discussion, and dozens of style exercises based on the readings.

Though I am editing the book solo in this edition and writing (or rewriting) the entire instructor's manual myself, I continue to be deeply indebted to Carolyn Perry and Melody Daily for many years of involvement with the book. I have benefited enormously from their friendship and their intelligence, and their ideas have now become thoroughly intertwined with my own.

Thanks also go to the supportive editors at Cengage Learning—to Janet Young and Becky Wong; to Rosemary Jaffe who oversaw production; and to Jill Dougan, who handled some thorny problems with permissions. I am also grateful to the following colleagues for their reviews:

Jesse Airaudi, Baylor University
James Allen, College of DuPage
Anna Bourgeois, University of Wyoming
Robert Cosgrove, Saddleback College
Carol Franks, Portland State University
Sharon S. Gibson, Towson University
Dennis Keen, Spokane Community College
Charles Lewis, Westminster College
Jeffrey N. Nelson, University of Alabama in Huntsville
Frank G. Novak, Jr., Pepperdine University
James Persoon, Grand Valley State University
Mary S. Pollock, Stetson University
Joseph Powell, Central Washington University
Kathy Stein, The University of Texas at El Paso
Burt Thorp, University of North Dakota
Mary L. Tobin, Rice University
Kenneth R. Wright, James Madison University

Douglas Hunt

THE
DOLPHIN
READER

Introduction: About the Essay

Douglas Hunt

Understanding at Three Levels

When I was about ten, I used to watch a television show called *Learn to Draw with Jon Gnagy*. Gnagy assured his viewers that they could draw if they mastered four basic shapes: ball, cone, cube, and cylinder. After you practiced sketching these shapes, you recognized them—bent and stretched, highlighted and shaded—as the building blocks of everything in sight. After a few weeks you began to see your sister's nose as a cone (base down, point tilted back between the eyes) embedded in the elongated ball of her head, which rested on the cylinder of her neck, and so on down to her toes (cylinder, cylinder, ball). Once you saw the world this way, drawing became, if not easy, at least possible.

If we could identify the underlying "shapes" or elements of the essay, we might become better readers and writers, but people disagree about what the elements are. My seventh-grade teacher favored the patterns of sentences: subject+verb+object, subject+verb+indirect object+object, and so on. My eleventh-grade teacher saw the thesis, the supporting details, and the transitions as the key elements. What I learned from these teachers benefits me every day, but I can't say that they taught me to read or write essays. Instead, I learned to write exercises in sentence variety and organization—shells into which we all hoped a real essay would be poured someday.

More fruitful has been Aristotle's statement that a persuasive speech reaches the audience through three "appeals": the logical, the ethical, and the emotional. Here is a thought that can be adapted to the very broad range of things we call essays (including many articles, letters, and reports). Changing Aristotle's terms slightly, we'll say that the three crucial elements of an essay are its levels of meaning: the logical, the social, and the visceral.

The logical level involves statements that require proof: proof that the defendant is guilty as charged, proof that a design flaw caused the bridge to collapse, proof that a college education is a good (or bad) financial investment. Proofs can take many different forms, but the most basic is *generalization and specification*. This may sound like two processes, but logically the two are inseparable, like breathing in and breathing out.

A clear example of the relation between generalization and specification comes from Nazi Germany, where Hitler's propaganda machine made sweeping statements about the superiority of the Aryan race and the threat posed to it by Jews and Judaism. The reaction of many intelligent and well-educated Germans was to examine the logic of these claims. For every generalization, they reasoned, there ought to be specification. To justify the generalization that the Jews were conspiring to undermine the Aryan race, the Nazis should offer specific evidence, specific examples. A historian tells me that the call for "specification" (in German, *Spezifizierung*) became so closely identified with resistance to the Nazi "big lie" that Hitler's agents would sit in bars, restaurants, and other public places, listening for the word *Spezifizierung* and prepared to arrest and interrogate those who said it too loudly or too often. That no questionable generalization should stand without adequate specification is one of the rules of the road in the logical level of an essay.

When the generalization is new or controversial, logical people will usually want the writer to provide several examples. Take, for example, the way historian Daniel Boorstin supports his generalization that technology has produced a "removal of distinctions" in our ordinary experience:

> One of the consequences of our success in technology, of our wealth, of our energy and our imagination, has been the removal of distinctions, not just between people but between everything and everything else, between every place and every other place, between every time and every other time. For example, television removes the distinction between being here and being there. And the same kind of process, of thinning out, of removing distinctions, has appeared in one area after another of our lives.
>
> For instance, in the seasons. One of the great unheralded achievements of American civilization was the rise of transportation and refrigeration, the development of techniques of canning and preserving meat, vegetables, and fruits in such a way that it became possible to enjoy strawberries in winter, to enjoy fresh meat at seasons when the

meat was not slaughtered, to thin out the difference between the diet of winter and the diet of summer.[1]

Boorstin's essay goes on to talk about central heating and air conditioning (which thin the distinction between summer and winter), plate glass windows (which lessen the difference between indoors and outdoors), and easy-to-use cameras (which mix the past into the present). The generalization that technology "thins" our experience by removing distinctions may never have occurred to us before, but Boorstin's specification makes it relatively clear and convincing.

Of course, *disputing* generalizations is as much a logical action as *proposing* them. Couldn't we write a short essay challenging Boorstin's generalization by offering a few counterexamples of our own? We could point out that when a family flies from Minneapolis to southern Florida for a midwinter vacation, the contrast between winter and summer is not diminished for them, but sharpened. Or we could argue that in our own experience, sitting snug by a window during a thunderstorm doesn't diminish our awareness of the difference between being outdoors and indoors, but heightens it.

That Boorstin's generalization can be disputed does not weaken his essay; in fact it adds spice. Readers are more likely to be engaged by the logic of the essay if there is a real chance of dispute, a real need to show a connection between generalization and specifics. Offer the generalization that "Goldfish are easy pets to keep" and few readers will wait, breathless, to hear the predictable specifics about water temperature, food, and aeration.

Much more, of course, could be said about the logical aspect of writing, but for now we can conclude that it involves making connections between generalizations and specific cases. The writer who offers a sweeping generalization without specifics has done nothing at the logical level; likewise, the writer who offers a list of details unconnected to any general idea has done nothing. We should also say, however, that the logical level of an essay is not the only one; in some fine essays it is far from the most important. Developing the logical level alone is acting as if we were severed heads, kept alive by tubes and machines and

1. "Technology and Democracy," *Democracy and Its Discontents* (New York, 1974), pp. 103–104.

interacting with society only by analyzing data. The essayist remembers that we are alive from the neck down and that we have an almost inexhaustible interest in the lives of those around us.

*   *   *

Let's leave the logic behind for now and move to the social level of our lives and of the essay. I'll begin indelicately by putting you in my shoes on the day I composed this page, and putting those shoes into a stall in the men's rest room of the public library. To our left is another stall, occupied by a man wearing a pair of brown Kangaroos who is puffing noisily as he hauls himself to his feet and slowly walks out. As he opens the stall door, we hear him say, "They ought to make these stalls wider; you can hardly turn around in there." Into the newly vacated stall walks a pair of Adidas, and as the outer door closes behind the Kangaroos, the man in the Adidas says, apparently to us, "That guy ought to lose some weight."

The scene reminds us that humans are a gossipy, judgmental race, always ready to give and take opinions about the proper management of society (*"They* ought to make these stalls wider") or about the proper management of the individual life (*"That guy* ought to lose some weight"). As Aristotle said, we are all creatures of the *polis* (the community), and one of our life's great projects is to contribute to the community's consensus on what behavior is good or bad, noble or base, cool or uncool. You may remember reading a children's magazine that contained a comic strip called "Gufus and Gallant." Week after week, the cartoonist would produce a scenario in which Gufus would show us how not to behave and Gallant would behave with a shining nobility. From childhood forward, we think incessantly about what behavior is Gufus and what is Gallant.

Among the earliest surviving essays are thirty short sketches by Theophrastus, Aristotle's pupil. These "characters," as he called them, explore the social side of life as directly as "Gufus and Gallant" did. Here, for instance, is a Gufus piece usually called "The Faultfinder":

> Faultfinding is being unreasonably critical of your portion in life. For example, a friend sends over a serving of the main dinner course with

his compliments: the faultfinder is the kind who says to the messenger, "You can go tell your master I said that he didn't want me to have a taste of his soup and his third-rate wine—that's why he wouldn't give me a dinner invitation." And even while his mistress is kissing him he will complain, "I wonder if you really love me the way you say you do." He gets angry at the weather, too, not because it rained but because it didn't rain soon enough.

If he comes on a wallet in the street, his comment is "Always this—never a real find!" Let him get a slave at bargain prices, moreover, after begging and pleading, and what does he say but, "I really wonder if the fellow can be in sound shape, seeing that he was so cheap." Or supposing somebody announces, "You've got a baby boy!" He meets this good news with: "You might as well have told me half my estate's down the drain—that's what it really means." What's more, he can win a case with every single ballot in his favor; he will still claim that his lawyer passed over a lot of sound arguments. And when friends have raised a loan to help him out and one of them asks him, "Aren't you pleased?" his answer is "How can I be, when I have to pay everybody back and then act grateful besides?"

This essay makes the modest logical claim that there exists in society (or at least there existed in ancient Athens) a recognizable category of people who can be called faultfinders. The point, however, is less to show that the group exists than to remind us that we don't want to belong to it. For a day or two after reading "The Faultfinder," we may be less likely to complain about the food someone cooks for us, less likely to be critical of the present a friend gives us.

As "The Faultfinder" reminds us, the social level of our thinking inevitably involves matters of style, tone, and sensitivity. Consider this passage about Dick Cavett in Naomi Wolf's essay "The Rites of Sisterhood."[2] Cavett, a talk-show host known for his intelligence and his liberal views, was the commencement speaker when Wolf graduated from Yale.

Cavett took the microphone and seemed visibly to pale at the sight of two thousand female about-to-be Yale graduates. "When I was an undergraduate," he said, "there were no women here. The women went to Vassar. At Vassar," he said, "they had nude photographs taken of the women to check their posture in gym class. One year

2. *Next: Young American Writers on the New Generation,* ed. Eric Liv (New York, 1984), p. 188.

some of the photos were stolen, and they showed up for sale in New Haven's red-light district." His punch line? "The photos found no buyers."

Even this short passage should give you some sense of Wolf's reaction to Cavett's speech, but the statements that follow do much more to develop the social level of Wolf's essay:

> I will never forget that moment. There were our parents and grand-parents, many of whom had come long distances at great expense to be with us on our special day. There were we, silent in our black gowns, our tassels, our new shoes. We did not break the silence with boos or hisses, out of respect for our families who had given so much to make that day a success; and they in turn kept silent out of the same concern for us.

Wolf's objection is not to Cavett's logic, but to his behavior. Wolf couldn't convince us by logical argument to favor respect over disrespect, fair play over bias, sensitivity over insensitivity. She presumably doesn't *need* to convince us. She needs only to show us that Cavett's speech was disrespectful, unfair, and insensitive. This showing isn't an open-and-shut business, of course; we can imagine another writer setting out to show that Cavett's speech wasn't as boorish as Wolf makes it out to be, and that Wolf is herself being disrespectful, unfair, and insensitive. The debate about such matters is one way that the community and the nation gradually form and change their shared values.

Since we are thinking now as essayists, it is worth noting that Wolf criticizes Cavett for the words he chose to write and read on a particular occasion for a particular audience. We may accept her criticism or not, but since essays inevitably have a social dimension, their tone *is* a serious issue. Some writers swagger or whine, insult or patronize, and yet somehow expect that the reader will listen with patience and respect. They ought to make those essays wider; you can hardly turn around in there.

＊   ＊   ＊

Our educational system does less to alert us to the visceral (bodily) level of writing than to the logical or social levels, perhaps because teachers tend to see the body as a natural enemy. Let me introduce the visceral level by telling you about my baby daughter Kate and her first word, *kitty*. She learned the word early because her baby sitter Nancy used to lure a neighbor's cat onto the porch on summer days to pet it. After winter set in, we would show Kate a photograph and ask her where the kitty was, and she would smile, coo, and wiggle all over as she pointed to the cat and said, "Kitty." For her, the word must have been the key that unlocked a number of bodily experiences. It probably summoned up memories of summer days on the porch, the silky feel of the fur, the purring, the comfort of being held on Nancy's lap. As the rhetorician Kenneth Burke put it, the word "glowed" for her; it had emotional and physical associations no dictionary maker records. She reacted to these associations as a whole creature, not merely as a logical or social being.

This creaturely reaction to words, phrases, and images may become dulled as we grow older—it may be overlayered by the development of our logical and social responses to what we read—but it never goes away. My reaction to words like *lake, sandpaper,* and *baby* is not as dramatic as Kate's response to *kitty* (I can read them and sit still), but it is not different in kind. And, of course, it is not just words, but phrases and whole sentences that may have a bodily impact on us. The other day, in the midst of an abstract discussion of social policy, I heard one speaker quote the Buddhist proverb "You can't water a tree by watering each individual leaf." The escape from this dry discussion of hard issues to the familiar and tangible world of trees and water had great appeal to me, for reasons my body probably understood better than my mind ever will.

The writer of a scientific paper or a mathematical proof may ignore the body's "reasoning," but the skillful writer of essays doesn't. Take, for example, the first sentence of George Orwell's "Marrakech": "As the corpse went past, the flies left the restaurant table in a cloud and rushed after it, but they came back a few minutes later." The sentence might have no effect on an android with a stainless steel gut, but it is enough to make a human's skin crawl. It probably *does* make our skins crawl, as a clever physiologist with a galvanometer might demonstrate. Or consider this paragraph from Carol Bly's "Getting Tired":

> The second day I was promoted from elevating corncobs at the corn pile to actual plowing. Hour after hour I sat up there on the old

Alice, as she was called (an Allis-Chalmer WC that looked rusted from the Flood). You have to sit twisted part way around, checking that the plowshares are scouring clean, turning over and dropping the dead crop and soil, not clogging. For the first two hours I was very political. I thought about what would be good for American farming—stronger marketing organizations, or maybe a law like the Norwegian Odal law, preventing the breaking up of small farms or selling them to business interests. Then the sun got high, and each time I reached the headlands area at the field's end I dumped off something else, now my cap, next my jacket, finally my sweater.

Few of us, these days, have plowed with an open tractor, but our muscles have probably been in the twisted posture Bly describes, and we probably remember stripping off layers of clothing on days that start out cold and then heat with the rising sun. These bodily memories are evoked, however briefly, as we read. Those who have been around farms may associate Bly's language—*plowshares, scouring, headlands*—with the sights and sounds and solid objects they remember, objects that carry with them memories and emotions, pleasant or unpleasant. Writing that points us to objects and sensations—to tastes, textures, smells, temperatures, sounds, colors, shapes, motions—will ordinarily involve us more deeply than writing that is merely logical or merely social.

*   *   *

I don't want to leave the impression that our visceral responses depend entirely on the relation between words and past physical experience. Language is also, itself, a *present* physical experience. Perhaps half a dozen times in the last decade I have passed through a room where Martin Luther King Jr.'s "I Have a Dream" speech was playing on radio or television. It has always stopped me cold. Listen to the following passage, a series of sentences that are rhythmically perfect in themselves and that are joined rhythmically by the repetition of "I have a dream":

> I say to you today, my friends, that in spite of the difficulties and frustrations of the moment I still have a dream tonight. It is a dream deeply rooted in the American dream.
> I have a dream that one day this nation will rise up and live out the true meaning of its creed: "We hold those truths to be self-evident, that all men are created equal."

I have a dream that one day on the red hills of Georgia the sons of former slaves and the sons of former slaveowners will be able to sit down together at the table of brotherhood.

I have a dream that one day even the state of Mississippi, a desert state sweltering with the heat of injustice and oppression, will be transformed into an oasis of freedom and justice.

I have a dream that my four little children will one day live in a nation where they will not be judged by the color of their skin but by the content of their character.

Listen to the beat of the *k* sounds in the last sentence (*color, skin, content, character*) and think how much would be lost if King had said, "where they will be judged by their character, rather than their skin tone." The speech moves us partly because of the way the language moves. Essays are not speeches, but when we read closely, we register the sounds in our mental ear and even (researchers tell us) subconsciously form them with our vocal cords. Rhythm, assonance, alliteration, onomatopoeia—the whole palette of verbal sound effects—create visceral responses.

*   *   *

What difference does it make if we read essays with increased consciousness that they work on three levels? If my experience is typical, we begin to *see* essays more clearly, to become more consciously aware of what essayists have accomplished. When I graduated from high school as part of a post-*Sputnik,* scientifically oriented generation of students, I was fixated on the logical level of writing and simply missed the other two in most of what I read. I was like an artist attempting to see all objects as balls, and so dismissing cones, cylinders, and cubes as balls that failed the test of roundness. Eventually I broadened my range and learned to recognize that writing could be excellent because it engaged us socially and viscerally. And eventually I learned to recognize a type of excellence I had not suspected: the excellence of balance achieved when an essay works on all three levels and so appeals to mind, body, and character at once.

Have we exhausted the truth about the essay when we recognize that it has three levels? Certainly not. The harder we look, the more levels we are likely to see: four, six, ten, who can say? The well-written essay, like a ray of clear light, contains a whole spectrum of colors. The important thing is to recognize both its complexity and its unity.

The Three Levels and Revision

Being aware as we write that an essay can develop at three levels is both a blessing and a challenge. It is a blessing because it gives us three channels through which to reach the reader. It is a challenge because we must now

1. Think what the subject means logically. (How can its details be connected to generalizations or generalizations to details?)
2. Think what the subject means socially. (How can it be related to a standard for admirable or dishonorable behavior?)
3. Think what the subject means viscerally. (How can it be connected to the senses and the emotions that are evoked by the senses?)

The struggle to work at three levels is part of the hidden drama behind drafting and revision.

Those who have written very little are generally surprised at the amount of revision experienced writers do. The economist John Kenneth Galbraith, equally famous for the subtlety of his theories and for the clarity of his prose, put it this way:

> There may be inspired writers for whom the first draft is just right. But anyone who is not certifiably a Milton had better assume that the first draft is a very primitive thing. The reason is simple: writing is very difficult work. . . . Thinking, as Voltaire avowed, is also a very tedious process which men and women will do anything to avoid. So all first drafts are deeply flawed by the need to combine composition with thought. Each later one is less demanding in this regard; hence the writing can be better.

Galbraith tells us that on bad days he writes so poorly that "no fewer than five revisions are required. However, when I'm greatly inspired, only four are needed before, as I've often said, I put in that note of spontaneity which even my meanest critics concede."[3]

3. "Writing, Typing, and Economics," *The Atlantic Monthly* (March 1978), p. 103.

Great writers rarely preserve the four or five (or more) drafts that led them to a finished product. By good fortune, however, we do have access to six drafts of a *New Yorker* "comment" by E. B. White, one of the best American essayists of this century. In this section we will take a short tour through three of White's drafts, watching the way that he develops the logical, social, and visceral levels. I am not, of course, saying that White wrote with these levels consciously in his mind (any more than a bicyclist consciously thinks about balance, velocity, and centrifugal force as she rounds a corner), but I think we can see their presence in the decisions White makes.

First, a word about the nature of the writing and the writer. "Comments" are unsigned essays in miniature; in *The New Yorker* they have traditionally been written using the "editorial *we*," a practice that irritated White because it tends to make the writer sound like a Siamese twin. White began writing comments in 1927, and so had more than forty years of experience with them by 1969, when the magazine asked him to comment on *Apollo 11*'s landing on the moon.

The deadline pressure on White was more intense than usual. Neil Armstrong took his historic "small step" to the lunar surface at 10:56 P.M. on July 20, and the television broadcast of the moon walk lasted until 1:00 A.M.; White, who lived on a farm in Maine, had to cable his comment to New York in time for it to go to press at noon.

The visceral level, for this writer and this subject, posed a problem. White's best writing generally evoked the places and activities he loved best—ball games, circuses, zoos, farming, camping, canoeing. He was by disposition and habit an outdoorsman, capable of describing barns, pigs, and spiders affectionately (as you will know if you have read *Charlotte's Web*) and passionate about the sights, sounds, and smells of sailing. A few years before he wrote the moon-landing comment, he wrote these sentences in "The Sea and the Wind That Blows":

> My first encounter with the sea was a case of hate at first sight. I was taken, at the age of four, to a bathing beach in New Rochelle. Everything about the experience frightened and repelled me: the taste of salt in my mouth, the foul chill of the wooden bathhouse, the littered sand, the stench of the tide flats. I came away hating and fearing the

sea. Later, I found that what I had hated and feared, I now feared and loved.[4]

In the wide outdoors world, White could find the keys that unlock visceral responses, the connections between the senses and the emotions. Now, however, he was being asked to write about what is to the senses a much narrower world—the images and sounds produced by his television set. This situation presented him with a handicap that he had difficulty overcoming.

The logical level presented White with another sort of difficulty. Here there was generalization to connect the event with, but the nature of the connection wasn't clear. World War II had convinced White that in a world of electronic communication, long-range bombers, and nuclear weaponry, nationalism was irrational and dangerous.

> Whether we wish it or not, we may soon have to make a clear choice between the special nation to which we pledge our allegiance and the broad humanity of which we are born a part. The choice is implicit in the world to come. We have a little time in which we can make that choice intelligently. Failing that, the choice will be made for us in the confusion of war, from which the world will emerge unified—the unity of total desolation.[5]

Logic taught White that nationalism was a thing of the past, and (as we will see) this generalization shaped his view of the particular event he witnessed.

At the social level, the moon landing presented White the familiar struggle between pride and modesty, between boasting about our accomplishments and keeping them in perspective. In this struggle, White consistently favored modesty. Much of the humor in his writing comes from his tendency to find himself slightly ridiculous, and many of his essays aim to "keep Man in a mood of decent humility," particularly when people are crowing about their conquest of nature. "I am pessimistic about the human race," he once said, "because it is too ingenious for its own good. Our approach to nature is to beat it into submission." To the degree that the moon landing became an occasion for crowing and strutting, therefore, it went against the grain of White's character.

4. *Ford Times* (June 1963), pp. 2–6.
5. *The Wild Flag* (Cambridge, MA, 1946) pp. x–xi.

If we look at White's very rough first draft, we can see his struggle to make one coherent statement that combines his visceral, logical, and social responses to the event.

Planning a trip to the moon differs in no essential respect from planning a trip to the beach. You have to decide what to take along, what to leave behind. Should the thermos jug go? The child's rubber horse? The dill pickles? These are the sometimes fateful decisions on which the success or failure of the whole outing turns. Something goes along that spoils everything because it is always in the way. Something gets left behind that is desperately needed for comfort or safety. The men who had to decide what to take along to the moon must have pondered long and hard, drawn up many a list. We're not sure they planned well, when they included the little telescoped flagpole and the American flag, artificially stiffened so that it would fly to the breeze that didn't blow. As we watched the Stars and Stripes planted on the surface of the moon, we experienced the same sensations of pride that must have filled the hearts of millions of Americans. But the emotion soon turned to   This was our great chance, and we muffed it. The men who stepped out onto the surface of the moon are in a class by themselves—pioneers of what is universal. They saw the earth whole—just as it is, a round ball in   But they colored the moon red, white, and blue—good colors all—but out of place in that setting. The moon still influences the tides, and the tides lap on every shore, right around the globe. The moon still belongs to lovers, and lovers are everywhere—not just in America. What a pity we couldn't have planted some emblem that precisely expressed this unique, this incredible occasion, even if it were nothing more than a white banner, with the legend: "At last!"

White clearly didn't intend this to be a final draft: He twice began sentences that he couldn't end. *What* exactly did our emotions turn to? A round ball in *what*? Having no adequate answers, he left spaces and went on. His aim was to discover the general shape of the comment, to see what he had to say.

I mentioned before that the subject was difficult for White because it offered so little visceral interest, and he knew that he needed to engage his own senses and emotions if he wanted to engage his readers'. In this draft, you can see the attempts to overcome the difficulty. One comes directly from the television screen: "the American flag, artificially stiffened so that it would fly to the breeze that didn't blow." Here is a visual image most of White's readers would have remembered, one that jars us a little by reminding us that there is no *air* up there. Another attempt is the analogy with the beach trip. This analogy gives White access to objects and sense impressions: a Thermos jug (with its suggestion of hot liquid), a rubber horse (an interesting item for those who think about the feel of it), and dill pickles (a pungent taste). The third attempt is the mention of the moon's effects here on earth, on the tides and on lovers. Here we have some footholds for visceral reactions.

Of course, the flag is related to White's key logical concern: the outdated nature of nationalism. The astronauts are "pioneers of what is universal"; they can see "the earth whole"; they are standing on the moon, creator of tides that "lap on every shore." In this draft, White wants us to see that for them to plant a *national* flag is a case of invoking antiquated patriotism in an international age.

The most serious difficulty in the draft is social. White is clearly uneasy about the amount of boasting and strutting associated with the moon landing, but he can't seem to find the right alternative posture. The opening sentences seem determined to take the whole occasion lightly. Later, he criticizes the planners harshly: "We're not sure they planned well. . . . This was our great chance, and we muffed it." In these passages he sounds like Theophrastus' faultfinder. On the other hand, he sometimes bends over backward to sound like a patriot and enthusiast: "As we watched the Stars and Stripes planted on the surface of the moon, we experienced the same sensations of pride that must have filled the hearts of millions of Americans. . . . red, white, and blue—good colors all. . . . this unique, this incredible occasion." It would be hard for readers to trust (or even understand) a man who seems to have three sides to his mouth and seems to talk out of all three in a single paragraph.

The changes White made in the next two drafts show him working at the social level, trying to find the proper tone. Since some of the changes are slight, we'll find them easier to detect if we look at drafts one and three side by side, section by section. The first section in both drafts presents the analogy to the beach trip.

DRAFT ONE	DRAFT THREE
Planning a trip to the moon differs in no essential respect from planning a trip to the beach. You have to decide what to take along, what to leave behind. Should the thermos jug go? The child's rubber horse? The dill pickles? These are the sometimes fateful decisions on which the success or failure of the whole outing turns. Something goes along that spoils everything because it is always in the way. Something gets left behind that is desperately needed for comfort or safety. The men who had to decide what to take along to the moon must have pondered long and hard, drawn up many a list.	Planning a trip to the moon differs in no essential respect from planning a trip to the beach. You have to decide what to take along, what to leave behind. Should the thermos jug go? The child's rubber horse? The dill pickles? These are the sometimes fateful decisions on which the success or failure of the whole outing turns. Something goes along that spoils everything because it is always in the way; something gets left behind that is desperately needed for comfort or for safety. The men who drew up the moon list for the astronauts planned long and hard and well. (Should the vacuum cleaner go to suck up moondust?)

"Do not adjust your set," as they say on television. The two columns are nearly identical until we get to the last sentence or two. There we get some changes that soften White's scolding tone. Now the planners don't just work "long" and "hard"; they work "well." The parenthetical sentence about the vacuum cleaner is apparently intended as an example of the sort of planning they did well, though it seems a lame joke. (In draft two it had been lamer still: "Should they take along a vacuum cleaner to suck up moondust and save the world?") Notice, too, that White separates the astronauts from the planners. This distinction will be useful to him as he continues to rewrite and rethink.

In the middle section, the complaint about the presence of the flag, the drafts differ more sharply.

We're not sure they planned well, when they included the little telescoped flagpole and the American flag, artificially stiffened so that it would fly to the breeze that didn't blow. As we watched the Stars and Stripes planted on the surface of the moon, we experienced the same sensations of pride that must have filled the hearts of millions of Americans. But the emotion soon turned to

This was our great chance, and we muffed it. The men who stepped out onto the surface of the moon are in a class by themselves—pioneers of what is universal. They saw the earth whole—just as it is, a round ball in

But they colored the moon red, white, and blue—good colors all—but out of place in that setting.

Among the items they sent along, of course, was the little jointed flag that could be stiffened to the breeze that did not blow. (It is traditional for explorers to plant the flag.) Yet the two men who stepped out on the surface of the moon were in a class by themselves and should have been equipped accordingly; they were of the new breed of men, those who had seen the earth whole. When, following instructions, they colored the moon red, white, and blue, they were fumbling with the past—or so it seemed to us who watched, trembling with awe and admiration and pride. This was the last chapter in the long book of nationalism, one that could well have been omitted.

Most of the changes affect White's tone, bringing out a less cantankerous, more sympathetic side of his character. In the first draft, White directly challenged NASA's decision to plant the flag ("We're not sure they planned well"). Now he is understanding: "Of course," the planners send along the flag, since it is "traditional" for explorers to plant one. White has been more generous toward the astronauts, especially. In draft one, they were lumped with the planners who had "muffed" our "great chance." Anyone who has played baseball knows the sting of being told that you have "muffed it." In draft three, they are "following instructions" and "fumbling with the past" (a ball too large for anyone to catch neatly). Notice that in the last sentence of this section, White states his logical point more clearly than ever before: "This was the last chapter in the long book of nationalism, one that could well have been omitted." The relation between

White's logical position and his social posture is now considerably clearer. This draft says, "Look, I am convinced that nationalism is outdated, and I don't intend to hide my conviction, but I don't intend to be a spoilsport either. It was a shining moment, and I felt its wonder, though I wish we could have used it for a better purpose."

The final section in both drafts reminds us that the moon is international property and argues that the right "flag" to plant would have been one that represented the entire world. White has reworked the passage considerably by the time he gets to draft three.

Draft one	Draft three
The moon still influences the tides, and the tides lap on every shore, right around the globe. The moon still belongs to lovers, and lovers are everywhere—not just in America. What a pity we couldn't have planted some emblem that precisely expressed this unique, this incredible occasion, even if it were nothing more than a white banner, with the legend: "At last!"	But the moon still holds the key to madness, which is universal, still controls the tides that lap on shores everywhere, and guards lovers that kiss in every land, under no banner but the sky. What a pity we couldn't have forsworn our little Iwo Jima scene and planted instead a banner acceptable to all—a simple white handkerchief, perhaps, symbol of the common cold, which, like the moon, affects us all.

Partly because of the forceful verbs, the first sentence in the new draft has more visceral effect than the old version:

> *But the moon*
>> *still* holds *the key to madness,*
>>> *which is universal,*
>> *still* controls *the tides that lap on shores everywhere,*
>> *and* guards *lovers that kiss in every land,*
>>> *under no banner but the sky.*

The moon sounds like a strong ruler here, stronger than any mere superpower. A more dramatic change happens in the final sentence of the new draft. By mentioning Iwo Jima, White conjures up memories of the most famous photograph of World War II, an object that "glows" with associations. And in contrast to this image of embattled marines planting a flag on a conquered hilltop, White offers a white handkerchief, "symbol of the common cold, which . . . affects us all." Again we have an object that "glows" with visceral associations, but very different ones. Rather than encouraging stiff-necked pride, the handkerchief "keeps Man in a mood of decent humility." White has brought the visceral level and the social level together.

By common standards, this third draft seems a finished product; White telegraphed it to *The New Yorker,* but when the heat of composition began to cool, he saw there was more work to be done at both the social and logical levels. By beginning with the beach comparison and ending with the handkerchief, White had trivialized the moon landing, and he now saw that this trivializing was unfair and shoddy. By hinging his essay on the generalization that nationalism was out of date, he had demanded that his readers accept an enormous assumption without any reasoning or evidence. Time was very short, but White took the paragraph through three more drafts before telegraphing *The New Yorker* that the comment was "no good as is" and offering to dictate over the phone "a shorter one on the same theme but different in tone." Here, for comparison, are draft three and draft six, the one that appeared on page one of the magazine on July 26:

DRAFT THREE

Planning a trip to the moon differs in no essential respect from planning a trip to the beach. You have to decide what to take along, what to leave behind. Should the thermos jug go? The child's rubber horse? The dill pickles? These are the sometimes fateful decisions on which the success or failure of the whole outing turns. Something goes along that spoils everything because it is always in the way; something gets left behind that is desperately needed for comfort or for safety. The

DRAFT SIX

The moon, it turns out, is a great place for men. One-sixth gravity must be a lot of fun, and when Armstrong and Aldrin went into their bouncy little dance, like two happy children, it was a moment not only of triumph, but of gaiety.

men who drew up the moon
list for the astronauts planned
long and hard and well.
(Should the vacuum cleaner go
to suck up moondust?)

Among the items they sent
along, of course, was the little
jointed flag that could be stiffened to the breeze that did not
blow. (It is traditional for
explorers to plant the flag.) Yet
the two men who stepped out
on the surface of the moon
were in a class by themselves
and should have been equipped
accordingly; they were of the
new breed of men, those who
had seen the earth whole.
When, following instructions,
they colored the moon red,
white, and blue, they were
fumbling with the past—or so
it seemed to us who watched,
trembling with awe and admiration and pride. This was the
last chapter in the long book of
nationalism, one that could
well have been omitted.

But the moon still holds the
key to madness, which is
universal, still controls the
tides that lap on shores everywhere, and guards lovers that
kiss in every land, under no
banner but the sky. What a
pity we couldn't have for-
sworn our little Iwo Jima
scene and planted instead a
banner acceptable to all—a
simple white handkerchief,
perhaps, symbol of the common cold, which, like the
moon, affects us all.

The moon, on the other hand,
is a poor place for flags. Ours
looked stiff and awkward,
trying to float on the breeze
that does not blow. (There
must be a lesson here somewhere.) It is traditional, of
course, for explorers to plant
the flag, but it struck us, as
we watched with awe and
admiration and pride, that
our two fellows were universal men, not national men,
and should have been
equipped accordingly.

Like every great river and
every great sea, the moon
belongs to none and belongs
to all. It still holds the key to
madness, still controls the
tides that lap on shores everywhere, still guards the lovers
that kiss in every land under
no banner but the sky. What a
pity in our moment of triumph we couldn't have for-
sworn the familiar Iwo Jima
scene and planted instead a
device acceptable to all: a limp
white handkerchief, perhaps,
symbol of the common cold,
which, like the moon, affects
us all, unites us all.

What has happened here? Socially, White has stopped being a killjoy, stopped being the one person at the party who intends to spend the evening complaining. Once he gets the chip off his shoulder, he is able to recall a detail that appeals to all of us on the visceral level—the "bouncy little dance" of the astronauts.

He is also able to clarify and strengthen his logical point. Rather than insist on the controversial generalization that nationalism is anachronistic, he builds on the widely acceptable generalization that some things belong to all humankind: "Like every great river and every great sea, the moon belongs to none and belongs to all." If the high seas are regarded as beyond nationalism, how much more so the moon, which "still holds the key to madness, still controls the tides that lap on shores everywhere"? And with the little addition of "unites us all" at the very end, White brings the three dimensions of the essay together. The visceral things that affect us all—tides, kisses, the common cold, the moon—also unite us all, as logic should tell us; as social creatures we should behave accordingly. No flags for the moon, no sniping in the essay. White has come to terms with his subject.

*   *   *

You will find many more changes in White's drafts than I have mentioned: Of the 305 words in the first draft, only 15 remain to the end, a survival rate lower than we find in most airline crashes. But the small changes in the essay are less important than the changes of mind that go with them. An essay is not just a finished product. For the writer, it is a process that leads to changes, not only on paper, but in the logical, social, and visceral levels of the self.

Our word *essay,* any dictionary will tell you, is derived from the French word *essai,* "a trial, an attempt, a test." The attempt begins with the blank page and ends when the writer declares some draft final. In this sense, we don't see a living essay in a book, any more than we see a living butterfly in the collector's case. To read well, we have to bring the essay back to life. We have to enter the writer's mind far enough to understand what his or her "attempt" was and against what resistances it made its way forward. Even if we finally disagree with the writer, we should use our intelligence and imagination to see the distance traveled since the page was blank.

As writers, we travel the same road in the other direction. Faced with the blank sheet, we must feel the pull of the completed essay, which is partly the pull of all the essays we have read, understood, and admired. When E. B. White was nearly fifty, his brother gave him a box of white typing paper. Writing back his thanks, White said, "I'm glad to report that even now, at this late day, a blank sheet of paper holds the greatest excitement there is for me—more promising than a silver cloud, prettier than a little red wagon. It holds all the hope there is, all fears." To learn what our own blank sheets may hold is one of the reasons to read.

1

SOME WAYS
OF KNOWING

This photograph is my proof. There was that afternoon when things were still good between us, and we embrased and were so happy. She did love me. It had happened. Look, see for yourself.

This photograph is my proof. © DUANE MICHALS.

OVERVIEW

In the opening pages of his novel *Hard Times,* Charles Dickens presents us with two neatly contrasted characters. Sitting in a classroom are a girl named Sissy Jupe and a boy named Bitzer. Sissy is a picture of health, robust and tanned from her life with a troupe of traveling entertainers who specialize in tricks of horsemanship. Yet even though she has been surrounded by horses all her life and undoubtedly knows how to groom, feed, and ride them, she is stumped when the superintendent of the school, Thomas Gradgrind, asks her to define a horse. "Girl number twenty," Gradgrind announces, "possessed of no facts in reference to one of the commonest animals!" He turns to Bitzer, a pale student who may never have touched a horse but who has learned the facts very well: "Quadruped. Gramnivorous. Forty teeth, namely twenty-four grinders, four eye-teeth, and twelve incisive. Sheds coat in the spring; in marshy country, sheds hoofs, too. Hoofs hard, but requiring to be shod by iron. Age known by marks in the mouth."

"Now, girl number twenty," Gradgrind says, "you know what a horse is."

In Gradgrind's mind, and in the minds of many other people, understanding means no more than the accumulation of facts. Occasionally you may hear a politician, for instance, complaining about the number of high school seniors who don't know who the sixteenth president of the United States was or in what year Columbus discovered America. But as many educators have pointed out, there comes a point in a student's education where accumulating facts is no longer enough. "College," as William G. Perry Jr. puts it, "raises other questions: by whose calendar is it proper to say that Columbus discovered America in 1492? How, when, and by whom was the year 1 established in this calendar? What of other calendars? In view of the evidence for Leif Ericson's previous visit (and the American Indians), what historical ethnocentrism is suggested by the word "discover" in this sentence? As for Leif Ericson, in accord with what assumptions do you order the evidence?"

No longer is "knowing" something merely a matter of memorizing it. Now students have to ask how facts are arrived at, how they fit into systems of thought and *depend* on systems of thought. Better (or worse!) still, students have to understand how different systems of thought—different ways of knowing—relate to one another and what kinds of truths they are capable of producing.

Experiencing various ways of knowing is one of the large functions of the college curriculum. It can hardly be accomplished in a single class or a single book. Nonetheless, the selection of readings that follow may serve as a useful introduction:

- Adrienne Rich, addressing the students of a women's college, warns them (and us) not to mistake the knowledge dispensed by professors for the objective Truth.
- Entomologist Samuel Scudder tells us how a lesson from a great biologist trained him to observe nature as he never had before.
- Carol Bly reminds us that we need to see life as something more than a set of problems to be solved. We have to face some unsolvable realities: "love, death, injustice, and eternity."
- Jacob Bronowski, a man comfortable in both the scientific world and the world of the arts, explores the point where poetry and physics meet: "the search for unity in hidden likenesses."
- William G. Perry Jr., beginning with the curious story of a student who gets an A on an exam by putting out a line of bull, argues that a certain *kind* of bull is at the heart of a liberal education.
- Vincent G. Dethier, an entomologist and physiologist, gives us a lesson on experimental methods as he tests the tastebuds of a housefly.
- Native American poet Linda Hogan tells us how her heritage and her art urge her to deal with nature as something more than a lifeless mechanism.
- Anthropologist William L. Rodman shows how an apparently innocuous conversation between people from different cultures can set off ripples of unexpected meaning.

ADRIENNE RICH

Claiming an Education

Adrienne Rich's most recent books of poetry are *Midnight Salvage: Poems 1995–1998* and *Fox: Poems 1998–2000.* A new selection of her essays, *Arts of the Possible: Essays and Conversations,* was published in 2001. She has recently been the recipient of the Dorothea Tanning Prize of the Academy of American Poets "for mastery in the art of poetry," and the Lannen Foundation Lifetime Achievement Award. She lives in California. "Claiming an Education" was originally a speech delivered to the students of Douglass College, Rutgers University, in 1977. It later appeared in *Blood, Bread, and Poetry: Selected Prose 1979–1986* (1986).

For this convocation, I planned to separate my remarks into two parts: some thoughts about you, the women students here, and some thoughts about us who teach in a women's college. But ultimately, those two parts are indivisible. If university education means anything beyond the processing of human beings into expected roles, through credit hours, tests, and grades (and I believe that in a women's college especially it *might* mean much more), it implies an ethical and intellectual contract between teacher and student. This contract must remain intuitive, dynamic, unwritten; but we must turn to it again and again if learning is to be reclaimed from the depersonalizing and cheapening pressures of the present-day academic scene.   1

The first thing I want to say to you who are students, is that you cannot afford to think of being here to *receive* an education; you will do much better to think of yourselves as being here to *claim* one. One of the dictionary definitions of the verb "to claim" is: *to take as the rightful owner; to assert in the face of possible contradiction.* "To receive" is *to come into possession of; to act as receptacle or container for; to accept as authoritative or true.* The difference is that between acting and being acted-upon, and for women it can literally mean the difference between life and death.   2

One of the devastating weaknesses of university learning, of the store of knowledge and opinion that has been handed down   3 through academic training, has been its almost total erasure of women's experience and thought from the curriculum, and its exclusion of women as members of the academic community. Today, with increasing numbers of women students in nearly every branch of higher learning, we still see very few women in the upper levels of faculty and administration in most institutions. Douglass College itself is a women's college in a university administered overwhelmingly by men, who in turn are answerable to the state legislature, again composed predominantly of men. But the most significant fact for you is that what you learn here, the very texts you read, the lectures you hear, the way your studies are divided into categories and fragmented one from the other—all this reflects, to a very large degree, neither objective reality, nor an accurate picture of the past, nor a group of rigorously tested observations about human behavior. What you can learn here (and I mean not only at Douglass but any college in any university) is how *men* have perceived and organized their experience, their history, their ideas of social relationships, good and evil, sickness and health, etc. When you read or hear about "great issues," "major texts," "the mainstream of Western thought," you are hearing about what men, above all white men, in their male subjectivity, have decided is important.

Black and other minority peoples have for some time recognized that their racial and ethnic experience was not accounted for in the studies broadly labeled human; and that even the sciences can be racist. For many reasons, it has been more difficult for women to comprehend our exclusion, and to realize that even the sciences can be sexist. For one thing, it is only within the last hundred years that higher education has grudgingly been opened up to women at all, even to white, middle-class women. And many of us have found ourselves poring eagerly over books with titles like: *The Descent of Man; Man and His Symbols; Irrational Man; The Phenomenon of Man; The Future of Man; Man and the Machine; From Man to Man; May Man Prevail?; Man, Science and Society;* or *One-Dimensional Man*—books pretending to describe a "human" reality that does not include over one-half the human species.

Less than a decade ago, with the rebirth of a feminist movement in this country, women students and teachers in a number of universities began to demand and set up women's studies courses—to *claim* a woman-directed education. And, despite the inevitable accusations of "unscholarly," "group therapy," "faddism," etc., despite backlash and budget cuts, women's studies are still growing, offering to more and more women a new intellectual grasp on their lives, new understanding of our history, a fresh vision of the human experience, and also a critical basis for evaluating what they hear and read in other courses, and in the society at large.

But my talk is not really about women's studies, much as I believe in their scholarly, scientific, and human necessity. While I think that any Douglass student has everything to gain by investigating and enrolling in women's studies courses, I want to suggest that there is a more essential experience that you owe yourselves, one which courses in women's studies can greatly enrich, but which finally depends on you, in all your interactions with yourself and your world. This is the experience of *taking responsibility toward yourselves*. Our upbringing as women has so often told us that this should come second to our relationships and responsibilities to other people. We have been offered ethical models of the self-denying wife and mother; intellectual models of the brilliant but slapdash dilettante who never commits herself to anything the whole way, or the intelligent woman who denies her intelligence in order to seem more "feminine," or who sits in passive silence even when she disagrees inwardly with everything that is being said around her.

Responsibility to yourself means refusing to let others do your thinking, talking, and naming for you; it means learning to respect and use your own brains and instincts; hence, grappling with hard work. It means that you do not treat your body as a commodity with which to purchase superficial intimacy or economic security; for our bodies and minds are inseparable in this life, and when we allow our bodies to be treated as objects, our minds are in mortal danger. It means insisting that those to whom you give your friendship and love are able to respect your mind. It means being able to say, with Charlotte Brontë's *Jane Eyre:* "I have an inward treasure born with me, which can keep me alive if all the extraneous delights should be withheld or offered only at a price I cannot afford to give."

Responsibility to yourself means that you don't fall for shallow and easy solutions—predigested books and ideas, weekend

6

7

8

encounters guaranteed to change your life, taking "gut" courses instead of ones you know will challenge you, bluffing at school and life instead of doing solid work, marrying early as an escape from real decisions, getting pregnant as an evasion of already existing problems. It means that you refuse to sell your talents and aspirations short, simply to avoid conflict and confrontation. And this, in turn, means resisting the forces in society which say that women should be nice, play safe, have low professional expectations, drown in love and forget about work, live through others, and stay in the places assigned to us. It means that we insist on a life of meaningful work, insist that work be as meaningful as love and friendship in our lives. It means, therefore, the courage to be "different"; not to be continuously available to others when we need time for ourselves and our work; to be able to demand of others—parents, friends, roommates, teachers, lovers, husbands, children—that they respect our sense of purpose and our integrity as persons. Women everywhere are finding the courage to do this, more and more, and we are finding that courage both in our study of women in the past who possessed it, and in each other as we look to other women for comradeship, community, and challenge. The difference between a life lived actively, and a life of passive drifting and dispersal of energies, is an immense difference. Once we begin to feel committed to our lives, responsible to ourselves, we can never again be satisfied with the old, passive way.

Now comes the second part of the contract. I believe that in a women's college you have the right to expect your faculty to take you seriously. The education of women has been a matter of debate for centuries, and old, negative attitudes about women's role, women's ability to think and take leadership, are still rife both in and outside the university. Many male professors (and I don't mean only at Douglass) still feel that teaching in a women's college is a second-rate career. Many tend to eroticize their women students—to treat them as sexual objects—instead of demanding the best of their minds. (At Yale a legal suit [*Alexander* v. *Yale*] has been brought against the university by a group of women students demanding a stated policy against sexual advances toward female students by male professors.) Many teachers, both men and women, trained in the male-centered tradition, are still handing the ideas and texts of that tradition on to students without teaching them to criticize its antiwoman attitudes, its omission of women as part of the species. Too often, all of us fail to teach the most important thing, which is that clear thinking, active discussion, and excellent writing are all necessary for intellectual freedom, and that these require *hard work*. Sometimes, perhaps in discouragement with a culture which is both antiintellectual and antiwoman, we may resign ourselves to low expectations for our students before we have given them half a chance to become more thoughtful, expressive human beings. We need to take to heart the words of Elizabeth Barrett Browning, a poet, a thinking woman, and a feminist, who wrote in 1845 of her impatience with studies which cultivate a "passive recipiency" in the mind, and asserted that "women want to be made to *think actively:* their apprehension is quicker than that of men, but their defect lies for the most part in the logical faculty and in the higher mental activities." Note that she implies a defect which can be remedied by intellectual training; *not* an inborn lack of ability.

I have said that the contract on the student's part involves that you demand to be taken seriously so that you can also go on taking yourself seriously. This means seeking out criticism, recognizing that the most affirming thing anyone can do for you is demand that you push yourself further, show you the range of what you *can* do. It means rejecting attitudes of "take-it-easy," "why-be-so-serious," "why-worry-you'll-probably-get-married-anyway." It means assuming your share of responsibility for what happens in the classroom, because that affects the quality of your daily life here. It means that the student sees herself engaged *with* her teachers in an active, ongoing struggle for a real education. But for her to do this, her teachers must be committed to the belief that women's minds and experience are intrinsically valuable and indispensable to any civilization worthy the name; that there is no more exhilarating and intellectually fertile place in the academic world today than a women's college—*if* both students and teachers in large enough numbers are trying to fulfill this contract. The contract is really a pledge of mutual seriousness about women, about language, ideas, methods, and values. It is our shared commitment toward a world in which the inborn potentialities of so many women's minds will no longer be wasted, raveled-away, paralyzed, or denied.

10

SAMUEL SCUDDER

Learning to See

Samuel Scudder was one of the most productive biologists of his time. During his long career he published definitive descriptions of hundreds of species of living insects and also named more than a thousand species of fossil insects. "Learning to See," which was published anonymously in 1874, describes the beginning of his studies at Harvard under the celebrated zoologist and geologist Louis Agassiz, who laid the foundation for modern descriptive biology at the same time he opposed the theories of his great contemporary Charles Darwin.

It was more than fifteen years ago that I entered the laboratory of Professor Agassiz, and told him I had enrolled my name in the Scientific School as a student of natural history. He asked me a few questions about my object in coming, my antecedents generally, the mode in which I afterwards proposed to use the knowledge I might acquire, and, finally, whether I wished to study any special branch. To the latter I replied that, while I wished to be well grounded in all departments of zoology, I purposed to devote myself specially to insects.

"When do you wish to begin?" he asked.

"Now," I replied.

This seemed to please him, and with an energetic "Very well!" he reached from a shelf a huge jar of specimens in yellow alcohol.

"Take this fish," said he, "and look at it; we call it a haemulon; by and by I will ask what you have seen."

With that he left me, but in a moment returned with explicit instructions as to the care of the object entrusted to me.

"No man is fit to be a naturalist," said he, "who does not know how to take care of specimens."

I was to keep the fish before me in a tin tray, and occasionally moisten the surface with alcohol from the jar, always taking care to replace the stopper tightly. Those were not the days of ground-glass stoppers and elegantly shaped exhibition jars; all the old students will recall the huge necklace glass bottles with their leaky, wax-besmeared corks, half eaten by insects, and begrimed with cellar dust. Entomology was a cleaner science than ichthyology, but the example of the Professor, who had unhesitatingly plunged to the bottom of the jar to produce the fish, was infectious; and though this alcohol had a "very ancient and fish-like smell,"[1] I really dared not show any aversion within these sacred precincts, and treated the alcohol as though it were pure water. Still I was conscious of a passing feeling of disappointment, for gazing at a fish did not commend itself to an ardent entomologist. My friends at home, too, were annoyed when they discovered that no amount of eau-de-Cologne would drown the perfume which haunted me like a shadow.

In ten minutes I had seen all that could be seen in that fish, and started in search of the Professor—who had, however, left the Museum; and when I returned, after lingering over some of the odd animals stored in the upper apartment, my specimen was dry all over. I dashed the fluid over the fish as if to resuscitate the beast from a fainting-fit, and looked with anxiety for a return of the normal sloppy appearance. This little excitement over, nothing was to be done but to return to a steadfast gaze at my mute companion. Half an hour passed—an hour—another hour; the fish began to look loathsome. I turned it over and around; looked it in the face—ghastly; from behind, beneath, above, sideways, at a three-quarters' view—just as ghastly. I was in despair; at an early hour I concluded that lunch was necessary; so, with infinite relief, the fish was carefully replaced in the jar, and for an hour I was free.

On my return, I learned that Professor Agassiz had been at the Museum, but had gone, and would not return for several hours. My fellow-students were too busy to be disturbed by continued conversation. Slowly I drew forth that hideous fish, and with a feeling of desperation again looked at it. I might not use a magnifying-glass; instruments of all kinds were interdicted. My two hands, my two eyes, and the fish; it seemed a most limited field. I pushed my finger down its throat to feel how sharp the teeth were. I began to count the scales in the different rows, until I was convinced that that was nonsense. At last a happy thought struck me—I would draw the fish; and now with surprise I began to discover new features in the creature. Just then the Professor returned.

1. The quotation is from Shakespeare, *The Tempest*, II, ii, 25.

"That is right," he said; "a pencil is one of the best of eyes. I   11
am glad to notice, too, that you keep your specimen wet, and
your bottle corked."

With these encouraging words, he added: 12

"Well, what is it like?"   13

He listened attentively to my brief rehearsal of the structure of   14
parts whose names were still unknown to me: the fringed gill-
arches and movable operculum; the pores of the head, fleshy lips
and lidless eyes; the lateral line, the spinous fins and forked tail;
the compressed and arched body. When I had finished, he waited
as if expecting more, and then, with an air of disappointment:

"You have not looked very carefully; why," he continued   15
more earnestly, "you haven't even seen one of the most conspicuous features of the animal, which is as plainly before your eyes
as the fish itself; look again, look again!" and he left me to my
misery.

I was piqued; I was mortified. Still more of that wretched fish!   16
But now I set myself to my task with a will, and discovered one
new thing after another, until I saw how just the Professor's criticism had been. The afternoon passed quickly; and when,
toward its close, the Professor inquired:

"Do you see it yet?"   17

"No," I replied, "I am certain I do not, but I see how little I   18
saw before."

"That is next best," said he, earnestly, "but I won't hear you   19
now; put away your fish and go home; perhaps you will be ready
with a better answer in the morning. I will examine you before
you look at the fish."

This was disconcerting. Not only must I think of my fish all   20
night, studying, without the object before me, what this unknown but most visible feature might be; but also, without reviewing my discoveries, I must give an exact account of them the
next day. I had a bad memory; so I walked home by Charles
River in a distracted state, with my two perplexities.

The cordial greeting from the Professor the next morning was   21
reassuring; here was a man who seemed to be quite as anxious as
I that I should see for myself what he saw.

"Do you perhaps mean," I asked, "that the fish has symmet-   22
rical sides with paired organs?"

His thoroughly pleased "Of course! of course!" repaid the   23 wakeful hours of the previous night. After he had discoursed most happily and enthusiastically—as he always did—upon the importance of this point, I ventured to ask what I should do next.

"Oh, look at your fish!" he said, and left me again to my own   24
devices. In a little more than an hour he returned, and heard my new catalogue.

"That is good, that is good!" he repeated; "but that is not all;   25
go on"; and so for three long days he placed that fish before my eyes, forbidding me to look at anything else, or to use any artificial aid. "Look, look, look," was his repeated injunction.

This was the best entomological lesson I ever had—a lesson   26
whose influence has extended to the details of every subsequent study; a legacy the Professor has left to me, as he has left it to many others, of inestimable value, which we could not buy, with which we cannot part.

A year afterward, some of us were amusing ourselves with   27
chalking outlandish beasts on the Museum blackboard. We drew prancing starfishes; frogs in mortal combat; hydra-headed worms; stately crawfishes, standing on their tails, bearing aloft umbrellas; and grotesque fishes with gaping mouths and staring eyes. The Professor came in shortly after, and was as amused as any at our experiments. He looked at the fishes.

"Haemulons, every one of them," he said; "Mr. ____ drew   28
them."

True; and to this day, if I attempt a fish, I can draw nothing   29
but haemulons.

The fourth day, a second fish of the same group was placed   30
beside the first, and I was bidden to point out the resemblances and differences between the two; another and another followed, until the entire family lay before me, and a whole legion of jars covered the table and surrounding shelves; the odor had become a pleasant perfume; and even now, the sight of an old, six-inch, worm-eaten cork brings fragrant memories.

The whole group of haemulons was thus brought in review;   31
and, whether engaged upon the dissection of the internal organs, the preparation and examination of the bony framework, or the description of the various parts, Agassiz's training in the method of observing facts and their orderly arrangement was ever accompanied by the urgent exhortation not to be content with them.

"Facts are stupid things," he would say, "until brought into   32
connection with some general law."

At the end of eight months, it was almost with reluctance that   33
I left these friends and turned to insects; but what I had gained
by this outside experience has been of greater value than years of
later investigation in my favorite groups.

CAROL BLY

Growing Up Expressive

Though educated at a New England boarding school and at
Wellesley College, Carol Bly has lived most of her life in Minnesota, her home state. She teaches creative writing at the University of Minnesota and has a national reputation as a writer of
fiction, but some of her most memorable writing has been done
for local and regional publications and seems to be directly addressed to her practical neighbors. "Growing Up Expressive" was
originally published in *Minnesota Monthly* and later appeared as
the last of the *Letters from the Country* (1981).

Love, death, the cruelty of power, and time's curve past the   1
stars are what children want to look at. For convenience's sake,
let's say these are the four most vitally touching things in life. Little children ask questions about them with relish. Children, provided they are still little enough, have no eye to doing any
problem solving about love or death or injustice or the universe;
they are simply interested. I've noticed that as we read aloud literature to them, about Baba Yaga, and Dr. Dolittle, and Ivan and
the Firebird, and Rat and Mole, children are not only interested,
they are prepared to be vitally touched by the great things of life.
If you like the phrase, they are what some people call "being as
a little child." Another way of looking at it is to say that in our
minds we have two kinds of receptivity to life going on all the
time: first, being vitally touched and enthusiastic (grateful, enraged, puzzled—but, at all events, *moved*) and, second, having a
will to solve problems.

Our gritty society wants and therefore deliberately trains   2
problem solvers, however, not mystics. We teach human beings
to keep themselves conscious only of problems that *can* conceivably be solved. There must be no hopeless causes. Now this
means that some subjects, of which death and sexual love come
to mind straight off, should be kept at as low a level of consciousness as possible. Both resist problem solving. A single-
minded problem solver focuses his consciousness, of course, on
problems to be solved, but even he realizes there is a concentric,
peripheral band of other material around the problems. This
band appears to him as "issues." He is not interested in these issues for themselves; he sees them simply as impacting on the
problems. He will allow us to talk of love, death, injustice, and
eternity—he may even encourage us to do so because his group-
dynamics training advises him to let us have our say, thus dissi-
pating our willfulness—but his heart is circling, circling, looking
for an opening to *wrap up* these "issues" so he can return attention to discrete, solvable problems. For example, a physician
who has that mentality does not wish to be near dying patients
very much. They are definitely not a solvable problem. If he is
wicked, he will regard them as a present issue with impact on a
future problem: then he will order experimentation done on
them during their last weeks with us. It means his ethic is toward
the healing process only, but not toward the dying person. His
ethic is toward problem solving, not toward wonder. He will feel
quite conscientious while doing the experiments on the dying patient, because he feels he is saving lives of future patients.

To return to little children for a second: they simply like to   3
contemplate life and death. So our difficulty, in trying to educate
adults so they will be balanced but enthusiastic, is to keep both
streams going—the problem solving, which seems to be the mental genius of our species, and the fearless contemplation of gigantic things, the spiritual genius of our species.

The problem-solving mentality is inculcated no less in art and   4
English classes than in mathematics and science. Its snake oil is
hope of success: by setting very small topics in front of people,
for which it is easy for them to see the goals, the problems, the
solutions, their egos are not threatened. They feel hopeful of being effective. Therefore, to raise a generation of problem solvers,
you encourage them to visit the county offices (as our sixth-grade

teachers do) and you lead them to understand that this is citizenship. You carefully do not suggest that citizenship also means comparatively complex and hopeless activities like Amnesty International's pressure to get prisoners in far places released or at least no longer tortured. Small egos are threatened by huge, perhaps insoluble problems. Therefore, one feeds the small ego confidence by setting before it dozens and dozens of very simple situations. The ego is nourished by feeling it understands the relationship between the county recorder's office and the county treasurer's office; in later life, when young people find a couple of sticky places in county government, they will confidently work at smoothing them. How very different an experience such problem solving is from having put before one the spectacle of the United States' various stances and activities with respect to germ warfare. Educators regularly steer off all interest in national and international government to one side, constantly feeding our rural young people on questions to which one can hope for answers on a short timeline. We do not ask them to exercise that muscle which bears the weight of vast considerations—such as cruelty in large governments. By the time the average rural Minnesotan is eighteen, he or she expects to stay in cheerful places, devote some time to local government and civic work, and "win the little ones." Rural young people have a repertoire of pejorative language for hard causes: "opening that keg of worms," "no end to that once you get into it," "don't worry—you can't do anything about that from where you are," "we could go on about that forever!" They are right, of course: we could, and our species, at its most cultivated, does go on forever about love, death, power, time, the universe. But some of us, alas, have been conditioned by eighteen fashionably to despise those subjects because there are no immediate answers to all the questions they ask us.

The other way we negatively reinforce any philosophical bent 5 in children is to pretend we don't see the content in their artwork. We comment only on the technique, in somewhat the same way you can scarcely get a comment on rural preachers' sermon content: the response is always, He does a good (or bad) job of speaking. "Well, but what did he say?" "Oh, he talked really well. That man can preach!"

The way to devalue the content of a child's painting is to say, 6 "Wow, you sure can paint!" The average art teacher in Minnesota is at pains to find something to say to the third grader's painting of a space machine with complicated, presumably electronic equipment in it. Here is the drawing in words: A man is sitting at some controls. Outside his capsule, fire is flying from emission points on his ship toward another spaceship at right, hitting it. Explosions are coming out of its side and tail. What is an art teacher to do with this? Goodness knows. So he or she says, "My goodness, I can see there's a lot of action there!" It is said in a deliberately encouraging way but anyone can hear under the carefully supportive comment: "A lot of work going into nothing but more TV-inspired violence." One might as well have told the child, "Thank you for sharing."

I once attended a regional writers' group at which a young   7
poet wrote about his feelings of being a single parent and trying to keep his sanity as he cared for his children. In his poem, he raced up the staircase, grabbed a gun, and shot the clock. When he finished reading it aloud to us, someone told him, "I certainly am glad you shared with us. I'd like to really thank you for sharing."

If we are truly serious about life we are going to have to stop   8
thanking people for sharing. It isn't enough response to whatever has been offered. It is half ingenuous, and sometimes it is insincere, and often it is patronizing. It is the *dictum excrementi*[1] of our decade.

I would like to keep in mind for a moment the art works   9
described above: the child's painting of a spaceship assaulting another spaceship, and the harrowed father's racing up the staircase and shooting the clock. Here is a third. It is a twelve-year-old's theme for English class.

> They were their four days and nights before anyone found them. It was wet and cold down there. As little kids at the orphanage, they had been beaten every night until they could scarcely make it to bed. Now they were older. Duane and Ellen leaned together. "I love you forever," she told him. He asked her, "Even though my face is marked from getting scarlett fever and polio and small pox and newmonya and they wouldn't take decent care of me, not call the doctor or anything, so the marks will always be on me?" "You know I love you," Ellen told him. "You know that time they tortured me for information and I was there but I didn't talk and later I found out

1. *dictum excrementi:* The Latin translates roughly as "worthless expression."

it was your uncle who did it. I didn't talk because I remembered the American flag." Just then they heard someone shout, "Anyone alive down there in this mess?" You see a bomb had gone off destroying a entire U.S.A. city where they lived. Duane had lived with his cruel uncle who took him out of the orphanage to get cheap labor and Ellen lived at a boardinghouse where there were rats that ate pages of her diary all the time. Now they both looked up and shouted "We're here!" A head appeared at the top of the well into which they had fallen or they would of been in 6,500 pieces like all the other men and ladies even pregnant ones and little kids in that town. Now this head called down, "Oh—a boy and a girl!" then the head explained it was going for a ladder and ropes and it ducked away and where it had been they saw the beginnings of stars for that night, the stars still milky in front of the bright blue because the sky wasn't dark enough yet to show them up good.

The English teacher will typically comment on this story by observing that the spelling is uneven, and adjectives get used as adverbs. In rural Minnesota (if not elsewhere) an English teacher can spend every class hour on adjectives used as adverbs: it is meat and potatoes to a nag. But when we discuss spelling, syntax, and adverbs, we are talking method, not content. The child notices that nothing is said of the story's *plot*. No one remarks on the *feelings* in it. Now if this happens every time a child hands in fiction or a poem, the child will realize by the time he reaches twelfth grade that meaning or feelings are not worth anything, that "mechanics" (note the term) are all that matter. [10]

It is rare for a public school English teacher to comment on a child's content unless the material is *factual*. Minnesota teachers encourage writing booklets about the state, themes on ecology and county government, on how Dad strikes the field each autumn, on how Mom avoids open-kettle canning because the USDA advises against it. In this way, our children are conditioned to regard writing as problem solving instead of contemplation, as routine thinking instead of imaginative inquiry. [11]

How can we manage it otherwise? [12]

I would like to suggest some questions we can ask children about their artwork which will encourage them to grow up into lovers, lobby supporters, and Amnesty International members, instead of only township officers and annual protestors against daylight saving time. Let us gather all the elements of the three artworks presented in this Letter: the little boy's spaceship-war [13] painting, the young divorced father's narrative poem, and the twelve-year-old girl's story of love in a well. We have a set of images before us, then:

Man directing spaceship fire
Another aircraft being obliterated
Staircase, man shooting a clock; children
Cruel orphanage
Torture
Last survivors of a decimated city

Let us, instead of lending the great sneer to these images, be respectful of them. It may help to pretend the painting is by Picasso, that Flaubert[2] wrote the father/clock scene, and that Tolstoy[3] wrote the well story. It helps to remember that Picasso felt the assault of historical events on us—like Guernica;[4] Flaubert, as skillfully as Dostoyevsky[5] and with less self-pity, was an observer of violent detail; and the Tolstoy who wrote *Resurrection* or the scene of Pierre's imprisonment in *War and Peace* would turn to the well/love story without qualm.

We know we would never say to Picasso, Flaubert, or Tolstoy, "Why don't you draw something you know about from everyday life? Why don't you write about something you know about? You say Anna was smashed beneath a train? Thank you for sharing!"

The fact is that a child's feelings about orphanages and torture and love are things that he does know about. They are psychic realities inside him, and when he draws them, he is drawing something from everyday life. Sometimes they are from his night life of dreaming, but in any event they are images of passion and he is drawing from his genuine if garbled experience. A few years ago there was a stupid movement to discourage children's reading of Grimms' fairy tales. Later, with a more sophisticated psychology, we learned that the stepmother who is hostile and overweening is a reality to all children; the cutting-off of the hero's right hand and replacing of it with a hand of silver is a reality to

2. Gustave Flaubert (1821–1880): French author of such "realist" novels as *Madame Bovary*.
3. Leo Tolstoy (1828–1910): Russian novelist.
4. Guernica: a Spanish fishing village whose bombing by fascist forces in 1937 inspired a painting by Pablo Picasso (1881–1973).
5. Feodor Dostoyevsky (1821–1881): Russian novelist.

all children. Spaceships, witches' gingerbread houses, orphanages, being the last two people to survive on earth—all these are part of the inner landscape, something children know about. Therefore, in examining their artwork, we need better sets of questions to ask them. Young people who are not repressed are going to lay their wild stuff in front of adults (hoping for comment of some kind, praise if possible) until the sands of life are run, so we had better try to be good at responding to them. And unless we want to raise drones suitable only for conveyor-belt shifts, we had better be at least half as enthusiastic as when they tell us, Mama, I got the mowing finished.

Here are some questions to ask our young artist. How much   17
of that electronic equipment is used for firepower and how much just to run the ship? After the other spaceship is blown up and the people in it are dead, what will this man do? Will he go home somewhere? Were the stars out that night? You said he'll go home to his parents. Did the other man have parents? How soon will that man's parents find out that his spaceship was destroyed? Could you draw in the stars? You said they were out— could you draw them into the picture some way? but don't ruin anything you've got in there now. Also, that wire you said ran to the solar plates, will you darken it so it shows better? Don't change it—just make it clearer. Yes—terrific! Can you see the planet where the other man would have returned to if he had lived till morning?

The young father's story: There is an obvious psychic compli-   18
cation to this story: the violence in his shooting out the clock face is gratuitous, and the plea for attention on the part of the author directed at the reader is glaring: clock faces as psychological symbols are in the public domain. Anyone who tells a friend (or a group of strangers) I am going to shoot up a clock face at 11 P.M. is asking for psychological attention. In a civil world, to ask is to receive, so if we are civilized we have to pay attention and ask the young author: Why does the father in the story blast the clock? And, when he replies, we have to ask some more. If there was ever an instance in which it was O.K. to say, "Thanks for sharing," this is not it.

I should like to add that this will be especially difficult for ru-   19
ral teachers because the traditional country way to treat any kind of mental problem is to stare it down. It didn't happen. I didn't hear that insane thing you just said, and you know you

don't really hate your mother. What nice parent would shoot a clock? We uniformly do what Dr. Vaillant in *Adaptations to Life*[6] would call a denial adaptation. It takes a brave questioner when the young person brings in a crazy story.

The well/love story: Did you know there really are such or- [20] phanages? There are orphanages where the children have to get up at four-thirty to work in the dairy, and the girls work hours and hours in the kitchens, and the children's growth is stunted. Did you make the girl so brave on purpose? Were they a lucky couple or an unlucky couple, or is that the sort of a question you can't ask? You made a point of telling us they'd been through a lot of hardship. What would it have been like for them if they hadn't? Do you want to talk about what blew up in the city? Did you imagine yourself in the well?

Those are not brilliant questions; they are simply respectful, [21] because the art works described are concerned with death by violence; cruelty by institutions; treachery by relations; bravery (or cowardice—either one is important); sexual love, either despite or encouraged by dreadful circumstances.

They are some of the subjects in *War and Peace,* in Dürer's[7] [22] etchings, paintings, and woodcuts, and in *Madame Bovary.*

It is a moot question in my mind which of two disciplines will [23] be the more useful in helping people stay vitally touched by the Great Things: psychology might do it—and English literature in high school might do it (instruction on the college level is generally so dutiful to methodology that it seems a lost cause to me. "How did D. H. Lawrence foreshadow this event?" and "What metaphors does Harold Rosenberg use in his discussion of Action Painting?" are the questions of technocrats, not preservers of spirit. It is as if we got home from church and the others said, "How was church?" "We had Eucharist," we tell them. "Well, how was it?" they ask. "Pretty good," we reply. "Bishop Anderson was there. He held the chalice eight inches above the rail so no one spilled, then he turned and wiped the chalice after each use so no germs were passed along. People who had already communed returned to their benches using the north aisle so there was no bottlenecking at the chancel.")

---

6. The author is referring to a book published in 1977 by Dr. George E. Vaillant, studying the ways people succeed or fail in coping with various life changes.
7. Albrecht Dürer (1471–1528): German artist.

I don't think churches will be helpful in preserving the mysti-   24
cal outlook as long as they see life and death as a *problem*—a
problem of salvation—with a solution to be worked at. Churches
have an axe to grind. They might take the father running up the
staircase to be an impact subject: they would wish to use their
program to solve his problem. Churchmen often appear to be
companionable counselors, but the appearance is largely manner
and habit. Under the manner, the clergyman's mindset is nearly
always to see a disturbed or grieving person's imagery as *the issues*. From there, he swings into psychological problem solving.

I would like to commend this responsibility to our English   25
teachers: that they help our children preserve pity, happiness,
and grief inside themselves. They can enhance those feelings by
having young children both write and draw pictures. They can
be very enthusiastic about the children's first drawings of death
in the sky. Adults, particularly mature ones who have *not* got
children in school at the moment, should make it clear that we
expect this of English teachers and that we don't give a damn if
LeRoy and Merv never in their lives get the sentence balance of
past conditional and perfect subjunctive clauses right. We need
to protect some of the Things Invisible inside LeRoy and Merv
and the rest of us.

This is my last Letter from the Country. That is why it is so   26
shrill. Gadflies are always looking out a chance to be shrill anyway, so I jumped to this one and have shouted my favorite hope:
that we can educate children not to be problem solvers but to be
madly expressive all their lives.

JACOB BRONOWSKI

The Creative Mind

Born in Poland, Jacob Bronowski took his Ph.D. in mathematics
at Cambridge University and then published a number of books
about the very unmathematical poet William Blake. As a member
of the scientific team studying the effects of the atomic bombing
of Japan, Bronowski was jolted into a high level of concern about
the role of science in his times. The rest of his career was spent la-

boring to help his readers and listeners see that science—so deeply implicated in the horrors of the twentieth century—also had a human face. "The Creative Mind," originally delivered as a lecture at the Massachusetts Institute of Technology in 1953, later became the first chapter of *Science and Human Values* (1956).

I

On a fine November day in 1945, late in the afternoon, I was   1 landed on an airstrip in southern Japan. From there a jeep was to take me over the mountains to join a ship which lay in Nagasaki Harbor. I knew nothing of the country or the distance before us. We drove off; dusk fell; the road rose and fell away, the pine woods came down to the road, straggled on and opened again. I did not know that we had left the open country until unexpectedly I heard the ship's loudspeakers broadcasting dance music. Then suddenly I was aware that we were already at the center of damage in Nagasaki. The shadows behind me were the skeletons of the Mitsubishi factory buildings, pushed backwards and sideways as if by a giant hand. What I had thought to be broken rocks was a concrete power house with its roof punched in. I could now make out the outline of two crumpled gasometers; there was a cold furnace festooned with service pipes; otherwise nothing but cockeyed telegraph poles and loops of wire in a bare waste of ashes. I had blundered into this desolate landscape as instantly as one might wake among the craters of the moon. The moment of recognition when I realized that I was already in Nagasaki is present to me as I write, as vividly as when I lived it. I see the warm night and the meaningless shapes; I can even remember the tune that was coming from the ship. It was a dance tune which had been popular in 1945, and it was called "Is You Is Or Is You Ain't Ma Baby?"

These essays, which I have called *Science and Human Values,*   2 were born at that moment. For the moment I have recalled was a universal moment; what I met was, almost as abruptly, the experience of mankind. On an evening like that evening, some time in 1945, each of us in his own way learned that his imagination had been dwarfed. We looked up and saw the power of which we had been proud loom over us like the ruins of Nagasaki.

The power of science for good and for evil has troubled other   3 minds than ours. We are not here fumbling with a new dilemma;

our subject and our fears are as old as the toolmaking civilizations. Men have been killed with weapons before now: what happened at Nagasaki was only more massive (for 40,000 were killed there by a flash which lasted seconds) and more ironical (for the bomb exploded over the main Christian community in Japan). Nothing happened in 1945 except that we changed the scale of our indifference to man; and conscience, in revenge, for an instant became immediate to us. Before this immediacy fades in a sequence of televised atomic tests, let us acknowledge our subject for what it is: civilization face to face with its own implications. The implications are both the industrial slum which Nagasaki was before it was bombed, and the ashy desolation which the bomb made of the slum. And civilization asks of both ruins, "Is You Is Or Is You Ain't Ma Baby?"

2

The man whom I imagine to be asking this question, wrily   4
with a sense of shame, is not a scientist; he is civilized man. It is of course more usual for each member of civilization to take flight from its consequences by protesting that others have failed him. Those whose education and perhaps tastes have confined them to the humanities protest that the scientists alone are to blame, for plainly no mandarin[1] ever made a bomb or an industry. The scientists say, with equal contempt, that the Greek scholars and the earnest cataloguers of cave paintings do well to wash their hands of blame; but what in fact are they doing to help direct the society whose ills grow more often from inaction than from error?

This absurd division reached its *reductio ad absurdum,* I   5
think, when one of my teachers, G. H. Hardy, justified his great life work on the ground that it could do no one the least harm— or the least good. But Hardy was a mathematician; will humanists really let him opt out of the conspiracy of scientists? Or are scientists in their turn to forgive Hardy because, protest as he might, most of them learned their indispensable mathematics from his books?

1. mandarin: sometimes used to mean a person influential in intellectual or literary circles.

There is no comfort in such bickering. When Shelley pictured 6
science as a modern Prometheus[2] who would wake the world to
a wonderful dream of Godwin,[3] he was alas too simple. But it is
as pointless to read what has happened since as a nightmare.
Dream or nightmare, we have to live our experience as it is, and
we have to live it awake. We live in a world which is penetrated
through and through by science, and which is both whole and
real. We cannot turn it into a game simply by taking sides.

And this make-believe game might cost us what we value 7
most: the human content of our lives. The scholar who disdains
science may speak in fun, but his fun is not quite a laughing matter. To think of science as a set of special tricks, to see the scientist as the manipulator of outlandish skills—this is the root of the
poison mandrake which flourishes rank in the comic strips.
There is no more threatening and no more degrading doctrine
than the fancy that somehow we may shelve the responsibility
for making the decisions of our society by passing it to a few scientists armored with a special magic. This is another dream, the
dream of H. G. Wells, in which the tall elegant engineers rule,
with perfect benevolence, a humanity which has no business except to be happy. To H. G. Wells, this was a dream of heaven—a
modern version of the idle, harp-resounding heaven of other
childhood pieties. But in fact it is the picture of a slave society,
and should make us shiver whenever we hear a man of sensibility dismiss science as someone else's concern. The world today is
made, it is powered by science; and for any man to abdicate an
interest in science is to walk with open eyes towards slavery.

My aim in this book is to show that the parts of civilization 8
make a whole: to display the links which give society its coher-
ence, and, more, which give it life. In particular, I want to show
the place of science in the canons of conduct which it has still to
perfect.

This subject falls into three parts. The first is a study of the na- 9
ture of the scientific activity, and with it of all those imaginative
acts of understanding which exercise "The Creative Mind." After this it is logical to ask what is the nature of the truth, as we

2. Prometheus: a Titan of Greek mythology who gave humans the gift of fire.
3. William Godwin (1756–1836): a utopian socialist who dreamed of a world of
perfect personal freedom in small, self-sufficient communities.

seek it in science and in social life; and to trace the influence which this search for empirical truth has had on conduct. This influence has prompted me to call the second part "The Habit of Truth." Last I shall study the conditions for the success of science, and find in them the values of man which science would have had to invent afresh if man had not otherwise known them: the values which make up "The Sense of Human Dignity."

This, then, is a high-ranging subject which is not to be held in   10 the narrow limits of a laboratory. It disputes the prejudice of the humanist who takes his science sourly and, equally, the petty view which many scientists take of their own activity and that of others. When men misunderstand their own work, they cannot understand the work of others; so that it is natural that these scientists have been indifferent to the arts. They have been content, with the humanists, to think science mechanical and neutral; they could therefore justify themselves only by the claim that it is practical. By this lame criterion they have of course found poetry and music and painting at least unreal and often meaningless. I challenge all these judgments.

3

There is a likeness between the creative acts of the mind in art   11 and in science. Yet, when a man uses the word science in such a sentence, it may be suspected that he does not mean what the headlines mean by science. Am I about to sidle away to those riddles in the Theory of Numbers which Hardy loved, or to the heady speculations of astrophysicists, in order to make claims for abstract science which have no bearing on its daily practice?

I have no such design. My purpose is to talk about science as   12 it is, practical and theoretical. I define science as the organization of our knowledge in such a way that it commands more of the hidden potential in nature. What I have in mind therefore is both deep and matter of fact; it reaches from the kinetic theory of gases to the telephone and the suspension bridge and medicated toothpaste. It admits no sharp boundary between knowledge and use. There are of course people who like to draw a line between pure and applied science; and oddly, they are often the same people who find art unreal. To them, the word *useful* is a final arbiter, either for or against a work; and they use this word as if it can mean only what makes a man feel heavier after meals.

There is no sanction for confining the practice of science in 13 this or another way. True, science is full of useful inventions. And its theories have often been made by men whose imagination was directed by the uses to which their age looked. Newton turned naturally to astronomy because it was the subject of his day, and it was so because finding one's way at sea had long been a practical preoccupation of the society into which he was born. It should be added, mischievously, that astronomy also had some standing because it was used very practically to cast horoscopes. (Kepler used it for this purpose; in the Thirty Years' War he cast the horoscope of Wallenstein which wonderfully told his character, and he predicted a universal disaster for 1634 which proved to be the murder of Wallenstein.)

In a setting which is more familiar, Faraday worked all his life 14 to link electricity with magnetism because this was the glittering problem of his day; and it was so because his society, like ours, was on the lookout for new sources of power. Consider a more modest example today: the new mathematical methods of automatic control, a subject sometimes called cybernetics, have been developed now because this is a time when communication and control have in effect become forms of power. These inventions have been directed by social needs, and they are useful inventions; yet it was not their usefulness which dominated and set light to the minds of those who made them. Neither Newton nor Faraday, nor yet Norbert Wiener, spent their time in a scramble for patents.

What a scientist does is compounded of two interests: the in- 15 terest of his time and his own interest. In this his behavior is no different from any other man's. The need of the age gives its shape to scientific progress as a whole. But it is not the need of the age which gives the individual scientist his sense of pleasure and of adventure, and that excitement which keeps him working late into the night when all the useful typists have gone home at five o'clock. He is personally involved in his work, as the poet is in his, and as the artist is in the painting. Paints and painting too much have been made for useful ends; and language was developed, from whatever beginnings, for practical communication. Yet you cannot have a man handle paints or language or the symbolic concepts of physics, you cannot even have him stain a microscope slide, without instantly waking in him a pleasure in the very language, a sense of exploring his own activity. This sense lies at the heart of creation.

4

The sense of personal exploration is as urgent, and as delight-   16
ful, to the practical scientist as to the theoretical. Those who think otherwise are confusing what is practical with what is humdrum. Good humdrum work without originality is done every day by everyone, theoretical scientists as well as practical, and writers and painters too, as well as truck drivers and bank clerks. Of course the unoriginal work keeps the world going; but it is not therefore the monopoly of practical men. And neither need the practical man be unoriginal. If he is to break out of what has been done before, he must bring to his own tools the same sense of pride and discovery which the poet brings to words. He cannot afford to be less radical in conceiving and less creative in designing a new turbine than a new world system.

And this is why in turn practical discoveries are not made only   17
by practical men. As the world's interest has shifted, since the Industrial Revolution, to the tapping of new springs of power, the theoretical scientist has shifted his interests too. His speculations about energy have been as abstract as once they were about astronomy; and they have been profound now as they were then, because the man loved to think. The Carnot cycle[4] and the dynamo grew equally from this love, and so did nuclear physics and the German V[5] weapons and Kelvin's interest in low temperatures. Man does not invent by following either use or tradition; he does not invent even a new form of communication by calling a conference of communication engineers. Who invented the television set? In any deep sense, it was Clerk Maxwell who foresaw the existence of radio waves, and Heinrich Hertz who proved it, and J. J. Thomson who discovered the electron. This is

4. Carnot cycle: the cycle of heat and work exchanges in an ideal steam engine, conceived by the nineteenth-century French engineer Sadi Carnot.
5. German V: the rockets with which Hitler bombarded England in World War II.

not said in order to rob any practical man of the invention, but from a sad sense of justice; for neither Maxwell nor Hertz nor J. J. Thomson would take pride in television just now.

Man masters nature not by force but by understanding. This is why science has succeeded when magic failed: because it has looked for no spell to cast over nature. The alchemist and the magician in the Middle Ages thought, and the addict of comic strips is still encouraged to think, that nature must be mastered by a device which outrages her laws. But in four hundred years since the Scientific Revolution we have learned that we gain our ends only *with* the laws of nature; we control her only by understanding her laws. We cannot even bully nature by any insistence that our work shall be designed to give power over her. We must be content that power is the byproduct of understanding. So the Greeks said that Orpheus played the lyre with such sympathy that wild beasts were tamed by the hand on the strings. They did not suggest that he got this gift by setting out to be a lion tamer.

18

5

What is the insight with which the scientist tries to see into nature? Can it indeed be called either imaginative or creative? To the literary man the question may seem merely silly. He has been taught that science is a large collection of facts; and if this is true, then the only seeing which scientists need do is, he supposes, seeing the facts. He pictures them, the colorless professionals of science, going off to work in the morning into the universe in a neutral, unexposed state. They then expose themselves like a photographic plate. And then in the darkroom or laboratory they develop the image, so that suddenly and startlingly it appears, printed in capital letters, as a new formula for atomic energy.

19

Men who have read Balzac and Zola[6] are not deceived by the claims of these writers that they do no more than record the facts. The readers of Christopher Isherwood do not take him literally when he writes "I am a camera." Yet the same readers

20

6. Honoré de Balzac (1799–1850) and Émile Zola (1840–1902) were literary realists.

solemnly carry with them from their school days this foolish picture of the scientist fixing by some mechanical process the facts of nature. I have had of all people a historian tell me that science is a collection of facts, and his voice had not even the ironic rasp of one filing cabinet reproving another.

It seems impossible that this historian had ever studied the beginnings of a scientific discovery. The Scientific Revolution can be held to begin in the year 1543 when there was brought to Copernicus, perhaps on his deathbed, the first printed copy of the book he had finished about a dozen years earlier. The thesis of this book is that the earth moves around the sun. When did Copernicus go out and record this fact with his camera? What appearance in nature prompted his outrageous guess? And in what odd sense is this guess to be called a neutral record of fact? 21

Less than a hundred years after Copernicus, Kepler published (between 1609 and 1619) the three laws which described the paths of the planets. The work of Newton and with it most of our mechanics spring from these laws. They have a solid, matter of fact sound. For example, Kepler says that if one squares the year of a planet, one gets a number which is proportional to the cube of its average distance from the sun. Does anyone think that such a law is found by taking enough readings and then squaring and cubing everything in sight? If he does, then as a scientist, he is doomed to a wasted life; he has as little prospect of making a scientific discovery as an electronic brain has. 22

It was not this way that Copernicus and Kepler thought, or that scientists think today. Copernicus found that the orbits of the planets would look simpler if they were looked at from the sun and not from the earth. But he did not in the first place find this by routine calculation. His first step was a leap of imagination—to lift himself from the earth, and put himself wildly, speculatively into the sun. "The earth conceives from the sun," he wrote; and "the sun rules the family of stars." We catch in his mind an image, the gesture of the virile man standing in the sun, with arms outstretched, overlooking the planets. Perhaps Copernicus took the picture from the drawings of the youth with outstretched arms which the Renaissance teachers put into their books on the proportions of the body. Perhaps he had seen Leonardo's drawings of his loved pupil Salai. I do not know. To me, the gesture of Copernicus, the shining youth looking outward from the sun, is still vivid in a drawing which William 23

Blake in 1780 based on all these: the drawing which is usually called *Glad Day*.

Kepler's mind, we know, was filled with just such fanciful 24 analogies; and we know what they were. Kepler wanted to relate the speeds of the planets to the musical intervals. He tried to fit the five regular solids into their orbits. None of these likenesses worked, and they have been forgotten; yet they have been and they remain the stepping stones of every creative mind. Kepler felt for his laws by way of metaphors, he searched mystically for likenesses with what he knew in every strange corner of nature. And when among these guesses he hit upon his laws, he did not think of their numbers as the balancing of a cosmic bank account, but as a revelation of the unity of all nature. To us, the analogies by which Kepler listened for the movement of the planets in the music of the spheres are farfetched. Yet are they more so than the wild leap by which Rutherford and Bohr in our own century found a model for the atom in, of all places, the planetary system?

6

No scientific theory is a collection of facts. It will not even do 25 to call a theory true or false in the simple sense in which every fact is either so or not so. The Epicureans held that matter is made of atoms two thousand years ago and we are now tempted to say that their theory was true. But if we do so we confuse their notion of matter with our own. John Dalton in 1808 first saw the structure of matter as we do today, and what he took from the ancients was not their theory but something richer, their image: the atom. Much of what was in Dalton's mind was as vague as the Greek notion, and quite as mistaken. But he suddenly gave life to the new facts of chemistry and the ancient theory together, by fusing them to give what neither had: a coherent picture of how matter is linked and built up from different kinds of atoms. The act of fusion is the creative act.

All science is the search for unity in hidden likenesses. The 26 search may be on a grand scale, as in the modern theories which try to link the fields of gravitation and electromagnetism. But we do not need to be browbeaten by the scale of science. There are discoveries to be made by snatching a small likeness from the air too, if it is bold enough. In 1935 the Japanese physicist Hideki Yukawa wrote a paper which can still give heart to a young scientist. He took as his starting point the known fact that waves of light can sometimes behave as if they were separate pellets. From this he reasoned that the forces which held the nucleus of an atom together might sometimes also be observed as if they were solid pellets. A schoolboy can see how thin Yukawa's analogy is, and his teacher would be severe with it. Yet Yukawa without a blush calculated the mass of the pellet he expected to see, and waited. He was right; his meson was found, and a range of other mesons, neither the existence nor the nature of which had been suspected before. The likeness had borne fruit.

The scientist looks for order in the appearance of nature by   27 exploring such likenesses. For order does not display itself of itself; if it can be said to be there at all, it is not there for the mere looking. There is no way of pointing a finger or a camera at it; order must be discovered and, in a deep sense, it must be created. What we see, as we see it, is mere disorder.

This point has been put trenchantly in a fable by Karl Popper.   28 Suppose that someone wished to give his whole life to science. Suppose that he therefore sat down, pencil in hand, and for the next twenty, thirty, forty years recorded in notebook after notebook everything that he could observe. He may be supposed to leave out nothing: today's humidity, the racing results, the level of cosmic radiation and the stock-market prices and the look of Mars, all would be there. He would have compiled the most careful record of nature that has ever been made; and, dying in the calm certainty of a life well spent, he would of course leave his notebooks to the Royal Society. Would the Royal Society thank him for the treasure of a lifetime of observation? It would not. The Royal Society would treat his notebooks exactly as the English bishops have treated Joanna Southcott's box.[7] It would refuse to open them at all, because it would know without looking that the notebooks contain only a jumble of disorderly and meaningless items.

---

7. Joanna Southcott (1750–1814) claimed to have transcribed divinely inspired messages concerning the Second Coming of Christ. At her death she left a locked box, instructing that it should be opened in the presence of all the bishops in a time of national emergency. It was opened, in the presence of one bishop, in 1928; nothing in it was deemed of interest, which further convinced the English religious establishment that she had merely been a crank.

7

Science finds order and meaning in our experience, and sets   29
about this in quite a different way. It sets about it as Newton did
in the story which he himself told in his old age, and of which the
schoolbooks give only a caricature. In the year 1665, when Newton was twenty-two, the plague broke out in southern England,
and the University of Cambridge was closed. Newton therefore
spent the next eighteen months at home, removed from traditional learning, at a time when he was impatient for knowledge
and, in his own phrase, "I was in the prime of my age for invention." In this eager, boyish mood, sitting one day in the garden of
his widowed mother, he saw an apple fall. So far the books have
the story right; we think we even know the kind of apple; tradition has it that it was a Flower of Kent. But now they miss the
crux of the story. For what struck the young Newton at the sight
was not the thought that the apple must be drawn to the earth by
gravity; that conception was older than Newton. What struck
him was the conjecture that the same force of gravity, which
reaches to the top of the tree, might go on reaching out beyond
the earth and its air, endlessly into space. Gravity might reach the
moon: this was Newton's new thought; and it might be gravity
which holds the moon in her orbit. There and then he calculated
what force from the earth (falling off as the square of the distance) would hold the moon, and compared it with the known
force of gravity at tree height. The forces agreed; Newton says
laconically, "I found them answer pretty nearly." Yet they agreed
only nearly: the likeness and the approximation go together, for
no likeness is exact. In Newton's sentence modern science is full
grown.

It grows from a comparison. It has seized a likeness between   30
two unlike appearances; for the apple in the summer garden and
the grave moon overhead are surely as unlike in their movements
as two things can be. Newton traced in them two expressions of
a single concept, gravitation: and the concept (and the unity) are
in that sense his free creation. The progress of science is the discovery at each step of a new order which gives unity to what had
long seemed unlike. Faraday did this when he closed the link between electricity and magnetism. Clerk Maxwell did it when he
linked both with light. Einstein linked time with space, mass
with energy, and the path of light past the sun with the flight of

a bullet; and spent his dying years in trying to add to these likenesses another, which would find a single imaginative order between the equations of Clerk Maxwell and his own geometry of gravitation.

8

When Coleridge tried to define beauty, he returned always to   31
one deep thought: beauty, he said, is "unity in variety." Science is
nothing else than the search to discover unity in the wild variety
of nature—or more exactly, in the variety of our experience. Poetry, painting, the arts are the same search, in Coleridge's phrase,
for unity in variety. Each in his own way looks for likenesses under the variety of human experience. What is a poetic image but
the seizing and the exploration of a hidden likeness, in holding
together two parts of a comparison which are to give depth each
to the other? When Romeo finds Juliet in the tomb, and thinks
her dead, he uses in his heartbreaking speech the words,

> *Death that hath suckt the honey of thy breath.*

The critic can only haltingly take to pieces the single shock
which this image carries. The young Shakespeare admired Marlowe, and Marlowe's Faustus had said of the ghostly kiss of Helen
of Troy that it sucked forth his soul. But that is a pale image; what
Shakespeare has done is to fire it with the single word honey.
Death is a bee at the lips of Juliet, and the bee is an insect that
stings; the sting of death was a commonplace phrase when
Shakespeare wrote. The sting is there, under the image; Shakespeare has packed it into the word honey; but the very word
rides powerfully over its own undertones. Death is a bee that
stings other people, but it comes to Juliet as if she were a flower;
this is the moving thought under the instant image. The creative
mind speaks in such thoughts.

The poetic image here is also, and accidentally, heightened by   32
the tenderness which town dwellers now feel for country ways.
But it need not be; there are likenesses to conjure with, and
images as powerful, within the man-made world. The poems of
Alexander Pope belong to this world. They are not countrified,
and therefore readers today find them unemotional and often ar-

tificial. Let me then quote Pope: here he is in a formal satire face to face, towards the end of his life, with his own gifts. In eight lines he looks poignantly forward towards death and back to the laborious years which made him famous.

Years foll'wing Years, steal something ev'ry day,
At last they steal us from our selves away;
In one our Frolicks, one Amusements end,
In one a Mistress drops, in one a Friend:
This subtle Thief of Life, this paltry Time,
What will it leave me, if it snatch my Rhime?
If ev'ry Wheel of that unweary'd Mill
That turn'd ten thousand Verses, now stands still.

The human mind had been compared to what the eighteenth century called a mill, that is to a machine, before; Pope's own idol Bolingbroke had compared it to a clockwork. In these lines the likeness goes deeper, for Pope is thinking of the ten thousand Verses which he had translated from Homer: what he says is sad and just at the same time, because this really had been a mechanical and at times a grinding task. Yet the clockwork is present in the image too; when the wheels stand still, time for Pope will stand still for ever; we feel that we already hear, over the horizon, Faust's defiant reply to Mephistopheles, which Goethe had not yet written—"let the clock strike and stop, let the hand fall, and time be at an end."

Werd ich zum Augenblicke sagen:
Verweile doch! du bist so schön!
Dann magst du mich in Fesseln schlagen,
Dann will ich gern zugrunde gehn!
Dann mag die Totenglocke schallen,
Dann bist du deines Dienstes frei,
Die Uhr mag stehn, der Zeiger fallen
Es sei die Zeit für mich vorbei![8]

I have quoted Pope and Goethe because their metaphor here   33
is not poetic; it is rather a hand reaching straight into experience and arranging it with new meaning. Metaphors of this kind need

8. "If ever I say to the passing moment: / Stay a while! Thou art so fair! / Then may you cast me into chains, / Then will I gladly perish! / Then may the death-bell toll, / Then are you freed from my service, / Let the clock strike and stop, let the hand fall / and time be at an end!" (German)

not always be written in words. The most powerful of them all is simply the presence of King Lear and his Fool in the hovel of a man who is shamming madness, while lightning rages outside.[9] Or let me quote another clash of two conceptions of life, from a modern poet. In his later poems W. B. Yeats was troubled by the feeling that in shutting himself up to write, he was missing the active pleasures of life; and yet it seemed to him certain that the man who lives for these pleasures will leave no lasting work behind him. He said this at times very simply, too:

> The intellect of man is forced to choose
> Perfection of the life, or of the work.

This problem, whether a man fulfills himself in word or in play, is of course more common than Yeats allowed; and it may be more commonplace. But it is given breadth and force by the images in which Yeats pondered it.

> Get all the gold and silver that you can,
> Satisfy ambition, or animate
> The trivial days and ram them with the sun,
> And yet upon these maxims meditate:
> All women dote upon an idle man
> Although their children need a rich estate;
> No man has ever lived that had enough
> Of children's gratitude or woman's love.

The love of women, the gratitude of children: the images fix two philosophies as nothing else can. They are tools of creative thought, as coherent and as exact as the conceptual images with which science works: as time and space, or as the proton and the neutron.

9

The discoveries of science, the works of art are explorations— more, are explosions, of a hidden likeness. The discoverer or the artist presents in them two aspects of nature and fuses them into one. This is the act of creation, in which an original thought is

34

9. In Act III, scene iv of Shakespeare's *King Lear*, psychological, moral, familial, and political disorder all find a metaphor in the storm that batters these three vulnerable men.

born, and it is the same act in original science and original art. But it is not therefore the monopoly of the man who wrote the poem or who made the discovery. On the contrary, I believe this view of the creative act to be right because it alone gives a meaning to the act of appreciation. The poem or the discovery exists in two moments of vision: the moment of appreciation as much as that of creation; for the appreciator must see the movement, wake to the echo which was started in the creation of the work. In the moment of appreciation we live again the moment when the creator saw and held the hidden likeness. When a simile takes us aback and persuades us together, when we find a juxtaposition in a picture both odd and intriguing, when a theory is at once fresh and convincing, we do not merely nod over someone else's work. We re-enact the creative act, and we ourselves make the discovery again. At bottom, there is no unifying likeness there until we too have seized it, we too have made it for ourselves.

How slipshod by comparison is the notion that either art or science sets out to copy nature. If the task of the painter were to copy for men what they see, the critic could make only a single judgment: either that the copy is right or that it is wrong. And if science were a copy of fact, then every theory would be either right or wrong, and would be so for ever. There would be nothing left for us to say but this is so, or is not so. No one who has read a page by a good critic or a speculative scientist can ever again think that this barren choice of yes or no is all that the mind offers. 35

Reality is not an exhibit for man's inspection, labelled "Do not touch." There are no appearances to be photographed, no experiences to be copied, in which we do not take part. Science, like art, is not a copy of nature but a re-creation of her. We remake nature by the act of discovery, in the poem or in the theorem. And the great poem and the deep theorem are new to every reader, and yet are his own experiences, because he himself re-creates them. They are the mark of unity in variety; and in the instant when the mind seizes this for itself, in art or in science, the heart misses a beat. 36

WILLIAM G. PERRY JR.

Examsmanship and the Liberal Arts

For many years William G. Perry Jr. was associated with the Bureau of Study Counsel at Harvard University, where he combined the role of a counseling psychologist with that of teacher of reading and studying skills. This practical work with students connected naturally with his academic research on the gradual maturation of students' thinking during the college years. "Examsmanship and the Liberal Arts," first published in *Examining at Harvard College* (1967), grew out of a five-year study in which Perry interviewed students to learn why some thrived at Harvard, while others of equal intelligence were unsuccessful and unhappy there.

"But sir, I don't think I really deserve it, it was mostly bull,   1
really." This disclaimer from a student whose examination we have awarded a straight "A" is wondrously depressing. Alfred North Whitehead invented its only possible rejoinder: "Yes sir, what you wrote is nonsense, utter nonsense. But ah! Sir! It's the right *kind* of nonsense!"

Bull, in this university, is customarily a source of laughter, or   2
a problem in ethics. I shall step a little out of fashion to use the subject as a take-off point for a study in comparative epistemology. The phenomenon of bull, in all the honor and opprobrium with which it is regarded by students and faculty, says something, I think, about our theories of knowledge. So too, the grades which we assign on examinations communicate to students what these theories may be.

We do not have to be out-and-out logical-positivists[1] to sup-   3
pose that we have something to learn about "what we think knowledge is" by having a good look at "what we do when we go about measuring it." We know the straight "A" examination

1. Logical positivists like Bertrand Russell (1872–1970) insist that philosophical speculation be tightly checked by reference to the "positive" data of experience. This position links them to the psychological behaviorists.

when we see it, of course, and we have reason to hope that the student will understand why his work receives our recognition. He doesn't always. And those who receive lesser honor? Perhaps an understanding of certain anomalies in our customs of grading good bull will explain the students' confusion.

I must beg patience, then, both of the reader's humor and of   4
his morals. Not that I ask him to suspend his sense of humor but that I shall ask him to go beyond it. In a great university the picture of a bright student attempting to outwit his professor while his professor takes pride in not being outwitted is certainly ridiculous. I shall report just such a scene, for its implications bear upon my point. Its comedy need not present a serious obstacle to thought.

As for the ethics of bull, I must ask for a suspension of judg-   5
ment. I wish that students could suspend theirs. Unlike humor, moral commitment is hard to think beyond. Too early a moral judgment is precisely what stands between many able students and a liberal education. The stunning realization that the Harvard Faculty will often accept, as evidence of knowledge, the cerebrations of a student who has little data at his disposal, confronts every student with an ethical dilemma. For some it forms an academic focus for what used to be thought of as "adolescent disillusion." It is irrelevant that rumor inflates the phenomenon to mythical proportions. The students know that beneath the myth there remains a solid and haunting reality. The moral "bind" consequent on this awareness appears most poignantly in serious students who are reluctant to concede the competitive advantage to the bullster and who yet feel a deep personal shame when, having succumbed to "temptation," they themselves receive a high grade for work they consider "dishonest."

I have spent many hours with students caught in this unwel-   6
come bitterness. These hours lend an urgency to my theme. I have found that students have been able to come to terms with the ethical problem, to the extent that it is real, only after a refined study of the true nature of bull and its relation to "knowledge." I shall submit grounds for my suspicion that we can be found guilty of sharing the student's confusion of moral and epistemological issues.

I

I present as my "premise," then, an amoral *fabliau*. Its hero-   7
villain is the Abominable Mr. Metzger '47. Since I celebrate his
virtuosity, I regret giving him a pseudonym, but the peculiar style
of his bravado requires me to honor also his modesty. Bull in
pure form is rare; there is usually some contamination by data.
The community has reason to be grateful to Mr. Metzger for
having created an instance of laboratory purity, free from any
adulteration by matter. The more credit is due him, I think, because his act was free from premeditation, deliberation, or hope
of personal gain.

Mr. Metzger stood one rainy November day in the lobby of   8
Memorial Hall. A junior, concentrating in mathematics, he was
fond of diverting himself by taking part in the drama, a penchant
which may have had some influence on the events of the next
hour. He was waiting to take part in a rehearsal in Sanders Theatre, but, as sometimes happens, no other players appeared. Perhaps the rehearsal had been canceled without his knowledge? He
decided to wait another five minutes.

Students, meanwhile, were filing into the Great Hall opposite,   9
and taking seats at the testing tables. Spying a friend crossing the
lobby toward the Great Hall's door, Metzger greeted him and extended appropriate condolences. He inquired, too, what course
his friend was being tested in. "Oh, Soc. Sci. something-or-
other." "What's it all about?" asked Metzger, and this, as Homer
remarked of Patroclus, was the beginning of evil for him.

"It's about Modern Perspectives on Man and Society and All   10
That," said his friend. "Pretty interesting, really."

"Always wanted to take a course like that," said Metzger.   11
"Any good reading?"

"Yeah, great. There's this book"—his friend did not have time   12
to finish.

"Take your seats please" said a stern voice beside them. The   13
idle conversation had somehow taken the two friends to one of
the tables in the Great Hall. Both students automatically obeyed;
the proctor put blue books before them; another proctor presented them with copies of the printed hour-test.

Mr. Metzger remembered afterwards a brief misgiving that   14
was suddenly overwhelmed by a surge of curiosity and puckish

glee. He wrote "George Smith" on the blue book, opened it, and addressed the first question.

I must pause to exonerate the Management. The Faculty has 15 a rule that no student may attend an examination in a course in which he is not enrolled. To the wisdom of this rule the outcome of this deplorable story stands witness. The Registrar, charged with the enforcement of the rule, has developed an organization with procedures which are certainly the finest to be devised. In November, however, class rosters are still shaky, and on this particular day another student, named Smith, was absent. As for the culprit, we can reduce his guilt no further than to suppose that he was ignorant of the rule, or, in the face of the momentous challenge before him, forgetful.

We need not be distracted by Metzger's performance on the 16 "objective" or "spot" questions on the test. His D on these sections can be explained by those versed in the theory of probability. Our interest focuses on the quality of his essay. It appears that when Metzger's friend picked up his own blue book a few days later, he found himself in company with a large proportion of his section in having received on the essay a C. When he quietly picked up "George Smith's" blue book to return it to Metzger, he observed that the grade for the essay was A. In the margin was a note in the section man's hand. It read "Excellent work. Could you have pinned these observations down a bit more closely? Compare . . . in . . . pp. . . . ."

Such news could hardly be kept quiet. There was a leak, and 17 the whole scandal broke on the front page of Tuesday's *Crimson*. With the press Metzger was modest, as becomes a hero. He said that there had been nothing to it at all, really. The essay question had offered a choice of two books, Margaret Mead's *And Keep Your Powder Dry* or Geoffrey Gorer's *The American People*. Metzger reported that having read neither of them, he had chosen the second "because the title gave me some notion as to what the book might be about." On the test, two critical comments were offered on each book, one favorable, one unfavorable. The students were asked to "discuss." Metzger conceded that he had played safe in throwing his lot with the most laudatory of the two comments, "but I did not forget to be balanced."

I do not have Mr. Metzger's essay before me except in vivid 18 memory. As I recall, he took his first cue from the name Geoffrey, and committed his strategy to the premise that Gorer was born into an "Anglo-Saxon" culture, probably English, but certainly "English speaking." Having heard that Margaret Mead was a social anthropologist, he inferred that Gorer was the same. He then entered upon his essay, centering his inquiry upon what he supposed might be the problems inherent in an anthropologist's observation of a culture which was his own, or nearly his own. Drawing in part from memories of table-talk on cultural relativity[2] and in part from creative logic, he rang changes on the relation of observer to observed, and assessed the kind and degree of objectivity which might accrue to an observer through training as an anthropologist. He concluded that the book in question did in fact contribute a considerable range of "'objective,' and even 'fresh,'" insights into the nature of our culture. "At the same time," he warned, "these observations must be understood within the context of their generation by a person only partly freed from his embeddedness in the culture he is observing, and limited in his capacity to transcend those particular tendencies and biases which he has himself developed as a personality in his interaction with this culture since his birth. In this sense the book portrays as much the character of Geoffrey Gorer as it analyzes that of the American people." It is my regrettable duty to report that at this moment of triumph Mr. Metzger was carried away by the temptations of parody and added, "We are thus much the richer."

In any case, this was the essay for which Metzger received his 19 honor grade and his public acclaim. He was now, of course, in serious trouble with the authorities.

I shall leave him for the moment to the mercy of the Adminis- 20 trative Board of Harvard College and turn the reader's attention to the section man who ascribed the grade. He was in much worse trouble. All the consternation in his immediate area of the Faculty and all the glee in other areas fell upon his unprotected head. I shall now undertake his defense.

I do so not simply because I was acquainted with him and feel 21 a respect for his intelligence; I believe in the justice of his grade! Well, perhaps "justice" is the wrong word in a situation so man-

2. "An important part of Harvard's education takes place during meals in the Houses." An Official Publication. [author's note] Houses are dormitories for upper-division students.

ifestly absurd. This is more a case in "equity." That is, the grade is equitable if we accept other aspects of the situation which are equally absurd. My proposition is this: if we accept as valid those C grades which were accorded students who, like Metzger's friend, demonstrated a thorough familiarity with the details of the book without relating their critique to the methodological problems of social anthropology, then "George Smith" deserved not only the same, but better.

The reader may protest that the C's given to students who   22
showed evidence only of diligence were indeed not valid and that both these students and "George Smith" should have received E's. To give the diligent E is of course not in accord with custom. I shall take up this matter later. For now, were I to allow the protest, I could only restate my thesis: that "George Smith's" E would, in a college of liberal arts, be properly a "better" E.

At this point I need a short-hand. It is a curious fact that there   23
is no academic slang for the presentation of evidence of diligence alone. "Parroting" won't do; it is possible to "parrot" bull. I must beg the reader's pardon, and, for reasons almost too obvious to bear, suggest "cow."

Stated as nouns, the concepts look simple enough: 24

cow (pure): data, however relevant, without relevancies.
bull (pure): relevancies, however relevant, without data.

The reader can see all too clearly where this simplicity would   25
lead. I can assure him that I would not have imposed on him this way were I aiming to say that knowledge in this university is definable as some neuter compromise between cow and bull, some infertile hermaphrodite. This is precisely what many diligent students seem to believe: that what they must learn to do is to "find the right mean" between "amounts" of detail and "amounts" of generalities. Of course this is not the point at all. The problem is not quantitative, nor does its solution lie on a continuum between the particular and the general. Cow and bull are not poles of a single dimension. A clear notion of what they really are is essential to my inquiry, and for heuristic purposes I wish to observe them further in the celibate state.

When the pure concepts are translated into verbs, their com-   26
plexities become apparent in the assumptions and purposes of the students as they write:

To cow (*v. intrans.*) or the act of cowing:
    To list data (or perform operations) without awareness of, or
comment upon, the contexts, frames of reference, or points of observation which determine the origin, nature, and meaning of the data
(or procedures). To write on the assumption that "a fact is a fact."
To present evidence of hard work as a substitute for understanding,
without any intent to deceive.

To bull (*v. intrans.*) or the act of bulling:
    To discourse upon the contexts, frames of reference and points of
observation which would determine the origin, nature, and meaning
of data if one had any. To present evidence of an understanding of
form in the hope that the reader may be deceived into supposing a familiarity with content.

At the level of conscious intent, it is evident that cowing is   27
more moral, or less immoral, than bulling. To speculate about
unconscious intent would be either an injustice or a needless
elaboration of my theme. It is enough that the impression left by
cow is one of earnestness, diligence, and painful naiveté. The
grader may feel disappointment or even irritation, but these feelings are usually balanced by pity, compassion, and a reluctance to
hit a man when he's both down and moral. He may feel some challenge to his teaching, but none whatever to his one-ups-manship.
He writes in the margin: "See me."

We are now in a position to understand the anomaly of cus-   28
tom: As instructors, we always assign bull an E, *when we detect
it;* whereas we usually give a cow a C, *even though it is always
obvious.*

After all, we did not ask to be confronted with a choice be-   29
tween morals and understanding (or did we?). We evince a
charming humanity, I think, in our decision to grade in favor of
morals and pathos. "I simply *can't* give this student an E after he
has *worked* so hard." At the same time we tacitly express our respect for the bullster's strength. We recognize a colleague. If he
knows so well how to dish it out, we can be sure that he can also
take it.

Of course it is just possible that we carry with us, perhaps   30
from our own school-days, an assumption that if a student is
willing to work hard and collect "good hard facts" he can always be taught to understand their relevance, whereas a student
who has caught onto the forms of relevance without working at
all is a lost scholar.

But this is not in accord with our experience.   31

It is not in accord either, as far as I can see, with the stated   32
values of a liberal education. If a liberal education should teach
students "how to think," not only in their own fields but in fields
outside their own—that is, to understand "how the other fellow
orders knowledge," then bulling, even in its purest form, expresses an important part of what a pluralist university holds
dear, surely a more important part than the collecting of "facts
that are facts" which schoolboys learn to do. Here then, good
bull appears not as ignorance at all but as an aspect of knowledge. It is both relevant and "true." In a university setting good
bull is therefore of more value than "facts," which, without a
frame of reference, are not even "true" at all.

Perhaps this value accounts for the final anomaly: as instructors,   33
we are inclined to reward bull highly, *where we do not detect its
intent,* to the consternation of the bullster's acquaintances. And
often we do not examine the matter too closely. After a long
evening of reading blue books full of cow, the sudden meeting
with a student who at least understands the problems of one's
field provides a lift like a draught of refreshing wine, and a
strong disposition toward trust.

This was, then, the sense of confidence that came to our un-   34
fortunate section man as he read "George Smith's" sympathetic
considerations.

II

In my own years of watching over students' shoulders as they   35
work, I have come to believe that this feeling of trust has a firmer
basis than the confidence generated by evidence of diligence
alone. I believe that the theory of a liberal education holds. Students who have dared to understand man's real relation to his
knowledge have shown themselves to be in a strong position to
learn content rapidly and meaningfully, and to retain it. I have
learned to be less concerned about the education of a student
who has come to understand the nature of man's knowledge,
even though he has not yet committed himself to hard work,
than I am about the education of the student who, after one or
two terms at Harvard, is working desperately hard and still believes that collected "facts" constitute knowledge. The latter,

when I try to explain to him, too often understands me to be saying that he "doesn't *put in enough generalities.*" Surely he has "put in *enough* facts."

I have come to see such quantitative statements as expressions   36
of an entire, coherent epistemology. In grammar school the student is taught that Columbus discovered America in 1492. The *more* such items he gets "right" on a given test the more he is credited with "knowing." From years of this sort of thing it is not unnatural to develop the conviction that knowledge consists of the accretion of hard facts by hard work.

The student learns that the more facts and procedures he can   37
get "right" in a given course, the better will be his grade. The more courses he takes, the more subjects he has "had," the more credits he accumulates, the more diplomas he will get, until, after graduate school, he will emerge with his doctorate, a member of the community of scholars.

The foundation of this entire life is the proposition that a fact   38
is a fact. The necessary correlate of this proposition is that a fact is either right or wrong. This implies that the standard against which the rightness or wrongness of a fact may be judged exists *someplace*—perhaps graven upon a tablet in a Platonic world outside and above *this* cave of tears. In grammar school it is evident that the tablets which enshrine the spelling of a word or the answer to an arithmetic problem are visible to my teacher who need only compare my offerings to it. In high school I observe that my English teachers disagree. This can only mean that the tablets in such matters as the goodness of a poem are distant and obscured by clouds. They surely exist. The pleasing of befuddled English teachers degenerates into assessing their prejudices, a game in which I have no protection against my competitors more glib of tongue. I respect only my science teachers, authorities who *really know.* Later I learn from them that "this is only what we think *now.*" But eventually, surely . . . Into this epistemology of education, apparently shared by teachers in such terms as "credits," "semester hours" and "years of French," the student may invest his ideals, his drive, his competitiveness, his safety, his self-esteem, and even his love.

College raises other questions: by whose calendar is it proper   39
to say that Columbus discovered America in 1492? How, when, and by whom was the year 1 established in this calendar? What of other calendars? In view of the evidence for Leif Ericson's pre-

vious visit (and the American Indians), what historical ethnocentrism is suggested by the use of the word "discover" in this sentence? As for Leif Ericson, in accord with what assumptions do you order the evidence?

These questions and their answers are not "more" knowledge. 40 They are devastation. I do not need to elaborate upon the epistemology, or rather epistemologies, they imply. A fact has become at last "an observation or an operation performed in a frame of reference." A liberal education is founded in an awareness of frame of reference even in the most immediate and empirical examination of data. Its acquirement involves relinquishing hope of absolutes and of the protection they afford against doubt and the glib-tongued competitor. It demands an ever widening sophistication about systems of thought and observation. It leads, not away from him, but *through* the arts of gamesmanship to a new trust.

This trust is in the value and integrity of systems, their varied 41 character, and the way their apparently incompatible metaphors enlighten, from complementary facets, the particulars of human experience. As one student said to me: "I used to be cynical about intellectual games. Now I want to know them thoroughly. You see I came to realize that it was only when I knew the rules of the game cold that I could tell whether what I was saying was tripe."

We too often think of the bullster as cynical. He can be, and 42 not always in a light-hearted way. We have failed to observe that there can lie behind cow the potential of a deeper and more dangerous despair. The moralism of sheer work and obedience can be an ethic that, unwilling to face a despair of its ends, glorifies its means. The implicit refusal to consider the relativity of both ends and means leaves the operator in an unconsidered proprietary absolutism. History bears witness that in the pinches this moral superiority has no recourse to negotiation, only to force.

A liberal education proposes that man's hope lies elsewhere: 43 in the negotiability that can arise from an understanding of the integrity of systems and of their origins in man's address to his universe. The prerequisite is the courage to accept such a definition of knowledge. From then on, of course, there is nothing incompatible between such an epistemology and hard work. Rather the contrary.

I can now at last let bull and cow get together. The reader   44
knows best how a productive wedding is arranged in his own
field. This is the nuptial he celebrates with a straight A on examinations. The masculine context must embrace the feminine
particular, though itself "born of woman." Such a union is
knowledge itself, and it alone can generate new contexts and
new data which can unite in their turn to form new knowledge.

In this happy setting we can congratulate in particular the   45
Natural Sciences, long thought to be barren ground to the bullster. I have indeed drawn my examples of bull from the Social
Sciences, and by analogy from the Humanities. Essay-writing in
these fields has long been thought to nurture the art of bull to its
prime. I feel, however, that the Natural Sciences have no reason
to feel slighted. It is perhaps no accident that Metzger was a
mathematician. As part of my researches for this paper, furthermore, a student of considerable talent has recently honored me
with an impressive analysis of the art of amassing "partial credits" on examinations in advanced physics. Though beyond me in
some respects, his presentation confirmed my impression that instructors of Physics frequently honor on examinations opera-
tions structurally similar to those requisite in a good essay.

The very qualities that make the Natural Sciences fields of de-   46
light for the eager gamesman have been essential to their marvelous fertility.

III

As priests of these mysteries, how can we make our rites more   47
precisely expressive? The student who merely cows robs himself,
without knowing it, of his education and his soul. The student
who only bulls robs himself, as he knows full well, of the joys of
inductive discovery—that is, of engagement. The introduction of
frames of reference in the new curricula of Mathematics and
Physics in the schools is a hopeful experiment. We do not know
yet how much of these potent revelations the very young can
stand, but I suspect they may rejoice in them more than we have
supposed. I can't believe they have never wondered about Leif
Ericson and that word "discovered," or even about 1492. They
have simply been too wise to inquire.

Increasingly in recent years better students in the better high schools and preparatory schools are being allowed to inquire. In fact they appear to be receiving both encouragement and training in their inquiry. I have the evidence before me. [48]

Each year for the past five years all freshmen entering Harvard and Radcliffe have been asked in freshman week to "grade" two essays answering an examination question in History. They are then asked to give their reasons for their grades. One essay, filled with dates, is 99% cow. The other, with hardly a date in it, is a good essay, easily mistaken for bull. The "official" grades of these essays are, for the first (alas!) C "because he has worked so hard," and for the second (soundly, I think) B. Each year a larger majority of freshmen evaluate these essays as would the majority of the faculty, and for the faculty's reasons, and each year a smaller minority give the higher honor to the essay offering data alone. Most interesting, a larger number of students each year, while not overrating the second essay, award the first the straight E appropriate to it in a college of liberal arts. [49]

For us who must grade such students in a university, these developments imply a new urgency, did we not feel it already. Through our grades we describe for the students, in the showdown, what we believe about the nature of knowledge. The subtleties of bull are not peripheral to our academic concerns. That they penetrate to the center of our care is evident in our feelings when a student whose good work we have awarded a high grade reveals to us that he does not feel he deserves it. Whether he disqualifies himself because "there's too much bull in it," or worse because "I really don't think I've worked that hard," he presents a serious educational problem. Many students feel this sleaziness; only a few reveal it to us. [50]

We can hardly allow a mistaken sense of fraudulence to undermine our students' achievements. We must lead students beyond their concept of bull so that they may honor relevancies that are really relevant. We can willingly acknowledge that, in lieu of the date 1492, a consideration of calendars and of the word "discovered," may well be offered with intent to deceive. We must insist that this does not make such considerations intrinsically immoral, and that, contrariwise, the date 1492 may be no substitute for them. Most of all, we must convey the impression that we grade understanding qua understanding. To be [51] convincing, I suppose we must concede to ourselves in advance that a bright student's understanding is understanding even if he achieved it by osmosis rather than by hard work in our course.

These are delicate matters. As for cow, its complexities are not   52
what need concern us. Unlike good bull, it does not represent partial knowledge at all. It belongs to a different theory of knowledge entirely. In our theories of knowledge it represents total ignorance, or worse yet, a knowledge downright inimical to understanding. I even go so far as to propose that we award no more C's for cow. To do so is rarely, I feel, the act of mercy it seems. Mercy lies in clarity.

The reader may be afflicted by a lingering curiosity about the   53
fate of Mr. Metzger. I hasten to reassure him. The Administrative Board of Harvard College, whatever its satanic reputation, is a benign body. Its members, to be sure, were on the spot. They delighted in Metzger's exploit, but they were responsible to the Faculty's rule. The hero stood in danger of probation. The debate was painful. Suddenly one member, of a refined legalistic sensibility, observed that the rule applied specifically to "examinations" and that the occasion had been simply an hour-test. Mr. Metzger was merely "admonished."

VINCENT G. DETHIER

Extracting Information from a Fly

An expert on insect physiology and behavior, Vincent Dethier was a distinguished research scientist who taught at such institutions as Princeton and Johns Hopkins. Most of his publications were, of course, written for other scientists in his field, but he wrote three successful books about science for the general public, including *To Know a Fly* (1962), from which the following chapter is taken. As a reviewer for the *Journal of the American Medical Association* noted, *To Know a Fly*, though disarmingly easy to read, is full of acute observations about the methods of scientific experimentation.

A properly conducted experiment is a beautiful thing. It is 1
an adventure, an expedition, a conquest. It commences with an
act of faith, faith that the world is real, that our senses generally
can be trusted, that effects have causes, and that we can discover meaning by reason. It continues with an observation and a
question. An experiment is a scientist's way of asking nature a
question. He alters a condition, observes a result, and draws
a conclusion. It is no game for a disorderly mind (although the
ranks of Science are replete with confused thinkers). There are
many ways of going astray. The mention of two will suffice.

The most commonly committed scientific sin is the lack of 2
proper experimental control. The scientist must be certain that
the result he obtains is a consequence of the specific alteration he
introduced and not of some other coincidental one. There is the
case of the gentleman who had trained a flea to leap at the command "Jump!"

"Now," said the clever gentleman, "I shall do an experiment 3
to discover where the flea's ears are located. First I shall ampu-
tate his feelers." Whereupon, the operation having been completed and the flea having recovered, the command "Jump!" was
given. The flea jumped. "Ah," said the gentleman obviously
pleased, "he does not hear with his antennae. I shall now ampu-
tate his forelegs." With each succeeding operation the flea leaped
on command until only the hindmost legs remained. When they
were removed, the flea failed to jump. "You see," concluded the
gentleman triumphantly, "he hears with his hind legs."

Or there is the well-known case of the chap who wondered 4
which component of his mixed drink caused his inevitable in-
toxication. He tried bourbon and water, rum and water, scotch
and water, rye and water, gin and water and concluded, since
every drink had water as a constant, that water caused his
drunkenness. He then gritted his teeth and tried water alone—
with negative results. When I last saw him he had concluded that
the glass was the intoxicating agent, and he was about to begin
another series of experiments employing paper cups.

Of course even controls can be carried to absurd extremes 5
as in the case of the atheistic scientist who seized upon the
opportunity afforded by the birth of twins to test the efficacy of
religion. He had one baby baptized and kept the other as a
control.

Another common fallacy is that of confusing correlation with　6
cause and effect. This is exemplified by the case of the gentleman
who was extricated from the rubble of an apartment house immediately after an earthquake. "Do you know what happened?"
his rescuers inquired.

"I am not certain," replied the survivor. "I remember pulling　7
down the window shade and it caused the whole building to
collapse."

The kind of question asked of nature is a measure of a scien-　8
tist's intellectual stature. Too many research workers have no
questions at all to ask, but this does not deter them from doing
experiments. They become enamored of a new instrument, acquire it, then ask only "What can I do with this beauty?" Others
ask such questions as "How many leaves are there this year on
the ivy on the zoology building?" And having counted them do
not know what to do with the information. But some questions
can be useful and challenging. And meaningful questions can be
asked of a fly.

Between the fly and the biologist, however, there is a language　9
barrier that makes getting direct answers to questions difficult.
With a human subject it is only necessary to ask: what color is
this? does that hurt? are you hungry? The human subject may, of
course, lie; the fly cannot. However, to elicit information from
him it is necessary to resort to all kinds of trickery and legerde-
main. This means pitting one's brain against that of the fly—a
risk some people are unwilling to assume. But then, experimentation is only for the adventuresome, for the dreamers, for the
brave.

It is risky even at higher levels. I am reminded of the eminent　10
professor who had designed experiments to test an ape's capacity to use tools. A banana was hung from a string just out of
reach. An assortment of tools, that is, boxes to pile up, bamboo
poles to fit together, etc., were provided, and the ape's ability was
to be judged by his choice of method. To the chagrin of the professor, the ape chose a method that had never even occurred to
that learned gentleman.

Extracting information from a fly can be equally challenging.　11
Take the question of taste, for example. Does a fly possess a
sense of taste? Is it similar to ours? How sensitive is it? What
does he prefer?

The first fruitful experimental approach to this problem be-   12
gan less than fifty years ago with a very shrewd observation;
namely, that flies (and bees and butterflies) walked about in their
food and constantly stuck out their tongues. The next time you
dine with a fly (and modern sanitary practice has not greatly diminished the opportunities), observe his behavior when he
gavots across the top of the custard pie. His proboscis, which is
normally carried retracted into his head like the landing gear of
an airplane, will be lowered, and like a miniature vacuum
cleaner he will suck in food. For a striking demonstration of this,
mix some sugared water and food coloring and paint a sheet of
paper. The first fly to find it will leave a beautiful trail of lip
prints, hardly the kind suitable for lipstick ads but nonetheless
instructive.

Proboscis extension has been seen thousands of times by   13
thousands of people but few have been either struck by the sanitary aspects of the act or ingenious enough to figure out how
they might put the observation to use to learn about fly behavior.

The brilliant idea conceived by the biologist who first specu-   14
lated on why some insects paraded around in their food was that
they tasted with their feet. In retrospect it is the simplest thing in
the world to test this idea. It also makes a fine parlor trick for
even the most blasé gathering.

The first step is to provide a fly with a handle since Nature   15
failed to do so. Procure a stick about the size of a lead pencil. (A
lead pencil will do nicely. So will an applicator stick, the kind
that a physician employs when swabbing a throat.) Dip one
end repeatedly into candle wax or paraffin until a fly-sized gob
accumulates. Next anaesthetize a fly. The least messy method
is to deposit him in the freezing compartment of a refrigerator
for several minutes. Then, working very rapidly, place him back-
side down on the wax and seal his wings onto it with a hot
needle.

Now for the experimental proof. Lower the fly gently over a   16
saucer of water until his feet just touch. Chances are he is thirsty.
If so, he will lower his proboscis as soon as his feet touch and
will suck avidly. When thirst has been allayed, the proboscis will
be retracted compactly into the head. This is a neat arrangement
because a permanently extended proboscis might flop about uncomfortably during flight or be trod upon while walking.

Next, lower the fly into a saucer of sugared water. In a frac-   17
tion of a second the proboscis is flicked out again. Put him back
into water (this is the control), and the proboscis is retracted.
Water, in; sugar, out. The performance continues almost indefinitely. Who can doubt that the fly can taste with his feet? The
beauty of this proboscis response, as it is called, is that it is a reflex action, almost as automatic as a knee jerk. By taking advantage of its automatism, one can learn very subtle things about a
fly's sense of taste.

For example, who has the more acute sense of taste, you or   18
the fly? As the cookbooks say, take ten saucers. Fill the first with
water and stir in one teaspoon of sugar. Now pour half the contents of the saucer into another which should then be filled with
water. After stirring, pour half of the contents of the second
saucer into a third and fill it with water. Repeat this process until you have a row of ten saucers. Now take a fly (having made
certain that he is not thirsty) and lower him gently into the most
dilute mixture. Then try him in the next and so on up the series
until his proboscis is lowered. This is the weakest sugar solution
that he can taste.

Now test yourself. If you are the sort of person who does   19
not mind kissing his dog, you can use the same saucers as the
fly. Otherwise make up a fresh series. You will be surprised, perhaps chagrined, to discover that the fly is unbelievably more sensitive than you. In fact, a starving fly is ten million times more
sensitive.

You console yourself with the thought that he may be less ver-   20
satile, less of a gourmet, than you. Well, this too can be tested.
Try him on other sugars; there are any number of sugars: cane
sugar, beet sugar, malt sugar, milk sugar, grape sugar. Each is
chemically different; each has for you a different sweetness. It is
only necessary to determine for each the most dilute solution
that will cause the fly to lower his proboscis. Then when the sugars are listed in order of decreasing effectiveness, it turns out that
the order is the same for you and the fly: grape sugar, cane sugar,
malt sugar, milk sugar, beet sugar. In one respect the fly is less
gullible; he is not fooled by saccharine or any other artificial
sweeteners.

But, you may argue, I can distinguish many other kinds of   21
tastes. This is only partly correct. You can distinguish many
kinds of flavors, but to assist you in this you recruit your nose.

Flavor is a mixture of tastes, odors, and textures. With taste alone you are pretty much restricted to sweet, salt, sour, and bitter.

The old adage that one can catch more flies with honey than   22
with vinegar has a sound basis in physiology. Leaving aside for the moment the fact that flies react differently to different odors, the truth remains that flies accept materials that taste sweet to us and reject those that taste salt, sour, or bitter to us. This fact, too, can be demonstrated with the proboscis response, but the only way for a fly to say "No" is to retract his proboscis, and it can be retracted only if it is first extended. Accordingly, one prepares several saucers of sugared water. A pinch of salt is added to one, two pinches to another, three pinches to a third, and so on. As before, the fly is lowered gently into the saucer with the least salt. He responds, as expected, by extending his proboscis. He is then allowed to taste the next dish, and the next, and the next. At one of these dishes he will stubbornly refuse to extend his proboscis. Since this dish contains the same amount of sugar as the rest, one must conclude that it is the salt that is being rejected. The test can be repeated with vinegar, lemon juice, or quinine water. It can even be tried with aspirin, whiskey, bicarbonate of soda, tobacco juice—anything that will dissolve in water. If you wish to be really sophisticated, you can test the relative sensitivity of his legs and mouth by standing him in one solution and allowing his proboscis to come down into a different one. A friend of mine who once wished to study the stomach of the fly and to color it so it could be seen more easily under the microscope hit upon the idea of standing a fly in sugar but arranging for its mouth to come down in dye. As a result the fly's insides were stained beautifully. This is one example of a physiological way to coat a pill.

LINDA HOGAN

Hearing Voices

A Chickasaw essayist, poet, playwright, and novelist, Linda Hogan currently teaches creative writing at the University of Colorado at Boulder. Her writing, she told and interviewer for *Contemporary Authors,* "comes from and goes back to the community, both the human and the global community. I am interested in the deepest questions, those of spirit, of shelter, of growth and movement toward peace and liberation, inner and outer." The following essay first appeared in *The Writer and Her World* (Janet Sternburg, ed.) in 1992.

When Barbara McClintock[1] was awarded a Nobel Prize for her work on gene transposition in corn plants, the most striking thing about her was that she made her discoveries by listening to what the corn spoke to her, by respecting the life of the corn and "letting it come."   1

McClintock says she learned "the stories" of the plants. She "heard" them. She watched the daily green journeys of growth from earth toward sky and sun. She knew her plants in the way a healer or mystic would have known them, from the inside, the inner voices of corn and woman speaking to one another.   2

As an Indian woman, I come from a long history of people who have listened to the language of this continent, people who have known that corn grows with the songs and prayers of the people, that it has a story to tell, that the world is alive. Both in oral traditions and in mythology—the true language of inner life—account after account tells of the stones giving guidance, the trees singing, the corn telling of inner earth, the dragonfly offering up a tongue. This is true in the European traditions as well: Psyche received direction from the reeds and the ants, Orpheus[2] knew the languages of earth, animals, and birds.   3

This intuitive and common language is what I seek for my writing, work in touch with the mystery and force of life, work that speaks a few of the many voices around us, and it is important to me that McClintock listened to the voices of corn. It is important to the continuance of life that she told the truth of her method and that it reminded us all of where our strength, our knowing, and our sustenance come from.   4

1. Barbara McClintock (1902–1992): a geneticist whose discovery that genes can transfer their positions on chromosomes contributed greatly to the understanding of hereditary processes. She won the Nobel Prize in 1983.
2. In Greek mythology, Psyche lost her lover Cupid when she insisted on seeing his face; after years of hardship—during which she received assistance from nature—she was reunited with him and made immortal. Orpheus's music celebrated the sounds of nature.

It is also poetry, this science, and I note how often scientific theories lead to the world of poetry and vision, theories telling us how atoms that were stars have been transformed into our living, breathing bodies. And in these theories, or maybe they should be called stories, we begin to understand how we are each many people, including the stars we once were, and how we are in essence the earth and the universe, how what we do travels clear around the earth and returns. In a single moment of our living, there is our ancestral and personal history, our future, even our deaths planted in us and already growing toward their fulfillment. The corn plants are there, and like all the rest we are forever merging our borders with theirs in the world collective.

Our very lives might depend on this listening. In the Chernobyl nuclear accident,[3] the wind told the story that was being suppressed by the people. It gave away the truth. It carried the story of danger to other countries. It was a poet, a prophet, a scientist.

Sometimes, like the wind, poetry has its own laws speaking for the life of the planet. It is a language that wants to bring back together what the other words have torn apart. It is the language of life speaking through us about the sacredness of life.

This life speaking life is what I find so compelling about the work of poets such as Ernesto Cardenal, who is also a priest and was the Nicaraguan Minister of Culture. He writes: "The armadillos are very happy with this government. / . . . Not only humans desired liberation / the whole ecology wanted it." Cardenal has also written "The Parrots," a poem about caged birds who were being sent to the United States as pets for the wealthy, how the cages were opened, the parrots allowed back into the mountains and jungles, freed like the people, "and sent back to the land we were pulled from."

How we have been pulled from the land! And how poetry has worked hard to set us free, uncage us, keep us from split tongues that mimic the voices of our captors. It returns us to our land. Poetry is a string of words that parades without a permit. It is a lockbox of words to put an ear to as we try to crack the safe of

3. The world's worst nuclear-reactor accident (April 26, 1986) occurred at a nuclear power plant in Ukraine. The worldwide effects of the fallout have yet to be determined.

language, listening for the right combination, the treasure inside. It is life resonating. It is sometimes called Prayer, Soothsaying, Complaint, Invocation, Proclamation, Testimony, Witness. Writing is and does all these things. And like that parade, it is illegitimately insistent on going its own way, on being part of the miracle of life, telling the story about what happened when we were cosmic dust, what it means to be stars listening to our human atoms.

But don't misunderstand me. I am not just a dreamer. I am also the practical type. A friend's father, watching the United States stage another revolution in another Third World country, said, "Why doesn't the government just feed people and then let the political chips fall where they may?" He was right. It was easy, obvious, even financially more reasonable to do that, to let democracy be chosen because it feeds hunger. I want my writing to be that simple, that clear and direct. Likewise, I feel it is not enough for me just to write, but I need to live it, to be informed by it. I have found over the years that my work has more courage than I do. It has more wisdom. It teaches me, leads me places I never knew I was heading. And it is about a new way of living, of being in the world.

I was on a panel recently where the question was raised whether we thought literature could save lives. The audience, book people, smiled expectantly with the thought. I wanted to say, Yes, it saves lives. But I couldn't speak those words. It saves spirits maybe, hearts. It changes minds, but for me writing is an incredible privilege. When I sit down at the desk, there are other women who are hungry, homeless. I don't want to forget that, that the world of matter is still there to be reckoned with. This writing is a form of freedom most other people do not have. So, when I write, I feel a responsibility, a commitment to other humans and to the animal and plant communities as well.

Still, writing has changed me. And there is the powerful need we all have to tell a story, each of us with a piece of the whole pattern to complete. As Alice Walker[4] says, we are all telling part of the same story, and as Sharon Olds[5] has said, Every writer is a cell on the body politic of America.

4. Alice Walker: (1944–   ): See headnote to "Everyday Use."
5. Sharon Olds (1942–   ): American poet.

Another Nobel Prize laureate is Betty Williams,[6] a Northern 13
Ireland co-winner of the 1977 Peace Prize. I heard her speak
about how, after witnessing the death of children, she stepped
outside in the middle of the night and began knocking on doors
and yelling, behaviors that would have earned her a diagnosis of
hysteria in our own medical circles. She knocked on doors that
might have opened with weapons pointing in her face, and she
cried out, "What kind of people have we become that we would
allow children to be killed on our streets?" Within four hours the
city was awake, and there were sixteen thousands names on petitions for peace. Now, that woman's work is a lesson to those of
us who deal with language, and to those of us who are dealt into
silence. She used language to begin the process of peace. This is
the living, breathing power of the word. It is poetry. So are the
names of those who signed the petitions. Maybe it is this kind of
language that saves lives.

Writing begins for me with survival, with life and with freeing 14
life, saving life, speaking life. It is work that speaks what can't be
easily said. It originated from a compelling desire to live and be
alive. For me, it is sometimes the need to speak for other forms
of life, to take the side of human life, even our sometimes frivolous living, and our grief-filled living, our joyous living, our violent living, busy living, our peaceful living. It is about possibility.
It is based in the world of matter. I am interested in how something small turns into an image that is large and strong with res-
onance, where the ordinary becomes beautiful. I believe the
divine, the magic, is here in the weeds at our feet, unacknowledged. What a world this is. Where else could water rise up to
the sky, turn into snow crystals, magnificently brought together,
fall from the sky all around us, pile up billions deep, and catch
the small sparks of sunlight as they return again to water?

These acts of magic happen all the time; in Chaco Canyon,[7] 15
my sister has seen a kiva, a ceremonial room in the earth, that is
in the center of the canyon. This place has been uninhabited for
what seems like forever. It has been without water. In fact, there

6. Betty Williams (1943–   ): activist who shared the 1976 Nobel Peace Prize
with Mairead Corrigan for leadership of the peace movement in Northern Ireland.
7. Chaco Canyon: in northwest New Mexico, site of ruins of the prehistoric
Anasazi culture.

are theories that the ancient people disappeared when they jour-
neyed after water. In the center of it a corn plant was growing. It
was all alone and it had been there since the ancient ones, the old
ones who came before us all, those people who wove dog hair
into belts, who witnessed the painting of flute players on the
seeping canyon walls, who knew the stories of corn. And there
was one corn plant growing out of the holy place. It planted itself yearly. With no water, no person to care for it, no overturn-
ing of the soil, this corn plant rises up to tell its story, and that's
what this poetry is.

WILLIAM L. RODMAN

When Questions Are Answers

William Rodman, a professor of anthropology at McMaster University in Ontario, has conducted research in the South Pacific for
nearly three decades. Rodman has published several articles
about the culture of Ambae, an isolated island just twenty miles
long, located in the small nation of Vanuatu (formerly called New
Hebrides). In recent years he has been particularly interested in
the role of narrative in the human sciences and the problems of interpretive anthropology. "When Questions Are Answers" was
published in *American Anthropologist* in June 1991.

AN INTRODUCTION

This is what I think happened, my reconstruction of an event   1
that occurred over thirty years ago on a remote island in the
South Pacific. What follows is a fiction, but it's as true a fiction
as I can write on the basis of my own experience on the island
and the information available to me. Minor details in my account might be incorrect but what is important is that today
people on the island believe that the meeting between the anthropologist and the teenager took place, and that from that

meeting they discovered the message of anthropology to the native peoples of the world. What I found, many years after the event, is that their interpretation of the message of anthropology had played a critical role in changing their way of life.

In the late 1950s, an anthropologist spent a few days as the guest of an Australian couple who maintained a trade store on the weather coast of Aoba, a northern island in the New Hebrides archipelago. The anthropologist had just completed ten months of fieldwork on the neighboring island of Pentecost; he was on his way home—Aoba was just a stopover, a place to wait for a boat that would take him to a place to wait for a plane back to North America.

At some point during the anthropologist's brief stay on the island, a young man named Andrew Namala walked down to the coast from his inland village.[1] He was a quiet young man, the brother of a schoolteacher but the son of a chief. He was close to his father, a man who had killed many pigs and gained high rank in the graded society *(hungwe)* before Church of Christ missionaries in the 1940s convinced their followers on the island to give up all customary activities. Andrew's father remained a traditional chief, for not even a missionary can strip a man of his rank in the graded society, but he was a nonpracticing chief, a chief in cultural exile who had become a proper Christian in the Church of Christ.

The day that Andrew walked down to the coast, the wife of the trader was tending store. She was a big, friendly woman, fluent in the local Pidgin English—Bislama—and knowledgeable about the personal lives of almost everyone who visited her store. She knew Andrew, and she knew his father, too. One thing she knew about Andrew's father was that the old chief was one of the few men in the Church of Christ skilled in the art of sand drawing.

Sand drawings have an irresistible appeal for ethnographers. Copies of the drawings can be found in the works of Codrington, Rivers, Deacon, Layard, Harrisson, and almost every other ethnographer with an interest in material culture who has

1. All names in this essay are pseudonyms. However, all the statements of the pseudonymous Ambaens (including Andrew Namala's story in the section entitled "Text") are translated versions of comments I tape-recorded in Bislama. [author's note]

Figure 1

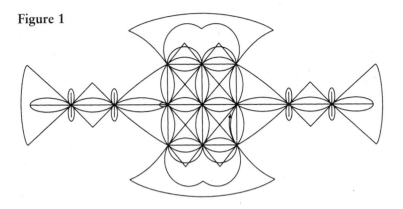

worked in the northern New Hebrides.[2] (See Figure 1.) It's not hard to explain why the drawings have attracted so much attention. They excite the basic ethnographic impulse to record and preserve. The artist's medium is fine sand or dirt as soft as talcum powder; if the artist is skillful, he creates a thing of beauty that cannot last beyond a single afternoon. Sand drawings are symbolically charged filigree that the wind blows away, myths in pictures that the tide wipes clean. The trader's wife knew that the anthropologist had collected some sand drawings on Pentecost, so she introduced him to Andrew, the son of a local expert.

The anthropologist and the teenager went outside the trade store to talk. It was hot in the store, and there were shade trees just outside—a wild mango, a rose apple, and some others. Moreover, there was a breeze off the sea.

At first, the anthropologist's questions concerned sand drawings, and then, when that subject ran dry, he asked the young man about a range of other topics—magic, supernatural power, subsistence techniques, the experiences of local people in World War II, and recent changes in patterns of nutrition, all topics on which he had collected information during his recent fieldwork.

2. The man I called "Andrew Namala" drew the sand drawing represented in Figure 1. The name of the sand drawing is "The War-Club of the Spirits" (*Rungwe Bulana Tamate*). As much of a sand drawing as possible is drawn in one continuous line. I use the masculine pronoun in my description of the drawings because, on Ambae, the person who works the sand drawings always is male. [author's note]

In a casual way, he seems to have been seeking information concerning Aoba that he could compare with data he gathered on Pentecost. Yet it's hard to consider the encounter an "interview." It wasn't planned; it lacked formality; from the anthropologist's point of view, it may even have lacked a sense of occasion. It was a way to pass the time before dinner, a pleasant way to decompress from fieldwork.

The anthropologist left Aoba a few days later. During the decades that were to follow, he never published anything that derived from his talk with the teenager. It's unlikely the conversation changed his life in any significant way.   8

To Andrew, however, the encounter *was* a meaningful event. It puzzled him. Who was the outsider? Why was he interested in the local way of life? What did his questions *mean?* In 1982, Andrew spoke to me of the interview as if it happened yesterday. As I listened, I found that most of the anthropologist's questions have an air of plausibility. I recognized them as legitimate questions for an ethnographer to ask, as questions I might ask someone in an unfamiliar locale.   9

Andrew's life was changed as a result of his encounter with the outsider and so, at least indirectly, was the way of life of the people with whom he lived. They included the 343 members of the Church of Christ in the Longana district of the island, now called Ambae, in the new Pacific nation that changed its name from "New Hebrides" to "Vanuatu" at the time of Independence in 1980 (see Figure 2). Andrew discovered an implicit pattern in the questions the anthropologist asked, and once the hidden meaning of the questions was revealed to him, the meeting took on new and deeper significance. Andrew's memory of his encounter with the anthropologist became instrumental knowledge, *used* knowledge, a key ideological justification for a profound change in the practice of a people's social affaairs.   10

What follows here is primarily an account of how members of the Church of Christ on the island where I conduct fieldwork discovered the true meaning of anthropology and what that knowledge did to their lives. They shared their interpretation of the meaning of anthropology with me for a reason—because they wanted to teach me a lesson. So this is my story too, my explanation of how and why a group of chiefs on Ambae decided that the time had come to teach me the message of anthropology.   11

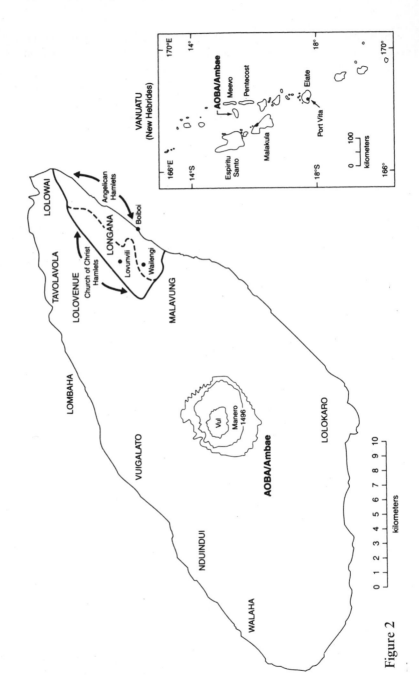

Figure 2

PRETEXT

In 1982, early in my third term of fieldwork in the district of   12
Longana on Ambae, a young man brought me a message from a
friend who lives in a hill village some distance away from the
hamlet where I stay on the island. The message was in Bislama
and was handwritten in pencil on part of a page torn from a
school exercise book: "Come see me Friday afternoon," the note
said, and it was signed "Nicodemus." I turned the scrap of paper
over and scrawled "Friday's fine. See you then," and gave it back
to the messanger. I didn't add, but I felt, that wild boars couldn't
keep me away.

Nicodemus Wai (as anyone in Longana will tell you—and the   13
phrase never varies) is "different from other men." One way in
which he differs is that he talks differently: sometimes, even in
private conversation, he sounds like he learned how to talk by
listening to Churchill's speeches on shortwave radio. He seems to
think in rhetoric; his mind pumps metaphors as naturally as water issues from a spring; his stories have all the shadings of vivid
dreams. But Nicodemus isn't just a dreamer. He expresses himself in action as well as words. In the late 1960s, he became an
early supporter of Jimmy Stevens, a.k.a. President Moses, the
charismatic descendant of a Tongan princess and a Scottish sea-
man who founded a political movement with millenarian overtones called "Na Griamel."[3] Na Griamel began on the island of
Espiritu Santo, 30 miles across the sea from Aoba/Ambae. Partly
through Nicodemus's efforts, the entire population of the
Church of Christ of the district of Longana on Aoba became
supporters of the movement. Then, in the mid-1970s, Nicodemus became the voice of Radio Vanafo, Jimmy Stevens's illegal
radio station, located deep in the Santo bush. In those days,
Nicodemus sometimes referred to himself as "a revolutionary
pussycat," "pussycat" being a reference not to his disposition
but to his ability to slip away from trouble unseen.

I had last seen Nicodemus in 1979. A year later, the Anglo-   14
French Condominium of the New Hebrides became the independent Republic of Vanuatu. Achieving independence wasn't easy
for the nationalists who opposed British and French rule: two

3. John Besant's (1984) *The Santo Rebellion: An Imperial Reckoning* provides a
detailed account of the career of Jimmy Stevens, Na Griamel, the Rebellion, and
its aftermath.

months before the date set for independence, Jimmy Stevens led a rebellion against the central government. When Vanuatu became a new nation, Na Griamel was firmly in control of Espiritu Santo (known locally simply as "Santo"), the largest island in the archipelago. Jimmy Stevens renamed Santo "Vermarana" and declared the island independent of the rest of the country. Since I had last seen Nicodemus, troops from Papua New Guinea had smashed Na Griamel's radio transmitter, the Santo Rebellion had failed, and Jimmy Stevens had been tried and sentenced to prison, escaped, and attempted unsuccessfully to make a run for New Caledonia in a glass-bottomed boat he stole from a guided tour company in the capital, Port Vila.

Nicodemus and I lived in villages only a few miles apart, but we seldom met because my hosts and his kin were political enemies who also belonged to rival religions. Longana runs about eight kilometers along a coastal track, which ends at a dry riverbed that marks one boundary of the district. There, the road turns and begins to rise abruptly for one-and-a-half kilometers into the foothills of the interior of the island. Two groups live in the district. The coastal population are Anglicans, followers of tradition, and supporters of the majority political party and the central government. They are the people with whom I have worked since my first fieldwork on the island in 1969. The 549 Anglicans live in scattered hamlets separate from those of the 343 members of the Church of Christ, all of whom live in the hills and most of whom at the time of independence were among the most loyal supporters of Jimmy Stevens and Na Griamel. Like most of the people with whom I was in daily contact, I seldom ventured into the Church of Christ area, and never without an invitation. 15

I heard from my Anglican adoptive kinsmen that Nicodemus had been implicated in the theft of a large quantity of medical supplies from the Santo hospital during the Rebellion. I heard he had surrendered to police, been pardoned, found God, and started his own church, which lacked a name, the idea being that labels such as "Anglican" and "Church of Christ" only serve to create conflict and obscure the essential unity of Christians everywhere. I heard all these things as rumors and I badly wanted to see him: the "revolutionary pussycat" was leading one of the most interesting lives of anyone I knew. 16

On Friday, when I crested the hill that led into Nicodemus's village, I saw him walking toward me, a big, broken-toothed smile on his face. I also saw something else, a sight to which I ascribed no particular significance at the time: Nicodemus's brother, Andrew Namala, sitting in front of the village's men's house in the company of a number of older men. Andrew was carving a *rungwe*, a traditional fighting-club that men of rank now use as a walking stick. He saw me, grinned, and waved. I waved back. He then returned to whittling and conversation with the other men.

I expected Nicodemus to take me to his house, a place where we would not be disturbed. Instead, he directed me to a small house with walls of split and woven bamboo that stood on the edge of a clearing, about a hundred feet away from the men's house. He explained to me that it was a house the village had built for visitors; inside, it was cool and clean, a good place to talk.

Nicodemus and I seated ourselves on benches and faced each other across a bare table. We chatted about our families as I set up my tape recorder. I tested the microphone and then I asked him: "Have you been back to Jimmy Stevens's headquarters on Santo since the Rebellion?"

"Yes, just once," he replied in a thoughtful voice. "It used to be a pretty place, but it's not anymore." His tone was that of a man evoking memories within himself, trying to see the scene as it was. "The soldiers ruined everything, the people's way of life, the gardens, everything. All that's left there now is a French school." He paused and then took a deep breath. "The reason I went back there is that an old friend of mine had died. . . ." And at that instant the storyteller in Nicodemus took over. He told me about the end of the Rebellion, about the dawn raid on Jimmy Stevens's headquarters, about murders reported as accidents, about the secret involvement of Americans belonging to the Phoenix Foundation in the Rebellion. I found out why he had been accused of the theft of the medical supplies and why he was never charged with the crime. He told me the story of his surrender to the government troops and why they let him go. He seemed to me much older than the last time I had seen him, and he told me how tired he was of being a "diver in deep waters"; now, he said, he had "come to the surface for air." His only wish

17

18

19

20

was to lead a quiet life, as a husband, as a father to his five children, and as pastor to his flock in the Church-With-No-Name.

The packed earth beneath my bare feet became cooler, and the shadows within the house deepened. We had been talking for about three hours when a boy scurried into the house, climbed into Nicodemus's lap and whispered in his ear. Nicodemus nodded and lowered the boy to the ground. He slapped his hands on the table with an air of finality: the spell was broken, the interview over. He rose in a way that indicated he expected me to do the same. "Bill," he said, "the chiefs are waiting for you. Your kava is ready." 21

Kava *(Piper mythysticum)* is a drug about which I feel profound ambivalence. It is a bitter brew that everyone on Ambae admits tastes awful: one of its several origin myths attributes its taste to the fact that it first grew from the decaying vagina of a murdered woman. That myth makes sense of why, today, Ambaen men hawk and spit after every shell. It's also a powerful enough drug to alter perception in fundamental ways. Once I drank a shell so strong that everything I saw for the next 20 minutes flickered, just like an old-time movie. Most often, however, one or two draughts of kava merely numbs the tongue, eases the mind, and generates companionship and goodwill among the drinkers. For a male fieldworker, accepting a host's invitation of kava is a social necessity; it's better to accept and throw up than to refuse, however smilingly. 22

The men's house was filled. Every man of rank in the Church of Christ area was there. Andrew Namala greeted me at the doorway, and then I went from man to man, shaking hands in greeting, my body bent slightly from the waist in a position of respect. In the center of the clubhouse, there were five split coconut shells filled with kava. The chief of highest rank in the men's house told me which shell of kava I was to drink. He glanced around the men's house. "Thaddeus, you come drink with us," he said. "You too, Sam . . . and you, Andrew." He then took a twig and passed down the line of shells, dipping the stick in the kava, raising it to his mouth and tasting it, and then moving on to the next shell. I'd seen this done before, though not often, and until I learned better I'd always assumed that the chief was testing the kava for poison, symbolically if not actually. In fact, the trajectory of the twig is from the chief's mouth to each cup, not 23 the reverse: the ritual is done so that guests will absorb some knowledge from their host.

I drank my kava, stepped outside the men's house, spat, made other terrible sounds, then came back inside, passed around a pack of Camels and settled against a bamboo wall. It was strong stuff, and I began to feel the hum and glow of the kava working on me. I smoked a cigarette, pleasantly stoned, listening, watching as other men drank their shells of kava. *24*

When everyone in the men's house had downed a shell of kava, the quality of sound in the room changed, became softer, quieter, and someone began to tell a story. It was a few minutes before I realized that I was listening to something more than idle men's house conversation. With some difficulty, I switched on my tape recorder. Andrew squatted a few feet away, still working on his club in the semi-darkness. There was a moment of silence as one story ended, then he began to speak. *25*

TEXT

"There was a man who came here shortly after World War II ended." (He confers with others in the men's house about the visitor's name. Someone suggests "Mr. Allen," but Andrew shakes his head and continues.) "We don't remember his name but he came here to find out about our sand drawings and about the messages we leave for each other on the ground. Before he came here, he visited the island of Pentecost, and then he arrived at Boi Boi, the landing down on the coast. He stayed in the house of the trader who lived there—Mr. Mueller. *26*

"At that time, I was a young man, maybe seventeen or eighteen. Sometimes, I would walk down to the coast to visit the Muellers' trade store. One day, as I approached the store, Mrs. Mueller saw me coming, and she yelled to me: *27*

'Hey! Isn't your father the chief who knows about sand drawings?' *28*

'Yes,' I said, 'and so do I.' *29*

'Aww, you're just a kid; you don't know any sand drawings.' *30*

'Oh yes I do,' I said. . . . Now I remember! Mr. Jones! Mr. Jones was his name. Mrs. Mueller introduced me to him. *31*

'Do you know any sand drawings?' he asked me. 'A few,' I replied. *32*

We went outside the store and sat down. Mr. Jones opened his 33
book and showed me a drawing.
'Do you know this one?' he asked. 'It's from Pentecost.' 34
'Yes,' I said, 'I know it.' 35
'What is it called?' 36
I told him. 37
He showed me another drawing. 'What's this one?' 38
'It's called fresh coconuts,' I said. 39
Altogether, Mr. Jones asked me if I knew four different draw- 40
ings. I knew each one.
'Enough,' he said. 'I want to ask you some questions. In the 41
past, did some men around here know how to make thunder?'
'Yes,' I said. 'They did.' 42
'What about now?' 43
'No longer.' 44
'O.K.,' he said, 'let me ask you about something else: in the 45
past, did some men around here know how to make earth-
quakes?'
'Yes,' I said. 'They did.' 46
'What about now?' 47
'No longer.' 48
'What about cyclones? Did men know how to make them?' 49
'Yes.' 50
'Now?' 51
'No.' 52
'Why do such men no longer exist?' he asked me. 53
Well, I didn't really know, so I just told him the first thing that 54
came to mind. I said: 'What happened was that the missionaries
arrived. They showed us the Bible and told us to leave our hea-
then ways. They told us to burn or throw away our magical sub-
stances and to forget about them.'
Then Mr. Jones asked me: 'Did you go to Santo during the 55
war?'
'No,' I told him. 'I was too young. When the men of my vil- 56
lage returned from Santo, they told us: "It's over: the war has
ended."'
'How do you think America managed to win the war?' he 57
asked.
'I don't know,' I said. 58
'Do you drink tea?' asked Mr. Jones. 59
'Yes.' 60

'When you drink tea, do you eat anything?'   61

'Yes. Sometimes cabin biscuits, sometimes bread.'   62

'Do you like the taste of tea, biscuits, and bread?'   63

'Yes.'   64

'Fine,' said Mr. Jones. 'Do you eat rice?'   65

'Yes.'   66

'When you eat rice, do you eat any other food at the same   67
time?'

'Sometimes meat, sometimes tinned fish.'   68

'Do you like the taste of rice, meat, and tinned fish?'   69

'Yes.'   70

'All right,' said Mr. Jones, 'I have another question: do you   71
know how to make a garden?'

'Yes.'   72

'Then tell me how you do it. What do you do when you want   73
to clear land?'

I showed him how I held my bush-knife and how I used the   74
knife to clear land.

It was then that I realized that he was teaching me a lesson, a   75
lesson about the value of traditional culture *[kastom]*.

'Look,' he said, 'rain drives sunlight away. Night replaces day.   76
Think again about the reason why the Americans won the war.
Have you figured it out? I'll tell you. It's because the soldiers carried the Bible with them. The Bible provides White men with
their *kastom*. Why have you people lost *your kastom*?'

My word! Then I understood.   77

I shared with Mr. Jones my knowledge of sand drawings and   78
I showed him the signs we write on the ground, the four main
ones, the one that tells your friends to wait for you, the one that
says: 'I'm tired of waiting—I've gone in this direction.' But I
knew that there were many other signs I didn't know, that nobody knew anymore.

Before Mr. Jones departed from the island, he told me he   79
would put the signs I had shown him into a book he would write
after he returned to America. 'I'll put the signs in a book,' he
said, 'and then it won't matter if I die or if you die. Even when
we both are dead, the signs will remain in the book for our children to see.'

You know, Bill, I think the kinds of things I've been talking   80
about—sand drawings, signs, that sort of thing—are the real
kastom of Longana. Lots of people who don't know much about

kastom just talk about pigs. Pigs, pigs, pigs. But pigs aren't the backbone of *kastom*. Pigs are just a kind of money."

CONTEXT

Even at the time, bone-tired, the kava still working on my 81
brain, I had the feeling that Andrew was trying to tell me something of importance to him, something much more than merely an anecdote about his encounter with a White man many years ago. When he finished the story, he lapsed into silence, and returned to chip, chip, chipping away at his fighting-club. The light in the men's house was dim and fallow, the golden last light of late afternoon. Andrew worked on his club, his shoulders hunched, his face a dark and pensive mask. The time did not seem right to ask him questions. Soon, men seated in the shadows of the men's house returned to quiet conversation and then later we all went to another hill village where a mortuary feast was in progress. My "father"—old Mathias Tari—was there. We drank a shell of kava together, my second, his first, and waited for the bundles of food to come out of the earth oven. When we received our food, we set off down the hill toward home, the old man leading, me following behind, slipping, sliding, but somehow never quite falling.

Days passed, then weeks, and eventually I transcribed the tape 82
of my interview with Nicodemus. There, on the end of the last tape in the Nicodemus series, was Andrew Namala telling his story. This time, listening to him, I began to notice details—the way in which he knitted the segments of the narrative together, the progressions in the encounter between the anthropologist and the teenager, the apparent revelation at the climax of the story: "My word! Then I understood." But *what* had he understood? Why, then, did he share his knowledge willingly, even joyously, with the outsider? What was the lesson about *kastom* that he thought the anthropologist had taught him?

From these questions came others. I reflected on the occasion, 83
and I began to wonder about the context in which Andrew told me his story. The recounting of the tale had been truly a performance, and Andrew had played to a packed (men's) house: Why had so many chiefs gathered in his village on a work day, a Friday in the cool season? Then, too, there was the puzzle of why

he had told me the story. Why in public? What was the significance of the last bit, the part he directed at me as if underlining
the story's message: things like sand drawings are the backbone
of *kastom* of Longana, pigs are not. Now *there's* an unorthodox
view! When men speak of *kastom* in Longana, they mean pig-
killing, rank-taking, the graded society *(hungwe)*: I'd heard men
use *kastom* as a synonym for "pig-killing" hundreds of times.[4]
Andrew himself had been an important catalyst in the recent revival of pig-killing in the Church of Christ area in Longana. In
1979, I'd seen him take the second-highest rank, killing tusked
boars in the midst of a thunderstorm, a man radiant with energy,
in complete control of his body, his every movement clean and
precise; Andrew's was the best of the many rank-takings I'd seen.
That was then, three years ago, but now he was taking the line
that "lots of people who don't know much about *kastom* just
talk about pigs." Hell, everybody in Longana who engages in
kastom talks about pigs. So what was he trying to tell me?

Some mysteries, if you dream on them enough and have 84
enough context, reveal themselves. It took me a while, but eventually I understood. The key to understanding Andrew's interpretation of his talk with the anthropologist (and also the key to
the way in which he told me the story) is *qaltavalu*, literally "hidden talk," a form of communication based on a system of implicit meanings. People sometimes *qaltavalu* in everyday life; for
example, a man may ask a woman for a plate of rice and not
have food in mind at all. More commonly, it occurs as a rhetorical device in speeches: rival chiefs use *qaltavalu* against each
other to devastating effect. "Hidden talk" is the process; shame
is the product. *Qaltavalu* says to a rival: "Look, I am speaking
about you in public, and *you* understand my meaning, even if
everyone else does not. Shall I make my meaning explicit, or will
you change your way of acting?" Or, perhaps, ". . . provide me
with the support I need?" The threat of public exposure often is
sanction (or blackmail) enough in a society in which people
dread public humiliation.

Qaltavalu has a third use: it's one of the most important cus- 85
tomary techniques of instruction. Teachers on Ambae seldom

4. Rodman inserts a note here citing other anthropological accounts of the
graded society on Ambae. For economy's sake, we have deleted the citations.
Those interested in this scholarly apparatus should consult the version of Rodman's article in *American Anthropologist*.

state the obvious. Instead, they teach by parable, by indirection raised to the level of a fine art. They figure that a student is most apt to remember a lesson if he has to work to figure out what the lesson is.[5]

Andrew's encounter with the anthropologist made little sense   86 to the hill people in terms of their prior dealings with Europeans. By the 1950s, Longanans in the Church of Christ area had had limited experience with White people: in fact, most people's knowledge of Whites resulted exclusively from their contacts with the Australian trader and his wife (who were the only resident Whites in the district), missionaries, and very, *very* rarely, a government official. Longanan followers of the Church of Christ had heard missionaries preach against *kastom* as a mark of moral backwardness, as beliefs to be uprooted, substances to be destroyed, and behaviors to be transformed. In contrast to missionaries, traders and the occasional district agent didn't seem to regard *kastom* as immoral, but they didn't take local traditions very seriously either: to them, *kastom* is play, a harmless set of activities that waste time and money.

In contrast to missionaries, traders, and district agents, the   87 anthropologist clearly was interested in *kastom*. Andrew, the son of a chief, chose to interpret his meeting with the outsider in terms of a category of Ambaen culture, *qaltavalu*. What was the hidden meaning of the encounter? What was the anthropologist (cast in the role of "teacher") *really* saying? Viewed within the framework of ordinary conversation, the questions communicate little information. What, after all, does winning a war have to do with the taste of tea? But as *qaltavalu*—aiiyahhh!—patterns begin to emerge, and implicit links between the questions appear. Andrew puzzled over the meaning of the questions until

---

5. Parallels to the Ambaean notion of *qaltavalu* can be found elsewhere in Oceania and in other parts of the world. Strathern, for example, discusses the "veiled speech" *(ik ek)* that Melpa of Highland New Guinea use in a number of contexts, including children's games, love songs, public argument and debate, and formal oratory. The Melpa also have a concept of "hidden truth" similar to that of Ambae. Unlike Ambae, however, Melpa figurative speech apparently is not used in education as a formal means for the transmission of knowledge. Outside Oceania, "hidden talk" as a pedagogical device sometimes occurs in places where a person's knowledge is supposed to grow in small increments, as among the Saramaka of Surinam, where old men teach their younger kinsmen in a style marked by ellipsis, concealment, and partial disclosure. [author's note]

they provided him with an answer to the problem of the anomalous White man.

He opens his narrative with the incident involving the trader's 88
wife. He depicts her as *assuming* that members of the younger
generation no longer know their own traditions. Andrew proves
her wrong when he correctly identifies the Pentecost sand drawings. By so doing, he demonstrates to the anthropologist his interest in *kastom* and qualifies himself as a worthy recipient of the
anthropologist's message.

The next section of the narrative consists of a set of questions 89
that have in common the theme of lost power. The storyteller has
the anthropologist establish an implicit relationship between lost
power and the loss of tradition. The "teacher" is drawing his
"student's" attention to the fact that, in the past, men possessed
great supernatural powers: no one today knows how to make
thunder, earthquakes, and cyclones. Then, abruptly, the anthropologist asks: "Why do such men no longer exist?" and Andrew,
free-associating, is forced to confront the fact that missionaries
were responsible for the loss of the knowledge and magical substances that had been the source of customary power.

The conversation appears to change course when the anthro- 90
pologist asks Andrew: "Did you go to Santo during the war?" In
fact, in his questions about World War II, Mr. Jones reveals his
true intent, but not in an obvious way. "How do you think
America managed to win the war?" is another question probing
the theme of power. It's an extension of his previous questions,
but Andrew doesn't catch the drift of his "teacher's" line of reasoning: "I don't know," he replies.

So Mr. Jones tries another tack: "Do you drink tea?" he asks. 91
All the next set of questions concern diet. In a broader sense,
however, the questions elicit information about change and the
presence of foreign elements in Longana; Andrew is made to
come face to face with his alienation from tradition. He is forced
to admit he not only eats White people's food; he *likes* it.

All is not lost, however. Mr. Jones is a good teacher, a master 92
of *qaltavalu,* so he nudges his student with yet another question:
"Do you know how to make a garden?" This most straightforward of questions, reconsidered *qaltavalu,* is transformed into
something like: "Do you remember the most fundamental traditional skill of all—how to make a living from the earth?" Andrew responds affirmatively. This allows the "teacher" to lead

him in the direction of a reconsideration of his essential values. He asks Andrew to demonstrate the skills that bind him to the land. Andrew does so, and at last he understands that Mr. Jones is using customary means to make a point about *kastom.* But what *is* the point? Andrew still is not sure, so Mr. Jones steps out of character and makes his message explicit: in effect, he tells the young man that Americans are strong because their *kastom,* which can be found in the Bible, is powerful; Americans remain strong because they remain true to the traditional values associated with their own way of life. Missionaries deprived the islanders of indigenous *kastom*s and, as a result, people lost much of their power.

So what was the anthropologist's hidden message? What was the true meaning of the encounter and the questions he asked? The answer in the questions isn't hard to discover. The anthropologist made Andrew work toward an understanding that *kastom is* important: it is the way to power; those who lose their *kastom*s are powerless. By the end of the narrative, Andrew has discovered the "true" message of anthropology: anthropologists are an equal and opposing force in the world to certain kinds of missionaries. They are a counter to anti-*kastom* Christianity and those missionaries who urge people to abandon their traditional ways. The aim of anthropology is to teach all peoples to value their traditional ways.

The anthropologist's message to Andrew became Andrew's message to his people. At first, no one listened. For 15 years, he lived as an outsider in his own society, a man with a passionate concern for *kastom* in a Christian community that believed (with equal fervor) that *kastom* is anti-Christian. He learned from his father, and then, when his father died and there was no one else in the Church of Christ who could teach him *kastom,* he sought out chiefs in the Anglican sector of the district. It took courage to go to those chiefs. At that time, Anglicans and members of the Church of Christ regarded each other with mutual suspicion and hostility. He went to the chiefs, and he learned from them. Gradually, he became a master of tradition.

Then the times changed. In the 1970s, with the waning of colonialism, *kastom* became a symbol of national identity in the New Hebrides, a rallying cry of the pro-independence movement. The Anglicans in Longana all joined the Vanuaku Pati,

which promoted *kastom* in the interests of national unity. Everyone in the Church of Christ joined Na Griamel, which claimed
that the majority political party "pays only lip service to . . . customs, while Nagriamel made the respect for them a basic part of
its party's philosophy." Not only politicians rode the pro-*kastom*
bandwagon; missionaries with an eye to the future did too.
Church of Christ missionaries now maintained a cautious silence
on matters of *kastom:* in the hill country of Longana, no one
mistook the church's new attitude as one of approval or even tolerance; some men, however—and Andrew was one of them—
thought that the church would no longer interfere in customary
activities such as pig-killing and kava drinking. In this time of
uncertainty, when men were still trying to interpret their changed
circumstances, Andrew used the story of his meeting with the anthropologist as an ideological resource. He found a willing audience for its message. Men now were willing to listen to the idea
that *kastom* is a path to power—nationally, locally, and personally. After a hiatus of forty years, members of the Church of
Christ in Longana began to take rank again, and Andrew was
one of the first. He started on the lowest level of the graded society (as was proper) and, within seven years, he had climbed to
the second-highest rank.

    I went to four pig-killings in the Church of Christ area in the
late 1970s, when I spent 12 months in Longana. I went, but
without much enthusiasm. I went mainly because people expected me to go, because if I stayed home it would have been an
insult to the rank-taker and his sponsor. I had seen close to forty
ranks taken in the Anglican area and I had written a Ph.D. dissertation on the topic. I had been there, done that, knew the
moves, and wanted to get on to something else. What really interested me at the time was the fact that colonial authorities had
withdrawn from participation in local legal affairs. People in
Longana were beginning to codify their own laws and develop
their own courts: that was what I wanted to study, not rank-
taking. I stayed in the Anglican area of Longana, and I visited the
Church of Christ mainly to see friends, like Nicodemus Wai, and
to attend the occasional rank-taking.

    When I next visited Longana, in 1982, I found that the pace
of rank-taking in the Church of Christ had accelerated. Suddenly,
everybody in the hills seemed to be killing pigs—grandfathers,

church leaders, teenagers wearing Sony Walkman headsets. Pig-killing had become a fad, a craze, a way to wow your neighbors. Abuses were common: some men were skipping ranks, others were holding ceremonies with little or no preparation in the complex rituals. The first Church of Christ rank-taking I saw in 1982 was awful: the kid taking the rank clearly didn't know what he was doing, his resources were minimal, and the pigs died hard, screaming like babies. Andrew was one of the teenager's sponsors, a secondary sponsor without much say, and there was little he could do to improve the situation. At one point, he raced by the grassy hill where I was sitting and he yelled over his shoulder: "Hemia i kastom ya, be i kastom olbaot!" The phrase doesn't translate easily, but it means something like: "I guess this is *kastom,* but it's sure a mess!" It wasn't long after that ceremony that Nicodemus invited me to his village.

There's no doubt in my mind that Nicodemus's invitation was   98
a pretext, a way to get me to the village without arousing my sus-picions, and that Andrew told me the story of his encounter as a *qaltavalu.* In fact, the *qaltavalu* was multi-leveled and complex.

In a sense, Andrew was trying to teach me the same lesson   99
that the anthropologist had taught him. He had seen me mainly in two contexts: at rank-takings and in his brother's company. As far as he could tell, I was interested in pigs and in certain kinds of radical change. Somehow, I had lost the grand vision of anthropology: obviously, I needed rerouting. He was saying to me: *kastom* is the true interest of anthropology; there is much *kastom* you do not know; don't listen to the people who equate pigs with *kastom;* pigs are business, *kastom* is art, and art endures.

He was shaming me, in a sense, but he was also flattering me,   100
trusting my local knowledge; a novice wouldn't catch the *qal-tavalu.* Writing this paper, it occurs to me that I wasn't the only target of his *qaltavalu* that afternoon. Quite possibly, he had a larger purpose, an aim rather more important than teaching an athropologist the meaning of anthropology. *Qaltavalu* is a sub-tle system of meaning, and Andrew was a master of the form, and quite capable of sending a message to two audiences at once. I think now that I was Andrew's pretext for aiming a *qaltavalu* at the other men in the men's house. They—not me—were his monster, his creation made of parts of the old culture, slugging

back kava as if there had never been years of abstinence, killing pigs with a passion for prestige but without skill, without grace, with no respect. They needed to slow down, to relearn the lesson that *kastom* is various and subtle, a matter of the mind as well as public display. They too needed to relearn the hidden message of anthropology that Mr. Jones taught so many years ago.

CONCLUSIONS

I returned to Ambae in 1985, just in time to attend Andrew   101
Namala's mortuary feast. He died suddenly, of uncertain causes, precisely 100 days before I returned to the island. Some people— perhaps most—attributed his death to sorcery. Indeed, there were men with knowledge of magical spells who had a good mo- tive to try to kill him. Andrew was ambitious, much admired, much envied, and a master of *qaltavalu*. If *qaltavalu* poses the question, then sometimes men in danger of public humiliation find an answer in sorcery.[6]

At the mortuary feast, Andrew's widow asked me to photo-   102
graph his ceremonial regalia, which she laid out over his grave. There was the bustle in which I saw him kill pigs, the armbands he'd earned, the thick belt he'd made himself lined with cowrie shells, and also a traditional fighting-club, the one he'd been carving that afternoon in the clubhouse when he told me the *qal- tavalu*. I stood there with my camera, and I was aware of his widow behind me, weeping softly and saying her dead husband's name over and over. Then I took the shot, and moved back to where the men were drinking kava.

That ends my narrative, and you may have realized that I, too,   103
have been engaging in *qaltavalu*, but my point is not what some may think, that we have lost our vision and should return to our roots and study "tradition." That was Andrew's *qaltavalu* to me, not my *qaltavalu* to you. My *qaltavalu* concerns our hidden talk to each other, in writing, in narratives buried in the text of our

---

6. Sorcery is part of *kastom*; it's the dark twin of benevolent magic, the magic that brings gentle rains and cures the ill and makes pigs grow tusks as round as ridgepoles and as big as a big-man's palm. You can't have the one without the possibility of the other. [author's note]

ethnographies. This essay presents a narrative explanation, "an account of the linkages among events as a process one seeks to explain." Embedded in the narrative is an allegory about several kinds of interpretive quest. The anthropologist I call "Mr. Jones" was "as much the question as the questioner." So was I, and so are all fieldworkers: the people we study study us, even in moments when we do not seek to study them. We are not just observers observed; we are interpreters interpreted. To figure out what the devil they think they are up to requires us to try to figure out what they think *we* are up to—our motivation, purposes, and (sometimes) the moral message we bring with us. This is an Other side to reflexivity, one crucial to understanding the dialogics of encounters in field research, and one that anthropologists have only begun to explore.[7]

7. Despite the growing interest in reflexive and dialogical perspectives in anthropology, anthropologists have devoted little attention to the Other's view of anthropology and the anthropological Self. Some notable exceptions to the general lack of consideration of the topic include Dumont, Dwyer, Feld, Stoller, and Page. Despite the efforts of such scholars, it still can reasonably be said that "rarely have we heard much of how the anthropologist was perceived by the people he or she studied, or of the impact that participating in anthropological research may have had on their lives." In a similar vein, Rosaldo points out that "anthropologists often talk about seeing things from the native point of view. . . . Yet we have given little thought to how members of other cultures conceive the translation of cultures." [author's note]

2

SOME REASONS
FOR WRITING

Child refugee studies in a warehouse school in Hong Kong, 1965. Reproduced with permission. *All Mankind*, copyright © 1983 The Christian Science Publishing Society. All rights reserved.

OVERVIEW

"I'm not a writer," a student told me recently. "If I have something to say, I use the telephone." She was angry with a teacher who had just given her a low grade on a paper, and her anger had forced a good question to the surface—why would anyone write these days? If the people we want to talk with aren't available for a face-to-face conversation, the electronic media give us increasingly convenient ways to carry our voices (and our faces, too) anywhere, without all the fuss and inconvenience of writing.

What I might have pointed out was that life doesn't consist entirely of a series of one-to-one conversations. Unless you plan to live a very sheltered life, you will sometimes speak not only to individuals, but also to groups who may find your extemporaneous comments confusing or dull. Sometimes you will have to make yourself clear on a particularly difficult matter, weighing every word. Sometimes you will need to address a "public": an audience of strangers whose only way of judging you and your cause will be what you present them in a few hundred words. Sometimes you will face a difficult problem that no one else can solve for you, and writing will prove to be the best way for you to reason your way through to a conclusion. Unrehearsed conversation, face to face or on the telephone, is a wonderful thing, and writing can never replace it. But there are occasions that are more public *and* more private than a personal conversation, and for these, the process of drafting, revising, and polishing is crucial. I might have *said* all this if I had had time to *write* it first. But it was a face-to-face conversation, and I didn't have time to compose a proper answer.

In the essays collected in this unit, five writers discuss some of the public and private motives that compel them to write:

- George Orwell talks with his usual frankness about his mixed motives for writing, including "sheer egotism," but also including a desire "to alter other people's idea of the kind of society they should strive after."
- David Bradley traces his involvement with writing to the example of his father, an editor, writer, and preacher who

taught him not only the pleasures of writing, but also the hidden cost.

- Richard Rodriguez, who grew up in a close-knit family with a strong sense of privacy, talks about the difficulty of becoming a public writer, someone who works in silence and reveals himself in "words that someone far from home can understand."
- Adrienne Rich traces the evolution of her poetry, showing how the writing both reflected her emerging understanding of sexual politics and helped her come to that understanding.
- In his second essay in this unit George Orwell surveys ways that writing can prevent and corrupt thought, and recommends some rules to prevent this from happening.
- In an essay that begins with an allusion to Orwell, Joan Didion presents herself as a writer whose motives are only partly related to his: "I write entirely to find out what I'm thinking, what I'm looking at, what I see and what it means."

GEORGE ORWELL

Why I Write

Eric Arthur Blair, who took the pen name George Orwell, was the son of a minor colonial official. Born in India, Orwell was sent to England for his education. There he attended exclusive schools where his relative poverty made him feel like an outsider. Though he might have gone on to Cambridge University, he elected instead to join the Indian Imperial Police in Burma, a job that made him, he later said, "part of that evil despotism" he came to despise. Thereafter he became a journalist exploring life among the working poor. He fought fascism as part of the Republican Army during the Spanish Civil War, and he worked for the British Broadcasting Corporation during World War II. Though his fame in his own lifetime came largely through his novels, his long-lasting influence has come through his nonfiction. "Why I Write" was first published in *Gangrel*, summer 1946.

From a very early age, perhaps the age of five or six, I knew that when I grew up I should be a writer. Between the ages of about seventeen and twenty-four I tried to abandon this idea, but I did so with the consciousness that I was outraging my true nature and that sooner or later I should have to settle down and write books.

I was the middle child of three, but there was a gap of five years on either side, and I barely saw my father before I was eight. For this and other reasons I was somewhat lonely, and I soon developed disagreeable mannerisms which made me unpopular throughout my schooldays. I had the lonely child's habit of making up stories and holding conversations with imaginary persons, and I think from the very start my literary ambitions were mixed up with the feeling of being isolated and undervalued. I knew that I had a facility with words and a power of facing unpleasant facts, and I felt that this created a sort of private world in which I could get my own back for my failure in everyday life. Nevertheless the volume of serious—*i.e.* seriously intended—writing which I produced all through my childhood and boyhood would not amount to half a dozen pages. I wrote my first poem at the age of four or five, my mother taking it

down to dictation. I cannot remember anything about it except
that it was about a tiger and the tiger had "chair-like teeth"—a
good enough phrase, but I fancy the poem was a plagiarism of
Blake's "Tiger, Tiger." At eleven, when the war of 1914–18
broke out, I wrote a patriotic poem which was printed in the local newspaper, as was another, two years later, on the death of
Kitchener.[1] From time to time, when I was a bit older, I wrote
bad and usually unfinished "nature poems" in the Georgian
style. I also, about twice, attempted a short story which was a
ghastly failure. That was the total of the would-be serious work
that I actually set down on paper during all those years.

However, throughout this time I did in a sense engage in liter-   3
ary activities. To begin with there was the made-to-order stuff
which I produced quickly, easily and without much pleasure to
myself. Apart from school work, I wrote *vers d'occasion*, semi-
comic poems which I could turn out at what now seems to me
astonishing speed—at fourteen I wrote a whole rhyming play, in
imitation of Aristophanes,[2] in about a week—and helped to edit
school magazines, both printed and in manuscript. These magazines were the most pitiful burlesque stuff that you could imagine, and I took far less trouble with them than I now would with
the cheapest journalism. But side by side with all this, for fifteen
years or more, I was carrying out a literary exercise of a quite
different kind: this was the making up of a continuous "story"
about myself, a sort of diary existing only in the mind. I believe
this is a common habit of children and adolescents. As a very
small child I used to imagine that I was, say, Robin Hood, and
picture myself as the hero of thrilling adventures, but quite soon
my "story" ceased to be narcissistic in a crude way and became
more and more a mere description of what I was doing and the
things I saw. For minutes at a time this kind of thing would be
running through my head: "He pushed the door open and entered the room. A yellow beam of sunlight, filtering through the
muslin curtains, slanted on to the table, where a match-box, half
open, lay beside the inkpot. With his right hand in his pocket he
moved across to the window. Down in the street a tortoiseshell
cat was chasing a dead leaf," etc., etc. This habit continued till I
was about twenty-five, right through my non-literary years. Al-

1. Herbert Horatio Kitchener (1850–1916): British general and politician lost at
sea in military action.
2. Aristophanes (ca. 448–380 B.C.): Greek playwright.

though I had to search, and did search, for the right words, I seemed to be making this descriptive effort almost against my will, under a kind of compulsion from outside. The "story" must, I suppose, have reflected the styles of the various writers I admired at different ages, but so far as I remember it always had the same meticulous descriptive quality.

When I was about sixteen I suddenly discovered the joy of 4 mere words, *i.e.*, the sounds and associations of words. The lines from *Paradise Lost*—

> *So hee with difficulty and labour hard*
> *Moved on: with difficulty and labour hee,*

which do not now seem to me so very wonderful, sent shivers down my backbone; and the spelling "hee" for "he" was an added pleasure. As for the need to describe things, I knew all about it already. So it is clear what kind of books I wanted to write, in so far as I could be said to want to write books at that time. I wanted to write enormous naturalistic novels with unhappy endings, full of detailed descriptions and arresting similes, and also full of purple passages in which words were used partly for the sake of their sound. And in fact my first completed novel, *Burmese Days*, which I wrote when I was thirty but projected much earlier, is rather that kind of book.

I give all this background information because I do not think 5 one can assess a writer's motives without knowing something of his early development. His subject matter will be determined by the age he lives in—at least this is true in tumultuous, revolutionary ages like our own—but before he ever begins to write he will have acquired an emotional attitude from which he will never completely escape. It is his job, no doubt, to discipline his temperament and avoid getting stuck at some immature stage, or in some perverse mood: but if he escapes from his early influences altogether, he will have killed his impulse to write. Putting aside the need to earn a living, I think there are four great motives for writing, at any rate for writing prose. They exist in different degrees in every writer, and in any one writer the proportions will vary from time to time, according to the atmosphere in which he is living. They are:

1. Sheer egoism. Desire to seem clever, to be talked about, 6
   to be remembered after death, to get your own back on

grown-ups who snubbed you in childhood, etc., etc. It is humbug to pretend that this is not a motive, and a strong one. Writers share this characteristic with scientists, artists, politicians, lawyers, soldiers, successful business-men—in short, with the whole top crust of humanity. The great mass of human beings are not acutely selfish. After the age of about thirty they abandon individual ambi-tion—in many cases, indeed, they almost abandon the sense of being individuals at all—and live chiefly for oth-ers, or are simply smothered under drudgery. But there is also the minority of gifted, wilful people who are deter-mined to live their own lives to the end, and writers belong in this class. Serious writers, I should say, are on the whole more vain and self-centered than journalists, though less interested in money.

2. Aesthetic enthusiasm. Perception of beauty in the external world, or, on the other hand, in words and their right arrangement. Pleasure in the impact of one sound on an-other, in the firmness of good prose or the rhythm of a good story. Desire to share an experience which one feels is valuable and ought not to be missed. The aesthetic mo-tive is very feeble in a lot of writers, but even a pamphlet-eer or a writer of textbooks will have pet words and phrases which appeal to him for non-utilitarian reasons; or he may feel strongly about typography, width of margins, etc. Above the level of a railway guide, no book is quite free from aesthetic considerations. 7

3. Historical impulse. Desire to see things as they are, to find out true facts and store them up for the use of posterity. 8

4. Political purpose—using the word "political" in the widest possible sense. Desire to push the world in a certain direc-tion, to alter other people's idea of the kind of society that they should strive after. Once again, no book is genuinely free from political bias. The opinion that art should have nothing to do with politics is itself a political attitude. 9

It can be seen how these various impulses must war against one another, and how they must fluctuate from person to person and from time to time. By nature—taking your "nature" to be the state you have attained when you are first adult—I am a per- 10 son in whom the first three motives would outweigh the fourth. In a peaceful age I might have written ornate or merely descriptive books, and might have remained almost unaware of my political loyalties. As it is I have been forced into becoming a sort of pamphleteer. First I spent five years in an unsuitable profession (the Indian Imperial Police, in Burma), and then I underwent poverty and the sense of failure. This increased my natural hatred of authority and made me for the first time fully aware of the existence of the working classes, and the job in Burma had given me some understanding of the nature of imperialism: but these experiences were not enough to give me an accurate political orientation. Then came Hitler, the Spanish civil war, etc. By the end of 1935 I had still failed to reach a firm decision. I remember a little poem that I wrote at that date, expressing my dilemma:

> A happy vicar I might have been
> Two hundred years ago,
> To preach upon eternal doom
> And watch my walnuts grow;
>
> But born, alas, in an evil time,
> I missed that pleasant haven,
> For the hair has grown on my upper lip
> And the clergy are all clean-shaven.
>
> And later still the times were good,
> We were so easy to please,
> We rocked our troubled thoughts to sleep
> On the bosoms of the trees.
>
> All ignorant we dared to own
> The joys we now dissemble;
> The greenfinch on the apple bough
> Could make my enemies tremble.
>
> But girls' bellies and apricots,
> Roach in a shaded stream,
> Horses, ducks in flight at dawn,
> All these are a dream.
>
> It is forbidden to dream again;
> We maim our joys or hide them;
> Horses are made of chromium steel
> And little fat men shall ride them.

I am the worm who never turned,
The eunuch without a harem;
Between the priest and the commissar
I walk like Eugene Aram;

And the commissar is telling my fortune
While the radio plays,
But the priest has promised an Austin Seven,
For Duggie always pays.

I dreamed I dwelt in marble halls,
And woke to find it true;
I wasn't born for an age like this;
Was Smith? Was Jones? Were you?

The Spanish war and other events in 1936–7 turned the scale and thereafter I knew where I stood. Every line of serious work that I have written since 1936 has been written, directly or indirectly, *against* totalitarianism and *for* democratic socialism, as I understand it. It seems to me nonsense, in a period like our own, to think that one can avoid writing of such subjects. Everyone writes of them in one guise or another. It is simply a question of which side one takes and what approach one follows. And the more one is conscious of one's political bias, the more chance one has of acting politically without sacrificing one's aesthetic and intellectual integrity.

What I have most wanted to do throughout the past ten years is to make political writing into an art. My starting point is always a feeling of partisanship, a sense of injustice. When I sit down to write a book, I do not say to myself, "I am going to produce a work of art." I write it because there is some lie that I want to expose, some fact to which I want to draw attention, and my initial concern is to get a hearing. But I could not do the work of writing a book, or even a long magazine article, if it were not also an aesthetic experience. Anyone who cares to examine my work will see that even when it is downright propaganda it contains much that a full-time politician would consider irrelevant. I am not able, and I do not want, completely to abandon the world view that I acquired in childhood. So long as I remain alive and well I shall continue to feel strongly about prose style, to love the surface of the earth, and to take a pleasure in solid objects and scraps of useless information. It is no use trying to suppress that side of myself. The job is to reconcile my ingrained likes and dislikes with the essentially public, non-individual activities that this age forces on all of us.

It is not easy. It raises problems of construction and of language, and it raises in a new way the problem of truthfulness. Let me give just one example of the cruder kind of difficulty that arises. My book about the Spanish civil war, *Homage to Catalonia*, is, of course, a frankly political book, but in the main it is written with a certain detachment and regard for form. I did try very hard in it to tell the whole truth without violating my literary instincts. But among other things it contains a long chapter, full of newspaper quotations and the like, defending the Trotskyists who were accused of plotting with Franco. Clearly such a chapter, which after a year or two would lose its interest for any ordinary reader, must ruin the book. A critic whom I respect read me a lecture about it. "Why did you put in all that stuff?" he said. "You've turned what might have been a good book into journalism." What he said was true, but I could not have done otherwise. I happened to know, what very few people in England had been allowed to know, that innocent men were being falsely accused. If I had not been angry about that I should never have written the book.

In one form or another this problem comes up again. The problem of language is subtler and would take too long to discuss. I will only say that of late years I have tried to write less picturesquely and more exactly. In any case I find that by the time you have perfected any style of writing, you have always outgrown it. *Animal Farm* was the first book in which I tried, with full consciousness of what I was doing, to fuse political purpose and artistic purpose into one whole. I have not written a novel for seven years, but I hope to write another fairly soon. It is bound to be a failure, every book is a failure, but I do know with some clarity what kind of book I want to write. Looking back through the last page or two, I see that I have made it appear as though my motives in writing were wholly public-spirited. I don't want to leave that as the final impression. All writers are vain, selfish, and lazy, and at the very bottom of their motives there lies a mystery. Writing a book is a horrible, exhausting struggle, like a long bout of some painful illness. One would never undertake such a thing if one were not driven on by some

12

13

demon whom one can neither resist nor understand. For all one knows that demon is simply the same instinct that makes a baby squall for attention. And yet it is also true that one can write nothing readable unless one constantly struggles to efface one's own personality. Good prose is like a windowpane. I cannot say with certainty which of my motives are the strongest, but I know which of them deserve to be followed. And looking back through my work, I see that it is invariably where I lacked a *political* purpose that I wrote lifeless books and was betrayed into purple passages, sentences without meaning, decorative adjectives, and humbug generally.

DAVID BRADLEY

The Faith

David Bradley grew up in rural Pennsylvania, "perilously close," as he puts it, "to the Mason-Dixon line." While an undergraduate he completed a novel based on the life stories he had heard at a local bar and he began work on a second novel, *The Chaneyville Incident* (1981). *Chaneyville* explored an incident Bradley had learned about from his mother: the capture, killing, and burial of thirteen runaway slaves on a farm near Bradley's home. It took him ten years and four full drafts to complete this prize-winning novel. "The Faith" was first published in *In Praise of What Persists* (Stephen Berg, ed.) in 1983.

One evening not long ago I found myself sitting on a stage in front of a live audience, being asked questions about life and art. I was uncomfortable, as I always am in such circumstances. Still, things were going pretty well on this occasion, until the interviewer noted that my father had been a minister, and asked what influence religion, the church, and the faith of my father, had had on my development as a writer. After a moment of confusion, I responded that since I had, at various times and with more than a modicum of accuracy, been labeled a heretic, a pagan, a heathen, and a moral degenerate, all things considered, the faith of my father had had very little to do with my writing. Which was, depending on how cynical you want to be, either a total lie or as

close as I could get to the truthful answer—which would have
been: "Practically everything."

The history of my relationship to religion cannot be stated so   2
simply as "My father was a minister." In fact, I am descended
from a long line of ministers. The first was my great-grandfather,
a freedman named Peter Bradley, who, in the early part of the
nineteenth century, was licensed to preach by the African
Methodist Episcopal Zion Church, one of two denominations
formed at that time by blacks who were tired of the discrimination they were forced to endure in the regular Methodist Church.
Peter's son, Daniel Francis, followed in his father's footsteps and
then went a step further, becoming a presiding elder with administrative and spiritual responsibility over a number of churches
in western Pennsylvania and Ohio. Daniel Francis's son, David,
followed his father's footsteps, and then added a step of his own:
he was elected a general officer of the denomination (a rank just
below that of bishop), with the dual responsibility of traveling
the country to run conferences and workshops in Christian education and of publishing the church's quasi-academic journal,
the *A. M. E. Zion Quarterly Review,* tasks he performed without
interruption for nearly thirty years. Since David was my father, it
would seem reasonable to expect that I would carry on the family tradition. That I did not was a fact that was viewed with great
relief by all those who knew me—including David senior. Nevertheless, my apostasy had its origins in the church. For because of
my father's editorial functions, I grew up in a publishing house.

My earliest memories of excitement, bustle, and tension cen-   3
ter on the process of mailing the 1,400- or 1,500-copy press run
of the *Quarterly Review.* The books came in sweet-smelling and
crisp from the printer, were labeled, bundled, and shipped out
again in big gray-green musty mailbags labeled with the names
of far-off states, a process that was sheer heaven to a three- or
four-year-old and sheer hell for everybody else, especially my
mother, who did the bulk of the work and had to give up a chunk
of her house to the process.

In fact, the work of publishing the *Review* took up the whole   4
house most of the time; it was just that work usually went on at
a less frenetic rate. While my father was away, my mother, who
was the subscription and shipping department, spent some time
cleaning the lists (a constant task, since ministers, the main sub-
scribers, were regularly being moved around) and typing names

and addresses onto labels. When my father returned home, the tempo picked up. He spent a good bit of time in the study, writing to other ministers and prominent lay people to solicit articles and publishable sermons, and editing those that had already arrived. At that same time, he would be writing a bit himself, composing the two or three editorials that graced each issue.

The *Review*, while it was called a quarterly, was not published every three months, but rather four times a year; my father took it to the printer when he was home long enough to get it ready, and when the printer had time to do the work. The date for that was sometimes fixed only a week or so in advance, and once it was set, the tempo became fairly furious; my father spent more and more time in the study, selecting cover art, editing the late-arriving articles, rewriting the press releases from the National Council of Churches that he used for filler. Then, on the date designated, with the copy in one hand, and my hand in the other, my father would go to the printer. 5

I looked forward to going to the printer with my father, in part because of the printer himself, a venerable gentleman named George, the perfect image of a chapelman all the way down to his ink-stained knuckles and honest-to-God green eyeshade. The chapel over which he presided was no mere print shop, but the printing plant of the local daily, a dark cavern with an ink-impregnated wood floor and air that smelled of hot metal and chemicals, crowded with weirdly shaped machines. On the left a bank of linotypes spewed hot type and spattered molten lead onto the floor. On the right were machines to do the tasks that at home I saw done by hand—address labels, tie bundles, stuff envelopes. At the back, dominating the entire scene, was the great press on which the paper was printed, a big, black, awkward-looking thing that towered to the ceiling and descended into the bowels of the earth. Once George invited my father to bring me down at night to see the press roll, a sight that proved to be so exciting I could not tell if all the shaking was due to the awesome turning of the rollers or to the weakness in my knees; but usually we went to the printer during the day, and the big press was simply a silent presence. 6

During the visits to the printer, my father and George would be closeted in the little cubbyhole that served as George's office, while I had the run of the chapel. It was on one of those occa- 7 sions, I believe, that any chance I would follow in the family footsteps was lost. For on this one day, while George and my father muttered of ems and ens, one of the linotype operators paused in his work and invited me to write my name on a scrap of paper, and after I had done so, let me watch as he punched my name out in hot lead. I think that was the moment when my personal die was cast.

Of course, it might have had no lasting effect had not my father, at about the same time, inadvertently introduced me to the corrupting pleasure of having written a book. 8

A few years before I was born, my father abandoned his studies at New York University, where he had been working for a Ph.D. in history. Five years later, for no reason other than desire, he took up the writing of what would have been his dissertation: "A History of the A. M. E. Zion Church." 9

I do not remember what it was like being around him while he wrote—I was, after all, less than five. I recall his methodology, which was to write a fairly detailed outline in a flowing longhand on lined paper, which he would store in a big loose-leaf binder until he was ready to turn it into a messy typescript which a typist—often my mother—later rendered as clean copy. (For one reason or another, this is the method I now use to write nonfiction.) I believe there was a certain heightening of tension during the time he was sending the typescript off to publishers; I know that he eventually entered into a cooperative arrangement with a press in Tennessee, a measure which forced him to take out a second mortgage—something I know he felt guilty about, since years later he would explain that we were not in better financial shape because of the book, but something he did not really regret, since he did it again in order to publish the second volume. 10

At the time the first volume was published, I was only six, but already I was in love with books. I had my own card at the public library, and I had read everything they had that was suitable for a child my age, and a lot that was not. Moreover, I had reread much of it many times, and the characters and stories had become so familiar, that my imagination was no longer a participant in the process; as a result, I had taken to imagining the people behind the characters. I was not old enough for literary biographies (the biographies written for children at that time went heavy on Clara Barton and Thomas Alva Edison and the 11 like, and concentrated on the time when they were children; I loathed the things). And so I made up my own, based on bits of story I had picked up here and there. I was fascinated with Herman Melville and Richard Henry Dana, Jr., both of whom my mother said had actually gone to sea. And I was captivated by Jack London, who, my father told me, had really gone hunting gold in the frozen Yukon.

But even though I was taken with these people, I felt removed   12 from them; they were not real—not as real, anyway, as the characters about whom they wrote. For I could imagine myself standing before the mast or trekking the frozen tundra, but I simply could not imagine myself writing a book.

But then one day a big tractor-trailer pulled up in the drive-   13 way and began to unload cartons, and my father, normally not an impulsive or a demonstrative man, took the first carton and ripped it open and pulled out a book that had his name stamped on the front board in gold foil, and suddenly the men behind the books I'd read were as real to me as my father. And suddenly I began to see that slug of type, which I had kept safe, mounted and inked, imprinting my name on a book.

I have always been uncertain about the importance of some of   14 the things that have happened to me, suspecting that if one thing had not pushed me in the direction of writing, then probably something else would have. But I know the importance of that moment. For time and time again, people have said to me that the writing of a book is an impossible task, even to comprehend. For me, though, it was not only comprehensible, it was visible. And so, by the age of six or seven, I had firmly turned away from the family tradition. Ironically enough, at about the same time I began to discover the majesty and beauty of the Christian worship service.

When I was four or five, my father had started taking me with   15 him on some of his travels, usually in the summer, when his work took him mostly to the Southeast. The first place I went with him—and it became a regular trip—was Dinwiddie, Virginia, where, in an aging ramshackle three-story building, the church operated an "Institute"—a combination Christian education workshop, summer camp, and revival meeting.

The Institute ran for three weeks—a week each for children,   16 teenagers (what the church called "young people"), and adults. The format for all was basically the same: a day of classes punctuated by morning and noon chapel services, an afternoon recreation period, and three meals of good plain food—corn bread, grits, chicken, pork, greens—and climaxed by evening worship. The morning and afternoon worship services were short and pretty plain affairs. The evening service was pageantry, if for no other reason than that it was the focal point of everybody's day. My father's involvement was primarily with the "young people," and so I spent more time at the Institute when they were there. Evening worship was important to them because it was the closest they could get to a dating situation, and they made the most of it. It was important to the ministers, who shared the various offices of the service on a rotating basis, competing eagerly for the choice assignments, preaching and praying. It was important to the people in the community, who used the evening worship as a kind of camp meeting. And it was important to me, because the Institute was not equipped with a radio or a TV, and worse, had a limited number of books. (I was so desperate for reading matter I practically memorized the begats.) For me, evening worship was a source of entertainment.

It began with the arrival of the audience, the scrubbed youths   17 and their chaperones, followed closely by the people from the community: the older ladies in out-of-fashion but immaculate dresses and toilet water; the men, seeming all of an age, with big rough hands poking out of the cuffs of suit coats worn awkwardly; the younger girls, in light dresses, casting flirtatious glances at the young men at the Institute (who were usually from cities, and therefore seen as sophisticated) and sharp challenging looks at the institute's young women (who were also usually from the city, and therefore seen as probably a little wild). They would all troop into the dilapidated auditorium, filling the rows of ragtag seating—trestle benches, tip-up seats from abandoned theaters, folding chairs mended with cardboard, even a couple of mismatched church pews—and wait impatiently for the ministers.

The ministers entered from the front, moving more or less in   18 time to the sound that came from an off-key, beaten-up piano. They were not unfamiliar figures—they were around all day, teaching classes, arguing points of theology and church politics, and playing Chinese checkers beneath the trees. Now they were solemn and dignified in black suits and clerical collars, each intent on performing his role, no matter how minor, with as much style as he could muster.

Performance was the word, for the service was high drama,   19
from the solemnly intoned ritual invocation, to the rolling
hymns sung by a hundred people who needed no hymnals, in
passionate voices that overpowered the doubtful leadership of
the gap-toothed piano, to the hucksterish importunings over the
collection plate, as a minister would announce the total and then
proceed to cajole, shame, or bully the audience into bringing it
higher. There was no applause, of course, but the performance of
each minister was rewarded with responses from the worshipers;
the preaching and praying being applauded with a spontaneous
chorus of "Amen, amen," "Yes, yes, yes," and the ultimate ac-
colade, "Preach on, preach on." Which they did, sometimes until midnight.

I was overwhelmed by the worship services, not because I   20
was religious, but because there was something innately compelling about the form and pacing and order of it: the slow,
solemn beginning, the rhythms of song and responsive reading,
the spontaneous lyricism, the sense of wholeness and cohesion
and abandon when a preacher really got going, the perfection
of catharsis when the end of the service flowed swiftly and
smoothly to the benediction.

I have often wondered why my initial emotional response did   21
not manifest itself as some kind of visible expression of faith—
why, while I sang the hymns and was moved by the pageantry, I
never gave myself over to witnessing or even made a journey to
the altar to accept Jesus as my savior. I believe this was due to the
example of my father, who found emotional religious expression
embarrassing, and took an intellectual approach to religion, to
anything. In any case, my love of worship expressed itself in an
analytical way—I began to see it as a critical paradigm. The order of service, with its variations in pacing and mood, its combination of poetic and prosaic elements, of mysticism and
hucksterism, became, to me, the model of what a dramatic experience should be. This led to my development of a critical consciousness: I began to judge worship services as good, or not so
good. More important, from the point of view of a writer, I saw
enough services that were not so good to develop an editorial
sense, a feeling for when the prayer was becoming repetitive,
when the hymn was wrong, when the minister failed to create a
sermon that expanded upon the text. But more important than

even that, I learned that the analytical, critical approach, while a useful means, was not, for me, an end.

For I had on a very few occasions seen a preacher, sometimes not a usually good preacher, create, perhaps with the aid of divine inspiration, a service or a sermon that defied criticism. Once I saw it happen to my father.   22

The year was 1965. By that time, our summer travels had taken my father and me beyond Virginia into North and South Carolina. Nevertheless, the format of the Christian education conventions we attended was the same as that at the Dinwiddie Institute. In one place, that year, they asked my father to preach.   23

I was not overly excited by the prospect, since I had heard him preach two or three hundred times, and had always found his sermons to be rather dry, tending, as he tended, to focus on the head rather than the heart. The text was Isaiah 30:21: "And thine ears shall hear a word behind thee, saying, This *is* the way, walk ye in it," and as my father read it, I realized that I had heard the sermon he was beginning at least four times, liking it less each time. When he began to speak I expected the textual analysis and explication by definition that marked his style. But this night he abandoned that—something got hold of him. He followed the reading of the text with the telling of a tale.   24

He had, he said, been in high school, sitting in a classroom, when a man had come to the school asking for volunteers to go up to fight a forest fire that raged on a nearby mountain. My father and some others agreed to go, and were taken up by wagon, then went on foot a mile or two farther, to a point where they had been told to dig a firebreak. The fire, my father said, seemed a long way away; not sensing the danger, they allowed themselves to become absorbed in their task. When finally they looked up from it, they found that the fire had swept about them—they were surrounded by flames.   25

They reacted as one would have expected. My father told of his panic, how he had at first cried hysterically, then begun to curse, using words he had not realized he knew, had finally collapsed into desperate prayer, all, it seemed, to no avail. But then, when the smoke was at its thickest, when he was about to lose sight of his companions, when the very sound of their wailing was lost in the roaring of the flames, there came a voice calling to them to follow. They followed that voice, escaping with its   26 guidance through what must have been the last gap in the fire. Afterward they asked who it had been who risked himself to save them, but no one could tell them who it was.

From the tale my father moved to the obvious but eloquent equation, exchanging that unknown savior for a known one, who called the same message, and who led all who followed him clear of the flames. And then, almost abruptly, and far sooner than anyone expected, he stopped. And he brought down the house. 27

That sermon shocked me. Because I knew my father, knew that he had hidden that story for forty years, had kept it out of previous versions of the same sermon because he was the kind of man who hated to admit weakness, or indecision, or helplessness. I knew that to relive that time on the mountainside had cost him greatly, and to admit his own helplessness had cost him even more. But I realized that the sermon had been something beyond that which was usual for him, and I believed, for no reason I could express, but nevertheless believed, that it was the paying of the price that had made the sermon possible. I believed that in confessing his own weakness he had found access to a hidden source of power inside, or perhaps outside, himself—in any case, a source of power that was magical, mystical. 28

Until that night I had not understood what it meant to write. I had known that the writer's goal was to reveal truths in words manipulated so effectively as to cause a movement in the minds and hearts of those who read them. But I had not understood that it would cost anything. I had believed that I could do those things while remaining secure and safe in myself—I had even believed that writing fiction was a way to conceal my true feelings and weaknesses. That night, I found out better. That night, I realized that no matter how good I became in the manipulation of symbols, I could never hope to move anyone without allowing myself to be moved, that I could reveal only slight truths unless I was willing to reveal the truths about myself. I did not enjoy the realization. For I was no fonder of self-revelation than my father, and though I knew I would love to do with written words what my father had done in speech, I was not sure I could pay the price. I was not sure I wanted to. 29

I do not know why my career as a writer did not end there. All I know is that, in fact, it began there. For out of that night came 30 the only idea I have that could truly be called an aesthetic standard: expensiveness. When I ask myself, as all writers do, whether to write something this way or that way, whether to keep this bit, or throw it away, I ask myself, along with all the practical, technical, editorial questions, Does it cost? Is it possible that someone reading might discover something about me that I would rather not have him know? Is there something truly private here, something I would never admit face to face, unless, perhaps, I was drunk?

I would like to say that if the answer to those questions is No, 31 I go back and dig down inside myself until I do find something it will cost me to say; the truth is I do not always do that. But I believe I should. And I believe that someday, when I am good enough, not as a manipulator of words and phrases but as a human being, I will. And I believe that each time I work, and make the effort, I get closer to that ideal.

I doubt that could be called a religious expression. That I act 32 upon it is, however, a matter of faith. For I cannot prove that there is anything to be gained from writing with that sort of aesthetic in mind. I cannot show that my work will be read by more people, that my books will sell more copies, that I will make more money, get better reviews. I cannot truly say that the work is better—I believe it is, but I cannot prove it. Despite the fact that I cannot prove it, however, I believe this aesthetic of cost does make a difference in my writing and the reception of it. This belief is important. For without it I would not be able to pay the price of writing in the way that pleases me. I would write, but, by my standards, I would do it badly. Eventually I would give it up, or become a prostitute, in it only for the money. I need not fear this, because I do believe. The capacity for belief is something I acquired from being so much in contact with others who believed. This, perhaps, is the most important influence on me from the faith of my father.

RICHARD RODRIGUEZ

Mr. Secrets

The son of Mexican-American immigrants, Richard Rodriguez entered public school in Sacramento, California, knowing little English. He proved to be an excellent student, eventually taking degrees at Stanford and Columbia University. While studying in London for a Ph.D. in English Renaissance literature, he abandoned academic life and began to publish autobiographical essays and books focused on his situation as a double outsider—uneasy among English and American academics because of his ethnic background, uneasy around his family because of his emerging identity as a writer. "Mr. Secrets" is the sixth chapter of *Hunger of Memory* (1981).

I am writing about those very things my mother has asked me   1
not to reveal. Shortly after I published my first autobiographical
essay seven years ago, my mother wrote me a letter pleading
with me never again to write about our family life. "Write about
something else in the future. Our family life is private." And besides: "Why do you need to tell the *gringos* about how 'divided'
you feel from the family?"

I sit at my desk now, surrounded by versions of paragraphs   2
and pages of this book, considering that question.

When I decided to compose this intellectual autobiography, a   3
New York editor told me that I would embark on a lonely journey. Over the noise of voices and dishes in an East Side restaurant, he said, "There will be times when you will think the entire
world has forgotten you. Some mornings you will yearn for a
phone call or a letter to assure you that you still are connected to
the world." There *have* been mornings when I've dreaded the
isolation this writing requires. Mornings spent listless in silence
and in fear of confronting the blank sheet of paper. There have
been times I've rushed away from my papers to answer the
phone; gladly gotten up from my chair, hearing the mailman outside. Times I have been frustrated by the slowness of words, the
way even a single paragraph never seemed done.

I had known a writer's loneliness before, working on my dis-   4

sertation in the British Museum. But that experience did not prepare me for the task of writing these pages where my own life is
the subject. Many days I feared I had stopped living by commit-
ting myself to remember the past. I feared that my absorption
with events in my past amounted to an immature refusal to live
in the present. Adulthood seemed consumed by memory. I would
tell myself otherwise. I would tell myself that the act of remembering is an act of the present. (In writing this autobiography, I
am actually describing the man I have become—the man in the
present.)

Times when the money ran out, I left writing for temporary 5
jobs. Once I had a job for over six months. I resumed something
like a conventional social life. But then I have turned away, come
back to my San Francisco apartment to closet myself in the silence I both need and fear.

I stay away from late-night parties. (To be clearheaded in the 6
morning.) I disconnect my phone for much of the day. I must
avoid complex relationships—a troublesome lover or a troubled
friend. The person who knows me best scolds me for escaping
from life. (*Am* I evading adulthood?) People I know get promotions at jobs. Friends move away. Friends get married. Friends
divorce. One friend tells me she is pregnant. Then she has a baby.
Then the baby has the formed face of a child. Can walk. Talk.
And still I sit at this desk laying my words like jigsaw pieces, a
fellow with ladies in housecoats and old men in slippers who
watch TV. Neighbors in my apartment house rush off to work
about nine. I hear their steps on the stairs. (They will be back at
six o'clock.) Somewhere planes are flying. The door slams behind them.

"Why?" My mother's question hangs in the still air of memory. 7

The loneliness I have felt many mornings, however, has not 8
made me forget that I am engaged in a highly public activity. I
sit here in silence writing this small volume of words, and it
seems to me the most public thing I ever have done. My mother's
letter has served to remind me: I am making my personal life
public. Probably I will never try to explain my motives to my
mother and father. My mother's question will go unanswered to
her face. Like everything else on these pages, my reasons for
writing will be revealed instead to public readers I expect never
to meet.

I

It is to those whom my mother refers to as the *gringos* that I write. The *gringos*. The expression reminds me that she and my father have not followed their children all the way down the path to full Americanization. They were changed—became more easy in public, less withdrawn and uncertain—by the public success of their children. But something remained unchanged in their lives. With excessive care they continue today to note the difference between private and public life. And their private society remains only their family. No matter how friendly they are in public, no matter how firm their smiles, my parents never forget when they are in public. My mother must use a high-pitched tone of voice when she addresses people who are not relatives. It is a tone of voice I have all my life heard her use away from the house. Coming home from grammar school with new friends, I would hear it, its reminder: My new intimates were strangers to her. Like my sisters and brother, over the years, I've grown used to hearing that voice. Expected to hear it. Though I suspect that voice has played deep in my soul, sounding a lyre, to recall my "betrayal," my movement away from our family's intimate past. It is the voice I hear even now when my mother addresses her son- or daughter-in-law. (They remain public people to her.) She speaks to them, sounding the way she does when talking over the fence to a neighbor.

It was, in fact, the lady next door to my parents—a librarian—who first mentioned seeing my essay seven years ago. My mother was embarrassed because she hadn't any idea what the lady was talking about. But she had heard enough to go to a library with my father to find the article. They read what I wrote. And then she wrote her letter.

It is addressed to me in Spanish, but the body of the letter is in English. Almost mechanically she speaks of her pride at the start. ("Your dad and I are very proud of the brilliant manner you have to express yourself.") Then the matter of most concern comes to the fore. "Your dad and I have only one objection to what you write. You say too much about the family. . . . Why do you have to do that? . . . Why do you need to tell the *gringos*? . . . Why do you think we're so separated as a family? Do you really think this, Richard?"

A new paragraph changes the tone. Soft, maternal. Worried   12
for me she adds, "Do not punish yourself for having to give up
our culture in order to 'make it' as you say. Think of all the wonderful achievements you have obtained. You should be proud.
Learn Spanish better. Practice it with your dad and me. Don't
worry so much. Don't get the idea that I am mad at you either.

"Just keep one thing in mind. Writing is one thing, the family   13
is another. I don't want *tus hermanos*[1] hurt by your writings.
And what do you think the cousins will say when they read
where you talk about how the aunts were maids? Especially I
don't want the *gringos* knowing about our private affairs. Why
should they? Please give this some thought. Please write about
something else in the future. Do me this favor."

Please.   14

To the adult I am today, my mother needs to say what she   15
would never have needed to say to her child: the boy who faithfully kept family secrets. When my fourth-grade teacher made
our class write a paper about a typical evening at home, it never
occurred to me actually to do so. "Describe what you do with
your family," she told us. And automatically I produced a fic-
tionalized account. I wrote that I had six brothers and sisters; I
described watching my mother get dressed up in a red-sequined
dress before she went with my father to a party; I even related
how the imaginary baby sitter ("a high school student") taught
my brother and sisters and me to make popcorn and how, later,
I fell asleep before my parents returned. The nun who read what
I wrote would have known that what I had written was completely imagined. But she never said anything about my contrivance. And I never expected her to either. I never thought she
really wanted me to write about my family life. In any case, I
would have been unable to do so.

I was very much the son of parents who regarded the most in-   16
nocuous piece of information about the family to be secret. Although I had, by that time, grown easy in public, I felt that my
family life was strictly private, not to be revealed to unfamiliar
ears or eyes. Around the age of ten, I was held by surprise listening to my best friend tell me one day that he "hated" his father.
In a furious whisper he said that when he attempted to kiss his

1. "Your [Rodriguez's] brother and sisters."

father before going to bed, his father had laughed: "Don't you think you're getting too old for that sort of thing, son?" I was intrigued not so much by the incident as by the fact that the boy would relate it to *me*.

In those years I was exposed to the sliding-glass-door informality of middle-class California family life. Ringing the doorbell of a friend's house, I would hear someone inside yell out, "Come on in, Richie; door's not locked." And in I would go to discover my friend's family undisturbed by my presence. The father was in the kitchen in his underwear. The mother was in her bathrobe. Voices gathered in familiarity. A parent scolded a child in front of me; voices quarreled, then laughed; the mother told me something about her son after he had stepped out of the room and she was sure he wouldn't overhear; the father would speak to his children and to me in the same tone of voice. I was one of the family, the parents of several good friends would assure me. (Richie.)   17

My mother sometimes invited my grammar school friends to stay for dinner or even to stay overnight. But my parents never treated such visitors as part of the family, never told them they were. When a school friend ate at our table, my father spoke less than usual. (Stray, distant words.) My mother was careful to use her "visitor's voice." Sometimes, listening to her, I would feel annoyed because she wouldn't be more herself. Sometimes I'd feel embarrassed that I couldn't give to a friend at my house what I freely accepted at his.   18

I remained, nevertheless, my parents' child. At school, in sixth grade, my teacher suggested that I start keeping a diary. ("You should write down your personal experiences and reflections.") But I shied away from the idea. It was the one suggestion that the scholarship boy couldn't follow. I would not have wanted to write about the minor daily events of my life; I would never have been able to write about what most deeply, daily, concerned me during those years: I was growing away from my parents. Even if I could have been certain that no one would find my diary, even if I could have destroyed each page after I had written it, I would have felt uncomfortable writing about my home life. There seemed to me something intrinsically public about written words.   19

Writing, at any rate, was a skill I didn't regard highly. It was a grammar school skill I acquired with comparative ease. I do not   20 remember struggling to write the way I struggled to learn how to read. The nuns would praise student papers for being neat—the handwritten letters easy for others to read; they promised that my writing style would improve as I read more and more. But that wasn't the reason I became a reader. Reading was for me the key to "knowledge"; I swallowed facts and dates and names and themes. Writing, by contrast, was an activity I thought of as a kind of report, evidence of learning. I wrote down what I heard teachers say. I wrote down things from my books. I wrote down all I knew when I was examined at the end of the school year. Writing was performed after the fact; it was not the exciting experience of learning itself. In eighth grade I read several hundred books, the titles of which I still can recall. But I cannot remember a single essay I wrote. I only remember that the most frequent kind of essay I wrote was the book report.

In high school there were more "creative" writing assign- 21 ments. English teachers assigned the composition of short stories and poems. One sophomore story I wrote was a romance set in the Civil War South. I remember that it earned me a good enough grade, but my teacher suggested with quiet tact that next time I try writing about "something you know more about— something closer to home." Home? I wrote a short story about an old man who lived all by himself in a house down the block. That was as close as my writing ever got to my house. Still, I won prizes. When teachers suggested I contribute articles to the school literary magazine, I did so. And when I was asked to join the school newspaper, I said yes. I did not feel any great pride in my writings, however. (My mother was the one who collected my prize-winning essays in a box she kept in her closet.) Though I remember seeing my by-line in print for the first time, and dwelling on the printing press letters with fascination: RICHARD RODRIGUEZ. The letters furnished evidence of a vast public identity writing made possible.

When I was a freshman in college, I began typing all my as- 22 signments. My writing speed decreased. Writing became a struggle. In high school I had been able to handwrite ten- and twenty-page papers in little more than an hour—and I never revised what I wrote. A college essay took me several nights to prepare. Suddenly everything I wrote seemed in need of revision. I became a self-conscious writer. A stylist. The change, I suspect, was the result of seeing my words ordered by the even, impersonal, anonymous typewriter print. As arranged by a machine, the words that I typed no longer seemed mine. I was able to see them with a new appreciation for how my reader would see them.

From grammar school to graduate school I could always name my reader. I wrote for my teacher. I could consult him or her before writing, and after. I suppose that I knew other readers could make sense of what I wrote—that, therefore, I addressed a general reader. But I didn't think very much about it. Only toward the end of my schooling and only because political issues pressed upon me did I write, and have published in magazines, essays intended for readers I never expected to meet. Now I am struck by the opportunity. I write today for a reader who exists in my mind only phantasmagorically. Someone with a face erased; someone of no particular race or sex or age or weather. A gray presence. Unknown, unfamiliar. All that I know about him is that he has had a long education and that his society, like mine, is often public *(un gringo)*.

23

2

"What is psychiatry?" my mother asks. She is standing in her kitchen at the ironing board. We have been talking about nothing very important. ("Visiting.") As a result of nothing we have been saying, her question has come. But I am not surprised by it. My mother and father ask me such things. Now that they are retired they seem to think about subjects they never considered before. My father sits for hours in an armchair, wide-eyed. After my mother and I have finished discussing obligatory family news, he will approach me and wonder: When was Christianity introduced to the Asian continent? How does the brain learn things? Where is the Garden of Eden?

24

Perhaps because they consider me the family academic, my mother and father expect me to know. They do not, in any case, ask my brother and sisters the questions wild curiosity shapes. (That curiosity beats, unbeaten by age.)

25

Psychiatry? I shrug my shoulders to start with, to tell my mother that it is very hard to explain. I go on to say something about Freud. And analysis. Something about the function of a

26

clinically trained listener. (I study my mother's face as I speak, to see if she follows.) I compare a psychiatrist to a Catholic priest hearing Confession. But the analogy is inexact. My mother can easily speak to a priest in a darkened confessional; can easily make an act of self-revelation using the impersonal formula of ritual contrition: "Bless me, father, for I have sinned. . . ." It would be altogether different for her to address a psychiatrist in unstructured conversation, revealing those events and feelings that burn close to the heart.

"You mean that people tell a psychiatrist about their personal lives?"

27

Even as I begin to respond, I realize that she cannot imagine ever doing such a thing. She shakes her head sadly, bending over the ironing board to inspect a shirt with the tip of the iron she holds in her hand. Then she changes the subject. She is talking to me about one of her sisters, my aunt, who is seriously ill. Whatever it is that prompted her question about psychiatry has passed.

28

I stand there. I continue thinking about what she has asked me—and what she cannot comprehend. My parents seem to me possessed of great dignity. An aristocratic reserve. Like the very rich who live behind tall walls, my mother and father are always mindful of the line separating public from private life. Watching a celebrity talk show on television, they listen for several minutes as a movie star with bright teeth recounts details of his recent divorce. And I see my parents grow impatient. Finally, my mother gets up from her chair. Changing the channel, she says with simple disdain, "Cheap people."

29

My mother and my father are not cheap people. They never are tempted to believe that public life can also be intimate. They remain aloof from the modern temptation that captivates many in America's middle class: the temptation to relieve the anonymity of public life by trying to make it intimate. They do not understand, consequently, what so pleases the television audience listening to a movie star discuss his divorce with bogus private language. My father opens a newspaper to find an article by a politician's wife in which she reveals (actually, renders merely as gossip) intimate details of her marriage. And he looks up from the article to ask me, "Why does she do this?"

30

I find his question embarrassing. Although I know that he does not intend to embarrass me, I am forced to think about this

31

book I have been writing. And I realize that my parents will be as puzzled by my act of self-revelation as they are by the movie star's revelations on the talk show. They never will call me cheap for publishing an autobiography. But I can well imagine their faces tightened by incomprehension as they read my words.

(Why does he do this?)   32

Many mornings at my desk I have been paralyzed by the   33 thought of their faces, their eyes. I imagine their eyes moving slowly across these pages. That image has weakened my resolve. Finally, however, it not stopped me. Despite the fact that my parents remain even now in my mind a critical, silent chorus, standing together, I continue to write. I do not make my parents' sharp distinction between public and private life. With my mother and father I scorn those who attempt to create in experience of intimacy in public. But unlike my parents, I have come to think that there is a place for the deeply personal in public life. This is what I have learned by trying to write this book: There are things so deeply personal that they can be revealed only to strangers. I believe this. I continue to write.

"What is psychiatry?" my mother asks. And I wish I could tell   34 her. (I wish she could imagine it.) "There are things that are so personal that they can only be said to someone who is not close. Someone you don't know. A person who is not an intimate friend or a relation. There are things too personal to be shared with intimates."

She stands at the ironing board, her tone easy because she is   35 speaking to me. (I am her son.) For my mother that which is personal can only be said to a relative—her only intimates. She makes the single exception of confessing her sins to a Catholic priest. Otherwise, she speaks of her personal life only at home. The same is true of my father—though he is silent even with family members. Of those matters too jaggedly personal to reveal to intimates, my parents will never speak. And that seems to me an extraordinary oppression. The unspoken may well up within my mother and cause her to sigh. But beyond that sigh nothing is heard. There is no one she can address. Words never form. Silence remains to repress them. She remains quiet. My father in his chair remains quiet.

I wonder now what my parents' silence contains. What would   36 be their version of the past we once shared? What memories do they carry about me? What were their feelings at many of the moments I recollect on these pages? What did my father—who had dreamed of Australia—think of his children once they forced him to change plans and remain in America? What contrary feelings did he have about our early success? How does he regard the adults his sons and daughters have become? And my mother. At what moments has she hated me? On what occasions has she been embarrassed by me? What does she recall feeling during these difficult, sullen years of my childhood? What would be her version of this book? What are my parents unable to tell me today? What things are too personal? What feelings so unruly they dare not reveal to other intimates? Or even to each other? Or to themselves?

Some people have told me how wonderful it is that I am the 37 first in my family to write a book. I stand on the edge of a long silence. But I do not give voice to my parents by writing about their lives. I distinguish myself from them by writing about the life we once shared. Even when I quote them accurately, I profoundly distort my parents' words. (They were never intended to be read by the public.) So my parents do not truly speak on my pages. I may force their words to stand between quotation marks. With every word, however, I change what was said only to me.

"What is new with you?" My mother looks up from her iron- 38 ing to ask me. (In recent years she has taken to calling me Mr. Secrets, because I tell her so little about my work in San Francisco—this book she must suspect I am writing.)

Nothing much. I respond. 39

I write very slowly because I write under the obligation to 40 make myself clear to someone who knows nothing about me. It is a lonely adventure. Each morning I make my way along a narrowing precipice of written words. I hear an echoing voice—my own resembling another's. Silent! The reader's voice silently trails every word I put down. I reread my words, and again it is the reader's voice I hear in my mind, sounding my prose.

When I wrote my first autobiographical essay, it was no coin- 41 cidence that, from the first page, I expected to publish what I wrote. I didn't consciously determine the issue. Somehow I knew, however, that my words were meant for a public reader. Only because of that reader did the words come to the page. The reader became my excuse, my reason for writing.

It had taken me a long time to come to this address. There are   42
remarkable children who very early are able to write publicly
about their personal lives. Some children confide to a diary those
things—like the first shuddering of sexual desire—too private to
tell a parent or brother. The youthful writer addresses a stranger,
the Other, with "Dear Diary" and tries to give public expression
to what is intensely, privately felt. In so doing, he attempts to
evade the guilt of repression. And the embarrassment of solitary
feeling. For by rendering feelings in words that a stranger can
understand—words that belong to the public, this Other—the
young diarist no longer need feel all alone or eccentric. His feelings are capable of public intelligibility. In turn, the act of revelation helps the writer better understand his own feelings. Such
is the benefit of language: By finding public words to describe
one's feelings, one can describe oneself to oneself. One names
what was previously only darkly felt.

I have come to think of myself as engaged in writing graffiti.   43
Encouraged by physical isolation to reveal what is most personal; determined at the same time to have my words seen by
strangers. I have come to understand better why works of literature—while never intimate, never individually addressed to the
reader—are so often among the most personal statements we
hear in our lives. Writing, I have come to value written words as
never before. One can use *spoken* words to reveal one's personal
self to strangers. But *written* words heighten the feeling of privacy. They permit the most thorough and careful exploration.
(In the silent room, I prey upon that which is most private. Behind the closed door, I am least reticent about giving those memories expression.) The writer is freed from the obligation of
finding an auditor in public. (As I use words that someone far
from home can understand, I create my listener. I imagine her
listening.)

My teachers gave me a great deal more than I knew when they   44
taught me to write public English. I was unable then to use the
skill for deeply personal purposes. I insisted upon writing impersonal essays. And I wrote always with a specific reader in mind.
Nevertheless, the skill of public writing was gradually developed
by the many classroom papers I had to compose. Today I *can*
address an anonymous reader. And this seems to me important
to say. Somehow the inclination to write about my private life in

public is related to the ability to do so. It is not enough to say that my mother and father do not want to write their autobiographies. It needs also to be said that they are unable to write to a public reader. They lack the skill. Though both of them can write in Spanish and English, they write in a hesitant manner. Their syntax is uncertain. Their vocabulary limited. They write well enough to communicate "news" to relatives in letters. And they can handle written transactions in institutional America. But the man who sits in his chair so many hours, and the woman at the ironing board—"keeping busy because I don't want to get old"—will never be able to believe that any description of their personal lives could be understood by a stranger far from home.

3

When my mother mentioned seeing my article seven years 45 ago, she *wrote* to me. And I responded to her letter with one of my own. (I wrote: "I am sorry that my article bothered you. . . . I had not meant to hurt. . . . I think, however, that education has divided the family. . . . That is something which happens in most families, though it is rarely discussed. . . . I had meant to praise what I have lost. . . . I continue to love you both very much.") I wrote to my mother because it would have been too difficult, too painful to hear her voice on the phone. Too unmanageable a confrontation of voices. The impersonality of the written word made it the easiest means of exchange. The remarkable thing is that nothing has been spoken about this matter by either of us in the years intervening. I know my mother suspects that I continue to write about the family. She knows that I spend months at a time "writing," but she does not press me for information. (Mr. Secrets.) She does not protest.

The first time I saw my mother after she had received my let- 46 ter, she came with my father to lunch. I opened the door to find her smiling slightly. In an instant I tried to gather her mood. (She looked as nervous and shy as I must have seemed.) We embraced. And she said that my father was looking for a place to park the car. She came into my apartment and asked what we were having for lunch. Slowly, our voices reverted to tones we normally sound with each other. (Nothing was said of my article.) I think my mother sensed that afternoon that the person whose essay she saw in a national magazine was a person unfamiliar to her, some Other. The public person—the writer, Richard Rodriguez—would remain distant and untouchable. She never would hear his public voice across a dining room table. And that afternoon she seemed to accept the idea, granted me the right, the freedom so crucial to adulthood, to become a person very different in public from the person I am at home.

Intimates are not always so generous. One close friend calls to tell me she has read an essay of mine. "All that Spanish angst," she laughs. "It's not really you." Only someone very close would be tempted to say such a thing—only a person who knows who I am. From such an intimate one must sometimes escape to the company of strangers, to the liberation of the city, in order to form new versions of oneself.　47

In the company of strangers now, I do not reveal the person I am among intimates. My brother and sisters recognize a different person, not the Richard Rodriguez in this book. I hope, when they read this, they will continue to trust the person they have known me to be. But I hope too that, like our mother, they will understand why it is that the voice I sound here I have never sounded to them. All those faraway childhood mornings in Sacramento, walking together to school, we talked but never mentioned a thing about what concerned us so much: the great event of our schooling, the change it forced on our lives. Years passed. Silence grew thicker, less penetrable. We grew older without ever speaking to each other about any of it. Intimacy grooved our voices in familiar notes; familiarity defined the limits of what could be said. Until we became adults. And now we see each other most years at noisy family gatherings where there is no place to stop the conversation, no right moment to turn the heads of listeners, no way to essay this, my voice.　48

I see them now, my brother and sisters, two or three times every year. We do not live so very far from one another. But as an entire family, we only manage to gather for dinner on Easter. And Mother's Day. Christmas. It is usually at our parents' house that these dinners are held. Our mother invariably organizes things. Well before anyone else has the chance to make other arrangements, her voice will sound on the phone to remind us of an upcoming gathering.　49

Lately, I have begun to wonder how the family will gather   50
even three times a year when she is not there with her phone to
unite us. For the time being, however, she presides at the table.
She—not my father, who sits opposite her—says the Grace before Meals. She busies herself throughout the meal. "Sit down
now," somebody tells her. But she moves back and forth from
the dining room table to the kitchen. Someone needs more food.
(What's missing?) Something always is missing from the table.
When she is seated, she listens to the conversation. But she seems
lonely. (Does she think things would have been different if one of
her children had brought home someone who could speak Spanish?) She does not know how or where to join in when her children are talking about Woody Allen movies or real estate tax
laws or somebody's yoga class. (Does she remember how we vied
with each other to sit beside her in a movie theatre?) Someone remembers at some point to include her in the conversation. Someone asks how many pounds the turkey was this year. She
responds in her visitor's voice. And soon the voices ride away.
She is left with the silence.

Sitting beside me, as usual, is my younger sister. We gossip.   51
She tells me about her trip last week to Milan; we laugh; we talk
about clothes, mutual friends in New York.

Other voices intrude: I hear the voices of my brother and sis-   52
ter and the people who have married into our family. I am the
loudest talker. I am the one doing most of the talking. I talk, having learned from hundreds of cocktail parties and dinner parties
how to talk with great animation about nothing especially. I
sound happy. I talk to everyone about something. And I become
shy only when my older sister wonders what I am doing these
days. Working in Los Angeles? Or writing again? When will she
be able to see something I've published?

I try to change the subject.   53

"Are you writing a book?"   54

I notice, out of the corner of my eye, that my mother is ner-   55
vously piling dishes and then getting up to take them out to the
kitchen.

I say yes.   56

"Well, well, well. Let's see it. Is it going to be a love story? A   57
romance? What's it about?"

She glances down at her thirteen-year-old son, her oldest.   58
"Tommy reads and reads, just like you used to."

I look over at him and ask him what sort of books he likes   59
best.

"Everything!" his mother answers with pride.   60

He smiles. I wonder: Am I watching myself in this boy? In this   61
face where I can scarcely trace a family resemblance? Have I
foreseen his past? He lives in a world of Little League and Pop
Warner. He has spoken English all his life. His father is of German descent, a fourth-generation American. And he does not go
to a Catholic school, but to a public school named after a dead
politician. Still, he is someone who reads. . . .

"He and I read all the same books," my sister informs me.   62
And with that remark, my nephew's life slips out of my grasp to
imagine.

Dinner progresses. There is dessert. Four cakes. Coffee. The   63
conversation advances with remarkable ease. Talk is cheerful,
the way talk is among people who rarely see one another and then
are surprised that they have so much to say. Sometimes voices
converge from various points around the table. Sometimes
voices retreat to separate topics, two or three conversations.

My mother interrupts. She speaks and gets everyone's atten-   64
tion. Some cousin of ours is getting married next month. (Already.) And some other relative is now the mother of a
nine-pound baby boy. (Already?) And some relative's son is
graduating from college this year. (We haven't seen him since he
was five.) And somebody else, an aunt, is retiring from her job in
that candy store. And a friend of my mother's from Sacramento—Do we remember her after all these years?—died of cancer just last week. (Already!)

My father remains a witness to the evening. It is difficult to   65
tell what he hears (his hearing is bad) or cannot understand (his
English is bad). His face stays impassive, unless he is directly addressed. In which case he smiles and nods, too eagerly, too
quickly, at what has been said. (Has he really heard?) When he
has finished eating, I notice, he sits back in his chair. And his eyes
move from face to face. Sometimes I feel that he is looking at me.
I look over to see him, and his eyes dart away the second after I
glance.

When Christmas dinner is finished, there are gifts to exchange   66
in the front room. Tradition demands that my brother, the oldest, play master of ceremonies, "Santa's helper," handing out

presents with a cigar in his hand. It is the chore he has come to assume, making us laugh with his hammy asides. "This is for Richard," he says, rattling a box next to his ear, rolling his eyes. "And this one is for Mama Rodriguez." (There is the bright snap of a camera.)

Nowadays there is money enough for buying useless and slightly ludicrous gifts for my mother and father. (They will receive an expensive backgammon set. And airplane tickets to places they haven't the energy or the desire to visit. And they will be given a huge silver urn—"for chilling champagne.") 67

My mother is not surprised that her children are well-off. Her two daughters are business executives. Her oldest son is a lawyer. She predicted it all long ago. "Someday," she used to say when we were young, "you will all grow up and all be very rich. You'll have lots of money to buy me presents. But I'll be a little old lady. I won't have any teeth or hair. So you'll have to buy me soft food and put a blue wig on my head. And you'll buy me a big fur coat. But you'll only be able to see my eyes." 68

Every Christmas now the floor around her is carpeted with red and green wrapping paper. And her feet are wreathed with gifts. 69

By the time the last gift is unwrapped, everyone seems very tired. The room has become uncomfortably warm. The talk grows listless. ("Does anyone want coffee or more cake?" Somebody groans.) Children are falling asleep. Someone gets up to leave, prompting others to leave. ("We have to get up early tomorrow.") 70

"Another Christmas," my mother says. She says that same thing every year, so we all smile to hear it again. 71

Children are bundled up for the fast walk to the car. My mother stands by the door calling good-bye. She stands with a coat over her shoulders, looking into the dark where expensive foreign cars idle sharply. She seems, all of a sudden, very small. She looks worried. 72

"Don't come out, it's too cold," somebody shouts at her or at my father, who steps out onto the porch. I watch my younger sister in a shiny mink jacket bend slightly to kiss my mother before she rushes down the front steps. My mother stands waving toward no one in particular. She seems sad to me. How sad? Why? (Sad that we all are going home? Sad that it was not quite, can never be, the Christmas one remembers having had once?) I 73 am tempted to ask her quietly if there is anything wrong. (But these are questions of paradise, Mama.)

My brother drives away.   74

"Daddy shouldn't be outside," my mother says. "Here, take   75
this jacket out to him."

She steps into the warmth of the entrance hall and hands me   76
the coat she has been wearing over her shoulders.

I take it to my father and place it on him. In that instant I feel   77
the thinness of his arms. He turns. He asks if I am going home now too. It is, I realize, the only thing he has said to me all evening.

ADRIENNE RICH

When We Dead Awaken: Writing as Re-Vision

Adrienne Rich's most recent books of poetry are *Midnight Salvage: Poems 1995–1998,* and *Fox: Poems 1998–2000.* A new selection of her essays, *Arts of the Possible: Essays and Conversations,* was published in 2001. She has recently been the recipient of the Dorothea Tanning Prize of the Academy of American Poets "for mastery in the art of poetry," and the Lannen Foundation Lifetime Achievement Award. She lives in California. "When We Dead Awaken" was first published in *College English* in 1972.

Ibsen's *When We Dead Awaken* is a play about the use that   1
the male artist and thinker—in the process of creating culture as we know it—has made of women, in his life and in his work; and about a woman's slow struggling awakening to the use to which her life has been put. Bernard Shaw wrote in 1900 of this play:

> [Ibsen] shows us that no degradation ever devized or permitted is as disastrous as this degradation; that through it women can die into luxuries for men and yet can kill them; that men and women are becoming conscious of this; and that what remains to be seen as per-

haps the most interesting of all imminent social developments is what will happen "when we dead awaken."[1]

It's exhilarating to be alive in a time of awakening conscious-   2
ness; it can also be confusing, disorienting, and painful. This awakening of dead or sleeping consciousness has already affected the lives of millions of women, even those who don't know it yet. It is also affecting the lives of men, even those who deny its claims upon them. The argument will go on whether an oppressive economic class system is responsible for the oppressive nature of male/female relations, or whether, in fact, patriarchy—the domination of males—is the original model of oppression on which all others are based. But in the last few years the women's movement has drawn inescapable and illuminating connections between our sexual lives and our political institutions. The sleepwalkers are coming awake, and for the first time this awakening has a collective reality; it is no longer such a lonely thing to open one's eyes.

Re-vision—the act of looking back, of seeing with fresh eyes,   3
of entering an old text from a new critical direction—is for women more than a chapter in cultural history: it is an act of survival. Until we can understand the assumptions in which we are drenched we cannot know ourselves. And this drive to self-knowledge, for women, is more than a search for identity: it is part of our refusal of the self-destructiveness of male-dominated society. A radical critique of literature, feminist in its impulse, would take the work first of all as a clue to how we live, how we have been living, how we have been led to imagine ourselves, how our language has trapped as well as liberated us, how the very act of naming has been till now a male prerogative, and how we can begin to see and name—and therefore live—afresh. A change in the concept of sexual identity is essential if we are not going to see the old political order reassert itself in every new revolution. We need to know the writing of the past, and know it differently than we have ever known it; not to pass on a tradition but to break its hold over us.

For writers, and at this moment for women writers in partic-   4
ular, there is the challenge and promise of a whole new psychic

1. G. B. Shaw, *The Quintessence of Ibsenism* (New York: Hill & Wang, 1922), p. 139. [author's note]

geography to be explored. But there is also a difficult and dangerous walking on the ice, as we try to find language and images for a consciousness we are just coming into, and with little in the past to support us. I want to talk about some aspects of this difficulty and this danger.

Jane Harrison, the great classical anthropologist, wrote in 1914 in a letter to her friend Gilbert Murray:

> By the by, about "Women," it has bothered me often—why do women never want to write poetry about Man as a sex—why is Woman a dream and a terror to man and not the other way around? . . . Is it mere convention and propriety, or something deeper?[2]

I think Jane Harrison's question cuts deep into the myth-making tradition, the romantic tradition; deep into what women and men have been to each other; and deep into the psyche of the woman writer. Thinking about that question, I began thinking of the work of two twentieth-century women poets, Sylvia Plath and Diane Wakoski. It strikes me that in the work of both Man appears as, if not a dream, a fascination and a terror; and that the source of the fascination and the terror is, simply, Man's power—to dominate, tyrannize, choose, or reject the woman. The charisma of Man seems to come purely from his power over her and his control of the world by force, not from anything fertile or life-giving in him. And, in the work of both these poets, it is finally the woman's sense of *herself*—embattled, possessed— that gives the poetry its dynamic charge, its rhythms of struggle, need, will, and female energy. Until recently this female anger and this furious awareness of the Man's power over her were not available materials to the female poet, who tended to write of Love as the source of her suffering, and to view that victimization by Love as an almost inevitable fate. Or, like Marianne Moore and Elizabeth Bishop,[3] she kept sexuality at a measured and chiseled distance in her poems.

One answer to Jane Harrison's question has to be that historically men and women have played very different parts in each others' lives. Where woman has been a luxury for man, and has

2. J. G. Stewart, *Jane Ellen Harrison: A Portrait from Letters* (London: Merlin, 1959), p. 140. [author's note]
3. Marianne Moore (1887–1972) and Elizabeth Bishop (1911–1979) are two of the most prominent American poets of the twentieth century.

served as the painter's model and the poet's muse, but also as comforter, nurse, cook, bearer of his seed, secretarial assistant, and copyist of manuscripts, man has played a quite different role for the female artist. Henry James repeats an incident which the writer Prosper Mérimée described, of how, while he was living with George Sand,

> he once opened his eyes, in the raw winter dawn, to see his compan-
> ion, in a dressing-gown, on her knees before the domestic hearth, a
> candlestick beside her and a red *madras* round her head, making
> bravely, with her own hands the fire that was to enable her to sit
> down betimes to urgent pen and paper. The story represents him as
> having felt that the spectacle chilled his ardor and tried his taste; her
> appearance was unfortunate, her occupation an inconsequence, and
> her industry a reproof—the result of all which was a lively irritation
> and an early rupture.[4]

The specter of this kind of male judgment, along with the mis-naming and thwarting of her needs by a culture controlled by males, has created problems for the woman writer: problems of contact with herself, problems of language and style, problems of energy and survival.

In rereading Virginia Woolf's *A Room of One's Own* (1929)[5] for the first time in some years, I was astonished at the sense of effort, of pains taken, of dogged tentativeness, in the tone of that essay. And I recognized that tone. I had heard it often enough, in myself and in other women. It is the tone of a woman almost in touch with her anger, who is determined not to appear angry, who is *willing* herself to be calm, detached, and even charming in a roomful of men where things have been said which are attacks on her very integrity. Virginia Woolf is addressing an audience of women, but she is acutely conscious—as she always was—of being overheard by men; by Morgan and Lytton and Maynard Keynes[6] and for that matter by her father, Leslie

---

4. Henry James, "Notes on Novelists," in *Selected Literary Criticism of Henry James*, Morris Shapira, ed. (London: Heinemann, 1963), pp. 157–58. [author's note]
5. Virginia Woolf: British novelist and essayist (1882–1941).
6. Novelist and essayist Edward Morgan Forster (1879–1970), biographer and essayist Lytton Strachey (1880–1932), and economist Maynard Keynes (1883–1946) were, along with Woolf, members of the Bloomsbury Group, a cir-cle of English writers and intellectuals who met for several years at the beginning of this century in the Bloomsbury section of London.

Stephen.[7] She drew the language out into an exacerbated thread in her determination to have her own sensibility yet protect it from those masculine presences. Only at rare moments in that essay do you hear the passion in her voice; she was trying to sound as cool as Jane Austen, as Olympian as Shakespeare, because that is the way the men of the culture thought a writer should sound.

No male writer has written primarily or even largely for women, or with the sense of women's criticism as a consideration when he chooses his materials, his theme, his language. But to a lesser or greater extent, every woman writer has written for men even when, like Virginia Woolf, she was supposed to be addressing women. If we have come to the point when this balance might begin to change, when women can stop being haunted, not only by "convention and propriety" but by internalized fears of being and saying themselves, then it is an extraordinary moment for the woman writer—and reader.

I have hesitated to do what I am going to do now, which is to use myself as an illustration. For one thing, it's a lot easier and less dangerous to talk about other women writers. But there is something else. Like Virginia Woolf, I am aware of the women who are not with us here because they are washing the dishes and looking after the children, Nearly fifty years after she spoke, that fact remains largely unchanged. And I am thinking also of women whom she left out of the picture altogether—women who are washing other people's dishes and caring for other people's children, not to mention women who went on the streets last night in order to feed their children. We seem to be special women here, we have liked to think of ourselves as special, and we have known that men would tolerate, even romanticize us as special, as long as our words and actions didn't threaten their privilege of tolerating or rejecting us and our work according to *their* ideas of what a special woman ought to be. An important insight of the radical women's movement has been

---

7. *A.R., 1978:* This intuition of mine was corroborated when, early in 1978, I read the correspondence between Woolf and Dame Ethel Smyth (Henry W. and Albert A. Berg Collection, The New York Public Library, Astor, Lenox and Tilden Foundations); in a letter dated June 8, 1933, Woolf speaks of having kept her own personality out of *A Room of One's Own* lest she not be taken seriously: ". . . how personal, so will they say, rubbing their hands with glee, women always are; *I even hear them as I write.*" (Italics mine.) [author's note]

how divisive and how ultimately destructive is this myth of the special woman, who is also the token woman. Every one of us here in this room has had great luck—we are teachers, writers, academicians; our own gifts could not have been enough, for we all know women whose gifts are buried or aborted. Our struggles can have meaning and our privileges—however precarious under patriarchy—can be justified only if they can help to change the lives of women whose gifts—and whose very being—continue to be thwarted and silenced.

My own luck was being born white and middle-class into a   10 house full of books, with a father who encouraged me to read and write. So for about twenty years I wrote for a particular man, who criticized and praised me and made me feel I was indeed "special." The obverse side of this, of course, was that I tried for a long time to please him, or rather, not to displease him. And then of course there were other men—writers, teachers—the Man, who was not a terror or a dream but a literary master and a master in other ways less easy to acknowledge. And there were all those poems about women, written by men: it seemed to be a given that men wrote poems and women frequently inhabited them. These women were almost always beautiful, but threatened with the loss of beauty, the loss of youth—the fate worse than death. Or, they were beautiful and died young, like Lucy and Lenore.[8] Or, the woman was like Maud Gonne,[9] cruel and disastrously mistaken, and the poem reproached her because she had refused to become a luxury for the poet.

A lot is being said today about the influence that the myths   11 and images of women have on all of us who are products of culture. I think it has been a peculiar confusion to the girl or woman who tries to write because she is peculiarly susceptible to language. She goes to poetry or fiction looking for *her* way of being in the world, since she too has been putting words and images together; she is looking eagerly for guides, maps, possibilities; and over and over in the "words' masculine persuasive force" of

8. Lucy, "a child of nature," is the idealized subject of William Wordsworth's "Lucy" poems (1799); Lenore is the beautiful maiden whose death is lamented in Edgar Allan Poe's poem "Lenore."
9. Maud Gonne (1866–1953): her beauty and activism in Irish politics inspired the poet W. B. Yeats, who, though she continually refused him, proposed to her several times.

literature she comes up against something that negates everything she is about: she meets the image of Woman in books written by men. She finds a terror and a dream, she finds a beautiful pale face, she finds La Belle Dame Sans Merci, she finds Juliet or Tess or Salomé,[10] but precisely what she does not find is that absorbed, drudging, puzzled, sometimes inspired creature, herself, who sits at a desk trying to put words together.

So what does she do? What did I do? I read the older women   12
poets with their peculiar keenness and ambivalence: Sappho, Christina Rossetti, Emily Dickinson, Elinor Wylie, Edna Millay, H.D. I discovered that the woman poet most admired at the time (by men) was Marianne Moore, who was maidenly, elegant, intellectual, discreet. But even in reading these women I was looking in them for the same things I had found in the poetry of men, because I wanted women poets to be the equals of men, and to be equal was still confused with sounding the same.

I know that my style was formed first by male poets: by the   13
men I was reading as an undergraduate—Frost, Dylan Thomas, Donne, Auden, MacNiece, Stevens, Yeats. What I chiefly learned from them was craft.[11] But poems are like dreams: in them you put what you don't know you know. Looking back at poems I wrote before I was twenty-one, I'm startled because beneath the conscious craft are glimpses of the split I even then experienced between the girl who wrote poems, who defined herself in writing poems, and the girl who was to define herself by her relationships with men. "Aunt Jennifer's Tigers" (1951), written while I was a student, looks with deliberate detachment at this split.[12]

10. Rich's list defines women as destroyers or the destroyed: La Belle Dame Sans Merci (the lovely lady without pity) is the title character of an 1819 poem by John Keats that retells the myth of a mortal ravaged by his love for a supernatural *femme fatale;* Juliet is one of the star-crossed lovers of Shakespeare's 1595 play *Romeo and Juliet;* Tess is the doomed woman of Thomas Hardy's *Tess of the D'Urbervilles* (1891); and Salomé, from Oscar Wilde's 1894 play *Salomé,* demands the beheading of John the Baptist.
11. *A.R., 1978:* Yet I spent months, at sixteen, memorizing and writing imitations of Millay's sonnets; and in notebooks of that period I find what are obviously attempts to imitate Dickinson's metrics and verbal compression. I knew H.D. only through anthologized lyrics; her epic poetry was not then available to me. [author's note]
12. *A.R., 1978:* Texts of poetry quoted herein can be found in A. R., *Poems Selected and New: 1950–1974* (New York: Norton, 1975). [author's note]

Aunt Jennifer's tigers stride across a screen,
Bright topaz denizens of a world of green.
They do not fear the men beneath the tree;
They pace in sleek chivalric certainty.

Aunt Jennifer's fingers fluttering through her wool
Find even the ivory needle hard to pull.
The massive weight of Uncle's wedding band
Sits heavily upon Aunt Jennifer's hand.

When Aunt is dead, her terrified hands will lie
Still ringed with ordeals she was mastered by.
The tigers in the panel that she made
Will go on striding, proud and unafraid.

In writing this poem, composed and apparently cool as it is, I thought I was creating a portrait of an imaginary woman. But this woman suffers from the opposition of her imagination, worked out in tapestry, and her life-style, "ringed with ordeals she was mastered by." It was important to me that Aunt Jennifer was a person as distinct from myself as possible—distanced by the formalism of the poem, by its objective, observant tone—even by putting the woman in a different generation.

In those years formalism was part of the strategy—like asbestos gloves, it allowed me to handle materials I couldn't pick up bare-handed. A later strategy was to use the persona of a man, as I did in "The Loser" (1958):

A man thinks of the woman he once loved: first, after her
wedding, and then nearly a decade later.

I
I kissed you, bride and lost, and went
home from that bourgeois sacrament,
your cheek still tasting cold upon
my lips that gave you benison
with all the swagger that they knew—
as losers somehow learn to do.

Your wedding made my eyes ache; soon
the world would be worse off for one
more golden apple dropped to ground
without the least protesting sound,
and you would windfall lie, and we
forget your shimmer on the tree.

14

Beauty is always wasted: if
not Mignon's song sung to the deaf,
at all events to the unmoved.
A face like yours cannot be loved
long or seriously enough.
Almost, we seem to hold it off.

II
Well, you are tougher than I thought.
Now when the wash with ice hangs taut
this morning of St. Valentine,
I see you strip the squeaking line,
your body weighed against the load,
and all my groans can do no good.

Because you are still beautiful,
though squared and stiffened by the pull
of what nine windy years have done.
You have three daughters, lost a son.
I see all your intelligence
flung into that unwearied stance.

My envy is of no avail.
I turn my head and wish him well
who chafed your beauty into use
and lives forever in a house
lit by the friction of your mind.
You stagger in against the wind.

I finished college, published my first book by a fluke, as it   15
seemed to me, and broke off a love affair. I took a job, lived
alone, went on writing, fell in love. I was young, full of energy,
and the book seemed to mean that others agreed I was a poet.
Because I was also determined to prove that as a woman poet
I could also have what was then defined as a "full" woman's
life, I plunged in my early twenties into marriage and had three
children before I was thirty. There was nothing overt in the environment to warn me: these were the fifties, and in reaction to
the earlier wave of feminism, middle-class women were making
careers of domestic perfection, working to send their husbands
through professional schools, then retiring to raise large families.
People were moving out to the suburbs, technology was going
to be the answer to everything, even sex; the family was in its
glory. Life was extremely private; women were isolated from

each other by the loyalties of marriage. I have a sense that women didn't talk to each other much in the fifties—not about their secret emptinesses, their frustrations. I went on trying to write; my second book and first child appeared in the same month. But by the time that book came out I was already dissatisfied with those poems, which seemed to me mere exercises for poems I hadn't written. The book was praised, however, for its "gracefulness"; I had a marriage and a child. If there were doubts, if there were periods of null depression or active despairing, these could only mean that I was ungrateful, insatiable, perhaps a monster.

About the time my third child was born, I felt that I had either to consider myself a failed woman and a failed poet, or to try to find some synthesis by which to understand what was happening to me. What frightened me most was the sense of drift, of being pulled along on a current which called itself my destiny, but in which I seemed to be losing touch with whoever I had been, with the girl who had experienced her own will and energy almost ecstatically at times, walking around a city or riding a train at night or typing in a student room. In a poem about my grandmother I wrote (of myself): "A young girl, thought sleeping, is certified dead" ("Halfway"). I was writing very little, partly from fatigue, that female fatigue of suppressed anger and loss of contact with my own being; partly from the discontinuity of female life with its attention to small chores, errands, work that others constantly undo, small children's constant needs. What I did write was unconvincing to me; my anger and frustration were hard to acknowledge in or out of poems because in fact I cared a great deal about my husband and my children. Trying to look back and understand that time I have tried to analyze the real nature of the conflict. Most, if not all, human lives are full of fantasy—passive day-dreaming which need not be acted on. But to write poetry or fiction, or even to think well, is not to fantasize, or to put fantasies on paper. For a poem to coalesce, for a character or an action to take shape, there has to be an imaginative transformation of reality which is in no way passive. And a certain freedom of the mind is needed—freedom to press on, to enter the currents of your thought like a glider pilot, knowing that your motion can be sustained, that the buoyancy of your attention will not be suddenly snatched away. Moreover, if the imagination is to transcend and transform experience it has to

16

question, to challenge, to conceive of alternatives, perhaps to the very life you are living at that moment. You have to be free to play around with the notion that day might be night, love might be hate; nothing can be too sacred for the imagination to turn into its opposite or to call experimentally by another name. For writing is re-naming. Now, to be maternally with small children all day in the old way, to be with a man in the old way of marriage, requires a holding-back, a putting-aside of that imaginative activity, and demands instead a kind of conservatism. I want to make it clear that I am *not* saying that in order to write well, or think well, it is necessary to become unavailable to others, or to become a devouring ego. This has been the myth of the masculine artist and thinker; and I do not accept it. But to be a female human being trying to fulfill traditional female functions in a traditional way *is* in direct conflict with the subversive function of the imagination. The word traditional is important here. There must be ways, and we will be finding out more and more about them, in which the energy of creation and the energy of relation can be united. But in those years I always felt the conflict as a failure of love in myself. I had thought I was choosing a full life: the life available to most men, in which sexuality, work, and parenthood could coexist. But I felt, at twenty-nine, guilt toward the people closest to me, and guilty toward my own being.

I wanted, then, more than anything, the one thing of which   17
there was never enough: time to think, time to write. The fifties and early sixties were years of rapid revelations: the sit-ins and marches in the South, the Bay of Pigs, the early antiwar movement,[13] raised large questions—questions for which the masculine world of the academy around me seemed to have expert and fluent answers. But I needed to think for myself—about pacifism and dissent and violence, about poetry and society, and about my own relationship to all these things. For about ten years I was reading in fierce snatches, scribbling in notebooks, writing poetry in fragments; I was looking desperately for clues, because if

13. Sit-ins . . . antiwar movement: sit-ins and freedom marches were nonviolent approaches to the struggle for civil rights advocated by Martin Luther King Jr.; in 1962 the CIA ordered an invasion at the Cuban Bay of Pigs in a failed attempt to overthrow Fidel Castro; and protesters opposed the involvement of the U.S. in the Vietnam War.

there were no clues then I thought I might be insane. I wrote in a notebook about this time:

> Paralyzed by the sense that there exists a mesh of relationships—e.g., between my anger at the children, my sensual life, pacifism, sex (I mean sex in its broadest significance, not merely sexual desire)—an interconnectedness which, if I could see it, make it valid, would give me back myself, make it possible to function lucidly and passionately. Yet I grope in and out among these dark webs.

I think I began at this point to feel that politics was not something "out there" but something "in here" and of the essence of my condition.

In the late fifties I was able to write, for the first time, directly about experiencing myself as a woman. The poem was jotted in fragments during children's naps, brief hours in a library, or at 3:00 A.M. after rising with a wakeful child. I despaired of doing any continuous work at this time. Yet I began to feel that my fragments and scraps had a common consciousness and a common theme, one which I would have been very unwilling to put on paper at an earlier time because I had been taught that poetry should be "universal," which meant, of course, nonfemale. Until then I had tried very much *not* to identify myself as a female poet. Over two years I wrote a ten-part poem called "Snapshots of a Daughter-in-Law" (1958–1960), in a longer looser mode than I'd ever trusted myself with before. It was an extraordinary relief to write that poem. It strikes me now as too literary, too dependent on allusion; I hadn't found the courage yet to do without authorities, or even to use the pronoun "I"—the woman in the poem is always "she." One section of it, No. 2, concerns a woman who thinks she is going mad; she is haunted by voices telling her to resist and rebel, voices which she can hear but not obey.

2.
Banging the coffee-pot into the sink
she hears the angels chiding, and looks out
past the raked gardens to the sloppy sky.
Only a week since They said: Have no patience!

The next time it was: Be insatiable.
Then: Save yourself; others you cannot save.
Sometimes she's let the tapstream scald her arm,
a match burn to her thumbnail,

or held her hand above the kettle's snout
right in the woolly steam. They are probably angels,
since nothing hurts her anymore, except
each morning's grit blowing into her eyes.

The poem "Orion," written five years later, is a poem of re- 19
connection with a part of myself I had felt I was losing—the active principle, the energetic imagination, the "half-brother"
whom I projected, as I had for many years, into the constellation
Orion. It's no accident that the words "cold and egotistical" appear in this poem, and are applied to myself.

Far back when I went zig-zagging
through tamarack pastures
you were my genius, you
my cast-iron Viking, my helmed
lion-heart king in prison.
Years later now you're young

my fierce half-brother, staring
down from that simplified west
your breast open, your belt dragged down
by an oldfashioned thing, a sword
the last bravado you won't give over
though it weighs you down as you stride

and the stars in it are dim
and maybe have stopped burning.
But you burn, and I know it;
as I throw back my head to take you in
an old transfusion happens again:
divine astronomy is nothing to it.

Indoors I bruise and blunder,
break faith, leave ill enough
alone, a dead child born in the dark.
Night cracks up over the chimney,
pieces of time, frozen geodes
come showering down in the grate.

A man reaches behind my eyes
and finds them empty
a woman's head turns away
from my head in the mirror
children are dying my death
and eating crumbs of my life.

Pity is not your forte.
Calmly you ache up there
pinned aloft in your crow's nest,
my speechless pirate!
You take it all for granted
and when I look you back

it's with a starlike eye
shooting its cold and egotistical spear
where it can do least damage.
Breathe deep! No hurt, no pardon
out here in the cold with you
you with your back to the wall.

The choice still seemed to be between "love"—womanly, maternal love, altruistic love—a love defined and ruled by the weight of an entire culture; and egotism—a force directed by men into creation, achievement, ambition, often at the expense of others, but justifiably so. For weren't they men, and wasn't that their destiny as womanly, selfless love was ours? We know now that the alternatives are false ones—that the word "love" is itself in need of re-vision.

There is a companion poem to "Orion," written three years later, in which at last the woman in the poem and the woman writing the poem become the same person. It is called "Planetarium," and it was written after a visit to a real planetarium, where I read an account of the work of Caroline Herschel, the astronomer, who worked with her brother William, but whose name remained obscure, as his did not. 20

Thinking of Caroline Herschel, 1750–1848, astronomer,
sister of William; and others

A woman in the shape of a monster
a monster in the shape of a woman
the skies are full of them

a woman   "in the snow
among the Clocks and instruments
or measuring the ground with poles"

in her 98 years to discover
8 comets

she whom the moon ruled
like us

levitating into the night sky
riding the polished lenses

Galaxies of women, there
doing penance for impetuousness
ribs chilled
in those spaces   of the mind
An eye,
        "virile, precise and absolutely certain"
        from the mad webs of Uranisborg

                        encountering the NOVA

every impulse of light exploding
from the core
as life flies out of us

                Tycho whispering at last
                "Let me not seem to have lived in vain"

What we see, we see
and seeing is changing

the light that shrivels a mountain
and leaves a man alive

Heartbeat of the pulsar
heart sweating through my body

The radio impulse
pouring in from Taurus

                I am bombarded yet   I stand

I have been standing all my life in the
direct path of a battery of signals
the most accurately transmitted most
untranslateable language in the universe
I am a galactic cloud so deep   so invo-
luted that a light wave could take 15
years to travel through me   And has
taken   I am an instrument in the shape
of a woman trying to translate pulsations
into images   for the relief of the body
and the reconstruction of the mind.

    In closing I want to tell you about a dream I had last summer. 21
I dreamed I was asked to read my poetry at a mass women's
meeting, but when I began to read, what came out were the lyrics

of a blues song. I share this dream with you because it seemed to me to say something about the problems and the future of the woman writer, and probably of women in general. The awakening of consciousness is not like the crossing of a frontier—one step and you are in another country. Much of woman's poetry has been of the nature of the blues song: a cry of pain, of victimization, or a lyric of seduction.[14] And today, much poetry by women—and prose for that matter—is charged with anger. I think we need to go through that anger, and we will betray our own reality if we try, as Virginia Woolf was trying, for an objectivity, a detachment, that would make us sound more like Jane Austen or Shakespeare. We know more than Jane Austen or Shakespeare knew: more than Jane Austen because our lives are more complex, more than Shakespeare because we know more about the lives of women—Jane Austen and Virginia Woolf included.

Both the victimization and the anger experienced by women   22
are real, and have real sources, everywhere in the environment, built into society, language, the structures of thought. They will go on being tapped and explored by poets, among others. We can neither deny them, nor will we rest there. A new generation of women poets is already working out of the psychic energy released when women begin to move out towards what the feminist philosopher Mary Daly has described as the "new space" on the boundaries of patriarchy.[15] Women are speaking to and of women in these poems, out of a newly released courage to name, to love each other, to share risk and grief and celebration.

To the eye of a feminist, the work of Western male poets now   23
writing reveals a deep, fatalistic pessimism as to the possibilities of change, whether societal or personal, along with a familiar and threadbare use of women (and nature) as redemptive on the one hand, threatening on the other; and a new tide of phallocentric sadism and overt woman-hating which matches the sexual brutality of recent films. "Political" poetry by men remains stranded amid the struggles for power among male groups; in condemning U.S. imperialism or the Chilean junta the poet can

14. *A. R., 1978:* When I dreamed that dream, was I wholly ignorant of the tradition of Bessie Smith and other women's blues lyrics which transcended victimization to sing of resistance and independence? [author's note]
15. Mary Daly, *Beyond God the Father: Toward a Philosophy of Women's Liberation* (Boston: Beacon, 1973). [author's note]

claim to speak for the oppressed while remaining, as male, part
of a system of sexual oppression. The enemy is always outside
the self, the struggle somewhere else. The mood of isolation, self-
pity, and self-imitation that pervades "nonpolitical" poetry suggests that a profound change in masculine consciousness will
have to precede any new male poetic—or other—inspiration.
The creative energy of patriarchy is fast running out; what remains is its self-generating energy for destruction. As women, we
have our work cut out for us.

GEORGE ORWELL

Politics and the
English Language

George Orwell is best known to the general public for two novels—one humorous, one grim. *Animal Farm* (1945) satirizes totalitarian politics; *1984* (1949) presents a totalitarian future in which
politicians control information and language so that it becomes
nearly impossible for citizens to think. Orwell's life from boyhood
forward was a struggle against one form of totalitarianism or another. Several of his works, fiction and nonfiction, have become
touchstones for those who are concerned about the preservation of
civil liberties and freedom of thought. "Politics and the English
Language" was first published in *Horizon,* April 1946.

Most people who bother with the matter at all would admit   1
that the English language is in a bad way, but it is generally assumed that we cannot by conscious action do anything about it.
Our civilization is decadent and our language—so the argument
runs—must inevitably share in the general collapse. It follows
that any struggle against the abuse of language is a sentimental
archaism, like preferring candles to electric light or hansom cabs
to aeroplanes. Underneath this lies the half-conscious belief that
language is a natural growth and not an instrument which we
shape for our own purposes.

Now, it is clear that the decline of a language must ultimately   2
have political and economic causes: it is not due simply to the
bad influence of this or that individual writer. But an effect can
become a cause, reinforcing the original cause and producing the
same effect in an intensified form, and so on indefinitely. A man
may take to drink because he feels himself to be a failure, and
then fail all the more completely because he drinks. It is rather
the same thing that is happening to the English language. It becomes ugly and inaccurate because our thoughts are foolish, but
the slovenliness of our language makes it easier for us to have
foolish thoughts. The point is that the process is reversible. Modern English, especially written English, is full of bad habits which
spread by imitation and which can be avoided if one is willing to
take the necessary trouble. If one gets rid of these habits one can
think more clearly, and to think clearly is a necessary first step
towards political regeneration: so that the fight against bad English is not frivolous and is not the exclusive concern of professional writers. I will come back to this presently, and I hope that
by the time the meaning of what I have said here will have become clearer. Meanwhile, here are five specimens of the English
language as it is now habitually written.

These five passages have not been picked out because they are   3
especially bad—I could have quoted far worse if I had chosen—
but because they illustrate various of the mental vices from
which we now suffer. They are a little below the average, but are
fairly representative samples. I number them so that I can refer
back to them when necessary:

> (1) I am not, indeed, sure whether it is not true to say that the
> Milton who once seemed not unlike a seventeenth-century Shelley
> had not become, out of an experience ever more bitter in each year,
> more alien [*sic*] to the founder of that Jesuit sect which nothing could
> induce him to tolerate.
>
> Professor Harold Laski (Essay in *Freedom of Expression*).

> (2) Above all, we cannot play ducks and drakes with a native bat-
> tery of idioms which prescribes such egregious collocations of voca-
> bles as the Basic *put up with* for *tolerate* or *put at a loss* for *bewilder.*
>
> Professor Lancelot Hogben (*Interglossa*).

(3) On the one side we have the free personality: by definition it is not neurotic, for it has neither conflict nor dream. Its desires, such as they are, are transparent, for they are just what institutional approval keeps in the forefront of consciousness; another institutional pattern would alter their number and intensity; there is little in them that is natural, irreducible, or culturally dangerous. But *on the other side,* the social bond itself is nothing but the mutual reflection of these self-secure integrities. Recall the definition of love. Is not this the very picture of a small academic? Where is there a place in this hall of mirrors for either personality or fraternity?

Essay on psychology in *Politics* (New York).

(4) All the "best people" from the gentlemen's clubs, and all the frantic fascist captains, united in common hatred of Socialism and bestial horror of the rising tide of the mass revolutionary movement, have turned to acts of provocation, to foul incendiarism, to medieval legends of poisoned wells, to legalize their own destruction of proletarian organizations, and rouse the agitated petty-bourgeoisie to chauvinistic fervour on behalf of the fight against the revolutionary way out of the crisis.

Communist pamphlet.

(5) If a new spirit *is* to be infused into this old country, there is one thorny and contentious reform which must be tackled, and that is the humanization and galvanization of the B.B.C. Timidity here will bespeak cancer and atrophy of the soul. The heart of Britain may be sound and of strong beat, for instance, but the British lion's roar at present is like that of Bottom in Shakespeare's *Midsummer Night's Dream*—as gentle as any sucking dove. A virile new Britain cannot continue indefinitely to be traduced in the eyes or rather ears, of the world by the effete languors of Langham Place, brazenly masquerading as "standard English." When the Voice of Britain is heard at nine o'clock, better far and infinitely less ludicrous to hear aitches honestly dropped than the present priggish, inflated, inhibited, schoolma'amish arch braying of blameless bashful mewing maidens!

Letter in *Tribune.*

Each of these passages has faults of its own, but, quite apart 4 from avoidable ugliness, two qualities are common to all of them. The first is staleness of imagery: the other is lack of precision. The writer either has a meaning and cannot express it, or he inadvertently says something else, or he is almost indifferent as to whether his words mean anything or not. This mixture of vagueness and sheer incompetence is the most marked characteristic of modern English prose, and especially of any kind of political writing. As soon as certain topics are raised, the concrete melts into the abstract and no one seems able to think of turns of speech that are not hackneyed: prose consists less and less of *words* chosen for the sake of their meaning, and more and more of *phrases* tacked together like the sections of a prefabricated hen-house. I list below, with notes and examples, various of the tricks by means of which the work of prose-construction is habitually dodged.

DYING METAPHORS

A newly invented metaphor assists thought by evoking a visual image, while on the other hand a metaphor which is technically "dead" (e.g. *iron resolution*) has in effect reverted to being an ordinary word and can generally be used without loss of vividness. But in between these two classes there is a huge dump of worn-out metaphors which have lost all evocative power and are merely used because they save people the trouble of inventing phrases for themselves. Examples are: *Ring the changes on, take up the cudgels for, toe the line, ride roughshod over, stand shoulder to shoulder with, play into the hands of, no axe to grind, grist to the mill, fishing in troubled waters, on the order of the day, Achilles' heel, swan song, hotbed.* Many of these are used without knowledge of their meaning (what is a "rift," for instance?), and incompatible metaphors are frequently mixed, a sure sign that the writer is not interested in what he is saying. Some metaphors now current have been twisted out of their original meaning without those who use them even being aware of the fact. For example, *toe the line* is sometimes written *tow the line.* Another example is *the hammer and the anvil,* now always used with the implication that the anvil gets the worst of it. In real life it is always the anvil that breaks the hammer, never the other way about: a writer who stopped to think what he was saying would be aware of this, and would avoid perverting the original phrase.

OPERATORS OR VERBAL FALSE LIMBS

These save the trouble of picking out appropriate verbs and   6
nouns, and at the same time pad each sentence with extra syllables which give it an appearance of symmetry. Characteristic
phrases are: *render inoperative, militate against, make contact
with, be subjected to, give rise to, give grounds for, have the effect
of, play a leading part (role) in, make itself felt, take effect, exhibit a tendency to, serve the purpose of, etc., etc.* The keynote is
the elimination of simple verbs. Instead of being a single word, such
as *break, stop, spoil, mend, kill,* a verb becomes a *phrase,* made
up of a noun or adjective tacked on to some general-purposes
verb such as *prove, serve, form, play, render.* In addition, the passive voice is wherever possible used in preference to the active,
and noun constructions are used instead of gerunds *(by examination of* instead of *by examining).* The range of verbs is further
cut down by means of the *-ize* and *de-* formation, and the banal
statements are given an appearance of profundity by means of
the *not un-* formation. Simple conjunctions and prepositions are
replaced by such phrases as *with respect to, having regard to, the
fact that, by dint of, in view of, in the interests of, on the hypothesis that;* and the ends of sentences are saved from anticli-
max by such resounding commonplaces as *greatly to be desired,
cannot be left out of account, a development to be expected in
the near future, deserving of serious consideration, brought to a
satisfactory conclusion,* and so on and so forth.

PRETENTIOUS DICTION

Words like *phenomenon, element, individual* (as noun), *ob-*   7
*jective, categorical, effective, virtual, basic, primary, promote,
constitute, exhibit, exploit, utilize, eliminate, liquidate,* are used
to dress up simple statements and give an air of scientific impar-
tiality to biased judgments. Adjectives like *epoch-making, epic,
historic, unforgettable, triumphant, age-old, inevitable, inexorable, veritable,* are used to dignify the sordid processes of international politics, while writing that aims at glorifying war
usually takes on an archaic colour, its characteristic words being:
*realm, throne, chariot, mailed fist, trident, sword, shield, buck-
ler, banner, jackboot, clarion.* Foreign words and expressions

such as *cul de sac, ancien régime, deus ex machina, mutatis mutandis, status quo, gleichschaltung, weltanschauung,* are used to give an air of culture and elegance. Except for the useful abbreviations *i.e., e.g.,* and *etc.,* there is no real need for any of the hundreds of foreign phrases now current in English. Bad writers, and especially scientific, political and sociological writers, are nearly always haunted by the notion that Latin or Greek words are grander than Saxon ones, and unnecessary words like *expedite, ameliorate, predict, extraneous, deracinated, clandestine, subaqueous* and hundreds of others constantly gain ground from their Anglo-Saxon opposite numbers.[1] The jargon peculiar to Marxist writing (*hyena, hangman, cannibal, petty bourgeois, these gentry, lacquey, flunkey, mad dog, White Guard,* etc.) consists largely of words and phrases translated from Russian, German or French; but the normal way of coining a new word is to use a Latin or Greek root with the appropriate affix and, where necessary, the *-ize* formation. It is often easier to make up words of this kind (*deregionalize, impermissible, extramarital, nonfragmentatory* and so forth) than to think up the English words that will cover one's meaning. The result, in general, is an increase in slovenliness and vagueness.

MEANINGLESS WORDS

In certain kinds of writing, particularly in art criticism and literary criticism, it is normal to come across long passages which are almost completely lacking in meaning.[2] Words like *romantic, plastic, values, human, dead, sentimental, natural, vitality,* as used in art criticism, are strictly meaningless in the sense that

1. An interesting illustration of this is the way in which the English flower names which were in use till very recently are being ousted by Greek ones, *snapdragon* becoming *antirrhinum, forget-me-not* becoming *myosotis,* etc. It is hard to see any practical reason for this change of fashion: it is probably due to an instinctive turning-away from the more homely word and a vague feeling that the Greek word is scientific. [author's note]
2. Example: "Comfort's catholicity of perception and image, strangely Whitmanesque in range, almost the exact opposite in aesthetic compulsion, continues to evoke that trembling atmospheric accumulative hinting at a cruel, an inexorably serene timelessness. . . . Wrey Gardiner scores by aiming at simple bull's-eyes with precision. Only they are not so simple, and through this contented sadness runs more than the surface bitter-sweet of resignation" *(Poetry Quarterly).* [author's note]

they not only do not point to any discoverable object, but are hardly ever expected to do so by the reader. When one critic writes, "The outstanding feature of Mr. X's work is its living quality," while another writes, "The immediately striking thing about Mr. X's work is its peculiar deadness," the reader accepts this as a simple difference of opinion. If words like *black* and *white* were involved, instead of the jargon words *dead* and *living*, he would see at once that language was being used in an improper way. Many political words are similarly abused. The word *Fascism* has now no meaning except in so far as it signifies "something not desirable." The words *democracy, socialism, freedom, patriotic, realistic, justice*, have each of them several different meanings which cannot be reconciled with one another. In the case of a word like *democracy*, not only is there no agreed definition, but the attempt to make one is resisted from all sides. It is almost universally felt that when we call a country democratic we are praising it: consequently the defenders of every kind of régime claim that it is a democracy, and fear that they might have to stop using the word if it were tied down to any one meaning. Words of this kind are often used in a consciously dishonest way. That is, the person who uses them has his own private definition but allows his hearer to think he means something quite different. Statements like *Marshal Pétain was a true patriot, The Soviet Press is the freest in the world, The Catholic Church is opposed to persecution*, are almost always made with intent to deceive. Other words used in variable meanings, in most cases more or less dishonestly, are: *class, totalitarian, science, progressive, reactionary, bourgeois, equality.*

Now that I have made this catalogue of swindles and perversions, let me give another example of the kind of writing that they lead to. This time it must of its nature be an imaginary one. I am going to translate a passage of good English into modern English of the worst sort. Here is a well-known verse from *Ecclesiastes*:

> I returned and saw under the sun, that the race is not to the swift, nor the battle to the strong, neither yet bread to the wise, nor yet riches to men of understanding, nor yet favour to men of skill; but time and chance happeneth to them all.

Here it is in modern English:

> Objective consideration of contemporary phenomena compels the conclusion that success or failure in competitive activities exhibits no ten-

dency to be commensurate with innate capacity, but that a considerable element of the unpredictable must invariably be taken into account.

This is a parody, but not a very gross one. Exhibit (3), above, for instance, contains several patches of the same kind of English. It will be seen that I have not made a full translation. The beginning and ending of the sentence follow the original meaning fairly closely, but in the middle the concrete illustrations— race, battle, bread—dissolve into the vague phrase "success or failure in competitive activities." This had to be so, because no modern writer of the kind I am discussing—no one capable of using phrases like "objective consideration of contemporary phenomena"—would ever tabulate his thoughts in that precise and detailed way. The whole tendency of modern prose is away from concreteness. Now analyse the two sentences a little more closely. The first contains forty-nine words but only sixty syllables, and all its words are those of everyday life. The second contains thirty-eight words of ninety syllables: eighteen of its words are from Latin roots, and one from Greek. The first sentence contains six vivid images, and only one phrase ("time and chance") that could be called vague. The second contains not a single fresh, arresting phrase, and in spite of its ninety syllables it gives only a shortened version of the meaning contained in the first. Yet without a doubt it is the second kind of sentence that is gaining ground in modern English. I do not want to exaggerate. This kind of writing is not yet universal, and outcrops of simplicity will occur here and there in the worst-written page. Still, if you or I were told to write a few lines on the uncertainty of human fortunes, we should probably come much nearer to my imaginary sentence than to the one from *Ecclesiastes*.

As I have tried to show, modern writing at its worst does not consist in picking out words for the sake of their meaning and inventing images in order to make the meaning clearer. It consists in gumming together long strips of words which have already been set in order by someone else, and making the results presentable by sheer humbug. The attraction of this way of writing is that it is easy. It is easier—even quicker, once you have the habit—to say *In my opinion it is not unjustifiable assumption that* than to say *I think*. If you use ready-made phrases, you not only don't have to hunt about for words; you also don't have to bother with the rhythms of your sentences, since these phrases are generally so arranged as to be more or less euphonious. When you are composing in a hurry—when you are dictating to a stenographer, for instance, or making a public speech—it is natural to fall into a pretentious, Latinized style. Tags like *a consideration which we should do well to bear in mind* or *a conclusion to which all of us would readily assent* will save many a sentence from coming down with a bump. By using stale metaphors, similes and idioms, you save much mental effort, at the cost of leaving your meaning vague, not only for your reader but for yourself. This is the significance of mixed metaphors. The sole aim of a metaphor is to call up a visual image. When these images clash—as in *The Fascist octopus has sung its swan song, the jackboot is thrown into the melting pot*—it can be taken as certain that the writer is not seeing a mental image of the objects he is naming; in other words he is not really thinking. Look again at the examples I gave at the beginning of this essay. Professor Laski (1) uses five negatives in fifty-three words. One of these is superfluous, making nonsense of the whole passage, and in addition there is the slip *alien* for akin, making further nonsense, and several avoidable pieces of clumsiness which increase the general vagueness. Professor Hogben (2) plays ducks and drakes with a battery which is able to write prescriptions, and, while disapproving of the everyday phrase *put up with,* is unwilling to look *egregious* up in the dictionary and see what it means. (3), if one takes an uncharitable attitude towards it, is simply meaningless: probably one could work out its intended meaning by reading the whole of the article in which it occurs. In (4), the writer knows more or less what he wants to say, but an accumulation of stale phrases chokes him like tea leaves blocking a sink. In (5), words and meaning have almost parted company. People who write in this manner usually have a general emotional meaning—they dislike one thing and want to express solidarity with another—but they are not interested in the detail of what they are saying. A scrupulous writer, in every sentence that he writes, will ask himself at least four questions, thus: What am I trying to say? What words will express it? What image or idiom will make it clearer? Is this image fresh enough to have an effect? And he will probably ask himself two more: Could I put it more shortly? Have I said anything that is avoidably ugly? But you are not obliged to go to all this trouble: You can shirk it by simply throwing your mind open and letting the ready-made phrases come crowding in. They will construct your sentences for you—even think your thoughts for you, to a certain extent—and at need they will perform the important service of partially concealing your meaning even from yourself. It is at this point that the special connection between politics and the debasement of language becomes clear.

In our time it is broadly true that political writing is bad writing. Where it is not true, it will generally be found that the writer is some kind of rebel, expressing his private opinions and not a "party line." Orthodoxy, of whatever colour, seems to demand a lifeless, imitative style. The political dialects to be found in pamphlets, leading articles, manifestos, White Papers and the speeches of under-secretaries do, of course, vary from party to party, but they are all alike in that one almost never finds in them a fresh, vivid, home-made turn of speech. When one watches some tired hack on the platform mechanically repeating the familiar phrases—*bestial atrocities, iron heel, bloodstained tyranny, free peoples of the world, stand shoulder to shoulder*—one often has a curious feeling that one is not watching a live human being but some kind of dummy: a feeling which suddenly becomes stronger at moments when the light catches the speaker's spectacles and turns them into blank discs which seem to have no eyes behind them. And this is not altogether fanciful. A speaker who uses that kind of phraseology has gone some distance towards turning himself into a machine. The appropriate noises are coming out of his larynx, but his brain is not involved as it would be if he were choosing his words for himself. If the speech he is making is one that he is accustomed to make over and over again, he may be almost unconscious of what he is saying, as one is when one utters the responses in church. And this reduced state of consciousness, if not indispensable, is at any rate favourable to political conformity.

In our time, political speech and writing are largely the defense of the indefensible. Things like the continuance of British rule in India, the Russian purges and deportations, the dropping of the atom bombs on Japan, can indeed be defended, but only by arguments which are too brutal for most people to face, and which do not square with the professed aims of political parties. Thus political language has to consist largely of euphemism, question-begging and sheer cloudy vagueness. Defenseless villages are bombarded from the air, the inhabitants driven out into the countryside, the cattle machine-gunned, the huts set on fire with incendiary bullets: this is called *pacification*. Millions of peasants are robbed of their farms and sent trudging along the roads with no more than they can carry: this is called *transfer of population* or *rectification of frontiers*. People are imprisoned for years without trial, or shot in the back of the neck or sent to die of scurvy in Arctic lumber camps: this is called *elimination of unreliable elements*. Such phraseology is needed if one wants to name things without calling up mental pictures of them. Consider for instance some comfortable English professor defending Russian totalitarianism. He cannot say outright, "I believe in killing off your opponents when you can get good results by doing so." Probably, therefore, he will say something like this:

"While freely conceding that the Soviet régime exhibits certain features which the humanitarian may be inclined to deplore, we must, I think, agree that a certain curtailment of the right to political opposition is an unavoidable concomitant of transitional periods, and that the rigours which the Russian people have been called upon to undergo have been amply justified in the sphere of concrete achievement." 15

The inflated style is itself a kind of euphemism. A mass of Latin words falls upon the facts like soft snow, blurring the outlines and covering up all the details. The great enemy of clear language is insincerity. When there is a gap between one's real and one's declared aims, one turns as it were instinctively to long words and exhausted idioms, like a cuttlefish squirting out ink. In our age there is no such thing as "keeping out of politics." All issues are political issues, and politics itself is a mass of lies, evasions, folly, hatred and schizophrenia. When the general atmosphere is bad, language must suffer. I should expect to find—this is a guess which I have not sufficient knowledge to verify—that the German, Russian and Italian languages have all deteriorated in the last ten or fifteen years, as a result of dictatorship. 16

But if thought corrupts language, language can also corrupt thought. A bad usage can spread by tradition and imitation, even among people who should and do know better. The debased language that I have been discussing is in some ways very convenient. Phrases like *a not unjustifiable assumption, leaves much to* 17 *be desired, would serve no good purpose, a consideration which we should do well to bear in mind,* are a continuous temptation, a packet of aspirins always at one's elbow. Look back through this essay, and for certain you will find that I have again and again committed the very faults I am protesting against. By this morning's post I have received a pamphlet dealing with conditions in Germany. The author tells me that he "felt impelled" to write it. I open it at random, and here is almost the first sentence that I see: "(The Allies) have an opportunity not only of achieving a radical transformation of Germany's social and political structure in such a way as to avoid a nationalistic reaction in Germany itself, but at the same time of laying the foundations of a co-operative and unified Europe." You see, he "feels impelled" to write—feels, presumably, that he has something new to say— and yet his words, like cavalry horses answering the bugle, group themselves automatically into the familiar dreary pattern. This invasion of one's mind by ready-made phrases *(lay the foundations, achieve a radical transformation)* can only be prevented if one is constantly on guard against them, and every such phrase anesthetizes a portion of one's brain.

I said earlier that the decadence of our language is probably curable. Those who deny this would argue, if they produced an argument at all, that language merely reflects existing social conditions, and that we cannot influence its development by any direct tinkering with words and constructions. So far as the general tone or spirit of a language goes, this may be true, but it is not true in detail. Silly words and expressions have often disappeared, not through any evolutionary process but owing to the conscious action of a minority. Two recent examples were *explore every avenue* and *leave no stone unturned,* which were killed by the jeers of a few journalists. There is a long list of fly-blown metaphors which could similarly be got rid of if enough people would interest themselves in the job; and it should also be possible to laugh the *not un-* formation out of existence,[3] to reduce the amount of Latin and Greek in the average sentence, to drive out foreign phrases and strayed scientific words, and, in general, to make pretentiousness unfashionable. But all these are

3. One can cure oneself of the *not un-* formation by memorizing this sentence: *A not unblack dog was chasing a not unsmall rabbit across a not ungreen field.* [author's note]

minor points. The defence of the English language implies more than this, and perhaps it is best to start by saying what it does *not* imply.

To begin with it has nothing to do with archaism, with the salvaging of obsolete words and turns of speech, or with the setting up of a "standard English" which must never be departed from. On the contrary, it is especially concerned with the scrapping of every word or idiom which has outworn its usefulness. It has nothing to do with correct grammar and syntax, which are of no importance so long as one makes one's meaning clear, or with the avoidance of Americanisms, or with having what is called a "good prose style." On the other hand it is not concerned with fake simplicity and the attempt to make written English colloquial. Nor does it even imply in every case preferring the Saxon word to the Latin one, though it does imply using the fewest and shortest words that will cover one's meaning. What is above all needed is to let the meaning choose the word, and not the other way about. In prose, the worst thing one can do with words is to surrender to them. When you think of a concrete object, you think wordlessly, and then, if you want to describe the thing you have been visualizing you probably hunt about till you find the exact words that seem to fit. When you think of something abstract you are more inclined to use words from the start, and unless you make a conscious effort to prevent it, the existing dialect will come rushing in and do the job for you, at the expense of blurring or even changing your meaning. Probably it is better to put off using words as long as possible and get one's meaning as clear as one can through pictures or sensations. Afterwards one can choose—not simply *accept*—the phrases that will best cover the meaning, and then switch round and decide what impression one's words are likely to make on another person. This last effort of the mind cuts out all stale or mixed images, all prefabricated phrases, needless repetitions, and humbug and vagueness generally. But one can often be in doubt about the effect of a word or a phrase, and one needs rules that one can rely on when instinct fails. I think the following rules will cover most cases:

i. Never use a metaphor, simile or other figure of speech which you are used to seeing in print.

ii. Never use a long word where a short one will do.
iii. If it is possible to cut a word out, always cut it out.
iv. Never use the passive where you can use the active.
v. Never use a foreign phrase, a scientific word or a jargon word if you can think of an everyday English equivalent.
vi. Break any of these rules sooner than say anything outright barbarous.

These rules sound elementary, and so they are, but they demand a deep change of attitude in anyone who has grown used to writing in the style now fashionable. One could keep all of them and still write bad English, but one could not write the kind of stuff that I quoted in those five specimens at the beginning of this article.

I have not here been considering the literary use of language, but merely language as an instrument for expressing and not for concealing or preventing thought. Stuart Chase and others have come near to claiming that all abstract words are meaningless, and have used this as a pretext for advocating a kind of political quietism. Since you don't know what Fascism is, how can you struggle against Fascism? One need not swallow such absurdities as this, but one ought to recognize that the present political chaos is connected with the decay of language, and that one can probably bring about some improvement by starting at the verbal end. If you simplify your English, you are freed from the worst follies of orthodoxy. You cannot speak any of the necessary dialects, and when you make a stupid remark its stupidity will be obvious, even to yourself. Political language—and with variations this is true of all political parties, from Conservatives to Anarchists—is designed to make lies sound truthful and murder respectable, and to give an appearance of solidity to pure wind. One cannot change this all in a moment, but one can at least change one's own habits, and from time to time one can even, if one jeers loudly enough, send some worn-out and useless phrase—some *jackboot, Achilles' heel, hotbed, melting pot, acid test, veritable inferno* or other lump of verbal refuse—into the dustbin where it belongs.

JOAN DIDION

Why I Write

About the time Joan Didion graduated from the University of California at Berkeley in 1956, she won *Vogue* magazine's essay contest for young writers. The prize gave her an internship at the magazine and led her directly to a career as a professional writer. She quickly established herself as a successful novelist, essayist, columnist, and—eventually—screenwriter. "Why I Write" was initially delivered as a speech at the University of California, where Didion's audience included several of her former professors. It was published in the *New York Times Book Review* in December 1976.

Of course I stole the title for this talk, from George Orwell. 1 One reason I stole it was that I like the sound of the words: Why I Write. There you have three short unambiguous words that share a sound, and the sound they share is this:

I

I

I

In many ways writing is the act of saying *I*, of imposing one- 2 self upon other people, of saying *listen to me, see it my way, change your mind*. It's an aggressive, even a hostile act. You can disguise its aggressiveness all you want with veils of subordinate clauses and qualifiers and tentative subjunctives, with ellipses and evasions—with the whole manner of intimating rather than claiming, of alluding rather than stating—but there's no getting around the fact that setting words on paper is the tactic of a se- cret bully, an invasion, an imposition of the writer's sensibility on the reader's most private space.

I stole the title not only because the words sounded right but 3 because they seemed to sum up, in a no-nonsense way, all I have to tell you. Like many writers I have only this one "subject," this one "area": the act of writing. I can bring you no reports from any other front. I may have other interests: I am "interested," for example, in marine biology, but I don't flatter myself that you would come out to hear me talk about it. I am not a scholar. I am not in the least an intellectual, which is not to say that when I hear the word "intellectual" I reach for my gun, but only to say that I do not think in abstracts. During the years when I was an undergraduate at Berkeley I tried, with a kind of hopeless late-adolescent energy, to buy some temporary visa into the world of ideas, to forge for myself a mind that could deal with the abstract.

In short I tried to think. I failed. My attention veered inexorably back to the specific, to the tangible, to what was generally considered, by everyone I knew then and for that matter have known since, the peripheral. I would try to contemplate the Hegelian dialectic and would find myself concentrating instead on a flowering pear tree outside my window and the particular way the petals fell on my floor. I would try to read linguistic theory and would find myself wondering instead if the lights were on in the bevatron up the hill. When I say that I was wondering if the lights were on in the bevatron you might immediately suspect, if you deal in ideas at all, that I was registering the bevatron as a political symbol, thinking in shorthand about the military-industrial complex and its role in the university community, but you would be wrong. I was only wondering if the lights were on in the bevatron, and how they looked. A physical fact.

I had trouble graduating from Berkeley, not because of this inability to deal with ideas—I was majoring in English, and I could locate the house-and-garden imagery in *The Portrait of a Lady* as well as the next person, "imagery" being by definition the kind of specific that got my attention—but simply because I had neglected to take a course in Milton. For reasons which now sound baroque I needed a degree by the end of that summer, and the English department finally agreed, if I would come down from Sacramento every Friday and talk about the cosmology of *Paradise Lost,* to certify me proficient in Milton. I did this. Some Fridays I took the Greyhound bus, other Fridays I caught the Southern Pacific's City of San Francisco on the last leg of its transcontinental trip. I can no longer tell you whether Milton put the sun or the earth at the center of his universe in *Paradise Lost,* the central question of at least one century and a topic about which I wrote 10,000 words that summer, but I can still recall the exact rancidity of the butter in the City of San Francisco's dining car, and the way the tinted windows on the Greyhound bus cast the oil refineries around Carquinez Straits into a grayed and obscurely sinister light. In short my attention was always on the periphery, on what I could see and taste and touch, on the butter, and the Greyhound bus. During those years I was traveling on what I knew to be a very shaky passport, forged papers: I knew that I was no legitimate resident in any world of ideas. I knew I couldn't think. All I knew then was what I couldn't do. All I knew then was what I wasn't, and it took me some years to discover what I was.

Which was a writer. 6

By which I mean not a "good" writer or a "bad" writer but 7 simply a writer, a person whose most absorbed and passionate hours are spent arranging words on pieces of paper. Had my credentials been in order I would never have become a writer. Had I been blessed with even limited access to my own mind there would have been no reason to write. I write entirely to find out what I'm thinking, what I'm looking at, what I see and what it means. What I want and what I fear. Why did the oil refineries around Carquinez Straits seem sinister to me in the summer of 1956? Why have the night lights in the bevatron burned in my mind for twenty years? *What is going on in these pictures in my mind?*

When I talk about pictures in my mind I am talking, quite 8 specifically, about images that shimmer around the edges. There used to be an illustration in every elementary psychology book showing a cat drawn by a patient in varying stages of schizophrenia. This cat had a shimmer around it. You could see the molecular structure breaking down at the very edges of the cat: the cat became the background and the background the cat, everything interacting, exchanging ions. People on hallucinogens describe the same perception of objects. I'm not a schizophrenic, nor do I take hallucinogens, but certain images do shimmer for me. Look hard enough, and you can't miss the shimmer. It's there. You can't think too much about these pictures that shimmer. You just lie low and let them develop. You stay quiet. You don't talk to many people and you keep your nervous system from shorting out and you try to locate the cat in the shimmer, the grammar in the picture.

Just as I meant "shimmer" literally I mean "grammar" liter- 9 ally. Grammar is a piano I play by ear, since I seem to have been out of school the year the rules were mentioned. All I know about grammar is its infinite power. To shift the structure of a sentence alters the meaning of that sentence, as definitely and in-flexibly as the position of a camera alters the meaning of the ob-ject photographed. Many people know about camera angles now, but not so many know about sentences. The arrangement of the words matters, and the arrangement you want can be found in the picture in your mind. The picture dictates the arrangement. The picture dictates whether this will be a sentence with or without clauses, a sentence that ends hard or a dying-fall sentence, long or short, active or passive. The picture tells you how to arrange the words and the arrangement of the words tells you, or tells me, what's going on in the picture. *Nota bene.*[1]

It tells you.

You don't tell it.

Let me show you what I mean by pictures in the mind. I began *Play It as It Lays* just as I have begun each of my novels, with no notion of "character" or "plot" or even "incident." I had only two pictures in my mind, more about which later, and a techni-cal intention, which was to write a novel so elliptical and fast that it would be over before you noticed it, a novel so fast that it would scarcely exist on the page at all. About the pictures: the first was of white space. Empty space. This was clearly the pic-ture that dictated the narrative intention of the book—a book in which anything that happened would happen off the page, a "white" book to which the reader would have to bring his or her own bad dreams—and yet this picture told me no "story," sug-gested no situation. The second picture did. This second picture was of something actually witnessed. A young woman with long hair and a short white halter dress walks through the casino at the Riviera in Las Vegas at one in the morning. She crosses the casino alone and picks up a house telephone. I watch her because I have heard her paged, and recognize her name: she is a minor actress I see around Los Angeles from time to time, in places like Jax and once in a gynecologist's office in the Beverly Hills Clinic, but have never met. I know nothing about her. Who is paging her? Why is she here to be paged? How exactly did she come to this? It was precisely this moment in Las Vegas that made *Play It as It Lays* begin to tell itself to me, but the moment appears in the novel only obliquely, in a chapter which begins:

1. "Note well." (Latin)

"Maria made a list of things she would never do. She would   13
never: walk through the Sands or Caesar's alone after midnight.
She would never: ball at a party, do S-M unless she wanted to,
borrow furs from Abe Lipsey, deal. She would never: carry a
Yorkshire in Beverly Hills."

That is the beginning of the chapter and that is also the end of   14
the chapter, which may suggest what I meant by "white space."

I recall having a number of pictures in my mind when I began   15
the novel I just finished, *A Book of Common Prayer.* As a matter
of fact one of these pictures was of that bevatron I mentioned, although I would be hard put to tell you a story in which nuclear
energy figures. Another was a newspaper photograph of a hijacked 707 burning on the desert in the Middle East. Another
was the night view from a room in which I once spent a week
with paratyphoid, a hotel room on the Colombian coast. My
husband and I seemed to be on the Colombian coast represent-
ing the United States of America at a film festival (I recall invoking the name "Jack Valenti" a lot, as if its reiteration could make
me well), and it was a bad place to have fever, not only because
my indisposition offended our hosts but because every night in
this hotel the generator failed. The lights went out. The elevator
stopped. My husband would go to the event of the evening and
make excuses for me and I would stay alone in this hotel room,
in the dark. I remember standing at the window trying to call Bogotá (the telephone seemed to work on the same principle as the
generator) and watching the night wind come up and wondering
what I was doing eleven degrees off the equator with a fever of
103. The view from that window definitely figures in *A Book of
Common Prayer,* as does the burning 707, and yet none of these
pictures told me the story I needed.

The picture that did, the picture that shimmered and made   16
these other images coalesce, was the Panama airport at 6 A.M. I
was in this airport only once, on a plane to Bogotá that stopped
for an hour to refuel, but the way it looked that morning remained superimposed on everything I saw until the day I finished
A Book of Common Prayer, I lived in that airport for several
years. I can still feel the hot air when I step off the plane, can see
the heat already rising off the tarmac at 6 A.M. I can feel my skirt
damp and wrinkled on my legs. I can feel the asphalt stick to my
sandals. I remember the big tail of a Pan American plane floating

motionless down at the end of the tarmac. I remember the sound of a slot machine in the waiting room. I could tell you that I remember a particular woman in the airport, an American woman, *a norteamericana,* a thin *norteamericana* about forty who wore a big square emerald in lieu of a wedding ring, but there was no such woman there.

I put this woman in the airport later. I made this woman up, just as I later made up a country to put the airport in, and a family to run the country. This woman in the airport is neither catching a plane nor meeting one. She is ordering tea in the airport coffee shop. In fact she is not simply "ordering" tea but insisting that the water be boiled, in front of her, for twenty minutes. Why is this woman in this airport? Why is she going nowhere, where has she been? Where did she get that big emerald? What derangement, or disassociation, makes her believe that her will to see the water boiled can possibly prevail?

"She had been going to one airport or another for four months, one could see it, looking at the visas on her passport. All those airports where Charlotte Douglas's passport had been stamped would have looked alike. Sometimes the sign on the tower would say 'Bienvenidos' and sometimes the sign on the tower would say 'Bienvenue,' some places were wet and hot and others dry and hot, but at each of these airports the pastel concrete walls would rust and stain and the swamp off the runway would be littered with the fuselages of cannibalized Fairchild F-227's and the water would need boiling.

"I knew why Charlotte went to the airport even if Victor did not.

"I knew about airports."

These lines appear about halfway through *A Book of Common Prayer,* but I wrote them during the second week I worked on the book, long before I had any idea where Charlotte Douglas had been or why she went to airports. Until I wrote these lines I had no character called "Victor" in mind: the necessity for mentioning a name, and the name "Victor," occurred to me as I wrote the sentence. *I knew why Charlotte went to the airport* sounded incomplete. *I knew why Charlotte went to the airport even if Victor did not* carried a little more narrative drive. Most important of all, until I wrote these lines I did not know who "I" was, who was telling the story. I had intended until then that the

"I" be no more than the voice of the author, a nineteenth-century omniscient narrator, But there it was:

"I knew why Charlotte went to the airport even if Victor did not.   22

"I knew about airports."   23

This "I" was the voice of no author in my house. This "I" was   24 someone who not only knew why Charlotte went to the airport but also knew someone called "Victor." Who was Victor? Who was this narrator? Why was this narrator telling me this story? Let me tell you one thing about why writers write: had I known the answer to any of these questions I would never have needed to write a novel.

3

COMMUNITY

Barn Raising. © 2002 ANDREW STAWICKI.

Overview

In "The Common Life" Scott Russell Sanders writes about the sense of belonging to a community, "the sense of being utterly in place," as he puts it. For our ancestors living a thousand years ago, the sense of having a place in a community must have been inescapable and therefore unremarkable. Most people were born within a day's walk of the place they would die, in or near a village where a stranger's face was a novelty. In this kind of community, everyone had a recognizable face and a role in the local gossip.

Today we live differently. Millions of Americans rise in the morning, listen to news reports about events thousands of miles away, commute to work along streets inhabited by strangers, and work all day with people about whose "private life" (a rather modern concept) they know almost nothing. And many of us relocate so often—moving from city to city for the sake of education and careers—that we have periods of feeling even more profoundly out of place.

Of course, not everyone wants to belong to a close-knit community. Sometimes the ability to disconnect from our old communities and our old identities within them is exhilarating. For good or ill, though, the change from our old life as village-dwelling species to our new life of cities and relocations is a dramatic one—an experiment whose results we don't yet know. How do we build communities when we are so often on the move and living among strangers? What makes a modern community strong or weak, safe or dangerous, welcoming or unwelcoming?

The selection of readings that follow offers several perspectives on these questions:

- Scott Russell Sanders, in the most openly personal essay of the group, offers his ideal of a healthy community and encourages us to reconsider our relation not only to our human neighbors, but also to our natural surroundings.
- Robert Putnam, in an academic essay that led to a popular book, expresses his concern that our increasing isolation is diminishing the "social capital" needed for true democracy.

179

- Katha Pollitt rejects Robert Putnam's assumptions and evidence, and she doubts the significance of "social capital." "Love your neighbor if you can," she advises, "but forget civic trust."
- H. D. F. Kitto explains why he thinks that the community life of the ancient Greek *polis* (the small city-state) was superior to the community life we moderns experience.
- James Baldwin describes "wide, filthy, hostile Fifth Avenue" and the neighborhood around it, a ghetto made worse by attempts to improve it.
- Jane Jacobs, in a passage from *The Death and Life of Great American Cities,* discusses some circumstances that allow people who hardly know each other to live together with a sense of community and mutual responsibility.
- Susan Glaspell, in a play set in the kitchen of an isolated farmhouse, shows a community struggling to understand a murder for which it might have itself to blame.

SCOTT RUSSELL SANDERS

The Common Life

Currently teaching at Indiana University, Scott Sanders has said of his writing, "In all my work, regardless of period or style, I am concerned with the practical problems of living on a small planet, in nature and in communities. I am concerned with the life people make together, in marriages and families and towns, more than with the life of isolated individuals." The following essay is from *Writing from the Center* (1995).

One delicious afternoon while my daughter Eva was home from college for spring vacation, she invited two neighbor girls to help her make bread. The girls are sisters, five-year-old Alexandra and ten-year-old Rachel, both frolicky, with eager dark eyes and shining faces. They live just down the street from us here in Bloomington, Indiana, and whenever they see me pass by, on bicycle or on foot, they ask about Eva, whom they adore.   1

I was in the yard that afternoon mulching flower beds with compost, and I could hear the girls chattering as Eva led them up the sidewalk to our door. I had plenty of other chores to do in the yard, where every living thing was urgent with April. But how could I stay outside, when so much beauty and laughter and spunk were gathered in the kitchen?   2

I kept looking in on the cooks, until Eva finally asked, "Daddy, you wouldn't like to knead some dough, would you?"   3

"I'd love to," I said. "You sure there's room for me?"   4

"There's room," Eva replied, "but you'll have to wash in the basement."   5

Hands washed, I took my place at the counter beside Rachel and Alexandra, who perched on a stool I had made for Eva when she was a toddler. Eva had still needed that stool when she learned to make bread on this counter; and my son, now six feet tall, had balanced there as well for his own first lessons in cooking. I never needed the stool, but I needed the same teacher—my wife Ruth, a woman with eloquent fingers.   6

Our kitchen is small; Ruth and I share that cramped space by moving in a kind of dance we have been practicing for years.   7

When we bump one another, it is usually for the pleasure of bumping. But Eva and the girls and I jostled like birds too numerous for a nest. We spattered flour everywhere. We told stories. We joked. All the while I bobbed on a current of bliss, delighting in the feel of live dough beneath my fingers, the smell of yeast, the piping of child-voices so much like the birdsong cascading through our open windows, the prospect of whole-wheat loaves hot from the oven.

An artist might paint this kitchen scene in pastels for a poster, with a tender motto below, as evidence that all is right with the world. All is manifestly *not* right with the world. The world, most of us would agree, is a mess: rife with murder and mayhem, abuse of land, extinction of species, lying and theft and greed. There are days when I can see nothing but a spectacle of cruelty and waste, and the weight of dismay pins me to my chair. On such days I need a boost merely to get up, uncurl my fists, and go about my work. The needed strength may come from family, from neighbors, from a friend's greeting in the mail, from the forked leaves of larkspur breaking ground, from rainstorms and music and wind, from the lines of a handmade table or the lines in a well-worn book, from the taste of an apple or the brash trill of finches in our backyard trees. Strength also comes to me from memories of times when I have felt a deep and complex joy, a sense of being exactly where I should be and doing exactly what I should do, as I felt on that breadmaking afternoon.

I wish to reflect on the sources of that joy, that sense of being utterly in place, because I suspect they are the sources of all that I find authentic in my life. So much in life seems to me unauthentic, I cannot afford to let the genuine passages slip by without considering what makes them ring true. It is as though I spend my days wandering about, chasing false scents, lost, and then occasionally, for a few ticks of the heart, I stumble onto the path. While making bread with my daughter and her two young friends, I was on the path. So I recall that time now as a way of keeping company with Eva, who has gone back to college, but also as a way of discovering in our common life a reservoir of power and hope.

What is so powerful, so encouraging, in that kitchen scene? To begin with, I love my three fellow cooks; I relish every tilt of their heads and turn of their voices. In their presence I feel more alive and alert, as if the rust had been knocked off my nerves. The armor of self dissolves, ego relaxes its grip, and I am simply there, on the breeze of the moment.

Rachel and Alexandra belong to the Abed family, with whom 11 we often share food and talk and festivities. We turn to the Abeds for advice, for starts of plants, for cheer, and they likewise turn to us. Not long ago they received troubling news that may force them to move away, and we have been sharing in their distress. So the Abed girls brought into our kitchen a history of neighborliness, a history all the more valuable because it might soon come to an end.

The girls also brought a readiness to learn what Eva had to 12 teach. Eva, as I mentioned, had learned from Ruth how to make bread, and Ruth had learned from a Canadian friend, and our friend had learned from her grandmother. As Rachel and Alexandra shoved their hands into the dough, I could imagine the rope of knowledge stretching back and back through generations, to folks who ground their grain with stones and did their baking in wood stoves or fireplaces or in pits of glowing coals.

If you have made yeast bread, you know how at first the 13 dough clings to your fingers, and then gradually, as you knead in more flour, it begins to pull away and take on a life of its own, becoming at last as resilient as a plump belly. If you have not made yeast bread, no amount of hearing or reading about it will give you that knowledge, because you have to learn through your body, through fingers and wrists and aching forearms, through shoulders and backs. Much of what we know comes to us that way, passed on from person to person, age after age, surviving in muscle and bone. I learned from my mother how to transplant a seedling, how to sew on a button; I learned from my father how to saw a board square, how to curry a horse, how to change the oil in a car. The pleasure I take in sawing or currying, in planting or sewing, even in changing oil, like my pleasure in making bread, is bound up with the affection I feel for my teachers and the respect I feel for the long, slow accumulation of knowledge that informs our simplest acts.

Those simple acts come down to us because they serve real 14 needs. You plant a tree or sweep a floor or rock a baby without asking the point of your labors. You patch the roof to stop a leak, patch a sweater to keep from having to throw it out. You pluck the banjo because it tickles your ears and rouses Grandpa to dance. None of us can live entirely by such meaningful acts; our jobs, if nothing else, often push us through empty motions. But unless at least some of what we do has a transparent purpose, answering not merely to duty or fashion but to actual needs, then the heart has gone out of our work. What art could be more plainly valuable than cooking? The reason for baking bread is as palpable as your tongue. After our loaves were finished, Eva and I delivered two of them to the Abeds, who showed in their faces a perfect understanding of the good of bread.

When I compare the dough to a plump belly, I hear the sexual 15 overtones, of course. By making the comparison, I do not wish to say, with Freud, that every sensual act is a surrogate for sex; on the contrary, I believe sex comes closer to being a stand-in, rather brazen and obvious, like a ham actor pretending to be the whole show, when it is only one player in the drama of our sensual life. That life flows through us constantly, so long as we do not shut ourselves off. The sound of birds and the smell of April dirt and the brush of wind through the open door were all ingredients in the bread we baked.

Before baking, the yeast was alive, dozing in the refrigerator. 16 Scooped out of its jar, stirred into warm water, fed on sugar, it soon bubbled out gas to leaven the loaves. You have to make sure the water for the yeast, like milk for a baby, is neither too hot nor too cold, and so, as for a baby's bottle, I test the temperature on my wrist. The flour, too, had been alive not long before as wheat thriving in sun and rain. Our nourishment is borrowed life. You need not be a Christian to feel, in a bite of bread, a sense of communion with the energy that courses through all things. The lump in your mouth is a chunk of earth; there is nothing else to eat. In our house we say grace before meals, to remind ourselves of that gift and that dependence.

The elements of my kitchen scene—loving company, neigh- 17 borliness, inherited knowledge and good work, shared purpose, sensual delight, and union with the creation—sum up for me what is vital in community. Here is the spring of hope I have been led to by my trail of bread. In our common life we may find the strength not merely to carry on in face of the world's bad news, but to resist cruelty and waste. I speak of it as common because it is ordinary, because we make it together, because it binds us through time to the rest of humanity and through our bodies to the rest of nature. By honoring this common life, nurturing it, carrying it steadily in mind, we might renew our households and neighborhoods and cities, and in doing so might redeem ourselves from the bleakness of private lives spent in frenzied pursuit of sensation and wealth.

Ever since the eclipse of our native cultures, the dominant American view has been more nearly the opposite: that we should cultivate the self rather than the community; that we should look to the individual as the source of hope and the center of value, while expecting hindrance and harm from society. [18]

What other view could have emerged from our history? The first Europeans to reach America were daredevils and treasure seekers, as were most of those who mapped the interior. Many colonists were renegades of one stripe or another, some of them religious nonconformists, some political rebels, more than a few of them fugitives from the law. The trappers, hunters, traders, and freebooters who pushed the frontier westward seldom recognized any authority beyond the reach of their own hands. Coast to coast, our land has been settled and our cities have been filled by generations of immigrants more intent on leaving behind old tyrannies than on seeking new social bonds. [19]

Our government was forged in rebellion against alien control. Our economy was founded on the sanctity of private property, and thus our corporations have taken on a sacred immunity through being defined under the law as persons. Our criminal justice system is so careful to protect the rights of individuals that it may require years to convict a bank robber who killed a bystander in front of a crowd, or a bank official who left a trail of embezzlement as wide as the Mississippi. [20]

Our religion has been marked by an evangelical Protestantism that emphasizes personal salvation rather than social redemption. To "Get Right with God," as signs along the roads here in the Midwest gravely recommend, does not mean to reconcile your fellow citizens to the divine order, but to make a separate peace, to look after the eternal future of your own singular soul. True, we have a remarkable history of communal experiments, most of them religiously inspired—from Plymouth Colony, through the Shaker villages, Robert Owen's New Harmony, the settlements at Oneida, Amana, and countless other places, to the [21] communes in our own day. But these are generally known to us, if they are known at all, as utopian failures.

For much of the present century, Americans have been fighting   22 various forms of collectivism—senile empires during World War I, then Nazism, communism, and now fundamentalist theocracies— and these wars, the shouting kind as well as the shooting kind, have only strengthened our commitment to individualism. We have understood freedom for the most part negatively rather than positively, as release from constraints rather than as the condition for making a decent life in common. Hands off, we say; give me elbow room; good fences make good neighbors; my home is my castle; don't tread on me. I'm looking out for number one, we say; I'm doing my own thing. We have a Bill of Rights, which protects each of us from a bullying society, but no Bill of Responsibilities, which would oblige us to answer the needs of others.

Even where America's founding documents clearly address   23 the public good, they have often been turned to private ends. Consider just one notorious example, the Second Amendment to the Constitution:

> As well regulated Militia, being necessary to the security of a free State, the right of the people to keep and bear Arms, shall not be infringed.

It would be difficult to say more plainly that arms are to be kept for the sake of a militia, and a militia is to be kept for defense of the country. In our day, a reasonable person might judge that the Pentagon deploys quite enough weapons, without requiring any supplement from household arsenals. Yet this lucid passage has been construed to justify a domestic arms race, until we now have in America more gun shops than gas stations, we have nearly as many handguns as hands, and we have concentrated enough firepower in the average city to carry on a war—which is roughly what, in some cities, is going on. Thus, by reading the Second Amendment through the lens of our obsessive individualism, we have turned a provision for public safety into a guarantee of public danger.

Observe how zealously we have carved up our cities and   24 paved our land and polluted our air and burned up most of the earth's petroleum within a single generation—all for the sake of the automobile, a symbol of personal autonomy even more potent than the gun. There is a contemptuous ring to the word "mass" in mass transportation, as if the only alternative to private cars were cattle cars. Motorcycles and snowmobiles and three-wheelers fill our public lands with the din of engines and tear up the terrain, yet any effort to restrict their use is denounced as an infringement of individual rights. Millions of motorists exercise those rights by hurling the husks of their pleasures onto the roadside, boxes and bottles and bags. Ravines and ditches in my part of the country are crammed with rusty cars and refrigerators, burst couches and stricken TVs, which their former owners would not bother to haul to the dump. Meanwhile, advertisers sell us everything from jeeps to jeans as tokens of freedom, and we are so infatuated with the sovereign self that we fall for the spiel, as if by purchasing one of a million identical products we could distinguish ourselves from the herd.

The cult of the individual shows up everywhere in American lore, which celebrates drifters, rebels, and loners, while pitying or reviling the pillars of the community. The backwoods explorer like Daniel Boone, the riverboat rowdy like Mike Fink, the lumberjack, the prospector, the rambler and gambler, the daring crook like Jesse James and the resourceful killer like Billy the Kid, along with countless lonesome cowboys, all wander, unattached, through the great spaces of our imagination. When society begins to close in, making demands and asking questions, our heroes hit the road. Like Huckleberry Finn, they are forever lighting out for the Territory, where nobody will tell them what to do. Huck Finn ran away from what he called civilization in order to leave behind the wickedness of slavery, and who can blame him, but he was also running away from church and school and neighbors, from aunts who made him wash before meals, from girls who cramped his style, from chores, from gossip, from the whole nuisance of living alongside other people. 25

In our literature, when community enters at all, it is likely to appear as a conspiracy against the free soul of a hero or heroine. Recall how restless Natty Bumppo becomes whenever Cooper drags him in from the woods to a settlement. Remember how strenuously Emerson preaches against conforming to society and in favor of self-reliance, how earnestly Hawthorne warns us about the tyranny of those Puritan villages. Think of Thoreau running errands in Concord, rushing in the front door of a house and out the back, then home to his cabin in the woods, never pausing, lest he be caught in the snares of the town. Think of the revulsion Edna Pontellier feels toward the Creole society of New 26

Orleans in Kate Chopin's *The Awakening*. Think of Willa Cather's or Toni Morrison's or James Baldwin's high-spirited women and men who can only thrive by fleeing their home communities. Think of Spoon River, Winesburg, Gopher Prairie, Zenith, all those oppressive fictional places, the backward hamlets and stifling suburbs and heartless cities that are fit only for drones and drudges and mindless Babbitts.

In *The Invasion of the Body Snatchers*, a film from my child-   27
hood that still disturbs my dreams, an alien life form takes over one person after another in a small town, merging them into a single creature with a single will, until just one freethinking individual remains, and even he is clearly doomed. Along with dozens of other invasion tales, the film was a warning against communism, I suppose, but it was also a caution against the perils of belonging, of losing your one sweet self in the group, and thus it projected a fear as old as America.

Of course you can find American books and films that speak   28
as passionately for the virtues of our life together as for the virtues of our lives apart. To mention only a few novels from the past decade, I think of Gloria Naylor's *Mama Day,* Wendell Berry's *A Place on Earth,* Ursula Le Guin's *Always Coming Home,* and Ernest Gaines's *A Gathering of Old Men.* But they represent a minority opinion. The majority opinion fills bestseller lists and cinema screens and billboards with isolated, alienated, rebellious figures who are too potent or sensitive for membership in any group.

I have been shaped by this history, and I, too, am uneasy   29
about groups, especially large ones, above all those that are glued together by hatred, those that use a color of skin or a cut of clothes for admission tickets, and those that wrap themselves in scriptures or flags. I have felt a chill from blundering into company where I was not wanted. I have known women and men who were scorned because they refused to fit the molds their neighbors had prepared for them. I have seen Klansmen parading in white hoods, their crosses burning on front lawns. I have seen a gang work its way through a subway car, picking on the old, the young, the weak. Through film I have watched the Nuremberg rallies, watched policemen bashing demonstrators in Chicago, missiles parading in Red Square, tanks crushing dissidents in Tiananmen Square. Like everyone born since World War

II, I have grown up on television images of atrocities carried out, at home and abroad, with the blessing of governments or revolutionary armies or charismatic thugs.

In valuing community, therefore, I do not mean to approve of 30 any and every association of people. Humans are drawn together by a variety of motives, some of them worthy, some of them ugly. Anyone who has spent recess on a school playground knows the terror of mob rule. Anyone who has lived through a war knows that mobs may pretend to speak for an entire nation. I recently saw, for the first time in a long while, a bumper sticker that recalled for me the angriest days of the Vietnam War: AMERICA— LOVE IT OR LEAVE IT. What loving America seemed to mean, for those who brandished that slogan back around 1970, was the approval of everything the government said or the army did in our name. "All those who seek to destroy the liberty of a democratic nation ought to know," Alexis de Tocqueville observed in *Democracy in America,* "that war is the surest and the shortest means to accomplish it." As a conscientious objector, with a sister who studied near my home in Ohio on a campus where National Guardsmen killed several protestors, I felt the force of despotism in that slogan.

Rather than give in to despotism, some of my friends went to 31 jail and others into exile. My wife and I considered staying in England, where we had been studying for several years and where I had been offered a job. But instead we chose to come home, here to the Midwest where we had grown up, to work for change. In our idealism, we might have rephrased that bumper sticker to read: AMERICA—LOVE IT AND REDEEM IT. For us, loving America had little to do with politicians and even less with soldiers, but very much to do with what I have been calling the common life: useful work, ordinary sights, family, neighbors, ancestors, our fellow creatures, and the rivers and woods and fields that make up our mutual home.

During the more than twenty years since returning to America, 32 I have had some of the idealism knocked out of me, but I still believe that loving your country or city or neighborhood may require you to resist, to call for change, to speak on behalf of what you believe in, especially if what you believe in has been neglected.

What we have too often neglected, in our revulsion against 33 tyranny and our worship of the individual, is the common good. The results of that neglect are visible in the decay of our cities, the despoiling of our land, the fouling of our rivers and air, the haphazard commercial sprawl along our highways, the gluttonous feeding at the public trough, the mortgaging of our children's and grandchildren's future through our refusal to pay for current consumption. Only a people addicted to private pleasure would allow themselves to be defined as consumers—rather than conservers or restorers—of the earth's abundance.

In spite of the comforting assurances, from Adam Smith onward, that the unfettered pursuit of private wealth should result in unlimited public good, we all know that to be mostly a lie. If we needed reminders of how great that lie is, we could look at the savings and loan industry, where billions of dollars were stolen from small investors by rich managers who yearned to be richer; we could look at the Pentagon, where contracts are routinely encrusted with graft, or at Wall Street, where millionaires finagle to become billionaires through insider trading; we could look at our national forests, where logging companies buy timber for less than the cost to taxpayers of harvesting it; or we could look at our suburbs, where palaces multiply, while downtown more and more people are sleeping in cardboard boxes. Wealth does not precipitate like dew from the air; it comes out of the earth and from the labor of many hands. When a few hands hold onto great wealth, using it only for personal ease and display, that is a betrayal of the common life, the sole source of riches. 34

Fortunately, while our tradition is heavily tilted in favor of private life, we also inherit a tradition of caring for the community. Although Tocqueville found much to fear and quite a bit to despise in this raw democracy, he praised Americans for having "carried to the highest perfection the art of pursuing in common the object of their common desires." Writing of what he had seen in the 1830s, Tocqueville judged Americans to be avaricious, self-serving, and aggressive; but he was also amazed by our eagerness to form clubs, to raise barns or town halls, to join together in one cause or another: "In no country in the world, do the citizens make such exertions for the common weal. I know of no people who have established schools so numerous and efficacious, places of public worship better suited to the wants on the inhabitants, or roads kept in better repair." 35

Today we might revise his estimate of our schools or roads, but we can still see all around us the fruits of that concern for the 36 common weal—the libraries, museums, courthouses, hospitals, orphanages, universities, parks, on and on. Born as most of us are into places where such amenities already exist, we may take them for granted; but they would not be there for us to use had our forebears not cooperated in building them. No matter where we live, our home places have also benefited from the Granges and unions, the volunteer fire brigades, the art guilds and garden clubs, the charities, food kitchens, homeless shelters, soccer and baseball teams, the Scouts and 4-H, the Girls and Boys Clubs, the Lions and Elks and Rotarians, the countless gatherings of people who saw a need and responded to it.

This history of local care hardly ever makes it into our litera- 37 ture, for it is less glamorous than rebellion, yet it is a crucial part of our heritage. Any of us could cite examples of people who dug in and joined with others to make our home places better places. Women and men who invest themselves in their communities, fighting for good schools or green spaces, paying attention to where they are, seem to me as worthy of celebration as those adventurous loners who keep drifting on, prospecting for pleasure.

A few days after our breadmaking, Eva and I went to a con- 38 cert in Bloomington's newly opened arts center. The old limestone building had once been the town hall, then a fire station and jail, then for several years an abandoned shell. Volunteers bought the building from the city for a dollar, then renovated it with materials, labor, and money donated by local people. Now we have a handsome facility that is in constant use for pottery classes, theater productions, puppet shows, art exhibits, poetry readings, and every manner of musical event.

The music Eva and I heard was *Hymnody of Earth,* for ham- 39 mer dulcimer, percussion, and children's choir. Composed by our next-door neighbor, Malcolm Dalglish, and featuring lyrics by our Ohio Valley neighbor, Wendell Berry, it was performed that night by Malcolm, percussionist Glen Velez, and the Bloomington Youth Chorus. As I sat there with Eva in a sellout crowd—about a third of whom I knew by name, another third by face—I listened to music that had been elaborated within earshot of my house, and I heard my friend play his instrument, and I watched those children's faces shining with the colors of the human spectrum, and I felt the restored building clasping us all like the cupped hands of our community. I knew once more that I was in the right place, a place created and filled and inspired by our lives together.

*   *   *

A woman who recently moved from Los Angeles to Bloom- 40
ington told me that she would not be able to stay here long, because she was already beginning to recognize people in the
grocery stores, on the sidewalks, in the library. Being surrounded
by familiar faces made her nervous, after years in a city where
she could range about anonymously. Every traveler knows the
sense of liberation that comes from journeying to a place where
nobody expects anything of you. Everyone who has gone to college knows the exhilaration of slipping away from the watchful
eyes of Mom and Dad. We all need seasons of withdrawal from
responsibility. But if we make a career of being unaccountable,
we have lost something essential to our humanity, and we may
well become a burden or a threat to those around us. A community can support a number of people who are just passing
through, or who care about no one's needs but their own; the
greater the proportion of such people, however, the more vulnerable the community, until eventually it breaks down. That is
true on any scale, from a household to a planet.

The words *community, communion,* and *communicate* all de- 41
rive from *common,* and the two syllables of *common* grow from
separate roots, the first meaning "together" or "next to," the
second having to do with barter or exchange. Embodied in that
word is a sense of our shared life as one of giving and receiving—
music, touch, ideas, recipes, stories, medicine, tools, the whole
range of artifacts and talents. After twenty-five years with Ruth,
that is how I have come to understand marriage, as a constant
exchange of labor and love. We do not calculate who gives how
much; if we had to, the marriage would be in trouble. Looking
outward from this community of two, I see my life embedded in
ever larger exchanges—those of family and friendship, neighborhood and city, countryside and country—and on every scale
there is giving and receiving, calling and answering.

Many people shy away from community out of a fear that it 42
may become suffocating, confining, even vicious; and of course it
may, if it grows rigid or exclusive. A healthy community is dynamic, stirred up by the energies of those who already belong,
open to new members and fresh influences, kept in motion by the
constant bartering of gifts. It is fashionable just now to speak of
this open quality as "tolerance," but that word sounds too grudging to me—as though, to avoid strife, we must grit our teeth and

ignore whatever is strange to us. The community I desire is not grudging; it is exuberant, joyful, grounded in affection, pleasure, and mutual aid. Such a community arises not from duty or money but from the free interchange of people who share a place, share work and food, sorrows and hope. Taking part in the common life means dwelling in a web of relationships, the many threads tugging at you while also holding you upright.

I have told elsewhere the story of a man who lived in the Ohio township where I grew up, a builder who refused to join the volunteer fire department. Why should he join, when his house was brick, properly wired, fitted out with new appliances? Well, one day that house caught fire. The wife dialed the emergency number, the siren wailed, and pretty soon the volunteer firemen, my father among them, showed up with the pumper truck. But they held back on the hoses, asking the builder if he still saw no reason to join, and the builder said he could see a pretty good reason to join right there and then, and the volunteers let the water loose.   43

I have also told before the story of a family from that township whose house burned down. The fire had been started accidentally by the father, who came home drunk and fell asleep smoking on the couch. While the place was still ablaze, the man took off, abandoning his wife and several young children. The local people sheltered the family, then built them a new house. This was a poor township. But nobody thought to call in the government or apply to a foundation. These were neighbors in a fix, and so you helped them, just as you would harvest corn for an ailing farmer or pull a flailing child from the creek or put your arm around a weeping friend.   44

I am not harking back to some idyllic past, like the one embalmed in the *Saturday Evening Post* covers by Norman Rockwell or the prints of Currier and Ives. The past was never golden. As a people, we still need to unlearn some of the bad habits formed during the long period of settlement. One good habit we might reclaim, however, is that of looking after those who live nearby. For much of our history, neighbors have kept one another going, kept one another sane. Still today, in town and country, in apartment buildings and barrios, even in suburban estates, you are certain to lead a narrower life without the steady presence of neighbors. It is neither quaint nor sentimental to advocate neighborliness; it is far more sentimental to suggest that we can do without such mutual aid.   45

Even Emerson, preaching self-reliance, knew the necessity of   46
neighbors. He lived in a village, gave and received help, and delivered his essays as lectures for fellow citizens whom he hoped
to sway. He could have left his ideas in his journals, where they
first took shape, but he knew those ideas would only have effect
when they were shared. I like to think he would have agreed with
the Lakota shaman, Black Elk, that "a man who has a vision is
not able to use the power of it until after he has performed the
vision on earth for the people to see." If you visit Emerson's
house in Concord, you will find leather buckets hanging near the
door, for he belonged to the village fire brigade, and even in the
seclusion of his study, in the depths of thought, he kept his ears
open for the alarm bell.

We should not have to wait until our houses are burning be-   47
fore we see the wisdom of facing our local needs by joining in
common work. We should not have to wait until gunfire breaks
out in our schools, rashes break out on our skin, dead fish float in
our streams, or beggars sleep on our streets before we act on behalf of the community. On a crowded planet, we had better learn
how to live well together, or we will live miserably apart.

In cultural politics these days there is much talk of diversity and   48
difference. This is all to the good, insofar as it encourages us to welcome the many distinctive traditions and visions that have flowed
into America from around the world. But if, while respecting how
we differ, we do not also recognize how much we have in common,
we will have climbed out of the melting pot into the fire. Every
day's newspaper brings word of people suffering and dying in the
name of one distinction or another. We have never been slow to notice differences—of accent, race, dress, habits. If we merely change
how those differences are valued, celebrating what had formerly
been despised or despising what had been celebrated, we continue
to define ourselves and one another in the old divisive ways.

Ethnic labels are especially dangerous, for, while we pin them   49
on as badges of pride, we may have difficulty taking them off
when others decide to use them as targets. The larger the group
identified by a label, the less likely it is to be a genuine community. Haste or laziness may lead us to speak of blacks and whites,
of Christians and Muslims and Jews, of Armenians and Mexicans, yet the common life transcends such categories. Sharing a

national anthem, a religion, or a skin color may be grounds for holding rallies or waging war, but community is more intimate than nationality, more subtle than race or creed, arising not from abstract qualities but from the daily give-and-take among particular people in a particular place.

It is also dangerous to separate a concern for human diversity   50 from a concern for natural diversity. Since Europeans arrived in North America, we have been drawing recklessly on beaver and bison, trees and topsoil, petroleum, coal, iron and copper ore, clean air and water. Many of the achievements on which we pride ourselves are the result not of our supposed virtues but of this plundered bounty. We do not have another continent to use up; unless we learn to inhabit this one more conservingly, we will see our lives, as well as the land, swiftly degraded. There is no contradiction between caring for our fellow human beings and caring for the rest of nature; on the contrary, only by attending to the health of the land can we measure our true needs or secure a lasting home.

Just before Eva was to leave again for college, she and I went   51 for a hike in a nature preserve along Clear Creek, near Bloomington, to look at the hepatica and bloodroot and listen to the spring-high water. At the edge of the preserve, a wooden sign declared that the riding of horses was prohibited. The trail had been freshly gouged by horseshoes and was eroding badly. Trash snagged in the roots of sycamores along the stream. Much of the soil and its cover of wildflowers had washed from the slopes where people scrambled up to picnic on the limestone bluff. Some of the cans they had left behind glinted among white stars of trillium.

I wondered what it would take to persuade the riders to get   52 down off their horses and go on foot. What would it take to discourage people from dumping their worn-out washing machines in ditches? What would convince farmers to quit spraying poisons on their fields, suburbanites to quit spraying poisons on their lawns? What power in heaven or earth could stop loggers from seeing every tree as lumber, stop developers from seeing every acre of land as real estate, stop oil-company executives from seeing our last few scraps of wilderness as pay dirt waiting to be drilled? What would it take to persuade all of us to eat what we need, rather than what we can hold; to buy what we need, rather than what we can afford; to draw our pleasure from inexhaustible springs?

Signs will not work that change of mind, for in a battle of signs   53
the billboards always win. Police cannot enforce it. Tongue lash-
ings and sermons and earnest essays will not do it, nor will laws
alone bring it about. The framers of the Constitution may have
assumed that we did not need a Bill of Responsibilities because religion and reason and the benign impulses of our nature would
lead us to care for one another and for our home. At the end of a
bloody century, on the eve of a new millennium that threatens to
be still bloodier, few of us now feel much confidence in those re-
deeming influences. Only a powerful ethic might restrain us, re-
train us, restore us. Our survival is at stake, yet worrying about
our survival alone is too selfish a motive to carry us as far as we
need to go. Nothing short of reimagining where we are and what
we are will be radical enough to transform how we live.

Aldo Leopold gave us the beginnings of this new ethic nearly   54
half a century ago, in *A Sand Country Almanac,* where he described the land itself as a community made up of rock, water,
soil, plants, and animals—including Homo sapiens, the only
species clever enough to ignore, for a short while, the conditions
of membership. "We abuse land because we see it as a commodity belonging to us," Leopold wrote. "When we see land as a
community to which we belong, we may begin to use it with love
and respect." To use our places with love and respect demands
from us the same generosity and restraint that we show in our
dealings with a wife or husband, a child or parent, a neighbor, a
stranger in trouble.

Once again this spring, the seventy-seventh of her life, my   55
mother put out lint from her clothes dryer for the birds to use in
building their nests. "I know how hard it is to make a home from
scratch," she says, "I've done it often enough myself." That is not
anthropomorphism; it is fellow feeling, the root of all kindness.

Doctors the world over study the same physiology, for we are   56
one species, woven together by strands of DNA that stretch back
to the beginnings of life. There is, in fact, only one life, one pulse
animating the dust. Sycamores and snakes, grasshoppers and
grass, hawks and humans all spring from the same source and all
return to it. We need to make of this common life not merely a
metaphor, although we live by metaphors, and not merely a
story, although we live by stories; we need to make the common
life a fact of the heart. That awareness, that concern, that love
needs to go as deep in us as the feeling we have when a child

dashes into the street and we hear a squeal of brakes, or when a piece of our home ground goes under concrete, or when a cat purrs against our palms or rain sends shivers through our bones or a smile floats back to us from another face.

With our own population booming, with frogs singing in the April ponds, with mushrooms cracking the pavement, life may seem the most ordinary of forces, like hunger or gravity; it may seem cheap, since we see it wasted every day. But in truth life is expensive, life is extraordinary, having required five billion years of struggle and luck on one stony, watery planet to reach its present precarious state. And so far as we have been able to discover from peering out into the great black spaces, the life that is common to all creatures here on earth is exceedingly uncommon, perhaps unique, in the universe. How, grasping that, can we remain unchanged? *57*

It may be that we will not change, that nothing can restrain us, that we are incapable of reimagining our relations to one another or our place in creation. So many alarm bells are ringing, we may be tempted to stuff our ears with cotton. Better that we should keep ears and eyes open, take courage as well as joy from our common life, and work for what we love. What I love is curled about a loaf of bread, a family, a musical neighbor, a building salvaged for art, a town of familiar faces, a creek and a limestone bluff and a sky full of birds. Those may seem like frail threads to hold anyone in place while history heaves us about, and yet, when they are braided together, I find them to be amazingly strong. *58*

Robert D. Putnam

Bowling Alone: America's Declining Social Capital

A professor at Harvard University, Robert Putnam has focused on the ways that voluntary associations—choral music groups, service clubs, churches, and so forth—encourage democracy. The following essay from the *Journal of Democracy* (January 1995) received sudden attention when it became a source of ideas for President Clinton's State of the Union address in January 1996.

Many students of the new democracies that have emerged   1
over the past decade and a half have emphasized the importance
of a strong and active civil society to the consolidation of democracy. Especially with regard to the postcommunist countries,
scholars and democratic activists alike have lamented the absence or obliteration of traditions of independent civic engagement and a widespread tendency toward passive reliance on the
state. To those concerned with the weakness of civil societies in
the developing or postcommunist world, the advanced Western
democracies and above all the United States have typically been
taken as models to be emulated. There is striking evidence, however, that the vibrancy of American civil society has notably declined over the past several decades.

Ever since the publication of Alexis de Tocqueville's *Democ-*   2
racy in America, the United States has played a central role in
systematic studies of the links between democracy and civil society. Although this is in part because trends in American life are
often regarded as harbingers of social modernization, it is also
because America has traditionally been considered unusually
"civic" (a reputation that, as we shall later see, has not been entirely unjustified).

When Tocqueville visited the United States in the 1830s, it   3
was the Americans' propensity for civic association that most
impressed him as the key to their unprecedented ability to make
democracy work. "Americans of all ages, all stations in life, and
all types of disposition," he observed, "are forever forming associations. There are not only commercial and industrial associations in which all take part, but others of a thousand different
types—religious, moral, serious, futile, very general and very
limited, immensely large and very minute. . . . Nothing, in my
view, deserves more attention than the intellectual and moral
associations in America."[1]

Recently, American social scientists of a neo-Tocquevillean   4
bent have unearthed a wide range of empirical evidence that the
quality of public life and the performance of social institutions
(and not only in America) are indeed powerfully influenced by
norms and networks of civic engagement. Researchers in such
fields as education, urban poverty, unemployment, the control of

---

1. Alexis de Tocqueville, *Democracy in America,* ed. J. P. Maier, trans. George
Lawrence (Garden City, N.Y.: Anchor Books, 1969), 513–17. [author's note]

crime and drug abuse, and even health have discovered that successful outcomes are more likely in civically engaged communities. Similarly, research on the varying economic attainments of
different ethnic groups in the United States has demonstrated the
importance of social bonds within each group. These results are
consistent with research in a wide range of settings that demonstrates the vital importance of social networks for job placement
and many other economic outcomes.

Meanwhile, a seemingly unrelated body of research on the so-   5
ciology of economic development has also focused attention on
the role of social networks. Some of this work is situated in the
developing countries, and some of it elucidates the peculiarly
successful "network capitalism" of East Asia.[2] Even in less exotic Western economies, however, researchers have discovered
highly efficient, highly flexible "industrial districts" based on
networks of collaboration among workers and small entrepreneurs. Far from being paleoindustrial anachronisms, these dense
interpersonal and interorganizational networks undergird ultra-
modern industries, from the high tech of Silicon Valley to the
high fashion of Benetton.

The norms and networks of civic engagement also powerfully   6
affect the performance of representative government. That, at

2. On social networks and economic growth in the developing world, see Milton
J. Esman and Norman Uphoff, *Local Organizations: Intermediaries in Rural De-
velopment* (Ithaca: Cornell University Press, 1984), esp. 15–42 and 99–180; and
Albert O. Hirschman, *Getting Ahead Collectively: Grassroots Experiences in
Latin America* (Elmsford, N.Y.: Pergamon Press, 1984), esp. 42–77. On East
Asia, see Gustav Papanek, "The New Asian Capitalism: An Economic Portrait,"
in Peter L. Berger and Hsin-Huang Michael Hsiao, eds., *In Search of an East
Asian Development Model* (New Brunswick, N.J.: Transaction, 1987), 27–80;
Peter B. Evans, "The State as Problem and Solution: Predation, Embedded Au-
tonomy and Structural Change," in Stephan Haggard and Robert R. Kaufman,
eds., *The Politics of Economic Adjustment* (Princeton: Princeton University
Press, 1992), 139–81; and Gary G. Hamilton, William Zeile, and Wan-Jin Kim,
"Network Structure of East Asian Economies," in Stewart R. Clegg and S. Gor-
don Redding, eds., *Capitalism in Contrasting Cultures* (Hawthorne, N.Y.: De
Gruyter, 1990), 105–29. See also Gary G. Hamilton and Nicole Woolsey Biggart,
"Market, Culture, and Authority: A Comparative Analysis of Management and
Organization in the Far East," *American Journal of Sociology* (Supplement) 94
(1988): S52–S94; and Susan Greenhalgh, "Families and Networks in Taiwan's
Economic Development," in Edwin Winckler and Susan Greenhalgh, eds., *Con-
tending Approaches to the Political Economy of Taiwan* (Armonk, N.Y.: M. E.
Sharpe, 1987), 224–45. [author's note]

least, was the central conclusion of my own 20-year, quasi-experimental study of subnational governments in different regions of Italy.[3] Although all these regional governments seemed identical on paper, their levels of effectiveness varied dramatically. Systematic inquiry showed that the quality of governance was determined by longstanding traditions of civic engagement (or its absence). Voter turnout, newspaper readership, membership in choral societies and football clubs—these were the hallmarks of a successful region. In fact, historical analysis suggested that these networks of organized reciprocity and civic solidarity, far from being an epiphenomenon of socioeconomic modernization, were a precondition for it.

No doubt the mechanisms through which civic engagement   7
and social connectedness produce such results—better schools, faster economic development, lower crime, and more effective government—are multiple and complex. While these briefly recounted findings require further confirmation and perhaps qualification, the parallels across hundreds of empirical studies in a dozen disparate disciplines and subfields are striking. Social scientists in several fields have recently suggested a common framework for understanding these phenomena, a framework that rests on the concept of *social capital*.[4] By analogy with notions of physical capital and human capital—tools and training that enhance individual productivity—"social capital" refers to features of social organization such as networks, norms, and social trust that facilitate coordination and cooperation for mutual benefit.

For a variety of reasons, life is easier in a community blessed   8
with a substantial stock of social capital. In the first place, net-

3. Robert D. Putnam, *Making Democracy Work: Civic Traditions in Modern Italy* (Princeton: Princeton University Press, 1993). [author's note]
4. James S. Coleman deserves primary credit for developing the "social capital" theoretical framework. See his "Social Capital in the Creation of Human Capital," *American Journal of Sociology* (Supplement) 94 (1988): S95–S120, as well as his *The Foundations of Social Theory* (Cambridge: Harvard University Press, 1990), 300–21. See also Mark Granovetter, "Economic Action and Social Structure: The Problem of Embeddedness," *American Journal of Sociology* 91 (1985): 481–510; Glenn C. Loury, "Why Should We Care About Group Inequality?" *Social Philosophy and Policy* 5 (1987): 249–71; and Robert D. Putnam, "The Prosperous Community: Social Capital and Public Life," *American Prospect* 13 (1993): 35–42. To my knowledge, the first scholar to use the term "social capital" in its current sense was Jane Jacobs, in *The Death and Life of Great American Cities* (New York: Random House, 1961), 138. [author's note]

works of civic engagement foster sturdy norms of generalized reciprocity and encourage the emergence of social trust. Such networks facilitate coordination and communication, amplify reputations, and thus allow dilemmas of collective action to be resolved. When economic and political negotiation is embedded in dense networks of social interaction, incentives for opportunism are reduced. At the same time, networks of civic engagement embody past success at collaboration, which can serve as a cultural template for future collaboration. Finally, dense networks of interaction probably broaden the participants' sense of self, developing the "I" into the "we," or (in the language of rational-choice theorists) enhancing the participants' "taste" for collective benefits.

I do not intend here to survey (much less contribute to) the development of the theory of social capital. Instead, I use the central premise of that rapidly growing body of work—that social connections and civic engagement pervasively influence our public life, as well as our private prospects—as the starting point for an empirical survey of trends in social capital in contemporary America. I concentrate here entirely on the American case, although the developments I portray may in some measure characterize many contemporary societies.

WHATEVER HAPPENED TO CIVIC ENGAGEMENT?

We begin with familiar evidence on changing patterns of political participation, not least because it is immediately relevant to issues of democracy in the narrow sense. Consider the well-known decline in turnout in national elections over the last three decades. From a relative high point in the early 1960s, voter turnout had by 1990 declined by nearly a quarter; tens of millions of Americans had forsaken their parents' habitual readiness to engage in the simplest act of citizenship. Broadly similar trends also characterize participation in state and local elections.

It is not just the voting booth that has been increasingly deserted by Americans. A series of identical questions posed by the Roper Organization to national samples ten times each year over the last two decades reveals that since 1973 the number of Americans who report that "in the past year" they have "attended a public meeting on town or school affairs" has fallen by more

202   ROBERT D. PUTNAM

than a third (from 22 percent in 1973 to 13 percent in 1993). Similar (or even greater) relative declines are evident in responses to questions about attending a political rally or speech, serving on a committee of some local organization, and working for a political party. By almost every measure, Americans' direct engagement in politics and government has fallen steadily and sharply over the last generation, despite the fact that average levels of education—the best individual-level predictor of political participation—have risen sharply throughout this period. Every year over the last decade or two, millions more have withdrawn from the affairs of their communities.

Not coincidentally, Americans have also disengaged psychologically from politics and government over this era. The proportion of Americans who reply that they "trust the government in Washington" only "some of the time" or "almost never" has risen steadily from 30 percent in 1966 to 75 percent in 1992.   12

These trends are well known, of course, and taken by themselves would seem amenable to a strictly political explanation. Perhaps the long litany of political tragedies and scandals since the 1960s (assassinations, Vietnam, Watergate, Irangate, and so on) has triggered an understandable disgust for politics and government among Americans, and that in turn has motivated their withdrawal. I do not doubt that this common interpretation has some merit, but its limitations become plain when we examine trends in civic engagement of a wider sort.   13

Our survey of organizational membership among Americans can usefully begin with a glance at the aggregate results of the General Social Survey, a scientifically conducted, national-sample survey that has been repeated 14 times over the last two decades. Church-related groups constitute the most common type of organization joined by Americans; they are especially popular with women. Other types of organizations frequently joined by women include school-service groups (mostly parent-teacher associations), sports groups, professional societies, and literary societies. Among men, sports clubs, labor unions, professional societies, fraternal groups, veterans' groups, and service clubs are all relatively popular.   14

Religious affiliation is by far the most common associational membership among Americans. Indeed, by many measures America continues to be (even more than in Tocqueville's time)   15 an astonishingly "churched" society. For example, the United States has more houses of worship per capita than any other nation on Earth. Yet religious sentiment in America seems to be becoming somewhat less tied to institutions and more self-defined.

How have these complex crosscurrents played out over the last three or four decades in terms of Americans' engagement with organized religion? The general pattern is clear: The 1960s witnessed a significant drop in reported weekly churchgoing—from roughly 48 percent in the late 1950s to roughly 41 percent in the early 1970s. Since then, it has stagnated or (according to some surveys) declined still further. Meanwhile, data from the General Social Survey show a modest decline in membership in all "church-related groups" over the last 20 years. It would seem, then, that net participation by Americans, both in religious services and in church-related groups, has declined modestly (by perhaps a sixth) since the 1960s. 16

For many years, labor unions provided one of the most common organizational affiliations among American workers. Yet union membership has been falling for nearly four decades, with the steepest decline occurring between 1975 and 1985. Since the mid-1950s, when union membership peaked, the unionized portion of the nonagricultural work force in America has dropped by more than half, falling from 32.5 percent in 1953 to 15.8 percent in 1992. By now, virtually all of the explosive growth in union membership that was associated with the New Deal has been erased. The solidarity of union halls is now mostly a fading memory of aging men.[5] 17

The parent-teacher association (PTA) has been an especially important form of civic engagement in twentieth-century America because parental involvement in the educational process represents a particularly productive from of social capital. It is, therefore, dismaying to discover that participation in parent-teacher organizations has dropped drastically over the last generation, from more than 12 million in 1964 to barely 5 million in 1982 before recovering to approximately 7 million now. 18

5. Any simplistically political interpretation of the collapse of American unionism would need to confront the fact that the steepest decline began more than six years before the Reagan administration's attack on PATCO. Data from the General Social Survey show a roughly 40-percent decline in reported union membership between 1975 and 1991. [author's note]

Next, we turn to evidence on membership in (and volunteer-   19
ing for) civic and fraternal organizations. These data show some
striking patterns. First, membership in traditional women's
groups has declined more or less steadily since the mid-1960s.
For example, membership in the national Federation of Women's
Clubs is down by more than half (59 percent) since 1964, while
membership in the League of Women Voters (LWV) is off 42 percent since 1969.[6]

Similar reductions are apparent in the numbers of volunteers   20
for mainline civic organizations, such as the Boy Scouts (off by
26 percent since 1970) and the Red Cross (off by 61 percent
since 1970). But what about the possibility that volunteers have
simply switched their loyalties to other organizations? Evidence
on "regular" (as opposed to occasional or "drop-by") volunteering is available from the Labor Department's Current Population Surveys of 1974 and 1989. These estimates suggest that
serious volunteering declined by roughly one-sixth over these 15
years, from 24 percent of adults in 1974 to 20 percent in 1989.
The multitudes of Red Cross aides and Boy Scout troop leaders
now missing in action have apparently not been offset by equal
numbers of new recruits elsewhere.

Fraternal organizations have also witnessed a substantial   21
drop in membership during the 1980s and 1990s. Membership is
down significantly in such groups as the Lions (off 12 percent
since 1983), the Elks (off 18 percent since 1979), the Shriners
(off 27 percent since 1979), the Jaycees (off 44 percent since
1979), and the Masons (down 39 percent since 1959). In sum,
after expanding steadily throughout most of this century, many
major civic organizations have experienced a sudden, substantial, and nearly simultaneous decline in membership over the last
decade or two.

The most whimsical yet discomfiting bit of evidence of social   22
disengagement in contemporary America that I have discovered is

6. Data for the LWV are available over a longer time span and show an interesting pattern: a sharp slump during the Depression, a strong and sustained rise after World War II that more than tripled membership between 1945 and 1969,
and then the post-1969 decline, which has already erased virtually all the post-
war gains and continues still. This same historical pattern applies to those men's
fraternal organizations for which comparable data are available—steady increases for the first seven decades of the century, interrupted only by the Great
Depression, followed by a collapse in the 1970s and 1980s that has already
wiped out most of the postwar expansion and continues apace. [author's note]

this: more Americans are bowling today than ever before, but bowling in organized leagues has plummeted in the last decade or so. Between 1980 and 1993 the total number of bowlers in America increased by 10 percent, while league bowling decreased by 40 percent. (Lest this be thought a wholly trivial example, I should note that nearly 80 million Americans went bowling at least once during 1993, *nearly a third more than voted in the 1994 congressional elections* and roughly the same number as claim to attend church regularly. Even after the 1980s' plunge in league bowling, nearly 3 percent of American adults regularly bowl in leagues.) The rise of solo bowling threatens the livelihood of bowling-lane proprietors because those who bowl as members of leagues consume three times as much beer and pizza as solo bowlers, and the money in bowling is in the beer and pizza, not the balls and shoes. The broader social significance, however, lies in the social interaction and even occasionally civic conversations over beer and pizza that solo bowlers forgo. Whether or not bowling beats balloting in the eyes of most Americans, bowling teams illustrate yet another vanishing form of social capital.

COUNTERTRENDS

At this point, however, we must confront a serious counterar-   23
gument. Perhaps the traditional forms of civic organization whose decay we have been tracing have been replaced by vibrant new organizations. For example, national environmental organizations (like the Sierra Club) and feminist groups (like the National Organization for Women) grew rapidly during the 1970s and 1980s and now count hundreds of thousands of dues-paying members. An even more dramatic example is the American Association of Retired Persons (AARP), which grew exponentially from 400,000 card-carrying members in 1960 to 33 million in 1993, becoming (after the Catholic Church) the largest private organization in the world. The national administrators of these organizations are among the most feared lobbyists in Washington, in large part because of their massive mailing lists of presumably loyal members.

These new mass-membership organizations are plainly of   24
great political importance. From the point of view of social connectedness, however, they are sufficiently different from classic

"secondary associations" that we need to invent a new label—
perhaps "tertiary associations." For the vast majority of their
members, the only act of membership consists in writing a check
for dues or perhaps occasionally reading a newsletter. Few ever
attend any meetings of such organizations, and most are unlikely
ever (knowingly) to encounter any other member. The bond between any two members of the Sierra Club is less like the bond
between any two members of a gardening club and more like the
bond between any two Red Sox fans (or perhaps any two devoted Honda owners): they root for the same team and they
share some of the same interests, but they are unaware of each
other's existence. Their ties, in short, are to common symbols,
common leaders, and perhaps common ideals, but not to one another. The theory of social capital argues that associational
membership should, for example, increase social trust, but this
prediction is much less straightforward with regard to membership in tertiary associations. From the point of view of social
connectedness, the Environmental Defense Fund and a bowling
league are just not in the same category.

If the growth of tertiary organizations represents one poten-   25
tial (but probably not real) counterexample to my thesis, a second countertrend is represented by the growing prominence of
nonprofit organizations, especially nonprofit service agencies.
This so-called third sector includes everything from Oxfam and
the Metropolitan Museum of Art to the Ford Foundation and
the Mayo Clinic. In other words, although most secondary associations are nonprofits, most nonprofit agencies are not secondary associations. To identify trends in the size of the nonprofit
sector with trends in social connectedness would be another fundamental conceptual mistake.[7]

A third potential countertrend is much more relevant to an as-   26
sessment of social capital and civic engagement. Some able researchers have argued that the last few decades have witnessed a

7. Cf. Lester M. Salamon, "The Rise of the Nonprofit Sector," *Foreign Affairs*
73 (July-August 1994): 109–22. See also Salamon, "Partners in Public Service:
The Scope and Theory of Government-Nonprofit Relations," in Walter W. Powell, ed., *The Nonprofit Sector: A Research Handbook* (New Haven: Yale University Press, 1987), 99–117. Salamon's empirical evidence does not sustain his
broad claims about a global "associational revolution" comparable in significance to the rise of the nation-state several centuries ago. [author's note]

rapid expansion in "support groups" of various sorts. Robert Wuthnow reports that fully 40 percent of all Americans claim to be "currently involved in [a] small group that meets regularly and provides support or caring for those who participate in it."[8] Many of these groups are religiously affiliated, but many others are not. For example, nearly 5 percent of Wuthnow's national sample claim to participate regularly in a "self-help" group, such as Alcoholics Anonymous, and nearly as many say they belong to book-discussion groups and hobby clubs.

The groups described by Wuthnow's respondents unquestionably represent an important form of social capital, and they need to be accounted for in any serious reckoning of trends in social connectedness. On the other hand, they do not typically play the same role as traditional civic associations. As Wuthnow emphasizes,

27

> Small groups may not be fostering community as effectively as many of their proponents would like. Some small groups merely provide occasions for individuals to focus on themselves in the presence of others. The social contract binding members together asserts only the weakest of obligations. Come if you have time. Talk if you feel like it. Respect everyone's opinion. Never criticize. Leave quietly if you become dissatisfied. . . . We can imagine that [these small groups] really substitute for families, neighborhoods, and broader community attachments that may demand lifelong commitments, when, in fact, they do not.[9]

All three of these potential countertrends—tertiary organizations, nonprofit organizations, and support groups—need somehow to be weighed against the erosion of conventional civic organizations. One way of doing so is to consult the General Social Survey.

Within all educational categories, total associational membership declined significantly between 1967 and 1993. Among the college-educated, the average number of group memberships per person fell from 2.8 to 2.0 (a 26-percent decline); among high-school graduates, the number fell from 1.8 to 1.2 (32 percent); and among those with fewer than 12 years of education, the number fell from 1.4 to 1.1 (25 percent). In other words, at *all*

28

8. Robert Wuthnow, *Sharing the Journey: Support Groups and America's New Quest for Community* (New York: The Free Press, 1994), 45.
9. Ibid., 3–6.

educational (and hence social) levels of American society, and counting *all* sorts of group memberships, *the average number of associational memberships has fallen by about a fourth over the last quarter-century.* Without controls for educational levels, the trend is not nearly so clear, but the central point is this: *more Americans than ever before are in social circumstances that foster associational involvement (higher education, middle age, and so on), but nevertheless aggregate associational membership appears to be stagnant or declining.*

Broken down by type of group, the downward trend is most marked for church-related groups, for labor unions, for fraternal and veterans' organizations, and for school-service groups. Conversely, membership in professional associations has risen over these years, although less than might have been predicted, given sharply rising educational and occupational levels. Essentially the same trends are evident for both men and women in the sample. In short, the available survey evidence confirms our earlier conclusion: American social capital in the form of civic associations has significantly eroded over the last generation. [29]

Good Neighborliness and Social Trust

I noted earlier that most readily available quantitative evidence on trends in social connectedness involves formal settings, such as the voting booth, the union hall, or the PTA. One glaring exception is so widely discussed as to require little comment here: the most fundamental form of social capital is the family, and the massive evidence of the loosening of bonds within the family (both extended and nuclear) is well known. This trend, of course, is quite consistent with—and may help to explain—our theme of social decapitalization. [30]

A second aspect of informal social capital on which we happen to have reasonably reliable time-series data involves neighborliness. In each General Social Survey since 1974 respondents have been asked, "How often do you spend a social evening with a neighbor?" The proportion of Americans who socialize with their neighbors more than once a year has slowly but steadily declined over the last two decades, from 72 percent in 1974 to 61 percent in 1993. (On the other hand, socializing with "friends who do not live in your neighborhood" appears to be on the in- [31]

crease, a trend that may reflect the growth of workplace-based social connections.)

Americans are also less trusting. The proportion of Americans saying that most people can be trusted fell by more than a third between 1960, when 58 percent chose that alternative, and 1993, when only 37 percent did. The same trend is apparent in all educational groups; indeed, because social trust is also correlated with education and because educational levels have risen sharply, the overall decrease in social trust is even more apparent if we control for education.

Our discussion of trends in social connectedness and civic engagement has tacitly assumed that all the forms of social capital that we have discussed are themselves coherently correlated across individuals. This is in fact true. Members of associations are much more likely than nonmembers to participate in politics, to spend time with neighbors, to express social trust, and so on.

The close correlation between social trust and associational membership is true not only across time and across individuals, but also across countries. Evidence from the 1991 World Values Survey demonstrates the following:[10]

1. Across the 35 countries in this survey, social trust and civic engagement are strongly correlated; the greater the density of associational membership in a society, the more trusting its citizens. Trust and engagement are two facets of the same underlying factor—social capital.

2. America still ranks relatively high by cross-national standards on both these dimensions of social capital. Even in the 1990s, after several decades' erosion, Americans are more trusting and more engaged than people in most other countries of the world.

3. The trends of the past quarter-century, however, have apparently moved the United States significantly lower in the international rankings of social capital. The recent deterioration in American social capital has been sufficiently great that (if no other country changed its position in the meantime) another quarter-century of change at the same rate would bring

---

10. I am grateful to Ronald Inglehart, who directs this unique cross-national project, for sharing these highly useful data with me. See his "The Impact of Culture on Economic Development: Theory, Hypotheses, and Some Empirical Tests" (unpublished manuscript, University of Michigan, 1994). [author's note]

the United States, roughly speaking, to the midpoint among all these countries, roughly equivalent to South Korea, Belgium, or Estonia today. Two generations' decline at the same rate would leave the United States at the level of today's Chile, Portugal, and Slovenia.

WHY IS U.S. SOCIAL CAPITAL ERODING?

As we have seen, something has happened in America in the last two or three decades to diminish civic engagement and social connectedness. What could that "something" be? Here are several possible explanations, along with some initial evidence on each. [38]

The movement of women into the labor force. Over these same two or three decades, many millions of American women have moved out of the home into paid employment. This is the primary, though not the sole, reason why the weekly working hours of the average American have increased significantly during these years. It seems highly plausible that this social revolution should have reduced the time and energy available for building social capital. For certain organizations, such as the PTA, the League of Women Voters, the Federation of Women's Clubs, and the Red Cross, this is almost certainly an important part of the story. The sharpest decline in women's civic participation seems to have come in the 1970s; membership in such "women's" organizations as these has been virtually halved since the late 1960s. By contrast, most of the decline in participation in men's organizations occurred about ten years later; the total decline to date has been approximately 25 percent for the typical organization. On the other hand, the survey data imply that the aggregate declines for men are virtually as great as those for women. It is logically possible, of course, that the male declines might represent the knock-on effect of women's liberation, as dishwashing crowded out the lodge, but time-budget studies suggest that most husbands of working wives have assumed only a minor part of the housework. In short, something besides the women's revolution seems to lie behind the erosion of social capital. [39]

Mobility: The "re-potting" hypothesis. Numerous studies of organizational involvement have shown that residential stability and [40] such related phenomena as homeownership are clearly associated with greater civic engagement. Mobility, like frequent re-potting of plants, tends to disrupt root systems, and it takes time for an up-rooted individual to put down new roots. It seems plausible that the automobile, suburbanization, and the movement to the Sun Belt have reduced the social rootedness of the average American, but one fundamental difficulty with this hypothesis is apparent: the best evidence shows that residential stability and homeownership in America have risen modestly since 1965, and are surely higher now than during the 1950s, when civic engagement and social con-nectedness by our measures was definitely higher.

Other demographic transformations. A range of additional changes have transformed the American family since the 1960s— fewer marriages, more divorces, fewer children, lower real wages, and so on. Each of these changes might account for some of the slackening of civic engagement, since married, middle-class par-ents are generally more socially involved than other people. Moreover, the changes in scale that have swept over the Ameri-can economy in these years—illustrated by the replacement of the corner grocery by the supermarket and now perhaps of the supermarket by electronic shopping at home, or the replacement of community-based enterprises by outposts of distant multina-tional firms—may perhaps have undermined the material and even physical basis for civic engagement. [41]

The technological transformation of leisure. There is reason to believe that deep-seated technological trends are radically "privatizing" or "individualizing" our use of leisure time and thus disrupting many opportunities for social-capital formation. The most obvious and probably the most powerful instrument of this revolution is television. Time-budget studies in the 1960s showed that the growth in time spent watching television dwarfed all other changes in the way Americans passed their days and nights. Television has made our communities (or, rather, what we experience as our communities) wider and shal-lower. In the language of economics, electronic technology en-ables individual tastes to be satisfied more fully, but at the cost of the positive social externalities associated with more primitive forms of entertainment. The same logic applies to the replace-ment of vaudeville by the movies and now of movies by the VCR. The new "virtual reality" helmets that we will soon don to [42] be entertained in total isolation are merely the latest extension of this trend. Is technology thus driving a wedge between our individual interests and our collective interests? It is a question that seems worth exploring more systematically.

WHAT IS TO BE DONE?

The last refuge of a social-scientific scoundrel is to call for   43 more research. Nevertheless, I cannot forbear from suggesting some further lines of inquiry.

- We must sort out the dimensions of social capital, which   44 clearly is not a unidimensional concept, despite language (even in this essay) that implies the contrary. What types of organizations and networks most effectively embody—or generate— social capital, in the sense of mutual reciprocity, the resolution of dilemmas of collective action, and the broadening of social identities? In this essay I have emphasized the density of associational life. In earlier work I stressed the structure of networks, arguing that "horizontal" ties represented more productive social capital than vertical ties.[11]

- Another set of important issues involves macrosociological   45 crosscurrents that might intersect with the trends described here. What will be the impact, for example, of electronic networks on social capital? My hunch is that meeting in an electronic forum is not the equivalent of meeting in a bowling alley—or even in a saloon—but hard empirical research is needed. What about the development of social capital in the workplace? Is it growing in counterpoint to the decline of civic engagement, reflecting some social analogue of the first law of thermodynamics—social capital is neither created nor destroyed, merely redistributed? Or do the trends described in this essay represent a deadweight loss?

- A rounded assessment of changes in American social capital   46 over the last quarter-century needs to count the costs as well as the benefits of community engagement. We must not romanticize small-town, middle-class civic life in the America of the 1950s. In addition to the deleterious trends emphasized in this essay, recent decades have witnessed a substantial decline in intolerance and probably also in overt discrimination, and those

11. See my *Making Democracy Work*, esp. ch. 6. [author's note]

beneficent trends may be related in complex ways to the erosion of traditional social capital. Moreover, a balanced accounting of the social-capital books would need to reconcile
the insights of this approach with the undoubted insights offered by Mancur Olson and others who stress that closely knit
social, economic, and political organizations are prone to inefficient cartelization and to what political economists term "rent
seeking" and ordinary men and women call corruption.[12]

- Finally, and perhaps most urgently, we need to explore creatively how public policy impinges on (or might impinge on)
social-capital formation. In some well-known instances, public policy has destroyed highly effective social networks and
norms. American slum-clearance policy of the 1950s and
1960s, for example, renovated physical capital, but at a very
high cost to existing social capital. The consolidation of country post offices and small school districts has promised administrative and financial efficiencies, but full-cost accounting for
the effects of these policies on social capital might produce a
more negative verdict. On the other hand, such past initiatives
as the county agricultural-agent system, community colleges,
and tax deductions for charitable contributions illustrate that
government can encourage social-capital formation. Even a
recent proposal in San Luis Obispo, California, to require that
all new houses have front porches illustrates the power of government to influence where and how networks are formed.

The concept of "civil society" has played a central role in the
recent global debate about the preconditions for democracy and
democratization. In the newer democracies this phrase has properly focused attention on the need to foster a vibrant civic life in
soils traditionally inhospitable to self-government. In the established democracies, ironically, growing numbers of citizens are
questioning the effectiveness of their public institutions at the
very moment when liberal democracy has swept the battlefield,
both ideologically and geopolitically. In America, at least, there
is reason to suspect that this democratic disarray may be linked
to a broad and continuing erosion of civic engagement that began a quarter-century ago. High on our scholarly agenda should

47

48

12. See Mancur Olson, *The Rise and Decline of Nations: Economic Growth,
Stagflation, and Social Rigidities* (New Haven: Yale University Press, 1982), 2.
[author's note]

be the question of whether a comparable erosion of social capital may be under way in other advanced democracies, perhaps in different institutional and behavioral guises. High on America's agenda should be the question of how to reverse these adverse trends in social connectedness, thus restoring civic engagement and civic trust.

KATHA POLLITT

For Whom the Ball Rolls

Poet and essayist Katha Pollitt has been a contributing editor at *The Nation* for nearly two decades. Irritated, as one critic has observed, with all forms of "intellectual sloppiness," she has published social criticism in a number of national magazines, including *The New Yorker* and *The Atlantic Monthly*. The following rejoinder to Robert Putnam's "Bowling Alone" appeared in *The Nation* on April 15, 1996.

The only things I like about bowling are the shoes and the beer. Maybe that's why I can't get excited about Robert Putnam, the Harvard political scientist whose slender article "Bowling Alone: America's Declining Social Capital" in the January 1995 *Journal of Democracy,* has spawned more commentary than *Hamlet,* including a profile in *People,* and brought him tête-à-tête with President Clinton, whose State of the Union address he helped inspire. Putnam argues that declining membership in such venerable civic institutions as bowling leagues, the P.T.A., the League of Women Voters, the Boy Scouts, the Elks and the Shriners is an index of a weakened "civil society," the zone of social engagement between the family and the state. Why should you care about the leagues? Because, says Putnam, they bowl for thee: A weak civil society means less "trust" in each other, and that means a less vigorous democracy, as evidenced in declining electoral turnouts.

It's the sort of thesis academics and pundits adore, a big woolly argument that's been pre-reduced to a soundbite of genius. Bowling alone—it's wistful, comical, nostalgic, sad, a tiny haiku of post-industrial loneliness. Right-wingers like Francis Fukuyama and George Will like it because it can be twisted to support their absurd contention that philanthropy has been strangled by big government. Clintonians and communitarians like it because it moralizes a middle-class, apolitical civic-mindedness that recognizes no hard class or race inequalities shaping individual choice: We are all equally able to volunteer for the Red Cross, as we are all equally able to vote. Putnam's prime culprit in the decline of civic America—television—is similarly beyond the reach of structural change. It's as though America were all one big leafy suburb, in which the gladhanders and do-gooders had been bewitched by the evil blue light of *Seinfeld* and *Friends*.

At least Putnam doesn't blame working mothers. Still, the discussion around "Bowling Alone" is peculiar in a number of ways. How many of those who praise its thesis fit either half of his theory, I wonder: Is Bill Bradley a Shriner? Does *The Washington Post*'s David Broder bake cookies for the P.T.A.? If not, is the boob tube to blame? As Theda Skocpol noted in her politely devastating rejoinder to Putnam's follow-up article, "The Strange Disappearance of Civic America," in *The American Prospect* (Winter 1996), Putnam seems to place both the burden of civic engagement and responsibility for its collapse on the non-elite classes. Tenured professors may be too busy to sing in a choir (Putnam's former avocation): The rest of us are just couch potatoes.

Although Putnam is careful to disclaim nostalgia for the fifties, his picture of healthy civic life is remarkably, well, square. I've been a woman all my life, but I've never heard of the Federation of Women's Clubs. And what politically minded female, in 1996, would join the bland and matronly League of Women Voters, when she could volunteer with Planned Parenthood or NOW or Concerned Women of America, and shape the debate instead of merely keeping it polite? It's probably going too far to argue that the decline of the Boy Scouts is directly related to its barring of gay and nonbelieving lads. But should it really surprise us that such a stodgy organization has a hard time finding volunteers?

Or take those bowling leagues. Putnam treats these as if they arose merely from the appetite of individuals for fellowship and tenpins. But in fact they came out of specific forms of working-class and lower-middle-class life: stable blue-collar or office employment (businesses and unions often started and sponsored teams) that fostered group solidarity, a marital ethos that permitted husbands plenty of boys' nights out, a lack of cultural and entertainment alternatives. It would be amazing if league bowling survived the passing of the way of life that brought it into being, nor am I so sure we need mourn it. People still bowl, after all. In fact they bowl more than ever, although they consume less beer and pizza, which is why league decline bothers the owners of bowling alleys. And despite Putnam's title, they don't bowl alone. They bowl with friends, on dates, with their kids, with other families. The bowling story could be told as one of happy progress: from a drink-sodden night of spouse avoidance with the same old faces from work to temperate and spontaneous fun with one's intimate friends and relations.

No, the whole theory is seriously out of touch with the complexities of contemporary life. If church membership is down (good news in my book), it's hardly because people are staying home to watch TV. More likely, organized religion doesn't speak to their spiritual needs the way (for example) self-help programs do. Putnam dismisses the twelve-step movement much too quickly. At the very least, its popularity calls the TV-time-drain theory into question. I know people who've gone to A.A. every day, for years. As for building social capital, my own brief experience with Alanon more than fifteen years ago is still my touchstone of ordinary human decency and kindness. What's that if not "trust"? My membership in the P.T.A., by contrast, is motivated mostly by mistrust: As another parent put it, we join the P.T.A. to keep our kids from being shafted by the school system. 6

Putnam's theory may not explain much about the way we live now, but its warm reception speaks volumes. The bigfoot journalists and academic superstars, opinion manufacturers and wise men of both parties are worried, and it isn't about bowling or Boy Scouts. It's about that loss of "trust," a continuum that begins with one's neighbor and ends with the two parties, government, authority. It makes sense for the political and opinion elites to feel this trust—for them, the system works. It's made them rich and famous. But how much faith can a rational and disinterested person have in the set-up that's produced our current crop of leaders? 7

Love your neighbor if you can, but forget civic trust. What we need is more civic skepticism. Especially about people who want you to do their bowling for them. 8

H. D. F. KITTO

The Polis

H. D. F. Kitto, a British professor of classics, established his scholarly reputation with books on Greek drama. His witty and energetic style eventually won a large audience for his argument that, despite its relative poverty, ancient Athens really *was* a better place to live than a British or American city. The chapter reproduced here is from *The Greeks* (1951), a book that has been continuously in print since 1951 and that has been translated into six languages.

"Polis" is the Greek word which we translate "city-state." It is a bad translation, because the normal polis was not much like a city, and was very much more than a state. But translation, like politics, is the art of the possible; since we have not got the thing which the Greeks called "the polis," we do not possess an equivalent word. From now on, we will avoid the misleading term "city-state," and use the Greek word instead. In this chapter we will first inquire how this political system arose, then we will try to reconstitute the word "polis" and recover its real meaning by watching it in action. It may be a long task, but all the time we shall be improving our acquaintance with the Greeks. Without a clear conception what the polis was, and what it meant to the Greeks, it is quite impossible to understand properly Greek history, the Greek mind, or the Greek achievement.

First then, what was the polis? In the *Iliad* we discern a political structure that seems not unfamiliar—a structure that can be called an advanced or a degenerate form of tribalism, according to taste. There are kings, like Achilles, who rule their people, and there is the great king, Agamemnon, King of Men, who is something like a feudal overlord. He is under obligation, whether of right or of custom, to consult the other kings or chieftains in matters of common interest. They form a regular council, and in its debates the sceptre, symbol of authority, is held by the speaker for the time being. This is recognizably European, not Oriental; Agamemnon is no despot, ruling with the unquestioned authority of a god. There are also signs of a shadowy Assembly of the People, to be consulted on important occasions:

though Homer, a courtly poet, and in any case not a constitutional historian, says little about it.

Such, in outline, is the tradition about pre-conquest Greece. 3 When the curtain goes up again after the Dark Age we see a very different picture. No longer is there a "wide-ruling Agamemnon" lording it in Mycenae. In Crete, where Idomeneus had been ruling as sole king, we find over fifty quite independent poleis, fifty small "states" in the place of one. It is a small matter that the kings have disappeared; the important thing is that the kingdoms have gone too. What is true of Crete is true of Greece in general, or at least of those parts which play any considerable part in Greek history—Ionia, the islands, the Peloponnesus except Arcadia, Central Greece except the western parts, and South Italy and Sicily when they became Greek. All these were divided into an enormous number of quite independent and autonomous political units.

It is important to realize their size. The modern reader picks 4 up a translation of Plato's *Republic* or Aristotle's *Politics;* he finds Plato ordaining that his ideal city shall have 5,000 citizens, and Aristotle that each citizen should be able to know all the others by sight; and he smiles, perhaps, at such philosophic fantasies. But Plato and Aristotle are not fantasts. Plato is imagining a polis on the normal Hellenic scale; indeed he implies that many existing Greek poleis are too small—for many had less than 5,000 citizens. Aristotle says, in his amusing way—Aristotle sometimes sounds very like a don[1]—that a polis of ten citizens would be impossible, because it could not be self-sufficient, and that a polis of a hundred thousand would be absurd, because it could not govern itself properly. And we are not to think of these "citizens" as a "master-class" owning and dominating thousands of slaves. The ordinary Greek in these early centuries was a farmer, and if he owned a slave he was doing pretty well. Aristotle speaks of a hundred thousand citizens; if we allow each to have a wife and four children, and then add a liberal number of slaves and resident aliens, we shall arrive at something like a million—the population of Birmingham; and to Aristotle an independent "state" as populous as Birmingham is a lecture-room joke. Or we may turn from the philosophers to a practical man,

---

1. A tutor or fellow of one of the colleges at Oxford or Cambridge. That is, Aristotle sounds professorial.

Hippodamas, who laid out the Piraeus in the most up-to-date American style; he said that the ideal number of citizens was ten thousand, which would imply a total population of about 100,000.

In fact, only three poleis had more than 20,000 citizens— Syracuse and Acragas (Girgenti) in Sicily, and Athens. At the outbreak of the Peloponnesian War the population of Attica was probably about 350,000, half Athenian (men, women and children), about a tenth resident aliens, and the rest slaves. Sparta, or Lacedaemon, had a much smaller citizen-body, though it was larger in area. The Spartans had conquered and annexed Messenia, and possessed 3,200 square miles of territory. By Greek standards this was an enormous area: it would take a good walker two days to cross it. The important commercial city of Corinth had a territory of 330 square miles—about the size of Huntingdonshire. The island of Ceos, which is about as big as Bute, was divided into four poleis. It had therefore four armies, four governments, possibly four different calendars, and, it may be, four different currencies and systems of measures—though this is less likely. Mycenae was in historical times a shrunken relic of Agamemnon's capital, but still independent. She sent an army to help the Greek cause against Persia at the battle of Plataea; the army consisted of eighty men. Even by Greek standards this was small, but we do not hear that any jokes were made about an army sharing a cab.

To think on this scale is difficult for us, who regard a state of ten million as small, and are accustomed to states which, like the U.S.A. and the U.S.S.R., are so big that they have to be referred to by their initials; but when the adjustable reader has become accustomed to the scale, he will not commit the vulgar error of confusing size with significance. The modern writer is sometimes heard to speak with splendid scorn of "those petty Greek states, with their interminable quarrels." Quite so; Plataea, Sicyon, Aegina and the rest are petty, compared with modern states. The Earth itself is petty, compared with Jupiter—but then, the atmosphere of Jupiter is mainly ammonia, and that makes a difference. We do not like breathing ammonia—and the Greeks would not much have liked breathing the atmosphere of the vast modern State. They knew of one such, the Persian Empire—and thought it very suitable, for barbarians. Difference of scale, when it is great enough, amounts to difference of kind.

But before we deal with the nature of the polis, the reader   7
might like to know how it happened that the relatively spacious
pattern of pre-Dorian Greece became such a mosaic of small
fragments. The Classical scholar too would like to know; there
are no records, so that all we can do is to suggest plausible reasons. There are historical, geographical and economic reasons;
and when these have been duly set forth, we may conclude perhaps that the most important reason of all is simply that this is
the way in which the Greeks preferred to live.

The coming of the Dorians was not an attack made by one or-   8
ganized nation upon another. The invaded indeed had their organization, loose though it was; some of the invaders—the main
body that conquered Lacedaemon—must have been a coherent
force; but others must have been small groups of raiders, profit-
ing from the general turmoil and seizing good land where they
could find it. A sign of this is that we find members of the same
clan in different states. Pindar, for example, was a citizen of
Thebes and a member of the ancient family of the Aegidae. But
there were Aegidae too in Aegina and Sparta, quite independent
poleis, and Pindar addresses them as kinsmen. This particular
clan therefore was split up in the invasions. In a country like
Greece this would be very natural.

In a period so unsettled the inhabitants of any valley or island   9
might at a moment's notice be compelled to fight for their fields.
Therefore a local strong-point was necessary, normally a defen-
sible hill-top somewhere in the plain. This, the "acropolis"
("high-town"), would be fortified, and here would be the resi-
dence of the king. It would also be the natural place of assembly,
and the religious centre.

This is the beginning of the town. What we have to do is to   10
give reasons why the town grew, and why such a small pocket of
people remained an independent political unit. The former task
is simple. To begin with, natural economic growth made a central market necessary. We saw that the economic system implied
by Hesiod and Homer was "close household economy"; the estate, large or small, produced nearly everything that it needed,
and what it could not produce it did without. As things became
more stable a rather more specialized economy became possible:
more goods were produced for sale. Hence the growth of a
market.

At this point we may invoke the very sociable habits of the   11
Greeks, ancient or modern. The English farmer likes to build his
house on his land, and to come into town when he has to. What
little leisure he has he likes to spend on the very satisfying occupation of looking over a gate. The Greek prefers to live in the
town or village, to walk out to his work, and to spend his rather
ampler leisure talking in the town or village square. Therefore
the market becomes a market-town, naturally beneath the
Acropolis. This became the centre of the communal life of the
people—and we shall see presently how important that was.

But why did not such towns form larger units? This is the im-   12
portant question.

There is an economic point. The physical barriers which   13
Greece has so abundantly made the transport of goods difficult,
except by sea, and the sea was not yet used with any confidence.
Moreover, the variety of which we spoke earlier enabled quite a
small area to be reasonably self-sufficient for a people who made
such small material demands on life as the Greek. Both of these
facts tend in the same direction; there was in Greece no great
economic interdependence, no reciprocal pull between the different parts of the country, strong enough to counteract the desire of the Greek to live in small communities.

There is a geographical point. It is sometimes asserted that   14
this system of independent poleis was imposed on Greece by the
physical character of the country. The theory is attractive, especially to those who like to have one majestic explanation of any
phenomenon, but it does not seem to be true. It is of course obvious that the physical subdivision of the country helped; the system could not have existed, for example, in Egypt, a country
which depends entirely on the proper management of the Nile
flood, and therefore must have a central government. But there
are countries cut up quite as much as Greece—Scotland, for instance—which have never developed the polis-system; and conversely there were in Greece many neighbouring poleis, such as
Corinth and Sicyon, which remained independent of each other
although between them there was no physical barrier that would
seriously incommode a modern cyclist. Moreover, it was precisely the most mountainous parts of Greece that never developed poleis, or not until later days—Arcadia and Aetolia, for
example, which had something like a canton-system. The polis

flourished in those parts where communications were relatively easy. So that we are still looking for our explanation.

Economics and geography helped, but the real explanation is   15 the character of the Greeks—which those determinists may explain who have the necessary faith in their omniscience. As it will take some time to deal with this, we may first clear out of the way an important historical point. How did it come about that so preposterous a system was able to last for more than twenty minutes?

The ironies of history are many and bitter, but at least this   16 must be put to the credit of the gods, that they arranged for the Greeks to have the Eastern Mediterranean almost to themselves long enough to work out what was almost a laboratory-experiment to test how far, and in what conditions, human nature is capable of creating and sustaining a civilization. In Asia, the Hittite Empire had collapsed, the Lydian kingdom was not aggressive, and the Persian power, which eventually overthrew Lydia, was still embryonic in the mountainous recesses of the continent; Egypt was in decay; Macedon, destined to make nonsense of the polis-system, was and long remained in a state of ineffective semi-barbarism; Rome had not yet been heard of, nor any other power in Italy. There were indeed the Phoenicians, and their western colony, Carthage, but these were traders first and last. Therefore this lively and intelligent Greek people was for some centuries allowed to live under the apparently absurd system which suited and developed its genius instead of becoming absorbed in the dull mass of a large empire, which would have smothered its spiritual growth, and made it what it afterwards became, a race of brilliant individuals and opportunists. Obviously some day somebody would create a strong centralized power in the Eastern Mediterranean—a successor to the ancient sea-power of King Minos. Would it be Greek, Oriental, or something else? This question must be the theme of a later chapter, but no history of Greece can be intelligible until one has understood what the polis meant to the Greek; and when we have understood that, we shall also understand why the Greeks developed it, and so obstinately tried to maintain it. Let us then examine the word in action.

It meant at first that which was later called the Acropolis, the   17 stronghold of the whole community and the centre of its public life. The town which nearly always grew up around this was designated by another word, "asty." But "polis" very soon meant either the citadel or the whole people which, as it were, "used" this citadel. So we read in Thucydides, "Epidamnus is a polis on the right as you sail into the Ionian gulf." This is not like saying "Bristol is a city on the right as you sail up the Bristol Channel," for Bristol is not an independent state which might be at war with Gloucester, but only an urban area with a purely local administration. Thucydides' words imply that there is a town—though possibly a very small one—called Epidamnus, which is the political centre of the Epidamnians, who live in the territory of which the town is the centre—not the "capital"—and are Epidamnians whether they live in the town or in one of the villages in this territory.

Sometimes the territory and the town have different names. Thus, Attica is the territory occupied by the Athenian people; it comprised Athens—the "polis" in the narrower sense—the Piraeus, and many villages; but the people collectively were Athenians, not Attics, and a citizen was an Athenian in whatever part of Attica he might live.   18

In this sense "polis" is our "state." In Sophocles' *Antigone* Creon comes forward to make his first proclamation as king. He begins, "Gentlemen, as for the polis, the gods have brought it safely through the storm, on even keel." It is the familiar image of the Ship of State, and we think we know where we are. But later in the play he says what we should naturally translate, "Public proclamation has been made . . ." He says in fact, "It has been proclaimed to the polis . . ."—not to the "state," but to the "people." Later in the play he quarrels violently with his son: "What?" he cries, "is anyone but me to rule in this land?" Haemon answers, "It is no polis that is ruled by one man only." The answer brings out another important part of the whole conception of a polis, namely that it is a community, and that its affairs are the affairs of all. The actual business of governing might be entrusted to a monarch, acting in the name of all according to traditional usages, or to the heads of certain noble families, or to a council of citizens owning so much property, or to all the citizens. All these, and many modifications of them, were natural forms of "polity"; all were sharply distinguished by the Greek from Oriental monarchy, in which the monarch is irresponsible,   19 not holding his powers in trust by the grace of god, but being himself a god. If there was irresponsible government there was no polis. Haemon is accusing his father of talking like a "tyranos"[2] and thereby destroying the polis—but not "the State."

To continue our exposition of the word. The chorus in Aristophanes' *Acharnians,* admiring the conduct of the hero, turns to the audience with an appeal which I render literally, "Dost thou see, O whole polis?" The last words are sometimes translated "thou thronging city," which sounds better, but obscures an essential point, namely that the size of the polis made it possible for a member to appeal to all his fellow-citizens in person, and this he naturally did if he thought that another member of the polis had injured him. It was the common assumption of the Greeks that the polis took its origin in the desire for Justice. Individuals are lawless, but the polis will see to it that wrongs are redressed. But not by an elaborate machinery of state-justice, for such a machine could not be operated except by individuals, who may be as unjust as the original wrongdoer. The injured party will be sure of obtaining justice only if he can declare his wrongs to the whole polis. The word therefore now means "people" in actual distinction from "state." 20

Iocasta, the tragic Queen in the *Oedipus,* will show us a little more of the range of the word. It becomes a question if Oedipus her husband is not after all the accursed man who had killed the previous king Laius. "No, no," cries Iocasta, "it cannot be! The slave said it was 'brigands' who had attacked them, not a 'brigand.' He cannot go back on his word now. The polis heard him, not I alone." Here the word is used without any "political" association at all; it is, as it were, off duty, and signifies "the whole people." This is a shade of meaning which is not always so prominent, but is never entirely absent. 21

Then Demosthenes the orator talks of a man who, literally, "avoids the city"—a translation which might lead the unwary to suppose that he lived in something corresponding to the Lake District, or Purley. But the phrase "avoids the polis" tells us nothing about his domicile; it means that he took no part in pub- 22

2. I prefer to use the Greek form of this (apparently) Oriental word. It is the Greek equivalent of "dictator," but it does not necessarily have the colour of our word "tyrant." [author's note]

lic life—and was therefore something of an oddity. The affairs of the community did not interest him.

We have now learned enough about the word polis to realize 23 that there is no possible English rendering of such a common phrase as, "It is everyone's duty to help the polis." We cannot say "help the state," for that arouses no enthusiasm; it is "the state" that takes half our incomes from us. Not "the community," for with us "the community" is too big and too various to be grasped except theoretically. One's village, one's trade union, one's class, are entities that mean something to us at once, but "work for the community," though an admirable sentiment, is to most of us vague and flabby. In the years before the war, what did most parts of Great Britain know about the depressed areas? How much do bankers, miners and farmworkers understand each other? But the "polis" every Greek knew; there it was, complete, before his eyes. He could see the fields which gave it its sustenance—or did not, if the crops failed; he could see how agriculture, trade and industry dove-tailed into one another; he knew the frontiers, where they were strong and where weak; if any malcontents were planning a *coup,* it was difficult for them to conceal the fact. The entire life of the polis, and the relation between its parts, were much easier to grasp, because of the small scale of things. Therefore to say "It is everyone's duty to help the polis" was not to express a fine sentiment but to speak the plainest and most urgent common sense.[3] Public affairs had an immediacy and a concreteness which they cannot possibly have for us.

One specific example will help. The Athenian democracy 24 taxed the rich with as much disinterested enthusiasm as the British, but this could be done in a much more gracious way, simply because the State was so small and intimate. Among us, the payer of super-tax (presumably) pays much as the income-tax payer does: he writes his cheque and thinks, "There! *That's* gone down the drain!" In Athens, the man whose wealth exceeded a certain sum had, in a yearly rota, to perform certain "liturgies"—literally, "folk-works." He had to keep a warship in commission for one year (with the privilege of commanding it, if

3. It did not, of course, follow that the Greek obeyed common sense any oftener than we do. [author's note]

he chose), or finance the production of plays at the Festival, or equip a religious procession. It was a heavy burden, and no doubt unwelcome, but at least some fun could be got out of it and some pride taken in it. There was satisfaction and honour to be gained from producing a trilogy worthily before one's fellow-citizens. So, in countless other ways, the size of the polis made vivid and immediate, things which to us are only abstractions or wearisome duties. Naturally this cut both ways. For example, an incompetent or unlucky commander was the object not of a diffused and harmless popular indignation, but of direct accusation; he might be tried for his life before an Assembly, many of whose past members he had led to death.

Pericles' Funeral Speech, recorded or recreated by Thucydides, will illustrate this immediacy, and will also take our conception of the polis a little further. Each year, Thucydides tells us, if citizens had died in war—and they had, more often than not—a funeral oration was delivered by "a man chosen by the polis." Today, that would be someone nominated by the Prime Minister, or the British Academy, or the B.B.C. In Athens it meant that someone was chosen by the Assembly who had often spoken to that Assembly; and on this occasion Pericles spoke from a specially high platform, that his voice might reach as many as possible. Let us consider two phrases that Pericles used in that speech. 25

He is comparing the Athenian polis with the Spartan, and makes the point that the Spartans admit foreign visitors only grudgingly, and from time to time expel all strangers, "while we make our polis common to all." "Polis" here is not the political unit; there is no question of naturalizing foreigners—which the Greeks did rarely, simply because the polis was so intimate a union. Pericles means here: "We throw open to all our common cultural life," as is shown by the words that follow, difficult though they are to translate: "nor do we deny them any instruction or spectacle"—words that are almost meaningless until we realize that the drama, tragic and comic, the performance of choral hymns, public recitals of Homer, games, were all necessary and normal parts of "political" life. This is the sort of thing Pericles has in mind when he speaks of "instruction and spectacle," and of "making the polis open to all." 26

But we must go further than this. A perusal of the speech will show that in praising the Athenian polis Pericles is praising more 27 than a state, a nation, or a people: he is praising a way of life; he means no less when, a little later, he calls Athens the "school of Hellas."—And what of that? Do not we praise "the English way of life"? The difference is this; we expect our State to be quite indifferent to "the English way of life"—indeed, the idea that the State should actively try to promote it would fill most of us with alarm. The Greeks thought of the polis as an active, formative thing, training the minds and characters of the citizens; we think of it as a piece of machinery for the production of safety and convenience. The training in virtue, which the medieval state left to the Church, and the polis made its own concern, the modern state leaves to God knows what.

"Polis," then, originally "citadel," may mean as much as "the whole communal life of the people, political, cultural, moral"— even "economic," for how else are we to understand another phrase in this same speech, "the produce of the whole world comes to us, because of the magnitude of our polis"? This must mean "our national wealth." 28

Religion too was bound up with the polis—though not every form of religion. The Olympian gods were indeed worshipped by Greeks everywhere, but each polis had, if not its own gods, at least its own particular cults of these gods. Thus, Athena of the Brazen House was worshipped at Sparta, but to the Spartans Athena was never what she was to the Athenians, "Athena Polias," Athena guardian of the City. So Hera, in Athens, was a goddess worshipped particularly by women, as the goddess of hearth and home, but in Argos "Argive Hera" was the supreme deity of the people. We have in these gods tribal deities, like Jehovah, who exist as it were on two levels at once, as gods of the individual polis, and gods of the whole Greek race. But beyond these Olympians, each polis had its minor local deities, "heroes" and nymphs, each worshipped with his immemorial rite, and scarcely imagined to exist outside the particular locality where the rite was performed. So that in spite of the panhellenic Olympian system, and in spite of the philosophic spirit which made merely tribal gods impossible for the Greek, there is a sense in which it is true to say that the polis is an independent religious, as well as political, unit. The tragic poets at least could make use of the old belief that the gods desert a city which is about to be captured. The gods are the unseen partners in the city's welfare. 29

How intimately religious and "political" thinking were con-   30
nected we can best see from the *Oresteia* of Aeschylus. This trilogy is built around the idea of Justice. It moves from chaos to
order, from conflict to reconciliation; and it moves on two planes
at once, the human and the divine. In the *Agamemnon* we see
one of the moral Laws of the universe, that punishment must follow crime, fulfilled in the crudest possible way; one crime evokes
another crime to avenge it, in apparently endless succession—
but always with the sanction of Zeus. In the *Choephori* this series of crimes reaches its climax when Orestes avenges his father
by killing his mother. He does this with repugnance, but he is
commanded to do it by Apollo, the son and the mouthpiece of
Zeus—Why? Because in murdering Agamemnon the King and
her husband, Clytemnestra has committed a crime which, un-
punished, would shatter the very fabric of society. It is the concern of the Olympian gods to defend Order; they are particularly
the gods of the Polis. But Orestes' matricide outrages the deepest
human instincts; he is therefore implacably pursued by other
deities, the Furies. The Furies have no interest in social order, but
they cannot permit this outrage on the sacredness of the blood-
tie, which it is their office to protect. In the *Eumenides* there is a
terrific conflict between the ancient Furies and the younger
Olympians over the unhappy Orestes. The solution is that
Athena comes with a new dispensation from Zeus. A jury of
Athenian citizens is empanelled to try Orestes on the Acropolis
where he has fled for protection—this being the first meeting of
the Council of the Areopagus. The votes on either side are equal;
therefore, as an act of mercy, Orestes is acquitted. The Furies,
cheated of their legitimate prey, threaten Attica with destruction,
but Athena persuades them to make their home in Athens, with
their ancient office not abrogated (as at first they think) but enhanced, since henceforth they will punish violence within the polis, not only within the family.

So, to Aeschylus, the mature polis becomes the means by   31
which the Law is satisfied without producing chaos, since public
justice supersedes private vengeance; and the claims of authority
are reconciled with the instincts of humanity. The trilogy ends
with an impressive piece of pageantry. The awful Furies exchange their black robes for red ones, no longer Furies, but
"Kindly Ones" (Eumenides); no longer enemies of Zeus, but his

willing and honoured agents, defenders of his now perfected social order against intestine violence. Before the eyes of the Athenian citizens assembled in the theatre just under the Acropolis—and indeed guided by citizen-marshals—they pass out of the theatre to their new home on the other side of the Acropolis. Some of the most acute of man's moral and social problems have been solved, and the means of the reconciliation is the Polis.

A few minutes later, on that early spring day of 458 B.C., the citizens too would leave the theatre, and by the same exits as the Eumenides. In what mood? Surely no audience has had such an experience since. At the time, the Athenian polis was confidently riding the crest of the wave. In this trilogy there was exaltation, for they had seen their polis emerge as the pattern of Justice, of Order, of what the Greeks called Cosmos; the polis, they saw, was—or could be—the very crown and summit of things. They had seen their goddess herself acting as President of the first judicial tribunal—a steadying and sobering thought. But there was more than this. The rising democracy had recently curtailed the powers of the ancient Court of the Areopagus, and the reforming statesman had been assassinated by his political enemies. What of the Eumenides, the awful inhabitants of the land, the transformed Furies, whose function it was to avenge the shedding of a kinsman's blood? There was warning here, as well as exaltation, in the thought that the polis had its divine as well as its human members. There was Athena, one of those Olympians who had presided over the formation of ordered society, and there were the more primitive deities who had been persuaded by Athena to accept this pattern of civilized life, and were swift to punish any who, by violence from within, threatened its stability.

To such an extent was the religious thought of Aeschylus intertwined with the idea of the polis; and not of Aeschylus alone, but of many other Greek thinkers too—notably of Socrates, Plato, and Aristotle. Aristotle made a remark which we most inadequately translate "Man is a political animal." What Aristotle really said is "Man is a creature who lives in a polis"; and what he goes on to demonstrate, in his *Politics,* is that the polis is the only framework within which man can fully realize his spiritual, moral and intellectual capacities.

Such are some of the implications of this word: we shall meet more later, for I have deliberately said little about its purely "political" side—to emphasize the fact that it is so much more than a form of political organization. The polis was a living community, based on kinship, real or assumed—a kind of extended family, turning as much as possible of life into family life, and of course having its family quarrels, which were the more bitter because they were family quarrels.

This it is that explains not only the polis but also much of what the Greek made and thought, that he was essentially social. In the winning of his livelihood he was essentially individualist: in the filling of his life he was essentially "communist." Religion, art, games, the discussion of things—all these were needs of life that could be fully satisfied only through the polis—not, as with us, through voluntary associations of like-minded people, or through *entrepreneurs* appealing to individuals. (This partly explains the difference between Greek drama and the modern cinema.) Moreover, he wanted to play his own part in running the affairs of the community. When we realize how many of the necessary, interesting and exciting activities of life the Greek enjoyed through the polis, all of them in the open air, within sight of the same acropolis, with the same ring of mountains or of sea visibly enclosing the life of every member of the state—then it becomes possible to understand Greek history, to understand that in spite of the promptings of common sense the Greek could not bring himself to sacrifice the polis, with its vivid and comprehensive life, to a wider but less interesting unity. We may perhaps record an Imaginary Conversation between an Ancient Greek and a member of the Athenaeum. The member regrets the lack of political sense shown by the Greeks. The Greek replies, "How many clubs are there in London?" The member, at a guess, says about five hundred. The Greek then says, "Now, if all these combined, what splendid premises they could build. They could have a club-house as big as Hyde Park." "But," says the member, "that would no longer be a club." "Precisely," says the Greek, "and a polis as big as yours is no longer a polis."

After all, modern Europe, in spite of its common culture, common interests, and ease of communication, finds it difficult to accept the idea of limiting national sovereignty, though this would increase the security of life without notably adding to its dullness; the Greek had possibly more to gain by watering down the polis—but how much more to lose. It was not common sense that made Achilles great, but certain other qualities.

JAMES BALDWIN

Fifth Avenue, Uptown: A Letter from Harlem

James Baldwin was born and raised in Harlem. The stepson of an evangelical preacher, he became a preacher himself during his high school years. Later he worked as a handyman, dishwasher, and waiter before writer Richard Wright helped him win the first of a series of literary fellowships that allowed him to develop his talent as a novelist. From 1948 to 1957 he lived in Paris to avoid the segregated culture of the United States. "Fifth Avenue, Uptown" appeared in *Esquire* in 1960.

There is a housing project standing now where the house in   1
which we grew up once stood, and one of those stunted city trees is snarling where our doorway used to be. This is on the rehabilitated side of the avenue. The other side of the avenue—for progress takes time—has not been rehabilitated yet and it looks exactly as it looked in the days when we sat with our noses pressed against the windowpane, longing to be allowed to go "across the street." The grocery store which gave us credit is still there, and there can be no doubt that it is still giving credit. The people in the project certainly need it—far more, indeed, than they ever needed the project. The last time I passed by, the Jewish proprietor was still standing among his shelves, looking sadder and heavier but scarcely any older. Farther down the block stands the shoe-repair store in which our shoes were repaired until reparation became impossible and in which, then, we bought all our "new" ones. The Negro proprietor is still in the window, head down, working at the leather.

These two, I imagine, could tell a long tale if they would (perhaps they would be glad to if they could), having watched so   2
many, for so long, struggling in the fishhooks, the barbed wire, of this avenue.

The avenue is elsewhere the renowned and elegant Fifth. The   3
area I am describing, which, in today's gang parlance, would be called "the turf," is bound by Lenox Avenue on the west, the Harlem River on the east, 135th Street on the north, and 130th

Street on the south. We never lived beyond these boundaries; this is where we grew up. Walking along 145th Street—for example—familiar as it is, and similar, does not have the same impact because I did not know any of the people on the block. But when I turn east on 131st Street and Lenox Avenue, there is first a soda-pop joint, then a shoeshine "parlor," then a grocery store, then a dry cleaners', then the houses. All along the street there are people who watched me grow up, people who grew up with me, people I watched grow up along with my brothers and sisters; and, sometimes in my arms, sometimes underfoot, sometimes at my shoulder—or on it—their children, a riot, a forest of children, who include my nieces and nephews.

When we reach the end of this long block, we find ourselves 4 on wide, filthy, hostile Fifth Avenue, facing that project which hangs over the avenue like a monument to the folly, and the cowardice, of good intentions. All along the block, for anyone who knows it, are immense human gaps, like craters. These gaps are not created merely by those who have moved away, inevitably into some other ghetto; or by those who have risen, almost always into a greater capacity for self-loathing and self-delusion; or yet by those who, by whatever means—War II, the Korean war, a policeman's gun or billy, a gang war, a brawl, madness, an overdose of heroin, or, simply, unnatural exhaustion—are dead. I am talking about those who are left, and I am talking principally about the young. What are they doing? Well, some, a minority, are fanatical churchgoers, members of the more extreme of the Holy Roller sects. Many, many more are "moslems," by affiliation or sympathy, that is to say that they are united by nothing more—and nothing less—than a hatred of the white world and all its works. They are present, for example, at every Buy Black street-corner meeting—meetings in which the speaker urges his hearers to cease trading with white men and establish a separate economy. Neither the speaker nor his hearers can possibly do this, of course, since Negroes do not own General Motors or RCA or the A & P, nor, indeed, do they own more than a wholly insufficient fraction of anything else in Harlem (those who *do* own anything are more interested in their profits than in their fellows). But these meetings nevertheless keep alive in the participators a certain pride of bitterness without which, however futile this bitterness may be, they could scarcely remain alive at all. Many have given up. They stay home and watch the TV screen, living on the earnings of their parents, cousins, brothers, or uncles, and only leave the house to go to the movies or to the nearest bar. "How're you making it?" one may ask, running into them along the block, or in the bar. "Oh, I'm TV-ing it"; with the saddest, sweetest, most shame-faced of smiles, and from a great distance. This distance one is compelled to respect; anyone who has traveled so far will not easily be dragged again into the world. There are further retreats, of course, than the TV screen or the bar. There are those who are simply sitting on their stoops, "stoned," animated for a moment only, and hideously, by the approach of someone who may lend them the money for a "fix." Or by the approach of someone from whom they can purchase it, one of the shrewd ones, on the way to prison or just coming out.

And the others, who have avoided all of these deaths, get up ⁵ in the morning and go downtown to meet "the man." They work in the white man's world all day and come home in the evening to this fetid block. They struggle to instill in their children some private sense of honor or dignity which will help the child survive. This means, of course, that they must struggle, stolidly, incessantly, to keep this sense alive in themselves, in spite of the insults, the indifference, and the cruelty they are certain to encounter in their working day. They patiently browbeat the landlord into fixing the heat, the plaster, the plumbing; this demands prodigious patience; nor is patience usually enough. In trying to make their hovels habitable, they are perpetually throwing good money after bad. Such frustration, so long endured, is driving many strong, admirable men and women whose only crime is color to the very gates of paranoia.

One remembers them from another time—playing handball in ⁶ the playground, going to church, wondering if they were going to be promoted at school. One remembers them going off to war—gladly, to escape this block. One remembers their return. Perhaps one remembers their wedding day. And one sees where the girl is now—vainly looking for salvation from some other embittered, trussed, and struggling boy—and sees the all-but-abandoned children in the streets.

Now I am perfectly aware that there are other slums in which ⁷ white men are fighting for their lives, and mainly losing. I know

that blood is also flowing through those streets and that the human damage there is incalculable. People are continually pointing out to me the wretchedness of white people in order to
console me for the wretchedness of blacks. But an itemized account of the American failure does not console me and it should
not console anyone else. That hundreds of thousands of white
people are living, in effect, no better than the "niggers" is not a
fact to be regarded with complacency. The social and moral
bankruptcy suggested by this fact is of the bitterest, most terrifying kind.

The people, however, who believe that this democratic anguish has some consoling value are always pointing out that So-
and-So, white, and So-and-So, black, rose from the slums into
the big time. The existence—the public existence—of, say, Frank
Sinatra and Sammy Davis, Jr. proves to them that America is still
the land of opportunity and that inequalities vanish before the
determined will. It proves nothing of the sort. The determined
will is rare—at the moment, in this country, it is unspeakably
rare—and the inequalities suffered by the many are in no way
justified by the rise of a few. A few have always risen—in every
country, every era, and in the teeth of regimes which can by no
stretch of the imagination be thought of as free. Not all of these
people, it is worth remembering, left the world better than they
found it. The determined will is rare, but it is not invariably
benevolent. Furthermore, the American equation of success with
the big times reveals an awful disrespect for human life and human achievement. This equation has placed our cities among the
most dangerous in the world and has placed our youth among
the most empty and most bewildered. The situation of our youth
is not mysterious. Children have never been very good at listening to their elders, but they have never failed to imitate them.
They must, they have no other models. That is exactly what our
children are doing. They are imitating our immorality, our disrespect for the pain of others.

All other slum dwellers, when the bank account permits it,
can move out of the slum and vanish altogether from the eye of
persecution. No Negro in this country has ever made that much
money and it will be a long time before any Negro does. The Negroes in Harlem, who have no money, spend what they have on
such gimcracks as they are sold. These include "wider" TV

screens, more "faithful" hi-fi sets, more "powerful" cars, all of which, of course, are obsolete long before they are paid for. Anyone who has ever struggled with poverty knows how extremely expensive it is to be poor; and if one is a member of a captive population, economically speaking, one's feet have simply been placed on the treadmill forever. One is victimized, economically, in a thousand ways—rent, for example, or car insurance. Go shopping one day in Harlem—for anything—and compare Harlem prices and quality with those downtown.

The people who have managed to get off this block have only got as far as a more respectable ghetto. This respectable ghetto does not even have the advantages of the disreputable one— friends, neighbors, a familiar church, and friendly tradesmen; and it is not, moreover, in the nature of any ghetto to remain respectable long. Every Sunday, people who have left the block take the lonely ride back, dragging their increasingly discontented children with them. They spend the day talking, not always with words, about the trouble they've seen and the trouble—one must watch their eyes as they watch their children—they are only too likely to see. For children do not like ghettos. It takes them nearly no time to discover exactly why they are there. ₁₀

The projects in Harlem are hated. They are hated almost as much as policemen, and this is saying a great deal. And they are hated for the same reason: both reveal, unbearably, the real attitude of the white world, no matter how many liberal speeches are made, no matter how many lofty editorials are written, no matter how many civil-rights commissions are set up. ₁₁

The projects are hideous, of course, there being a law, apparently respected throughout the world, that popular housing shall be as cheerless as a prison. They are lumped all over Harlem, colorless, bleak, high, and revolting. The wide windows look out on Harlem's invincible and indescribable squalor: the Park Avenue railroad tracks, around which, about forty years ago, the present dark community began; the unrehabilitated houses, bowed down, it would seem, under the great weight of frustration and bitterness they contain; the dark, the ominous schoolhouses from which the child may emerge maimed, blinded, hooked, or enraged for life; and the churches, churches, block ₁₂

upon block of churches, niched in the walls like cannon in the walls of a fortress. Even if the administration of the projects were not so insanely humiliating (for example: one must report raises in salary to the management, which will then eat up the profit by raising one's rent; the management has the right to know who is staying in your apartment; the management can ask you to leave, at their discretion), the projects would still be hated because they are an insult to the meanest intelligence.

Harlem got its first private project, Riverton[1]—which is now, naturally, a slum—about twelve years ago because at that time Negroes were not allowed to live in Stuyvesant Town. Harlem watched Riverton go up, therefore, in the most violent bitterness of spirit, and hated it long before the builders arrived. They began hating it at about the time people began moving out of their condemned houses to make room for this additional proof of how thoroughly the white world despised them. And they had scarcely moved in, naturally, before they began smashing windows, defacing walls, urinating in the elevators, and fornicating in the playgrounds. Liberals, both white and black, were appalled at the spectacle. I was appalled by the liberal innocence— or cynicism, which comes out in practice as much the same thing. Other people were delighted to be able to point to proof positive that nothing could be done to better the lot of the colored people. They were, and are, right in one respect: that nothing can be done as long as they are treated like colored people. The people in Harlem know they are living there because white people do not think they are good enough to live anywhere else. No amount of "improvement" can sweeten this fact. Whatever money is now being earmarked to improve this, or any other ghetto, might as well be burnt. A ghetto can be improved in one way only: out of existence.

13

1. The inhabitants of Riverton were much embittered by this description; they have, apparently, forgotten how their project came into being; and have repeatedly informed me that I cannot possibly be referring to Riverton, but to another housing project which is directly across the street. It is quite clear, I think, that I have no interest in accusing any individuals or families of the depredations herein described: but neither can I deny the evidence of my own eyes. Nor do I blame anyone in Harlem for making the best of a dreadful bargain. But anyone who lives in Harlem and imagines that he has *not* struck this bargain, or that what he takes to be his status (in whose eyes?) protects him against the common pain, demoralization, and danger, is simply self deluded. [author's note]

Similarly, the only way to police a ghetto is to be oppressive.   14
None of the Police Commissioner's men, even with the best will
in the world, have any way of understanding the lives led by the
people they swagger about in twos and threes controlling. Their
very presence is an insult, and it would be, even if they spent
their entire day feeding gumdrops to children. They represent the
force of the white world, and the world's real intentions are, simply, for the world's criminal profit and ease, to keep the black
man corraled up here, in his place. The badge, the gun in the hol-
ster, and the swinging club make vivid what will happen should
his rebellion become overt. Rare, indeed, is the Harlem citizen,
from the most circumspect church member to the most shiftless
adolescent, who does not have a long tale to tell of police incompetence, injustice, or brutality. I myself have witnessed and
endured it more than once. The businessmen and racketeers also
have a story. And so do the prostitutes. (And this is not, perhaps,
the place to discuss Harlem's very complex attitude toward black
policemen, nor the reasons, according to Harlem, that they are
nearly all downtown.)

It is hard, on the other hand, to blame the policeman, blank,   15
good-natured, thoughtless, and insuperably innocent, for being
such a perfect representative of the people he serves. He, too, believes in good intentions and is astounded and offended when
they are not taken for the deed. He has never, himself, done anything for which to be hated—which of us has?—and yet he is facing, daily and nightly, people who would gladly see him dead,
and he knows it. There is no way for him not to know it: there
are few things under heaven more unnerving than the silent, accumulating contempt and hatred of a people. He moves through
Harlem, therefore, like an occupying soldier in a bitterly hostile
country; which is precisely what, and where, he is, and is the reason he walks in twos and threes. And he is not the only one who
knows why he is always in company: the people who are watching him know why, too. Any street meeting, sacred or secular,
which he and his colleagues uneasily cover has as its explicit or
implicit burden the cruelty and injustice of the white domination. And these days, of course, in terms increasingly vivid and
jubilant, it speaks of the end of that domination. The white policeman standing on a Harlem street corner finds himself at the
very center of the revolution now occurring in the world. He is

not prepared for it—naturally, nobody is—and, what is possibly much more to the point, he is exposed, as few white people are, to the anguish of the black people around him. Even if he is gifted with the merest mustard grain of imagination, something must seep in. He cannot avoid observing that some of the children, in spite of their color, remind him of children he has known and loved, perhaps even of his own children. He knows that he certainly does not want *his* children living this way. He can retreat from his uneasiness in only one direction: into a callousness which very shortly becomes second nature. He becomes more callous, the population becomes more hostile, the situation grows more tense, and the police force is increased. One day, to everyone's astonishment, someone drops a match in the powder keg and everything blows up. Before the dust has settled or the blood congealed, editorials, speeches, and civil-rights commissions are loud in the land, demanding to know what happened. What happened is that Negroes want to be treated like men.

Negroes want to be treated like men: a perfectly straightfor-   16
ward statement, containing only seven words. People who have mastered Kant, Hegel, Shakespeare, Marx, Freud, and the Bible find this statement utterly impenetrable. The idea seems to threaten profound, barely conscious assumptions. A kind of panic paralyzes their features, as though they found themselves trapped on the edge of a steep place. I once tried to describe to a very well-known American intellectual the conditions among Negroes in the South. My recital disturbed him and made him indignant; and he asked me in perfect innocence, "Why don't all the Negroes in the South move North?" I tried to explain what *has* happened, unfailingly, whenever a significant body of Negroes move North. They do not escape Jim Crow: they merely encounter another, not-less-deadly variety. They do not move to Chicago, they move to the South Side; they do not move to New York, they move to Harlem. This pressure within the ghetto causes the ghetto walls to expand, and this expansion is always violent. White people hold the line as long as they can, and in as many ways as they can, from verbal intimidation to physical violence. But inevitably the border which has divided the ghetto from the rest of the world falls into the hands of the ghetto. The white people fall back bitterly before the black horde; the landlords make a tidy profit by raising the rent, chopping up the

rooms, and all but dispensing with the upkeep; and what has once been a neighborhood turns into a "turf." This is precisely what happened when the Puerto Ricans arrived in their thousands—and the bitterness thus caused is, as I write, being fought out all up and down those streets.

Northerners indulge in an extremely dangerous luxury. They seem to feel that because they fought on the right side during the Civil War, and won, they have earned the right merely to deplore what is going on in the South, without taking any responsibility for it; and that they can ignore what is happening in Northern cities because what is happening in Little Rock or Birmingham is worse. Well, in the first place, it is not possible for anyone who has not endured both to know which is "worse." I know Negroes who prefer the South and white Southerners, because "At least there, you haven't got to play any guessing games!" The guessing games referred to have driven more than one Negro into the narcotics ward, the madhouse, or the river. I know another Negro, a man very dear to me, who says with conviction and with truth, "The spirit of the South is the spirit of America." He was born in the North and did his military training in the South. He did not, as far as I can gather, find the South "worse"; he found it, if anything, all too familiar. In the second place, though, even if Birmingham *is* worse, no doubt Johannesburg, South Africa, beats it by several miles, and Buchenwald was one of the worst things that ever happened in the entire history of the world. The world has never lacked for horrifying examples; but I do not believe that these examples are meant to be used as justification for our own crimes. This perpetual justification empties the heart of all human feeling. The emptier our hearts become, the greater will be our crimes. Thirdly, the South is not merely an embarrassingly backward region, but a part of this country, and what happens there concerns every one of us.

As far as the color problem is concerned, there is but one difference between the Southern white and the Northerner: the Southerner remembers, historically and in his own psyche, a kind of Eden in which he loved black people and they loved him. Historically, the flaming sword laid across this Eden is the Civil War. Personally, it is the Southerner's sexual coming of age, when, without any warning, unbreakable taboos are set up between himself and his past. Everything, thereafter, is permitted him except the love he remembers and has never ceased to need. The resulting, indescribable torment affects every Southern mind and is the basis of the Southern hysteria.

None of this is true for the Northerner. Negroes represent   19 nothing to him personally, except, perhaps, the dangers of car- nality. He never sees Negroes. Southerners see them all the time. Northerners never think about them whereas Southerners are never really thinking of anything else. Negroes are, therefore, ig- nored in the North and are under surveillance in the South, and suffer hideously in both places. Neither the Southerner nor the Northerner is able to look on the Negro simply as a man. It seems to be indispensable to the national self-esteem that the Ne- gro be considered either as a kind of ward (in which case we are told how many Negroes, comparatively, bought Cadillacs last year and how few, comparatively, were lynched), or as a victim (in which case we are promised that he will never vote in our as- semblies or go to school with our kids). They are two sides of the same coin and the South will not change—*cannot* change—until the North changes. The country will not change until it re- examines itself and discovers what it really means by freedom. In the meantime, generations keep being born, bitterness is in- creased by incompetence, pride, and folly, and the world shrinks around us.

It is a terrible, an inexorable, law that one cannot deny the hu-   20 manity of another without diminishing one's own: in the face of one's victim, one sees oneself. Walk through the streets of Harlem and see what we, this nation, have become.

JANE JACOBS

The Uses of Sidewalks

Jane Jacobs is a college dropout who became one of the most in- fluential urban theorists in the second half of the twentieth cen- tury. She is best known for her opposition to the "urban renewal" programs of the 1950s and 1960s, which often involved the bull- dozing of older, poorer neighborhoods. The following selection is drawn from *The Death and Life of Great American Cities* (1961).

This is something everyone already knows: A well-used city 1 street is apt to be a safe street. A deserted city street is apt to be unsafe. But how does this work, really? And what makes a city street well used or shunned? Why is the sidewalk mall in Washington Houses, which is supposed to be an attraction, shunned? Why are the sidewalks of the old city just to its west not shunned? What about streets that are busy part of the time and then empty abruptly?

A city street equipped to handle strangers, and to make a 2 safety asset, in itself, out of the presence of strangers, as the streets of successful city neighborhoods always do, must have three main qualities:

First, there must be a clear demarcation between what is pub- 3 lic space and what is private space. Public and private spaces cannot ooze into each other as they do typically in suburban settings or in projects.

Second, there must be eyes upon the street, eyes belonging to 4 those we might call the natural proprietors of the street. The buildings on a street equipped to handle strangers and to insure the safety of both residents and strangers, must be oriented to the street. They cannot turn their backs or blank sides on it and leave it blind.

And third, the sidewalk must have users on it fairly continu- 5 ously, both to add to the number of effective eyes on the street and to induce the people in buildings along the street to watch the sidewalks in sufficient numbers. Nobody enjoys sitting on a stoop or looking out a window at an empty street. Almost nobody does such a thing. Large numbers of people entertain themselves, off and on, by watching street activity.

In settlements that are smaller and simpler than big cities, con- 6 trols on acceptable public behavior, if not on crime, seem to operate with greater or lesser success through a web of reputation, gossip, approval, disapproval and sanctions, all of which are powerful if people know each other and word travels. But a city's streets, which must control not only the behavior of the people of the city but also of visitors from suburbs and towns who want to have a big time away from the gossip and sanctions at home, have to operate by more direct, straightforward methods. It is a wonder cities have solved such an inherently difficult problem at all. And yet in many streets they do it magnificently.

It is futile to try to evade the issue of unsafe city streets by   7
attempting to make some other features of a locality, say interior
courtyards, or sheltered play spaces, safe instead. By definition
again, the streets of a city must do most of the job of handling
strangers, for this is where strangers come and go. The streets must
not only defend the city against predatory strangers, they must
protect the many, many peaceable and well-meaning strangers
who use them, insuring their safety too as they pass through.
Moreover, no normal person can spend his life in some artificial haven, and this includes children. Everyone must use the
streets.

On the surface, we seem to have here some simple aims: To try   8
to secure streets where the public space is unequivocally public,
physically unmixed with private or with nothing-at-all space, so
that the area needing surveillance has clear and practicable limits; and to see that these public street spaces have eyes on them
as continuously as possible.

But it is not so simple to achieve these objects, especially the   9
latter. You can't make people use streets they have no reason to
use. You can't make people watch streets they do not want to
watch. Safety on the streets by surveillance and mutual policing
of one another sounds grim, but in real life it is not grim. The
safety of the street works best, most casually, and with least frequent taint of hostility or suspicion precisely where people are
using and most enjoying the city streets voluntarily and are least
conscious, normally, that they are policing.

The basic requisite for such surveillance is a substantial quan-   10
tity of stores and other public places sprinkled along the sidewalks of a district; enterprises and public places that are used by
evening and night must be among them especially. Stores, bars
and restaurants, as the chief examples, work in several different
and complex ways to abet sidewalk safety.

First, they give people—both residents and strangers—concrete   11
reasons for using the sidewalks on which these enterprises face.

Second, they draw people along the sidewalks past places   12
which have no attractions to public use in themselves but which
become traveled and peopled as routes to somewhere else; this influence does not carry very far geographically, so enterprises must
be frequent in a city district if they are to populate with walkers
those other stretches of street that lack public places along the

sidewalk. Moreover, there should be many different kinds of enterprises, to give people reasons for crisscrossing paths.

Third, storekeepers and other small businessmen are typically strong proponents of peace and order themselves; they hate broken windows and holdups; they hate having customers made nervous about safety. They are great street watchers and sidewalk guardians if present in sufficient numbers.   13

Fourth, the activity generated by people on errands, or people aiming for food or drink, is itself an attraction to still other people.   14

This last point, that the sight of people attracts still other people, is something that city planners and city architectural designers seem to find incomprehensible. They operate on the premise that city people seek the sight of emptiness, obvious order and quiet. Nothing could be less true. People's love of watching activity and other people is constantly evident in cities everywhere. This trait reaches an almost ludicrous extreme on upper Broadway in New York, where the street is divided by a narrow central mall, right in the middle of traffic. At the cross-street intersections of this long north-south mall, benches have been placed behind big concrete buffers and on any day when the weather is even barely tolerable these benches are filled with people at block after block after block, watching the pedestrians who cross the mall in front of them, watching the traffic, watching the people on the busy sidewalks, watching each other. Eventually Broadway reaches Columbia University and Barnard College, one to the right, the other to the left. Here all is obvious order and quiet. No more stores, no more activity generated by the stores, almost no more pedestrians crossing—and no more watchers. The benches are there but they go empty in even the finest weather. I have tried them and can see why. No place could be more boring. Even the students of these institutions shun the solitude. They are doing their outdoor loitering, outdoor homework and general street watching on the steps overlooking the busiest campus crossing.   15

It is just so on city streets elsewhere. A lively street always has both its users and pure watchers. Last year I was on such a street in the Lower East Side of Manhattan, waiting for a bus. I had not been there longer than a minute, barely long enough to begin taking in the street's activity of errand goers, children playing,   16 and loiterers on the stoops, when my attention was attracted by a woman who opened a window on the third floor of a tenement across the street and vigorously yoo-hooed at me. When I caught on that she wanted my attention and responded, she shouted down, "The bus doesn't run here on Saturdays!" Then by a combination of shouts and pantomime she directed me around the corner. This woman was one of thousands upon thousands of people in New York who casually take care of the streets. They notice strangers. They observe everything going on. If they need to take action, whether to direct a stranger waiting in the wrong place or to call the police, they do so. Action usually requires, to be sure, a certain self-assurance about the actor's proprietorship of the street and the support he will get if necessary, matters which will be gone into later in this book. But even more fundamental than the action and necessary to the action, is the watching itself.

Not everyone in cities helps to take care of the streets, and many a city resident or city worker is unaware of why his neighborhood is safe. The other day an incident occurred on the street where I live, and it interested me because of this point. [17]

My block of the street, I must explain, is a small one, but it contains a remarkable range of buildings, varying from several vintages of tenements to three- and four-story houses that have been converted into low-rent flats with stores on the ground floor, or returned to single-family use like ours. Across the street there used to be mostly four-story brick tenements with stores below. But twelve years ago several buildings, from the corner to the middle of the block, were converted into one building with elevator apartments of small size and high rents. [18]

The incident that attracted my attention was a suppressed struggle going on between a man and a little girl of eight or nine years old. The man seemed to be trying to get the girl to go with him. By turns he was directing a cajoling attention to her, and then assuming an air of nonchalance. The girl was making herself rigid, as children do when they resist, against the wall of one of the tenements across the street. [19]

As I watched from our second-floor window, making up my mind how to intervene if it seemed advisable, I saw it was not going to be necessary. From the butcher shop beneath the tenement had emerged the woman who, with her husband, runs the shop; she was standing within earshot of the man, her arms folded and [20] a look of determination on her face. Joe Cornacchia, who with his sons-in-law keeps the delicatessen, emerged about the same moment and stood solidly to the other side. Several heads poked out of the tenement windows above, one was withdrawn quickly and its owner reappeared a moment later in the doorway behind the man. Two men from the bar next to the butcher shop came to the doorway and waited. On my side of the street, I saw that the locksmith, the fruit man and the laundry proprietor had all come out of their shops and that the scene was also being surveyed from a number of windows besides ours. That man did not know it, but he was surrounded. Nobody was going to allow a little girl to be dragged off, even if nobody knew who she was.

I am sorry—sorry purely for dramatic purposes—to have to report that the little girl turned out to be the man's daughter.   21

Throughout the duration of the little drama, perhaps five minutes in all, no eyes appeared in the windows of the high-rent, small-apartment building. It was the only building of which this was true. When we first moved to our block, I used to anticipate happily that perhaps soon all the buildings would be rehabilitated like that one. I know better now, and can only anticipate with gloom and foreboding the recent news that exactly this transformation is scheduled for the rest of the block frontage adjoining the high-rent building. The high-rent tenants, most of whom are so transient we cannot even keep track of their faces,[1] have not the remotest idea of who takes care of the street, or how. A city neighborhood can absorb and protect a substantial number of these birds of passage, as our neighborhood does. But if and when the neighborhood finally *becomes* them, they will gradually find the streets less secure, they will be vaguely mystified about it, and if things get bad enough they will drift away to another neighborhood which is mysteriously safer.   22

In some rich city neighborhoods, where there is little do-it-yourself surveillance, such as residential Park Avenue or upper Fifth Avenue in New York, street watchers are hired. The monotonous sidewalks of residential Park Avenue, for example, are surprisingly little used; their putative users are populating, instead, the interesting store-, bar- and restaurant-filled sidewalks of Lexington Avenue and Madison Avenue to east and west, and   23

1. Some, according to the storekeepers, live on beans and bread and spend their sojourn looking for a place to live where all their money will not go for rent. [author's note]

the cross streets leading to these. A network of doormen and superintendents, of delivery boys and nursemaids, a form of hired neighborhood, keeps residential Park Avenue supplied with eyes. At night, with the security of the doormen as a bulwark, dog walkers safely venture forth and supplement the doormen. But this street is so blank of built-in eyes, so devoid of concrete reasons for using or watching it instead of turning the first corner off of it, that if its rents were to slip below the point where they could support a plentiful hired neighborhood of doormen and elevator men, it would undoubtedly become a woefully dangerous street.

Once a street is well equipped to handle strangers, once it has   24
both a good, effective demarcation between private and public spaces and has a basic supply of activity and eyes, the more strangers the merrier.

Strangers become an enormous asset on the street on which I   25
live, and the spurs off it, particularly at night when safety assets are most needed. We are fortunate enough, on the street, to be gifted not only with a locally supported bar and another around the corner, but also with a famous bar that draws continuous troops of strangers from adjoining neighborhoods and even from out of town. It is famous because the poet Dylan Thomas used to go there, and mentioned it in his writing. This bar, indeed, works two distinct shifts. In the morning and early afternoon it is a social gathering place for the old community of Irish longshoremen and other craftsmen in the area, as it always was. But beginning in midafternoon it takes on a different life, more like a college bull session with beer, combined with a literary cocktail party, and this continues until the early hours of the morning. On a cold winter's night, as you pass the White Horse, and the doors open, a solid wave of conversation and animation surges out and hits you; very warming. The comings and goings from this bar do much to keep our street reasonably populated until three in the morning, and it is a street always safe to come home to. The only instance I know of a beating in our street occurred in the dead hours between the closing of the bar and dawn. The beating was halted by one of our neighbors who saw it from his window and, unconsciously certain that even at night he was part of a web of strong street law and order, intervened.

A friend of mine lives on a street uptown where a church   26
youth and community center, with many night dances and other

activities, performs the same service for his street that the White Horse bar does for ours. Orthodox planning is much imbued with puritanical and Utopian conceptions of how people should spend their free time, and in planning, these moralisms on people's private lives are deeply confused with concepts about the workings of cities. In maintaining city street civilization, the White Horse bar and the church-sponsored youth center, different as they undoubtedly are, perform much the same public street civilizing service. There is not only room in cities for such differences and many more in taste, purpose and interest of occupation; cities also have a need for people with all these differences in taste and proclivity. The preferences of Utopians, and of other compulsive managers of other people's leisure, for one kind of legal enterprise over others is worse than irrelevant for cities. It is harmful. The greater and more plentiful the range of all legitimate interests (in the strictly legal sense) that city streets and their enterprises can satisfy, the better for the streets and for the safety and civilization of the city.

Bars, and indeed all commerce, have a bad name in many city districts precisely because they do draw strangers, and the strangers do not work out as an asset at all.   27

This sad circumstance is especially true in the dispirited gray belts of great cities and in once fashionable or at least once solid inner residential areas gone into decline. Because these neighborhoods are so dangerous, and the streets typically so dark, it is commonly believed that their trouble may be insufficient street lighting. Good lighting is important, but darkness alone does not account for the gray areas' deep, functional sickness, the Great Blight of Dullness.   28

The value of bright street lights for dispirited gray areas rises from the reassurance they offer to some people who need to go out on the sidewalk, or would like to, but lacking the good light would not do so. Thus the lights induce these people to contribute their own eyes to the upkeep of the street. Moreover, as is obvious, good lighting augments every pair of eyes, makes the eyes count for more because their range is greater. Each additional pair of eyes, and every increase in their range, is that much to the good for dull gray areas. But unless eyes are there, and unless in the brains behind those eyes is the almost unconscious reassurance of general street support in upholding civilization,   29 lights can do no good. Horrifying public crimes can, and do, occur in well-lighted subway stations when no effective eyes are present. They virtually never occur in darkened theaters where many people and eyes are present. Street lights can be like that famous stone that falls in the desert where there are no ears to hear. Does it make a noise? Without effective eyes to see, does a light cast light? Not for practical purposes.

Suppose we continue with building, and with deliberate rebuilding, of unsafe cities. How do we live with this insecurity? From the evidence thus far, there seem to be three modes of living with it; maybe in time others will be invented but I suspect these three will simply be further developed, if that is the word for it.   30

The first mode is to let danger hold sway, and let those unfortunate enough to be stuck with it take the consequences. This is the policy now followed with respect to low-income housing projects, and to many middle-income housing projects.   31

The second mode is to take refuge in vehicles. This is a technique practiced in the big wild-animal reservations of Africa, where tourists are warned to leave their cars under no circumstances until they reach a lodge. It is also the technique practiced in Los Angeles. Surprised visitors to that city are forever recounting how the police of Beverly Hills stopped them, made them prove their reasons for being afoot, and warned them of the danger. This technique of public safety does not seem to work too effectively yet in Los Angeles, as the crime rate shows, but in time it may. And think what the crime figures might be if more people without metal shells were helpless upon the vast, blind-eyed reservation of Los Angeles.   32

People in dangerous parts of other cities often use automobiles as protection too, of course, or try to. A letter to the editor in the *New York Post,* reads, "I live on a dark street off Utica Avenue in Brooklyn and therefore decided to take a cab home even though it was not late. The cab driver asked that I get off at the corner of Utica, saying he did not want to go down the dark street. If I had wanted to walk down the dark street, who needed him?"   33

The third mode . . . was developed by hoodlum gangs and has been adopted widely by developers of the rebuilt city. This mode is to cultivate the institution of Turf.   34

Under the Turf system in its historical form, a gang appropri-   35
ates as its territory certain streets or housing projects or parks—
often a combination of the three. Members of other gangs
cannot enter this Turf without permission from the Turf-owning
gang, or if they do so it is at peril of being beaten or run off. In
1956, the New York City Youth Board, fairly desperate because
of gang warfare, arranged through its gang youth workers a series of truces among fighting gangs. The truces were reported to
stipulate, among other provisions, a mutual understanding of
Turf boundaries among the gangs concerned and agreement not
to trespass.

The city's police commissioner, Stephen P. Kennedy, there-   36
upon expressed outrage at agreements respecting Turf. The police, he said, aimed to protect the right of every person to walk
any part of the city in safety and with impunity as a basic right.
Pacts about Turf, he indicated, were intolerably subversive both
of public rights and public safety.

I think Commissioner Kennedy was profoundly right. How-   37
ever, we must reflect upon the problem facing the Youth Board
workers. It was a real one, and they were trying as well as they
could to meet it with whatever empirical means they could. The
safety of the city, on which public right and freedom of movement
ultimately depend, was missing from the unsuccessful streets,
parks and projects dominated by these gangs. Freedom of the city,
under these circumstances, was a rather academic ideal.

Now consider the redevelopment projects of cities: the middle-   38
and upper-income housing occupying many acres of city, many
former blocks, with their own grounds and their own streets to
serve these "islands within the city," "cities within the city," and
"new concepts in city living," as the advertisements for them
say. The technique here is also to designate the Turf and fence the
other gangs out. At first the fences were never visible. Patrolling
guards were sufficient to enforce the line. But in the past few
years the fences have become literal.

Perhaps the first was the high cyclone fence around a Radiant   39
Garden City project adjoining Johns Hopkins Hospital in Baltimore (great educational institutions seem to be deplorably inventive with Turf devices). In case anyone mistakes what the
fence means, the signs on the project street also say "Keep Out.
No Trespassing." It is uncanny to see a city neighborhood, in a
civilian city, walled off like this. It looks not only ugly, in a deep

sense, but surrealistic. You can imagine how it sits with the neighbors, in spite of the antidote message on the project church's bulletin board: "Christ's Love Is The Best Tonic Of All."

New York has been quick to copy the lesson of Baltimore, in its own fashion. Indeed, at the back of Amalgamated Houses on the Lower East Side, New York has gone further. At the northern end of the project's parklike central promenade, an iron-bar gate has been permanently padlocked and is crowned not with mere metal netting but with a tangle of barbed wire. And does this defended promenade give out on depraved old megalopolis? Not at all. Its neighbor is a public playground and beyond this more project housing for a different income class.

In the rebuilt city it takes a heap of fences to make a balanced neighborhood. The "juncture" between two differently price-tagged populations, again in the rebuilt Lower East Side, that between middle-income cooperative Corlears Hook and low-income Vladeck Houses, is especially elaborate. Corlears Hook buffers its Turf against its next-door neighbors with a wide parking lot running the full width of the super-block juncture, next a spindly hedge and a six-foot-high cyclone fence, next a completely fenced-in no man's land some thirty feet wide consisting mainly of dirty blowing papers and deliberately inaccessible to anything else. Then begins the Vladeck Turf.

Similarly, on the Upper West Side, the rental agent of the Park West Village, "Your Own World in the Heart of New York," on whom I have foisted myself as a prospective tenant, tells me reassuringly, "Madam, as soon as the shopping center is completed, the entire grounds will be fenced in."

"Cyclone fences?"

"That is correct, madam. And eventually"—waving his hand at the city surrounding his domain—"all that will go. Those people will go. We are the pioneers here."

I suppose it is rather like pioneer life in a stockaded village, except that the pioneers were working toward greater security for their civilization, not less.

Some members of the gangs on the new Turfs find this way of life hard to take. Such was one who wrote a letter to the *New York Post* in 1959: "The other day for the first time my pride at being a resident of Stuyvesant Town and of New York City was replaced by indignation and shame. I noticed two boys about 12 years old sitting on a Stuyvesant Town bench. They were deep in conversation, quiet, well-behaved—and Puerto Rican. Suddenly two Stuyvesant Town guards were approaching—one from the north and one from the south. The one signaled the other by pointing to the two boys. One went up to the boys and after several words, quietly spoken on both sides, the boys rose and left. They tried to look unconcerned. . . . How can we expect people to have dignity and self-respect if we rip it from them even before they reach adulthood? How really poor are we of Stuyvesant Town and of New York City, too, that we can't share a bench with two boys."

The Letters Editor gave this communication the headline, "Stay in Your Own Turf."

But on the whole, people seem to get used very quickly to living in a Turf with either a figurative or a literal fence, and to wonder how they got on without it formerly. This phenomenon was described, before the Turf fences came into the city, by the *New Yorker,* with reference not to fenced city but to fenced town. It seems that when Oak Ridge, Tennessee, was de-militarized after the war, the prospect of losing the fence that went with the militarization drew frightened and impassioned protests from many residents and occasioned town meetings of high excitement. Everyone in Oak Ridge had come, not many years before, from unfenced towns or cities, yet stockade life had become normal and they feared for their safety without the fence.

Just so, my ten-year-old nephew David, born and brought up in Stuyvesant Town, "A City Within a City," comments in wonder that anyone at all can walk on the street outside our door. "Doesn't anybody keep track whether they pay rent on this street?" he asks. "Who puts them out if they don't belong here?"

The technique of dividing the city into Turfs is not simply a New York solution. It is a Rebuilt American City solution. At the Harvard Design Conference of 1959, one of the topics pondered by city architectural designers turned out to be the puzzle of Turf, although they did not use that designation. The examples discussed happened to be the Lake Meadows middle-income project of Chicago and the Lafayette Park high-income project of Detroit. Do you keep the rest of the city out of these blind-eyed purlieus? How difficult and how unpalatable. Do you invite the rest of the city in? How difficult and how impossible.

Like the Youth Board workers, the developers and residents   51
of Radiant City and Radiant Garden City and Radiant Garden
City Beautiful have a genuine difficulty and they have to do the
best they can with it by the empirical means at their disposal.
They have little choice. Wherever the rebuilt city rises the bar-
baric concept of Turf must follow, because the rebuilt city has
junked a basic function of the city street and with it, necessarily,
the freedom of the city.

Under the seeming disorder of the old city, wherever the old   52
city is working successfully, is a marvelous order for maintaining
the safety of the streets and the freedom of the city. It is a complex order. Its essence is intricacy of sidewalk use, bringing with
it a constant succession of eyes. This order is all composed of
movement and change, and although it is life, not art, we may
fancifully call it the art form of the city and liken it to the
dance—not to a simple-minded precision dance with everyone
kicking up at the same time, twirling in unison and bowing off
en masse, but to an intricate ballet in which the individual
dancers and ensembles all have distinctive parts which miraculously reinforce each other and compose an orderly whole. The
ballet of the good city sidewalk never repeats itself from place
to place, and in any one place is always replete with new im-
provisations.

The stretch of Hudson Street where I live is each day the scene   53
of an intricate sidewalk ballet. I make my own first entrance into
it a little after eight when I put out the garbage can, surely a prosaic occupation, but I enjoy my part, my little clang, as the
droves of junior high school students walk by the center of the
stage dropping candy wrappers. (How do they eat so much
candy so early in the morning?)

While I sweep up the wrappers I watch the other rituals of   54
morning: Mr. Halpert unlocking the laundry's handcart from its
mooring to a cellar door, Joe Cornacchia's son-in-law stacking
out the empty crates from the delicatessen, the barber bringing
out his sidewalk folding chair. Mr. Goldstein arranging the coils
of wire which proclaim the hardware store is open, the wife of
the tenement's superintendent depositing her chunky three-year-
old with a toy mandolin on the stoop, the vantage point from
which he is learning the English his mother cannot speak. Now
the primary children, heading for St. Luke's, dribble through to

the south; the children for St. Veronica's cross, heading to the west, and the children for P.S. 41, heading toward the east. Two new entrances are being made from the wings: well-dressed and even elegant women and men with briefcases emerge from doorways and side streets. Most of these are heading for the bus and subways, but some hover on the curbs, stopping taxis which have miraculously appeared at the right moment, for the taxis are part of a wider morning ritual: having dropped passengers from midtown in the downtown financial district, they are now bringing downtowners up to midtown. Simultaneously, numbers of women in housedresses have emerged and as they crisscross with one another they pause for quick conversations that sound with either laughter or joint indignation, never, it seems, anything between. It is time for me to hurry to work too, and I exchange my ritual farewell with Mr. Lofaro, the short, thick-bodied, white-aproned fruit man who stands outside his doorway a little up the street, his arms folded, his feet planted, looking solid as earth itself. We nod; we each glance quickly up and down the street, then look back to each other and smile. We have done this many a morning for more than ten years, and we both know what it means: All is well.

The heart-of-the-day ballet I seldom see, because part of the nature of it is that working people who live there, like me, are mostly gone, filling the roles of strangers on other sidewalks. But from days off, I know enough of it to know that it becomes more and more intricate. Longshoremen who are not working that day gather at the White Horse or the Ideal or the International for beer and conversation. The executives and business lunchers from the industries just to the west throng the Dorgene restaurant and the Lion's Head coffee house; meat-market workers and communications scientists fill the bakery lunchroom. Character dancers come on, a strange old man with strings of old shoes over his shoulders, motor-scooter riders with big beards and girl friends who bounce on the back of the scooters and wear their hair long in front of their faces as well as behind, drunks who follow the advice of the Hat Council and are always turned out in hats, but not hats the Council would approve. Mr. Lacey, the locksmith, shuts up his shop for a while and goes to exchange the time of day with Mr. Slube at the cigar store. Mr. Koochagian, the tailor, waters the luxuriant jungle of plants in his window, gives them a critical look from the outside, accepts a compliment on them from two passers-by, fingers the leaves on the plane tree in front of our house with a thoughtful gardener's appraisal, and crosses the street for a bite at the Ideal where he can keep an eye on customers and wigwag across the message that he is coming. The baby carriages come out, and clusters of everyone from toddlers with dolls to teen-agers with homework gather at the stoops.

When I get home after work, the ballet is reaching its 56 crescendo. This is the time of roller skates and stilts and tricycles, and games in the lee of the stoop with bottletops and plastic cowboys; this is the time of bundles and packages, zigzagging from the drug store to the fruit stand and back over to the butcher's; this is the time when teen-agers, all dressed up, are pausing to ask if their slips show or their collars look right; this is the time when beautiful girls get out of MG's; this is the time when the fire engines go through; this is the time when anybody you know around Hudson Street will go by.

As darkness thickens and Mr. Halpert moors the laundry cart 57 to the cellar door again, the ballet goes on under lights, eddying back and forth but intensifying at the bright spotlight pools of Joe's sidewalk pizza dispensary, the bars, the delicatessen, the restaurant and the drug store. The night workers stop now at the delicatessen, to pick up salami and a container of milk. Things have settled down for the evening but the street and its ballet have not come to a stop.

I know the deep night ballet and its seasons best from waking 58 long after midnight to tend a baby and, sitting in the dark, seeing the shadows and hearing the sounds of the sidewalk. Mostly it is a sound like infinitely pattering snatches of party conversation and, about three in the morning, singing, very good singing. Sometimes there is sharpness and anger or sad, sad weeping, or a flurry of search for a string of beads broken. One night a young man came roaring along, bellowing terrible language at two girls whom he had apparently picked up and who were disappointing him. Doors opened, a wary semicircle formed around him, not too close, until the police came. Out came the heads, too, along Hudson Street, offering opinion, "Drunk . . . Crazy . . . A wild kid from the suburbs."[2]

2. He turned out to be a wild kid from the suburbs. Sometimes, on Hudson Street, we are tempted to believe the suburbs must be a difficult place to bring up children. [author's note]

Deep in the night, I am almost unaware how many people are   59
on the street unless something calls them together, like the bagpipe. Who the piper was and why he favored our street I have no
idea. The bagpipe just skirled out in the February night, and as if
it were a signal the random, dwindled movements of the sidewalk
took on direction. Swiftly, quietly, almost magically a little crowd
was there, a crowd that evolved into a circle with a Highland fling
inside it. The crowd could be seen on the shadowy sidewalk, the
dancers could be seen, but the bagpiper himself was almost invisible because his bravura was all in his music. He was a very little
man in a plain brown overcoat. When he finished and vanished,
the dancers and watchers applauded, and applause came from the
galleries too, half a dozen of the hundred windows on Hudson
Street. Then the windows closed, and the little crowd dissolved
into the random movements of the night street.

The strangers on Hudson Street, the allies whose eyes help us   60
natives keep the peace of the street, are so many that they always
seem to be different people from one day to the next. That does
not matter. Whether they are so many always-different people as
they seem to be, I do not know. Likely they are. When Jimmy Ro-
gan fell through a plate-glass window (he was separating some
scuffling friends) and almost lost his arm, a stranger in an old T
shirt emerged from the Ideal bar, swiftly applied an expert tourni-
quet and, according to the hospital's emergency staff, saved
Jimmy's life. Nobody remembered seeing the man before and no
one has seen him since. The hospital was called in this way: a
woman sitting on the steps next to the accident ran over to the
bus stop, wordlessly snatched the dime from the hand of a
stranger who was waiting with his fifteen-cent fare ready, and
raced into the Ideal's phone booth. The stranger raced after her to
offer the nickel too. Nobody remembered seeing him before, and
no one has seen him since. When you see the same stranger three
or four times on Hudson Street, you begin to nod. This is almost
getting to be an acquaintance, a public acquaintance, of course.

I have made the daily ballet of Hudson Street sound more fre-   61
netic than it is, because writing it telescopes it. In real life, it is
not that way. In real life, to be sure, something is always going
on, the ballet is never at a halt, but the general effect is peaceful
and the general tenor even leisurely. People who know well such
animated city streets will know how it is. I am afraid people who
do not will always have it a little wrong in their heads—like the

old prints of rhinoceroses made from travelers' descriptions of rhinoceroses.

   On Hudson Street, the same as in the North End of Boston or   62 in any other animated neighborhoods of great cities, we are not innately more competent at keeping the sidewalk safe than are the people who try to live off the hostile truce of Turf in a blind-eyed city. We are the lucky possessors of a city order that makes it relatively simple to keep the peace because there are plenty of eyes on the street. But there is nothing simple about that order itself, or the bewildering number of components that go into it. Most of those components are specialized in one way or another. They unite in their joint effect upon the sidewalk, which is not specialized in the least. That is its strength.

SUSAN GLASPELL

Trifles

Susan Glaspell was born in Davenport, Iowa, the daughter of a feed dealer and an immigrant Irishwoman. After two years working as a journalist in Davenport and several more writing sentimental short stories for popular magazines, she helped to found the Provincetown Players, a Massachusetts theater group that immediately became associated with the literary avante-garde. *Trifles* was performed by the group in 1916.

Characters

GEORGE HENDERSON, *County Attorney*   MRS. PETERS
HENRY PETERS, *Sheriff*   MRS. HALE
LEWIS HALE, *A Neighboring Farmer*

SCENE

The kitchen in the now abandoned farmhouse of JOHN WRIGHT, *a gloomy kitchen, and left without having been put in order—unwashed pans under the sink, a loaf of bread outside the breadbox, a dish towel on the table—other signs of incompleted work. At*

*the rear the outer door opens and the sheriff comes in followed by
the* COUNTY ATTORNEY *and* HALE. *The* SHERIFF *and* HALE *are men
in middle life, the* COUNTY ATTORNEY *is a young man; all are much
bundled up and go at once to the stove. They are followed by two
women—the* SHERIFF'S *wife first; she is a slightly wiry woman, a
thin nervous face.* MRS. HALE *is larger and would ordinarily be
called more comfortable looking, but she is disturbed now and
looks fearfully about as she enters. The women have come in
slowly, and stand close together near the door.*

COUNTY ATTORNEY. [*Rubbing his hands.*] This feels good. Come   1
up to the fire, ladies.
MRS. PETERS. [*After taking a step forward.*] I'm not—cold.
SHERIFF. [*Unbuttoning his overcoat and stepping away from the
stove as if to mark the beginning of official business.*] Now,
Mr. Hale, before we move things about, you explain to Mr.
Henderson just what you saw when you came here yesterday
morning.
COUNTY ATTORNEY. By the way, has anything been moved? Are
things just as you left them yesterday?
SHERIFF. [*Looking about.*] It's just the same. When it dropped   5
below zero last night I thought I'd better send Frank out this
morning to make a fire for us—no use getting peneumonia
with a big case on, but I told him not to touch anything except
the stove—and you know Frank.
COUNTY ATTORNEY. Somebody should have been left here yesterday.
SHERIFF. Oh—yesterday. When I had to send Frank to Morris
Center for that man who went crazy—I want you to know I
had my hands full yesterday, I knew you could get back from
Omaha by today and as long as I went over everything here
myself—
COUNTY ATTORNEY. Well, Mr. Hale, tell just what happened
when you came here yesterday morning.
HALE. Harry and I had started to town with a load of potatoes.
We came along the road from my place and as I got here I
said, "I'm going to see if I can't get John Wright to go in with
me on a party telephone." I spoke to Wright about it once before and he put me off, saying folks talked too much anyway,
and all he asked was peace and quiet—I guess you know

about how much he talked himself; but I thought maybe if I
went to the house and talked about it before his wife, though
I said to Harry that I didn't know as what his wife wanted
made much difference to John—

COUNTY ATTORNEY. Let's talk about that later, Mr. Hale. I do   10
want to talk about that, but tell now just what happened
when you got to the house.

HALE. I didn't hear or see anything; I knocked at the door, and
still it was all quiet inside. I knew they must be up, it was past
eight o'-clock. So I knocked again, and I thought I heard
somebody say, "Come in." I wasn't sure, I'm not sure yet, but
I opened the door—this door [*Indicating the door by which
the two women are still standing*] and there in that rocker—
[*Pointing to it.*] sat Mrs. Wright. [*They all look at the rocker.*]

COUNTY ATTORNEY. What—was she doing?

HALE. She was rockin' back and forth. She had her apron in her
hand and was kind of—pleating it.

COUNTY ATTORNEY. And how did she—look?

HALE. Well, she looked queer.   15

COUNTY ATTORNEY. How do you mean—queer?

HALE. Well, as if she didn't know what she was going to do next.
And kind of done up.

COUNTY ATTORNEY. How did she seem to feel about your
coming?

HALE. Why, I don't think she minded—one way or other. She
didn't pay much attention. I said, "How do, Mrs. Wright, it's
cold, ain't it?" And she said, "Is it?"—and went on kind of
pleating at her apron. Well, I was surprised; she didn't ask me
to come up to the stove, or to set down, but just sat there, not
even looking at me, so I said, "I want to see John." And then
she—laughed. I guess you would call it a laugh. I thought of
Harry and the team outside, so I said a little sharp: "Can't I
see John?" "No," she says, kind o' dull like. "Ain't he home?"
says I. "Yes," says she, "he's home." "Then why can't I see
him?" I asked her, out of patience. "'Cause he's dead," says
she. "*Dead?*" says I. She just nodded her head, not getting a
bit excited, but rockin' back and forth. "Why—where is he?"
says I, not knowing what to say. She just pointed upstairs—
like that [*Himself pointing to the room above*]. I got up, with
the idea of going up there. I walked from there to here—then

I says, "Why, what did he die of?" "He died of a rope round his neck," says she, and just went on pleatin' at her apron. Well, I went out and called Harry. I thought I might—need help. We went upstairs and there he was lyin'—

COUNTY ATTORNEY. I think I'd rather have you go into that up-   20
stairs where you can point it all out. Just go on now with the rest of the story.

HALE. Well, my first thought was to get that rope off. It looked . . . [*Stops, his face twitches.*] . . . but Harry, he went up to him, and he said, "No, he's dead all right, and we'd better not touch anything." So we went back down stairs. She was still sitting that same way. "Has anybody been notified?" I asked. "No," says she, unconcerned. "Who did this, Mrs. Wright?" said Harry. He said it businesslike—and she stopped pleatin' of her apron. "I don't know," she says. "You don't *know?*" says Harry. "No," says she. "Weren't you sleepin' in the bed with him?" says Harry. "Yes," says she, "but I was on the inside." "Somebody slipped a rope round his neck and strangled him and you didn't wake up?" says Harry. "I didn't wake up," she said after him. We must 'a looked as if we didn't see how that could be, for after a minute she said, "I sleep sound." Harry was going to ask her more questions but I said maybe we ought to let her tell her story first to the coroner, or the sheriff, so Harry went fast as he could to Rivers' place, where there's a telephone.

COUNTY ATTORNEY. And what did Mrs. Wright do when she knew that you had gone for the coroner?

HALE. She moved from that chair to this one over here [*Pointing to a small chair in the corner.*] and just sat there with her hands held together and looking down. I got a feeling that I ought to make some conversation, so I said I had come in to see if John wanted to put in a telephone, and at that she started to laugh, and then she stopped and looked at me— scared. [*The* COUNTY ATTORNEY, *who has had his notebook out, makes a note.*] I dunno, maybe it wasn't scared. I wouldn't like to say it was. Soon Harry got back, and then Dr. Lloyd came, and you, Mr. Peters, and so I guess that's all I know that you don't.

COUNTY ATTORNEY. [*Looking around.*] I guess we'll go upstairs first—and then out to the barn and around there. [*To the*

SHERIFF] You're convinced that there was nothing important here—nothing that would point to any motive.

SHERIFF. Nothing here but kitchen things.   25

[*The* COUNTY ATTORNEY, *after looking around the kitchen, opens the door of a cupboard closet. He gets up on a chair and looks on a shelf. Pulls his hand away, sticky.*]

COUNTY ATTORNEY. Here's a nice mess.

[*The women draw nearer.*]

MRS. PETERS. [*To the other woman.*] Oh, her fruit; it did freeze. [*To the* COUNTY ATTORNEY] She worried about that when it turned so cold. She said the fire'd go out and her jars would break.

SHERIFF. Well, can you beat the women! Held for murder and worryin' about her preserves.

COUNTY ATTORNEY. I guess before we're through she may have something more serious than preserves to worry about.

HALE. Well, women are used to worrying over trifles.   30

[*The two women move a little closer together.*]

COUNTY ATTORNEY. [*With the gallantry of a young politician.*] And yet, for all their worries, what would we do without the ladies? [*The women do not unbend. He goes to the sink, takes a dipperful of water from the pail and pouring it into a basin, washes his hands. Starts to wipe them on the roller towel, turns it for a cleaner place.*] Dirty towels! [*Kicks his foot against the pans under the sink.*] Not much of a housekeeper, would you say, ladies?

MRS. HALE. [*Stiffly.*] There's a great deal of work to be done on a farm.

COUNTY ATTORNEY. To be sure. And yet [*With a little bow to her*] I know there are some Dickson county farmhouses which do not have such roller towels.

[*He gives it a pull to expose its full length again.*]

MRS. HALE. Those towels get dirty awful quick. Men's hands aren't always as clean as they might be.

COUNTY ATTORNEY. Ah, loyal to your sex, I see. But you and   35
Mrs. Wright were neighbors. I suppose you were friends, too.

MRS. HALE. [*Shaking her head.*] I've not seen much of her of late years. I've not been in this house—it's more than a year.

COUNTY ATTORNEY. And why was that? You didn't like her?

MRS. HALE. I liked her all well enough. Farmers' wives have their hands full, Mr. Henderson. And then—

COUNTY ATTORNEY. Yes—?

MRS. HALE. [*Looking about.*] It never seemed a very cheerful   40
place.

COUNTY ATTORNEY. No—it's not cheerful. I shouldn't say she
had the homemaking instinct.

MRS. HALE. Well, I don't know as Wright had, either.

COUNTY ATTORNEY. You mean that they didn't get on very well?

MRS. HALE. No, I don't mean anything. But I don't think a
place'd be any cheerfuller for John Wright's being in it.

COUNTY ATTORNEY. I'd like to talk more of that a little later. I   45
want to get the lay of things upstairs now.

[*He goes to the left, where three steps lead to a stair door.*]

SHERIFF. I suppose anything Mrs. Peters does'll be all right. She
was to take in some clothes for her, you know, and a few little
things. We left in such a hurry yesterday.

COUNTY ATTORNEY. Yes, but I would like to see what you take,
Mrs. Peters, and keep an eye out for anything that might be of
use to us.

MRS. PETERS. Yes, Mr. Henderson.

[*The women listen to the men's steps on the stairs, then look
about the kitchen.*]

MRS. HALE. I'd hate to have men coming into my kitchen,
snooping around and criticizing.

[*She arranges the pans under the sink which the* COUNTY AT-
TORNEY *had shoved out of place.*]

MRS. PETERS. Of course it's no more than their duty.   50

MRS. HALE. Duty's all right, but I guess that deputy sheriff that
came out to make the fire might have got a little of this on.
[*Gives the roller towel a pull.*] Wish I'd thought of that
sooner. Seems mean to talk about her for not having things
slicked up when she had to come away in such a hurry.

MRS. PETERS. [*Who has gone to a small table in the left rear corner of the room, and lifted one end of a towel that covers a
pan.*] She had bread set.
[*Stands still.*]

MRS. HALE. [*Eyes fixed on a loaf of bread beside the breadbox,
which is on a low shelf at the other side of the room. Moves
slowly toward it.*] She was going to put this in there. [*Picks up
loaf, then abruptly drops it. In a manner of returning to familiar things.*] It's a shame about her fruit. I wonder if it's all
gone. [*Gets up on the chair and looks.*] I think there's some

here that's all right, Mrs. Peters. Yes—here; [*Holding it toward the window.*] this is cherries, too. [*Looking again.*] I declare I believe that's the only one. [*Gets down, bottle in her hand. Goes to the sink and wipes it off on the outside.*] She'll feel awful bad after all her hard work in the hot weather. I remember the afternoon I put up my cherries last summer.

[*She puts the bottle on the big kitchen table, center of the room. With a sigh, is about to sit down in the rocking-chair. Before she is seated realizes what chair it is; with a slow look at it, steps back. The chair which she has touched rocks back and forth.*]

MRS. PETERS.   Well, I must get those things from the front room closet. [*She goes to the door at the right, but after looking into the other room, steps back.*] You coming with me, Mrs. Hale? You could help me carry them.

[*They go in the other room; reappear,* MRS. PETERS *carrying a dress and skirt,* MRS. HALE *following with a pair of shoes.*]

MRS. PETERS.   My, it's cold in there.   55

[*She puts the clothes on the big table, and hurries to the stove.*]

MRS. HALE.   [*Examining her skirt.*] Wright was close. I think maybe that's why she kept so much to herself. She didn't even belong to the Ladies Aid. I suppose she felt she couldn't do her part, and then you don't enjoy things when you feel shabby. She used to wear pretty clothes and be lively, when she was Minnie Foster, one of the town girls singing in the choir. But that—oh, that was thirty years ago. This all you was to take in?

MRS. PETERS.   She said she wanted an apron. Funny thing to want, for there isn't much to get you dirty in jail, goodness knows. But I suppose just to make her feel more natural. She said they was in the top drawer in this cupboard. Yes, here. And then her little shawl that always hung behind the door. [*Opens stair door and looks.*] Yes, here it is.

[*Quickly shuts door leading upstairs.*]

MRS. HALE.   [*Abruptly moving toward her.*] Mrs. Peters?

MRS. PETERS.   Yes, Mrs. Hale?

MRS. HALE.   Do you think she did it?   60

MRS. PETERS.   [*In a frightened voice.*] Oh, I don't know.

MRS. HALE.   Well, I don't think she did. Asking for an apron and her little shawl. Worrying about her fruit.

MRS. PETERS. [*Starts to speak, glances up, where footsteps are heard in the room above. In a low voice.*] Mr. Peters says it looks bad for her. Mr. Henderson is awful sarcastic in a speech and he'll make fun of her sayin' she didn't wake up.

MRS. HALE. Well, I guess John Wright didn't wake when they was slipping that rope under his neck.

MRS. PETERS. No, it's strange. It must have been done awful crafty and still. They say it was such a—funny way to kill a man, rigging it all up like that.

65

MRS. HALE. That's just what Mr. Hale said. There was a gun in the house. He says that's what he can't understand.

MRS. PETERS. Mr. Henderson said coming out that what was needed for the case was a motive; something to show anger, or—sudden feeling.

MRS. HALE. [*Who is standing by the table.*] Well, I don't see any signs of anger around here. [*She puts her hand on the dish towel which lies on the table, stands looking down at table, one half of which is clean, the other half messy.*] It's wiped to here. [*Makes a move as if to finish work, then turns and looks at loaf of bread outside the breadbox. Drops towel. In that voice of coming back to familiar things.*] Wonder how they are finding things upstairs. I hope she had it a little more red-up up there. You know, it seems kind of *sneaking*. Locking her up in town and then coming out here and trying to get her own house to turn against her!

MRS. PETERS. But Mrs. Hale, the law is the law.

MRS. HALE. I s'pose 'tis. [*Unbuttoning her coat.*] Better loosen up your things, Mrs. Peters. You won't feel them when you go out.

70

[MRS. PETERS *takes off her fur tippet, goes to hang it on hook at back of room, stands looking at the under part of the small corner table.*]

MRS. PETERS. She was piecing a quilt.

[*She brings the large sewing basket and they look at the bright pieces.*]

MRS. HALE. It's log cabin pattern. Pretty, isn't it? I wonder if she was goin' to quilt it or just knot it?

[*Footsteps have been heard coming down the stairs. The* SHERIFF *enters followed by* HALE *and the* COUNTY ATTORNEY.]

SHERIFF. They wonder if she was going to quilt it or just knot it!

[*The men laugh; the women look abashed.*]

COUNTY ATTORNEY. [*Rubbing his hands over the stove.*] Frank's fire didn't do much up there, did it? Well, let's go out to the barn and get that cleared up.

[*The men go outside.*]

MRS. HALE. [*Resentfully.*] I don't know as there's anything so   75 strange, our takin' up our time with little things while we're waiting for them to get the evidence. [*She sits down at the big table smoothing out a block with decision.*] I don't see as it's anything to laugh about.

MRS. PETERS. [*Apologetically.*] Of course they've got awful important things on their minds.

[*Pulls up a chair and joins* MRS. HALE *at the table.*]

MRS. HALE. [*Examining another block.*] Mrs. Peters, look at this one. Here, this is the one she was working on, and look at the sewing! All the rest of it has been so nice and even. And look at this! It's all over the place! Why, it looks as if she didn't know what she was about!

[*After she has said this they look at each other, then start to glance back at the door. After an instant* MRS. HALE *has pulled at a knot and ripped the sewing.*]

MRS. PETERS. Oh, what are you doing, Mrs. Hale?

MRS. HALE. [*Mildly.*] Just pulling out a stitch or two that's not sewed very good. [*Threading a needle.*] Bad sewing always made me fidgety.

MRS. PETERS. [*Nervously.*] I don't think we ought to touch   80 things.

MRS. HALE. I'll just finish up this end. [*Suddenly stopping and leaning forward.*] Mrs. Peters?

MRS. PETERS. Yes, Mrs. Hale?

MRS. HALE. What do you suppose she was so nervous about?

MRS. PETERS. Oh—I don't know. I don't know as she was nervous. I sometimes sew awful queer when I'm just tired. [MRS. HALE *starts to say something, looks at* MRS. PETERS; *then goes on sewing.*] Well, I must get these things wrapped up. They may be through sooner than we think. [*Putting apron and other things together.*] I wonder where I can find a piece of paper, and string.

MRS. HALE. In that cupboard, maybe.   85

MRS. PETERS. [*Looking in cupboard.*] Why, here's a birdcage. [*Holds it up.*] Did she have a bird, Mrs. Hale?

MRS. HALE. Why I don't know whether she did or not—I've not been here for so long. There was a man around last year selling canaries cheap, but I don't know as she took one; maybe she did. She used to sing real pretty herself.

MRS. PETERS. [*Glancing around.*] Seems funny to think of a bird here. But she must have had one, or why would she have a cage? I wonder what happened to it.

MRS. HALE. I s'pose maybe the cat got it.

MRS. PETERS. No, she didn't have a cat. She's got that feeling some people have about cats—being afraid of them. My cat got in her room and she was real upset and asked me to take it out.   90

MRS. HALE. My sister Bessie was like that. Queer, ain't it?

MRS. PETERS. [*Examining the cage.*] Why, look at this door. It's broke. One hinge is pulled apart.

MRS. HALE. [*Looking too.*] Looks as if someone must have been rough with it.

MRS. PETERS. Why, yes.

[*She brings the cage forward and puts it on the table.*]

MRS. HALE. I wish if they're going to find any evidence they'd be about it. I don't like this place.   95

MRS. PETERS. But I'm awful glad you came with me, Mrs. Hale. It would be lonesome for me sitting here alone.

MRS. HALE. It would, wouldn't it? [*Dropping her sewing.*] But I tell you what I do wish, Mrs. Peters. I wish I had come over sometimes when *she* was here. I—[*Looking around the room.*]—wish I had.

MRS. PETERS. But of course you were awful busy. Mrs. Hale— your house and your children.

MRS. HALE. I could've come. I stayed away because it weren't cheerful—and that's why I ought to have come. I—I've never liked this place. Maybe because it's down in a hollow and you don't see the road. I dunno what it is but it's a lonesome place and always was. I wish I had come over to see Minnie Foster sometimes. I can see now—[*Shakes her head.*]

MRS. PETERS. Well, you mustn't reproach yourself, Mrs. Hale. Somehow we just don't see how it is with other folks until— something comes up.   100

MRS. HALE. Not having children makes less work—but it makes a quiet house, and Wright out to work all day, and no company when he did come in. Did you know John Wright, Mrs. Peters?

MRS. PETERS. Not to know him; I've seen him in town. They say he was a good man.

MRS. HALE. Yes—good; he didn't drink, and kept his word as well as most, I guess, and paid his debts. But he was a hard man, Mrs. Peters. Just to pass the time of day with him— [*Shivers.*] Like a raw wind that gets to the bone. [*Pauses, her eye falling on the cage.*] I should think she would 'a wanted a bird. But what do you suppose went with it?

MRS. PETERS. I don't know, unless it got sick and died.
[*She reaches over and swings the broken door, swings it again. Both women watch it.*]

MRS. HALE. You weren't raised round here, were you? [MRS. PE-   105
TERS *shakes her head.*] You didn't know—her?

MRS. PETERS. Not till they brought her yesterday.

MRS. HALE. She—come to think of it, she was kind of like a bird herself—real sweet and pretty, but kind of timid and—fluttery. How—she—did—change. [*Silence; then as if struck by a happy thought and relieved to get back to every day things.*] Tell you what, Mrs. Peters, why don't you take the quilt in with you? It might take up her mind.

MRS. PETERS. Why, I think that's a real nice idea, Mrs. Hale. There couldn't possibly be any objection to it, could there? Now, just what would I take? I wonder if her patches are in here—and her things. [*They look in the sewing basket.*]

MRS. HALE. Here's some red. I expect this has got sewing things in it. [*Brings out a fancy box.*] What a pretty box. Looks like something somebody would give you. Maybe her scissors are in here. [*Opens box. Suddenly puts her hand to her nose.*] Why—[MRS. PETERS *bends nearer, then turns her face away.*] There's something wrapped up in this piece of silk.

MRS. PETERS. Why, this isn't her scissors.   110

MRS. HALE. [*Lifting the silk.*] Oh, Mrs. Peters—it's—
[MRS. PETERS *bends closer.*]

MRS. PETERS. It's the bird.

MRS. HALE. [*Jumping up.*] But, Mrs. Peters—look at it! Its neck! Look at its neck! It's all—other side *to*.

MRS. PETERS. Somebody—wrung—its—neck.

[*Their eyes meet. A look of growing comprehension, of horror. Steps are heard outside.* MRS. HALE *slips box under quilt pieces, and sinks into her chair. Enter* SHERIFF *and* COUNTY ATTORNEY. MRS. PETERS *rises.*]

COUNTY ATTORNEY. [*As one turning from serious things to little pleasantries.*] Well, ladies, have you decided whether she was going to quilt it or knot it?

MRS. PETERS. We think she was going to—knot it.

COUNTY ATTORNEY. Well, that's interesting, I'm sure. [*Seeing the birdcage.*] Has the bird flown?

MRS. HALE. [*Putting more quilt pieces over the box.*] We think the—cat got it.

COUNTY ATTORNEY. [*Preoccupied.*] Is there a cat?

[MRS. HALE *glances in a quick covert way at* MRS. PETERS.]

MRS. PETERS. Well, not *now*. They're superstitious, you know. They leave.

COUNTY ATTORNEY. [*To* SHERIFF PETERS, *continuing an interrupted conversation.*] No sign at all of anyone having come from the outside. Their own rope. Now let's go up again and go over it piece by piece. [*They start upstairs.*] It would have to have been someone who knew just the—

[MRS. PETERS *sits down. The two women sit there not looking at one another, but as if peering into something and at the same time holding back. When they talk now it is in the manner of feeling their way over strange ground, as if afraid of what they are saying, but as if they can not help saying it.*]

MRS. HALE. She liked the bird. She was going to bury it in that pretty box.

MRS. PETERS. [*In a whisper.*] When I was a girl—my kitten—there was a boy took a hatchet, and before my eyes—and before I could get there—[*Covers her face an instant.*] If they hadn't held me back I would have—[*Catches herself, looks upstairs where steps are heard, falters weakly.*]—hurt him.

MRS. HALE. [*With a slow look around her.*] I wonder how it would seem never to have had any children around. [*Pause.*] No, Wright wouldn't like the bird—a thing that sang. She used to sing. He killed that, too.

MRS. PETERS. [*Moving uneasily.*] We don't know who killed the bird.

MRS. HALE. I knew John Wright.

MRS. PETERS. It was an awful thing was done in this house that night, Mrs. Hale. Killing a man while he slept, slipping a rope around his neck that choked the life out of him.

MRS. HALE. His neck. Choked the life out of him.
[*Her hand goes out and rests on the birdcage.*]

MRS. PETERS. [*With rising voice.*] We don't know who killed him. We don't *know.*

MRS. HALE. [*Her own feeling not interrupted.*] If there'd been   130
years and years of nothing, then a bird to sing to you, it would be awful—still, after the bird was still.

MRS. PETERS. [*Something within her speaking.*] I know what stillness is. When we homesteaded in Dakota, and my first baby died—after he was two years old, and me with no other then—

MRS. HALE. [*Moving.*] How soon do you suppose they'll be through, looking for the evidence?

MRS. PETERS. I know what stillness is. [*Pulling herself back.*] The law has got to punish crime, Mrs. Hale.

MRS. HALE. [*Not as if answering that.*] I wish you'd seen Minnie Foster when she wore a white dress with blue ribbons and stood up there in the choir and sang. [*A look around the room.*] Oh, I *wish* I'd come over here once in a while! That was a crime! That was a crime! Who's going to punish that?

MRS. PETERS. [*Looking upstairs.*] We mustn't—take on.   135

MRS. HALE. I might have known she needed help! I know how things can be—for women. I tell you, it's queer, Mrs. Peters. We live close together and we live far apart. We all go through the same things—it's all just a different kind of the same thing. [*Brushes her eyes; noticing the bottle of fruit, reaches out for it.*] If I was you I wouldn't tell her her fruit was gone. Tell her it *ain't.* Tell her it's all right. Take this in to prove it to her. She—she may never know whether it was broke or not.

MRS. PETERS. [*Takes the bottle, looks about for something to wrap it in; takes petticoat from the clothes brought from the other room, very nervously begins winding this around the bottle. In a false voice.*] My, it's a good thing the men couldn't hear us. Wouldn't they just laugh! Getting all stirred up over a little thing like a—dead canary. As if that could have anything to do with—with—wouldn't they *laugh!*
[*The men are heard coming down stairs.*]

MRS. HALE. [*Under her breath.*] Maybe they would—maybe they wouldn't.

COUNTY ATTORNEY. No, Peters, it's all perfectly clear except a reason for doing it. But you know juries when it comes to women. If there was some definite thing. Something to show—something to make a story about—a thing that would connect up with this strange way of doing it—

[*The women's eyes meet for an instant. Enter* HALE *from outer door.*]

HALE. Well, I've got the team around. Pretty cold out there.   140

COUNTY ATTORNEY. I'm going to stay here a while by myself. [*To the* SHERIFF.] You can send Frank out for me, can't you? I want to go over everything. I'm not satisfied that we can't do better.

SHERIFF. Do you want to see what Mrs. Peters is going to take in?

[*The* COUNTY ATTORNEY *goes to the table, picks up the apron, laughs.*]

COUNTY ATTORNEY. Oh, I guess they're not very dangerous things the ladies have picked out. [*Moves a few things about, disturbing the quilt pieces which cover the box. Steps back.*] No, Mrs. Peters doesn't need supervising. For that matter, a sheriff's wife is married to the law. Ever think of it that way, Mrs. Peters?

MRS. PETERS. Not—just that way.

SHERIFF. [*Chuckling.*] Married to the law. [*Moves toward the   145 other room.*] I just want you to come in here a minute, George. We ought to take a look at these windows.

COUNTY ATTORNEY. [*Scoffingly.*] Oh, windows!

SHERIFF. We'll be right out, Mr. Hale.

[HALE *goes outside. The* SHERIFF *follows the* COUNTY ATTORNEY *into the other room. Then* MRS. HALE *rises, hands tight together, looking intensely at* MRS. PETERS, *whose eyes make a slow turn, finally meeting* MRS. HALE's. *A moment* MRS. HALE *holds her, then her own eyes point the way to where the box is concealed. Suddenly* MRS. PETERS *throws back quilt pieces and tries to put the box in the bag she is wearing. It is too big. She opens box, starts to take bird out, cannot touch it, goes to pieces, stands there helpless. Sound of a knob turning in the other room.* MRS. HALE *snatches the box and puts it in the pocket of her big coat. Enter* COUNTY ATTORNEY *and* SHERIFF.]

COUNTY ATTORNEY. [*Facetiously.*] Well, Henry, at least we found out that she was not going to quilt it. She was going to—what is it you call it, ladies?

MRS. HALE. [*Her hand against her pocket.*] We call it—knot it, Mr. Henderson.

CURTAIN

4

FEMININITY AND MASCULINITY

The Lady Mayor. THOMAS MCAVOY/TimePix.

OVERVIEW

Writing in the middle of the twentieth century and in the middle of her brilliant career as an anthropologist, Margaret Mead made the following observation about femininity and masculinity:

> Different cultures have styled the relationships between men and women differently. When they have styled the roles so that they fitted well together, so that law and custom, ideal and practical possibilities, were reasonably close together, the men and the women who lived within that society have been fortunate. But to the degree that there have been discrepancies in the two roles, to the degree that a style of beauty that was unobtainable by most people, or a style of bravery or initiative, modesty and responsiveness, was insisted upon although the culture had inadequate devices for developing such initiative or such responsiveness, then both men and women suffer.[1]

Mead's writing often suggests that in her lifetime, in this respect, Americans may not have been particularly fortunate, and that many may have suffered as a result. The readings collected in this section address the same concerns Mead raises. All deal with ways various generations have built onto the natural difference of the sexes' conceptions of masculinity and femininity that are fanciful, artistic, exasperating, degrading, or ennobling.

- Susan Brownmiller presents femininity as an "esthetic," a set of demanding artistic forms that many women choose to practice, and she weighs "as if in a ledger book" what practitioners of the art gain against what they lose.
- Annie Dillard's portrait of her mother reminds us that a woman whose energy and talent are confined to a housewife's role can react like "Samson in chains."
- Tom Wolfe's portrait of the Project Mercury astronauts captures a familiar masculine ideal—a blend of competence and courage that he calls simply "the Right Stuff."
- Katha Pollitt expresses alarm that wherever her "funny, clever, bold, adventurous" daughter looks in the American media,

---

1. *Male and Female.* New York: William Morrow, 1949, p. 298.

she will get the same message: "Girls exist only in relation to boys."

- Jan Morris, who chose to become a woman in the 1960s, recalls what it was like to live in a man's body during an endeavor that was strictly masculine: the famous Mt. Everest expedition of 1953.
- Noel Perrin, without dismissing the possibility that some men are "completely masculine," quite happily reports that he is not.
- JoAnn Wypijewski, investigating the background of the men who killed Matthew Shepard, suggests that at the heart of the crime is a tortured, but not a terribly unusual, sense of what it means to be manly in America.
- Gloria Steinem's account of the financial difficulties of *Ms.* magazine shows us that a business can go broke by fighting sexual stereotyping.
- John Steinbeck's story presents the world of Elisa Allen, a woman forced to think hard about what femininity requires of her and what it offers in return.

Susan Brownmiller

Femininity

Susan Brownmiller was one of America's most visible and active
feminists in the 1970s. *Against Our Will* (1975), in which she argued that "rape is nothing more or less than a conscious process
of intimidation by which *all men* keep *all women* in a state of
fear," was a best-seller, serialized in four magazines. *Femininity*
(1984), from which the following excerpt is drawn, surprised
some readers by taking a less polemical tone.

We had a game in our house called "setting the table" and I   1
was Mother's helper. Forks to the left of the plate, knives and
spoons to the right. Placing the cutlery neatly, as I recall, was one
of my first duties, and the event was alive with meaning. When a
knife or a fork dropped on the floor, that meant a man was unexpectedly coming to dinner. A falling spoon announced the surprise arrival of a female guest. No matter that these visitors
never arrived on cue, I had learned a rule of gender identification. Men were straight-edged, sharply pronged and formidable,
women were softly curved and held the food in a rounded well.
It made perfect sense, like the division of pink and blue that I
saw in babies, an orderly way of viewing the world. Daddy, who
was gone all day at work and who loved to putter at home with
his pipe, tobacco and tool chest, was knife and fork. Mommy
and Grandma, with their ample proportions and pots and pans,
were grownup soup spoons, large and capacious. And I was a
teaspoon, small and slender, easy to hold and just right for pudding, my favorite dessert.

Being good at what was expected of me was one of my earli-   2
est projects, for not only was I rewarded, as most children are,
for doing things right, but excellence gave pride and stability to
my childhood existence. Girls were different from boys, and the
expression of that difference seemed mine to make clear. Did my
loving, anxious mother, who dressed me in white organdy
pinafores and Mary Janes and who cried hot tears when I got
them dirty, give me my first instruction? Of course. Did my dot-
ing aunts and uncles with their gifts of pretty dolls and miniature

tea sets add to my education? Of course. But even without the appropriate toys and clothes, lessons in the art of being feminine lay all around me and I absorbed them all: the fairy tales that were read to me at night, the brightly colored advertisements I pored over in magazines before I learned to decipher the words, the movies I saw, the comic books I hoarded, the radio soap operas I happily followed whenever I had to stay in bed with a cold. I loved being a little girl, or rather I loved being a fairy princess, for that was who I thought I was.

As I passed through a stormy adolescence to a stormy maturity, femininity increasingly became an exasperation, a brilliant, subtle esthetic that was bafflingly inconsistent at the same time that it was minutely, demandingly concrete, a rigid code of appearance and behavior defined by do's and don't-do's that went against my rebellious grain. Femininity was a challenge thrown down to the female sex, a challenge no proud, self-respecting young woman could afford to ignore, particularly one with enormous ambition that she nursed in secret, alternately feeding or starving its inchoate life in tremendous confusion.

"Don't lose your femininity" and "Isn't it remarkable how she manages to retain her femininity?" had terrifying implications. They spoke of a bottom-line failure so irreversible that nothing else mattered. The pinball machine has registered "tilt," the game had been called. Disqualification was marked on the forehead of a woman whose femininity was lost. No records would be entered in her name, for she had destroyed her birthright in her wretched, ungainly effort to imitate a man. She walked in limbo, this hapless creature, and it occurred to me that one day I might see her when I looked in the mirror. If the danger was so palpable that warning notices were freely posted, wasn't it possible that the small bundle of resentments I carried around in secret might spill out and place the mark on my own forehead? Whatever quarrels with femininity I had I kept to myself; whatever handicaps femininity imposed, they were mine to deal with alone, for there was no women's movement to ask the tough questions, or to brazenly disregard the rules.

Femininity, in essence, is a romantic sentiment, a nostalgic tradition of imposed limitations. Even as it hurries forward in the 1980s, putting on lipstick and high heels to appear well dressed, it trips on the ruffled petticoats and hoopskirts of an era gone by.

Invariably and necessarily, femininity is something that women had more of in the past, not only in the historic past of prior generations, but in each woman's personal past as well—in the virginal innocence that is replaced by knowledge, in the dewy cheek that is coarsened by age, in the "inherent nature" that a woman seems to misplace so forgetfully whenever she steps out of bounds. Why should this be so? The XX chromosomal message has not been scrambled, the estrogen-dominated hormonal balance is generally as biology intended, the reproductive organs, whatever use one has made of them, are usually in place, the breasts of whatever size are most often where they should be. But clearly, biological femaleness is not enough.

Femininity always demands more. It must constantly reassure 6
its audience by a willing demonstration of difference, even when one does not exist in nature, or it must seize and embrace a natural variation and compose a rhapsodic symphony upon the notes. Suppose one doesn't care to, has other things on her mind, is clumsy or tone-deaf despite the best instruction and training? To fail at the feminine difference is to appear not to care about men, and to risk the loss of their attention and approval. To be insufficiently feminine is viewed as a failure in core sexual identity, or as a failure to care sufficiently about oneself, for a woman found wanting will be appraised (and will appraise herself) as mannish or neutered or simply unattractive, as men have defined these terms.

We are talking, admittedly, about an exquisite esthetic. Enor- 7
mous pleasure can be extracted from feminine pursuits as a creative outlet or purely as relaxation; indeed, indulgence for the sake of fun, or art, or attention, is among femininity's great joys. But the chief attraction (and the central paradox, as well) is the competitive edge that femininity seems to promise in the unending struggle to survive, and perhaps to triumph. The world smiles favorably on the feminine woman: it extends little courtesies and minor privilege. Yet the nature of this competitive edge is ironic, at best, for one works at femininity by accepting restrictions, by limiting one's sights, by choosing an indirect route, by scattering concentration and not giving one's all as a man would to his own, certifiably masculine, interests. It does not require a great leap of imagination for a woman to understand the feminine principle as a grand collection of compromises, large

and small, that she simply must make in order to render herself a successful woman. If she has difficulty in satisfying femininity's demands, if its illusions go against her grain, or if she is criticized for her shortcomings and imperfections, the more she will see femininity as a desperate strategy of appeasement, a strategy she may not have the wish or the courage to abandon, for failure looms in either direction.

It is fashionable in some quarters to describe the feminine and   8 masculine principles as polar ends of the human continuum, and to sagely profess that both polarities exist in all people. Sun and moon, yin and yang, soft and hard, active and passive, etcetera, may indeed be opposites, but a linear continuum does not illuminate the problem. (Femininity, in all its contrivances, is a very active endeavor.) What, then, is the basic distinction? The masculine principle is better understood as a driving ethos of superiority designed to inspire straightforward, confident success, while the feminine principle is composed of vulnerability, the need for protection, the formalities of compliance and the avoidance of conflict—in short, an appeal of dependence and good will that gives the masculine principle its romantic validity and its admiring applause.

Femininity pleases men because it makes them appear more   9 masculine by contrast; and, in truth, conferring an extra portion of unearned gender distinction on men, an unchallenged space in which to breathe freely and feel stronger, wiser, more competent, is femininity's special gift. One could say that masculinity is often an effort to please women, but masculinity is known to please by displays of mastery and competence while femininity pleases by suggesting that these concerns, except in small matters, are beyond its intent. Whimsy, unpredictability and patterns of thinking and behavior that are dominated by emotion, such as tearful expressions of sentiment and fear, are thought to be feminine precisely because they lie outside the established route to success.

If in the beginnings of history the feminine woman was de-   10 fined by her physical dependency, her inability for reasons of reproductive biology to triumph over the forces of nature that were the tests of masculine strength and power, today she reflects both an economic and emotional dependency that is still considered "natural," romantic and attractive. After an unsettling fifteen years in which many basic assumptions about the sexes were challenged, the economic disparity did not disappear. Large numbers of women—those with small children, those left high and dry after a mid-life divorce—need financial support. But even those who earn their own living share a universal need for connectedness (call it love, if you wish). As unprecedented numbers of men abandon their sexual interest in women, others, sensing opportunity, choose to demonstrate their interest through variety and a change in partners. A sociological fact of the 1980s is that female competition for two scarce resources— men and jobs—is especially fierce.

So it is not surprising that we are currently witnessing a renewed interest in femininity and an unabashed indulgence in feminine pursuits. Femininity serves to reassure men that women need them and care about them enormously. By incorporating the decorative and the frivolous into its definition of style, femininity functions as an effective antidote to the unrelieved seriousness, the pressure of making one's way in a harsh, difficult world. In its mandate to avoid direct confrontation and to smooth over the fissures of conflict, femininity operates as a value system of niceness, a code of thoughtfulness and sensitivity that in modern society is sadly in short supply.   11

There is no reason to deny that indulgence in the art of feminine illusion can be reassuring to a woman, if she happens to be good at it. As sexuality undergoes some dizzying revisions, evidence that one is a woman "at heart" (the inquisitor's question) is not without worth. Since an answer of sorts may be furnished by piling on additional documentation, affirmation can arise from such identifiable but trivial feminine activities as buying a new eyeliner, experimenting with the latest shade of nail color, or bursting into tears at the outcome of a popular romance novel. Is there anything destructive in this? Time and cost factors, a deflection of energy and an absorption in fakery spring quickly to mind, and they need to be balanced, as in a ledger book, against the affirming advantage.   12

ANNIE DILLARD

Samson in Chains

Annie Dillard is known to many Americans primarily for *Pilgrim at Tinker Creek* (1975), a Pulitzer Prize-winning book that resembles Thoreau's *Walden* both in its spirituality and in its depiction of the natural world. The following excerpt from *An American Childhood* (1987), which we have titled "Samson in Chains," is a thumbnail portrait of Pam Lambert Doak, Dillard's mother—a woman whose "energy and intelligence suited her for a greater role in a larger arena" than her life provided her.

One Sunday afternoon Mother wandered through our kitchen, where Father was making a sandwich and listening to the ball game. The Pirates were playing the New York Giants at Forbes Field. In those days, the Giants had a utility infielder named Wayne Terwilliger. Just as Mother passed through, the radio announcer cried—with undue drama—"Terwilliger bunts one!"

"Terwilliger bunts one?" Mother cried back, stopped short. She turned. "Is that English?"

"The player's name is Terwilliger," Father said. "He bunted."

"That's marvelous," Mother said. "'Terwilliger bunts one.' No wonder you listen to baseball. 'Terwilliger bunts one.'"

For the next seven or eight years, Mother made this surprising string of syllables her own. Testing a microphone, she repeated, "Terwilliger bunts one"; testing a pen or a typewriter, she wrote it. If, as happened surprisingly often in the course of various improvised gags, she pretended to whisper something else in my ear, she actually whispered, "Terwilliger bunts one." Whenever someone used a French phrase, or a Latin one, she answered solemnly, "Terwilliger bunts one." If Mother had had, like Andrew Carnegie, the opportunity to cook up a motto for a coat of arms, hers would have read simply and tellingly, "Terwilliger bunts one." (Carnegie's was "Death to Privilege.")

She served us with other words and phrases. On a Florida trip, she repeated tremulously, "That . . . is a royal poinciana." I don't remember the tree; I remember the thrill in her voice. She pronounced it carefully, and spelled it. She also liked to say "portulaca."

The drama of the words "Tamiami Trail" stirred her, we 7
learned on the same Florida trip. People built Tampa on one coast, and they built Miami on another. Then—the height of visionary ambition and folly—they piled a slow, tremendous road through the terrible Everglades to connect them. To build the road, men stood sunk in muck to their armpits. They fought off cottonmouth moccasins and six-foot alligators. They slept in boats, wet. They blasted muck with dynamite, cut jungle with machetes; they laid logs, dragged drilling machines, hauled dredges, heaped limestone. The road took fourteen years to build up by the shovelful, a Panama Canal in reverse, and cost hundreds of lives from tropical, mosquito-carried diseases. Then, capping it all, some genius thought of the word Tamiami: they called the road from Tampa to Miami, this very road under our spinning wheels, the Tamiami Trail. Some called it Alligator Alley. Anyone could drive over this road without a thought.

Hearing this, moved, I thought all the suffering of road build- 8
ing was worth it (it wasn't my suffering), now that we had this new thing to hang these new words on—Alligator Alley for those who liked things cute, and, for connoisseurs like Mother, for lovers of the human drama in all its boldness and terror, the Tamiami Trail.

Back home, Mother cut clips from reels of talk, as it were, and 9
played them back at leisure. She noticed that many Pittsburghers confuse "leave" and "let." One kind relative brightened our morning by mentioning why she'd brought her son to visit: "He wanted to come with me, so I left him." Mother filled in Amy and me on locutions we missed. "I can't do it on Friday," her pretty sister told a crowded dinner party, "because Friday's the day I lay in the stores."

(All unconsciously, though, we ourselves used some pure 10
Pittsburghisms. We said "tele pole," pronounced "telly pole," for that splintery sidewalk post I loved to climb. We said "slippy"—the sidewalks are "slippy." We said, "That's all the farther I could go." And we said, as Pittsburghers do say, "This glass needs washed," or "The dog needs walked"—a usage our father eschewed; he knew it was not standard English, nor even comprehensible English, but he never let on.)

"Spell 'poinsettia,'" Mother would throw out at me, smiling   11
with pleasure. "Spell 'sherbet.'" The idea was not to make us
whizzes, but, quite the contrary, to remind us—and I, especially,
needed reminding—that we didn't know it all just yet.

"There's a deer standing in the front hall," she told me one   12
quiet evening in the country.

"Really?"   13

"No. I just wanted to tell you something once without your   14
saying, 'I know.'"

Supermarkets in the middle 1950s began luring, or bothering,   15
customers by giving out Top Value Stamps or Green Stamps.
When, shopping with Mother, we got to the head of the check-
out line, the checker, always a young man, asked, "Save
stamps?"

"No," Mother replied genially, week after week, "I build   16
model airplanes." I believe she originated this line. It took me
years to determine where the joke lay.

Anyone who met her verbal challenges she adored. She had   17
surgery on one of her eyes. On the operating table, just before
she conked out, she appealed feelingly to the surgeon, saying, as
she had been planning to say for weeks, "Will I be able to play
the piano?" "Not on me," the surgeon said. "You won't pull that
old one on me."

It was, indeed, an old one. The surgeon was supposed to an-   18
swer, "Yes, my dear, brave woman, you will be able to play the
piano after this operation," to which Mother intended to reply,
"Oh, good, I've always wanted to play the piano." This pat scenario bored her; she loved having it interrupted. It must have
galled her that usually her acquaintances were so predictably
unalert; it must have galled her that, for the length of her life, she
could surprise everyone so continually, so easily, when she had
been the same all along. At any rate, she loved anyone who, as
she put it, saw it coming, and called her on it.

She regarded the instructions on bureaucratic forms as   19
straight lines. "Do you advocate the overthrow of the United
States government by force or violence?" After some thought she
wrote, "Force." She regarded children, even babies, as straight
men. When Molly learned to crawl, Mother delighted in buying
her gowns with drawstrings at the bottom, like Swee'pea's, be-

cause, as she explained energetically, you could easily step on the drawstring without the baby's noticing, so that she crawled and crawled and crawled and never got anywhere except into a small ball at the gown's top.

When we children were young, she mothered us tenderly and dependably; as we got older, she resumed her career of anarchism. She collared us into her gags. If she answered the phone on a wrong number, she told the caller, "Just a minute," and dragged the receiver to Amy or me, saying, "Here, take this, your name is Cecile," or, worse, just, "It's for you." You had to think on your feet. But did you want to perform well as Cecile, or did you want to take pity on the wretched caller? 20

During a family trip to the Highland Park Zoo, Mother and I were alone for a minute. She approached a young couple holding hands on a bench by the seals, and addressed the young man in dripping tones: "Where have you been? Still got those baby-blue eyes; always did slay me. And this"—a swift nod at the dumbstruck young woman, who had removed her hand from the man's—"must be the one you were telling me about. She's not so bad, really, as you used to make out. But listen, you know how I miss you, you know where to reach me, same old place. And there's Ann over there—see how she's grown? See the blue eyes?" 21

And off she sashayed, taking me firmly by the hand, and leading us around briskly past the monkey house and away. She cocked an ear back, and both of us heard the desperate man begin, in a high-pitched wail, "I swear, I never saw her before in my life. . . ." 22

On a long, sloping beach by the ocean, she lay stretched out sunning with Father and friends, until the conversation gradually grew tedious, when without forethought she gave a little push with her heel and rolled away. People were stunned. She rolled deadpan and apparently effortlessly, arms and legs extended and tidy, down the beach to the distant water's edge, where she lay at ease just as she had been, but half in the surf, and well out of earshot. 23

She dearly loved to fluster people by throwing out a game's rules at whim—when she was getting bored, losing in a dull sort of way, and when everybody else was taking it too seriously. If 24 you turned your back, she moved the checkers around on the board. When you got them all straightened out, she denied she'd touched them; the next time you turned your back, she lined them up on the rug or hid them under your chair. In a betting rummy game called Michigan, she routinely played out of turn, or called out a card she didn't hold, or counted backward, simply to amuse herself by causing an uproar and watching the rest of us do double takes and have fits. (Much later, when serious suitors came to call, Mother subjected them to this fast card game as a trial by ordeal; she used it as an intelligence test and a measure of spirit. If the poor man could stay a round without breaking down or running out, he got to marry one of us, if he still wanted to.)

She excelled at bridge, playing fast and boldly, but when the stakes were low and the hands dull, she bid slams for the devilment of it, or raised her opponents' suit to bug them, or showed her hand, or tossed her cards in a handful behind her back in a characteristic swift motion accompanied by a vibrantly innocent look. It drove our stolid father crazy. The hand was over before it began, and the guests were appalled. How do you score it, who deals now, what do you do with a crazy person who is having so much fun? Or they were down seven, and the guests were appalled. "Pam!" "Dammit, Pam!" He groaned. What ails such people? What on earth possesses them? He rubbed his face.

She was an unstoppable force; she never let go. When we moved across town, she persuaded the U.S. Post Office to let her keep her old address—forever—because she'd had stationery printed. I don't know how she did it. Every new post office worker, over decades, needed to learn that although the Doaks' mail is addressed to here, it is delivered to there.

Mother's energy and intelligence suited her for a greater role in a larger arena—mayor of New York, say—than the one she had. She followed American politics closely; she had been known to vote for Democrats. She saw how things should be run, but she had nothing to run but our household. Even there, small minds bugged her; she was smarter than the people who designed the things she had to use all day for the length of her life.

"Look," she said. "Whoever designed this corkscrew never used one. Why would anyone sell it without trying it out?" So she invented a better one. She showed me a drawing of it. The

spirit of American enterprise never faded in Mother. If capitaliz-
ing and tooling up had been as interesting as theorizing and
thinking up, she would have fired up a new factory every week,
and chaired several hundred corporations.

"It grieves me," she would say, "it grieves my heart," that the   29
company that made one superior product packaged it poorly, or
took the wrong tack in its advertising. She knew, as she held the
thing mournfully in her two hands, that she'd never find another.
She was right. We children wholly sympathized, and so did Father; what could she do, what could anyone do, about it? She
was Samson in chains. She paced.

She didn't like the taste of stamps so she didn't lick stamps;   30
she licked the corner of the envelope instead. She glued sandpaper to the sides of kitchen drawers, and under kitchen cabinets,
so she always had a handy place to strike a match. She designed,
and hounded workmen to build against all norms, doubly wide
kitchen counters and elevated bathroom sinks. To splint a finger,
she stuck it in a lightweight cigar tube. Conversely, to protect a
pack of cigarettes, she carried it in a Band-Aid box. She drew
plans for an over-the-finger toothbrush for babies, an oven rack
that slid up and down, and—the family favorite—Lendalarm.
Lendalarm was a beeper you attached to books (or tools) you
loaned friends. After ten days, the beeper sounded. Only the
rightful owner could silence it.

She repeatedly reminded us of P. T. Barnum's dictum: You   31
could sell anything to anybody if you marketed it right. The adman who thought of making Americans believe they needed underarm deodorant was a visionary. So, too, was the hero who
made a success of a new product, Ivory soap. The executives
were horrified, Mother told me, that a cake of this stuff floated.
Soap wasn't supposed to float. Anyone would be able to tell it
was mostly whipped-up air. Then some inspired adman made a
leap: Advertise that it floats. Flaunt it. The rest is history.

She respected the rare few who broke through to new ways.   32
"Look," she'd say, "here's an intelligent apron." She called upon
us to admire intelligent control knobs and intelligent pan handles, intelligent andirons and picture frames and knife sharpen-
ers. She questioned everything, every pair of scissors, every
knitting needle, gardening glove, tape dispenser. Hers was a restless mental vigor that just about ignited the dumb household
objects with its force.

*   *   *

Torpid conformity was a kind of sin; it was stupidity itself, the   33
mighty stream against which Mother would never cease to struggle. If you held no minority opinions, or if you failed to risk total ostracism for them daily, the world would be a better place
without you.

Always I heard Mother's emotional voice asking Amy and me   34
the same few questions: Is that your own idea? Or somebody
else's? "*Giant* is a good movie," I pronounced to the family at
dinner. "Oh, really?" Mother warmed to these occasions. She all
but rolled up her sleeves. She knew I hadn't seen it. "Is that your
considered opinion?"

She herself held many unpopular, even fantastic, positions.   35
She was scathingly sarcastic about the McCarthy hearings while
they took place, right on our living-room television; she frantically opposed Father's wait-and-see calm. "We don't know
enough about it," he said. "I do," she said. "I know all I need to
know."

She asserted, against all opposition, that people who lived in   36
trailer parks were not bad but simply poor, and had as much
right to settle on beautiful land, such as rural Ligonier, Pennsylvania, as did the oldest of families in the finest of hidden houses.
Therefore, the people who owned trailer parks, and sought zon-
ing changes to permit trailer parks, needed our help. Her profound belief that the country-club pool sweeper was a person,
and that the department-store saleslady, the bus driver, telephone
operator, and housepainter were people, and even in groups the
steelworkers who carried pickets and the Christmas shoppers
who clogged intersections were people—this was a conviction
common enough in democratic Pittsburgh, but not altogether
common among our friends' parents, or even, perhaps, among
our parents' friends.

Opposition emboldened Mother, and she would take on any-   37
body on any issue—the chairman of the board, at a cocktail
party, on the current strike; she would fly at him in a flurry of
passion, as a songbird selflessly attacks a big hawk.

"Eisenhower's going to win," I announced after school. She   38
lowered her magazine and looked me in the eyes: "How do you
know?" I was doomed. It was fatal to say, "Everyone says so."
We all knew well what happened. "Do you consult this Everyone
before you make your decisions? What if Everyone decided to

round up all the Jews?" Mother knew there was no danger of
cowing me. She simply tried to keep us all awake. And in fact it
was always clear to Amy and me, and to Molly when she grew
old enough to listen, that if our classmates came to cruelty, just
as much as if the neighborhood or the nation came to madness,
we were expected to take, and would be each separately capable
of taking, a stand.

TOM WOLFE

The Right Stuff

Tom Wolfe is one of the leading practitioners of the New Journalism, which combines, as he says, "the objective reality of journalism" with "the subjective reality that people have always gone
to the novel for." The following excerpt describes the flight training during the 1950s of the men who became the Project Mercury
astronauts of the 1960s. It is drawn from *The Right Stuff* (1979).

A young man might go into military flight training believing   1
that he was entering some sort of technical school in which he
was simply going to acquire a certain set of skills. Instead, he
found himself all at once enclosed in a fraternity. And in this fraternity, even though it was military, men were not rated by their
outward rank as ensigns, lieutenants, commanders, or whatever.
No, herein the world was divided into those who had it and
those who did not. This quality, this *it*, was never named, however, nor was it talked about in any way.

As to just what this ineffable quality was . . . well, it obvi-   2
ously involved bravery. But it was not bravery in the simple sense
of being willing to risk your life. The idea seemed to be that any
fool could do that, if that was all that was required, just as any
fool could throw away his life in the process. No, the idea here
(in the all-enclosing fraternity) seemed to be that a man should
have the ability to go up in a hurtling piece of machinery and put
his hide on the line and then have the moxie, the reflexes, the experience, the coolness, to pull it back in the last yawning moment—and then to go up again *the next day,* and the next day,

and every next day, even if the series should prove infinite—and, ultimately, in its best expression, do so in a cause that means something to thousands, to a people, a nation, to humanity, to God. Nor was there *a test* to show whether or not a pilot had this righteous quality. There was, instead, a seemingly infinite series of tests. A career in flying was like climbing one of those ancient Babylonian pyramids made up of a dizzy progression of steps and ledges, a ziggurat, a pyramid extraordinarily high and steep; and the idea was to prove at every foot of the way up that pyramid that you were one of the elected and anointed ones who had *the right stuff* and could move higher and higher and even— ultimately, God willing, one day—that you might be able to join that special few at the very top, that elite who had the capacity to bring tears to men's eyes, the very Brotherhood of the Right Stuff itself.

None of this was to be mentioned, and yet it was acted out in a way that a young man could not fail to understand. When a new flight (i.e., a class) of trainees arrived at Pensacola, they were brought into an auditorium for a little lecture. An officer would tell them: "Take a look at the man on either side of you." Quite a few actually swiveled their heads this way and that, in the interest of appearing diligent. Then the officer would say: "One of the three of you is not going to make it!"—meaning, not get his wings. That was the opening theme, the *motif* of primary training. We already know that one-third of you do not have the right stuff—it only remains to find out who.

Furthermore, that was the way it turned out. At every level in one's progress up that staggeringly high pyramid, the world was once more divided into those men who had the right stuff to continue the climb and those who had to be *left behind* in the most obvious way. Some were eliminated in the course of the opening classroom work, as either not smart enough or not hard-working enough, and were left behind. Then came the basic flight instruction, in single-engine, propeller-driven trainers, and a few more—even though the military tried to make this stage easy— were washed out and left behind. Then came more demanding levels, one after the other, formation flying, instrument flying, jet training, all-weather flying, gunnery, and at each level more were washed out and left behind. By this point easily a third of the original candidates had been, indeed, eliminated . . . from the ranks of those who might prove to have the right stuff.

In the Navy, in addition to the stages that Air Force trainees   5
went through, the neophyte always had waiting for him, out in
the ocean, a certain grim gray slab; namely, the deck of an aircraft
carrier; and with it perhaps the most difficult routine in military
flying, carrier landings. He was shown films about it, he heard
lectures about it, and he knew that carrier landings were haz-
ardous. He first practiced touching down on the shape of a flight
deck painted on an airfield. He was instructed to touch down and
gun right off. This was safe enough—the shape didn't move, at
least—but it could do terrible things to, let us say, the gyroscope
of the soul. *That shape!—it's so damned small!* And more candidates were washed out and left behind. Then came the day, without warning, when those who remained were sent out over the
ocean for the first of many days of reckoning with the slab. The
first day was always a clear day with little wind and a calm sea.
The carrier was so steady that it seemed, from up there in the air,
to be resting on pilings, and the candidate usually made his first
carrier landing successfully, with relief and even *élan*. Many
young candidates looked like terrific aviators up to that very
point—and it was not until they were actually standing on the
carrier deck that they first began to wonder if they had the proper
stuff, after all. In the training film the flight deck was a grand
piece of gray geometry, perilous, to be sure, but an amazing abstract shape as one looks down upon it on the screen. And yet
once the newcomer's two feet were on it . . . *Geometry*—my God,
man, this is a . . . skillet! It *heaved,* it moved up and down underneath his feet, it pitched up, it pitched down, it rolled to port (this
great beast *rolled!*) and it rolled to starboard, as the ship moved
into the wind and, therefore, into the waves, and the wind kept
sweeping across, sixty feet up in the air out in the open sea,
and there were no railings whatsoever. This was a *skillet!*—a fry-
ing pan!—a short-order grill!—not gray but black, smeared with
skid marks from one end to the other and glistening with pools
of hydraulic fluid and the occasional jet-fuel slick, all of it still
hot, sticky, greasy, runny, virulent from God knows what trau-
mas—still ablaze!—consumed in detonations, explosions, flames,
combustion, roars, shrieks, whines, blasts, horrible shudders,
fracturing impacts, as little men in screaming red and yellow and
purple and green shirts with black Mickey Mouse helmets over
their ears skittered about on the surface as if for their very lives
(you've said it now!), hooking fighter planes onto the catapult

shuttles so that they can explode their afterburners and be slung off the deck in a red-mad fury with a *kaboom!* that pounds through the entire deck—a procedure that seems absolutely controlled, orderly, sublime, however, compared to what he is about to watch as aircraft return to the ship for what is known in the engineering stoicisms of the military as "recovery and arrest." To say that an F–4 was coming back onto this heaving barbecue from out of the sky at a speed of 135 knots . . . that might have been the truth in the training lecture, but it did not begin to get across the idea of what the newcomer saw from the deck itself, because it created the notion that perhaps the plane was gliding in. On the deck one knew differently! As the aircraft came closer and the carrier heaved on into the waves and the plane's speed did not diminish and the deck did not grow steady—indeed, it pitched up and down five or ten feet per greasy heave—one experienced a neural alarm that no lecture could have prepared him for: This is not an *airplane* coming toward me, it is a brick with some poor sonofabitch riding it (*someone much like myself!*), and it is not *gliding,* it is *falling,* a thirty-thousand-pound brick, headed not for a stripe on the deck but for *me*—and with a horrible *smash!* it hits the skillet, and with a blur of momentum as big as a freight train's it hurtles toward the far end of the deck—another blinding storm!—another roar as the pilot pushes the throttle up to full military power and another smear of rubber screams out over the skillet—and this is nominal!—quite okay!—for a wire stretched across the deck has grabbed the hook on the end of the plane as it hit the deck tail down, and the smash was the rest of the fifteen-ton brute slamming onto the deck, as it tripped up, so that it is now straining against the wire at full throttle, in case it hadn't held and the plane had "boltered" off the end of the deck and had to struggle up into the air again. And already the Mickey Mouse helmets are running toward the fiery monster. . . .

And the candidate, looking on, begins to *feel* that great heaving sun-blazing deathboard of a deck wallowing in his own vestibular system—and suddenly he finds himself backed up against his own limits. He ends up going to the flight surgeon with so-called conversion symptoms. Overnight he develops blurred vision or numbness in his hands and feet or sinusitis so severe that he cannot tolerate changes in altitude. On one level the symptom is real. He really cannot see too well or use his fingers or stand the pain. But somewhere in his subconscious he knows it is a plea and a begoff; he shows not the slightest concern (the flight surgeon notes) that the condition might be permanent and affect him in whatever life awaits him outside the arena of the right stuff.

Those who remained, those who qualified for carrier duty— and even more so those who later on qualified for *night* carrier duty began to feel a bit like Gideon's warriors. *So many have been left behind!* The young warriors were now treated to a deathly sweet and quite unmentionable sight. They could gaze at length upon the crushed and wilted pariahs who had washed out. They could inspect those who did not have that righteous stuff.

The military did not have very merciful instincts. Rather than packing up these poor souls and sending them home, the Navy, like the Air Force and the Marines, would try to make use of them in some other role, such as flight controller. So the washout has to keep taking classes with the rest of his group, even though he can no longer touch an airplane. He sits there in the classes staring at sheets of paper with cataracts of sheer human mortification over his eyes while the rest steal looks at him . . . this man reduced to an ant, this untouchable, this poor sonofabitch. And in what test had he been found wanting? Why, it seemed to be nothing less than *manhood* itself. Naturally, this was never mentioned, either. Yet there it was. *Manliness, manhood, manly courage* . . . there was something ancient, primordial, irresistible about the challenge of this stuff, no matter what a sophisticated and rational age one might think he lived in.

Perhaps because it could not be talked about, the subject began to take on superstitious and even mystical outlines. A man either had it or he didn't! There was no such thing as having *most* of it. Moreover, it could blow at any seam. One day a man would be ascending the pyramid at a terrific clip, and the next— bingo!—he would reach his own limits in the most unexpected way. Conrad and Schirra met an Air Force pilot who had had a great pal at Tyndall Air Force Base in Florida. This man had been the budding ace of the training class; he had flown the hottest fighter-style trainer, the T–38, like a dream; and then he began the routine step of being checked out in the T–33. The T–33 was not nearly as hot an aircraft as the T–38; it was essentially the old P–80 jet fighter. It had an exceedingly small cockpit. The pilot could barely move his shoulders. It was the sort of airplane of which everybody said, "You don't get into it, you *wear* it." Once inside a T–33 cockpit this man, this budding ace, developed claustrophobia of the most paralyzing sort. He tried everything to overcome it. He even went to a psychiatrist, which was a serious mistake for a military officer if his superiors learned of it. But nothing worked. He was shifted over to flying jet transports, such as the C–135. Very demanding and necessary aircraft they were, too, and he was still spoken of as an excellent pilot. But as everyone knew—and, again, it was never explained in so many words—only those who were assigned to fighter squadrons, the "fighter jocks," as they called each other with a self-satisfied irony, remained in the true fraternity. Those assigned to transports were not humiliated like washouts—*somebody* had to fly those planes—nevertheless, they, too, had been *left behind* for lack of the right stuff.

Or a man could go for a routine physical one fine day, feeling like a million dollars, and be grounded for *fallen arches*. It happened!—just like that! (And try raising them.) Or for breaking his wrist and losing only *part* of its mobility. Or for a minor deterioration of eyesight, or for any of hundreds of reasons that would make no difference to a man in an ordinary occupation. As a result all fighter jocks began looking upon doctors as their natural enemies. Going to see a flight surgeon was a no-gain proposition; a pilot could only hold his own or lose in the doctor's office. To be grounded for a medical reason was no humiliation, looked at objectively. But it was a humiliation, nonetheless!—for it meant you no longer had that indefinable, unutterable, integral stuff. (It could blow at *any* seam.)

All the hot young fighter jocks began trying to test the limits themselves in a superstitious way. They were like believing Presbyterians of a century before who used to probe their own experience to see if they were truly among *the elect*. When a fighter pilot was in training, whether in the Navy or the Air Force, his superiors were continually spelling out strict rules for him, about the use of the aircraft and conduct in the sky. They repeatedly forbade so-called hot-dog stunts, such as outside loops, buzzing, flat-hatting, hedgehopping and flying under bridges. But somehow one got the message that the man who truly *had* it could ignore those rules—not that he should make a point of it, but that

he *could*—and that after all there was only one way to find out—
and that in some strange unofficial way, peeking through his fingers, his instructor halfway expected him to challenge all the
limits. They would give a lecture about how a pilot should never
fly without a good solid breakfast—eggs, bacon, toast, and so
forth—because if he tried to fly with his blood-sugar level too
low, it could impair his alertness. Naturally, the next day every
hot dog in the unit would get up and have a breakfast consisting
of one cup of black coffee and take off and go up into a vertical
climb until the weight of the ship exactly canceled out the upward thrust of the engine and his air speed was zero, and he
would hang there for one thick adrenal instant—and then fall
like a rock, until one of three things happened: he keeled over
nose first and regained his aerodynamics and all was well, he
went into a spin and fought his way out of it, or he went into a
spin and had to eject or crunch it, which was always supremely
possible.

Likewise, "hassling"—mock dogfighting—was strictly forbid-   12
den, and so naturally young fighter jocks could hardly wait to go
up in, say, a pair of F–100s and start the duel by making a pass
at each other at 800 miles an hour, the winner being the pilot
who could slip in behind the other one and get locked in on his
tail ("wax his tail"), and it was not uncommon for some eager
jock to try too tight an outside turn and have his engine flame
out, whereupon, unable to restart it, he has to eject . . . and he
shakes his fist at the victor as he floats down by parachute and
his million-dollar aircraft goes *kaboom!* on the palmetto grass or
the desert floor, and he starts thinking about how he can get together with the other guy back at the base in time for the two of
them to get their stories straight before the investigation: "I don't
know what happened, sir. I was pulling up after a target run, and
it just flamed out on me." Hassling was forbidden, and hassling
that led to the destruction of an aircraft was a serious court-
martial offense, and the man's superiors knew that the engine
hadn't *just flamed out,* but every unofficial impulse on the base
seemed to be saying: "Hell, we wouldn't give you a nickel for a
pilot who hasn't done some crazy rat-racing like that. It's all part
of the right stuff."

The other side of this impulse showed up in the reluctance of   13
the young jocks to admit it when they had maneuvered themselves into a bad corner they couldn't get out of. There were two

reasons why a fighter pilot hated to declare an emergency. First, it triggered a complex and very public chain of events at the field: all other incoming flights were held up, including many of one's comrades who were probably low on fuel; the fire trucks came trundling out to the runway like yellow toys (as seen from way up there), the better to illustrate one's hapless state; and the bureaucracy began to crank up the paper monster for the investigation that always followed. And second, to declare an emergency, one first had to reach that conclusion in his own mind, which to the young pilot was the same as saying: "A minute ago I still *had* it—now I need your help!" To have a bunch of young fighter pilots up in the air thinking this way used to drive flight controllers crazy. They would see a ship beginning to drift off the radar, and they couldn't rouse the pilot on the microphone for anything other than a few meaningless mumbles, and they would know he was probably out there with engine failure at a low altitude, trying to reignite by lowering his auxiliary generator rig, which had a little propeller that was supposed to spin in the slipstream like a child's pinwheel.

"Whiskey Kilo Two Eight, do you want to declare an emergency?"   14

This would rouse him!—to say: "Negative, negative, Whiskey Kilo Two Eight is not declaring an emergency."   15

Kaboom. Believers in the right stuff would rather crash and burn.   16

One fine day, after he had joined a fighter squadron, it would dawn on the young pilot exactly how the losers in the great fraternal competition were now being left behind. Which is to say, not by instructors or other superiors or by failures at prescribed levels of competence, but by death. At this point the essence of the enterprise would begin to dawn on him. Slowly, step by step, the ante had been raised until he was now involved in what was surely the grimmest and grandest gamble of manhood. Being a fighter pilot—for that matter, simply taking off in a single-engine jet fighter of the Century series, such as an F–102, or any of the military's other marvelous bricks with fins on them—presented a man, on a perfectly sunny day, with more ways to get himself killed than his wife and children could imagine in their wildest fears. If he was barreling down the runway at two hundred miles an hour, completing the takeoff run, and the board started light-   17 ing up red, should he (a) abort the takeoff (and try to wrestle with the monster, which was gorged with jet fuel, out in the sand beyond the end of the runway) or (b) eject (and hope that the goddamned human cannonball trick works at zero altitude and he doesn't shatter an elbow or a kneecap on the way out) or (c) continue the takeoff and deal with the problem aloft (knowing full well that the ship may be on fire and therefore seconds away from exploding)? He would have one second to sort out the options and act, and this kind of little workaday decision came up all the time. Occasionally a man would look coldly at the binary problem he was now confronting every day—Right Stuff/ Death—and decide it wasn't worth it and voluntarily shift over to transports or reconnaissance or whatever. And his comrades would wonder, for a day or so, what evil virus had invaded his soul . . . as they left him behind. More often, however, the reverse would happen. Some college graduate would enter Navy aviation through the Reserves, simply as an alternative to the Army draft, fully intending to return to civilian life, to some waiting profession or family business; would become involved in the obsessive business of ascending the ziggurat pyramid of flying; and, at the end of his enlistment, would astound everyone back home and very likely himself as well by signing up for another one. What on earth got into him? He couldn't explain it. After all, the very words for it had been amputated. A Navy study showed that two-thirds of the fighter pilots who were rated in the top rungs of their groups—i.e., the hottest young pilots—reenlisted when the time came, and practically all were college graduates. By this point, a young fighter jock was like the preacher in *Moby Dick* who climbs up into the pulpit on a rope ladder and then pulls the ladder up behind him; except the pilot could not use the words necessary to express the vital lessons. Civilian life, and even home and hearth, now seemed not only far away but far *below*, back down many levels of the pyramid of the right stuff.

A fighter pilot soon found he wanted to associate only with 18 other fighter pilots. Who else could understand the nature of the little proposition (right stuff/death) they were all dealing with? And what other subject could compare with it? It was riveting! To talk about it in so many words was forbidden, of course. The very words *death, danger, bravery, fear* were not to be uttered except in the occasional specific instance or for ironic effect. Nevertheless, the subject could be adumbrated in *code* or *by example*. Hence the endless evenings of pilots huddled together talking about flying. On these long and drunken evenings (the bane of their family life) certain theorems would be propounded and demonstrated—and all by *code* and *example*. One theorem was: There are no *accidents* and no fatal flaws in the machines; there are only pilots with the wrong stuff. (I.e., blind Fate can't kill me.) When Bud Jennings crashed and burned in the swamps at Jacksonville, the other pilots in Pete Conrad's squadron said: *How could he have been so stupid?* It turned out that Jennings had gone up in the SNJ with his cockpit canopy opened in a way that was expressly forbidden in the manual, and carbon monoxide had been sucked in from the exhaust, and he passed out and crashed. All agreed that Bud Jennings was a good guy and a good pilot, but his epitaph on the ziggurat was: *How could he have been so stupid?* This seemed shocking at first, but by the time Conrad had reached the end of that bad string at Pax River,[1] he was capable of his own corollary to the theorem: viz., no single factor ever killed a pilot; there was always a chain of mistakes. But what about Ted Whelan, who fell like a rock from 8,100 feet when his parachute failed? Well, the parachute was merely part of the chain: first, someone should have caught the structural defect that resulted in the hydraulic leak that triggered the emergency; second, Whelan did not check out his seat-parachute rig, and the drogue failed to separate the main parachute from the seat; but even after those two mistakes, Whelan had fifteen or twenty seconds, as he fell, to disengage himself from the seat and open the parachute manually. Why just stare at the scenery coming up to smack you in the face! And everyone nodded. (He failed—but I wouldn't have!) Once the theorem and the corollary were understood, the Navy's statistics about one in every four Navy aviators dying meant nothing. The figures were averages, and averages applied to those with average stuff.

A riveting subject, especially if it were one's own hide that was on the line. Every evening at bases all over America, there were military pilots huddled in officers clubs eagerly cutting the right

1. During the "bad string," ten of Conrad's close friends had been killed in accidents.

stuff up in coded slices so they could talk about it. What more compelling topic of conversation was there in the world? In the Air Force there were even pilots who would ask the tower for priority landing clearance so that they could make the beer call on time, at 4 P.M. sharp, at the Officers Club. They would come right out and state the reason. The drunken rambles began at four and sometimes went on for ten or twelve hours. Such conversations! They diced that righteous stuff up into little bits, bowed ironically to it, stumbled blindfolded around it, groped, lurched, belched, staggered, bawled, sang, roared, and feinted at it with self-deprecating humor. Nevertheless!—they never mentioned it by name. No, they used the approved codes, such as: "Like a jerk I got myself into a hell of a corner today." They told of how they "lucked out of it." To get across the extreme peril of his exploit, one would use certain oblique cues. He would say, "I looked over at Robinson"—who would be known to the listeners as a non-com who sometimes rode backseat to read radar—"and he wasn't talking any more, he was just staring at the radar, like this, giving it that *zombie* look. Then I *knew* I was in trouble!" Beautiful! Just right! For it would also be known to the listeners that the non-coms advised one another: "*Never* fly with a lieutenant. *Avoid* captains and majors. Hell, man, do yourself a favor: don't fly with anybody below colonel." Which in turn said: "Those young bucks shoot dice with death!" And yet once in the air the non-com had his own standards. He was determined to remain as outwardly cool as the pilot, so that when the pilot did something that truly petrified him, he would say nothing; instead, he would turn silent, catatonic, like a zombie. Perfect! *Zombie*. There you had it, compressed into a single word, all of the foregoing. I'm a hell of a pilot! I shoot dice with death! And now all you fellows know it! And I haven't spoken of that unspoken stuff even once!

The talking and drinking began at the beer call, and then the boys would break for dinner and come back afterward and get more wasted and more garrulous or else more quietly fried, drinking good cheap PX booze until 2 A.M. The night was young! Why not get the cars and go out for a little proficiency run? It seemed that every fighter jock thought himself an ace driver, and he would do anything to obtain a hot car, especially a sports car, and the drunker he was, the more convinced he would be about his driving skills, as if the right stuff, being indivisible, carried over into any enterprise whatsoever, under any conditions. A little proficiency run, boys! (There's only one way to find out!) And they would roar off in close formation from, say, Nellis Air Force Base, down Route 15, into Las Vegas, barreling down the highway, rat-racing, sometimes four abreast, jockeying for position, piling into the most listless curve in the desert flats as if they were trying to root each other out of the groove at the Rebel 500—and then bursting into downtown Las Vegas with a rude fraternal roar like the Hell's Angels—and the natives chalked it up to youth and drink and the bad element that the Air Force attracted. They knew nothing about the right stuff, of course.

KATHA POLLITT

The Smurfette Principle

Katha Pollitt, a poet and a featured essayist in *The Nation*, became particularly interested in the media's presentation of women when she began to hear her daughter talk about men and women in terms clearly not learned at home: "Suddenly it's like this little person is a radio station through which the culture is beaming itself." The following essay was published in *The New York Times Magazine* in 1991.

This Christmas, I finally caved in: I gave my 3-year-old daughter, Sophie, her very own cassette of "The Little Mermaid." Now, she, too, can sit transfixed by Ariel, the perky teen-ager with the curvy tail who trades her voice for a pair of shapely legs and a shot at marriage to a prince. ("On land it's much preferred for ladies not to say a word," sings the cynical sea witch, "and she who holds her tongue will get her man." Since she's the villain, we're not meant to notice that events prove her correct.)

Usually when parents give a child some item they find repellent, they plead helplessness before a juvenile filibuster. But "The Little Mermaid" was my idea. Ariel may look a lot like Barbie, and her adventure may be limited to romance and over with the wedding bells, but unlike, say, Cinderella or Sleeping Beauty, she's active, brave and determined, the heroine of her own life. She even rescues the prince. And that makes her a rare fish, indeed, in the world of preschool culture.

Take a look at the kids' section of your local video store. You'll find that features starring boys, and usually aimed at them, account for 9 out of 10 offerings. Clicking the television dial one recent week—admittedly not an encyclopedic study—I came across not a single network cartoon or puppet show starring a female. (Nickelodeon, the children's cable channel, has one of each.) Except for the crudity of the animation and the general air of witlessness and hype, I might as well have been back in my own 1950's childhood, nibbling Frosted Flakes in front of Daffy Duck, Bugs Bunny, Porky Pig and the rest of the all-male Warner Brothers lineup.

Contemporary shows are either essentially all-male, like "Garfield," or are organized on what I call the Smurfette principle: a group of male buddies will be accented by a lone female, stereotypically defined. In the worst cartoons—the ones that blend seamlessly into the animated cereal commercials—the female is usually a little-sister type, a bunny in a pink dress and hair ribbons who tags along with the adventurous bears and badgers. But the Smurfette principle rules the more carefully made shows, too. Thus, Kanga, the only female in "Winnie-the-Pooh," is a mother. Piggy, of "Muppet Babies," is a pint-size version of Miss Piggy, the camp glamour queen of the Muppet movies. April, of the wildly popular "Teen-Age Mutant Ninja Turtles," functions as a girl Friday to a quartet of male superheroes. The message is clear. Boys are the norm, girls the variation; boys are central, girls peripheral; boys are individuals, girls types. Boys define the group, its story and its code of values. Girls exist only in relation to boys.

Well, commercial television—what did I expect? The surprise is that public television, for all its superior intelligence, charm and commitment to worthy values, shortchanges preschool girls, too. Mister Rogers lives in a neighborhood populated mostly by middle-aged men like himself. "Shining Time Station" features a cartoon in which the male characters are train engines and the female characters are passenger cars. And then there's "Sesame Street." True, the human characters are neatly divided between the genders (and among the races, too, which is another rarity).

The film clips, moreover, are just about the only place on television in which you regularly see girls having fun together: practicing double Dutch, having a sleep-over. But the Muppets are the real stars of "Sesame Street," and the important ones—the ones with real personalities, who sing on the musical videos, whom kids identify with and cherish in dozens of licensed products—are *all* male. I know one little girl who was so outraged and heartbroken when she realized that even Big Bird—her last hope—was a boy that she hasn't watched the show since.

Well, there's always the library. Some of the best children's 6 books ever written have been about girls—Madeline, Frances the badger. It's even possible to find stories with funny, feminist messages, like "The Paper-bag Princess." (She rescues the prince from a dragon, but he's so ungrateful that she decides not to marry him, after all.) But books about girls are a subset in a field that includes a much larger subset of books about boys (12 of the 14 storybooks singled out for praise in last year's Christmas roundup in *Newsweek,* for instance) and books in which the sex of the child is theoretically unimportant—in which case it usually "happens to be" male. Dr. Seuss's books are less about individual characters than about language and imaginative freedom—but, somehow or other, only boys get to go on beyond Zebra or see marvels on Mulberry Street. Frog and Toad, Lowly Worm, Lyle the Crocodile, all *could* have been female. But they're not.

Do kids pick up on the sexism in children's culture? You bet. 7 Preschoolers are like medieval philosophers: the text—a book, a movie, a TV show—is more authoritative than the evidence of their own eyes. "Let's play weddings," says my little niece. We grownups roll our eyes, but face it: it's still the one scenario in which the girl is the central figure. "Women are *nurses,*" my friend Anna, a doctor, was informed by her then 4-year-old, Molly. Even my Sophie is beginning to notice the back-seat role played by girls in some of her favorite books. "Who's that?" she asks every time we reread "The Cat in the Hat." It's Sally, the timid little sister of the resourceful boy narrator. She wants Sally to matter, I think, and since Sally is really just a name and a hair ribbon, we have to say her name again and again.

The sexism in preschool culture deforms both boys and girls. 8 Little girls learn to split their consciousness, filtering their dreams and ambitions through boy characters while admiring the clothes of the princess. The more privileged and daring can dream of becoming exceptional women in a man's world—Smurfettes. The others are being taught to accept the more usual fate, which is to be a passenger car drawn through life by a masculine train engine. Boys, who are rarely confronted with stories in which males play only minor roles, learn a simpler lesson: girls just don't matter much.

How can it be that 25 years of feminist social changes have   9 made so little impression on preschool culture? Molly, now 6 and well aware that women can be doctors, has one theory: children's entertainment is mostly made by men. That's true, as it happens, and I'm sure it explains a lot. It's also true that, as a society, we don't seem to care much what goes on with kids, as long as they are reasonably quiet. Marshmallow cereal, junky toys, endless hours in front of the tube—a society that accepts all that is not going to get in a lather about a little gender stereotyping. It's easier to focus on the bright side. I had "Cinderella," Sophie has "The Little Mermaid"—that's progress, isn't it?

"We're working on it," Dulcy Singer, the executive producer   10 of "Sesame Street," told me when I raised the sensitive question of those all-male Muppets. After all, the show has only been on the air for a quarter of a century; these things take time. The trouble is, our preschoolers don't have time. My funny, clever, bold, adventurous daughter is forming her gender ideas right now. I do what I can to counteract the messages she gets from her entertainment, and so does her father—Sophie watches very little television. But I can see we have our work cut out for us. It sure would help if the bunnies took off their hair ribbons, and if half of the monsters were fuzzy, blue—and female.

JAN MORRIS

To Everest

Jan Morris, born James Morris, served in the British Army from 1943 to 1947, then became a reporter for *The Times* of London. In 1953 he accompanied Sir Edmund Hillary on an expedition to Mount Everest, climbing to the 22,000-foot level in order to be the first to report the news of the first successful attempt to reach the summit. Thereafter, he became an accomplished foreign correspondent and travel writer. In 1964, acting on a long-standing feeling that he "had been born into the wrong body," he began a course of hormone treatments and surgery that would eventually change him into a woman. "To Everest," a chapter from *Conundrum* (1974), gives us a picture of the type of masculinity Morris felt compelled to escape.

Though I resented my body, I did not dislike it. I rather admired it, as it happened. It might not be the body beautiful, but it was lean and sinewy, never ran to fat, and worked like a machine of quality, responding exuberantly to a touch of the throttle or a long haul home. Women, I think, never have quite this feeling about their bodies, and I shall never have it again. It is a male prerogative, and contributes no doubt to the male arrogance. In those days, though for that very reason I did not want it, still I recognized the merits of my physique, and had pleasure from its exercise.

I first felt its full power, as one might realize for the first time the potential of a run-in car, in 1953, when I was assigned by *The Times* to join the British expedition shortly to make the first ascent of Mount Everest. This was essentially a physical undertaking. The paper had exclusive rights to dispatches from the mountain, and I was to be the only correspondent with the team, my job being partly to see that dispatches from the expedition's leader got safely home to London, but chiefly to write dispatches of my own. The competition would be intense and very likely violent, communications were primitive to a degree, and the only way to do the job was to climb fairly high up the mountain myself and periodically, to put a complex operation simply, run down it again with the news. It was not particularly to my credit that I was given the assignment—at an agile twenty-six I was patently better suited for it than most of my colleagues at Printing House Square. I took exercise daily (as I still do), did not smoke (and still don't), and though excessively fond of wine, seldom drank spirits, not much liking the taste of them.

I was also, being some years out of the 9th Lancers, furiously keen.[1] There is something about the newspaper life, however

1. Morris soldiered with this British regiment from 1943 to 1947, rising to the rank of second lieutenant. Among these highly professional soldiers, shows of enthusiasm, or "keenness," were considered bad form.

specious its values and ridiculous its antics, that brings out the zest in its practitioners. It may be nonsense, but it is undeniably fun. I was not especially anxious to achieve fame in the trade, for I already felt instinctively that it would not be my life's occupation, but even so I would have stooped to almost any skulduggery to achieve what was, self-consciously even then, quaintly called a scoop. The news from Everest was to be mine, and anyone who tried to steal it from me should look out for trouble.

In such a mood, at such an age, at the peak of a young man's   4
physical condition, I found myself in May, 1953, high on the flank of the world's greatest mountain.

Let me try to describe the sensation for my readers, as it seems   5
to me today—and especially for my women readers, who are unlikely I now see to have experienced such a conjunction of energies.

Imagine first the setting. This is theatrically changeable. In the   6
morning it is like living, reduced to minuscule proportions, in a bowl of broken ice cubes in a sunny garden. Somewhere over the rim, one assumes, there are green trees, fields, and flowers; within the bowl everything is a brilliant white and blue. It is silent in there. The mountain walls deaden everything and cushion the hours in a disciplinary hush. The only noise is a drip of water sometimes, the howl of a falling boulder or the rumble of a distant avalanche. The sky above is a savage blue, the sun glares mercilessly off the snow and ice, blistering one's lips, dazzling one's eyes, and filling that mountain declivity with its substance.

In the afternoon everything changes. Then the sky scowls   7
down, high snow-clouds billow in from Tibet, a restless cruel wind blows up, and before long the snow is falling in slanted parallel across the landscape, blotting out sky, ridges, and all, and making you feel that your ice-bowl has been put back into the refrigerator. It is terribly cold. The afternoon is filled with sounds, the rush of wind, the flapping of tent-canvas, the squeak and creak of guy-ropes; and as the evening draws on the snow piles up around your tent, half burying it infinitesimally in the hulk of Everest, as though you have been prematurely incarcerated, or perhaps trapped in a sunken submarine—for you can see the line of snow slowly rising through the nylon walls of the tent, like water rising to submerge you.

But imagine now the young man's condition. First, he is con-   8
stant against this inconstant background. His body is running

not in gusts and squalls, but at a steady high speed. He actually tingles with strength and energy, as though sparks might fly from his skin in the dark. Nothing sags in him. His body has no spare weight upon it, only muscles made supple by exercise. When, in the bright Himalayan morning, he emerges from his tent to make the long trek down the mountain to the Khumbu glacier below, it is as though he could leap down there in gigantic strides, singing as he goes. And when, the same evening perhaps, he labors up again through the driving snow, it is not a misery but a challenge to him, something to be outfaced, something actually to be enjoyed, as the deep snow drags at his feet, the water trickles down the back of his neck, and his face thickens with cold, ice, and wind.

There is no hardship to it, for it is not imposed upon him. He   9 is the master. He feels that anything is possible to him, and that his relative position to events will always remain the same. He does not have to wonder what his form will be tomorrow, for it will be the same as it is today. His mind, like his body, is tuned to the job, and will not splutter or falter. It is this feeling of unfluctuating control, I think, that women cannot share, and it springs of course not from the intellect or the personality, nor even so much from upbringing, but specifically from the body. The male body may be ungenerous, even uncreative in the deepest kind, but when it is working properly it is a marvelous thing to inhabit. I admit it in retrospect more than I did at the time, and I look back to those moments of supreme male fitness as one remembers champagne or a morning swim. Nothing could beat me, I knew for sure; and nothing did.

I think for sheer exuberance the best day of my life was my   10 last on Everest. The mountain had been climbed, and I had already begun my race down the glacier towards Katmandu, leaving the expedition to pack its gear behind me. By a combination of cunning and ingenuity I had already sent a coded message through an Indian Army radio transmitter at Namche Bazar, twenty miles south of Everest, its operators being unaware of its meaning; but I did not know if it had reached London safely, so I was myself hastening back to Katmandu and the cable office with my own final dispatch. How brilliant I felt, as with a couple of Sherpa porters I bounded down the glacial moraine towards the green below! I was brilliant with the success of my friends on the mountain, I was brilliant with my knowledge of the event, brilliant with muscular tautness, brilliant with conceit, brilliant with awareness of the subterfuge, amounting very nearly to dishonesty, by which I hoped to have deceived my competitors and scooped the world. All those weeks at high altitude had suited me, too, and had given me a kind of heightened fervor, as though my brain had been quickened by drugs to keep pace with my body. I laughed and sang all the way down the glacier, and when next morning I heard from the radio that my news had reached London providentially on the eve of Queen Elizabeth's coronation, I felt as though I had been crowned myself.

11   I never mind the swagger of young men. It is their right to swank, and I know the sensation!

12   Once more on Everest I was the outsider—formally this time, as well as tacitly. None of the climbers would have guessed, I am sure, how irrevocably distinct I felt from them; but they were aware that I was not a climber, and had been attached to the expedition only to watch. At first I was supposed to provide my own victuals and equipment, but it seemed rather silly to maintain such segregation twenty thousand feet above nowhere, so I soon pooled my resources with theirs, and pitched my tent among them.

13   On Everest, nevertheless, I realized more explicitly some truths about myself. Though I was as fit as most of those men, I responded to different drives. I would have suffered almost anything to get those dispatches safely back to London, but I did not share the mountaineers' burning urge to see that mountain climbed. Perhaps it was too abstract an objective for me—certainly I was not animated by any respect for inviolate nature, which I have always disliked, preferring like George Leigh-Mallory a blend of tame and wild. I was pleased when they did climb Everest, but chiefly for a less than elevated reason—patriotic pride, which I knew to be unworthy of their efforts, but which I could not suppress.

14   I well understood the masochistic relish of challenge which impelled them, and which stimulated me too, but the blankness of the achievement depressed me. One of the older Everesters, H. W. Tilman, once quoted G. K. Chesterton to illustrate the urge of alpinism: "I think the immense act has something about it human and excusable; and when I endeavor to analyze the reason

of this feeling I find it to lie, not in the fact that the thing was big or bold or successful, but in the fact that the thing was perfectly useless to everybody, including the person who did it." Leigh-Mallory presumably meant much the same, when he talked of climbing Everest simply "because it was there." But this elusive prize, this snatching at air, this nothingness, left me dissatisfied, as I think it would leave most women. Nothing had been discovered, nothing made, nothing improved.

I have always discounted the beauty of clouds, because their airy impermanence seems to me to disqualify them from the truest beauty, just as I have never responded to kinetic art, and love the shifting light of nature only because it reveals new shapes and meaning in the solids down below. Nor do I like sea views, unless there is land to be seen beyond them. A similar distrust of the ephemeral or the un-finite weakened my response to the triumph of Everest in 1953. It was a grand adventure, I knew, and my part in relaying its excitements to the world was to transform my professional life, and dog me ever after; yet even now I dislike that emptiness at its climax, that perfect uselessness, and feel in a slightly ashamed and ungrateful way that it was really all rather absurd.

For it was almost like a military expedition—the colonel in command, not so long from Montgomery's staff, the little army of porters who wound their way bent-back with their loads over the hills from Katmandu, the meticulously packed and listed stores, the briefings, the air of ordered determination. It was a superbly successful expedition—nobody killed, nobody disgraced—and looking back upon it now I see its cohesion as a specifically male accomplishment. Again constancy was the key. Men more than women respond to the team spirit, and this is partly because, if they are of an age, of a kind, and in a similar condition, they work together far more like a mechanism. Elations and despondencies are not so likely to distract them. Since their pace is more regular, all can more easily keep to it. They are distinctly more rhythm than melody.

In 1953 the rhythm was steadier than it might be now, for it was conscious then as well as constitutional. Stiff upper lip and fair play were integral to the British masculine ethos, and shame was a powerful impulse towards achievement. Social empathy, too, strongly reinforced the sense of maleness. The functional efficiency of class I had already discovered in the Army, and it was the same on Everest. Hunt's climbers were men of the officer class, as they would then have been called, and they were bound by common tastes and values. They spoke the same language, shared the same kind of past, enjoyed the same pleasures. Three of them had been to the same school. In a social sense they formed a kind of club; in an imperial sense, and this was almost the last of the imperial adventures, they were a company of sahibs attended by their multitudinous servants.

One could not, I think, apply these categories to women of equal intelligence in similar circumstances, and less and less can one now apply them to men. Class has lost its binding function; patriotism has lost its elevating force; young men are no longer ashamed of weaknesses; the stiff upper lip is no longer an ideal, only a music hall sally. The barrier between the genders is flimsier now, and no expedition will ever again go to the Himalayas so thoroughly masculine as Hunt's. It embarrasses me rather to have to admit that from that day to this, none has gone there more successfully. 18

I need not belabor my sense of alienation from this formidable team. I liked most of its members very much, and have remained friends with some to this day, but my sense of detachment was extreme, and though I shamelessly accepted their help throughout the adventure, still I was always at pains to cherish my separateness. I hated to think of myself as one of them, and when in England we were asked to sign menus, maps, or autograph books, I used carefully to sign myself James Morris of *The Times*—until the climbers, fancying I fear altogether different motives in me, asked me not to. At the same time a wayward self-consciousness—for I was a child of the age, too— compelled me to keep up male appearances, perhaps as much for my own persuasion as for anyone else's. I even overdid it rather. I grew a beard, and when at the end of the expedition I walked into the communications room at the British Embassy in Katmandu with my tin mug jangling from the belt of my trousers, the wireless operator asked acidly if I *had* to look so jungly. He did not know how cruelly the jibe hurt, for in a few words it cut this way and that through several skins of self-protection. 19

Everest taught me new meanings of maleness, and emphasized once more my own inner dichotomy. Yet paradoxically my most evocative memory of the experience haunts me with a truth of an 20 altogether different kind. Often when there was a lull on the mountain I would go down the glacier and wander among the moraines. Sometimes I went south, towards the distant Buddhist temple at Thyangboehe where the deodars shaded the green turf, and the bells, gongs, and trumpets of the monks sounded from their shambled refectory. Sometimes I clambered into the snows of the north, towards the great wall of the Lho La, over whose ominous white ridge stood the peaks of Tibet. I vaguely hoped to catch a glimpse of an abominable snowman, and I was looking too for traces of the lemurs and mountain hares which sometimes, I had been told, penetrated those high deserts.

I saw no animals ever. What I found instead was a man. I saw   21
him first in the extreme distance, across an absolutely blank snowfield at about nineteen thousand feet, to which I had climbed from the glacier below for the sake of the view. At first I was frightened, for I could not make out what he was—only a small black swaying speck, indescribably alone in the desolation. As he came closer I saw that he could only be human, so I plunged through the loose snow to meet him, and presently, there near the top of the world, thousands of feet and many miles above the trees, the streams, or human habitation, we met face to face. It was the strangest encounter of my life.

He was a holy man, wandering in the mountains, I suppose,   22
for wandering's sake. His brown, crinkled, squashed-up face looked back at me expressionless from beneath a yellow hood, and found it seemed nothing strange in my presence there. He wore a long yellow cloak and hide boots, and from his waist there hung a spoon and a cloth satchel. He carried nothing else, and he wore no gloves. I greeted him as best I could, but he did not answer, only smiling at me distantly and without surprise. Perhaps he was in a trance. I offered him a piece of chocolate, but he did not take it, simply standing there before me, slightly smiling, almost as though he were made of ice himself. Presently we parted, and without a word he continued on his unfaltering journey, apparently making for Tibet without visible means of survival, and moving with a proud, gliding, and effortless motion that seemed inexorable. He did not appear to move fast, but when I looked around he had almost disappeared, and was no more than that small black speck again, inexplicably moving over the snows.

I envied him his insouciant speed, and wondered if he too felt   23
that tingling of the body, that sense of mastery, which had so
deepened my sense of duality upon the slopes of Everest. But the
more I thought about it, the more clearly I realized that he had
no body at all.

NOEL PERRIN

The Androgynous Man

Noel Perrin teaches English and environmental studies at Dart-
mouth College. He is also a farmer, and many of his published essays are about rural life. "The Androgynous Man" appeared in
The New York Times in 1984.

The summer I was 16, I took a train from New York to   1
Steamboat Springs, Colo., where I was going to be assistant
horse wrangler at a camp. The trip took three days, and since I
was much too shy to talk to strangers, I had quite a lot of time
for reading. I read all of *Gone With the Wind*. I read all the interesting articles in a couple of magazines I had, and then I went
back and read all the dull stuff. I also took all the quizzes, a thing
of which magazines were even fuller then than now.

The one that held my undivided attention was called "How   2
Masculine/Feminine Are You?" It consisted of a large number of
inkblots. The reader was supposed to decide which of four objects each blot most resembled. The choices might be a cloud, a
steam engine, a caterpillar and a sofa.

When I finished the test, I was shocked to find that I was   3
barely masculine at all. On a scale of 1 to 10, I was about 1.2.
Me, the horse wrangler? (And not just wrangler, either. That
summer, I had to skin a couple of horses that died—the camp
owner wanted the hides.)

The results of that test were so terrifying to me that for the   4
first time in my life I did a piece of original analysis. Having unlimited time on the train, I looked at the "masculine" answers
over and over, trying to find what it was that distinguished real

men from people like me—and eventually I discovered two very simple patterns. It was "masculine" to think the blots looked like man-made objects, and "feminine" to think they looked like natural objects. It was masculine to think they looked like things capable of causing harm, and feminine to think of innocent things.

Even at 16, I had the sense to see that the compilers of the test   5 were using rather limited criteria—maleness and femaleness are both more complicated than *that*—and I breathed a huge sigh of relief. I wasn't necessarily a wimp, after all.

That the test did reveal something other than the superficial-   6 ity of its makers I realized only many years later. What it revealed was that there is a large class of men and women both, to which I belong, who are essentially androgynous. That doesn't mean we're gay, or low in the appropriate hormones, or uncomfortable performing the jobs traditionally assigned our sexes. (A few years after that summer, I was leading troops in combat and, unfashionable as it now is to admit this, having a very good time. War is exciting. What a pity the 20th century went and spoiled it with high-tech weapons.)

What it does mean to be spiritually androgynous is a kind of   7 freedom. Men who are all-male, or he-man, or 100 percent red-blooded Americans, have a little biological set that causes them to be attracted to physical power, and probably also to dominance. Maybe even to watching football. I don't say this to criticize them. Completely masculine men are quite often wonderful people: good husbands, good (though sometimes overwhelming) fathers, good members of society. Furthermore, they are often so unself-consciously at ease in the world that other men seek to imitate them. They just aren't as free as us androgynes. They pretty nearly have to be what they are; we have a range of choices open.

The sad part is that many of us never discover that. Men who   8 are not 100 percent red-blooded Americans—say, those who are only 75 percent red-blooded—often fail to notice their freedom. They are too busy trying to copy the he-men ever to realize that men, like women, come in a wide variety of acceptable types. Why this frantic imitation? My answer is mere speculation, but not casual. I have speculated on this for a long time.

Partly they're just envious of the he-man's unconscious ease.   9 Mostly they're terrified of finding that there may be something wrong with them deep down, some weakness at the heart. To avoid discovering that, they spend their lives acting out the role that the he-man naturally lives. Sad.

One thing that men owe to the women's movement is that this kind of failure is less common than it used to be. In releasing themselves from the single ideal of the dependent woman, women have more or less incidentally released a lot of men from the single ideal of the dominant male. The one mistake the feminists have made, I think, is in supposing that *all* men need this release, or that the world would be a better place if all men achieved it. It wouldn't. It would just be duller.   10

So far I have been pretty vague about just what the freedom of the androgynous man is. Obviously it varies with the case. In the case I know best, my own, I can be quite specific. It has freed me most as a parent. I am, among other things, a fairly good natural mother. I like the nurturing role. It makes me feel good to see a child eat—and it turns me to mush to see a 4-year-old holding a glass with both small hands, in order to drink. I even enjoyed sewing patches on the knees of my daughter Amy's Dr. Dentons when she was at the crawling stage. All that pleasure I would have lost if I had made myself stick to the notion of the paternal role that I started with.   11

Or take a smaller and rather ridiculous example. I feel free to kiss cats. Until recently it never occurred to me that I would want to, though my daughters have been doing it all their lives. But my elder daughter is now 22, and in London. Of course, I get to look after her cat while she is gone. He's a big, handsome farm cat named Petrushka, very unsentimental, though used from kittenhood to being kissed on the top of the head by Elizabeth. I've gotten very fond of him (he's the adventurous kind of cat who likes to climb hills with you), and one night I simply felt like kissing him on the top of the head, and did. Why did no one tell me sooner how silky cat fur is?   12

Then there's my relation to cars. I am completely unembarrassed by my inability to diagnose even minor problems in whatever object I happen to be driving, and don't have to make some insider's remark to mechanics to try to establish that I, too, am a "Man With His Machine."   13

The same ease extends to household maintenance. I do it, of course. Service people are expensive. But for the last decade my   14 house had functioned better than it used to because I've had the aid of a volume called "Home Repairs Any Woman Can Do," which is pitched just right for people at my technical level. As a youth, I'd as soon have touched such a book as I would have become a transvestite. Even though common sense says there is really nothing sexual whatsoever about fixing sinks.

Or take public emotion. All my life I have easily been moved   15
by certain kinds of voices. The actress Siobhan McKenna's, to take a notable case. Give her an emotional scene in a play, and within 10 words my eyes are full of tears. In boyhood, my great dread was that someone might notice. I struggled manfully, you might say, to suppress this weakness. Now, of course, I don't see it as a weakness at all, but as a kind of fulfillment. I even suspect that the true he-men feel the same way, or one kind of them does, at least, and it's only the poor imitators who have to struggle to repress themselves.

Let me come back to the inkblots, with their assumption that   16
masculine equates with machinery and science, and feminine with art and nature. I have no idea whether the right pronoun for God is He, She, or It. But this I'm pretty sure of. If God could somehow be induced to take that test, God would not come out macho, and not feminismo, either, but right in the middle. Fellow androgynes, it's a nice thought.

JoAnn Wypijewski

A Boy's Life

Before JoAnn Wypijewski struck out on her own as a freelance writer, she spent two decades at *The Nation*, beginning as a copyeditor and working her way up to more creative work. After the 1998 murder of Matthew Shepard, a homosexual student at the University of Wyoming, she traveled to Laramie to study the killers. Those who want to read the full version of her long report can find it in the September 1999 issue of *Harper's Magazine*.

From the beginning there was something too awfully iconic   1
about the case. Matthew Shepard—young, small, gay, a college boy in the cowboy town of Laramie, Wyoming, a kid who, his

father says, didn't know how to make a fist until he was thirteen—lured out of a bar by two "rednecks" ("trailer trash," "drop-outs," every tabloid term has been applied), hijacked to a lonely spot outside of town, strung up like a scarecrow on a buck fence, bludgeoned beyond recognition, and left to die without his shoes, his ring, his wallet, or the $20 inside it. With that mix of real and fanciful detail, it has been called a trophy killing, a hate crime, a sacrifice. Press crews who had never before and have not since lingered over gruesome murders of homosexuals came out in force, reporting their brush with a bigotry so poisonous it could scarcely be imagined. County Attorney Cal Rerucha says death by injection is the just response. At the site where Shepard was murdered, in a field of prairie grass and sagebrush within eyeshot of suburban houses, a cross has been laid out in pink limestone rocks. In crotches of the killing fence, two stones have been placed; one bears the word "love"; the other, "forgive." The poignancy of those messages has been transmitted out and beyond via television; it is somewhat diminished if one knows that the stones were put there by a journalist, whose article about the murder for *Vanity Fair* was called "The Crucifixion of Matthew Shepard."

Torture is more easily imagined when masked in iconography 2 but no better understood. Perhaps it all will become clear in October, when one of the accused, Aaron McKinney, goes on trial for kidnapping, aggravated robbery, and capital murder (his companion, Russell Henderson, pled guilty on April 5 and avoided death with two consecutive life terms), but it seems unlikely. "The story" passed into myth even before the trials had been set, and at this point fact, rumor, politics, protective cover, and jailhouse braggadocio are so entangled that the truth may be elusive even to the protagonists.

What is known, though somehow elided, is that in the most 3 literal definition of the word, Matthew Shepard was not crucified. His hands were not outstretched, as has been suggested by all manner of media since October 7, 1998, when the twenty-one-year-old University of Wyoming student was discovered near death, but rather tied behind him as if in handcuffs, lashed to a pole four inches off the ground. His head propped on the lowest fence rail, his legs extending out to the east, he was lying almost flat on his back when Deputy Reggie Fluty of the Albany County Sheriff's Department found him at 6:22 P.M.,

eighteen hours, it's believed, after he was assaulted. It was Shepard's diminutive aspect—Fluty thought he was thirteen—and the
horrid condition of his face and head, mangled by eighteen
blows from a three-pound Smith & Wesson .357 magnum, that
most compelled her attention.

Shepard had encountered McKinney and Henderson, both   4
also twenty-one, at the Fireside Bar on October 6. They exchanged words that no one heard, then left the bar and got into
a truck belonging to McKinney's father. There Shepard was
robbed and hit repeatedly. Out by the fence came the fatal beating. Shepard must have been kicked too, because he was bruised
between his legs and elsewhere. Amid the blows he cried, "Please
don't." He was left alive but unconscious, as McKinney and
Henderson headed for an address they'd got out of him. En route
they ran into two local punks out puncturing tires, Emiliano
Morales and Jeremy Herrera, and started a fight. McKinney
cracked Morales's head open with the same gun he'd used on
Shepard, coating the weapon with still more blood. Herrera then
whacked McKinney's head with a stick. Police arrived, grabbed
Henderson (he and McKinney had run in different directions),
and found the truck, the gun, Shepard's shoes and credit card.
Police wouldn't put the crimes together until later, so Henderson
was cited for interference with a peace officer and released. Henderson then drove to Cheyenne with his girlfriend, Chasity
Pasley, and McKinney's girlfriend, Kristen LeAnn Price (both
later charged as accessories after the fact), to dispose of his
bloody clothes. McKinney, dazed from the gash in his head,
stayed home in bed, and Price hid Shepard's wallet in the dirty
diaper of her and McKinney's infant son, Cameron. Six days
later, on October 12, Shepard died.

Those are the facts as disclosed by court records and McKin-   5
ney's confession. (He has pleaded not guilty.) In response, the
Equality State—which enfranchised women long before anyplace else, which struck sodomy laws from the books in 1977—
has disowned McKinney and Henderson as monsters. So has the
rest of the country.

And yet McKinney and Henderson appear to be young men of   6
common prejudices, far more devastatingly human than is comfortable to consider. They acquired the gun a few days before the
murder in a trade for $100 in methamphetamine—crank, speed,

crystal meth—the drug of choice among white rural youth, cheaper than cocaine and more long-lasting, more relentless in its accelerating effects, more widely used in Wyoming, per capita, than in any state in the country. McKinney, says the friend who traded him for it, desired the gun for its badass beauty—eight-inch barrel, fine tooling, "the Dirty Harry thing." The trade occurred while these three fellows and their girlfriends were on a meth binge. Before it was over they would smoke or snort maybe $2,000 worth of the drug. By the time they met Matthew Shepard, says the friend, who saw them that day, Mc-Kinney and Henderson were on the fifth day of that binge. They had not slept, he says, since before October 2, payday, when the partying had begun.

Those unreported facts—to the extent that anything can be factually determined in Laramie these days, with everyone involved in the case under a gag order—may tell more about the crime, more about the everyday life of hate and hurt and heterosexual culture than all the quasi-religious characterizations of Matthew's passion, death, and resurrection as patron saint of hate-crime legislation. It's just possible that Matthew Shepard didn't die because he was gay; he died because Aaron McKinney and Russell Henderson are straight.   7

    "If you're telling your feelings, you're kind of a wuss." Brent Jones, a heterosexual who went to high school with McKinney and Henderson, was guiding me through the psychic terrain of a boy's life.   8

    "So what do you do when things hurt?"   9

    "That's why God created whiskey, don't you think? You get drunker than a pig and hope it drains away—or you go home and cry."   10

    "Is that true for most guys, do you think?"   11

    "Yeah, pretty much."   12

    "So secretly you're all wusses, and you know you're wusses, but you can't let anyone know, even though you all know you know."   13

    "You could say that."   14

    "Can you talk to girls about this stuff?"   15

    "Unless you know this is the one—like, you're going to get married, and then you're in so deep you can't help yourself—but   16

*if not, if you think she might break up with you, then no, be-
cause she might tell someone, and then it gets around, and then
everyone thinks you're a wuss. And you don't want people to
think you're a wuss, unless you are a wuss, and then you know
you're a wuss, and then it doesn't matter."*

Among the weighty files on the proceedings against McKin-   17
ney and Henderson in the Albany County Courthouse is a curious reference. The state had charged, as an "aggravating factor"
in the murder, that "the defendant[s] knew or should have
known that the victim was suffering from a physical or mental
disability." The court threw this out; Judge Jeffrey Donnell, who
presided over Henderson's case, told me he assumed it referred
to Shepard's size (five foot two, 105 pounds) but was legally irrelevant whatever its intent. In a sense, it is sociologically irrelevant as well whether the prosecution regarded Shepard as
crippled more by sexuality or size, since by either measure he
was, in the vernacular of Laramie's straight youth, a wuss.

Wussitude haunts a boy's every move. It must have haunted   18
Aaron McKinney most of his life. McKinney, too, is a little
thing—not as little as Shepard, but at about five foot six, 145
pounds, he doesn't cut a formidable figure. George Markle, who
roomed with him after they both dropped out of high school, describes McKinney as having "tiny arms, a tiny, tiny chest, no definition in his body." He affected a gangsta style—droopy jeans,
baggy shirt, Raiders jacket, gold chains, gold on all his fingers.
He'd ape hip-hop street talk, but "he couldn't get it going if he
tried." His nickname was Dopey, both for his oversized ears and
for his reputation as a serious drug dealer and user. His shoulder
bears a tattoo of the Disney character pouring a giant can of beer
on his mother's grave, an appropriation of a common rapper's
homage to a fallen brother: "Pour a forty ounce on my homey's
grave."

The prosecution contends that Shepard was lured out of the   19
bar as if on a sexual promise. County public defender Wyatt
Skaggs says that neither Henderson nor McKinney ever asserted
that they came on to Shepard. And in his confession, McKinney
said Shepard "did not hit on or make advances toward" him and
Henderson, according to Sheriff's Detective Sgt. Rob DeBree.
Perhaps McKinney said something different when he came home
that night and wept in the arms of Kristen Price, or perhaps, pre-

suming homophobia to be an acceptable alibi, she thought she was helping him when she told the press that he and Henderson "just wanted to beat [Shepard] up bad enough to teach him a lesson not to come on to straight people." But once at the Albany County Detention Center, McKinney seemed to take up the pose of fag-basher as a point of pride. At least five prisoners awaiting trial or sentencing have asked their lawyers if the things he's said to them might be leveraged to their own advantage. "Being a verry [*sic*] drunk homofobick [*sic*] I flipped out and began to pistol whip the fag with my gun," McKinney wrote in a letter to another inmate's wife. He didn't mean to kill Shepard, he wrote; he was turning to leave him, tied to the fence but still conscious, when Matthew "mouthed off to the point that I became angry enough to strike him more with my gun." Even then, he insists, his attitude toward homosexuals is not particularly venomous and the murder was unintentional.

McKinney's mother was a nurse; she died as a result of a botched operation when Aaron was sixteen. Markle says there was a kind of shrine to her in his house, but Aaron rarely spoke of her, and then only superficially and only when he was high: "He was always happy then. Once, on mushrooms, he said that if he would slide backward down a hill, he could see his mom in heaven." According to probate records, McKinney got $98,268.02 in a settlement of the wrongful-death lawsuit his stepfather brought against the doctors and the hospital. "After he got the money, he had a lot of friends," Markle told me. He bought cars and cracked them up, bought drugs and became an instant figure in town. He was engaged at one point—"she got the drugs, he got the sex; I guess it worked out for a while"—until the girl found a more attractive connection. "He wasn't a babe magnet," Brent Jones says. He might make a good first impression—he's funny, I was told, though no one could quite explain how—but he couldn't keep that up. Women were *bitches* and *hos,* just like other men, who might also be called *fag, wuss, queer, sissie, girly man, woman,* the standard straight-boy arsenal, which McKinney employed indiscriminately, says Markle, "about as much as anybody—you know, joking around—he never mentioned anything about hating gays." He talked about marrying Price, who is eighteen, but, according to more than one person who was acquainted with them, he wasn't faithful and didn't seem even to like her much.

20

He loves his son, I'm told. And what else? Blank. What did he   21
talk about? Blank. What did he fear? Blank. Who is he? None of
the boys can really say. Interior life is unexplored territory, even
when it's their own. Exterior life, well, "Actually, when he
wasn't high he was kind of a geek," says a guy who's done drugs
with him since high school. "He wasn't the sharpest tool in the
shed. He always wanted to seem bigger, badder, and tougher
than anybody," says Jones, a strongly built fellow who first noticed McKinney when the latter hit him from behind. "He usually didn't pick on anyone bigger than him. He could never do it
alone, and he couldn't do it toe-to-toe." Markle says nothing
much mattered to McKinney in picking a fight, except that if he
started to lose, his friends would honor the rule they had among
themselves and come in to save him.

A stock media image of McKinney and Henderson in this   22
tragedy has them counting out quarters and dimes with dirty fingers to buy a pitcher of beer at the Fireside. It is meant to indicate their distance from Shepard, who had clean hands and paid
for his Heinekens with bills, and to offer some class perspective
on the cheap. *They were poor, they were losers, they lived in
trailers, for God's sake!* McKinney, as it happens, didn't live in a
trailer, though he had when he was younger—a nice double one
with his stepfather, until recently program director at KRQU radio. His natural father is a long-haul truck driver whom he was
heard to call "Daddy" only a few years ago, and in Aaron's
childhood the family lived on Palomino Drive in the Imperial
Heights subdivision. As teenagers he and his friends would drink
and get high in the field behind it—"quite the hangout," according to Markle—where McKinney had played as a boy and where
he would later leave Shepard to die.

Henderson spent most of his childhood in the warmly ap-   23
pointed ranch house where his grandmother runs a day care and
to which his late grandfather would repair after work at the post
office. At the time of the murder, Russell lived with Pasley, a UW
art student, now serving fifteen to twenty-four months, in a
trailer court no uglier than most in Laramie and with the same
kinds of late-model cars, trucks, and four-wheel-drive vehicles
parked outside, the same proportion of people pulling in and out
wearing ties or nice coats or everyday workers' clothes, and
probably the same type of modest but comfortable interiors as in
the ones I visited. No matter, in the monumental condescension

of the press, "trailer" always means failure, always connotes "trash," and, however much it's wrapped up in socioculturoeconomico froufrou, always insinuates the same thing: What can you expect from trash?

McKinney and Henderson were workers. At the end of the day they had dirty hands, just like countless working men who head to the bars at quitting time. Dirt is symbolic only if manual labor is, and manual laborers usually find their symbolism elsewhere. The pair had drunk two pitchers of beer at the Library bar before going to the Fireside; no one remembers anything about them at the Library, presumably because they paid in dollars. Maybe they resented a college boy's clean hands and patent-leather loafers and moneyed confidence; they wouldn't have been the only people in town who do, though acquaintances ascribe no such sentiments to them. UW is a state school, the only university in Wyoming. It stands aloof from the town, but no more than usual. Poll a classroom, and about a fifth of the students are from Laramie, and half say their parents are manual workers. Shepard, originally from Casper but schooled abroad because his father is in the oil business, didn't need a job; Pasley, like most students, did. There's nothing unique here about the injuries of class. In a month at Laramie Valley Roofing, McKinney and Henderson each would gross around $1,200, roughly $7.50 an hour. With rent payments of $370 and $340, respectively, they were like a lot of people in Laramie, where the median household income is $26,000, the average monthly rent is $439, and the average family works two jobs, maybe more. [24]

*   *   *

Hatred is like pornography—hard to define, but you know it when you see it. On the morning before Russell Henderson pleaded guilty, the Reverend Fred Phelps of Topeka, Kansas, brought his flock to the county courthouse with signs declaring GOD HATES FAGS, FAG GOD=RECTUM, PHIL 3:19, SAVE THE GERBILS. Phelps cited as his guide for most of this (the Bible has nothing to say about gerbils) such scriptural passages as Leviticus 18:22, "Thou shalt not lie with mankind, as with womankind: it *is* abomination." I asked if he also subscribes to Moses' suggestion a bit further on in Leviticus 20:13, "If a man also lie with mankind, as he lieth with a woman, . . . they shall [25] surely be put to death." He said he thought all civil law should be based on biblical code, but "it's never going to happen. I'm a pragmatist, a visionary."

"So, if you could, though, you would execute homosexuals?"   26

"I wouldn't execute them. The government would execute them."   27

His only audience were police, press, and a ring of angels—   28 counterprotesters dressed in white robes, their great wings sweeping up before his gaudy placards. The next day the university's student newspaper covered the day's events, running in enlarged type the observation of freshman Kristen Allen that "they have no business using the Bible verses out of context. God hates the sin but loves the sinner." On campus, where Phelps later moved his protest, onlookers expressed disgust at his message and invoked "tolerance."

Before it came to signify the highest state to which straight so-   29 ciety could aspire, tolerance was something one had for a bad job or a bad smell or a nightmare relative who visited once a year. In its new guise, tolerance means straight people know of gay men and women, but there is no recognizable gay life, no clubs except a tiny one on campus, no bars or restaurants or bookstores flying the rainbow flag. It means the university might institute a Matthew Shepard Chair in Civil Liberties but has no antidiscrimination policy that applies to homosexuals and no employee benefit policy that extends to domestic partners. It means the public school curriculum does not say teachers must "avoid planning curriculum promoting perversion, homosexuality, contraception, promiscuity and abortion as healthy lifestyle choices"—the policy in Lincoln County, Wyoming—but it also does not include "homosexuality" among vocabulary terms for sex-ed classes at any grade level and mentions the word only once, for eighth grade, under "Topics to be Discussed . . . particularly as they relate to [sexually transmitted diseases]." It means a father tells his lesbian daughter, "If you have to do this you should do it in the closet," and the mother tells her, "Let's just pretend I don't know, okay?" It means her brother "tries to be as supportive as he can be—and he is—but if a man hit on him, he'd beat the shit out of him. He wouldn't beat up someone for another reason, and he thinks that's an accomplishment—and it is." It means Chasity Pasley's mother won her custody battle over the charge that as a lesbian she was unfit, but her children

had to call her partner "Aunt." It means if you're gay and out
and attend a company party with your boyfriend, the sense in
the room is "We know you're gay and that's okay, but do you
have to bring your boyfriend?" It means Fred Dahl, the straight
head of UW's Survey Research Center, accepts the university's
expression of outrage over Shepard's murder but tells a social
work master's candidate named Shannon Bell that her project to
poll Wyoming residents on their attitudes toward homosexuality
might amount to harassment of straight people, and anyway,
"one good rodeo season and Wyoming will be back to normal."

In a graduate-class discussion right after Shepard was found,   30
the high-minded talk was all of tolerance as students challenged
a woman who had said she abhorred violence but still . . . homosexuality, it's immoral. Amid the chatter, a cowboy who'd
been silent said plainly, "The issue isn't tolerance. We don't need
to learn tolerance; we need to learn love."

There may be, as the song goes, a thin line between love and   31
hate, but, however many twists it takes, it is life's defining line.
And people like Phelps are no more responsible for it than pop
music is responsible for the murders at Columbine High School.
What keeps that line so strong, like strands of the clothesline
used to tie Matthew Shepard's wrists, are all the little things of a
culture, mostly unnoticed and unremarked, like the way in
which the simplest show of affection is a decision about safety,
like the way in which a man entwined with a woman is the
stuff of everyday commerce but a man expressing vulnerability
is equivalent to a quaint notion of virginity—you save it for
marriage.

"Masks are no longer as protective as they used to be," John   32
Scagliotti, the maker of Before *(and now* After*) Stonewall,
was telling me. "If you're gay, no longer can you hide, because
straight people watch TV, and they see how people hide. And
also this has changed straight culture, so all the little things you
do might make you question whether you're straight, or straight
enough. Your own suspicions are suspicious.*

"It gets even more complicated now that all these things that   33
*represent maleness are very attractive to both gay and straight
men. The downside of this, in a way, is that straight male bonding,
and male bonding in general, especially in rural places, is going
to be a very confused thing. Already at gyms, eighteen-year-olds*

don't take showers anymore—or if they do, they take all their things in with them, like modest little girls. You're confused, you're eighteen, and you really like this guy; he's your best buddy, and you'd rather spend all your time with him than with this girl. And you are straight, but now you're worried too."

The Henderson trial was to have begun on the first Tuesday   34
after Easter. At the Harvest Foursquare full-gospel church that Sunday, people wore name tags and expressed a serene camaraderie. Then they sent the children downstairs to play while the "illustrated sermon"—a dramatization of Christ's Passion and death—took place. It was a stunning performance, beginning with the Jesus character racked with sorrow in the Garden of Gethsemane. The narrator said Jesus suffered like any man. Then he said, departing from the script, "Every time I see an image of a feminine Jesus, it makes my blood boil. Jesus wasn't a weakling. Jesus was a man. If Jesus was here today, he could take on any man in this room." Later, when the Jesus character was tied to a post, flogged by two men—soldiers who took "sensual pleasure" in every fall of the whip, the narrator said—"Jesus didn't cry out for mercy. . . . Jesus was a man. Jesus was a man's man." The Jesus character writhed in agony. After he stumbled offstage with the cross, and the only sounds were his moans amid the pounding of nails, the narrator described the tender caress of the hands now ripped by sharp iron. In the congregation, men as well as women were moved to weeping. By the end, they were all singing, swaying, proclaiming their weakness before the Lord.

GLORIA STEINEM

Sex, Lies, and Advertising

Gloria Steinem grew up in relative poverty, finishing high school with low grades while she lived in a slum in Toledo, Ohio. Exceptional entrace test scores, however, sent her to Smith College, where she proved to be an excellent student. In 1971, after a decade of work as a journalist, she became editor of *Ms.* magazine, a post she held until 1987. In addition to promoting the work of feminist writers while editing *Ms.*, Steinem has produced a significant body of her own work, including *Outrageous Acts and Everyday Rebellions* (1983), *Revolution from Within* (1992), and *Moving Beyond Words* (1994). The following article was published in the July/August 1990 issue of *Ms.*

About three years ago, as *glasnost* was beginning and *Ms.*   1
seemed to be ending. I was invited to a press lunch for a Soviet official. He entertained us with anecdotes about new problems of democracy in his country. Local Communist leaders were being criticized in their media for the first time, he explained, and they were angry.

"So I'll have to ask my American friends," he finished pointedly, "how more *subtly* to control the press." In the silence that   2
followed, I said, "Advertising."

The reporters laughed, but later, one of them took me aside: 3
How *dare* I suggest that freedom of the press was limited? How dare I imply that his newsweekly could be influenced by ads?

I explained that I was thinking of advertising's media-wide influence on most of what we read. Even newsmagazines use   4
"soft" cover stories to sell ads, confuse readers with "advertorials," and occasionally self-censor on subjects known to be a problem with big advertisers.

But, I also explained, I was thinking especially of women's   5
magazines. There, it isn't just a little content that's devoted to attracting ads, it's almost all of it. That's why advertisers—not readers—have always been the problem for *Ms.* As the only women's magazine that didn't supply what the ad world euphemistically describes as "supportive editorial atmosphere" or "complementary copy" (for instance, articles that praise food/fashion/beauty subjects to "support" and "complement" food/fashion/beauty ads), *Ms.* could never attract enough advertising to break even.

"Oh, *women's* magazines," the journalist said with contempt.   6
"Everybody knows they're catalogs—but who cares? They have nothing to do with journalism."

*   *   *

I can't tell you how many times I've had this argument in 25   7
years of working for many kinds of publications. Except as moneymaking machines—"cash cows" as they are so elegantly called
in the trade—women's magazines are rarely taken seriously.
Though changes being made by women have been called more
far-reaching than the industrial revolution—and though many
editors try hard to reflect some of them in the few pages left to
them after all the ad-related subjects have been covered—the
magazines serving the female half of this country are still far below the journalistic and ethical standards of news and general interest publications. Most depressing of all, this doesn't even rate
an exposé.

If *Time* and *Newsweek* had to lavish praise on cars in general   8
and credit General Motors in particular to get GM ads, there
would be a scandal—maybe a criminal investigation. When
women's magazines from *Seventeen* to *Lear's* praise beauty
products in general and credit Revlon in particular to get ads, it's
just business as usual.

I.

When *Ms.* began, we didn't consider *not* taking ads. The most   9
important reason was keeping the price of a feminist magazine
low enough for most women to afford. But the second and almost equal reason was providing a forum where women and advertisers could talk to each other and improve advertising itself.
After all, it was (and still is) as potent a source of information in
this country as news or TV and movie dramas.

We decided to proceed in two stages. First, we would con-   10
vince makers of "people products" used by both men and
women but advertised mostly to men—cars, credit cards, insurance, sound equipment, financial services, and the like—that
their ads should be placed in a women's magazine. Since they
were accustomed to the division between editorial and advertising in news and general interest magazines, this would allow our
editorial content to be free and diverse. Second, we would add
the best ads for whatever traditional "women's products"
(clothes, shampoo, fragrance, food, and so on) that surveys
showed *Ms.* readers used. But we would ask them to come in
without the usual quid pro quo of "complementary copy."

We knew the second step might be harder. Food advertisers 11
have always demanded that women's magazines publish recipes
and articles on entertaining (preferably ones that name their
products) in return for their ads; clothing advertisers expect to
be surrounded by fashion spreads (especially ones that credit
their designers); and shampoo, fragrance, and beauty products
in general usually insist on positive editorial coverage of beauty
subjects, plus photo credits besides. That's why women's magazines look the way they do. But if we could break this link between ads and editorial content, then we wanted good ads for
"women's products," too.

By playing their part in this unprecedented mix of *all* the 12
things our readers need and use, advertisers also would be rewarded: ads for products like cars and mutual funds would find
a new growth market; the best ads for women's products would
no longer be lost in oceans of ads for the same category; and
both would have access to a laboratory of smart and caring readers whose response would help create effective ads for other media as well.

I thought then that our main problem would be the imagery 13
in ads themselves. Carmakers were still draping blondes in
evening gowns over the hoods like ornaments. Authority figures
were almost always male, even in ads for products that only
women used. Sadistic, he-man campaigns even won industry
praise. (For instance, *Advertising Age* had hailed the infamous
Silva Thin cigarette theme, "How to Get a Woman's Attention:
Ignore Her," as "brilliant.") Even in medical journals, tranquil-
izer ads showed depressed housewives standing beside piles of
dirty dishes and promised to get them back to work.

Obviously, *Ms.* would have to avoid such ads and seek out the 14
best ones—but this didn't seem impossible. *The New Yorker* had
been selecting ads for aesthetic reasons for years, a practice that
only seemed to make advertisers more eager to be in its pages.
Ebony and *Essence* were asking for ads with positive black images, and though their struggle was hard, they weren't being
called unreasonable.

Clearly, what *Ms.* needed was a very special publisher and ad 15
sales staff. I could think of only one woman with experience on
the business side of magazines—Patricia Carbine, who recently
had become a vice president of *McCall's* as well as its editor in
chief—and the reason I knew her name was a good omen. She

had been managing editor at *Look* (really *the* editor, but its owner refused to put a female name at the top of his masthead) when I was writing a column there. After I did an early interview with Cesar Chavez, then just emerging as a leader of migrant labor, and the publisher turned it down because he was worried about ads from Sunkist, Pat was the one who intervened. As I learned later, she had told the publisher she would resign if the interview wasn't published. Mainly because *Look* couldn't afford to lose Pat, it *was* published (and the ads from Sunkist never arrived).

Though I barely knew this woman, she had done two things I   16
always remembered: put her job on the line in a way that editors often talk about but rarely do, and been so loyal to her colleagues that she never told me or anyone outside *Look* that she had done so.

Fortunately, Pat did agree to leave *McCall's* and take a huge   17
cut in salary to become publisher of *Ms.* She became responsible for training and inspiring generations of young women who joined the *Ms.* ad sales force, many of whom went on to become "firsts" at the top of publishing. When *Ms.* first started, however, there were so few women with experience selling space that Pat and I made the rounds of ad agencies ourselves. Later, the fact that *Ms.* was asking companies to do business in a different way meant our saleswomen had to make many times the usual number of calls—first to convince agencies and then client companies besides—and to present endless amounts of research. I was often asked to do a final ad presentation, or see some higher decision-maker, or speak to women employees so executives could see the interest of women they worked with. That's why I spent more time persuading advertisers than editing or writing for *Ms.* and why I ended up with an unsentimental education in the seamy underside of publishing that few writers see (and even fewer magazines can publish).

Let me take you with us through some experiences, just as   18
they happened:

• Cheered on by early support from Volkswagen and one or two   19
other car companies, we scrape together time and money to put on a major reception in Detroit. We know U.S. carmakers firmly believe that women choose the upholstery, not the car, but we are armed with statistics and reader mail to prove the contrary: a car

is an important purchase for women, one that symbolizes mobility and freedom.

But almost nobody comes. We are left with many pounds of 20
shrimp on the table, and quite a lot of egg on our face. We blame
ourselves for not guessing that there would be a baseball pennant play-off on the same day, but executives go out of their way
to explain they wouldn't have come anyway. Thus begins ten
years of knocking on hostile doors, presenting endless documentation, and hiring a full-time saleswoman in Detroit; all necessary before *Ms.* gets any real results.

This long saga has a semihappy ending: foreign and, later, do- 21
mestic carmakers eventually provided *Ms.* with enough advertising to make cars one of our top sources of ad revenue. Slowly,
Detroit began to take the women's market seriously enough to
put car ads in other women's magazines, too, thus freeing a few
pages from the hothouse of fashion-beauty-food ads.

But long after figures showed a third, even a half, of many car 22
models being bought by women, U.S. makers continued to be
uncomfortable addressing women. Unlike foreign carmakers.
Detroit never quite learned the secret of creating intelligent ads
that exclude no one, and then placing them in women's magazines to overcome past exclusion. (*Ms.* readers were so grateful
for a routine Honda ad featuring rack and pinion steering, for
instance, that they sent fan mail.) Even now, Detroit continues to
ask, "Should we make special ads for women?" Perhaps that's
why some foreign cars still have a disproportionate share of the
U.S. women's market.

• In the *Ms.* Gazette, we do a brief report on a congressional 23
hearing into chemicals used in hair dyes that are absorbed
through the skin and may be carcinogenic. Newspapers report
this too, but Clairol, a Bristol-Myers subsidiary that makes
dozens of products—a few of which have just begun to advertise
in *Ms.*—is outraged. Not at newspapers or newsmagazines, just
at us. It's bad enough that *Ms.* is the only women's magazine refusing to provide the usual "complementary" articles and beauty
photos, but to criticize one of their categories—*that* is going too
far.

We offer to publish a letter from Clairol telling its side of the 24
story. In an excess of solicitousness, we even put this letter in the
Gazette, not in Letters to the Editors where it belongs. Nonetheless—and in spite of surveys that show *Ms.* readers are active

women who use more of almost everything Clairol makes than do the readers of any other women's magazine—*Ms.* gets almost none of these ads for the rest of its natural life.

Meanwhile, Clairol changes its hair coloring formula, apparently in response to the hearings we reported.   25

• Our saleswomen set out early to attract ads for consumer electronics: sound equipment, calculators, computers, VCRs, and the like. We know that our readers are determined to be included in the technological revolution. We know from reader surveys that *Ms.* readers are buying this stuff in numbers as high as those of magazines like *Playboy*, or "men 18 to 34," the prime targets of the consumer electronics industry. Moreover, unlike traditional women's products that our readers buy but don't need to read articles about, these are subjects they want covered in our pages. There actually *is* a supportive editorial atmosphere.   26

"But women don't understand technology," say executives at the end of ad presentations. "Maybe not," we respond, "but neither do men—and we all buy it."   27

"If women *do* buy it," say the decision-makers, "they're asking their husbands and boyfriends what to buy first." We produce letters from *Ms.* readers saying how turned off they are when salesmen say things like "Let me know when your husband can come in."   28

After several years of this, we get a few ads for compact sound systems. Some of them come from JVC, whose vice president, Harry Elias, is trying to convince his Japanese bosses that there is something called a women's market. At his invitation, I find myself speaking at huge trade shows in Chicago and Las Vegas, trying to persuade JVC dealers that showrooms don't have to be locker rooms where women are made to feel unwelcome. But as it turns out, the shows themselves are part of the problem. In Las Vegas, the only women around the technology displays are semi-nude models serving champagne. In Chicago, the big attraction is Marilyn Chambers, who followed Linda Lovelace of *Deep Throat* fame as Chuck Traynor's captive and/or employee. VCRs are being demonstrated with her porn videos.   29

In the end, we get ads for a car stereo now and then, but no VCRs; some IBM personal computers, but no Apple or Japanese ones. We notice that office magazines like *Working Woman* and *Savvy* don't benefit as much as they should from office   30 equipment ads either. In the electronics world, women and technology seem mutually exclusive. It remains a decade behind even Detroit.

• Because we get letters from little girls who love toy trains, and who ask our help in changing ads and box-top photos that feature little boys only, we try to get toy-train ads from Lionel. It turns out that Lionel executives *have* been concerned about little girls. They made a pink train, and were surprised when it didn't sell.   31

Lionel bows to consumer pressure with a photograph of a boy *and* a girl—but only on some of their boxes. They fear that, if trains are associated with girls, they will be devalued in the minds of boys. Needless to say, *Ms.* gets no train ads, and little girls remain a mostly unexplored market. By 1986, Lionel is put up for sale.   32

But for different reasons, we haven't had much luck with other kinds of toys either. In spite of many articles in child-rearing; an annual listing of nonsexist, multi-racial toys by Letty Cottin Pogrebin; Stories for Free Children, a regular feature also edited by Letty; and other prizewinning features for or about children, we get virtually no toy ads. Generations of *Ms.* saleswomen explain to toy manufacturers that a larger proportion of *Ms.* readers have preschool children than do the readers of other women's magazines, but this industry can't believe feminists have or care about children.   33

• When *Ms.* begins, the staff decides not to accept ads for feminine hygiene sprays or cigarettes: they are damaging and carry no appropriate health warnings. Though we don't think we should tell our readers what to do, we do think we should provide facts so they can decide for themselves. Since the antismoking lobby has been pressing for health warnings on cigarette ads, we decide to take them only as they comply.   34

Philip Morris is among the first to do so. One of its brands, Virginia Slims, is also sponsoring women's tennis and the first national polls of women's opinions. On the other hand, the Virginia Slims theme, "You've come a long way, baby," has more than a "baby" problem. It makes smoking a symbol of progress for women.   35

We explain to Philip Morris that this slogan won't do well in our pages, but they are convinced its success with some women   36 means it will work with *all* women. Finally, we agree to publish an ad for a Virginia Slims calendar as a test. The letters from readers are critical—and smart. For instance: Would you show a black man picking cotton, the same man in a Cardin suit, and symbolize the antislavery and civil rights movements by smoking? Of course not. But instead of honoring the test results, the Philip Morris people seem angry to be proven wrong. They take away ads for *all* their many brands.

This costs *Ms.* about $250,000 the first year. After five years, 37 we can no longer keep track. Occasionally, a new set of executives listens to *Ms.* saleswomen, but because we won't take Virginia Slims, not one Philip Morris product returns to our pages for the next 16 years.

Gradually, we also realize our naiveté in thinking we *could* 38 decide against taking cigarette ads. They became a disproportionate support of magazines the moment they were banned on television, and few magazines could compete and survive without them; certainly not *Ms.*, which lacks so many other categories. By the time statistics in the 1980s showed that women's rate of lung cancer was approaching men's, the necessity of taking cigarette ads has become a kind of prison.

• General Mills, Pillsbury, Carnation, DelMonte, Dole, Kraft, 39 Stouffer, Hormel, Nabisco: you name the food giant, we try it. But no matter how desirable the *Ms.* readership, our lack of recipes is lethal.

We explain to them that placing food ads *only* next to recipes 40 associates food with work. For many women, it is a negative that works *against* the ads. Why not place food ads in diverse media without recipes (thus reaching more men, who are now a third of the shoppers in supermarkets anyway), and leave the recipes to specialty magazines like *Gourmet* (a third of whose readers are also men)?

These arguments elicit interest, but except for an occasional 41 ad for a convenience food, instant coffee, diet drinks, yogurt, or such extras as avocados and almonds, this mainstay of the publishing industry stays closed to us. Period.

• Traditionally, wines and liquors didn't advertise to women: 42 men were thought to make the brand decisions, even if women did the buying. But after endless presentations, we begin to make a dent in this category. Thanks to the unconventional Michel Roux of Carillon Importers (distributors of Grand Marnier, Ab-

solut Vodka, and others), who assumes that food and drink have
no gender, some ads are leaving their men's club.

Beermakers are still selling masculinity. It takes *Ms.* fully eight   43
years to get its first beer ad (Michelob). In general, however,
liquor ads are less stereotyped in their imagery—and far less controlling of the editorial content around them—than are women's
products. But given the underrepresentation of other categories,
these very facts tend to create a disproportionate number of alcohol ads in the pages of *Ms.* This in turn dismays readers worried about women and alcoholism.

• We hear in 1980 that women in the Soviet Union have been   44
producing feminist *samizdat* (underground, self-published books)
and circulating them throughout the country. As punishment,
four of the leaders have been exiled. Though we are operating on
our usual shoestring, we solicit individual contributions to send
Robin Morgan to interview these women in Vienna.

The result is an exclusive cover story that includes the first   45
news of a populist peace movement against the Afghanistan occupation, a prediction of *glasnost* to come, and a grass-roots, intimate view of Soviet women's lives. From the popular press to
women's studies courses, the response is great. The story wins a
Front Page award.

Nonetheless, this journalistic coup undoes years of efforts to   46
get an ad schedule from Revlon. Why? Because the Soviet
women on our cover *are not wearing makeup.*

• Four years of research and presentations go into convincing   47
airlines that women now make travel choices and business trips.
United, the first airline to advertise in *Ms.*, is so impressed with
the response from our readers that one of its executives appears
in a film for our ad presentations. As usual, good ads get great
results.

But we have problems unrelated to such results. For instance: 48
because American Airlines flight attendants include among their
labor demands the stipulation that they could choose to have
their last names preceded by "Ms." on their name tags—in a
long-delayed revolt against the standard, "I am your pilot, Captain Rothgart, and this is your flight attendant, Cindy Sue"—
American officials seem to hold the magazine responsible. We get
no ads.

There is still a different problem at Eastern. A vice president   49
cancels subscriptions for thousands of copies on Eastern flights.

Why? Because he is offended by ads for lesbian poetry journals in the *Ms.* Classified. A "family airline," as he explains to me coldly on the phone, has to "draw the line somewhere."

It's obvious that *Ms.* can't exclude lesbians and serve women. 50 We've been trying to make that point ever since our first issue included an article by and about lesbians, and both Suzanne Levine, our managing editor, and I were lectured by such heavy hitters as Ed Kosner, then editor of *Newsweek* (and now of *New York Magazine*), who insisted that *Ms.* should "position" itself *against* lesbians. But our advertisers have paid to reach a guaranteed number of readers, and soliciting new subscriptions to compensate for Eastern would cost $150,000 plus rebating money in the meantime.

Like almost everything ad-related, this presents an elaborate 51 organizing problem. After days of searching for sympathetic members of the Eastern board, Frank Thomas, president of the Ford Foundation, kindly offers to call Roswell Gilpatric, a director of Eastern. I talk with Mr. Gilpatric, who calls Frank Borman, then the president of Eastern. Frank Borman calls me to say that his airline is not in the business of censoring magazines: *Ms.* will be returned to Eastern flights.

• Women's access to insurance and credit is vital, but with the 52 exception of Equitable and a few other ad pioneers, such financial services address men. For almost a decade after the Equal Credit Opportunity Act passes in 1974, we try to convince American Express that women are a growth market—but nothing works.

Finally, a former professor of Russian named Jerry Welsh be- 53 comes head of marketing. He assumes that women should be cardholders, and persuades his colleagues to feature women in a campaign. Thanks to this 1980s series, the growth rate for female cardholders surpasses that for men.

For this article, I asked Jerry Welsh if he would explain why 54 American Express waited so long. "Sure," he said, "they were afraid of having a 'pink' card."

• Women of color read *Ms.* in disproportionate numbers. This is 55 a source of pride to *Ms.* staffers, who are also more racially representative than the editors of other women's magazines. But this reality is obscured by ads filled with enough white women to make a reader snowblind.

Pat Carbine remembers mostly "astonishment" when she re-   56
quested African American, Hispanic, Asian, and other diverse
images. Marcia Ann Gillespie, a *Ms.* editor who was previously
the editor in chief of *Essence,* witnesses ad bias a second time:
having tried for *Essence* to get white advertisers to use black images (Revlon did so eventually, but L'Oréal, Lauder, Chanel, and
other companies never did), she sees similar problems getting integrated ads for an integrated magazine. Indeed, the ad world often creates black and Hispanic ads only for black and Hispanic
media. In an exact parallel of the fear that marketing a product
to women will endanger its appeal to men, the response is usually, "But your [white] readers won't identify."

In fact, those we are able to get—for instance, a Max Factor   57
ad made for *Essence* that Linda Wachner gives us after she becomes president—are praised by white readers, too. But there
are pathetically few such images.

• By the end of 1986, production and mailing costs have risen   58
astronomically, ad income is flat, and competition for ads is
stiffer than ever. The 60/40 preponderance of edit over ads that
we promised to readers becomes 50/50; children's stories, most
poetry, and some fiction are casualties of less space; in order to
get variety into limited pages, the length (and sometimes the
depth) of articles suffers; and, though we do refuse most of the
ads that would look like a parody in our pages, we get so worn
down that some slip through. (See this issue's No Comment.)
Still, readers perform miracles. Though we haven't been able to
afford a subscription mailing in two years, they maintain our
guaranteed circulation of 450,000.

Nonetheless, media reports on *Ms.* often insist that our un-   59
profitability must be due to reader disinterest. The myth that advertisers simply follow readers is very strong. Not one reporter
notes that other comparable magazines our size (say, *Vanity Fair*
or *The Atlantic*) have been losing more money in one year
than *Ms.* has lost in 16 years. No matter how much never-to-be-
recovered cash is poured into starting a magazine or keeping one
going, appearances seem to be all that matter. (Which is why we
haven't been able to explain our fragile state in public. Nothing
causes ad-flight like the smell of nonsuccess.)

My healthy response is anger. My not-so-healthy response is   60
constant worry. Also an obsession with finding one more rescue.

There is hardly a night when I don't wake up with sweaty palms and pounding heart, scared that we won't be able to pay the printer or the post office; scared most of all that closing our doors will hurt the women's movement.

Out of chutzpah and desperation, I arrange a lunch with 61 Leonard Lauder, president of Estée Lauder. With the exception of Clinique (the brainchild of Carol Phillips), none of the Lauder's hundreds of products has been advertised in *Ms.* A year's schedule of ads for just three or four of them could save us. Indeed, as the scion of a family-owned company whose ad practices are followed by the beauty industry, he is one of the few men who could liberate many pages in all women's magazines just by changing his mind about "complementary copy."

Over a lunch that costs more than we can pay for some arti- 62 cles, I explain the need for his leadership. I also lay out the record of *Ms.*: more literary and journalistic prizes won, more new issues introduced into the mainstream, new writers discovered, and impact on society than any other magazine; more articles that became books, stories that became movies, ideas that became television series, and newly advertised products that became profitable; and, most important for him, a place for his ads to reach women who aren't reachable through any other women's magazine. Indeed, if there is one constant characteristic of the ever-changing *Ms.* readership, it is their impact as leaders. Whether it's waiting until later to have first babies, or pioneering PABA as sun protection in cosmetics, *whatever* they are doing today, a third to a half of American women will be doing three to five years from now. It's never failed.

But, he says, *Ms.* readers are not *our* women. They're not in- 63 terested in things like fragrance and blush-on. If they were, *Ms.* would write articles about them.

On the contrary, I explain, surveys show they are more likely 64 to buy such things than the readers of, say, *Cosmopolitan* or *Vogue.* They're good customers because they're out in the world enough to need several sets of everything: home, work, purse, travel, gym, and so on. They just don't need to read articles about these things. Would he ask a men's magazine to publish monthly columns on how to shave before he advertised Aramis products (his line for men)?

He concedes that beauty features are often concocted more 65 for advertisers than readers. But *Ms.* isn't appropriate for his ads anyway, he explains. Why? Because Estée Lauder is selling "a kept-woman mentality."

I can't quite believe this. Sixty percent of the users of his prod- 66
ucts are salaried, and generally resemble *Ms.* readers. Besides, his company has the appeal of having been started by a creative and hardworking woman, his mother, Estée Lauder.

That doesn't matter, he says. He knows his customers, and 67
they would *like* to be kept women. That's why he will never advertise in *Ms.*

In November 1987, by vote of the Ms. Foundation for Edu- 68
cation and Communication (*Ms.*'s owner and publisher, the media subsidiary of the Ms. Foundation for Women), *Ms.* was sold to a company whose officers, Australian feminists Sandra Yates and Anne Summers, raised the investment money in their country that *Ms.* couldn't find in its own. They also started *Sassy* for teenage women.

In their two-year tenure, circulation was raised to 550,000 by 69
investment in circulation mailings, and, to the dismay of some readers, editorial features on clothes and new products made a more traditional bid for ads. Nonetheless, ad pages fell below previous levels. In addition, *Sassy*, whose fresh voice and sexual frankness were an unprecedented success with young readers, was targeted by two mothers from Indiana who began, as one of them put it, "calling every Christian organization I could think of." In response to this controversy, several crucial advertisers pulled out.

Such links between ads and editorial content were a problem 70
in Australia, too, but to a lesser degree. "Our readers pay two times more for their magazines," Anne explained, "so advertisers have less power to threaten a magazine's viability."

"I was shocked," said Sandra Yates with characteristic direct- 71
ness. "In Australia, we think you have freedom of the press—but you don't."

Since Anne and Sandra had not met their budget's projections 72
for ad revenue, their investors forced a sale. In October 1989, *Ms.* and *Sassy* were bought by Dale Lang, owner of *Working Mother, Working Woman,* and one of the few independent publishing companies left among the conglomerates. In response to a request from the original *Ms.* staff—as well as to reader letters urging that *Ms.* continue, plus his own belief that *Ms.* would benefit his other magazines by blazing a trail—he agreed to try

the ad-free, reader-supported *Ms.* you hold now and to give us complete editorial control.

II.

Do you think, as I once did, that advertisers make decisions   73
based on solid research? Well, think again. "Broadly speaking,"
says Joseph Smith of Oxtoby-Smith, Inc., a consumer research
firm, "there is no persuasive evidence that the editorial context
of an ad matters."

Advertisers who demand such "complementary copy," even   74
in the absence of respectable studies, clearly are operating under
a double standard. The same food companies place ads in *People*
with no recipes. Cosmetics companies support *The New Yorker*
with no regular beauty columns. So where does this habit of controlling the content of women's magazines come from?

Tradition. Ever since *Ladies Magazine* debuted in Boston in   75
1828, editorial copy directed to women has been informed by
something other than its readers' wishes. There were no ads
then, but in an age when married women were legal minors with
no right to their own money, there was another revenue source
to be kept in mind: husbands. "Husbands may rest assured,"
wrote editor Sarah Josepha Hale, "that nothing found in these
pages shall cause her [his wife] to be less assiduous in preparing
for his reception or encourage her to 'usurp station' or encroach
upon prerogatives of men."

Hale went on to become the editor of *Godey's Lady's Book,* a   76
magazine featuring "fashion plates": engravings of dresses for
readers to take to their seamstresses or copy themselves. Hale
added "how to" articles, which set the tone for women's service
magazines for years to come: how to write politely, avoid sun-
burn, and—in no fewer than 1,200 words—how to maintain a
goose quill pen. She advocated education for women but
avoided controversy. Just as most women's magazines now avoid
politics, poll their readers on issues like abortion but rarely take
a stand, and praise socially approved lifestyles, Hale saw to it
that *Godey's* avoided the hot topics of its day: slavery, abolition,
and women's suffrage.

What definitively turned women's magazines into catalogs,   77
however, were two events: Ellen Butterick's invention of the

clothing pattern in 1863 and the mass manufacture of patent medicines containing everything from colored water to cocaine. For the first time, readers could purchase what magazines encouraged them to want. As such magazines became more profitable, they also began to attract men as editors. (Most women's magazines continued to have men as top editors until the feminist 1970s.) Edward Bok, who became editor of *The Ladies' Home Journal* in 1889, discovered the power of advertisers when he rejected ads for patent medicines and found that other advertisers canceled in retribution. In the early 20th century, *Good Housekeeping* started its Institute to "test and approve" products. Its Seal of Approval became the grandfather of current "value added" programs that offer advertisers such bonuses as product sampling and department store promotions.

By the time suffragists finally won the vote in 1920, women's magazines had become too entrenched as catalogs to help women learn how to use it. The main function was to create a desire for products, teach how to use products, and make products a crucial part of gaining social approval, pleasing a husband, and performing as a homemaker. Some related articles and short stories were included to persuade women to pay for these catalogs. But articles were neither consumerist nor rebellious. Even fiction was usually subject to formula: if a woman had any sexual life outside marriage, she was supposed to come to a bad end.

In 1965, Helen Gurley Brown began to change part of that formula by bringing "the sexual revolution" to women's magazines—but in an ad-oriented way. Attracting multiple men required even more consumerism, as the Cosmo Girl made clear, than finding one husband.

In response to the workplace revolution of the 1970s, traditional women's magazines—that is, "trade books" for women working at home—were joined by *Savvy, Working Woman,* and other trade books for women working in offices. But by keeping the fashion/beauty/entertaining articles necessary to get traditional ads and then adding career articles besides, they inadvertently produced the antifeminist stereotype of Super Woman. The male-imitative, dress-for-success woman carrying a briefcase became the media image of a woman worker, even though a blue-collar woman's salary was often higher than her glorified secretarial sister's, and though women at a real briefcase level are statistically rare. Needless to say, these dress-for-success women were also thin, white, and beautiful.

In recent years, advertisers' control over the editorial content   81
of women's magazines has become so institutionalized that it is written into "insertion orders" or dictated to ad salespeople as official policy. The following are recent typical orders to women's magazines:

• Dow's Cleaning Products stipulates that ads for its Vivid and   82
Spray 'n Wash products should be adjacent to "children or fashion editorial"; ads for Bathroom Cleaner should be next to "home furnishing/family" features; and so on for other brands. "If a magazine fails for ½ the brands or more," the Dow order warns, "it will be omitted from further consideration."

• Bristol-Myers, the parent of Clairol, Windex, Drano, Bufferin,   83
and much more, stipulates that ads be placed next to "a full page of compatible editorial."

• S. C. Johnson & Son, makers of Johnson Wax, lawn and laun-   84
dry products, insect sprays, hair sprays, and so on, orders that its ads *should not be opposite extremely controversial features or material antithetical to the nature/copy of the advertised product.*" (Italics theirs.)

• Maidenform, manufacturer of bras and other apparel, leaves a   85
blank for the particular product and states: "The creative concept of the ___ campaign, and the very nature of the product itself appeal to the positive emotions of the reader/consumer. Therefore, it is imperative that all editorial adjacencies reflect that same positive tone. The editorial must not be negative in content or lend itself contrary to the ___ product imagery/message (e.g., *editorial relating to illness, disillusionment, large size fashion, etc.*)." (Italics mine.)

• The De Beers diamond company, a big seller of engagement   86
rings, prohibits magazines from placing its ads with "adjacencies to hard news or anti/love-romance themed editorial."

• Procter & Gamble, one of this country's most powerful and   87
diversified advertisers, stands out in the memory of Anne Summers and Sandra Yates (no mean feat in this context): its products were not to be placed in *any* issue that included *any* material on gun control, abortion, the occult, cults, or the disparagement of religion. Caution was also demanded in any issue covering sex or drugs, even for educational purposes.

Those are the most obvious chains around women's maga- 88
zines. There are also rules so clear they needn't be written down:
for instance, an overall "look" compatible with beauty and fashion ads. Even "real" nonmodel women photographed for a
woman's magazine are usually made up, dressed in credited
clothes, and retouched out of all reality. When editors do include
articles on less-than cheerful subjects (for instance, domestic violence), they tend to keep them short and unillustrated. The
point is to be "upbeat." Just as women in the street are asked,
"Why don't you smile, honey?" women's magazines acquire an
institutional smile.

Within the text itself, praise for advertisers' products has be- 89
come so ritualized that fields like "beauty writing" have been invented. One of its frequent practitioners explained seriously that
"It's a difficult art. How many new adjectives can you find? How
much greater can you make a lipstick sound? The FDA restricts
what companies can say on labels, but we create illusion. And ad
agencies are on the phone all the time pushing you to get their
product in. A lot of them keep the business based on how many
editorial clippings they produce every month. The worst are
products," like Lauder's as the writer confirmed, "with their
own name involved. It's all ego."

Often, editorial becomes one giant ad. Last November, for in- 90
stance, *Lear's* featured an elegant woman executive on the cover.
On the contents page, we learned she was wearing Guerlain
makeup and Samsara, a new fragrance by Guerlain. Inside were
full-page ads for Samsara and Guerlain antiwrinkle cream. In the
cover profile, we learned that this executive was responsible for
launching Samsara and is Guerlain's director of public relations.
When the *Columbia Journalism Review* did one of the few articles to include women's magazines in coverage of the influence of
ads, editor Frances Lear was quoted as defending her magazine
because "this kind of thing is done all the time."

Often, advertisers also plunge odd-shaped ads into the text, 91
no matter what the cost to the readers. At *Woman's Day*, a magazine originally founded by a supermarket chain, editor in chief
Ellen Levine said, "The day the copy had to rag around a
chicken leg was not a happy one."

Advertisers are also adamant about where in a magazine their 92
ads appear. When Revlon was not placed as the first beauty ad in
one Hearst magazine, for instance, Revlon pulled its ads from *all*

Hearst magazines. Ruth Whitney, editor in chief of *Glamour,* attributes some of these demands to "ad agencies wanting to prove to a client that they've squeezed the last drop of blood out of a magazine." She also is, she says, "sick and tired of hearing that women's magazines are controlled by cigarette ads." Relatively speaking, she's right. To be as censoring as are many advertisers for women's products, tobacco companies would have to demand articles in praise of smoking and expect glamorous photos of beautiful women smoking their brands.

I don't mean to imply that the editors I quote here share my objections to ads: most assume that women's magazines have to be the way they are. But it's also true that only former editors can be completely honest. "Most of the pressure came in the form of direct product mentions," explains Sey Chassler, who was editor in chief of *Redbook* from the sixties to the eighties. "We got threats from the big guys, the Revlons, blackmail threats. They wouldn't run ads unless we credited them.

"But it's not fair to single out the beauty advertisers because these pressures came from everybody. Advertisers want to know two things: What are you going to charge me? What *else* are you going to do for me? It's a holdup. For instance, management felt that fiction took up too much space. They couldn't put any advertising in that. For the last ten years, the number of fiction entries into the National Magazine Awards had declined.

"And pressures are getting worse. More magazines are more bottom-line oriented because they have been taken over by companies with no interest in publishing.

"I also think advertisers do this to women's magazines especially," he concluded, "because of the general disrespect they have for women."

Even media experts who don't give a damn about women's magazines are alarmed by the spread of this ad-edit linkage. In a climate *The Wall Street Journal* describes as an unacknowledged Depression for media, women's products are increasingly able to take their low standards wherever they go. For instance: newsweeklies publish uncritical stories on fashion and fitness. *The New York Times Magazine* recently ran an article on "firming creams," complete with mentions of advertisers. *Vanity Fair* published a profile of one major advertiser, Ralph Lauren, illustrated by the same photographer who does his ads, and turned the lifestyle of another, Calvin Klein, into a cover story. Even the outrageous *Spy* has toned down since it began to go after fashion ads.

And just to make us really worry, films and books, the last 98 media that go directly to the public without having to attract ads first, are in danger, too. Producers are beginning to depend on payments for displaying products in movies, and books are now being commissioned by companies like Federal Express.

But the truth is that women's products—like women's maga- 99 zines—have never been the subjects of much serious reporting anyway. News and general interest publications, including the "style" or "living" sections of newspapers, write about food and clothing as cooking and fashion, and almost never evaluate such products by brand name. Though chemical additives, pesticides, and animal fats are major health risks in the United States, and clothes, shoddy or not, absorb more consumer dollars than cars, this lack of information is serious. So is ignoring the contents of beauty products that are absorbed into our bodies through our skins, and that have profit margins so big they would make a loan shark blush.

III.

What could women's magazines be like if they were as free as 100 books? as realistic as newspapers? as creative as films? as diverse as women's lives? We don't know.

But we'll only find out if we take women's magazines seri- 101 ously. If readers were to act in a concerted way to change traditional practices of *all* women's magazines and the marketing of *all* women's products, we could do it. After all, they are operating on our consumer dollars; money that we now control. You and I could:

• write to editors and publishers (with copies to advertisers) that we're willing to pay *more* for magazines with editorial independence, but will *not* continue to pay for those that are just editorial extensions of ads;

• write to advertisers (with copies to editors and publishers) that we want fiction, political reporting, consumer reporting—whatever is, or is not, supported by their ads;

• put as much energy into breaking advertising's control over content as into changing the images in ads, or protesting ads for harmful products like cigarettes.;
• support only those women's magazines and products that take *us* seriously as readers and consumers.

Those of us in the magazine world can also use the carrot-and-stick technique. For instance: pointing out that, if magazines were a regulated medium like television, the demands of advertisers would be against FCC rules. Payola and extortion could be punished. As it is, there are probably illegalities. A magazine's postal rates are determined by the ratio of ad to edit pages, and the former costs more than the latter. So much for the stick.   102

The carrot means appealing to enlightened self-interest. For instance: there are many studies showing that the greatest factor in determining an ad's effectiveness is the credibility of its surroundings. The "higher the rating of editorial believability," concluded a 1987 survey by the *Journal of Advertising Research*, "the higher the rating of the advertising." Thus, an impenetrable wall between edit and ads would also be in the best interest of advertisers.   103

Unfortunately, few agencies or clients hear such arguments. Editors often maintain the false purity of refusing to talk to them at all. Instead, they see ad salespeople who know little about editorial, are trained in business as usual, and are usually paid by commission. Editors might also band together to take on controversy. That happened once when all the major women's magazines did articles in the same month on the Equal Rights Amendment. It could happen again.   104

It's almost three years away from life between the grindstones of advertising pressures and readers' needs. I'm just beginning to realize how edges got smoothed down—in spite of all our resistance.   105

I remember feeling put upon when I changed "Porsche" to "car" in a piece about Nazi imagery in German pornography by Andrea Dworkin—feeling sure Andrea would understand that Volkswagen, the distributor of Porsche and one of our few supportive advertisers, asked only to be far away from Nazi subjects. It's taken me all this time to realize that Andrea was the one with a right to feel put upon.   106

Even as I write this, I get a call from a writer for *Elle*, who is   107 doing a whole article on where women part their hair. Why, she wants to know, do I part mine in the middle?

It's all so familiar. A writer trying to make something of a nothing assignment; an editor laboring to think of new ways to attract ads; readers assuming that other women must want this ridiculous stuff; more women suffering for lack of information, insight, creativity, and laughter that could be on these same pages. 108

I ask you: Can't we do better than this? 109

JOHN STEINBECK

The Chrysanthemums

John Steinbeck was born in the Salinas Valley in California where "The Chrysanthemums" takes place, and worked there for several years as a hired hand, laborer, and occasional reporter. His most enduring works—those that eventually led to the Nobel Prize in 1962—were written during the Great Depression. "The Chrysanthemums" is a story from *The Long Valley* (1938).

The high grey-flannel fog of winter closed off the Salinas Valley from the sky and from all the rest of the world. On every side it sat like a lid on the mountains and made of the great valley a closed pot. On the broad, level land floor the gang plows bit deep and left the black earth shining like metal where the shares had cut. On the foothill ranches across the Salinas River, the yellow stubble fields seemed to be bathed in pale cold sunshine, but there was no sunshine in the valley now in December. The thick willow scrub along the river flamed with sharp and positive yellow leaves. 1

It was a time of quiet and of waiting. The air was cold and tender. A light wind blew up from the southwest so that the farmers were mildly hopeful of a good rain before long; but fog and rain do not go together. 2

Across the river, on Henry Allen's foothill ranch there was little work to be done, for the hay was cut and stored and the 3 orchards were plowed up to receive the rain deeply when it should come. The cattle on the higher slopes were becoming shaggy and rough-coated.

Elisa Allen, working in her flower garden, looked down   4 across the yard and saw Henry, her husband, talking to two men in business suits. The three of them stood by the tractor shed, each man with one foot on the side of the little Fordson. They smoked cigarettes and studied the machine as they talked.

Elisa watched them for a moment and then went back to her   5 work. She was thirty-five. Her face was lean and strong and her eyes were as clear as water. Her figure looked blocked and heavy in her gardening costume, a man's black hat pulled low down over her eyes, clodhopper shoes, a figured print dress almost completely covered by a big corduroy apron with four big pockets to hold the snips, the trowel and scratcher, the seeds and the knife she worked with. She wore heavy leather gloves to protect her hands while she worked.

She was cutting down the old year's chrysanthemum stalks   6 with a pair of short and powerful scissors. She looked down toward the men by the tractor shed now and then. Her face was eager and mature and handsome; even her work with the scissors was over-eager, over-powerful. The chrysanthemum stems seemed too small and easy for her energy.

She brushed a cloud of hair out of her eyes with the back of   7 her glove, and left a smudge of earth on the cheek in doing it. Behind her stood the neat white farm house with red geraniums close-banked around it as high as the windows. It was a hard-swept looking little house, with hard-polished windows, and a clean mud-mat on the front steps.

Elisa cast another glance toward the tractor shed. The   8 strangers were getting into their Ford coupe. She took off a glove and put her strong fingers down into the forest of new green chrysanthemum sprouts that were growing around the old roots. She spread the leaves and looked down among the close-growing stems. No aphids were there, no sowbugs or snails or cutworms. Her terrier fingers destroyed such pests before they could get started.

Elisa started at the sound of her husband's voice. He had   9 come near quietly, and he leaned over the wire fence that protected her flower garden from cattle and dogs and chickens.

"At it again," he said. "You've got a strong new crop coming."   10

Elisa straightened her back and pulled on the gardening glove   11
again. "Yes. They'll be strong this coming year." In her tone and
on her face there was a little smugness.

"You've got a gift with things," Henry observed. "Some of   12
those yellow chrysanthemums you had this year were ten inches
across. I wish you'd work out in the orchard and raise some apples that big."

Her eyes sharpened. "Maybe I could do it, too. I've a gift with   13
things, all right. My mother had it. She could stick anything in
the ground and make it grow. She said it was having planters'
hands that knew how to do it."

"Well, it sure works with flowers," he said.   14

"Henry, who were those men you were talking to?"   15

"Why, sure, that's what I came to tell you. They were from the   16
Western Meat Company. I sold those thirty head of three-year-old
steers. Got nearly my own price, too."

"Good," she said. "Good for you."   17

"And I thought," he continued, "I thought how it's Saturday   18
afternoon, and we might go into Salinas for dinner at a restaurant, and then to a picture show—to celebrate, you see."

"Good," she repeated. "Oh, yes. That will be good."   19

Henry put on his joking tone. "There's fights tonight. How'd   20
you like to go to the fights?"

"Oh, no," she said breathlessly. "No, I wouldn't like fights."   21

"Just fooling, Elisa. We'll go to a movie. Let's see. It's two   22
now. I'm going to take Scotty and bring down those steers from
the hill. It'll take us maybe two hours. We'll go in town about
five and have dinner at the Cominos Hotel. Like that?"

"Of course I'll like it. It's good to eat away from home."   23

"All right, then. I'll go get up a couple of horses."   24

She said, "I'll have plenty of time to transplant some of these   25
sets, I guess."

She heard her husband calling Scotty down by the barn. And   26
a little later she saw the two men ride up the pale yellow hillside
in search of the steers.

There was a little square sandy bed kept for rooting the   27
chrysanthemums. With her trowel she turned the soil over and
over, and smoothed it and patted it firm. Then she dug ten parallel trenches to receive the sets. Back at the chrysanthemum bed

she pulled out the little crisp shoots, trimmed off the leaves of each one with her scissors and laid it on a small orderly pile.

A squeak of wheels and plod of hoofs came from the road. 28 Elisa looked up. The country road ran along the dense bank of willows and cottonwoods that bordered the river, and up this road came a curious vehicle, curiously drawn. It was an old spring-wagon, with a round canvas top on it like the cover of a prairie schooner. It was drawn by an old bay horse and a little grey-and-white burro. A big stubble-bearded man sat between the cover flaps and drove the crawling team. Underneath the wagon, between the hind wheels, a lean and rangy mongrel dog walked sedately. Words were painted on the canvas in clumsy, crooked letters. "Pots, pans, knives, sisors, lawn mores. Fixed." Two rows of articles and the triumphantly definitive "Fixed" be-low. The black paint had run down in little sharp points beneath each letter.

Elisa, squatting on the ground, watched to see the crazy, loose- 29 jointed wagon pass by. But it didn't pass. It fumed into the farm road in front of her house, crooked old wheels skirling and squeaking. The rangy dog darted from between the wheels and ran ahead. Instantly the two ranch shepherds flew out at him. Then all three stopped, and with stiff and quivering tails, with taut straight legs, with ambassadorial dignity, they slowly cir-cled, sniffing daintily. The caravan pulled up to Elisa's wire fence and stopped. Now the newcomer dog, feeling out-numbered, towered his tail and retired under the wagon with raised hackles and bared teeth.

The man on the wagon seat called out. "That's a bad dog in a 30 fight when he gets started."

Elisa laughed. "I see he is. How soon does he generally get 31 started?"

The man caught up her laughter and echoed it heartily. 32 "Sometimes not for weeks and weeks," he said. He climbed stiffly down, over the wheel. The horse and the donkey drooped like unwatered flowers.

Elisa saw that he was a very big man. Although his hair and 33 beard were greying, he did not look old. His worn black suit was wrinkled and spotted with grease. The laughter had disappeared from his face and eyes the moment his laughing voice ceased. His eyes were dark, and they were full of the brooding that gets in the eyes of teamsters and of sailors. The calloused hands he rested on the wire fence were cracked, and every crack was a black line. He took off his battered hat.

"I'm off my general road, ma'am," he said. "Does this dirt road cut over across the river to the Los Angeles highway?" 34

Elisa stood up and shoved the thick scissors in her apron pocket. "Well, yes, it does, but it winds around and then fords the river. I don't think your team could pull through the sand." 35

He replied with some asperity. "It might surprise you what them beasts can pull through." 36

"When they get started?" she asked. 37

He smiled for a second. "Yes. When they get started." 38

"Well," said Elisa, "I think you'll save time if you go back to the Salinas road and pick up the highway there." 39

He drew a big finger down the chicken wire and made it sing. "I ain't in any hurry, ma'am. I go from Seattle to San Diego and back every year. Takes all my time. About six months each way. I aim to follow nice weather." 40

Elisa took off her gloves and stuffed them in the apron pocket with the scissors. She touched the under edge of her man's hat, searching for fugitive hairs. "That sounds like a nice kind of a way to live," she said. 41

He leaned confidently over the fence. "Maybe you noticed the writing on my wagon. I mend pots and sharpen knives and scissors. You got any of them things to do?" 42

"Oh, no," she said quickly. "Nothing like that." Her eyes hardened with resistance. 43

"Scissors is the worst thing," he explained. "Most people just ruin scissors trying to sharpen 'em but I know how. I got a special tool. It's a little bobbit kind of thing, and patented. But it sure does the trick." 44

"No. My scissors are all sharp." 45

"All right, then. Take a pot," he continued earnestly, "a bent pot, or a pot with a hole. I can make it like new so you don't have to buy no new ones. That's a saving for you." 46

"No," she said shortly. "I tell you I have nothing like that for you to do." 47

His face fell to an exaggerated sadness. His voice took on a whining undertone. "I ain't had a thing to do today. Maybe I won't have no supper tonight. You see I'm off my regular road. I 48 know folks on the highway clear from Seattle to San Diego. They save their things for me to sharpen up because they know I do it so good and save them money."

"I'm sorry," Elisa said irritably. "I haven't anything for you to do."   49

His eyes left her face and fell to searching the ground. They roamed about until they came to the chrysanthemum bed where she had been working. "What's them plants, ma'am?"   50

The irritation and resistance melted from Elisa's face. "Oh, those are chrysanthemums, giant whites and yellows. I raise them every year, bigger than anybody around here."   51

"Kind of a long-stemmed flower? Looks like a quick puff of colored smoke?" he asked.   52

"That's it. What a nice way to describe them."   53

"They smell kind of nasty till you get used to them," he said.   54

"It's a good bitter smell," she retorted, "not nasty at all."   55

He changed his tone quickly. "I like the smell myself."   56

"I had ten-inch blooms this year," she said.   57

The man leaned farther over the fence. "Look. I know a lady down the road a piece, has got the nicest garden you ever seen. Got nearly every kind of flower but no chrysanthemums. Last time I was mending a copper-bottom washtub for her (that's a hard job but I do it good), she said to me, 'If you ever run acrost some nice chrysanthemums I wish you'd try to get me a few seeds.' That's what she told me."   58

Elisa's eyes grew alert and eager. "She couldn't have known much about chrysanthemums. You can raise them from seed, but it's much easier to root the little sprouts you see there."   59

"Oh," he said. "I s'pose I can't take none to her, then."   60

"Why yes you can," Elisa cried. "I can put some in damp sand, and you can carry them right along with you. They'll take root in the pot if you keep them damp. And then she can transplant them."   61

"She'd sure like to have some, ma'am. You say they're nice ones?"   62

"Beautiful," she said. "Oh, beautiful." Her eyes shone. She tore off the battered hat and shook out her dark pretty hair. "I'll put them in a flower pot, and you can take them right with you. Come into the yard."   63

While the man came through the picket gate Elisa ran excitedly along the geranium-bordered path to the back of the house.   64

And she returned carrying a big red flower pot. The gloves were forgotten now. She kneeled on the ground by the starting bed and dug up the sandy soil with her fingers and scooped it into the bright new flower pot. Then she picked up the little pile of shoots she had prepared. With her strong fingers she pressed them into the sand and tamped around them with her knuckles. The man stood over her. "I'll tell you what to do," she said. "You remember so you can tell the lady."

"Yes, I'll try to remember."   65

"Well, look. These will take root in about a month. Then she   66
must set them out, about a foot apart in good rich earth like this,
see?" She lifted a handful of dark soil for him to look at. "They'll
grow fast and tall. Now remember this. In July tell her to cut
them down, about eight inches from the ground."

"Before they bloom?" he asked.   67

"Yes, before they bloom." Her face was tight with eagerness.   68
"They'll come right up again. About the last of September the
buds will start."

She stopped and seemed perplexed. "It's the budding that   69
takes the most care," she said hesitantly. "I don't know how to
tell you." She looked deep into his eyes, searchingly. Her mouth
opened a little, and she seemed to be listening. "I'll try to tell
you," she said. "Did you ever hear of planting hands?"

"Can't say I have, ma'am."   70

"Well, I can only tell you what it feels like. It's when you're   71
picking off the buds you don't want. Everything goes right down
into your fingertips. You watch your fingers work. They do it
themselves. You can feel how it is. They pick and pick the buds.
They never make a mistake. They're with the plant. Do you see?
Your fingers and the plant. You can feel that, right up your arm.
They know. They never make a mistake. You can feel it. When
you're like that you can't do anything wrong. Do you see that?
Can you understand that?"

She was kneeling on the ground looking up at him. Her breast   72
swelled passionately.

The man's eyes narrowed. He looked away, self-consciously.   73
"Maybe I know," he said. "Sometimes in the night in the wagon
there—"

Elisa's voice grew husky. She broke in on him. "I've never   74
lived as you do but I know what you mean. When the night is
dark—why, the stars are sharp-pointed, and there's quiet. Why,

you rise up and up! Every pointed star gets driven into your body. It's like that. Hot and sharp and—lovely."

Kneeling there, her hand went out toward his legs in the greasy black trousers. Her hesitant fingers almost touched the cloth. Then her hand dropped to the ground. She crouched low like a fawning dog.   75

He said, "It's nice, just like you say. Only when you don't have no dinner, it ain't."   76

She stood up then, very straight, and her face was ashamed. She held the flower pot out to him and placed it gently in his arms. "Here. Put it in your wagon, on the seat, where you can watch it. Maybe I can find something for you to do."   77

At the back of the house she dug in the can pile and found two old and battered aluminum saucepans. She carried them back and gave them to him. "Here, maybe you can fix these."   78

His manner changed. He became professional. "Good as new I can fix them." At the back of his wagon he set a little anvil, and out of an oily tool box dug a small machine hammer. Elisa came through the gate to watch him while he pounded out the dents in the kettles. His mouth grew sure and knowing. At a difficult part of the work he sucked his under-lip.   79

"You sleep right in the wagon?" Elisa asked.   80

"Right in the wagon, ma'am. Rain or shine I'm dry as a cow in there."   81

"It must be nice," she said. "It must be very nice. I wish women could do such things."   82

"It ain't the right kind of a life for a woman."   83

Her upper lip raised a little, showing her teeth. "How do you know? How can you tell?" she said.   84

"I don't know ma'am," he protested. "Of course I don't know. Now here's your kettles, done. You don't have to buy no new ones."   85

"How much?"   86

"Oh, fifty cents'll do. I keep my prices down and my work good. That's why I have all them satisfied customers up and down the highway."   87

Elisa brought him a fifty-cent piece from the house and dropped it in his hand. "You might be surprised to have a rival some time. I can sharpen scissors, too. And I can beat the dents out of little pots. I could show you what a woman might do."   88

He put his hammer back in the oily box and shoved the little   89
anvil out of sight. "It would be a lonely life for a woman, ma'am,
and a scary life, too, with animals creeping under the wagon all
night." He climbed over the singletree, steadying himself with a
hand on the burro's white rump. He settled himself in the seat,
picked up the lines. "Thank you kindly, ma'am," he said. "I'll do
like you told me; I'll go back and catch the Salinas road."

"Mind," she called, "if you're long in getting there, keep the   90
sand damp."

"Sand, ma'am? . . . Sand? Oh, sure. You mean round the   91
chrysanthemums. Sure I will." He clucked his tongue. The beasts
leaned luxuriously into their collars. The mongrel dog took his
place between the back wheels. The wagon turned and crawled
out the entrance road and back the way it had come, along the
river.

Elisa stood in front of her wire fence watching the slow   92
progress of the caravan. Her shoulders were straight, her head
thrown back, her eyes half-closed, so that the scene came vaguely
into them. Her lips moved silently, forming the words "Good-
bye—good-bye." Then she whispered. "That's a bright direction.
There's a glowing there." The sound of her whisper startled her.
She shook herself free and looked about to see whether anyone
had been listening. Only the dogs had heard. They lifted their
heads toward her from their sleeping in the dust, and then
stretched out their chins and settled asleep again. Elisa turned
and ran hurriedly into the house.

In the kitchen she reached behind the stove and felt the water   93
tank. It was full of hot water from the noonday cooking. In the
bathroom she tore off her soiled clothes and flung them into the
corner. And then she scrubbed herself with a little block of
pumice, legs and thighs, loins and chest and arms, until her skin
was scratched and red. When she had dried herself she stood in
front of a mirror in her bedroom and looked at her body. She
tightened her stomach and threw out her chest. She turned and
looked over her shoulder at her back.

After a while she began to dress, slowly. She put on her newest   94
underclothing and her nicest stockings and the dress which was
the symbol of her prettiness. She worked carefully on her hair,
pencilled her eyebrows and rouged her lips.

Before she was finished she heard the little thunder of hoofs   95 and the shouts of Henry and his helper as they drove the red steers into the corral. She heard the gate bang shut and set herself for Henry's arrival.

His step sounded on the porch. He entered the house calling   96
"Elisa, where are you?"

"In my room, dressing. I'm not ready. There's hot water for   97
your bath. Hurry up. It's getting late."

When she heard him splashing in the tub, Elisa laid his dark   98
suit on the bed, and shirt and socks and tie beside it. She stood
his polished shoes on the floor beside the bed. Then she went to
the porch and sat primly and stiffly down. She looked toward the
river road where the willow-line was still yellow with frosted
leaves so that under the high grey fog they seemed a thin band of
sunshine. This was the only color in the grey afternoon. She sat
unmoving for a long time. Her eyes blinked rarely.

Henry came banging out of the door, shoving his tie inside his   99
vest as he came. Elisa stiffened and her face grew tight. Henry
stopped short and looked at her. "Why—why, Elisa. You look so
nice!"

"Nice? You think I look nice? What do you mean by 'nice'?"   100

Henry blundered on. "I don't know. I mean you look differ-   101
ent, strong and happy."

"I am strong? Yes, strong. What do you mean 'strong'?"   102

He looked bewildered. "You're playing some kind of a   103
game," he said helplessly. "It's a kind of a play. You look strong
enough to break a calf over your knee, happy enough to eat it
like a watermelon."

For a second she lost her rigidity. "Henry! Don't talk like that.   104
You didn't know what you said." She grew complete again. "I'm
strong," she boasted. "I never knew before how strong."

Henry looked down toward the tractor shed, and when he   105
brought his eyes back to her, they were his own again. "I'll get
out the car. You can put on your coat while I'm starting."

Elisa went into the house. She heard him drive to the gate and   106
idle down his motor, and then she took a long time to put on her
hat. She pulled it here and pressed it there. When Henry turned
the motor off she slipped into her coat and went out.

The little roadster bounced along on the dirt road by the river,   107
raising the birds and driving the rabbits into the brush. Two
cranes flapped heavily over the willow-line and dropped into the
riverbed.

Far ahead on the road Elisa saw a dark speck. She knew.   108

She tried not to look as they passed it, but her eyes would not   109
obey. She whispered to herself sadly. "He might have thrown
them off the road. That wouldn't have been much trouble, not
very much. But he kept the pot," she explained. "He had to keep
the pot. That's why he couldn't get them off the road."

The roadster turned a bend and she saw the caravan ahead.   110
She swung full around toward her husband so she could not see
the little covered wagon and the mismatched team as the car
passed them.

In a moment they had left behind them the man who had not   111
known or needed to know what she said, the bargainer. She did
not look back.

To Henry, she said loudly, to be heard above the motor, "It   112
will be good, to-night, a good dinner."

"Now you're changed again," Henry complained. He took   113
one hand from the wheel and patted her knee. "I ought to take
you in to dinner oftener. It would be good for both of us. We get
so heavy out on the ranch."

"Henry," she asked, "could we have wine at dinner?"   114

"Sure. Say! That will be fine."   115

She was silent for a while; then she said, "Henry, at those   116
prize fights do the men hurt each other very much?"

"Sometimes a little, not often. Why?"   117

"Well, I've read how they break noses, and blood runs down   118
their chests. I've read how the fighting gloves get heavy and
soggy with blood."

He looked around at her. "What's the matter, Elisa? I didn't   119
know you read things like that." He brought the car to a stop,
then turned to the right over the Salinas River bridge.

"Do any women ever go to the fights?" she asked.   120

"Oh, sure, some. What's the matter, Elisa? Do you want to   121
go? I don't think you'd like it, but I'll take you if you really want
to go."

She relaxed limply in the seat. "Oh, no. I don't want to go. I'm   122
sure I don't." Her face was fumed away from him. "It will be
enough if we can have wine. It will be plenty." She turned up her
coat collar so he could not see that she was crying weakly—like
an old woman.

5

WHAT'S SO BAD
ABOUT BEING POOR?

At the time of the Louisville flood, 1937. MARGARET BOURKE-WHITE/TimePix.

OVERVIEW

Most Americans who lived before World War II, even if they were not themselves poor, saw enough poverty in their communities to recognize its gradations—from real destitution to mere difficulty paying the rent. Children who lived in families that could easily afford new clothes at the beginning of the school year knew other children who made do with old clothes. Girl Scouts and Boy Scouts learned to count thriftiness among the key virtues.

Americans who grew up in the second half of the twentieth century live in a different world. Poverty hasn't vanished, but most of us don't think of ourselves as living among the poor or of being likely to fall into poverty ourselves. Asked to list a dozen virtues, we wouldn't rank *thrift* alongside *courage*. We have become, conspicuously, a nation of consumers.

Our affluence has made the lives of the poor somewhat mysterious to us. The mystery sometimes produces pity, contempt, or fear of the poor; it doesn't often produce clear thinking or helpful action. The essays and the story collected in this section can hardly make the experience of poverty more comprehensible to those who have been insulated from it, but they do illustrate ways intelligent men and women have thought about what poverty means.

- Charles Murray, drawing on his experience as a Peace Corps worker in rural Thailand, invites us to consider the possibility that we would prefer poverty in a Thai village to relative affluence in a Bronx tenement.
- Gary Soto, drawing on his experience as a seventeen-year-old runaway working a dead-end job, shows us what work and life are like for those on the very margins of the economy.
- E. M. Forster, made prosperous by an inheritance and by sales of his books, considers the inevitable question "If you own things, what's their effect on you?"
- John Kenneth Galbraith, the leading liberal economist of his generation, summarizes the lines of thought by which conservative thinkers have avoided "compassion, along with the associated public effort" needed to help the poor.

- Clarence Darrow, famous principally as a brilliant defense attorney, tells the prisoners of Cook County jail that most of them are there not because of any moral defect, but because they have behaved rationally in the face of poverty.
- Sallie Tisdale considers why political liberals should do something they rarely do about the Salvation Army: "Take it seriously."
- Lars Eighner, a writer of considerable elegance who once made his living by picking through other people's garbage, looks at the American economy from the bottom up.
- Alice Walker, in a short story that brings poverty and affluence face to face in one family, helps us consider the difference between possessing something and owning it.

CHARLES MURRAY

What's So Bad About Being Poor?

After graduating from Harvard in 1965, Charles Murray spent five years as a Peace Corps worker in Thailand and stayed for a sixth to study the country's economic development. Returning to the United States, he took his Ph.D. in political science, focusing his attention on urban poverty and crime. His 1983 book, *Losing Ground: American Social Policy, 1950–1980, was* a cornerstone of Republican domestic policy during the Reagan years. "What's So Bad About Being Poor?" appeared in *The National Review* in 1988.

One of the great barriers to a discussion of poverty and social policy in the 1980s is that so few people who talk about poverty have ever been poor. The diminishing supply of the formerly poor in policy-making and policy-influencing positions is a side effect of progress. The number of poor households dropped dramatically from the beginning of World War II through the end of the 1960s. Despite this happy cause, however, it is a troubling phenomenon. From the beginning of American history through at least the 1950s, the new generation moving into positions of influence in politics, business, journalism, and academia was bound to include a large admixture of people who had grown up dirt-poor. People who had grown up in more privileged surroundings did not have to speculate about what being poor was like; someone sitting beside them, or at the head of the table, was likely to be able to tell them. It was easy to acknowledge then, as it is not now, that there is nothing so terrible about poverty *per se*. Poverty is not equivalent to destitution. Being poor does not necessarily mean being malnourished or ill-clothed. It does not automatically mean joylessness or despair. To be poor is not necessarily to be without dignity; it is not necessarily to be unhappy. When large numbers of people who were running the country had once been poor themselves, poverty could be kept in perspective.

Today, how many graduates of the Kennedy School of Government or of the Harvard Business School have ever been really poor? How many have ever had close friends who were? How many even have parents who were once poor? For those who have never been poor and never even known any people who were once poor, it is difficult to treat poverty as something other than a mystery. It is even more difficult to be detached about the importance of poverty, because to do so smacks of a "let them eat cake" mentality. By the same token, however, it is important that we who have never been poor be able to think about the relationship of poverty to social policy in a much more straightforward way than the nation's intellectuals and policy-makers have done for the past few decades. To that end, I propose a thought experiment based on the premise that tomorrow you had to be poor. I do not mean "low-income" by Western standards of affluence, but functioning near the subsistence level, as a very large proportion of the world's population still does.

In constructing this thought experiment, the first requirement   3
is to divorce yourself from certain reflexive assumptions. Do not think what it would be like to be poor while living in a community of rich people. I do not (yet) want to commingle the notions of absolute poverty and relative poverty, so you should imagine a community in which everyone else is as poor as you are, indeed, a world in which the existence of wealth is so far removed from daily life that it is not real.

The second requirement is to avoid constructing an imaginary   4
person. The point is not to try to imagine yourself in the shoes of "a poor person" but to imagine what *you*, with your particular personality, experiences, strengths, and limitations (including your middle-class upbringing and values), would do if you were suddenly thrust into this position.

To do all this in the American context is difficult. Any sce-   5
nario is filled with extraneous factors. So let me suggest one that I used as a way of passing the time when I was a researcher driving on the back roads of rural Thailand many years ago. What if, I would muse, I had to live for the rest of my life in the next village I came to (perhaps a nuclear war would have broken out, thereby keeping me indefinitely in Thailand; any rationalization would do)?

In some ways, the prospect was grim. I had never been charmed   6
by sleeping under mosquito netting nor by bathing with a few buckets of cloudy well water. When circumstances permitted, I

liked to end a day's work in a village by driving back to an air-conditioned hotel and a cold beer. But if I had no choice . . .

As it happens, Thailand has an attractive peasant culture. Survival itself is not a problem. The weather is always warm, so the requirements for clothes, fuel, and shelter are minimal. Village food is ample, if monotonous. But I would nonetheless be extremely poor, with an effective purchasing power of a few hundred dollars a year. The house I would live in would probably consist of a porch and one or two small, unlit, unfurnished rooms. The walls might be of wood, more probably of woven bamboo or leaf mats. I would have (in those years) no electricity and no running water. Perhaps I would have a bicycle or a transistor radio. Probably the nearest physician would be many kilometers away. In sum: If the criterion for measuring poverty is material goods, it would be difficult to find a community in deepest Appalachia or a neighborhood in the most depressed parts of South Chicago that even approaches the absolute material poverty of the average Thai village in which I would have to make my life.

On the other hand, as I thought about spending the next fifty years in a Thai village, I found myself wondering precisely what I would lack (compared to my present life) that would cause me great pain. The more I thought about the question, the less likely it seemed that I would be unhappy.

Since I lacked any useful trade, maybe I could swap the Jeep for a few *rai* of land and become a farmer. Learning how to farm well enough to survive would occupy my time and attention for several years. After that, I might try to become an affluent farmer. One of the assets I would bring from my Western upbringing and schooling would be a haphazardly acquired understanding of cash crops, markets, and entrepreneurial possibilities, and perhaps I could parlay that, along with hard work, into some income and more land. It also was clear to me that I probably would enjoy this "career." I am not saying I would *choose* it, but rather that I could find satisfaction in learning how to be a competent rice farmer, even though it was not for me the most desired of all possible careers.

What about my personal life? Thais are among the world's most handsome and charming people, and it was easy to imagine falling in love with a woman from the village, marrying her, and having a family with her. I could also anticipate the pleasure of watching my children grow up, probably at closer hand than I would in the United States. The children would not get the same education they would in the States, but I would have it within my power to see that they would be educated. A grade school is near every village. The priests in the local *wat* could teach them Buddhism. I could also become teacher to my children. A few basic textbooks in mathematics, science, and history; Plato and Shakespeare and the Bible; a dozen other well-chosen classics—all these could be acquired even in up-country Thailand. My children could reach adulthood literate, thoughtful, and civilized.

My children would do well in other ways too. They would   11 grow up in a "positive peer culture," as the experts say. Their Thai friends in the village would all be raised by their parents to be considerate, hard-working, pious, and honest—that's the way Thai villagers raise their children. My children would face few of the corrupting influences to be found in an American city.

Other personal pleasures? I knew I would find it easy to make   12 friends, and that some would become close. I would have other good times, too—celebrations on special occasions, but more often informal gatherings and jokes and conversation. If I read less, I would also read better. I would have great personal freedom as long as my behavior did not actively interfere with the lives of my neighbors (the tolerance for eccentric behavior in a Thai village is remarkably high). What about the physical condition of poverty? After a few months, I suspect that I would hardly notice.

You may conclude that this thought experiment is a transpar-   13 ent setup. First I ask what it would be like to be poor, then I proceed to outline a near-idyllic environment in which to be poor. I assume that I have a legacy of education experiences that would help me spend my time getting steadily less poor. And then I announce that poverty isn't so bad after all. But the point of the thought experiment is not to suggest that all kinds of poverty are tolerable, and even less that all peasant societies are pleasant places to live. When poverty means the inability to get enough food or shelter, it is every bit as bad as usually portrayed. When poverty means being forced to remain in that condition, with no way of improving one's situation, it is as bad as portrayed. When poverty is conjoined with oppression, be it a caste system or a hacienda system or a people's republic, it is as bad as portrayed. *My thought experiment is not a paean to peasant life, but a paean to communities of free people.* If poverty is defined in terms of money, everybody in the Thai village is poor. If poverty is defined as being unable to live a modest but decent existence, hardly anyone there is poor.

Does this thought experiment fail when it is transported to the United States? Imagine the same Thai village set down intact on the outskirts of Los Angeles. Surely its inhabitants must be miserable, living in their huts and watching the rest of the world live in splendor.   14

At this point in the argument, however, we need no longer think in terms of thought experiments. This situation is one that has been faced by hundreds of thousands of immigrants to the United States, whether they came from Europe at the end of World War II or from Vietnam in the mid-1970s. Lawyers found themselves working as janitors, professors found themselves working on assembly lines. Sometimes they worked their way up and out, but many had to remain janitors and factory workers, because they came here too late in life to retool their foreign-trained skills. But their children did not have to remain so, and they have not. A reading of their histories, in literature or in the oral testimony of their children, corroborates this pattern. Was a Latvian attorney forced to flee his country "happy" to have to work as a janitor? No. Was he prevented by his situation—specifically, by his poverty—from successfully pursuing happiness? Emphatically, no.   15

Let us continue the thought experiment nonetheless, with a slightly different twist. This time, you are given a choice. One choice is to be poor in rural Thailand, as I have described it, with just enough food and shelter and a few hundred dollars a year in cash: a little beyond bare subsistence, but not much. Or you may live in the United States, receive a free apartment, free food, free medical care, and a cash grant, the package coming to a total that puts you well above the poverty line. There is, however, a catch: you are *required* to live in a particular apartment, and this apartment is located in a public-housing project in one of the burned-out areas of the South Bronx. A condition of receiving the rest of the package is that you continue to live, and raise your children, in the South Bronx (you do not have the option of spending all of your waking hours in Manhattan, just as the village thought experiment did not give you the option of taking vacations in Bangkok). You still have all the assets you took to   16 the Thai village—once again, it is essential that you imagine not what it is like for an Alabama sharecropper to be transplanted to the South Bronx, but what it would be like *for you.*

In some ways, you would have much more access to distrac- 17 tions. Unlike the situation in the Thai village, you would have television you could watch all day, taking you vicariously into other worlds. And, for that matter, it would be much easier to get books than in a Thai village, and you would have much more money with which to buy them. You could, over time, fix up your apartment so that within its walls you would have an environment that looked and felt very like an apartment you could have elsewhere.

There is only one problem: You would have a terrible time 18 once you opened your door to the outside world. How, for example, are you going to raise your children in the South Bronx so that they grow up to be the adults you want them to be? (No, you don't have the option of sending them to live elsewhere.) How are you going to take a walk in the park in the evening? There are many good people in the South Bronx with whom you could become friends, just as in the village. But how are you to find them? And once they are found, how are you to create a functioning, mutually reinforcing community?

I suggest that as you think of answers to those questions, 19 you will find that, if you are to have much chance to be happy, the South Bronx needs to be changed in a way that the village did not—that, unlike the village as it stood, the South Bronx as it stands does not "work" as an environment for pursuing happiness. Let us ignore for the moment how these changes in environment could be brought about, by what combination of government's doing things and refraining from doing things. The fact is that hardly any of those changes involve greater income for you personally, but rather changes in the surrounding environment. There is a question that crystallizes the roles of personal *v.* environmental poverty in this situation: How much money would it take to persuade you to move self and family to this public-housing project in the South Bronx?

The purpose of the first two versions of the thought experi- 20 ment was to suggest a different perspective on one's own priorities regarding the pursuit of happiness, and by extension to suggest that perhaps public policy ought to reflect a different set of priorities as well. It is easy in this case, however, to assume that what one wants for oneself is not applicable to others. Thus, for example, it could be said that the only reason the thought experiments work (if you grant even that much) is that the central character starts out with enormous advantages of knowledge and values—which in themselves reflect the advantages of having grown up with plenty of material resources.

To explore that possibility, I ask you to bear with me for one 21 more thought experiment on this general topic, one I have found to be a touchstone. This time, the question is not what kinds of material resources you (with your fully developed set of advantages) need for your pursuit of happiness, but what a small child, without any developed assets at all, needs for his pursuit of happiness—specifically, what your own child needs.

Imagine that you are the parent of a small child, living in con- 22 temporary America, and in some way you are able to know that tomorrow you and your spouse will die and your child will be made an orphan. You do not have the option of sending the child to live with a friend or relative. You must select from among other and far-from-perfect choices. The choices, I assure you, are not veiled representations of anything else; the experiment is set up not to be realistic, but to evoke something about how you think.

Suppose first this choice: You may put your child with an ex- 23 tremely poor couple according to the official definition of "poor"— which is to say, poverty that is measured exclusively in money. This couple has so little money that your child's clothes will often be secondhand and there will be not even small luxuries to brighten his life. Life will be a struggle, often a painful one. But you also know that the parents work hard, will make sure your child goes to school and studies, and will teach your child that integrity and responsibility are primary values. Or you may put your child with parents who will be as affectionate to your child as the first couple but who have never worked, are indifferent to your child's education, think that integrity and responsibility (when they think of them at all) are meaningless words—but who have and will always have plenty of food and good clothes and amenities, provided by others.

Which couple do you choose? The answer is obvious to me 24 and I imagine to most readers: the first couple, of course. But if

you are among those who choose the first couple, stop and consider what the answer means. This is *your own child* you are
talking about, whom you would never let go hungry even if providing for your child meant going hungry yourself. And yet you
are choosing years of privation for that same child. Why?

Perhaps I set up the thought experiment too starkly. Let us re-   25
peat it, adding some ambiguity. This time, the first choice is again
the poor-but-virtuous couple. But the second couple is rich. They
are, we shall say, the heirs to a great fortune. They will not beat
your child or in any other way maltreat him. We may even assume affection on their part, as we will with the other couples.
But, once again, they have never worked and never will, are indifferent to your child's education, and think that integrity and
responsibility (when they think of them at all) are meaningless
words. They do, however, possess millions of dollars, more than
enough to last for the life of your child and of your child's children. Now, in whose care do you place your child? The poor
couple or the rich one?

This time, it seems likely that some people will choose the rich   26
couple—or more accurately, it is possible to think of ways in
which the decision might be tipped in that direction. For example,
a wealthy person who is indifferent to a child's education might
nonetheless ship the child off to an expensive boarding school at
the earliest possible age. In that case, it is conceivable that the
wealthy ne'er-do-wells are preferable to the poor-but-virtuous
couple, *if* they end up providing the values of the poor family
through the surrogate parenting of the boarding school—dubi-
ous, but conceivable. One may imagine other ways in which the
money might be used to compensate for the inadequacies of the
parents. But failing those very chancy possibilities, I suggest that
a great many parents on all sides of political fences would knowingly choose hunger and rags for their child rather than wealth.

Again, the question is: Why? What catastrophes are going to   27
befall the child placed in the wealthy home? What is the awful
fate? Would it be so terrible if he grew up to be thoughtlessly rich?
The child will live a life of luxury and have enough money to buy
himself out of almost any problem that might arise. Why not
leave it at that? Or let me put the question positively: In deciding
where to send the child, what is one trying to achieve by these calculations and predictions and hunches? What is the good that one
is trying to achieve? What is the criterion of success?

One may attach a variety of descriptors to the answer. Perhaps   28
you want the child to become a reflective, responsible adult. To
value honesty and integrity. To be able to identify sources of lasting satisfaction. Ultimately, if I keep pushing the question (Why is
honesty good? Why is being reflective good?), you will give the
answer that permits no follow-up: You want your child to be
happy. You are trying to choose the guardians who will best enable your child to pursue happiness. And, forced to a choice, material resources come very low on your list of priorities.

So far, I have limited the discussion to a narrow point: In de-   29
ciding how to enhance the ability of people to pursue happiness,
solutions that increase material resources beyond subsistence *in-
dependently of other considerations* are bound to fail. Money
per se is not very important. It quickly becomes trivial. Depending on other non-monetary conditions, poor people can have a
rich assortment of ways of pursuing happiness, or affluent people
can have very few.

The thought experiments were stratagems intended not to   30
convince you of any particular policy implications, but rather to
induce you to entertain this possibility: When a policy trade-off
involves (for example) imposing material hardship in return for
some other policy good, *it is possible* (I ask no more than that for
the time being) that imposing the material hardship is the right
choice. For example, regarding the "orphaned child" scenario: *If*
a policy leads to a society in which there are more of the first
kind of parents and fewer of the second, the sacrifices in material
resources available to the children involved might conceivably be
worth it.

The discussion, with its steady use of the concept of "near-   31
subsistence" as "enough material resources to pursue happiness,"
has also been intended to point up how little our concept of
poverty has to do with subsistence. Thus, for example, if one
simply looks at the end result of how people live, a natural observation concerning contemporary America might be that we
have large numbers of people who are living at a subsistence or
subsubsistence level. But I have been using "subsistence" in its
original sense: enough food to be adequately nourished, plus the
most basic shelter and clothing. The traditional Salvation Army
shelter provides subsistence, for example. In Western countries,
and perhaps especially the United States, two problems tend to

confuse the issue. One is that we have forgotten what subsistence means, so that an apartment with cockroaches, broken windows, and graffiti on the walls may be thought of as barely "subsistence level," even if it also has running water, electricity, heat, a television, and a pile of discarded fast-food cartons in the corner. It might be an awful place to live (for the reasons that the South Bronx can be an awful place to live), but it bears very little resemblance to what "subsistence" means to most of the world. Secondly, we tend to confuse the way in which some poor people *use* their resources (which indeed can often leave them in a near-subsistence state) with the raw purchasing power of the resources at their disposal. Take, for example, the apartment I just described and move a middle-class person with middle-class habits and knowledge into it, given exactly the same resources. Within days it would be still shabby but a different place. All of which is precisely the point of the thought experiments about Thailand and the South Bronx: Money has very little to do with living a poverty-stricken life. Similarly, "a subsistence income" has very little to do with what Americans think of as poverty.

That being the case, I am arguing that the job of designing 32 good public policy must be reconstrued. We do not have the option of saying, "First we will provide for the material base, then worry about the other necessary conditions for pursuing happiness." These conditions interact. The ways in which people go about achieving safety, self-respect, and self-fulfillment in their lives are inextricably bound up with each other and with the way in which people go about providing for their material well-being. We do not have the option of doing one good thing at a time.

In discussing the conditions for pursuing happiness I have put 33 material resources first only because that is where they have stood in the political debate. I am suggesting that properly they should be put last.

GARY SOTO

Black Hair

Gary Soto, who grew up among the working poor in Fresno, California, attended college at Fresno State. In the library there he read a modern poetry anthology and thought, "This is terrific. I'd like to do something like this." Twenty years later he decided to take a break from a successful career as a poet to "see if I could write prose." The result was *Living Up the Street* (1985), a memoir that won the American Book Award. "Black Hair' is a chapter from that book.

There are two kinds of work: One uses the mind and the other uses muscle. As a kid I found out about the latter. I'm thinking of the summer of 1969 when I was a seventeen-year-old runaway who ended up in Glendale, California, to work for Valley Tire Factory. To answer an ad in the newspaper I walked miles in the afternoon sun, my stomach slowly knotting on a doughnut that was breakfast, my teeth like bright candles gone yellow.

I walked in the door sweating and feeling ugly because my hair was still stiff from a swim at the Santa Monica beach the day before. Jules, the accountant and part owner, looked droopily through his bifocals at my application and then at me. He tipped his cigar in the ashtray, asked my age as if he didn't believe I was seventeen, but finally after a moment of silence, said, "Come back tomorrow. Eight-thirty."

I thanked him, left the office, and went around to the chain link fence to watch the workers heave tires into a bin; others carted uneven stacks of tires on hand trucks. Their faces were black from tire dust and when they talked—or cussed—their mouths showed a bright pink.

From there I walked up a commercial street, past a cleaners, a motorcycle shop, and a gas station where I washed my face and hands; before leaving I took a bottle that hung on the side of the Coke machine, filled it with water, and stopped it with a scrap of paper and a rubber band.

The next morning I arrived early at work. The assistant foreman, a potbellied Hungarian, showed me a timecard and how to punch in. He showed me the Coke machine, the locker room with its slimy shower, and also pointed out the places where I shouldn't go: The ovens where the tires were recapped and the customer service area, which had a slashed couch, a coffee table with greasy magazines, and an ashtray. He introduced me to Tully, a fat man with one ear, who worked the buffers that resurfaced the white walls. I was handed an apron and a face mask and shown how to use the buffer: Lift the tire and center, inflate it with a footpedal, press the buffer against the white band until cleaned, and then deflate and blow off the tire with an air hose.

With a paint brush he stirred a can of industrial preserver. 6 "Then slap this blue stuff on." While he was talking a co-worker came up quietly from behind him and goosed him with the air hose. Tully jumped as if he had been struck by a bullet and then turned around cussing and cupping his genitals in his hands as the other worker walked away calling out foul names. When Tully turned to me smiling his gray teeth, I lifted my mouth into a smile because I wanted to get along. He has to be on my side, I thought. He's the one who'll tell the foreman how I'm doing.

I worked carefully that day, setting the tires on the machine as 7 if they were babies, since it was easy to catch a finger in the rim that expanded to inflate the tire. At the day's end we swept up the tire dust and emptied the trash into bins.

At five the workers scattered for their cars and motorcycles 8 while I crossed the street to wash at a burger stand. My hair was stiff with dust and my mouth showed pink against the backdrop of my dirty face. I then ordered a hotdog and walked slowly in the direction of the abandoned house where I had stayed the night before. I lay under the trees and within minutes was asleep. When I woke my shoulders were sore and my eyes burned when I squeezed the lids together.

From the backyard I walked dully through a residential street, 9 and as evening came on, the TV glare in the living rooms and the headlights of passing cars showed against the blue drift of dusk. I saw two children coming up the street with snow cones, their tongues darting at the packed ice. I saw a boy with a peach and wanted to stop him, but felt embarrassed by my hunger. I walked for an hour only to return and discover the house lit brightly. Behind the fence I heard voices and saw a flashlight poking at the garage door. A man on the back steps mumbled something about the refrigerator to the one with the flashlight.

I waited for them to leave, but had the feeling they wouldn't   10
because there was the commotion of furniture being moved.
Tired, even more desperate, I started walking again with a great
urge to kick things and tear the day from my life. I felt weak
and my mind kept drifting because of hunger. I crossed the
street to a gas station where I sipped at the water fountain and
searched the Coke machine for change. I started walking again,
first up a commercial street, then into a residential area where
I lay down on someone's lawn and replayed a scene at home—
my Mother crying at the kitchen table, my stepfather yelling
with food in his mouth. They're cruel, I thought, and warned
myself that I should never forgive them. How could they do this
to me.

When I got up from the lawn it was late. I searched out a place   11
to sleep and found an unlocked car that seemed safe. In the back
seat, with my shoes off, I fell asleep but woke up startled about
four in the morning when the owner, a nurse on her way to
work, opened the door. She got in and was about to start the engine when I raised my head up from the backseat to explain my
presence. She screamed so loudly when I said "I'm sorry" that I
sprinted from the car with my shoes in hand. Her screams faded,
then stopped altogether, as I ran down the block where I hid behind a trash bin and waited for a police siren to sound. Nothing.
I crossed the street to a church where I slept stiffly on cardboard
in the balcony.

I woke up feeling tired and greasy. It was early and a few   12
street lights were still lit, the east growing pink with dawn. I
washed myself from a garden hose and returned to the church to
break into what looked like a kitchen. Paper cups, plastic spoons,
a coffee pot littered on a table. I found a box of Nabisco crackers which I ate until I was full.

At work I spent the morning at the buffer, but was then told   13
to help Iggy, an old Mexican, who was responsible for choosing
tires that could be recapped without the risk of exploding at high
speeds. Every morning a truck would deliver used tires, and after
I unloaded them Iggy would step among the tires to inspect them
for punctures and rips on the side walls.

With a yellow chalk he marked circles and Xs to indicate   14
damage and called out "junk." For those tires that could be recapped, he said "goody" and I placed them on my hand truck.
When I had a stack of eight I kicked the truck at an angle and

balanced them to another work area where Iggy again inspected
the tires, scratching Xs and calling out "junk."

Iggy worked only until three in the afternoon, at which time   15
he went to the locker room to wash and shave and to dress in a
two-piece suit. When he came out he glowed with a bracelet,
watch, rings, and a shiny fountain pen in his breast pocket. His
shoes sounded against the asphalt. He was the image of a banker
stepping into sunlight with millions on his mind. He said a few
low words to workers with whom he was friendly and none to
people like me.

I was seventeen, stupid because I couldn't figure out the dif-   16
ference between an F 78 14 and 750 14 at sight. Iggy shook his
head when I brought him the wrong tires, especially since I had
expressed interest in being his understudy. "Mexican, how can
you be so stupid?" he would yell at me, slapping a tire from my
hands. But within weeks I learned a lot about tires, from sizes
and makes to how they are molded in iron forms to how Valley
stole from other companies. Now and then we received a truck-
load of tires, most of them new or nearly new, and they were
taken to our warehouse in the back where the serial numbers
were ground off with a sander. On those days the foreman
handed out Cokes and joked with us as we worked to get the
numbers off.

Most of the workers were Mexican or black, though a few   17
redneck whites worked there. The base pay was a dollar sixty-
five, but the average was three dollars. Of the black workers, I
knew Sugar Daddy the best. His body carried two hundred and
fifty pounds, armfuls of scars, and a long knife that made me
jump when he brought it out from his boot without warning. At
one time he had been a singer, and had cut a record in 1967
called *Love's Chance*, which broke into the R and B charts. But
nothing came of it. No big contract, no club dates, no tours. He
made very little from the sales, only enough for an operation to
pull a steering wheel from his gut when, drunk and mad at a lady
friend, he slammed his Mustang into a row of parked cars.

"Touch it," he smiled at me one afternoon as he raised his   18
shirt, his black belly kinked with hair. Scared, I traced the scar
that ran from his chest to the left of his belly button, and I was
repelled but hid my disgust.

Among the Mexicans I had few friends because I was differ-   19
ent, a *pocho* who spoke bad Spanish. At lunch they sat in tires

and laughed over burritos, looking up at me to laugh even harder. I also sat in tires while nursing a Coke and felt dirty and sticky because I was still living on the street and had not had a real bath in over a week. Nevertheless, when the border patrol came to round up the nationals, I ran with them as they scrambled for the fence or hid among the tires behind the warehouse. The fore- man, who thought I was an undocumented worker, yelled at me to run, to get away. I did just that. At the time it seemed fun because there was no risk, only a goodhearted feeling of hide-and-seek, and besides it meant an hour away from work on com-pany time. When the police left we came back and some of the nationals made up stories of how they were almost caught—how they out-raced the police. Some of the stories were so convoluted and unconvincing that everyone laughed *mentiras,* especially when one described how he overpowered a policeman, took his gun away, and sold the patrol car. We laughed and he laughed, happy to be there to make up a story.

If work was difficult, so were the nights. I still had not gath- 20 ered enough money to rent a room, so I spent the nights sleeping in parked cars or in the balcony of a church. After a week I found a newspaper ad for a room for rent, phoned, and was given directions. Finished with work, I walked the five miles down Mission Road looking back into the traffic with my thumb out. No rides. After eight hours of handling tires I was frightening, I suppose, to drivers since they seldom looked at me; if they did, it was a quick glance. For the next six weeks I would try to hitch-hike, but the only person to stop was a Mexican woman who gave me two dollars to take the bus. I told her it was too much and that no bus ran from Mission Road to where I lived, but she insisted that I keep the money and trotted back to her idling car. It must have hurt her to see me day after day walking in the heat and looking very much the dirty Mexican to the many minds that didn't know what it meant to work at hard labor. That woman knew. Her eyes met mine as she opened the car door, and there was a tenderness that was surprisingly true—one for which you wait for years but when it comes it doesn't help. Nothing changes. You continue on in rags, with the sun still above you.

I rented a room from a middle-aged couple whose lives were 21 a mess. She was a school teacher and he was a fireman. A perfect set up, I thought. But during my stay there they would argue with one another for hours in their bedroom.

When I rang at the front door both Mr. and Mrs. Van Deusen   22
answered and didn't bother to disguise their shock at how awful
I looked. But they let me in all the same. Mrs. Van Deusen
showed me around the house, from the kitchen and bathroom to
the living room with its grand piano. On her fingers she counted
out the house rules as she walked me to my room. It was a girl's
room with lace curtains, scenic wallpaper of a Victorian couple
enjoying a stroll, canopied bed, and stuffed animals in a corner.
Leaving, she turned and asked if she could do laundry for me
and, feeling shy and hurt, I told her no; perhaps the next day. She
left and I undressed to take a bath, exhausted as I sat on the edge
of the bed probing my aches and my bruised places. With a towel
around my waist I hurried down the hallway to the bathroom
where Mrs. Van Deusen had set out an additional towel with a
tube of shampoo. I ran the water in the tub and sat on the toilet,
lid down, watching the steam curl toward the ceiling. When I
lowered myself into the tub I felt my body sting. I soaped a wash
cloth and scrubbed my arms until they lightened, even glowed
pink, but still I looked unwashed around my neck and face no
matter how hard I rubbed. Back in the room I sat in bed reading
a magazine, happy and thinking of no better luxury than a girl's
sheets, especially after nearly two weeks of sleeping on cardboard at the church.

I was too tired to sleep, so I sat at the window watching the   23
neighbors move about in pajamas, and, curious about the room,
looked through the bureau drawers to search out personal things—
snapshots, a messy diary, and a high school yearbook. I looked
up the Van Deusen's daughter, Barbara, and studied her face as if
I recognized her from my own school—a face that said "promise," "college," "nice clothes in the closet." She was a skater and
a member of the German Club; her greatest ambition was to sing
at the Hollywood Bowl.

After awhile I got into bed and as I drifted toward sleep I   24
thought about her. In my mind I played a love scene again and
again and altered it slightly each time. She comes home from college and at first is indifferent to my presence in her home, but finally I overwhelm her with deep pity when I come home hurt
from work, with blood on my shirt. Then there was another version: Home from college she is immediately taken with me, in
spite of my work-darkened face, and invites me into the family

car for a milkshake across town. Later, back at the house, we sit in the living room talking about school until we're so close I'm holding her hand. The truth of the matter was that Barbara did come home for a week, but was bitter toward her parents for taking in boarders (two others besides me). During that time she spoke to me only twice: Once, while searching the refrigerator, she asked if we had any mustard; the other time she asked if I had seen her car keys.

But it was a place to stay. Work had become more and more   25 difficult. I not only worked with Iggy, but also with the assistant foreman who was in charge of unloading trucks. After they backed in I hopped on top to pass the tires down by bouncing them on the tailgate to give them an extra spring so they would be less difficult to handle on the other end. Each truck was weighed down with more than two hundred tires, each averaging twenty pounds, so that by the time the truck was emptied and swept clean I glistened with sweat and my T-shirt stuck to my body. I blew snot threaded with tire dust onto the asphalt, indifferent to the customers who watched from the waiting room.

The days were dull. I did what there was to do from morning   26 until the bell sounded at five; I tugged, pulled, and cussed at tires until I was listless and my mind drifted and caught on small things, from cold sodas to shoes to stupid talk about what we would do with a million dollars. I remember unloading a truck with Hamp, a black man.

"What's better than a sharp lady?" he asked me as I stood   27 sweaty on a pile of junked tires. "Water. With ice," I said.

He laughed with his mouth open wide. With his fingers he   28 pinched the sweat from his chin and flicked at me. "You be too young, boy. A woman can make you a god."

As a kid I had chopped cotton and picked grapes, so I knew   29 work. I knew the fatigue and the boredom and the feeling that there was a good possibility you might have to do such work for years, if not for a lifetime. In fact, as a kid I imagined a dark fate: To marry Mexican poor, work Mexican hours, and in the end die a Mexican death, broke and in despair.

But this job at Valley Tire Company confirmed that there was   30 something worse than field work, and I was doing it. We were all doing it, from foreman to the newcomers like me, and what I felt heaving tires for eight hours a day was felt by everyone—black,

Mexican, redneck. We all despised those hours but didn't know what else to do. The workers were unskilled, some undocumented and fearful of deportation, and all struck with an uncertainty at what to do with their lives. Although everyone bitched about work, no one left. Some had worked there for as long as twelve years; some had sons working there. Few quit; no one was ever fired. It amazed me that no one gave up when the border patrol jumped from their vans, baton in hand, because I couldn't imagine any work that could be worse—or any life. What was out there, in the world, that made men run for the fence in fear?

Iggy was the only worker who seemed sure of himself. After 31 five hours of "junking," he brushed himself off, cleaned up in the washroom, and came out gleaming with an elegance that humbled the rest of us. Few would look him straight in the eye or talk to him in our usual stupid way because he was so much better. He carried himself as a man should—with that old world "dignity"—while the rest of us muffed our jobs and talked dully about dull things as we worked. From where he worked in his open shed he would now and then watch us with his hands on his hips. He would shake his head and click his tongue in disgust.

The rest of us lived dismally. I often wondered what the others' 32 homes were like; I couldn't imagine that they were much better than our work place. No one indicated that his outside life was interesting or intriguing. We all looked defeated and contemptible in our filth at the day's end. I imagined the average welcome at home: Rafael, a Mexican national who had worked at Valley for five years, returned to a beaten house of kids who were dressed in mismatched clothes and playing kick-the-can. As for Sugar Daddy, he returned home to a stuffy room where he would read and reread old magazines. He ate potato chips, drank beer, and watched TV. There was no grace in dipping socks into a wash basin where later he would wash his cup and plate.

There was no grace at work. It was all ridicule. The assistant 33 foreman drank Cokes in front of the newcomers as they laced tires in the afternoon sun. Knowing that I had a long walk home, Rudy, the college student, passed me waving and yelling "Hello," as I started down Mission Road on the way home to eat out of cans. Even our plump secretary got into the act by wearing short skirts and flaunting her milky legs. If there was love, it was ugly.

I'm thinking of Tully and an older man whose name I can no longer recall fondling one another in the washroom. I had come in cradling a smashed finger to find them pressed together in the shower, their pants undone and partly pulled down. When they saw me they smiled their pink mouths but didn't bother to push away.

How we arrived at such a place is a mystery to me. Why anyone would stay for years is even a deeper concern. You showed up, but from where? What broken life? What ugly past? The foreman showed you the Coke machine, the washroom, and the yard where you'd work. When you picked up a tire, you were amazed at the black it could give off. 34

E. M. FORSTER

My Wood

E. M. Forster, a brilliant English novelist and essayist, was able to pursue a career as a writer because of wealth inherited from a great aunt. The bequest troubled him: He never forgot that it was only good luck that had made him a wealthy man in a world where so many were poor. "My Wood," originally published in 1926, was reprinted in *Abinger Harvest* (1936).

A few years ago I wrote a book which dealt in part with the difficulties of the English in India. Feeling that they would have had no difficulties in India themselves, the Americans read the book freely. The more they read it the better it made them feel, and a cheque to the author was the result. I bought a wood with the cheque. It is not a large wood—it contains scarcely any trees, and it is intersected, blast it, by a public footpath. Still, it is the first property that I have owned, so it is right that other people should participate in my shame, and should ask themselves, in accents that will vary in horror, this very important question: What is the effect of property upon the character? Don't let's touch economics; the effect of private ownership upon the community as a whole is another question—a more important question, perhaps, but another one. Let's keep to psychology. If you 1

own things, what's their effect on you? What's the effect on me
of my wood?

In the first place, it makes me feel heavy. Property does have   2
this effect. Property produces men of weight, and it was a man
of weight who failed to get into the Kingdom of Heaven.[1] He
was not wicked, that unfortunate millionaire in the parable, he
was only stout; he stuck out in front, not to mention behind, and
as he wedged himself this way and that in the crystalline entrance and bruised his well-fed flanks, he saw beneath him a
comparatively slim camel passing through the eye of a needle
and being woven into the robe of God. The Gospels all through
couple stoutness and slowness. They point out what is perfectly
obvious, yet seldom realized: that if you have a lot of things
you cannot move about a lot, that furniture requires dusting,
dusters require servants, servants require insurance stamps, and
the whole tangle of them makes you think twice before you accept an invitation to dinner or go for a bathe in the Jordan.
Sometimes the Gospels proceed further and say with Tolstoy that
property is sinful; they approach the difficult ground of asceticism here, where I cannot follow them. But as to the immediate
effects of property on people, they just show straightforward
logic. It produces men of weight. Men of weight cannot, by definition, move like the lightning from the East unto the West, and
the ascent of a fourteen-stone[2] bishop into a pulpit is thus the exact antithesis of the coming of the Son of Man. My wood makes
me feel heavy.

In the second place, it makes me feel it ought to be larger.   3

The other day I heard a twig snap in it. I was annoyed at first,   4
for I thought that someone was blackberrying, and depreciating
the value of the undergrowth. On coming nearer, I saw it was not
a man who had trodden on the twig and snapped it, but a bird,
and I felt pleased. My bird. The bird was not equally pleased. Ignoring the relation between us, it took fright as soon as it saw
the shape of my face, and flew straight over the boundary hedge
into a field, the property of Mrs. Henessy, where it sat down with
a loud squawk. It had become Mrs. Henessy's bird. Something
seemed grossly amiss here, something that would not have oc-

1. Luke 18:18–25.
2. 196-pound.

curred had the wood been larger. I could not afford to buy Mrs. Henessy out, I dared not murder her, and limitations of this sort beset me on every side. Ahab did not want that vineyard[3]—he only needed it to round off his property, preparatory to plotting a new curve—and all the land around my wood has become necessary to me in order to round off the wood. A boundary protects. But—poor little thing—the boundary ought in its turn to be protected. Noises on the edge of it. Children throw stones. A little more, and then a little more, until we reach the sea. Happy Canute![4] Happier Alexander![5] And after all, why should even the world be the limit of possession? A rocket containing a Union Jack, will, it is hoped, be shortly fired at the moon. Mars. Sirius. Beyond which . . . But these immensities ended by saddening me. I could not suppose that my wood was the destined nucleus of universal dominion—it is so very small and contains no mineral wealth beyond the blackberries. Nor was I comforted when Mrs. Henessy's bird took alarm for the second time and flew clean away from us all, under the belief that it belonged to itself.

In the third place, property makes its owner feel that he ought to do something to it. Yet he isn't sure what. A restlessness comes over him, a vague sense that he has a personality to express—the same sense which, without any vagueness, leads the artist to an act of creation. Sometimes I think I will cut down such trees as remain in the wood, at other times I want to fill up the gaps between them with new trees. Both impulses are pretentious and empty. They are not honest movements towards money-making or beauty. They spring from a foolish desire to express myself and from an inability to enjoy what I have got. Creation, property, enjoyment form a sinister trinity in the human mind. Creation and enjoyment are both very very good, yet they are often unattainable without a material basis, and at such moments property pushes itself in as a substitute, saying, "Accept me instead—I'm good enough for all three." It is not enough. It is, as Shakespeare said of lust, "The expense of spirit in a waste of shame": it is "Before, a joy proposed; behind, a

3. 1 Kings 21.
4. Also spelled Cnute (994–1035): king of the English, Danes, and Norwegians.
5. Alexander the Great (356 B.C.–323 B.C.): king of Macedonia and conqueror of some of the richest countries of the Mideast.

dream." Yet we don't know how to shun it. It is forced on us by
our economic system as the alternative to starvation. It is also
forced on us by an internal defect in the soul, by the feeling that
in property may lie the germs of self-development and of exquisite or heroic deeds. Our life on earth is, and ought to be, material and carnal. But we have not yet learned to manage our
materialism and carnality properly; they are still entangled with
the desire for ownership, where (in the words of Dante) "Possession is one with loss."

And this brings us to our fourth and final point: the black-   6
berries.

Blackberries are not plentiful in this meagre grove, but they   7
are easily seen from the public footpath which traverses it, and
all too easily gathered. Foxgloves, too—people will pull up the
foxgloves, and ladies of an educational tendency even grub for
toadstools to show them on the Monday in class. Other ladies,
less educated, roll down the bracken in the arms of their gentlemen friends. There is paper, there are tins. Pray, does my wood
belong to me or doesn't it? And, if it does, should I not own it
best by allowing no one else to walk there? There is a wood near
Lyme Regis, also cursed by a public footpath, where the owner
has not hesitated on this point. He has built high stone walls
each side of the path, and has spanned it by bridges, so that the
public circulate like termites while he gorges on the blackberries
unseen. He really does own his wood, this able chap. Dives in
Hell did pretty well, but the gulf dividing him from Lazarus
could be traversed by vision,[6] and nothing traverses it here. And
perhaps I shall come to this in time. I shall wall in and fence out
until I really taste the sweets of property. Enormously stout, endlessly avaricious, pseudo-creative, intensely selfish, I shall weave
upon my forehead the quadruple crown of possession until those
nasty Bolshies come and take it off again and thrust me aside
into the outer darkness.

---

6. Luke 16:19–31.

John Kenneth Galbraith

How to Get the Poor Off Our Conscience

John Kenneth Galbraith is one of the leading economists of the last hundred years and one of the most controversial. Galbraith has argued repeatedly that the economy has become a treadmill, shaped by business interests to keep people working and consuming, regardless of what they might want if they were left to their own devices. Given this vision of the artificiality of affluence, he is naturally distressed by the existence of what he sees as equally artificial poverty. "How to Get the Poor Off Our Conscience" was published in *Harper's Magazine* in November 1985.

I would like to reflect on one of the oldest of human exercises,   1
the process by which over the years, and indeed over the centuries, we have undertaken to get the poor off our conscience.

Rich and poor have lived together, always uncomfortably and   2
sometimes perilously, since the beginning of time. Plutarch[1] was led to say: "An imbalance between the rich and poor is the oldest and most fatal ailment of republics." And the problems that arise from the continuing co-existence of affluence and poverty—and particularly the process by which good fortune is justified in the presence of the ill fortune of others—have been an intellectual preoccupation for centuries. They continue to be so in our own time.

One begins with the solution proposed in the Bible: the poor   3
suffer in this world but are wonderfully rewarded in the next. Their poverty is a temporary misfortune; if they are poor and also meek, they eventually will inherit the earth. This is, in some ways, an admirable solution. It allows the rich to enjoy their wealth while envying the poor their future fortune.

Much, much later, in the twenty or thirty years following the   4
publication in 1776 of *The Wealth of Nations*—the late dawn of the Industrial Revolution in Britain—the problem and its solution began to take on their modern form. Jeremy Bentham, a

1. Plutarch (46–120): Greek historian, biographer, and philosopher.

near contemporary of Adam Smith, came up with the formula that for perhaps fifty years was extraordinarily influential in British and, to some degree, American thought. This was utilitarianism. "By the principle of utility," Bentham said in 1789, "is meant the principle which approves or disapproves of every action whatsoever according to the tendency which it appears to have to augment or diminish the happiness of the party whose interest is in question." Virtue is, indeed must be, self-centered. While there were people with great good fortune and many more with great ill fortune, the social problem was solved as long as, again in Bentham's words, there was "the greatest good for the greatest number." Society did its best for the largest possible number of people; one accepted that the result might be sadly unpleasant for the many whose happiness was not served.

In the 1830s a new formula, influential in no slight degree to this day, became available for getting the poor off the public conscience. This is associated with the names of David Ricardo, a stockbroker, and Thomas Robert Malthus, a divine. The essentials are familiar: the poverty of the poor was the fault of the poor. And it was so because it was a product of their excessive fecundity: their grievously uncontrolled lust caused them to breed up to the full limits of the available subsistence.

This was Malthusianism. Poverty being caused in the bed meant that the rich were not responsible for either its creation or its amelioration. However, Malthus was himself not without a certain feeling of responsibility: he urged that the marriage ceremony contain a warning against undue and irresponsible sexual intercourse—a warning, it is fair to say, that has not been accepted as a fully effective method of birth control. In more recent times, Ronald Reagan has said that the best form of population control emerges from the market. (Couples in love should repair to R. H. Macy's, not their bedrooms.) Malthus, it must be said, was at least as relevant.

By the middle of the nineteenth century, a new form of denial achieved great influence, especially in the United States. The new doctrine, associated with the name of Herbert Spencer, was Social Darwinism. In economic life, as in biological development, the overriding rule was survival of the fittest. That phrase—"survival of the fittest"—came, in fact, not from Charles Darwin but from Spencer, and expressed his view of economic life. The elimination of the poor is nature's way of improving the race. The weak and unfortunate being extruded, the quality of the human family is thus strengthened.

One of the most notable American spokespersons of Social 8 Darwinism was John D. Rockefeller—the first Rockefeller—who said in a famous speech: "The American Beauty rose can be produced in the splendor and fragrance which bring cheer to its beholder only by sacrificing the early buds which grow up around it. And so it is in economic life. It is merely the working out of a law of nature and a law of God."

In the course of the present century, however, Social Darwinism 9 came to be considered a bit too cruel. It declined in popularity, and references to it acquired a condemnatory tone. We passed on to the more amorphous denial of poverty associated with Calvin Coolidge and Herbert Hoover. They held that public assistance to the poor interfered with the effective operation of the economic system—that such assistance was inconsistent with the economic design that had come to serve most people very well. The notion that there is something economically damaging about helping the poor remains with us to this day as one of the ways by which we get them off our conscience.

With the Roosevelt revolution (as previously with that of Lloyd 10 George in Britain), a specific responsibility was assumed by the government for the least fortunate people in the republic. Roosevelt and the presidents who followed him accepted a substantial measure of responsibility for the old through Social Security, for the unemployed through unemployment insurance, for the unemployable and the handicapped through direct relief, and for the sick through Medicare and Medicaid. This was a truly great change, and for a time, the age-old tendency to avoid thinking about the poor gave way to the feeling that we didn't need to try—that we were, indeed, doing something about them.

In recent years, however, it has become clear that the search 11 for a way of getting the poor off our conscience was not at an end; it was only suspended. And so we are now again engaged in this search in a highly energetic way. It has again become a major philosophical, literary, and rhetorical preoccupation, and an economically not unrewarding enterprise.

Of the four, maybe five, current designs we have to get the 12 poor off our conscience, the first proceeds from the inescapable

JOHN KENNETH GALBRAITH

fact that most of the things that must be done on behalf of the
poor must be done in one way or another by the government. It
is then argued that the government is inherently incompetent, except as regards weapons design and procurement and the overall
management of the Pentagon. Being incompetent and ineffective,
it must not be asked to succor the poor; it will only louse things
up or make things worse.

The allegation of government incompetence is associated in our   13
time with the general condemnation of the bureaucrat—again excluding those concerned with national defense. The only form
of discrimination that is still permissible—that is, still officially
encouraged in the United States today—is discrimination against
people who work for the federal government, especially on social
welfare activities. We have great corporate bureaucracies replete
with corporate bureaucrats, but they are good; only public bureaucracy and government servants are bad. In fact, we have in the
United States an extraordinarily good public service—one made
up of talented and dedicated people who are overwhelmingly honest and only rarely given to overpaying for monkey wrenches,
flashlights, coffee makers, and toilet seats. (When these aberra-
tions have occurred, they have, oddly enough, all been in the Pentagon.) We have nearly abolished poverty among the old, greatly
democratized health care, assured minorities of their civil rights,
and vastly enhanced educational opportunity. All this would seem
a considerable achievement for incompetent and otherwise ineffective people. We must recognize that the present condemnation
of government and government administration is really part of the
continuing design for avoiding responsibility for the poor.

The second design in this great centuries-old tradition is to argue   14
that any form of public help to the poor only hurts the poor. It destroys morale. It seduces people away from gainful employment. It
breaks up marriages, since women can seek welfare for themselves
and their children once they are without their husbands.

There is no proof of this—none, certainly, that compares that   15
damage with the damage that would be inflicted by the loss of
public assistance. Still, the case is made—and believed—that there
is something gravely damaging about aid to the unfortunate.
This is perhaps our most highly influential piece of fiction.

The third, and closely related, design for relieving ourselves of   16
responsibility for the poor is the argument that public-assistance

measures have an adverse effect on incentive. They transfer income from the diligent to the idle and feckless, thus reducing the effort of the diligent and encouraging the idleness of the idle. The modern manifestation of this is supply-side economics. Supply-side economics holds that the rich in the United States have not been working because they have too little income. So, by taking money from the poor and giving it to the rich, we increase effort and stimulate the economy. Can we really believe that any considerable number of the poor prefer welfare to a good job? Or that business people—corporate executives, the key figures in our time—are idling away their hours because of the insufficiency of their pay? This is a scandalous charge against the American businessperson, notably a hard worker. Belief can be the servant of truth—but even more of convenience.

The fourth design for getting the poor off our conscience is to 17 point to the presumed adverse effect on freedom of taking responsibility for them. Freedom consists of the right to spend a maximum of one's money by one's own choice, and to see a minimum taken and spent by the government. (Again, expenditure on national defense is excepted.) In the enduring words of Professor Milton Friedman, people must be "free to choose."

This is possibly the most transparent of all of the designs; no 18 mention is ordinarily made of the relation of income to the freedom of the poor. (Professor Friedman is here an exception; through the negative income tax, he would assure everyone a basic income.) There is, we can surely agree, no form of oppression that is quite so great, no constriction on thought and effort quite so comprehensive, as that which comes from having no money at all. Though we hear much about the limitation on the freedom of the affluent when their income is reduced through taxes, we hear nothing of the extraordinary enhancement of the freedom of the poor from having some money of their own to spend. Yet the loss of freedom from taxation to the rich is a small thing as compared with the gain in freedom from providing some income to the impoverished. Freedom we rightly cherish. Cherishing it, we should not use it as a cover for denying freedom to those in need.

Finally, when all else fails, we resort to simple psychological 19 denial. This is a psychic tendency that in various manifestations is common to us all. It causes us to avoid thinking about death. It causes a great many people to avoid thought of the arms race and the consequent rush toward a highly probable extinction. By the same process of psychological denial, we decline to think of the poor. Whether they be in Ethiopia, the South Bronx, or even in such an Elysium as Los Angeles, we resolve to keep them off our minds. Think, we are often advised, of something pleasant.

These are the modern designs by which we escape concern for   20 the poor. All, save perhaps the last, are in great inventive descent from Bentham, Malthus, and Spencer. Ronald Reagan and his colleagues are clearly in a notable tradition—at the end of a long history of effort to escape responsibility for one's fellow beings. So are the philosophers now celebrated in Washington: George Gilder, a greatly favored figure of the recent past, who tells to much applause that the poor must have the cruel spur of their own suffering to ensure effort; Charles Murray, who, to greater cheers, contemplates "scrapping the entire federal welfare and income-support structure for working and aged persons, including A.F.D.C., Medicaid, food stamps, unemployment insurance, Workers' Compensation, subsidized housing, disability insurance, and," he adds, "the rest. Cut the knot, for there is no way to untie it." By a triage, the worthy would be selected to survive; the loss of the rest is the penalty we should pay. Murray is the voice of Spencer in our time; he is enjoying, as indicated, unparalleled popularity in high Washington circles.

Compassion, along with the associated public effort, is the   21 least comfortable, the least convenient, course of behavior and action in our time. But it remains the only one that is consistent with a totally civilized life. Also, it is, in the end, the most truly conservative course. There is no paradox here. Civil discontent and its consequences do not come from contented people—an obvious point. To the extent that we can make contentment as nearly universal as possible, we will preserve and enlarge the social and political tranquillity for which conservatives, above all, should yearn.

CLARENCE DARROW

Address to the Prisoners in the Cook County Jail

Clarence Darrow was one of the most famous attorneys of the twentieth century. Early in his career he was a successful corporate lawyer, and eventually the attorney for the Chicago and Northwestern Railway. In 1894 he quit this lucrative post to defend (without fee) Eugene V. Debs, leader of a strike against the railroad. For nearly two decades thereafter Darrow was labor's most able advocate both in the courts and in testimony before Congress. In the final decades of his career he turned to criminal law, defending (among many others) John T. Scopes, who was charged with teaching evolution in the Tennessee schools. The following speech was delivered to the prisoners of the Cook County, Illinois, jail in 1902.

If I looked at jails and crimes and prisoners in the way the ordinary person does, I should not speak on this subject to you. The reason I talk to you on the question of crime, its cause and cure, is that I really do not in the least believe in crime. There is no such thing as a crime as the word is generally understood. I do not believe there is any sort of distinction between the real moral conditions of the people in and out of jail. One is just as good as the other. The people here can no more help being here than the people outside can avoid being outside. I do not believe that people are in jail because they deserve to be. They are in jail simply because they cannot avoid it on account of circumstances which are entirely beyond their control and for which they are in no way responsible.   1

I suppose a great many people on the outside would say I was doing you harm if they should hear what I say to you this afternoon, but you cannot be hurt a great deal anyway, so it will not matter. Good people outside would say that I was really teaching you things that were calculated to injure society, but it's worth while now and then to hear something different from what you ordinarily get from preachers and the like. These will tell you that you should be good and then you will get rich and be happy.   2

Of course we know that people do not get rich by being good, and that is the reason why so many of you people try to get rich some other way, only you do not understand how to do it quite as well as the fellow outside.

There are people who think that everything in this world is an 3 accident. But really there is no such thing as an accident. A great many folks admit that many of the people in jail ought to be there, and many who are outside ought to be in. I think none of them ought to be here. There ought to be no jails; and if it were not for the fact that people on the outside are so grasping and heartless in their dealings with the people on the inside, there would be no such institution as jails.

I do not want you to believe that I think all you people here 4 are angels. I do not think that. You are people of all kinds, all of you doing the best you can—and that is evidently not very well. You are people of all kinds and conditions and under all circumstances. In one sense everybody is equally good and equally bad. We all do the best we can under the circumstances. But as to the exact things for which you are sent here, some of you are guilty and did the particular act because you needed the money. Some of you did it because you are in the habit of doing it, and some of you because you are born to it, and it comes to be as natural as it does, for instance, for me to be good.

Most of you probably have nothing against me, and most of 5 you would treat me the same way as any other person would, probably better than some of the people on the outside would treat me, because you think I believe in you and they know I do not believe in them. While you would not have the least thing against me in the world, you might pick my pockets. I do not think all of you would, but I think some of you would. You would not have anything against me, but that's your profession, a few of you. Some of the rest of you, if my doors were unlocked, might come in if you saw anything you wanted—not out of any malice to me, but because that is your trade. There is no doubt there are quite a number of people in this jail who would pick my pockets. And still I know this—that when I get outside pretty nearly everybody picks my pocket. There may be some of you who would hold up a man on the street, if you did not happen to have something else to do, and needed the money; but when I want to light my house or my office the gas company holds me up. They charge me one dollar for something that is worth twenty-five cents. Still all these people are good people; they are pillars of society and support the churches, and they are respectable.

When I ride on the streetcars I am held up—I pay five cents for   6
a ride that is worth two and a half cents, simply because a body of men have bribed the city council and the legislature, so that all the rest of us have to pay tribute to them.

If I do not want to fall into the clutches of the gas trust and   7
choose to burn oil instead of gas, then good Mr. Rockefeller holds me up, and he uses a certain portion of his money to build universities and support churches which are engaged in telling us how to be good.

Some of you are here for obtaining property under false pre-   8
tenses—yet I pick up a great Sunday paper and read the advertisements of a merchant prince—"Shirtwaists for 39 cents, marked down from $3.00."

When I read the advertisement in the paper I see they are all   9
lies. When I want to get out and find a place to stand anywhere on the face of the earth, I find that it has all been taken up long ago before I came here, and before you came here, and somebody says, "Get off, swim into the lake, fly into the air; go anywhere, but get off." That is because these people have the police and they have the jails and the judges and the lawyers and the soldiers and all the rest of them to take care of the earth and drive everybody off that comes in their way.

A great many people will tell you that all this is true, but that   10
it does not excuse you. These facts do not excuse some fellow who reaches into my pocket and takes out a five-dollar bill. The fact that the gas company bribes the members of the legislature from year to year, and fixes the law, so that all you people are compelled to be "fleeced" whenever you deal with them; the fact that the streetcar companies and the gas companies have control of the streets; and the fact that the landlords own all the earth—this, they say, has nothing to do with you.

Let us see whether there is any connection between the crimes   11
of the respectable classes and your presence in the jail. Many of you people are in jail because you have really committed burglary; many of you, because you have stolen something. In the meaning of the law, you have taken some other person's property. Some of you have entered a store and carried off a pair of shoes because you did not have the price. Possibly some of you have committed murder. I cannot tell what all of you did. There

are a great many people here who have done some of these things who really do not know themselves why they did them. I think I know why you did them—every one of you; you did these things because you were bound to do them. It looked to you at the time as if you had a chance to do them or not, as you saw fit; but still, after all, you had no choice. There may be people here who had some money in their pockets and who still went out and got some more money in a way society forbids. Now, you may not yourselves see exactly why it was you did this thing, but if you look at the question deeply enough and carefully enough you will see that there were circumstances that drove you to do exactly the thing which you did. You could not help it any more than we outside can help taking the positions that we take. The reformers who tell you to be good and you will be happy, and the people on the outside who have property to protect—they think that the only way to do it is by building jails and locking you up in cells on weekdays and praying for you Sundays.

I think that all of this has nothing whatever to do with right   12
conduct. I think it is very easily seen what has to do with right conduct. Some so-called criminals—and I will use this word because it is handy, it means nothing to me—I speak of the criminals who get caught as distinguished from the criminals who catch them—some of these so-called criminals are in jail for their first offenses, but nine tenths of you are in jail because you did not have a good lawyer and, of course, you did not have a good lawyer because you did not have enough money to pay a good lawyer. There is no very great danger of a rich man going to jail.

Some of you may be here for the first time. If we would open   13
the doors and let you out, and leave the laws as they are today, some of you would be back tomorrow. This is about as good a place as you can get anyway. There are many people here who are so in the habit of coming that they would not know where else to go. There are people who are born with the tendency to break into jail every chance they get, and they cannot avoid it. You cannot figure out your life and see why it was, but still there is a reason for it; and if we were all wise and knew all the facts, we could figure it out.

In the first place, there are a good many more people who go   14
to jail in the wintertime than in the summer. Why is this? Is it because people are more wicked in winter? No, it is because the coal trust begins to get in its grip in the winter. A few gentlemen

take possession of the coal, and unless the people will pay seven or eight dollars a ton for something that is worth three dollars, they will have to freeze. Then there is nothing to do but to break into jail, and so there are many more in jail in the winter than in summer. It costs more for gas in the winter because the nights are longer, and people go to jail to save gas bills. The jails are electric-lighted. You may not know it, but these economic laws are working all the time, whether we know it or do not know it.

There are more people who go to jail in hard times than in   15 good times—few people, comparatively, go to jail except when they are hard up. They go to jail because they have no other place to go. They may not know why, but it is true all the same. People are not more wicked in hard times. That is not the reason. The fact is true all over the world that in hard times more people go to jail than in good times, and in winter more people go to jail than in summer. Of course it is pretty hard times for people who go to jail at any time. The people who go to jail are almost always poor people—people who have no other place to live, first and last. When times are hard, then you find large numbers of people who go to jail who would not otherwise be in jail.

Long ago, Mr. Buckle, who was a great philosopher and histo-   16 rian, collected facts, and he showed that the number of people who are arrested increased just as the price of food increased. When they put up the price of gas ten cents a thousand, I do not know who will go to jail, but I do know that a certain number of people will go. When the meat combine raises the price of beef, I do not know who is going to jail, but I know that a large number of people are bound to go. Whenever the Standard Oil Company raises the price of oil, I know that a certain number of girls who are seamstresses, and who work night after night long hours for somebody else, will be compelled to go out on the streets and ply another trade, and I know that Mr. Rockefeller and his associates are responsible and not the poor girls in the jails.

First and last, people are sent to jail because they are poor.   17 Sometimes, as I say, you may not need money at the particular time, but you wish to have thrifty forehanded habits, and do not always wait until you are in absolute want. Some of you people are perhaps plying the trade, the profession, which is called bur-glary. No man in his right senses will go into a strange house in the dead of night and prowl around with a dark lantern through unfamiliar rooms and take chances of his life, if he has plenty of the good things of the world in his own home. You would not take any such chances as that. If a man had clothes in his clothespress and beefsteak in his pantry and money in the bank, he would not navigate around nights in houses where he knows nothing about the premises whatever. It always requires experience and education for this profession, and people who fit themselves for it are no more to blame than I am for being a lawyer. A man would not hold up another man on the street if he had plenty of money in his own pocket. He might do it if he had one dollar or two dollars, but he wouldn't if he had as much money as Mr. Rockefeller has. Mr. Rockefeller has a great deal better hold-up game than that.

The more that is taken from the poor by the rich, who have   18
the chance to take it, the more poor people there are who are compelled to resort to these means for a livelihood. They may not understand it, they may not think so at once, but after all they are driven into that line of employment.

There is a bill before the legislature of this state to punish kid-   19
naping children with death. We have wise members of the legislature. They know the gas trust when they see it and they always see it—they can furnish light enough to be seen; and this legislature thinks it is going to stop kidnaping children by making a law punishing kidnapers of children with death. I don't believe in kidnaping children, but the legislature is all wrong. Kidnaping children is not a crime, it is a profession. It has been developed with the times. It has been developed with our modern industrial conditions. There are many ways of making money—many new ways that our ancestors knew nothing about. Our ancestors knew nothing about a billion-dollar trust; and here comes some poor fellow who has no other trade and he discovers the profession of kidnaping children.

This crime is born, not because people are bad; people don't   20
kidnap other people's children because they want the children or because they are devilish, but because they see a chance to get some money out of it. You cannot cure this crime by passing a law punishing by death kidnapers of children. There is one way to cure it. There is one way to cure all these offenses, and that is to give the people a chance to live. There is no other way, and there never was any other way since the world began; and the world is so blind and stupid that it will not see. If every man and woman and child in the world had a chance to make a decent,

fair, honest living, there would be no jails and no lawyers and no courts. There might be some persons here or there with some peculiar formation of their brain, like Rockefeller, who would do these things simply to be doing them; but they would be very, very few, and those should be sent to a hospital and treated, and not sent to jail; and they would entirely disappear in the second generation, or at least in the third generation.

I am not talking pure theory. I will just give you two or three illustrations.   21

The English people once punished criminals by sending them   22
away. They would load them on a ship and export them to Australia. England was owned by lords and nobles and rich people. They owned the whole earth over there, and the other people had to stay in the streets. They could not get a decent living. They used to take their criminals and send them to Australia—I mean the class of criminals who got caught. When these criminals got over there, and nobody else had come, they had the whole continent to run over, and so they could raise sheep and furnish their own meat, which is easier than stealing it. These criminals then became decent, respectable people because they had a chance to live. They did not commit any crimes. They were just like the English people who sent them there, only better. And in the second generation the descendants of those criminals were as good and respectable a class of people as there were on the face of the earth, and then they began building churches and jails themselves.

A portion of this country was settled in the same way, landing   23
prisoners down on the southern coast; but when they got here and had a whole continent to run over and plenty of chances to make a living, they became respectable citizens, making their own living just like any other citizen in the world. But finally the descendants of the English aristocracy who sent the people over to Australia found out they were getting rich, and so they went over to get possession of the earth as they always do, and they organized land syndicates and got control of the land and ores, and then they had just as many criminals in Australia as they did in England. It was not because the world had grown bad; it was because the earth had been taken away from the people.

Some of you people have lived in the country. It's prettier than   24
it is here. And if you have ever lived on a farm you understand that if you put a lot of cattle in a field, when the pasture is short

they will jump over the fence; but put them in a good field where there is plenty of pasture, and they will be law-abiding cattle to the end of time. The human animal is just like the rest of the animals, only a little more so. The same thing that governs in the one governs in the other.

Everybody makes his living along the lines of least resistance. 25 A wise man who comes into a country early sees a great undeveloped land. For instance, our rich men twenty-five years ago saw that Chicago was small and knew a lot of people would come here and settle, and they readily saw that if they had all the land around here it would be worth a good deal, so they grabbed the land. You cannot be a landlord because somebody has got it all. You must find some other calling. In England and Ireland and Scotland less than five per cent own all the land there is, and the people are bound to stay there on any kind of terms the landlords give. They must live the best they can, so they develop all these various professions—burglary, picking pockets, and the like.

Again, people find all sorts of ways of getting rich. These are 26 diseases like everything else. You look at people getting rich, organizing trusts and making a million dollars, and somebody gets the disease and he starts out. He catches it just as a man catches the mumps or the measles; he is not to blame, it is in the air. You will find men speculating beyond their means, because the mania of money-getting is taking possession of them. It is simply a disease—nothing more, nothing less. You cannot avoid catching it; but the fellows who have control of the earth have the advantage of you. See what the law is: when these men get control of things, they make the laws. They do not make the laws to protect anybody; courts are not instruments of justice. When your case gets into court it will make little difference whether you are guilty or innocent, but it's better if you have a smart lawyer. And you cannot have a smart lawyer unless you have money. First and last it's a question of money. Those men who own the earth make the laws to protect what they have. They fix up a sort of fence or pen around what they have, and they fix the law so the fellow on the outside cannot get in. The laws are really organized for the protection of the men who rule the world. They were never organized or enforced to do justice. We have no system for doing justice, not the slightest in the world.

Let me illustrate: Take the poorest person in this room. If 27 the community had provided a system of doing justice, the poorest person in this room would have as good a lawyer as the richest, would he not? When you went into court you would have just as long a trial and just as fair a trial as the richest person in Chicago. Your case would not be tried in fifteen or twenty minutes, whereas it would take fifteen days to get through with a rich man's case.

Then if you were rich and were beaten, your case would be 28
taken to the Appellate Court. A poor man cannot take his case to the Appellate Court; he has not the price. And then to the Supreme Court. And if he were beaten there he might perhaps go to the United States Supreme Court. And he might die of old age before he got into jail. If you are poor, it's a quick job. You are almost known to be guilty, else you would not be there. Why should anyone be in the criminal court if he were not guilty? He would not be there if he could be anywhere else. The officials have no time to look after all these cases. The people who are on the outside, who are running banks and building churches and making jails, they have no time to examine 600 or 700 prisoners each year to see whether they are guilty or innocent. If the courts were organized to promote justice the people would elect somebody to defend all these criminals, somebody as smart as the prosecutor—and give him as many detectives and as many assistants to help, and pay as much money to defend you as to prosecute you. We have a very able man for state's attorney, and he has many assistants, detectives, and policemen without end, and judges to hear the cases—everything handy.

Most all of our criminal code consists in offenses against 29
property. People are sent to jail because they have committed a crime against property. It is of very little consequence whether one hundred people more or less go to jail who ought not to go—you must protect property, because in this world property is of more importance than anything else.

How is it done? These people who have property fix it so they 30
can protect what they have. When somebody commits a crime it does not follow that he has done something that is morally wrong. The man on the outside who has committed no crime may have done something. For instance: to take all the coal in the United States and raise the price two dollars or three dollars when there is no need of it, and thus kill thousands of babies and send thousands of people to the poorhouse and tens of thousands to jail, as is done every year in the United States—this is a

greater crime than all the people in our jails ever committed; but the law does not punish it. Why? Because the fellows who control the earth make the laws. If you and I had the making of the laws, the first thing we would do would be to punish the fellow who gets control of the earth. Nature put this coal in the ground for me as well as for them and nature made the prairies up here to raise wheat for me as well as for them, and then the great railroad companies came along and fenced it up.

Most all of the crimes for which we are punished are property crimes. There are a few personal crimes, like murder—but they are very few. The crimes committed are mostly those against property. If this punishment is right the criminals must have a lot of property. How much money is there in this crowd? And yet you are all here for crimes against property. The people up and down the Lake Shore have not committed crime; still they have so much property they don't know what to do with it. It is perfectly plain why these people have not committed crimes against property; they make the laws and therefore do not need to break them. And in order for you to get some property you are obliged to break the rules of the game. I don't know but what some of you may have had a very nice chance to get rich by carrying a hod for one dollar a day, twelve hours. Instead of taking that nice, easy profession, you are a burglar. If you had been given a chance to be a banker you would rather follow that. Some of you may have had a chance to work as a switchman on a railroad where you know, according to statistics, that you cannot live and keep all your limbs more than seven years, and you can get fifty dollars or seventy-five dollars a month for taking your lives in your hands; and instead of taking that lucrative position you chose to be a sneak thief, or something like that. Some of you made that sort of choice. I don't know which I would take if I was reduced to this choice. I have an easier choice.

I will guarantee to take from this jail, or any jail in the world, five hundred men who have been the worst criminals and lawbreakers who ever got into jail, and I will go down to our lowest streets and take five hundred of the most abandoned prostitutes, and go out somewhere where there is plenty of land, and will give them a chance to make a living, and they will be as good people as the average in the community.

There is one remedy for the sort of condition we see here. The world never finds it out, or when it does find it out it does not enforce it. You may pass a law punishing every person with death for burglary, and it will make no difference. Men will commit it just the same. In England there was a time when one hundred different offenses were punishable with death, and it made no difference. The English people strangely found out that so fast as they repealed the severe penalties and so fast as they did away with punishing men by death, crime decreased instead of increased; that the smaller the penalty the fewer the crimes.

Hanging men in our county jails does not prevent murder. It makes murderers.   34

And this has been the history of the world. It's easy to see how   35
to do away with what we call crime. It is not so easy to do it. I will tell you how to do it. It can be done by giving the people a chance to live—by destroying special privileges. So long as big criminals can get the coal fields, so long as the big criminals have control of the city council and get the public streets for streetcars and gas rights—this is bound to send thousands of poor people to jail. So long as men are allowed to monopolize all the earth, and compel others to live on such terms as these men see fit to make, then you are bound to get into jail.

The only way in the world to abolish crime and criminals is to   36
abolish the big ones and the little ones together. Make fair conditions of life. Give men a chance to live. Abolish the right of private ownership of land, abolish monopoly, make the world partners in production, partners in the good things of life. Nobody would steal if he could get something of his own some easier way. Nobody will commit burglary when he has a house full. No girl will go out on the streets when she has a comfortable place at home. The man who owns a sweatshop or a department store may not be to blame himself for the condition of his girls, but when he pays them five dollars, three dollars, and two dollars a week, I wonder where he thinks they will get the rest of their money to live. The only way to cure these conditions is by equality. There should be no jails. They do not accomplish what they pretend to accomplish. If you would wipe them out there would be no more criminals than now. They terrorize nobody. They are a blot upon any civilization, and a jail is an evidence of the lack of charity of the people on the outside who make the jails and fill them with the victims of their greed.

SALLIE TISDALE

Good Soldiers

Sallie Tisdale began her prolific writing career while she worked
as a registered nurse in Portland, Oregon, publishing three award-
winning books about health and health care in three years. Thereafter she became a freelance writer whose contributions have
appeared in such periodicals as *Vogue, Esquire,* and *The New
Yorker.* "Good Soldiers," which appeared in *The New Republic*
in 1994, may have presented Tisdale with some unusual problems. What is Tisdale, a Buddhist, a leftist, and a woman who enjoys X-rated movies, to make of workers who have devoted their
lives to a Christian ideal and very conservative social values?

The red shield with a white letter "S," red kettles at Christ-   1
mas, fresh-faced young women in bonnets, street-corner brass
bands. Each image means only one thing, and each is likely to
evoke more amusement than respect. The Salvation Army is so
conspicuous as to be invisible to most people, almost as invisible
as the average person served in its kitchens and shelters. I've seen
the red shield on the big white building down the street from my
house, on the stately stonework of the New York headquarters
on Fourteenth Street, on the architectural gloss of a new building
in Santa Monica, and until recently I never paid attention. I
thought of the Salvation Army as little more than a chain of
thrift stores—a quaint and rather austere organization of inde-
terminate size.

I am not a Christian and never have been, but I think of Jesus   2
every time I pass a storefront mission and see men curled up in
doorways, families lined up outside. "The least among you," He
said. I am glad, when I pass the soup kitchens, that someone is
doing something. I am guilty because I do too little. I am puzzled
because I'm not always sure what I could and should do. But to
tackle homelessness and end-stage alcoholism with cornets and a
Bible reading, as I believed the Salvation Army to do, seemed
rather naive. What I mostly didn't do with the Salvation Army—
and do now—is take it seriously.

The Army is far larger than most people realize, claiming   3
more than 5 million members in ninety-nine countries. Last year,

it raised $726 million from private donations in the United States, more than any other nonprofit organization. (The Christmas kettles alone brought in $61 million.) All money raised locally is used locally. One of the principles of charity outlined in Army literature is that any social plan "must be on a scale commensurate with the situation with which it proposes to deal." In the United States last year the Army served at least 69 million free meals and provided shelter for 9.5 million homeless people.

These are, and should be, dazzling numbers, easily outstripping the income and services provided by other charities struggling directly with poverty. Certainly the Army is one of the most efficient, spending eighty-seven cents of every donated dollar on its service programs. In the name of bringing the poor and hungry up from the gutter to independence, the Salvation Army offers food and shelter, employment services, drug and alcohol recovery programs, a nationwide missing persons service, homes for pregnant women, shelter for battered women and their children, nursing care for people with AIDS, day-care centers, toy giveaways at Christmas, clothing, prison programs, hospitals, legal aid, various forms of counseling and, always, as much religion as anyone wants.

The Salvation Army is an evangelical church. Its charity is not simply service for service's sake, but service to people so much in need they cannot hear the word of the Salvationists' God. In 1992 the Army counted 133,833 "Decisions for Christ" by people attending worship or receiving charity. The Army's target has always been the most disadvantaged and the most reviled. In a way, the Salvation Army has tried to *be* the poor.

Though the Army can invoke in the thoughtful outsider an uncomfortable ambivalence, a careful reading of its policies reveals surprising layers of intelligence, tolerance and joy. My own cultural politics are far to the left of the Army's. My growing respect for it comes from the fact that the daily behavior of Salvationists is often more political and far to the left of my own. They preach and pray about the suffering of the world, but most of all, what Salvationists do in the face of suffering is act.

Captain Bill Dickinson runs the Seattle Temple Corps of the Salvation Army, a congregation of more than 400 members. He is 53 years old, mild, plainspoken, compact, graying. His voice is usually diffident, but now and then it will rise into the cantatory inflections of testimony. Bill and his wife, Mary, were childhood sweethearts in Walla Walla, Washington, where they both occasionally attended Salvation Army services. They married in 1960, a year after Bill finished his Navy Service. Bill eventually became a successful restaurant owner. He also became an alcoholic.

"I found early on that I'm the kind of person who can't take 8
just one drink. I was always trying to find satisfaction in *something*. I thought, if I work hard enough and make enough money, that way we'll find happiness. And we were very successful, and I felt no satisfaction. We had the financial means to do all kinds of stuff, and yet it was just an *empty* life." In Spokane, Washington, the Dickinsons began attending Army services for the first time since childhood.

Bill Dickinson told me of his resistance to the whispering call. 9
"I got to the point where I hated to go to church. The Holy Spirit had really been convicting me of my sin—my sins—and I had such a need to repent and come back to Him. But I wouldn't yield to the Holy Spirit because of my pride." He smiled, a little sheepish at the memory. "So finally it's Sunday morning and I'm sitting in the pew at church, and I couldn't wait for them to give the altar call. I thought, 'This is it, now or never.' August 29, 1982, at about 12:15, I went forward and accepted Christ as my Savior in the Lord. And I was delivered from the taste of alcohol."

Like Dickinson, many Army officers have had wide experi 10
ence in the secular world. Yet there is no typical Salvationist; prejudgment fails in this real world on which so many false stereotypes are based. Bill Dickinson is what he seems to be. Only in meeting a person whose internal life is so visible can we see how rare that quality is—the transparency that comes to each of us only when we are doing exactly what we want to do, and think we should be doing, with our lives.

On a Christmas visit I made to Dickinson's temple last year, 11
he introduced me to another kind of Salvationist, a tall, broad, laughing 35-year-old man named Ken Solts. Solts was then a second-year seminary student sent from California to help with the holiday kettle drive. Over cocoa in the Temple kitchen, Solts interrupted our conversation to ask me if I had accepted Jesus as my personal savior, accepted my refusal to discuss the matter with another laugh and went on. He eagerly told me of his own history of drug dealing and jail time. "Everything kind of caught up all at once, when I was 29." He shook his head. "There's something about what that drug—crank—does to you, some-

thing that makes you such an airhead, and it takes a long time for it to wear off. God has changed my life in such a short time, and if He can do it for me, He can do it for anyone.

"I'd made a lot of promises to God, and now I was really in a bad place. So I made another promise—that if He got me out of prison time, I would change my life. And somehow the courts ended up combining all my felonies into one, which was a miracle in itself, and then the judge suspended my sentence. I had three years probation, and all kinds of fines to pay, and there I was, with a big promise to keep.   12

"My parents are auxiliary captains in Sacramento. I knew if I moved there I'd have to go to church," he continued. "So, I went, but I wasn't ready to give in. One day I was just sitting there and I really felt the need to change my life. I prayed and asked Christ into my heart.   13

"When I was saved, I said, 'O.K., this is cool, but I'm *not* wearing that uniform.' So five months later I'm wearing a uniform, being sworn in as a senior soldier. Then my dad started talking to me about officership, and I said, 'I don't want to be an officer.' Besides, it's real strict. You can't be a cadet if you're on probation. Then the captain wrote to the probation officer, and the Army made a special grant to pay off my fines. They sent them a check. And the judge let me off."   14

People who join the Salvation Army church sign a covenant called the "Articles of War," and are then called soldiers. (Many people who attend Army services prefer not to sign the Articles, often because of the smoking restriction. These people are called "adherents.") Soldiers are enjoined against the use of alcohol, tobacco and other recreational drugs, and told to avoid gambling, debt and the use of profanity. They are encouraged to join trade unions and generally will side with labor during strikes. Soldiers are also urged to examine themselves for dishonesty, racism, sexism and arrogance. The Salvationist is admonished to see himself as a "stranger" on earth, and to see the church itself as "a band of pilgrims who are called to separate themselves from the oppressive patterns of the present." The death of a Salvationist is routinely referred to as a "promotion to Glory," and mourning is discouraged.   15

The Salvation Army's mix of social action and religion leads to a number of policies unexpected in fundamentalist Christianity. The Army *is* quaint, and austere; Salvationists are also   16 unflinchingly clear-headed about the state of the world. Naïveté, like the blush on the bonneted girl's cheek, is only an image. The Army combines radicalism and conservatism in a mix that should not work: since its inception it has been accused of being too conservative by some observers and too liberal by others—too religious in its charitable work, too secular in its religion.

Salvationists traditionally volunteer in war zones, and Army   17 officers are qualified as military chaplains. But any Salvationist who declares himself to be a conscientious objector will receive the church's backing. Contraception among Salvationists is not only a private matter between husband and wife, but, to a church intimate with the problems of overpopulation and poverty, also a matter of "informed responsibility."

Two issues stand out as the traditional thorns of fundamen-   18 talism—abortion and homosexuality. Abortion is strongly discouraged, but there are certain exceptions in which it is an acceptable choice. Homosexuality is considered one of several examples of "sexual misconduct," but the Doctrines of the Army are careful to distinguish between homosexual behavior and homosexual "tendencies." This doctrine is, in fact, the only example of real naïveté I've come across in Army literature. ("Some homosexuals achieve a happy heterosexual marriage," reads the position paper.) Absent from the Army's attitude toward homosexuality, however, is any trace of hate-mongering. In the words of the church, homosexuality is not "blameworthy and should not be allowed to create guilt."

Salvation Army officers receive no salary; the commitment to   19 the poor includes the experience of poverty. (William Booth, the Army's founder, told one class of newly trained officers, "I sentence you all to hard labor for the rest of your natural lives.") These days, Army officers are provided with modest housing, a car, a portion of the cost of their uniforms, 80 percent of their medical expenses and a living allowance. At the beginning of her career, a single officer will receive $138 per week; the amount gradually increases. A married couple receives between them a beginning allowance of $229 per week. A child under the age of 5 increases the couple's allowance by $23 per week. The most any officer or officer couple can make is $282 a week. (This is, approximately, all the compensation given to the Army's general, its worldwide leader.) Most officers tithe their allowance to the church. And the tithe is not all; from its inception, the Army has occasionally called on its members and officers for Self-Denial Funds for specific projects; in 1992 the Army raised more than $20 million from its own staff.

A Salvation Army officer is expected to be in uniform when- 20 ever he or she is on duty, and officers are almost always on duty. According to church literature, the navy blue uniform is "an invitation to the people to avail themselves" of officers for any kind of help. "I tell you, if I put my uniform on and go down the street and approach somebody," Dickinson told me one afternoon, "I'll have a very easy time striking up a conversation with them and even talking to them about the Lord. If I take my uniform off and just dress up in a suit or casual clothes, and do the same thing, chances are I'll be ignored. With the uniform they know they're safe. They're probably going to hear the Gospel story, but they'll accept that. They don't have to be afraid."

"People wave and smile at me. People will even stop and tell 21 me, 'Thank you for how you helped me out fifteen or twenty years ago, forty or fifty years ago,' or, 'Thank you for how you helped my parents.' They always told me that if I was ever in trouble, I could go to the Salvation Army and they would help me."

Army founder William Booth was born in Nottingham, En- 22 gland, in 1829 to severe poverty. He was a teetotaler, a vegetarian, the father of eight, often ill and depressed. He was called "General" wherever he went, and once was described as being "desperately in earnest all the time." He certainly looks earnest in his photographs, earnest and infinitely weary, with a long white beard, a frosting of snow-white hair, a prominent nose and uncommonly sad eyes.

Booth began preaching as a Wesleyan Methodist, but was 23 kicked out of the church because of his volatile outdoor sermons and his insistence on universal salvation—that God's saving grace was available to all people. (In Booth's time, the poor were either not allowed into church services or were required to stay hidden behind screens.) His sermons drew big crowds, and eventually mobs, riots and the police, especially after his young wife, Catherine Mumford, began to preach beside him. They converted hundreds of people at a time. In 1878 he changed the name of his Christian Mission to the Salvation Army, adopting as his motto "Blood and Fire."

Booth wanted the poor of London, he said, to have only what   24
cab horses could depend upon: adequate food, decent shelter,
gainful employment. He believed economic conditions held people
in thrall. In fact, reading his proposals today is a lesson in how
very different roads can lead to the same goal, because William
Booth steered close to a kind of Marxism in his love of Christ.
The Army, instead, arrived at a policy of strict nonpartisanship.
Only once, and not without internal dissension, has the Army
taken a public political position; in 1928 it briefly endorsed Herbert Hoover for president because he supported prohibition.

George Bernard Shaw, in his introduction to *Major Barbara*,   25
wrote that Booth "would take money from the Devil himself and
be only too glad to get it out of his hands and into God's." The
philosophy is akin to Booth's feeling about the joy of music,
which in the Army's hands is both irrepressible and reverent. "I
rather enjoy robbing the Devil of his choicest tunes," said Booth.

Once the Army was established, clients were expected to pay   26
for their meals. If the bowl of soup cost a penny to make, a man
should pay a penny, and if he didn't have a penny, the Army gave
him a penny's worth of work to do before he ate. This policy continued well into the 1950s, but today, sheer numbers make it impossible to let every hungry person work for his or her meal.
Instead, one officer told me simply, "If unemployment is the problem, we get them jobs." Eighty-two thousand jobs last year, in fact.

In the United States, the Salvation Army has seen its biggest   27
successes. The Army's first overseas missionaries, seven women
and a man, were sent to America in 1880. Only one of the
women was over the age of 20. A few days after docking in New
York (the first Salvation sermon being delivered on the dock), the
missionaries preached at Harry Hill's Variety, a saloon on the
corner of Crosby and Houston Streets. The *New York World*
duly reported the event as "A PECULIAR PEOPLE AMID QUEER
SURROUNDINGS." Within six months there were twelve American Salvation Army Corps; within ten years, the Army was in
forty-three states. And it grew, adding new Corps almost
monthly, and never failing to find new forms of spectacle and
display for its message—"Soup, Soap and Salvation!" The first
Salvation Army Christmas kettle was a crab pot put out on a
street in San Francisco, appropriated on an impulse by an officer
in 1891 and labeled "Keep the Pot Boiling!"

The first Army home for alcoholics, called the Church of the   28
Homeless Outcast, was started in Detroit in 1939. Now there
are 147, known as Adult Rehabilitation Centers (ARCS). The
clients in such programs, who must be considered unemployable
when they are admitted, receive free shelter, food, detoxification,
counseling and "work therapy"—training, advice, experience
and placement. Clients sort used clothes, pick up donations, help
with maintenance. In return, they receive a stipend of up to $15
a week.

The $726 million raised from individual donors in the United   29
States last year represents about two-thirds of the United States
Salvation Army's income. The rest comes from foundations,
income-producing programs (hospitals, day-care centers), corporations and federal and state governments. In recent years, the
amount of federal money accepted by the Army has dropped to
less than 1 percent of its annual budget. The Army considers it
"unnatural" to separate its secular work—charity—from its religious purpose. When the government pushes on the church-state
separation issue, the Army shoves back—it returns the money
and refuses any more with such a hitch attached. The Army now
requires its other donors to sign an agreement giving it the right
to keep its iconography visible.

A few months after his altar call, Bill Dickinson felt the call to   30
become an Army officer. "I'm sitting there saying, 'Lord, I'm 43,
and I know I'm too old to go into the training school, and so
there's no possible way to fulfill what you're telling me to do.'"
There was another complication, too: officers may only be married to another officer, or lose their rank altogether. Married couples always work together, in parallel roles or sharing the duties
of a single position. Bill could never become an officer without
Mary at his side.

Shortly after that Bill learned about something called an aux-   31
iliary commission that would enable him and Mary to become
officers without attending seminary. He approached Mary with
the idea. "She said, 'Absolutely not. There's no way that I'll ever
become a Salvation Army officer.' I knew it was either both of us
or neither of us."

Mary Dickinson, a shy woman who admits she "lacks confi-   32
dence," is an uncommon officer because she would have been

happy not to have become an officer at all. "I was very comfortable being at home, being a housewife. We had a good business, and three beautiful children, and grandchildren. Then he came to me and told me he wanted to be an officer. And I said, 'I *can't*. There's just no way.' Well, you never tell God *never*. It wasn't long after that, about a year, that God did speak in my heart." She laughs. "I said, 'Lord, you *really* don't mean that!' I struggled for some time, and I still struggle a lot."

When I asked Mary about the role of women in the Army she eyed me for a long moment before speaking. She had already told me she preferred to be addressed as "Mrs. Captain Bill Dickinson," rather than by her own name. "I have the feeling the women here . . . ," she trailed off, laughing. "You're not going to like this and most people don't like it when I say it, so I don't say it very often. I think women aren't equal to men. I feel the last word should be the husband's; it's a man's place behind the pulpit. People here, they get really angry with me sometimes. Because the women here *like* to be leaders." 33

Women have always been allowed to hold any position and have always outnumbered men in the Army both as soldiers and officers. For the past seven years (two years longer than the usual term) the general of the Salvation Army was a woman, an Australian named Eva Burrows. Until her retirement last July, she held the highest religious office of any woman in the world. 34

Catherine Mumford Booth openly advocated women's rights at a time of embryonic suffragism, and her influence on her husband was strong. William Booth wrote, "Women must be treated as equal with men in all intellectual and social relationships of life." Catherine Booth was openly condemned for preaching; in her day, women weren't allowed to hold religious office and were forbidden to take the pulpit. When a man at one of her open-air Bible meetings quoted Paul's advice to the Corinthians—"Let your women keep silence in the Churches"—she replied, "In the first place this is not a church, and in the second place I am not a Corinthian." 35

After physical and psychological testing and some education—a process lasting about a year—the Dickinsons were commissioned as auxiliary captains in November of 1985. They worked as assistants in Spokane, and then were transferred to a 36 small congregation in Idaho, then to a larger one in Kelso, Washington. When they became full captains in 1990, they moved to Seattle.

The Salvation Army is divided into Corps, which are evangelical units serving specific regions. As head of the Seattle Temple Corps, Bill functions largely as the pastor of any good-sized Protestant congregation does: writing and delivering sermons, ministering to the sick, conducting weddings and funerals, teaching and counseling. Mary cooks the Temple's weekly lunch for the elderly, helps clean the buildings, runs the Home League—a women's group—makes hospital visits, counsels women, designs the Sunday worship service around Bill's choice of topics, handles scheduling and, in the Christmas season, helps manage the kettle drive.

The Dickinsons work sixty to eighty hours a week. In its early days the Salvation Army had to force its officers to take vacations ("furloughs") because otherwise the officers worked themselves to exhaustion. "It's so difficult to find the time," says Dickinson, who, like every other Salvation Army officer I've met, seems to be in an organized hurry much of the time. "That's kind of a lame excuse, I guess, but I think we're in the last days, myself. There's so many things that need to be done, and so little time to do it in."

On a winter day in a cold, unceasing drizzle, Dickinson took me to Seattle's Harbor Light—the name typically given to the Army's shelters for the homeless. (A new social services building, the William Booth Center, has since replaced it.) Dickinson ran this program when he first came to Seattle, before being transferred to the Temple. We walked past the line of people waiting to enter, heads down in the rain, and were greeted all the way to the door. "Hey, Captain." "How are you, Captain?"

Inside, I watched a quiet crowd of 106 men and four women file into the dim chapel. Almost everyone was black or Hispanic. The so-called ethnic ministries of the Army, aimed at blacks, Asians and Hispanics, are its fastest-growing segments in the United States. Elsewhere in Seattle an entire Salvation Army Corps is devoted to the Laotian population. Many clients are from minority groups, many are immigrants, legal and otherwise, and many don't speak English.

I had heard clients in other programs refer to the church as the   41
"Starvation Army," in spite of the fact that this meal, like all
meals for the homeless, is free. I stood in the back talking to Major Eddie Reed, a retired officer who volunteered as chaplain.
Officers have to retire at 65, and in fact the Army maintains retirement homes for them if desired, but almost all volunteer back
into service.

Reed said that times had changed, that unlike the "hoboes" of   42
a few decades back, many of the homeless men he meets today
don't want to work for their meals. "Maybe they think the sermon is too high a price," he added. Earlier, a Harbor Light coun-
selor had told me that her clients were getting younger, and
frequently had multiple addictions. "We're seeing people who
had everything—car, job, apartment—and lost everything."

"Take off your hats!" yelled Vern, the doorman, an ex-ARC   43
client, and at his words several dozen baseball caps and cowboy
hats disappeared. Reed then delivered a five-minute sermon, taking as his theme the universal nature of God's love, and offering
an invitation to anyone wanting to accept the altar call. No one
did. "Let us pray. God, we ask that you bless the men in this
room. Bless the women in this room. We pray that you will touch
their hearts and their lives. These things we ask in the name of
Our Lord Jesus Christ. Amen." The room filled with a low mur-
mur of amens, and then Vern's loud, demanding voice: "Everybody, stay where you are! Sit down, please! Back row first!"

When Bill Dickinson was sent to the Temple Corps, Captain   44
Sherry McWhorter was transferred from Alaska to replace him
in the social services program, of which this Harbor Light is a
part. A divorced mother of four adopted children with a master's
degree, McWhorter had spent thirteen years running social welfare programs for the Army. She is a solid woman with steel-
gray, brush-cut hair and a brusque manner ruined by her silky
Texas accent: when I asked her about the need for social services
in Seattle and Alaska, she didn't hesitate.

"There's a whole generation of people now in their 20s and   45
30s who are a wasted generation. I've felt very frustrated ever
since the Reagan years, when they made so many cutbacks, especially in maternal and child health. People are so much worse
off now. I'm not picketing or anything, but in every community
the Salvation Army tries to help wherever we can to correct so-

cietal problems, and the helping process is often hindered by the government." The sight of Sherry McWhorter picketing in her navy blue uniform has tremendous appeal. The Army's policy of nonpartisanship is not always an equal match for the religiously inspired activism of its members.

When the health department ordered Dickinson to throw   46
away donated food, he threatened to have T.V. cameras film the event. The department backed off. Dickinson also publicly embarrassed the city of Seattle into allowing the homeless to sleep in the foyers of public buildings during a vicious cold snap. Such occasions of, as Dickinson puts it, "throwing our weight around when we have to," are in Booth's tradition. After all, Booth wanted brass bands because brass gets attention.

After Reed's brief sermon, the crowd hurried through the   47
basement lunch-line, taking bowls of soup, hunks of bread and apples back to long, bare tables. They ate hurriedly, coming back for seconds until the food was gone. Several men filled their pockets with apples and partial loaves of bread.

Last week I stood by a kettle in a big, crowded mall. (The ket-   48
tle on the street corner has become the kettle in the mall, although many malls forbid the kettles altogether. Those that allow them often won't permit a bell.) A four-person band, three men in jaunty caps and pressed slacks and one woman in a knee-length navy skirt, adjusted their music stands, lifted their polished golden instruments and burst into the familiar strains of "Joy to the World."

A small crowd gathered. A tall man with a cap pulled down   49
over his face strode by, dropping a handful of change into the kettle without looking up; two children sidled up and slipped in a bill; a cheerful young woman approached with both hands in front of her and emptied a pile of clanking coins. "See, I'm emptying my pockets!" she cheerfully called out. One traditional carol followed another. "Silent Night" giving way to "Here Comes Santa Claus" with extra, glittering trills. People stood nearby, smiling; the old man in a soldier's uniform, sitting by the kettle because he was too tired by then to stand, nodded in time to the trombone's beat.

And now it's me turning my pockets out. I don't have to   50
agree with its theology to know that in Salvationism, unlike

most religions, actions do speak louder than any number of words. If I want to help the poor and homeless with my money, this red kettle is a safe place to start.

LARS EIGHNER

On Dumpster Diving

Lars Eighner, grandson of a poet, began studying writing when he was eleven, but he found it impossible to make a living at writing. In 1987 he lost his job in Austin, Texas, and for three years was homeless. The letters he wrote to friends during this period eventually led him to publish "On Dumpster Diving" in *Threepenny Review* in 1991. The remarkable style of the essay, "almost classical," as one editor said, caused an immediate stir. "There are not many good writers digging in dumpsters," Eighner told an interviewer, "but there are good carpenters, good autoworkers, and good painters who have fallen on hard times."

Long before I began dumpster diving I was impressed with Dumpsters, enough so that I wrote the Merriam-Webster research service to discover what I could about the word "Dumpster." I learned from them that "Dumpster" is a proprietary word belonging to the Dempster Dumpster company.

Since then I have dutifully capitalized the word although it was lowercased in almost all of the citations Merriam-Webster photocopied for me. Dempster's word is too apt. I have never heard these things called anything but Dumpsters. I do not know anyone who knows the generic name for these objects. From time to time, however, I hear a wino or hobo give some corrupted credit to the original and call them Dipsy Dumpsters.

I began Dumpster diving about a year before I became homeless.

I prefer the term "scavenging," and use the word "scrounging" when I mean to be obscure. I have heard people, evidently meaning to be polite, use the word "foraging," but I prefer to reserve that word for gathering nuts and berries and such, which I do also according to the season and the opportunity. "Dumpster diving" seems to me to be a little too cute and, in my case, inaccurate because I lack the athletic ability to lower myself into the Dumpsters as the true divers do, much to their increased profit.

I like the frankness of the word "scavenging," which I can hardly think of without picturing a big black snail on an aquarium wall. I live from the refuse of others. I am a scavenger. I think it a sound and honorable niche, although if I could I would naturally prefer to live the comfortable consumer life, perhaps— and only perhaps—as a slightly less wasteful consumer owing to what I have learned as a scavenger.

While my dog Lizbeth and I were still living in the house on Avenue B in Austin, as my savings ran out, I put almost all my sporadic income into rent. The necessities of daily life I began to extract from Dumpsters. Yes, we ate from Dumpsters. Except for jeans, all my clothes came from Dumpsters. Boom boxes, candles, bedding, toilet paper, medicine, books, a typewriter, a virgin male love doll, change sometimes amounting to many dollars: I acquired many things from the Dumpsters.

I have learned much as a scavenger. I mean to put some of what I have learned down here, beginning with the practical art of Dumpster diving and proceeding to the abstract.

*   *   *

What is safe to eat?

After all, the finding of objects is becoming something of an urban art. Even respectable employed people will sometimes find something tempting sticking out of a Dumpster or standing beside one. Quite a number of people, not all of them of the bohemian type, are willing to brag that they found this or that piece in the trash. But eating from Dumpsters is the thing that separates the dilettanti from the professionals.

Eating safely from the Dumpsters involves three principles: using the senses and common sense to evaluate the condition of the found materials, knowing the Dumpsters of a given area and checking them regularly, and seeking always to answer the question, "Why was this discarded?"

Perhaps everyone who has a kitchen and a regular supply of groceries has, at one time or another, made a sandwich and eaten half of it before discovering mold on the bread or got a mouthful of milk before realizing the milk had turned. Nothing of the sort is likely to happen to a Dumpster diver because he is constantly reminded that most food is discarded for a reason. Yet a lot of perfectly good food can be found in Dumpsters.

Canned goods, for example, turn up fairly often in the Dumpsters I frequent. All except the most phobic people would be willing to eat from a can even if it came from a Dumpster. Canned goods are among the safest of foods to be found in Dumpsters, but are not utterly foolproof.   12

Although very rare with modern canning methods, botulism is a possibility. Most other forms of food poisoning seldom do lasting harm to a healthy person. But botulism is almost certainly fatal and often the first symptom is death. Except for carbonated beverages, all canned goods should contain a slight vacuum and suck air when first punctured. Bulging, rusty, dented cans and cans that spew when punctured should be avoided, especially when the contents are not very acidic or syrupy.   13

Heat can break down the botulin, but this requires much more cooking than most people do to canned goods. To the extent that botulism occurs at all, of course, it can occur in cans on pantry shelves as well as in cans from Dumpsters. Need I say that home-canned goods found in Dumpsters are simply too risky to be recommended.   14

From time to time one of my companions, aware of the source of my provisions, will ask, "Do you think these crackers are really safe to eat?" For some reason it is most often the crackers they ask about.   15

This question always makes me angry. Of course I would not offer my companion anything I had doubts about. But more than that, I wonder why he cannot evaluate the condition of the crackers for himself. I have no special knowledge and I have been wrong before. Since he knows where the food comes from, it seems to me he ought to assume some of the responsibility for deciding what he will put in his mouth.   16

For myself, I have few qualms about dry foods such as crackers, cookies, cereal, chips, and pasta if they are free of visible contaminates and still dry and crisp. Most often such things are found in the original packaging, which is not so much a positive sign as it is the absence of a negative one.   17

Raw fruits and vegetables with intact skins seem perfectly safe to me, excluding of course the obviously rotten. Many are discarded for minor imperfections which can be pared away. Leafy   18 vegetables, grapes, cauliflower, broccoli, and similar things may be contaminated by liquids and may be impractical to wash.

Candy, especially hard candy, is usually safe if it has not drawn ants. Chocolate is often discarded only because it has become discolored as the cocoa butter de-emulsified. Candying, after all, is one method of food preservation because pathogens do not like very sugary substances. 19

All of these foods might be found in any Dumpster and can be evaluated with some confidence largely on the basis of appearance. Beyond these are foods which cannot be correctly evaluated without additional information. 20

I began scavenging by pulling pizzas out of the Dumpster behind a pizza delivery shop. In general prepared food requires caution, but in this case I knew when the shop closed and went to the Dumpster as soon as the last of the help left. 21

Such shops often get prank orders, called "bogus." Because help seldom stays long at these places, pizzas are often made with the wrong topping, refused on delivery for being cold, or baked incorrectly. The products to be discarded are boxed up because inventory is kept by counting boxes: a boxed pizza can be written off; an unboxed pizza does not exist. 22

I never placed a bogus order to increase the supply of pizzas and I believe no one else was scavenging in this Dumpster. But the people in the shop became suspicious and began to retain their garbage in the shop overnight. 23

While it lasted I had a steady supply of fresh, sometimes warm pizza. Because I knew the Dumpster I knew the source of the pizza, and because I visited the Dumpster regularly I knew what was fresh and what was yesterday's. 24

The area I frequent is inhabited by many affluent college students. I am not here by chance; the Dumpsters in this area are very rich. Students throw out many good things, including food. In particular they tend to throw everything out when they move at the end of a semester, before and after breaks, and around midterm when many of them despair of college. So I find it advantageous to keep an eye on the academic calendar. 25

The students throw food away around the breaks because they do not know whether it has spoiled or will spoil before they return. A typical discard is a half jar of peanut butter. In fact nonorganic peanut butter does not require refrigeration and is unlikely to spoil 26 in any reasonable time. The student does not know that, and since it is Daddy's money, the student decides not to take a chance.

Opened containers require caution and some attention to the 27 question, "Why was this discarded?" But in the case of discards from student apartments, the answer may be that the item was discarded through carelessness, ignorance, or wastefulness. This can sometimes be deduced when the item is found with many others, including some that are obviously perfectly good.

Some students, and others, approach defrosting a freezer by 28 chucking out the whole lot. Not only do the circumstances of such a find tell the story, but also the mass of frozen goods stays cold for a long time and items may be found still frozen or freshly thawed.

Yogurt, cheese, and sour cream are items that are often thrown 29 out while they are still good. Occasionally I find a cheese with a spot of mold, which of course I just pare off, and because it is obvious why such a cheese was discarded, I treat it with less suspicion than an apparently perfect cheese found in similar circumstances. Yogurt is often discarded, still sealed, only because the expiration date on the carton had passed. This is one of my favorite finds because yogurt will keep for several days, even in warm weather.

Students throw out canned goods and staples at the end of 30 semesters and when they give up college at midterm. Drugs, pornography, spirits, and the like are often discarded when parents are expected—Dad's day, for example. And spirits also turn up after big party weekends, presumably discarded by the newly reformed. Wine and spirits, of course, keep perfectly well even once opened. My test for carbonated soft drinks is whether they still fizz vigorously. Many juices or other beverages are too acid or too syrupy to cause much concern provided they are not visibly contaminated. Liquids, however, require some care.

One hot day I found a large jug of Pat O'Brien's Hurricane 31 mix. The jug had been opened, but it was still ice cold. I drank three large glasses before it became apparent to me that someone had added the rum to the mix, and not a little rum. I never tasted the rum and by the time I began to feel the effects I had already ingested a very large quantity of the beverage. Some divers would have considered this is a boon, but being suddenly and thoroughly intoxicated in a public place in the early afternoon is not my idea of a good time.

I have heard of people maliciously contaminating discarded   32
food and even handouts, but mostly I have heard of this from people with vivid imaginations who have had no experience with the
Dumpsters themselves. Just before the pizza shop stopped discarding its garbage at night, jalapeños began showing up on most of
the discarded pizzas. If indeed this was meant to discourage me it
was a wasted effort because I am native Texan.

For myself, I avoid game, poultry, pork, and egg-based foods   33
whether I find them raw or cooked. I seldom have the means to
cook what I find, but when I do I avail myself of plentiful supplies of beef which is often in very good condition. I suppose fish
becomes disagreeable before it becomes dangerous. The dog is
happy to have any such thing that is past its prime and, in fact,
does not recognize fish as food until it is quite strong.

Home leftovers, as opposed to surpluses from restaurants, are   34
very often bad. Evidently, especially among students, there is a
common type of personality that carefully wraps up even the
smallest leftover and shoves it into the back of the refrigerator for
six months or so before discarding it. Characteristic of this type
are the reused jars and margarine tubs which house the remains.

I avoid ethnic foods I am unfamiliar with. If I do not know   35
what it is supposed to look like when it is good, I cannot be certain I will be able to tell if it is bad.

No matter how careful I am I still get dysentery at least once   36
a month, oftener in warm weather. I do not want to paint too
romantic a picture. Dumpster diving has serious drawbacks as a
way of life.

*   *   *

I learned to scavenge gradually, on my own. Since then I have   37
initiated several companions into the trade. I have learned that
there is a predictable series of stages a person goes through in
learning to scavenge.

At first the new scavenger is filled with disgust and self-   38
loathing. He is ashamed of being seen and may lurk around, trying to duck behind things, or he may try to dive at night.

(In fact, most people instinctively look away from a scavenger.   39
By skulking around, the novice calls attention to himself and
arouses suspicion. Diving at night is ineffective and needlessly
messy.)

Every grain of rice seems to be a maggot. Everything seems to 40
stink. He can wipe the egg yolk off the found can, but he cannot
erase the stigma of eating garbage out of his mind.

That stage passes with experience. The scavenger finds a pair 41
of running shoes that fit and look and smell brand new. He finds
a pocket calculator in perfect working order. He finds pristine ice
cream, still frozen, more than he can eat or keep. He begins to
understand: people do throw away perfectly good stuff, a lot of
perfectly good stuff.

At this stage, Dumpster shyness begins to dissipate. The diver, 42
after all, has the last laugh. He is finding all manner of good
things which are his for the taking. Those who disparage his profession are the fools, not he.

He may begin to hang onto some perfectly good things for 43
which he has neither a use nor a market. Then he begins to take
note of the things which are not perfectly good but are nearly so.
He mates a Walkman with broken earphones and one that is
missing a battery cover. He picks up things which he can repair.

At this stage he may become lost and never recover. Dump- 44
sters are full of things of some potential value to someone and
also of things which never had much intrinsic value but are interesting. All the Dumpster divers I have known come to the
point of trying to acquire everything they touch. Why not take it,
they reason, since it is all free?

This is, of course, hopeless. Most divers come to realize that 45
they must restrict themselves to items of relatively immediate
utility. But in some cases the diver simply cannot control himself.
I have met several of these pack-rat types. Their ideas of the values of various pieces of junk verge on the psychotic. Every bit of
glass may be a diamond, they think, and all that glisters, gold.

I tend to gain weight when I am scavenging. Partly this is be- 46
cause I always find far more pizza and doughnuts than water-
packed tuna, nonfat yogurt, and fresh vegetables.

Also I have not developed much faith in the reliability of 47
Dumpsters as a food source, although it has been proven to me
many times. I tend to eat as if I have no idea where my next meal
is coming from. But mostly I just hate to see food go to waste
and so I eat much more than I should. Something like this drives
the obsession to collect junk.

As for collecting objects, I usually restrict myself to collecting 48
one kind of small object at a time, such as pocket calculators,

sunglasses, or campaign buttons. To live on the street I must anticipate my needs to a certain extent: I must pick up and save warm bedding I find in August because it will not be found in Dumpsters in November. But even if I had a home with extensive storage space, I could not save everything that might be valuable in some contingency.

I have proprietary feelings about my Dumpsters. As I have 49 suggested, it is no accident that I scavenge from Dumpsters where good finds are common. But my limited experience with Dumpsters in other areas suggests to me that it is the population of competitors rather than the affluence of the dumpers that most affects the feasibility of survival by scavenging. The large number of competitors is what puts me off the idea of trying to scavenge in places like Los Angeles.

Curiously, I do not mind my direct competition, other scav- 50 engers, so much as I hate the can scroungers.

People scrounge cans because they have to have a little cash. I 51 have tried scrounging cans with an able-bodied companion. Afoot, a can scrounger simply cannot make more than a few dollars a day. One can extract the necessities of life from the Dumpsters directly with far less effort than would be required to accumulate the equivalent value in cans.

Can scroungers, then, are people who must have small amounts 52 of cash. These are drug addicts and winos, mostly the latter because the amounts of cash are so small.

Spirits and drugs do, like all other commodities, turn up in 53 Dumpsters, and the scavenger will from time to time have a half bottle of a rather good wine with his dinner. But the wino cannot survive on these occasional finds; he must have his daily dose to stave off the DTs. All the cans he can carry will buy about three bottles of Wild Irish Rose.

I do not begrudge them the cans, but can scroungers tend to 54 tear up the Dumpsters, mixing the contents and littering the area. They become so specialized that they can see only cans. They earn my contempt by passing up change, canned goods, and readily hockable items.

There are precious few courtesies among scavengers. But it is 55 a common practice to set aside surplus items: pairs of shoes, clothing, canned goods, and such. A true scavenger hates to see good stuff go to waste, and what he cannot use he leaves in good condition in plain sight.

Can scroungers lay waste to everything in their path and will   56
stir one of a pair of good shoes to the bottom of a Dumpster, to
be lost or ruined in the muck. Can scroungers will even go
through individual garbage cans, something I have never seen a
scavenger do.

Individual garbage cans are set out on the public easement   57
only on garbage days. On other days going through them requires trespassing close to a dwelling. Going through individual
garbage cans without scattering litter is almost impossible. Litter
is likely to reduce the public's tolerance of scavenging. Individual
garbage cans are simply not as productive as Dumpsters; people
in houses and duplexes do not move as often and for some reason do not tend to discard as much useful material. Moreover,
the time required to go through one garbage can that serves one
household is not much less than the time required to go through
a Dumpster that contains the refuse of twenty apartments.

But my strongest reservation about going through individual   58
garbage cans is that this seems to me a very personal kind of invasion to which I would object if I were a householder. Although
many things in Dumpsters are obviously meant never to come to
light, a Dumpster is somehow less personal.

*   *   *

I avoid trying to draw conclusions about the people who   59
dump in the Dumpsters I frequent. I think it would be unethical
to do so, although I know many people will find the idea of scavenger ethics too funny for words.

Dumpsters contain bank statements, bills, correspondence, and   60
other documents, just as anyone might expect. But there are also
less obvious sources of information. Pill bottles, for example. The
labels on pill bottles contain the name of the patient, the name of
the doctor, and the name of the drug. AIDS drugs and antipsy-
chotic medicines, to name but two groups, are specific and are seldom prescribed for any other disorders. The plastic compacts for
birth control pills usually have complete label information.

Despite all of this sensitive information, I have had only one   61
apartment resident object to my going through the Dumpster. In
that case it turned out the resident was a university athlete who was
taking bets and who was afraid I would turn up his wager slips.

Occasionally a find tells a story. I once found a small paper   62 bag containing some unused condoms, several partial tubes of flavored sexual lubricant, a partially used compact of birth control pills, and the torn pieces of a picture of a young man. Clearly she was through with him and planning to give up sex altogether.

Dumpster things are often sad—abandoned teddy bears, shred- 63 ded wedding books, despaired-of sales kits. I find many pets lying in state in Dumpsters. Although I hope to get off the streets so that Lizbeth can have a long and comfortable old age, I know this hope is not very realistic. So I suppose when her time comes she too will go into a Dumpster. I will have no better place for her. And after all, for most of her life her livelihood has come from the Dumpster. When she finds something I think is safe that has been spilled from the Dumpster, I let her have it. She already knows the route around the best Dumpsters. I like to think that if she survives me she will have a chance of evading the dogcatcher and of finding her sustenance on the route.

Silly vanities also come to rest in the Dumpsters. I am a rather 64 accomplished needleworker. I get a lot of materials from the Dumpsters. Evidently sorority girls, hoping to impress someone, perhaps themselves, with their mastery of a womanly art, buy a lot of embroider-by-number kits, work a few stitches horribly, and eventually discard the whole mess. I pull out their stitches, turn the canvas over, and work an original design. Do not think I refrain from chuckling as I make original gifts from these kits.

I find diaries and journals. I have often thought of compiling a 65 book of literary found objects. And perhaps I will one day. But what I find is hopelessly commonplace and bad without being, even unconsciously, camp. College students also discard their papers. I am horrified to discover the kind of paper which now merits an A in an undergraduate course. I am grateful, however, for the number of good books and magazines the students throw out.

In the area I know best I have never discovered vermin in the 66 Dumpsters, but there are two kinds of kitty surprise. One is alley cats which I meet as they leap, claws first, out of Dumpsters. This is especially thrilling when I have Lizbeth in tow. The other kind of kitty surprise is a plastic garbage bag filled with some ponderous, amorphous mass. This always proves to be used cat litter.

City bees harvest doughnut glaze and this makes the Dump- 67 ster at the doughnut shop more interesting. My faith in the instinctive wisdom of animals is always shaken whenever I see Lizbeth attempt to catch a bee in her mouth, which she does whenever bees are present. Evidently some birds find Dumpsters profitable, for birdie surprise is almost as common as kitty surprise of the first kind. In hunting season all kinds of small game turn up in Dumpsters, some of it, sadly, not entirely dead. Curiously, summer and winter, maggots are uncommon.

The worst of the living and near-living hazards of the Dump- 68
sters are the fire ants. The food that they claim is not much of a loss, but they are vicious and aggressive. It is very easy to brush against some surface of the Dumpster and pick up half a dozen or more fire ants, usually in some sensitive area such as the underarm. One advantage of bringing Lizbeth along as I make Dumpster rounds is that, for obvious reasons, she is very alert to ground-based fire ants. When Lizbeth recognizes the signs of fire ant infestation around our feet she does the Dance of the Zillion Fire Ants. I have learned not to ignore this warning from Lizbeth, whether I perceive the tiny ants or not, but to remove ourselves at Lizbeth's first *pas de bourrée*. All the more so because the ants are the worst in the months I wear flip-flops, if I have them.

(Perhaps someone will misunderstand the above. Lizbeth does 69
the Dance of the Zillion Fire Ants when she recognizes more fire ants than she cares to eat, not when she is being bitten. Since I have learned to react promptly, she does not get bitten at all. It is the isolated patrol of fire ants that falls in Lizbeth's range that deserves pity. Lizbeth finds them quite tasty.)

By far the best way to go through a Dumpster is to lower 70
yourself into it. Most of the good stuff tends to settle at the bottom because it is usually weightier than the rubbish. My more athletic companions have often demonstrated to me that they can extract much good material from a Dumpster I have already been over.

To those psychologically or physically unprepared to enter a 71
Dumpster, I recommend a stout stick, preferably with some barb or hook at one end. The hook can be used to grab plastic garbage bags. When I find canned goods or other objects loose at the bottom of a Dumpster I usually can roll them into a small bag that I can then hoist up. Much Dumpster diving is a matter of experience for which nothing will do except practice.

Dumpster diving is outdoor work, often surprisingly pleasant. 72
It is not entirely predictable; things of interest turn up every day, and some days there are finds of great value. I am always very

pleased when I can turn up exactly the thing I most wanted to find. Yet in spite of the element of chance, scavenging more than most other pursuits tends to yield returns in some proportion to the effort and intelligence brought to bear. It is very sweet to turn up a few dollars in change from a Dumpster that has just been gone over by a wino.

The land is now covered with cities. The cities are full of Dumpsters. I think of scavenging as a modern form of self-reliance. In any event, after ten years of government service, where everything is geared to the lowest common denominator, I find work that rewards initiative and effort refreshing. Certainly I would be happy to have a sinecure again, but I am not heartbroken not to have one anymore.   73

I find from the experience of scavenging two rather deep lessons. The first is to take what I can use and let the rest go by. I have come to think that there is no value in the abstract. A thing I cannot use or make useful, perhaps by trading, has no value however fine or rare it may be. I mean useful in a broad sense— so, for example, some art I would think useful and valuable, but other art might be otherwise for me.   74

I was shocked to realize that some things are not worth acquiring, but now I think it is so. Some material things are white elephants that eat up the possessor's substance.   75

The second lesson is of the transience of material being. This has not quite converted me to a dualist, but it has made some headway in that direction. I do not suppose that ideas are immortal, but certainly mental things are longer-lived than other material things.   76

Once I was the sort of person who invests material objects with sentimental value. Now I no longer have those things, but I have the sentiments yet.   77

Many times in my travels I have lost everything but the clothes I was wearing and Lizbeth. The things I find in Dumpsters, the love letters and ragdolls of so many lives, remind me of this lesson. Now I hardly pick up a thing without envisioning the time I will cast it away. This I think is a healthy state of mind. Almost everything I have now has already been cast out at least once, proving that what I own is valueless to someone.   78

Anyway, I find my desire to grab for the gaudy bauble has been largely sated. I think this is an attitude I share with the very   79 wealthy—we both know there is plenty more where what we have came from. Between us are the rat-race millions who have confounded their selves with the objects they grasp and who nightly scavenge the cable channels looking for they know not what.

I am sorry for them.   80

ALICE WALKER

Everyday Use

Alice Walker, best known to most Americans for her novel *The Color Purple* (1982), grew up in poverty in rural Georgia, the daughter of sharecroppers. The course of her education took her to New York City, where she worked for a time with the welfare department, but she maintained her ties to the rural South, working for civil rights in Mississippi during the 1960s. "Everyday Use" is from her 1973 collection, *In Love and Trouble: Stories of Black Women*.

for your grandmamma

I will wait for her in the yard that Maggie and I made so clean   1
and wavy yesterday afternoon. A yard like this is more comfortable than most people know. It is not just a yard. It is like an extended living room. When the hard clay is swept clean as a floor and the fine sand around the edges lined with tiny, irregular grooves, anyone can come and sit and look up into the elm tree and wait for the breezes that never come inside the house.

Maggie will be nervous until after her sister goes: she will stand   2
hopelessly in corners, homely and ashamed of the burn scars down her arms and legs, eying her sister with a mixture of envy and awe. She thinks her sister has held life always in the palm of one hand, that "no" is a word the world never learned to say to her.

You've no doubt seen those TV shows where the child who   3
has "made it" is confronted, as a surprise, by her own mother and father, tottering in weakly from backstage. (A pleasant surprise, of course: What would they do if parent and child came on

the show only to curse out and insult each other?) On TV mother and child embrace and smile into each other's faces. Sometimes the mother and father weep, the child wraps them in her arms and leans across the table to tell how she would not have made it without their help. I have seen these programs.

Sometimes I dream a dream in which Dee and I are suddenly brought together on a TV program of this sort. Out of a dark and soft-seated limousine I am ushered into a bright room filled with many people. There I meet a smiling, gray, sporty man like Johnny Carson who shakes my hand and tells me what a fine girl I have. Then we are on the stage and Dee is embracing me with tears in her eyes. She pins on my dress a large orchid, even though she has told me once that she thinks orchids are tacky flowers.

In real life I am a large, big-boned woman with rough, man-working hands. In the winter I wear flannel nightgowns to bed and overalls during the day. I can kill and clean a hog as mercilessly as a man. My fat keeps me hot in zero weather. I can work outside all day, breaking ice to get water for washing; I can eat pork liver cooked over the open fire minutes after it comes steaming from the hog. One winter I knocked a bull calf straight in the brain between the eyes with a sledge hammer and had the meat hung up to chill before nightfall. But of course all this does not show on television. I am the way my daughter would want me to be: a hundred pounds lighter, my skin like an uncooked barley pancake. My hair glistens in the hot bright lights. Johnny Carson has much to do to keep up with my quick and witty tongue.

But that is a mistake. I know even before I wake up. Who ever knew a Johnson with a quick tongue? Who can even imagine me looking a strange white man in the eye? It seems to me I have talked to them always with one foot raised in flight, with my head turned in whichever way is farthest from them. Dee, though. She would always look anyone in the eye. Hesitation was no part of her nature.

"How do I look, Mama?" Maggie says, showing just enough of her thin body enveloped in pink skirt and red blouse for me to know she's there, almost hidden by the door.

"Come out into the yard," I say.

Have you ever seen a lame animal, perhaps a dog run over by some careless person rich enough to own a car, sidle up to someone who is ignorant enough to be kind to him? That is the way my Maggie walks. She has been like this, chin on chest, eyes on ground, feet in shuffle, ever since the fire that burned the other house to the ground.

Dee is lighter than Maggie, with nicer hair and a fuller figure. 10 She's a woman now, though sometimes I forget. How long ago was it that the other house burned? Ten, twelve years? Sometimes I can still hear the flames and feel Maggie's arms sticking to me, her hair smoking and her dress falling off her in little black papery flakes. Her eyes seemed stretched open, blazed open by the flames reflected in them. And Dee. I see her standing off under the sweet gum tree she used to dig gum out of; a look of concentration on her face as she watched the last dingy gray board of the house fall in toward the red-hot brick chimney. Why don't you do a dance around the ashes? I'd wanted to ask her. She had hated the house that much.

I used to think she hated Maggie, too. But that was before we 11 raised the money, the church and me, to send her to Augusta to school. She used to read to us without pity; forcing words, lies, other folks' habits, whole lives upon us two, sitting trapped and ignorant underneath her voice. She washed us in a river of make-believe, burned us with a lot of knowledge we didn't necessarily need to know. Pressed us to her with the serious way she read, to shove us away at just the moment, like dimwits, we seemed about to understand.

Dee wanted nice things. A yellow organdy dress to wear to 12 her graduation from high school; black pumps to match a green suit she'd made from an old suit somebody gave me. She was determined to stare down any disaster in her efforts. Her eyelids would not flicker for minutes at a time. Often I fought off the temptation to shake her. At sixteen she had a style of her own: and knew what style was.

I never had an education myself. After second grade the 13 school was closed down. Don't ask me why: in 1927 colored asked fewer questions than they do now. Sometimes Maggie reads to me. She stumbles along good-naturedly but can't see well. She knows she is not bright. Like good looks and money, quickness passed her by. She will marry John Thomas (who has mossy teeth in an earnest face) and then I'll be free to sit here and I guess just sing church songs to myself. Although I never was a good singer. Never could carry a tune. I was always better at a man's job. I used to love to milk till I was hooked in the side in '49. Cows are soothing and slow and don't bother you, unless you try to milk them the wrong way.

I have deliberately turned my back on the house. It is three   14
rooms, just like the one that burned, except the roof is tin; they don't make shingle roofs any more. There are no real windows, just some holes cut in the sides, like the portholes in a ship, but not round and not square, with rawhide holding the shutters up on the outside. This house is in a pasture, too, like the other one. No doubt when Dee sees it she will want to tear it down. She wrote me once that no matter where we "choose" to live, she will manage to come see us. But she will never bring her friends. Maggie and I thought about this and Maggie asked me, "Mama, when did Dee ever *have* any friends?"

She had a few. Furtive boys in pink shirts hanging about on   15
washday after school. Nervous girls who never laughed. Impressed with her they worshiped the well-turned phrase, the cute shape, the scalding humor that erupted like bubbles in lye. She read to them.

When she was courting Jimmy T she didn't have much time to   16
pay to us, but turned all her faultfinding power on him. He *flew* to marry a cheap city girl from a family of ignorant flashy people. She hardly had time to recompose herself.

When she comes I will meet—but there they are!   17
Maggie attempts to make a dash for the house, in her shuf-   18
fling way, but I stay her with my hand. "Come back here," I say. And she stops and tries to dig a well in the sand with her toe.

It is hard to see them clearly through the strong sun. But even   19
the first glimpse of leg out of the car tells me it is Dee. Her feet were always neat-looking, as if God himself had shaped them with a certain style. From the other side of the car comes a short, stocky man. Hair is all over his head a foot long and hanging from his chin like a kinky mule tail. I hear Maggie suck in her breath. "Uhnnnh," is what it sounds like. Like when you see the wriggling end of a snake just in front of your foot on the road. "Uhnnnh."

Dee next. A dress down to the ground, in this hot weather. A   20
dress so loud it hurts my eyes. There are yellows and oranges enough to throw back the light of the sun. I feel my whole face warming from the heat waves it throws out. Earrings gold, too,

and hanging down to her shoulders. Bracelets dangling and making noises when she moves her arm up to shake the folds of the dress out of her armpits. The dress is loose and flows, and as she walks closer, I like it. I hear Maggie go "Uhnnnh" again. It is her sister's hair. It stands straight up like the wool on a sheep. It is black as night and around the edges are two long pigtails that rope about like small lizards disappearing behind her ears.

"Wa-su-zo-Tean-o!" she says, coming on in that gliding way   21
the dress makes her move. The short stocky fellow with the hair to his navel is all grinning and he follows up with "Asalamalakim,[1] my mother and sister!" He moves to hug Maggie but she falls back, right up against the back of my chair. I feel her trembling there and when I look up I see the perspiration falling off her chin.

"Don't get up," says Dee. Since I am stout it takes something   22
of a push. You can see me trying to move a second or two before I make it. She turns, showing white heels through her sandals, and goes back to the car. Out she peeks next with a Polaroid. She stoops down quickly and lines up picture after picture of me sitting there in front of the house with Maggie cowering behind me. She never takes a shot without making sure the house is included. When a cow comes nibbling around the edge of the yard she snaps it and me and Maggie *and* the house. Then she puts the Polaroid in the back seat of the car, and comes up and kisses me on the forehead.

Meanwhile Asalamalakim is going through motions with Maggie's hand. Maggie's hand is as limp as a fish, and probably as   23
cold, despite the sweat, and she keeps trying to pull it back. It looks like Asalamalakim wants to shake hands but wants to do it fancy. Or maybe he don't know how people shake hands. Anyhow, he soon gives up on Maggie.

"Well," I say. "Dee."   24

"No, Mama," she says. "Not 'Dee,' Wangero Leewanika Ke-   25
manjo!"

"What happened to 'Dee'?" I wanted to know.   26

"She's dead," Wangero said. "I couldn't bear it any longer, be-   27
ing named after the people who oppress me."

1. A Muslim greeting sounded phonetically. Likewise, Wa-su-zo-Tean-o is an African greeting.

"You know as well as me you was named after your aunt Di-   28
cie," I said. Dicie is my sister. She named Dee. We called her "Big
Dee" after Dee was born.

"But who was *she* named after?" asked Wangero.   29

"I guess after Grandma Dee," I said.   30

"And who was she named after?" asked Wangero.   31

"Her mother," I said, and saw Wangero was getting tired.   32
"That's about as far back as I can trace it," I said. Though, in
fact, I probably could have carried it back beyond the Civil War
through the branches.

"Well," said Asalamalakim, "there you are."   33

"Uhnnnh," I heard Maggie say.   34

"There I was not," I said, "before 'Dicie' cropped up in our   35
family, so why should I try to trace it that far back?"

He just stood there grinning, looking down on me like some-   36
body inspecting a Model A car. Every once in a while he and
Wangero sent eye signals over my head.

"How do you pronounce this name?" I asked.   37

"You don't have to call me by it if you don't want to," said   38
Wangero.

"Why shouldn't I?" I asked. "If that's what you want us to   39
call you, we'll call you."

"I know it might sound awkward at first," said Wangero.   40

"I'll get used to it," I said. "Ream it out again."   41

Well, soon we got the name out of the way. Asalamalakim had   42
a name twice as long and three times as hard. After I tripped over
it two or three times he told me to just call him Hakim-a-barber.
I wanted to ask him was he a barber, but I didn't really think he
was, so I didn't ask.

"You must belong to those beef-cattle peoples down the road,"   43
I said. They said "Asalamalakim" when they met you, too, but
they didn't shake hands. Always too busy: feeding the cattle, fixing the fences, putting up salt-lick shelters, throwing down hay.
When the white folks poisoned some of the herd the men stayed
up all night with rifles in their hands. I walked a mile and a half
just to see the sight.

Hakim-a-barber said, "I accept some of their doctrines, but   44
farming and raising cattle is not my style." (They didn't tell me,
and I didn't ask, whether Wangero (Dee) had really gone and
married him.)

We sat down to eat and right away he said he didn't eat col-   45
lards and pork was unclean. Wangero, though, went on through
the chitlins and corn bread, the greens and everything else. She
talked a blue streak over the sweet potatoes. Everything delighted her. Even the fact that we still used the benches her daddy
made for the table when we couldn't afford to buy chairs.

"Oh, Mama!" she cried. Then turned to Hakim-a-barber. "I   46
never knew how lovely these benches are. You can feel the rump
prints," she said, running her hands underneath her and along
the bench. Then she gave a sigh and her hand closed over Grandma
Dee's butter dish. "That's it!" she said. "I knew there was something I wanted to ask you if I could have." She jumped up from
the table and went over in the corner where the churn stood, the
milk in it clabber by now. She looked at the churn and looked
at it.

"This churn top is what I need," she said. "Didn't Uncle   47
Buddy whittle it out of a tree you all used to have?"

"Yes," I said.   48

"Uh huh," she said happily. "And I want the dasher, too."   49

"Uncle Buddy whittle that, too?" asked the barber.   50

Dee (Wangero) looked up at me.   51

"Aunt Dee's first husband whittled the dash," said Maggie so   52
low you almost couldn't hear her. "His name was Henry, but
they called him Stash."

"Maggie's brain is like an elephant's," Wangero said, laugh-   53
ing. "I can use the churn top as a centerpiece for the alcove
table," she said, sliding a plate over the churn, "and I'll think of
something artistic to do with the dasher."

When she finished wrapping the dasher the handle stuck out. I   54
took it for a moment in my hands. You didn't even have to look
close to see where hands pushing the dasher up and down to
make butter had left a kind of sink in the wood. In fact, there
were a lot of small sinks; you could see where thumbs and fingers
had sunk into the wood. It was beautiful light yellow wood, from
a tree that grew in the yard where Big Dee and Stash had lived.

After dinner Dee (Wangero) went to the trunk at the foot of   55
my bed and started rifling through it. Maggie hung back in the
kitchen over the dishpan. Out came Wangero with two quilts.
They had been pieced by Grandma Dee and then Big Dee and me
had hung them on the quilt frames on the front porch and quilted
them. One was in the Lone Star pattern. The other was Walk

Around the Mountain. In both of them were scraps of dresses Grandma Dee had worn fifty and more years ago. Bits and pieces of Grandpa Jarrell's Paisley shirts. And one teeny faded blue piece, about the size of a penny matchbox, that was from Great Grandpa Ezra's uniform that he wore in the Civil War.

"Mama," Wangero said sweet as a bird. "Can I have these old quilts?"   56

I heard something fall in the kitchen, and a minute later the kitchen door slammed.   57

"Why don't you take one or two of the others?" I asked. "These old things was just done by me and Big Dee from some tops your grandma pieced before she died."   58

"No," said Wangero. "I don't want those. They are stitched around the borders by machine."   59

"That'll make them last better," I said.   60

"That's not the point," said Wangero. "These are all pieces of dresses Grandma used to wear. She did all this stitching by hand. Imagine!" She held the quilts securely in her arms, stroking them.   61

"Some of the pieces, like those lavender ones, come from old clothes her mother handed down to her," I said, moving up to touch the quilts. Dee (Wangero) moved back just enough so that I couldn't reach the quilts. They already belonged to her.   62

"Imagine!" she breathed again, clutching them closely to her bosom.   63

"The truth is," I said, "I promised to give them quilts to Maggie, for when she marries John Thomas."   64

She gasped like a bee had stung her.   65

"Maggie can't appreciate these quilts!" she said. "She'd probably be backward enough to put them to everyday use."   66

"I reckon she would," I said. "God knows I been saving 'em for long enough with nobody using 'em. I hope she will!" I didn't want to bring up how I had offered Dee (Wangero) a quilt when she went away to college. Then she had told me they were old-fashioned, out of style.   67

"But they're *priceless!*" she was saying now, furiously; for she has a temper. "Maggie would put them on the bed and in five years they'd be in rags. Less than that!" "She can always make some more," I said. "Maggie knows how to quilt."   68

Dee (Wangero) looked at me with hatred. "You just will not understand. The point is these quilts, *these* quilts!"   69

"Well," I said, stumped. "What would you do with them?"   70

"Hang them," she said. As if that was the only thing you   71
could do with quilts.

Maggie by now was standing in the door. I could almost hear   72
the sound her feet made as they scraped over each other.

"She can have them, Mama," she said, like somebody used to   73
never winning anything, or having anything reserved for her. "I
can 'member Grandma Dee without the quilts."

I looked at her hard. She had filled her bottom lip with   74
checker-berry snuff and it gave her face a kind of dopey, hangdog
look. It was Grandma Dee and Big Dee who taught her how to
quilt herself. She stood there with her scarred hands hidden in
the folds of her skirt. She looked at her sister with something like
fear but she wasn't mad at her. This was Maggie's portion. This
was the way she knew God to work.

When I looked at her like that something hit me in the top of   75
my head and ran down to the soles of my feet. Just like when I'm
in church and the spirit of God touches me and I get happy and
shout. I did something I never had done before: hugged Maggie
to me, then dragged her on into the room, snatched the quilts out
of Miss Wangero's hands and dumped them into Maggie's lap.
Maggie just sat there on my bed with her mouth open.

"Take one or two of the others," I said to Dee.   76

But she turned without a word and went out to Hakim-a-   77
barber.

"You just don't understand," she said, as Maggie and I came   78
out to the car.

"What don't I understand?" I wanted to know.   79

"Your heritage," she said. And then she turned to Maggie,   80
kissed her, and said, "You ought to try to make something of
yourself, too, Maggie. It's really a new day for us. But from the
way you and Mama still live you'd never know it."

She put on some sunglasses that hid everything above the tip   81
of her nose and her chin.

Maggie smiled; maybe at the sunglasses. But a real smile, not   82
scared. After we watched the car dust settle I asked Maggie to
bring me a dip of snuff. And then the two of us sat there just enjoying, until it was time to go in the house and go to bed.

6

ON THE JOB

Women at Todd Shipyard, 1942. ELIOT ELISOFON/TimePix.

OVERVIEW

The hours are long, the pay is small
So take your time and buck them all.

This slogan from a Depression-era poster expresses an attitude all of us recognize. Most of us at some period of our lives view work as wage slavery: time subtracted from our real lives and justified only by the paycheck. Some of us hate work constantly: not just the particular job, but the whole system that keeps us on the treadmill. Even the rich, as Dorothy Sayers points out, may think of money primarily as something that saves them from the curse of work.

Most of us, however, have moments when we see work more positively. There is the story of the small farmer, hard-pressed financially and working from sunrise to sunset, who wins a fortune in the lottery. "What are you going to do with all that money?" a neighbor asks. "Well," he answers, "I suppose I'll keep on farming till it's gone." Some people love their work and feel that it is an essential part of their identity: "I go on working," the writer H. L. Mencken once said, "for the same reason that a hen goes on laying eggs."

Each essay or story in this section touches on the question of what makes work sometimes a curse and sometimes a blessing. Most include firsthand reports on the daily satisfactions and grievances of life on the job.

- Dorothy L. Sayers contrasts an older (and, as she says, a more religious) view of the nature of work with the modern tendency to measure the worth of a job by the paycheck it produces.
- In two interviews from Studs Terkel's book *Working*, a steelworker and a stonemason tell us how they feel about their jobs.
- Carol Bly describes work as a field hand on a Minnesota farm and gives us a sense of the "hidden psychology" of hard physical labor on someone else's land.
- Sue Hubbell, an independent beekeeper in the Ozark Mountains, also gives us a picture of physically demanding work, but work with quite a different psychology.

- Paul Roberts describes his descent from being a writer to being a producer of "info nuggets on whatever topics the multimedia companies believe will sell."
- Perri Klass, writing about her medical school education, shows that learning a job can mean absorbing a new vocabulary and the new set of attitudes that vocabulary encourages.
- William Carlos Williams's short story gives us the thoughts of a physician working with a hard case—"about the worst you'd expect to find anywhere"—an eleven-month-old girl dying under his care.

Dorothy L. Sayers

Living to Work

Dorothy Sayers, an Englishwoman, is best known for a series of crime novels featuring the aristocratic amateur detective Lord Peter Wimsey. In the 1940s, however, having freed herself from the "mystery formula," Sayers turned her attention to essays, religious drama, and verse translations—including a popular version of Dante's *Divine Comedy*. "Living to Work," written for radio broadcast during World War II, was suppressed by the BBC because it seemed too political and because "our public do not want to be admonished by a woman." The piece appeared, along with her similarly censored essays "Christian Morality" and "Forgiveness," in *Unpopular Opinions* (1946).

When I look at the world—not particularly at the world at war, but at our Western civilisation generally—I find myself dividing people into two main groups according to the way they think about work. And I feel sure that the new world after the war will be satisfactory or not according to the view we are all prepared to take about the work of the world. So let us look for a moment at these two groups of people. 1

One group—probably the larger and certainly the more discontented—look upon work as a hateful necessity, whose only use is to make money for them, so that they can escape from work and do something else. They feel that only when the day's labour is over can they really begin to live and be themselves. The other group—smaller nowadays, but on the whole far happier—look on their work as an opportunity for enjoyment and self-fulfilment. They only want to make money so that they may be free to devote themselves more single-mindedly to their work. Their work and their life are one thing; if they were to be cut off from their work, they would feel that they were cut off from life. You will realise that we have here a really fundamental difference of outlook, which is bound to influence all schemes about work, leisure and wages. 2

Now the first group—that of the work-haters—is not made up solely of people doing very hard, uninteresting and ill-paid 3 work. It includes a great many well-off people who do practically no work at all. The rich man who lives idly on his income, the man who gambles or speculates in the hope of getting money without working for it, the woman who marries for the mere sake of being comfortably established for life—all these people look on money in the same way: as something that saves them from the curse of work. Except that they have had better luck, their outlook is exactly the same as that of the sweated factory hand whose daily work is one long round of soul-and-body-destroying toil. For all of them, work is something hateful, only to be endured because it makes money; and money is desirable because it represents a way of escape from work. The only difference is that the rich have already made their escape, and the poor have not.

The second group is equally mixed. It includes the artists, scholars and scientists—the people really devoured with the passion for making and discovering things. It includes also the rapidly-diminishing band of old-fashioned craftsmen, taking a real pride and pleasure in turning out a good job of work. It includes also—and this is very important—those skilled mechanics and engineers who are genuinely in love with the complicated beauty of the machines they use and look after. Then there are those professional people in whom we recognize a clear, spiritual vocation—a call to what is sometimes very hard and exacting work—those doctors, nurses, priests, actors, teachers, whose work is something more to them than a mere means of livelihood; seamen who, for all they may grumble at the hardships of the sea, return to it again and again and are restless and unhappy on dry land; farmers and farm-workers who devotedly serve the land and the beasts they tend; airmen; explorers; and those comparatively rare women to whom the nurture of children is not merely a natural function but also a full-time and absorbing intellectual and emotional interest. A very mixed bag, you will notice, and not exclusively confined to the "possessing classes," or even to those who, individually or collectively, "own the means of production."

But we must also admit that, of late, the second group of workers has become more and more infected with the outlook of the first group. Agriculture—especially in those countries where farming is prosperous—has been directed, not to serving the land, but to bleeding it white in the interests of moneymaking.

Certain members of the medical profession—as you may read in Dr. Cronin's book, *The Citadel*—are less interested in preserving their patients' health than in exploiting their weaknesses for profit. Some writers openly admit that their sole aim is the manufacture of best-sellers. And if we are inclined to exclaim indignantly that this kind of conduct is bad for the work, bad for the individual, and bad for the community, we must also confess that we ourselves—the ordinary public—have been only too ready to acquiesce in these commercial standards, not only in trade and manufacture, but in the professions and public services as well.

For us, a "successful" author is one whose sales run into millions; any other standard of criticism is dismissed as "highbrow." We judge the skill of a physician or surgeon, not by his hospital record, but by whether or not he has many wealthy patients and an address in Harley Street.[1] The announcement that a new film has cost many thousands of pounds to make convinces us that it must be a good film; though very often these excessive production costs are evidence of nothing more than graft, incompetence and bad organisation in the studios. Also, it is useless to pretend that we do not admire and encourage the vices of the idle rich so long as our cinemas are crowded with young men and women gaping at film-stars in plutocratic surroundings and imbecile situations and wishing with all their hearts that they too could live like the heroes and heroines of these witless million-dollar screen stories. Just as it is idle to demand selfless devotion to duty in public servants, so long as we respect roguery in business, or so long as we say, with an admiring chuckle, about some fellow citizen who has pulled off some shady deal with our local borough authorities, that "Old So-and-so is hot stuff, and anybody would have to get up early to find any flies on *him*."

We have *all* become accustomed to rate the value of work by a purely money standard. The people who still cling to the old idea that work should be served and enjoyed for its own sake are diminishing and—what is worse—are being steadily pushed out of the control of public affairs and out of contact with the public. We find them odd and alien—and a subservient journalism (which we encourage by buying and reading it) persuades us to

1. Harley Street: the traditional address of London's most prosperous physicians.

consider them absurd and contemptible. It is only in times of emergency and national disaster that we realise how much we depend upon the man who puts the integrity of his job before money, before success, before self—before all those standards by which we have come to assess the value of work.

Consequently, in planning out our post-war economic para-   8
dise, we are apt to concentrate exclusively on questions of hours, wages and conditions, and to neglect the really fundamental question whether, in fact, we want work to be something in which a man can enjoy the exercise of his full natural powers; or merely a disagreeable task, with its hours as short as possible and its returns as high as possible, so that the worker may be released as quickly as possible to enjoy his life in his leisure. Mind, I do not say for a moment that hours, wages and conditions ought not to be dealt with; but we shall deal with them along different lines, according as we believe it right and natural that men should work to live or live to work.

At this point, many of you will be thinking: "Before we can do   9
anything about this, we must get rid of the capitalist system." But the much-abused "system" is precisely the system that arises when we think of work in terms of money-returns. The capitalist is faithfully carrying to its logical conclusion the opinion that work is an evil, that individual liberty means liberty to emancipate one's self from work, and that whatever pays best is right. And I see no chance of getting rid of "the system," or of the people who thrive on it, so long as in our hearts we accept the standards of that system, envy the very vices we condemn, build up with one hand what we pull down with the other, and treat with ridicule and neglect the people who acknowledge a less commercial—if you like, a more religious—conception of what work ought to be.

But now we are faced with a big difficulty. Suppose we decide   10
that we want work to provide our natural fulfilment and satisfaction, how are we to manage this in an age of industrial machinery? You will have noticed that all the workers in my second group possess three privileges. (1) Their work provides opportunity for individual initiative. (2) It is of a kind that, however laborious it may be in detail, allows them to view with satisfaction the final results of their labour. (3) It is of a kind that fits in with the natural rhythm of the human mind and body, since it in-

volves periods of swift, exacting energy, followed by periods of repose and recuperation, and does not bind the worker to the monotonous, relentless, deadly pace of an inhuman machine.

The factory hand has none of these advantages. He is not re-   11
quired to show initiative, but only to perform one unimaginative operation over and over again. He usually sees no step in the process of manufacture except that one operation, and so can take no interest in watching the thing he is making grow to its final perfection; often, indeed, it is some useless thing that only exists to create profits and wages, and which no worker could admire or desire for its own sake. Thirdly, it is the pace that kills—the subjection of the human frame to the unresting, unchanging, automatic movement of the machine. The other day, a journalist was talking to some miners. He says: "With one voice they told me that they think the machines are becoming monsters, draining their life-blood, and how they longed for the old days when they worked longer shifts, but with their hands, and the process of procuring the coal was less exhausting."

This last statement is very interesting, since it shows that the   12
regulation of hours and wages cannot by itself do away with the difficulty about certain kinds of work. The economic solution will not solve this problem, because it is not really an economic problem at all, but a problem about human nature and the nature of work.

Some people are so greatly depressed by these considerations   13
that they can see no way out of the difficulty except to do away with machines altogether, as things evil in themselves and destructive of all good living. But this is a counsel of despair. For one thing, it is not a practical proposition in the present state of things. Also, this suggestion takes no account of the real delight and satisfaction that the machines are capable of giving. It throws on the scrap-heap the skill and creative enthusiasm of the designer, the engineer's pride in his craft, the flying man's ecstasy in being air-borne, all the positive achievements of mechanical invention, and all those products—and they are many—which are actually *better* made by machinery than by hand. To renounce the machines means, at this time of day, to renounce the world and to retire to a kind of hermitage of the spirit. But society cannot be exclusively made of saints and solitaries; the average good citizen, like the average Christian, has to live *in* the

world; his task is not to run away from the machines but to learn to use them so that they work in harmony with human nature instead of injuring or oppressing it.

Now, I will not attempt, in the last few minutes of a short broadcast, to produce a cut-and-dried scheme for taming machinery to the service of man. I will only say that I believe it can be done, and (since my opinion would not carry very much weight) that there are many people, with personal experience of factory conditions, who have already worked out practical proposals for doing it. But it can only be done if we ourselves—all of us—know what we want and are united in wanting the same thing; if we are all prepared to revise our ideas about what work ought to be, and about what we mean by "having a good time." 14

For there is one fact we must face. Victory is the only possible condition upon which we can look forward to a "good time" of any kind; but victory will not leave us in a position where we can just relax all effort and enjoy ourselves in leisure and prosperity. We shall be living in a confused, exhausted and impoverished world, and there will be a great deal of work to do. Our best chance of having a good time will be to arrange our ideas, and our society, in such a way that everybody will have an opportunity to work hard and find happiness in doing *well* the work that will so desperately need to be done. 15

STUDS TERKEL

Two Prefaces from *Working*

Studs Terkel has worked as an actor, a movie theater manager, and a columnist, but it is as an interviewer of ordinary Americans that he has achieved widespread recognition. The host of a weekly interview program on a Chicago radio station since 1945, he has written a number of books in which his interviews are distilled into striking first-person narratives. The two interviews here were selected as prefaces to his 1974 book, *Working*.

The Steelworker: Mike Lefevre

It is a two-flat dwelling, somewhere in Cicero, on the out- 1
skirts of Chicago. He is thirty-seven. He works in a steel mill. On
occasion, his wife Carol works as a waitress in a neighborhood
restaurant; otherwise, she is at home, caring for their two small
children, a girl and a boy.

At the time of my first visit, a sculpted statuette of Mother and 2
Child was on the floor, head severed from body. He laughed
softly as he indicated his three-year-old daughter: "She Doctor
Spock'd it."

I'm a dying breed. A laborer. Strictly muscle work . . . pick it 3
up, put it down, pick it up, put it down. We handle between forty
and fifty thousand pounds of steel a day. (Laughs.) I know this is
hard to believe—from four hundred pounds to three- and four-
pound pieces. It's dying.

You can't take pride any more. You remember when a guy 4
could point to a house he built, how many logs he stacked. He
built it and he was proud of it. I don't really think I could be proud
if a contractor built a home for me. I would be tempted to get in
there and kick the carpenter in the ass (laughs), and take the saw
away from him. 'Cause I would have to be part of it, you know.

It's hard to take pride in a bridge you're never gonna cross, in 5
a door you're never gonna open. You're mass-producing things
and you never see the end result of it. (Muses.) I worked for a
trucker one time. And I got this tiny satisfaction when I loaded a
truck. At least I could see the truck depart loaded. In a steel mill,
forget it. You don't see where nothing goes.

I got chewed out by my foreman once. He said, "Mike, you're 6
a good worker but you have a bad attitude." My attitude is that
I don't get excited about my job. I do my work but I don't say
whoopee-doo. The day I get excited about my job is the day I go
to a head shrinker. How are you gonna get excited about pullin'
steel? How are you gonna get excited when you're tired and
want to sit down?

It's not just the work. Somebody built the pyramids. Some- 7
body's going to build something. Pyramids, Empire State Building—these things just don't happen. There's hard work behind it.
I would like to see a building, say, the Empire State, I would like

to see on one side of it a foot-wide strip from top to bottom with the name of every bricklayer, the name of every electrician, with all the names. So when a guy walked by, he could take his son and say, "See, that's me over there on the forty-fifth floor. I put the steel beam in." Picasso can point to a painting. What can I point to? A writer can point to a book. Everybody should have something to point to.

It's the not-recognition by other people. To say a woman is *just* a housewife is degrading, right? Okay. *Just* a housewife. It's also degrading to say *just* a laborer. The difference is that a man goes out and maybe gets smashed. 8

When I was single, I could quit, just split. I wandered all over the country. You worked just enough to get a poke, money in your pocket. Now I'm married and I got two kids . . . (trails off). I worked on a truck dock one time and I was single. The foreman came over and he grabbed my shoulder, kind of gave me a shove. I punched him and knocked him off the dock. I said, "Leave me alone. I'm doing my work, just stay away from me, just don't give me the with-the-hands business." 9

Hell, if you whip a damn mule he might kick you. Stay out of my way, that's all. Working is bad enough, don't bug me. I would rather work my ass off for eight hours a day with nobody watching me than five minutes with a guy watching me. Who you gonna sock? You can't sock General Motors, you can't sock anybody in Washington, you can't sock a system. 10

A mule, an old mule, that's the way I feel. Oh yeah. See. (Shows black and blue marks on arms and legs, burns.) You know what I heard from more than one guy at work? "If my kid wants to work in a factory, I am going to kick the hell out of him." I want my kid to be an effete snob. Yeah, mm-hmm. (Laughs.) I want him to be able to quote Walt Whitman, to be proud of it. 11

If you can't improve yourself, you improve your posterity. Otherwise life isn't worth nothing. You might as well go back to the cave and stay there. I'm sure the first caveman who went over the hill to see what was on the other side—I don't think he went there wholly out of curiosity. He went there because he wanted to get his son out of the cave. Just the same way I want to send my kid to college. 12

I work so damn hard and want to come home and sit down and lay around. *But I gotta get it out.* I want to be able to turn 13 around to somebody and say, "Hey, fuck you." You know? (Laughs.) The guy sitting next to me on the bus too. 'Cause all day I wanted to tell my foreman to go fuck himself, but I can't.

So I find a guy in a tavern. To tell him that. And he tells me   14 too. I've been in brawls. He's punching me and I'm punching him, because we actually want to punch somebody else. The most that'll happen is the bartender will bar us from the tavern. But at work, you lose your job.

This one foreman I've got, he's a kid. He's a college graduate.   15 He thinks he's better than everybody else. He was chewing me out and I was saying, "Yeah, yeah, yeah." He said, "What do you mean, yeah, yeah, yeah. Yes, *sir*." I told him, "Who the hell are you, Hitler? What is this '*Yes, sir*' bullshit? I came here to work, I didn't come here to crawl. There's a fuckin' difference." One word led to another and I lost.

I got broke down to a lower grade and lost twenty-five cents   16 an hour, which is a hell of a lot. It amounts to about ten dollars a week. He came over—after breaking me down. The guy comes over and smiles at me. I blew up. He didn't know it, but he was about two seconds and two feet away from a hospital. I said, "Stay the fuck away from me." He was just about to say something and was pointing his finger. I just reached my hand up and just grabbed his finger and I just put it back in his pocket. He walked away. I grabbed his finger because I'm married. If I'd a been single, I'd a grabbed his head. That's the difference.

You're doing this manual labor and you know that technol-   17 ogy can do it. (Laughs.) Let's face it, a machine can do the work of a man; otherwise they wouldn't have space probes. Why can we send a rocket ship that's unmanned and yet send a man in a steel mill to do a mule's work?

Automation? Depends how it's applied. It frightens me if it   18 puts me out on the street. It doesn't frighten me if it shortens my work week. You read that little thing: what are you going to do when this computer replaces you? Blow up computers. (Laughs.) Really. Blow up computers. I'll be goddamned if a computer is gonna eat before I do! I want milk for my kids and beer for me. Machines can either liberate man or enslave 'im, because they're pretty neutral. It's man who has the bias to put the thing one place or another.

If I had a twenty-hour workweek, I'd get to know my kids bet-   19 ter, my wife better. Some kid invited me to go on a college campus. On a Saturday. It was summertime. Hell, if I have a choice of taking my wife and kids to a picnic or going to a college campus, it's gonna be the picnic. But if I worked a twenty-hour week, I could go do both. Don't you think with that extra twenty hours people could really expand? Who's to say? There are some people in factories just by force of circumstance. I'm just like the colored people. Potential Einsteins don't have to be white. They could be in cotton fields, they could be in factories.

The twenty-hour week is a possibility today. The intellectuals, they always say there are potential Lord Byrons, Walt Whitmans, Roosevelts, Picassos working in construction or steel mills or factories. But I don't think they believe it. I think what they're afraid of is the potential Hitlers and Stalins that are there too. The people in power fear the leisure man. Not just the United States. Russia's the same way.

What do you think would happen in this country if, for one year, they experimented and gave everybody a twenty-hour week? How do they know that the guy who digs Wallace today doesn't try to resurrect Hitler tomorrow? Or the guy who is mildly disturbed at pollution doesn't decide to go to General Motors and shit on the guy's desk? You can become a fanatic if you had the time. The whole thing is time. That is, I think, one reason rich kids tend to be fanatic about politics: they have time. Time, that's the important thing.

It isn't that the average working guy is dumb. He's tired, that's all. I picked up a book on chess one time. That thing laid in the drawer for two or three weeks, you're too tired. During the weekends you want to take your kids out. You don't want to sit there and the kid comes up: "Daddy, can I go to the park?" You got your nose in a book? Forget it.

I know a guy fifty-seven years old. Know what he tells me? "Mike, I'm old and tired *all* the time." The first thing happens at work: when the arms start moving, the brain stops. I punch in about ten minutes to seven in the morning. I say hello to a couple of guys I like, I kid around with them. One guy says good morning to you and you say good morning. To another guy you say fuck you. The guy you say fuck you to is your friend.

I put on my hard hat, change into my safety shoes, put on my safety glasses, go to the bonderizer. It's the thing I work on. They rake the metal, they wash it, they dip it in a paint solution, and we take it off. Put it on, take it off, put it on, take it off, put it on, take it off. . . .

I say hello to everybody but my boss. At seven it starts. My arms get tired about the first half- hour. After that, they don't get tired any more until maybe the last half-hour at the end of the day. I work from seven to three thirty. My arms are tired at seven thirty and they're tired at three o'clock. I hope to God I never get broke in, because I always want my arms to be tired at seven thirty and three o'clock. (Laughs.) 'Cause that's when I know that there's a beginning and there's an end. That I'm not brainwashed. In between, I don't even try to think. 25

If I were to put you in front of a dock and I pulled up a skid in front of you with fifty hundred-pound sacks of potatoes and there are fifty more skids just like it, and this is what you're gonna do all day, what would you think about—potatoes? Unless a guy's a nut, he never thinks about work or talks about it. Maybe about baseball or about getting drunk the other night or he got laid or he didn't get laid. I'd say one out of a hundred will actually get excited about work. 26

Why is it that the communists always say they're for the workingman, and as soon as they set up a country, you got guys singing to tractors? They're singing about how they love the factory. That's where I couldn't buy communism. It's the intellectuals' utopia, not mine. I cannot picture myself singing to a tractor, I just can't. (Laughs.) Or singing to steel. (Singsongs.) Oh whoopdee-doo, I'm at the bonderizer, oh how I love this heavy steel. No thanks. Never hoppen. 27

Oh yeah, I daydream. I fantasize about a sexy blonde in Miami who's got my union dues. (Laughs.) I think of the head of the union the way I think of the head of my company. Living it up. I think of February in Miami. Warm weather, a place to lay in. When I hear a college kid say, "I'm oppressed," I don't believe him. You know what I'd like to do for one year? Live like a college kid. Just for one year. I'd love to. Wow! (Whispers.) Wow! Sports car! Marijuana! (Laughs.) Wild, sexy broads. I'd love that, hell yes, I would. 28

Somebody has to do this work. If my kid ever goes to college, I just want him to have a little respect, to realize that his dad is one of those somebodies. This is why even on—(muses) yeah, I 29 guess, sure—on the black thing . . . (Sighs heavily.) I can't really hate the colored fella that's working with me all day. The black intellectual I got no respect for. The white intellectual I got no use for. I got no use for the black militant who's gonna scream three hundred years of slavery to me while I'm busting my ass. You know what I mean? (Laughs.) I have one answer for that guy: go see Rockefeller. See Harriman. Don't bother me. We're in the same cotton field. So just don't bug me. (Laughs.)

After work I usually stop off at a tavern. Cold beer. Cold beer right away. When I was single, I used to go into hillbilly bars, get in a lot of brawls. Just to explode. I got a thing on my arm here (indicates scar). I got slapped with a bicycle chain. Oh, wow! (Softly) Mmm. I'm getting older. (Laughs.) I don't explode as much. You might say I'm broken in. (Quickly) No, I'll never be broken in. (Sighs.) When you get a little older, you exchange the words. When you're younger, you exchange the blows.

When I get home, I argue with my wife a little bit. Turn on TV, get mad at the news. (Laughs.) I don't even watch the news that much. I watch Jackie Gleason. I look for any alternative to the ten o'clock news. I don't want to go to bed angry. Don't hit a man with anything heavy at five o'clock. He just can't be bothered. This is his time to relax. The heaviest thing he wants is what his wife has to tell him.

When I come home, know what I do for the first twenty minutes? Fake it. I put on a smile. I got a kid three years old. Sometimes she says, "Daddy, where've you been?" I say, "Work." I could have told her I'd been in Disneyland What's work to a three-year-old kid? If I feel bad, I can't take it out on the kids. Kids are born innocent of everything but birth. You can't take it out on your wife either. This is why you go to a tavern. You want to release it there rather than do it at home. What does an actor do when he's got a bad movie? I got a bad movie every day.

I don't even need the alarm clock to get up in the morning. I can go out drinking all night, fall asleep at four, and bam! I'm up at six—no matter what I do. (Laughs.) It's a pseudo-death, more or less. Your whole system is paralyzed and you give all the appearance of death. It's an ingrown clock. It's a thing you just get used to. The hours differ. It depends. Sometimes my wife wants to do something crazy like play five hundred rummy or put a puzzle together. It could be midnight, could be ten o'clock, could be nine thirty.

What do you do weekends?   34

Drink beer, read a book. See that one? *Violence in America.*   35
It's one of them studies from Washington. One of them commit-
tees they're always appointing. A thing like that I read on a
weekend. But during the weekdays, gee . . . I just thought about
it. I don't do that much reading from Monday through Friday.
Unless it's a horny book. I'll read it at work and go home and do
my homework. (Laughs.) That's what the guys at the plant call
it—homework. (Laughs.) Sometimes my wife works on Saturday
and I drink beer at the tavern.

I went out drinking with one guy, oh, a long time ago. A col-   36
lege boy. He was working where I work now. Always preaching to me about how you need violence to change the system
and all that garbage. We went into a hillbilly joint. Some guy
there, I didn't know him from Adam, he said, "You think you're
smart." I said, "What's your pleasure?" (Laughs.) He said, "My
pleasure's to kick your ass." I told him I really can't be bothered. He said, "What're you, chicken?" I said, "No, I just don't
want to be bothered." He came over and said something to me
again. I said, "I don't beat women, drunks, or fools. Now leave
me alone."

The guy called his brother over. This college boy that was   37
with me, he came nudging my arm, "Mike, let's get out of here."
I said, "What are you worried about?" (Laughs.) This isn't unusual. People will bug you. You fend it off as much as you can
with your mouth and when you can't, you punch the guy out.

It was close to closing time and we stayed. We could have left,   38
but when you go into a place to have a beer and a guy challenges
you—if you expect to go in that place again, you don't leave. If
you have to fight the guy, you fight.

I got just outside the door and one of these guys jumped on   39
me and grabbed me around the neck. I grabbed his arm and
flung him against the wall. I grabbed him here (indicates throat),
and jiggled his head against the wall quite a few times. He kind
of slid down a little bit. This guy who said he was his brother
took a swing at me with a garrison belt. He just missed and hit
the wall. I'm looking around for my junior Stalin (laughs), who
loves violence and everything. He's gone. Split. (Laughs.) Next
day I see him at work. I couldn't get mad at him, he's a baby.

He saw a book in my back pocket one time and he was amazed.   40

He walked up to me and he said, "You read?" I said, "What do you mean, I read?" He said, "All these dummies read the sports pages around here. What are you doing with a book?" I got pissed off at the kid right away. I said, "What do you mean, all these dummies? Don't knock a man who's paying somebody else's way through college." He was a nineteen-year-old effete snob.

Yet you want your kid to be an effete snob?   41

Yes. I want my kid to look at me and say, "Dad, you're a nice   42
guy, but you're a fuckin' dummy." Hell yes, I want my kid to tell me that he's not gonna be like me. . . .

If I were hiring people to work, I'd try naturally to pay them a   43
decent wage. I'd try to find out their first names, their last names, keep the company as small as possible, so I could personalize the whole thing. All I would ask a man is a handshake, see you in the morning. No applications, nothing. I wouldn't be interested in the guy's past. Nobody ever checks the pedigree on a mule, do they? But they do on a man. Can you picture walking up to a mule and saying, "I'd like to know who his granddaddy was?"

I'd like to run a combination bookstore and tavern. (Laughs.) I   44
would like to have a place where college kids came and a steel-worker could sit down and talk. Where a workingman could not be ashamed of Walt Whitman and where a college professor could not be ashamed that he painted his house over the weekend.

If a carpenter built a cabin for poets, I think the least the po-   45
ets owe the carpenter is just three or four one-liners on the wall. A little plaque: Though we labor with our minds, this place we can relax in was built by someone who can work with his hands. And his work is as noble as ours. I think the poet owes something to the guy who builds the cabin for him.

I don't think of Monday. You know what I'm thinking about   46
on Sunday night? Next Sunday. If you work real hard, you think of a perpetual vacation. Not perpetual sleep . . . What do I think of on a Sunday night? Lord, I wish the fuck I could do something else for a living.

I don't know who the guy is who said there is nothing sweeter   47
than an unfinished symphony. Like an unfinished painting and an unfinished poem. If he creates this thing one day—let's say, Michelangelo's Sistine Chapel. It took him a long time to do this, this beautiful work of art. But what if he had to create this Sistine

Chapel a thousand times a year? Don't you think that would even dull Michelangelo's mind? Or if da Vinci had to draw his anatomical charts thirty, forty, fifty, sixty, eighty, ninety, a hundred times a day? Don't you think that would even bore da Vinci?

Way back, you spoke of the guys who built the pyramids, not the 48
pharaohs, the unknowns. You put yourself in their category?

Yes. I want my signature on 'em, too. Sometimes, out of pure 49
meanness, when I make something, I put a little dent in it. I like to do something to make it really unique. Hit it with a hammer. I deliberately fuck it up to see if it'll get by, just so I can say I did it. It could be anything. Let me put it this way: I think God invented the dodo bird so when we get up there we could tell Him, "Don't you ever make mistakes?" and He'd say, "Sure, look." (Laughs.) I'd like to make my imprint. My dodo bird. A mistake, *mine.* Let's say the whole building is nothing but red bricks. I'd like to have just the black one or the white one or the purple one. Deliberately fuck up.

This is gonna sound square, but my kid is my imprint. He's 50
my freedom. There's a line in one of Hemingway's books. I think it's from *For Whom the Bell Tolls.* They're behind the enemy lines, somewhere in Spain, and she's pregnant. She wants to stay with him. He tells her no. He says, "If you die, I die," knowing he's gonna die. But if you go, I go. Know what I mean? The mystics call it the brass bowl. Continuum. You know what I mean? This is why I work. Every time I see a young guy walk by with a shirt and tie and dressed up real sharp, I'm lookin' at my kid, you know? That's it.

THE MASON: CARL MURRAY BATES

We're in a tavern no more than thirty yards from the banks of 51
the Ohio. Toward the far side of the river, Alcoa smokestacks belch forth: an uneasy coupling of a bucolic past and an industrial present. The waters are polluted, yet the jobs out there offer the townspeople their daily bread.

He is fifty-seven years old. He's a stonemason who has pur- 52
sued his craft since he was seventeen. None of his three sons is in his trade.

As far as I know, masonry is older than carpentry, which goes   53
clear back to Bible times. Stonemason goes back way *before*
Bible time: the pyramids of Egypt, things of that sort. Anybody
that starts to build anything, stone, rock, or brick, start on the
northeast corner. Because when they built King Solomon's Temple, they started on the northeast corner. To this day, you look at
your courthouses, your big public buildings, you look at the cornerstone, when it was created, what year, it will be on the northeast corner. If I was gonna build a septic tank, I would start on
the northeast corner. (Laughs.) Superstition, I suppose.

With stone we build just about anything. Stone is the oldest   54
and best building material that ever was. Stone was being used
even by the cavemen that put it together with mud. They built
out of stone before they even used logs. He got him a cave, he
built stone across the front. And he learned to use dirt, mud, to
make the stones lay there without sliding around—which was
the beginnings of mortar, which we still call mud. The Romans
used mortar that's almost as good as we have today.

Everyone hears these things, they just don't remember 'em.   55
But me being in the profession, when I hear something in that
line, I remember it. Stone's my business. I, oh, sometimes talk to
architects and engineers that have made a study and I pick up the
stuff here and there.

Every piece of stone you pick up is different, the grain's a lit-   56
tle different and this and that. It'll split one way and break the
other. You pick up your stone and look at it and make an educated guess. It's a pretty good day layin' stone or brick. Not tir-
ing. Anything you like to do isn't tiresome. It's hard work; stone
is heavy. At the same time, you get interested in what you're doing and you usually fight the clock the other way. You're not
lookin' for quittin'. You're wondering you haven't got enough
done and it's almost quittin' time. (Laughs.) I ask the hod carrier
what time it is and he says two thirty. I say, "Oh, my Lord, I was
gonna get a whole lot more than this."

I pretty well work by myself. On houses, usually just one works.   57
I've got the hod carrier there, but most of the time I talk to myself,
"I'll get my hammer and I'll knock the chip off there." (Laughs.) A
good hod carrier is half your day. He won't work as hard as a poor
one. He knows what to do and make every move count makin' the
mortar. It has to be so much water, so much sand. His skill is to see

that you don't run out of anything. The hod carrier, he's above the laborer. He has a certain amount of prestige.

I think a laborer feels that he's the low man. Not so much   58
that he works with his hands, it's that he's at the bottom of the scale. He always wants to get up to a skilled trade. Of course he'd make more money. The main thing is the common laborer— even the word *common* laborer—just sounds so common, he's at the bottom. Many that works with his hands takes pride in his work.

I get a lot of phone calls when I get home: how about showin'   59
me how and I'll do it myself? I always wind up doin' it for 'em. (Laughs.) So I take a lot of pride in it and I do get, oh, I'd say, a lot of praise or whatever you want to call it. I don't suppose anybody, however much he's recognized, wouldn't like to be recognized a little more. I think I'm pretty well recognized.

One of my sons is an accountant and the other two are   60
bankers. They're mathematicians, I suppose you'd call 'em that. Air-conditioned offices and all that. They always look at the house I build. They stop by and see me when I'm aworkin'. Always want me to come down and fix somethin' on their house, too. (Laughs.) They don't buy a house that I don't have to look at it first. Oh sure, I've got to crawl under it and look on the roof, you know. . . .

I can't seem to think of any young masons. So many of 'em be-   61
fore, the man lays stone and his son follows his footsteps. Right now the only one of these sons I can think of is about forty, fifty years old.

I started back in the Depression times when there wasn't any   62
apprenticeships. You just go out and if you could hold your job, that's it. I was just a kid then. Now I worked real hard and carried all the blocks I could. Then I'd get my trowel and I'd lay one or two. The second day the boss told me: I think you could lay enough blocks to earn your wages. So I guess I had only one day of apprenticeship. Usually it takes about three years of being a hod carrier to start. And it takes another ten or fifteen years to learn the skill.

I admired the men that we had at that time that were stone-   63
masons. They knew their trade. So naturally I tried to pattern after them. There's been very little change in the work. Stone is still stone, mortar is still the same as it was fifty years ago. The style

of stone has changed a little. We use a lot more, we call it golf. A stone as big as a baseball up to as big as a basketball. Just round balls and whatnot. We just fit 'em in the wall that way.

Automation has tried to get in the bricklayer. Set 'em with a crane. I've seen several put up that way. But you've always got in-between the windows and this and that. It just doesn't seem to pan out. We do have a power saw. We do have an electric power mix to mix the mortar, but the rest of it's done by hand as it always was.   64

In the old days they all seemed to want it cut out and smoothed. It's harder now because you have no way to use your tools. You have no way to use a string, you have no way to use a level or a plumb. You just have to look at it because it's so rough and many irregularities. You have to just back up and look at it.   65

All construction, there's always a certain amount of injuries. A scaffold will break and so on. But practically no real danger. All I ever did do was work on houses, so we don't get up very high—maybe two stories. Very seldom that any more. Most of 'em are one story. And so many of 'em use stone for a trim. They may go up four, five feet and then paneling or something. There's a lot of skinned fingers or you hit your finger with a hammer. Practically all stone is worked with hammers and chisels. I wouldn't call it dangerous at all.   66

Stone's my life. I daydream all the time, most times it's on stone. Oh, I'm gonna build me a stone cabin down on the Green River. I'm gonna build stone cabinets in the kitchen. That stone door's gonna be awful heavy and I don't know how to attach the hinges. I've got to figure out how to make a stone roof. That's the kind of thing. All my dreams, it seems like it's got to have a piece of rock mixed in it.   67

If I got some problem that's bothering me, I'll actually wake up in the night and think of it. I'll sit at the table and get a pencil and paper and go over it, makin' marks on paper or drawin' or however . . . this way or that way. Now I've got to work this and I've only got so much. Or they decided they want it that way when you already got it fixed this way. Anyone hates tearing his work down. It's all the same price but you still don't like to do it.   68

These fireplaces, you've got to figure how they'll throw out heat, the way you curve the fireboxes inside. You have to draw a line so they reflect heat. But if you throw out too much of a   69 curve, you'll have them smoke. People in these fine houses don't want a puff of smoke coming out of the house.

The architect draws the picture and the plans, and the drafts-   70
man and the engineer, they help him. They figure the strength and so on. But when it comes to actually makin' the curves and doin' the work, you've got to do it with your hands. It comes right back to your hands.

When you get into stone, you're gettin' away from the pre-   71
fabs, you're gettin' into the better homes. Usually at this day and age they'll start into sixty to seventy thousand and run up to about half a million. We've got one goin' now that's mighty close, three or four hundred thousand. That type of house is what we build.

The lumber is not near as good as it used to be. We have bet-   72
ter fabricating material, such as plywood and sheet rock and things of that sort, but the lumber itself is definitely inferior. Thirty, forty years ago a house was almost entirely made of lumber, wood floors. . . . Now they have vinyl, they have carpet, everything, and so on. The framework wood is getting to be of very poor quality.

But stone is still stone and the bricks are actually more uni-   73
form than they used to be. Originally they took a clay bank. . . . I know a church been built that way. Went right on location, dug a hole in the ground and formed bricks with their hands. They made the bricks that built the building on the spot.

Now we've got modern kilns, modern heat, the temperature   74
don't vary. They got better bricks now than they used to have. We've got machines that make brick, so they're made true. Where they used to, they were pretty rough. I'm buildin' a big fireplace now out of old brick. They run wide, long, and it's a headache. I've been two weeks on that one fireplace.

The toughest job I ever done was this house, a hundred years   75
old plus. The lady wanted one room left just that way. And this doorway had to be closed. It had deteriorated and weathered for over a hundred years. The bricks was made out of broken pieces, none of 'em were straight. If you lay 'em crooked, it gets awful hard right there. You spend a lifetime tryin' to learn to lay bricks straight. And it took a half-day to measure with a spoon, to try to get the mortar to match. I'd have so much dirt, so much soot, so much lime, so when I got the recipe right I could make it in bigger

quantity. Then I made it with a coffee cup. Half a cup of this, half a cup of that . . . I even used soot out of a chimney and sweepin's off the floor. I was two days layin' up a little doorway, mixin' the mortar and all. The boss told the lady it couldn't be done. I said, "Give me the time, I believe I can do it." I defy you to find where that door is right now. That's the best job I ever done.

There's not a house in this country that I haven't built that I don't look at every time I go by. (Laughs.) I can set here now and actually in my mind see so many that you wouldn't believe. If there's one stone in there crooked, I know where it's at and I'll never forget it. Maybe thirty years, I'll know a place where I should have took that stone out and redone it but I didn't. I still notice it. The people who live there might not notice it, but I notice it. I never pass that house that I don't think of it. I've got one house in mind right now. (Laughs.) That's the work of my hands. 'Cause you see, stone, you don't prepaint it, you don't camouflage it. It's there, just like I left it forty years ago.

I can't imagine a job where you go home and maybe go by a year later and you don't know what you've done. My work, I can see what I did the first day I started. All my work is set right out there in the open and I can look at it as I go by. It's something I can see the rest of my life. Forty years ago, the first blocks I ever laid in my life, when I was seventeen years old. I never go through Eureka—a little town down there on the river—that I don't look thataway. It's always there.

Immortality as far as we're concerned. Nothin' in this world lasts forever, but did you know that stone—Bedford limestone, they claim—deteriorates one-sixteenth of an inch every hundred years? And it's around four or five inches for a house. So that's gettin' awful close. (Laughs.)

CAROL BLY

Getting Tired

Carol Bly has published short stories in such magazines as *The New Yorker,* and for more than a decade was herself an editor of a literary magazine. At the same time that she participated in the national literary scene however, she worked and lived in rural Minnesota and contributed essays—which she sometimes presented as "letters"—to local publications. "Getting Tired" is from her 1981 collection, *Letters from the Country*.

The men have left a gigantic 6600 combine a few yards from our grove, at the edge of the stubble. For days it was working around the farm; we heard it on the east, later on the west, and finally we could see it grinding back and forth over the windrows on the south. But now it has been simply squatting at the field's edge, huge, tremendously still, very professional, slightly dangerous.

We all have the correct feelings about this new combine: this isn't the good old farming where man and soil are dusted together all day; this isn't farming a poor man can afford, either, and therefore it further threatens his hold on the American "family farm" operation. We have been sneering at this machine for days, as its transistor radio, amplified well over the engine roar, has been grinding up our silence, spreading a kind of shrill ghetto evening all over the farm.

But now it is parked, and after a while I walk over to it and climb up its neat little John-Deere-green ladder on the left. Entering the big cab up there is like coming up into a large ship's bridge on visitors' day—heady stuff to see the inside workings of a huge operation like the Queen Elizabeth II. On the other hand I feel left out, being only a dumbfounded passenger. The combine cab has huge windows flaring wider at the top; they lean forward over the ground, and the driver sits so high behind the glass in its rubber moldings it is like a movie-set spaceship. He has obviously come to dominate the field, whether he farms it or not.

The value of the 66 is that it can do anything, and to change it from a combine into a cornpicker takes one man about half an hour, whereas most machine conversions on farms take several men a half day. It frees its owner from a lot of monkeying.

Monkeying, in city life, is what little boys do to clocks so they never run again. In farming it has two quite different meanings. The first is small side projects. You monkey with poultry, unless you're a major egg handler. Or you monkey with ducks or geese. If you have a very small milk herd, and finally decide that prices plus state regulations don't make your few Holsteins worthwhile, you "quit monkeying with them." There is a hidden dignity in this word: it precludes mention of money. It lets the wife of a very marginal farmer have a conversation with a woman who may be helping her husband run fifteen hundred acres. "How you coming with those geese?" "Oh, we've been real disgusted. We're thinking of quitting monkeying with them." It saves her having to say, "We lost our shirts on those darn geese."

The other meaning of monkeying is wrestling with and maintaining machinery, such as changing heads from combining to cornpicking. Farmers who cornpick the old way, in which the corn isn't shelled automatically during picking in the field but must be elevated to the top of a pile by belt and then shelled, put up with some monkeying.   6

Still, cornpicking and plowing is a marvelous time of the year on farms; one of the best autumns I've had recently had a few days of fieldwork in it. We were outside all day, from six in the morning to eight at night—coming in only for noon dinner. We ate our lunches on a messy truck flatbed. (For city people who don't know it: *lunch* isn't a noon meal; it is what you eat out of a black lunch pail at 9 A.M. and 3 P.M. If you offer a farmer a cup of coffee at 3:30 P.M. he or she is likely to say, "No thanks, I've already had lunch.") There were four of us hired to help—a couple to plow, Celia (a skilled farmhand who worked steady for our boss), and me. Lunch was always two sandwiches of white commercial bread with luncheon meat, and one very generous piece of cake-mix cake carefully wrapped in Saran Wrap. (I never found anyone around here self-conscious about using Saran Wrap when the Dow Chemical Company was also making napalm.)   7

It was very pleasant on the flatbed, squinting out over the yellow picked cornstalks—each time we stopped for lunch, a larger part of the field had been plowed black. We fell into the easy psychic habit of farmworkers: admiration of the boss. "Ja, I see he's buying one of those big 4010s," someone would say. We always perked up at inside information like that. Or "Ja," as the woman hired steady told us, "he's going to plow the home fields first this time, instead of the other way round." We temporary help were impressed by that, too. Then, with real flair, she brushed a crumb of luncheon meat off her jeans, the way you would make sure to flick a gnat off spotless tennis whites. It is the true feminine touch to brush a crumb off pants that are encrusted with Minnesota Profile A heavy loam, many swipes of SAE 40 oil, and grain dust.   8

All those days, we never tired of exchanging information on   9
how *he* was making out, what *he* was buying, whom *he* was going to let drive the new tractor, and so on. There is always something to talk about with the other hands, because farming is
genuinely absorbing. It has the best quality of work: nothing else
seems real. And everyone doing it, even the cheapest helpers like
me, can see the layout of the whole—from spring work, to cultivating, to small grain harvest, to cornpicking, to fall plowing.

The second day I was promoted from elevating corncobs at   10
the corn pile to actual plowing. Hour after hour I sat up there on
the old Alice, as she was called (an Allis-Chalmers WC that
looked rusted from the Flood). You have to sit twisted part way
around, checking that the plowshares are scouring clean, turning
over and dropping the dead crop and soil, not clogging. For the
first two hours I was very political. I thought about what would
be good for American farming—stronger marketing organizations, or maybe a law like the Norwegian Odal law, preventing
the breaking up of small farms or selling them to business interests. Then the sun got high, and each time I reached the headlands area at the field's end I dumped off something else, now my
cap, next my jacket, finally my sweater.

Since the headlands are the last to be plowed, they serve as a   11
field road until the very end. There are usually things parked
there—a pickup or a corn trailer—and things dumped—my
warmer clothing, our afternoon lunch pails, a broken furrow
wheel someone picked up.

By noon I'd dropped all political interest, and was thinking   12
only: how unlike this all is to Keats's picture of autumn, a "season of mists and mellow fruitfulness." This gigantic expanse of
horizon, with everywhere the easy growl of tractors, was simply
teeming with extrovert energy. It wouldn't calm down for another week, when whoever was lowest on the totem pole would
be sent out to check a field for dropped parts or to drive away
the last machines left around.

The worst hours for all common labor are the hours after   13
noon dinner. Nothing is inspiring then. That is when people
wonder how they ever got stuck in the line of work they've chosen for life. Or they wonder where the cool Indian smoke of secrets and messages began to vanish from their marriage. Instead
of plugging along like a cheerful beast working for me, the Allis
now smelled particularly gassy. To stay awake I froze my eyes

onto an indented circle in the hood around the gas cap. Someone had apparently knocked the screw cap fitting down into the hood, so there was a moat around it. In this moat some overflow gas leapt in tiny waves. Sometimes the gas cap was a castle, this was the moat; sometimes it was a nuclear-fission plant, this was the horrible hot-water waste. Sometimes it was just the gas cap on the old Alice with the spilt gas bouncing on the hot metal.

Row after row. I was stupefied. But then around 2:30 the   14 shadows appeared again, and the light, which had been dazing and white, grew fragile. The whole prairie began to gather itself for the cool evening. All of a sudden it was wonderful to be plowing again, and when I came to the field end, the filthy jackets and the busted furrow wheel were just benign mistakes: that is, if it chose to, the jacket could be a church robe, and the old wheel could be something with some pride to it, like a helm. And I felt the same about myself: instead of being someone with a half interest in literature and a half interest in farming doing a half-decent job plowing, I could have been someone desperately needed in Washington or Zurich. I drank my three o'clock coffee joyously, and traded the other plowman a Super-Valu cake-mix lemon cake slice for a Holsum baloney sandwich because it had garlic in it.

By seven at night we had been plowing with headlights for an   15 hour. I tried to make up games to keep going, on my second wind, on my third wind, but labor is labor after the whole day of it; the mind refuses to think of ancestors. It refuses to pretend the stalks marching up to the right wheel in the spooky light are men-at-arms, or to imagine a new generation coming along. It doesn't care. Now the Republicans could have announced a local meeting in which they would propose a new farm program whereby every farmer owning less than five hundred acres must take half price for his crop, and every farmer owning more than a thousand acres shall receive triple price for his crop, and I was so tired I wouldn't have shown up to protest.

A million hours later we sit around in a daze at the dining-   16 room table, and nobody says anything. In low, courteous mutters we ask for the macaroni hotdish down this way, please. Then we get up in ones and twos and go home. Now the farm help are all so tired we *are* a little like the various things left out on the headlands—some tools, a jacket, someone's thermos top—used up for that day. Thoughts won't even stick to us anymore.

Such tiredness must be part of farmers' wanting huge machin- 17
ery like the Deere 6600. That tiredness that feels so good to the
occasional laborer and the athlete is disturbing to a man destined
to it eight months of every year. But there is a more hidden psychology in the issue of enclosed combines versus open tractors. It
is this: one gets too many impressions on the open tractor. A
thousand impressions enter as you work up and down the rows:
nature's beauty or nature's stubbornness, politics, exhaustion, but
mainly the feeling that all this repetition—last year's cornpicking,
this year's cornpicking, next year's cornpicking—is taking up
your lifetime. The mere repetition reveals your eventual death.

When you sit inside a modern combine, on the other hand, 18
you are so isolated from field, sky, all the real world, that the
brain is dulled. You are not sensitized to your own mortality.
You aren't sensitive to anything at all.

This must be a common choice of our mechanical era: to hide 19
from life inside our machinery. If we can hide from life in there,
some idiotic part of the psyche reasons, we can hide from death
in there as well.

SUE HUBBELL

Beekeeper

After attending four universities and working for twelve years as a
bookstore manager and a librarian, Sue Hubbell moved to the
Missouri Ozarks, where she made a living tending eighteen million
honeybees and selling the honey they produced. In 1986 she published *A Country Year*, a book that won her an immediate national
audience. The following passage is excerpted from that book.

Anyone who has kept bees is a pushover for a swarm of them. 1
We always drop whatever we are doing and go off to pick one
up when asked to do so. It doesn't make sense, because from a
standpoint of serious beekeeping and honey production a swarm
isn't much good. Swarms are headed up by old queens with not
much vitality or egg-laying potential left, and so a beekeeper
should replace her with a new queen from a queen breeder. He
will probably have to feed and coddle the swarm through its first

year; it will seldom produce any extra honey the first season. And yet we always hive them.

There is something really odd about swarms, and I notice that   2
beekeepers don't talk about it much, probably because it is the sort of thing we don't feel comfortable about trying to put into words, something the other side of rationality.

The second year I kept bees, I picked up my first swarm. I was   3
in the middle of the spring beework, putting in ten to twelve hours a day, and very attuned to what the bees were doing out there in their hives. That day had begun with a heavy rainstorm, and so rather than working out in the beeyards, I was in the honey house making new equipment. By afternoon the rain had stopped, but the air was warm and heavy, charged and expectant. I began to feel odd, tense and anticipatory, and when the back of my neck began to prickle I decided to take a walk out to the new hives I had started. Near them, hanging pendulously from the branch of an apple tree, was a swarm of bees. Individual bees were still flying in from all directions, adding their numbers to those clinging around their queen.

In the springtime some colonies of bees, for reasons not well   4
understood, obey an impulse to split in two and thus multiply by swarming. The worker bees thoughtfully raise a new queen bee for the parent colony, and then a portion of the bees gather with the old queen, gorge themselves with honey and fly out of the hive, never to return, leaving all memory of their old home behind. They cluster somewhere temporarily, such as on the branch of my apple tree. If a beekeeper doesn't hive them, scout bees fly from the cluster and investigate nearby holes and spaces, and report back to the cluster on the suitability of new quarters.

We know about two forms of honeybee communication. One   5
is chemical: information about food sources and the wellbeing of the queen and colony is exchanged as bees continually feed one another with droplets of nectar which they have begun to process and chemically tag. The other form of communication is tactile: bees tell other bees about good things such as food or the location of a new home by patterned motions. These elaborate movements, which amount to a highly stylized map of landmarks, direction and the sun's position, are called the bee dance.

Different scout bees may find different locations for the swarm   6
and return to dance about their finds. Eventually, sometimes af-

ter several days, an agreement is reached, rather like the arrival of the Sense of the Meeting among Quakers, and all the bees in the cluster fly off to their new home.

I watched the bees on my apple tree for a while with delight 7 and pleasure, and then resumed to the barn to gather up enough equipment to hive them. As I did so, I glanced up at the sky. It was still dark from the receding thunderstorm, but a perfect and dazzling rainbow arched shimmering against the deep blue sky, its curve making a stunning and pleasing contrast with the sharp inverted V of the barn roof. I returned to the apple tree and shook the bees into the new beehive, noticing that I was singing snatches of one of Handel's coronation anthems. It seemed as appropriate music to hive a swarm by as any I knew.

Since then, I have learned to pay attention in the springtime 8 when the air feels electric and full of excitement. It was just so one day last week. I had been working quietly along the row of twelve hives in an outyard when the hair on the back of my neck began to stand on end. I looked up to see the air thick with bees flying in toward me from the north. The swarm was not from any of my hives, but for some reason bees often cluster near existing hives while they scout a new location. I closed up the hive I was working on and stood back to watch. I was near a slender post oak sapling, and the bees began to light on one of its lower limbs right next to my elbow. They came flying in, swirling as they descended, spiraling around me and the post oak until I was enveloped by the swarm, the air moving gently from the beat of their wings. I am not sure how long I stood there. I lost all sense of time and felt only elation, a kind of human emotional counterpart of the springlike, optimistic, burgeoning, state that the bees were in. I stood quietly; I was nothing more to the bees than an object to be encircled on their way to the spot where they had decided, in a way I could not know, to cluster. In another sense I was not remote from them at all, but was receiving all sorts of meaningful messages in the strongest way imaginable outside of human mental process and language. My skin was tingling as the bees brushed past and I felt almost a part of the swarm.

Eventually the bees settled down in the cluster. Regaining a 9 more suitable sense of my human condition and responsibilities, I went over to my pickup and got the empty hive that I always carry with me during swarming season. I propped it up so that

its entrance was just under the swarm. A frame of comb from another hive was inside and the bees in the cluster could smell it, so
they began to walk up into the entrance. I watched, looking for
the queen, for without her the swarm would die. It took perhaps
twenty minutes for all of them to file in, and the queen, a long,
elegant bee, was one of the last to enter.

I screened up the entrance and put the hive in the back of the   10
pickup. After I was finished with my work with the other hives
in the beeyard, I drove back home with my new swarm.

I should have ordered a new queen bee, killed the old one and   11
replaced her, but in doing that I would have destroyed the identity of the swarm. Every colony of bees takes its essence, character and personality from the queen who is mother to all its
members. As a commercial beekeeper, it was certainly my business to kill the old queen and replace her with a vigorous new
one so that the colony would become a good honey producer.

But I did not.   12

*   *   *

This week I have started cutting my firewood. It should be cut   13
months ahead of time to let it dry and cure, so that it will burn
hot in the winter. It is June now, and almost too late to be cutting
firewood, but during the spring I was working with the bees
from sunup until sundown and didn't have time. By midday it is
stifling back in the woods, so I go out at sunrise and cut wood
for a few hours, load it into the pickup and bring it back to stack
below the barn.

I like being out there early. The spiders have spun webs to   14
catch night-flying insects, and as the rising sun slants through the
trees, the dewdrops that line the webs are turned into exquisite,
delicate jewels. The woodlot smells of shade, leaf mold and
damp soil. Wild turkey have left fresh bare spots where they
scratched away the leaves looking for beetles and grubs. My
dogs like being there too, and today snuffled excitedly in a hollow at the base of a tree. The beagle shrieked into it, his baying
muffled. The squirrel who may have denned in the tree last night
temporarily escaped their notice and sat on a low limb eying the
two dogs suspiciously, tail twitching. A sunbeam lit up a tall this-
tle topped with a luxuriant purple blossom from which one but-

terfly and one honeybee sipped nectar. Red-eyed vireos sang high in the treetops where I could not see them.

For me their song ended when I started the chain saw. It makes a terrible racket, but I am fond of it. It is one of the first tools I learned to master on my own, and it is also important to me. My woodstove, a simple black cast-iron-and-sheet-metal affair, is the only source of heat for my cabin in the winter, and if I do not have firewood to burn in it, the dogs, cat, the houseplants, the water in my pipes and I will all freeze. It is wonderfully simple and direct: cut wood or die.

When Paul was here he cut the firewood and I, like all Ozark wives, carried the cut wood to the pickup. When he left, he left his chain saw, but it was a heavy, vibrating, ill-tempered thing. I weigh a hundred and five pounds, and although I could lift it, once I had it running it shook my hands so much that it became impossibly dangerous to use. One year I hired a man to cut my wood, but I was not pleased with the job he did, and so the next year, although I could not afford it, I bought the finest, lightest, best-made chain saw money could buy. It is a brand that many woodcutters use, and has an antivibration device built into even its smaller models.

The best chain saws are formidable and dangerous tools. My brother nearly cut off his arm with one. A neighbor who earns his living in timber just managed to kill the engine on his when he was cutting overhead and a branch snapped the saw back toward him. The chain did not stop running until it had cut through the beak of his cap. He was very solemn when I told him that I had bought my own chain saw, and he gave me a good piece of advice. "The time to worry about a chain saw," he said, "is when you stop being afraid of it."

I am cautious. I spend a lot of time sizing up a tree before I fell it. Once it is down, I clear away the surrounding brush before I start cutting it into lengths. That way I will not trip and lose my balance with the saw running. A dull chain and a poorly running saw are dangerous, so I've learned to keep mine in good shape and I sharpen the chain each time I use it.

This morning I finished sawing up a tree from the place where I had been cutting for the past week. In the process I lost, in the fallen leaves somewhere, my scrench—part screwdriver, part wrench—that I use to make adjustments on the saw. I shouldn't have been carrying it in my pocket, but the chain on the saw's bar had been loose; I had tightened it and had not walked back to the pickup to put it away. Scolding myself for being so careless, I began looking for another tree to cut, but stopped to watch a fawn that I had frightened from his night's sleeping place. He was young and his coat was still spotted, but he ran so quickly and silently that the two dogs, still sniffing after the squirrel, never saw him.

I like to cut the dead trees from my woodlot, leaving the ones   20 still alive to flourish, and I noticed a big one that had recently died. This one was bigger than I feel comfortable about felling. I've been cutting my own firewood for six years now, but I am still awed by the size and weight of a tree as it crashes to the ground, and I have to nerve myself to cut the really big ones.

I wanted this tree to fall on a stretch of open ground that was   21 free of other trees and brush, so I cut a wedge-shaped notch on that side of it. The theory is that the tree, thus weakened, will fall slowly in the direction of the notch when the serious cut, slightly above the notch on the other side, is made. The trouble is that trees, particularly dead ones that may have rot on the inside, do not know the theory and may fall in an unexpected direction. That is the way accidents happen. I was aware of this, and scared, besides, to be cutting down such a big tree; as a result, perhaps I cut too timid a wedge. I started sawing through on the other side, keeping an eye on the tree top to detect the characteristic tremble that signals a fall. I did not have time to jam the plastic wedge in my back pocket into the cut to hold it open because the tree began to fall in my direction, exactly opposite where I had intended. I killed the engine on the saw and jumped out of the way.

There was no danger, however. Directly in back of where I   22 had been standing were a number of other trees, which was why I had wanted to have the sawed one fall in the opposite direction; as my big tree started to topple, its upper branches snagged in another one, and it fell no further. I had sawed completely through the tree, but now the butt end had trapped my saw against the stump. I had cut what is descriptively called a "widow maker." If I had been cutting with someone else, we could have used a second saw to cut out mine and perhaps brought down the tree, but this is dangerous and I don't like to do it. I could not even free my saw by taking it apart, for I had lost my scrench, so I drove back to the barn and gathered up the tools I needed; a socket wrench, chains and a portable winch known as a come-along. A come-along is a cheery, sensible tool for a woman. It has a big hook at one end and another hook connected to a steel cable at the other. The cable is wound around a ratchet gear operated by a long handle to give leverage. It divides a heavy job up into small manageable bits that require no more than female strength, and I have used it many times to pull my pickup free from mud and snow.

The day was warming up and I was sweating by the time I got back to the woods, but I was determined to repair the botch I had made of the morning's woodcutting. Using the socket wrench, I removed the bar and chain from the saw's body and set it aside. The weight of the saw gone, I worked free the bar and chain pinched under the butt of the tree. Then I sat down on the ground, drank ice water from my thermos and figured out how I was going to pull down the tree. 23

Looking at the widow maker, I decided that if I could wind one of the chains around the butt of it, and another chain around a nearby standing tree, then connect the two with the come-along, I might be able to winch the tree to the ground. I attached the chains and come-along appropriately and began. Slowly, with each pump of the handle against the ratchet gear, the tree sank to the ground. 24

The sun was high in the sky, the heat oppressive and my shirt and jeans were soaked with sweat, so I decided to leave the job of cutting up the tree until tomorrow. I gathered my tools together, and in the process found the scrench, almost hidden in the leaf mold. Then I threw all the tools into the back of the pickup, and sat on the tailgate to finish off the rest of the ice water and listen to the red-eyed vireo singing. 25

It is satisfying, of course, to build up a supply of winter warmth, free except for the labor. But there is also something heady about becoming a part of the forest process. It sounds straightforward enough to say that when I cut firewood I cull and thin my woods, but that puts me in the business of deciding which trees should be encouraged and which should be taken. 26

I like my great tall black walnut, so I have cut the trees around it to give it the space and light it needs to grow generously. Dogwoods don't care. They frost the woods with white blossoms in the spring, and grow extravagantly in close company. If I clear a 27 patch, within a year or two pine seedlings move in, grow up exuberantly, compete and thin themselves to tolerable spacing. If I don't cut a diseased tree, its neighbors may sicken and die. If I cut away one half of a forked white oak, the remaining trunk will grow straight and sturdy. Sap gone, a standing dead tree like the one I cut today will make good firewood, and so invites cutting. But if I leave it, it will make a home for woodpeckers, and later for flying squirrels and screech owls. Where I leave a brush pile of top branches, rabbits make a home. If I leave a fallen tree, others will benefit: ants, spiders, beetles and wood roaches will use it for shelter and food, and lovely delicate fungi will grow out of it before it mixes with leaf mold to become a part of a new layer of soil.

One person with a chain saw makes a difference in the woods,   28
and by making a difference becomes part of the woodland cycle, a part of the abstraction that is the forest community.

* * *

I keep twenty hives of bees here in my home beeyard, but   29
most of my hives are scattered in outyards across the Ozarks, where I can find the thickest stands of wild blackberries and other good things for bees. I always have a waiting list of farmers who would like the bees on their land, for the clover in their pastures is more abundant when the bees are there to pollinate it.

One of the farmers, a third-generation Ozarker and a dairy-   30
man with a lively interest in bees, came over today for a look at what my neighbors call my honey factory. My honey house contains a shiny array of stainless-steel tanks with clear plastic tubing connecting them, a power uncapper for slicing open honeycomb, an extractor for spinning honey out of the comb, and a lot of machinery and equipment that whirs, thumps, hums and looks very special. The dairyman, shrewd in mountain ways, looked it all over carefully and then observed, "Well . . . ll . . . ll, wouldn't say for sure now, but it looks like a still to me."

There have been droughty years and cold wet ones when flow-   31
ers refused to bloom and I would have been better off with a still back up here on my mountain top, but the weather this past year was perfect from a bee's standpoint, and this August I ran 33,000 pounds of honey through my factory. This was nearly

twice the normal crop, and everything was overloaded, starting with me. Neither I nor my equipment is set up to handle this sort of harvest, even with extra help.

I always need to hire someone, a strong young man who is not afraid of being stung, to help me harvest the honey from the hives.   32

The honey I take is the surplus that the bees will not need for   33
the winter; they store it above their hives in wooden boxes called supers. To take it from them, I stand behind each hive with a gasoline-powered machine called a beeblower and blow the bees out of the supers with a jet of air. Meanwhile, the strong young man carries the supers, which weigh about sixty pounds each, and stacks them on pallets in the truck. There may be thirty to fifty supers in every outyard, and we have only about half an hour to get them off the hives, stacked and covered before the bees get really cross about what we are doing. The season to take the honey in this part of the country is summer's end, when the temperature is often above ninety-five degrees. The nature of the work and the temper of the bees require that we wear protective clothing while doing the job: a full set of coveralls, a zippered bee veil and leather gloves. Even a very strong young man works up a considerable sweat wrapped in a bee suit in hot weather hustling sixty-pound supers—being harassed by angry bees at the same time.

This year my helper has been Ky, my nephew, who wanted to   34
learn something about bees and beekeeping. He is a sweet, gentle, cooperative giant of a young man who, because of a series of physical problems, lacks confidence in his own ability to get on in the world.

As soon as he arrived, I set about to desensitize him to bee   35
stings. The first day, I put a piece of ice on his arm to numb it; then, holding the bee carefully by her head, I placed her abdomen on the numbed spot and let her sting him there. A bee's stinger is barbed and stays in the flesh, pulling loose from her body as she struggles to free herself. Lacking her stinger, the bee will live only a short time. The bulbous poison sac at the top of the stinger continues to pulsate after the bee has left, its muscles pumping the venom and forcing the barbed stinger deeper into the flesh.

I wanted Ky to have only a partial dose of venom that first   36
day, so after a minute I scraped the stinger out with my fingernail

and watched his reaction closely. A few people—about one percent of the population—are seriously sensitive to bee venom.
Each sting they receive can cause a more severe reaction than the
one before, reactions ranging from hives, difficulty in breathing
and accelerated heartbeat, to choking, anaphylactic shock and
death. Ky had been stung a few times in his life and didn't think
he was seriously allergic, but I wanted to make sure.

The spot where the stinger went in grew red and began to   37
swell. This was a normal reaction, and so was the itchiness that
Ky felt the next day. That time I let a bee sting him again, repeating the procedure, but leaving the stinger in his arm a full ten minutes, until the venom sac was emptied. Again the spot was red,
swollen and itchy, but had disappeared the next day. Thereafter
Ky decided that he didn't need the ice cube any more, and began
holding the bee himself to administer his own stings. I kept him at
one sting a day until he had no redness or swelling from the full
sting, and then had him increase to two stings daily. Again the
greater amount of venom caused redness and swelling, but soon
his body could tolerate them without an allergic reaction. I gradually had him build up to ten full stings a day with no reaction.

To encourage Ky, I had told him that what he was doing   38
might help protect him from the arthritis that runs in our family.
Beekeepers generally believe that getting stung by bees is a
healthy thing, and that bee venom alleviates the symptoms of
arthritis. When I first began keeping bees, I supposed this to be
just another one of the old wives' tales that make beekeeping
such an entertaining occupation, but after my hands were stung
the pain in my fingers disappeared and I too became a believer.
Ky was polite, amused and skeptical of what I told him, but he
welcomed my taking a few companionable stings on my knuckles along with him.

In desensitizing Ky to bee venom, I had simply been interested   39
in building up his tolerance to stings so that he could be an effective helper when we took the honey from the hives, for I knew
that he would be stung frequently. But I discovered that there
had been a secondary effect on Ky that was more important: he
was enormously pleased with himself for having passed through
what he evidently regarded as a rite of initiation. He was proud
and delighted in telling other people about the whole process. He
was now one tough guy.

I hoped he was prepared well enough for our first day of work.   40
I have had enough strong young men work for me to know what
would happen the first day: he would be stung royally.

Some beekeepers insist that bees know their keeper—that they   41
won't sting that person, but *will* sting a stranger. This is nonsense, for summertime bees live only six weeks and I often open
a particular hive less frequently than that, so I am usually a
stranger to my bees; yet I am seldom stung. Others say that bees
can sense fear or nervousness. I don't know if this is true or not,
but I do know that bees' eyes are constructed in such a way that
they can detect discontinuities and movement very well and sta-
tionary objects less well. This means that a person near their
hives who moves with rapid, jerky motions attracts their attention and will more often be blamed by the bees when their hives
are being meddled with than will the person whose motions are
calm and easy. It has been my experience that the strong young
man I hire for the honey harvest is always stung unmercifully for
the first few days while he is new to the process and a bit tense.
Then he learns to become easier with the bees and settles down
to his job. As he gains confidence and assurance, the bees calm
down too, and by the end of the harvest he usually is only stung
a few times a day.

I knew that Ky very much wanted to do a good job with me   42
that initial day working in the outyards. I had explained the procedures we would follow in taking the honey from the hives, but
of course they were new to him and he was anxious. The bees
from the first hive I opened flung themselves on him. Most of the
stingers could not penetrate his bee suit, but in the act of stinging
a bee leaves a chemical trace that marks the person stung as an
enemy, a chemical sign other bees can read easily. This sign was
read by the bees in each new hive I opened, and soon Ky's bee suit
began to look like a pincushion, bristling with stingers. In addition, the temperature was starting to climb and Ky was sweating.
Honey oozing from combs broken between the supers was running down the front of his bee suit when he carried them to the
truck. Honey and sweat made the suit cling to him, so that the
stingers of angry bees could penetrate the suit and he could feel
the prick of each one as it entered his skin. Hundreds of bees were
assaulting him and finally drove him out of the beeyard, chasing
him several hundred yards before they gave up the attack. There

was little I could do to help him but try to complete the job quickly, so I took the supers off the next few hives myself, carried them to the truck and loaded them. Bravely, Ky returned to finish the last few hives. We tied down the load and drove away. His face was red with exertion when he unzipped his bee veil. He didn't have much to say as we drove to the next yard, but sat beside me gulping down ice water from the thermos bottle.

At the second yard the bees didn't bother Ky as we set up the equipment. I hoped that much of the chemical marker the bees had left on him had evaporated, but as soon as I began to open the hives they were after him again. Soon a cloud of angry bees enveloped him, accompanying him to the truck and back. Because of the terrain, the truck had to be parked at an odd angle and Ky had to bend from the hips as he loaded it, stretching the fabric of the bee suit taut across the entire length of his back and rear, allowing the bees to sting through it easily. We couldn't talk over the noise of the beeblower's engine, but I was worried about how he was taking hundreds more stings. I was removing the bees from the supers as quickly as I could, but the yard was a good one and there were a lot of supers there.

In about an hour's time Ky carried and stacked what we later weighed in as a load of 2,500 pounds. The temperature must have been nearly a hundred degrees. After he had stacked the last super, I drove the truck away from the hives and we tied down the load. Ky's long hair was plastered to his face and I couldn't see the expression on it, but I knew he had been pushed to his limits and I was concerned about him. He tried to brush some of the stingers out of the seat of his bee suit before he sat down next to me in the truck in an uncommonly gingerly way. Unzipping his bee veil, he tossed it aside, pushed the hair back from his sweaty face, reached for the thermos bottle, gave me a sunny and triumphant grin and said, "If I ever get arthritis of the ass, I'll know all that stuff you've been telling me is a lot of baloney."

*   *   *

My farm lies north of town. After the first two miles, the black top gives way to a five-mile stretch of rocky road that shakes apart the pickups my neighbors and I drive. My mailbox is at the junction of this road and a mile-and-a-half gravel lane that meanders between it and the cabin, skirting the cliffs of the river that runs fast and clear below. Lichens, ferns and mosses grow there, and wind and rain have eroded caves and root holds for scrubby, twisted trees on the cliff faces. The thin soil at the top sustains a richer growth, and in the springtime the cliff top is abloom, first with serviceberry, then redbud and dogwood. In the summer, oaks shade the lane, grass grows in the middle of it, and black-eyed Susans grow beside it. In the winter, winds howl up out of the river gorge, driving snow across the lane in drifts so deep that sometimes I am marooned for a week or more.

I resumed yesterday from a honey-selling trip and was grateful, as I always am, to turn at the mailbox and head down my lane. I drive a big three-quarter ton white truck on these trips, one fitted out to carry a 5,000-pound load, a truck new enough to be repaired if it should break down in Hackensack without hours of poking around in a salvage yard, the source of parts for "Press on Regardless." 46

The white truck is commodious and dependable, and I am fond of it. It is a part of my life. One night I dropped off to sleep after reading about the nature of the soul. I dreamed about my own soul, and found that it is a female white truck, buoyant, impatient, one that speeds along, almost too fast in an exhilarating way, skimming slightly above the road, not quite keeping to the pathway. I rather enjoy having a soul of that sort. 47

Like many of my neighbors, I am poor. I live on an income well below the poverty line—although it does not seem like poverty when the redbud and dogwood are in bloom together—and when I travel I have to be careful about expenses. I eat in restaurants as little as possible, and I sleep in the truck: I pull into a truck stop, unroll my sleeping bag on the front seat and sleep there, as warm and comfortable as can be. In the morning I brush my teeth in the truck-stop restroom, and have my morning coffee in the restaurant. When I travel, people seldom notice or talk to me. I am unnoticeable in my ordinariness. If I were young and pretty, I might attract attention. But I am too old to be pretty, and rumpled besides, so I am invisible. This delights me, for I can sit in a booth at the truck stop, drink my coffee and watch without being watched. 48

One morning I was having coffee at 5:30 A.M., snugged up in a booth in a truck stop in New Mexico. The truckers were eating their breakfasts, straddling the stools at the horseshoe-shaped counter. A three-sided projection screen hung from the 49 ceiling, showing slides that changed every minute or so. The truckers watched, absorbed, as the slides alternated between the animate and the inanimate. A supertruck, dazzling in the sunshine, every tailpipe and chrome strip gleaming, was followed by a D-cup woman, pouring out of her teeny dress, provocatively pumping gasoline into a truck. The next slide was a low shot of a truck grille; this was followed by a scene with a plump blonde in a cute cop outfit, showing rather more breast and crotch than one would think regulation, arresting a naughty trucker.

I watched the truckers as they watched the screen, chewing   50
away on the leathery eggs-over-easy, their eyes glassy, as intent on chrome as on flesh. I finished my coffee and drove on unnoticed.

The trip I returned from yesterday was to Dallas, and as sales   51
trips go, it was a good one. Its maze of freeways make it easy to get around, and I was grateful to the food buyers, who placed Texas-sized orders.

On the way to Dallas I stopped for lunch at an Oklahoma   52
restaurant which had big windows facing the parking lot. Seeing the signs on my truck proclaiming my business and home town, the man at the cash register gave me a big grin when I walked inside and asked, "You the sweetest thing in Missouri?"

If there is one skill I have learned from living in the Ozarks, it   53
is how to talk Good Old Boy, so I quickly replied, "Shore am," and took my seat at a table to order a bowl of soup. As I paid the tab, my new friend inquired about the honey business; when he found out that my truck was loaded with honey for sale in Dallas, he bought a case for the restaurant gift shop and asked to be put on my mailing list. "Now that's Joe Ben Ponder, you hear? Joe *Ben*," he said in his soft southern Oklahoma drawl.

It seemed like an auspicious beginning for a sales trip, and I   54
badly needed a good one. I had just returned from Boston and New York, where sales had been poor, although the trip was good in some ways. In Boston I stayed with Liddy and Brian, and one evening they took me to the Harvard chapel, where Gustav Leonhardt played a program of baroque music on the chapel organ. It was beautiful and I enjoyed it; I also enjoyed seeing other friends and relatives whom I love and see too seldom, but I did not make any money. In New York there are stores on every corner that sell French bread, marvelous cheeses, imported salmon, exquisite delicacies and honey, some of it made by my honeybees. But then there is another such store in the middle of the

block. The customers are spread thin, and many places where I have sold honey for years have fired their managers and hired new ones, groping for a formula that will bring in the dollars once again. Macy's and Zabar's were having a war, and their buyers had no time for me. Sales elsewhere were poor, too, for it cut no French mustard with new managers that honey from my bees had been selling in the store for ten years. I drove up to Westchester and southern Connecticut to set up new accounts in the suburbs.

In my worn jeans and steel-toed work boots, one of which has 55 a hole in it from the time I dripped battery acid on it, I wandered through those fashionable towns peddling honey, towns filled with women out buying things to drape on themselves, and things to put in their houses, and things to take care of the things hanging on themselves and the things in their houses.

Twenty or twenty-five years ago I lived on the edge of lives 56 like these. In those days the women used to drive station wagons, and today they drive sleek little cars, but the look of strain on their faces is the same today as it was back then. I was glad to escape that life then and at the end of the sales day I was glad to escape in my white truck and head westward onto the Interstates with their green signs and truck stops, toward Missouri, toward my wild mountain top, toward home.

Paul Roberts

Virtual Grub Street

Paul Roberts was not a well-known writer when *Harper's Magazine* published "Virtual Grub Street" in 1996. Since then he has become a contributing editor to the magazine and has been publishing articles on environmental issues. One of these, "The Sweet Hereafter" (*Harper's*, 1997), was a National Magazine Award finalist.

It's Wednesday, late afternoon, and I'm writing about classical 1 composers—Bach, Beethoven, Mozart, and so on, thirty of them—for a multimedia product on European history. It's an odd assignment. I've never written about music or studied the people who make it. My specialty, before I started writing for CD-ROM companies, was environmental journalism, and what I know about classical composers is, basically, *Amadeus*. But ignorance, in the new electronic literature, isn't always an obstacle. The irony of the information revolution is that consumers neither like nor expect long, densely written texts on their computer screens. Long texts addle the eyes; they slow the rapid-fire "interactive" process, steal precious screen space from the animation, video, and multimedia's other, more marketable gewgaws. So we writers needn't be experts so much as filters whose task is to absorb and compress great gobs of information into small, easily digestible on-screen chunks. Brevity and blandness: these are the elements of the next literary style. Of roughly one thousand "essays" I've "written" for CD-ROM companies here in Seattle over the last year and a half, fewer than forty ran longer than two hundred words—about the length of the paragraph you're reading now—and most were much, much shorter.

I never expected to be working like this. I once earned a respectable living writing long, earnest articles about spotted owls, riparian buffer zones, even, on one occasion, a 10,000-word treatise on the Douglas fir, hero tree of the Pacific Northwest. Nowadays, whole months go by when I do nothing but crank out info-nuggets on whatever topics the multimedia companies believe will sell: dead composers, large African mammals, sports stars of yore. It is, without question, hack writing, the kind of pap (I used to think) only the feckless and unprincipled had the nerve or need to take. But if the emergence of the so-called new media has clarified anything, it's just how malleable literary standards and professional expectations are, how quickly they can wither or mutate or be ignored altogether in the presence of powerful novelty and cold cash. In early 1994, just before I joined the digital revolution, few of my writer friends had any understanding of what CD-ROM was, much less any desire to write for it. Today, half of the writers I know in this town are either working in electronic publishing or trying to.

> A brilliant performer from a young age, Austria's Wolfgang Amadeus Mozart (1756–1791) was perhaps the most influential composer of the eighteenth century. He wrote more than 130 works, including the operas *Don Giovanni* and *The Marriage of Figaro*, and is noted for his purity of form and melody. Despite such talents, Mozart struggled financially, earning a meager living as a pianist and tutor. He died a pauper at age thirty-five.

An economist might explain the current literary redeployment   3
as a simple shift in supply and demand. Between Christmas 1993
and Christmas 1995, consumer ownership of CD-ROM drives
jumped from fewer than 9 million to an estimated 40 million, with
another 17 million purchases projected by the end of 1996. What
was accurately described a few years ago as a garage industry is
now very much a mass market, and to keep it that way multimedia companies like Microsoft and Voyager and Broderbund are
spending billions of dollars developing thousands of new CD-ROM
titles in virtually every category one can imagine: games, naturally,
but also encyclopedias, interactive magazines, children's products,
how-tos, history, science, wildlife, even pornography. This title
wave has generated a massive demand for what multimedia executives glibly call "content," launching the industry on an enormous
hiring binge: software engineers and digital artists, of course, but
also legions of writers and editors, lured away from newspapers,
film companies, magazines, and publishing houses, plucked from
the ranks of the un- and underemployed (or "freelance," to use the
more generous term) and offered more money a week than many
previously had made in a month. For those of us raised to believe
that a career in writing meant a life at or near the poverty line,
multimedia feels like a gold rush, a wartime buildup, a massive
new government program.

But the new media's appeal to writers goes beyond dollars.   4
There's the allure of a sexy new technology, sharpened by a fear
of professional obsolescence. The fact is, multimedia can do
things the printed page never even dreamed about. It's digital,
which means that obscene amounts of data can be encoded and
stored on a four-inch, wafer-thin laser disc. It's also *interactive,*
which means that all those digitized artifacts—hundreds of photos and graphics, video clips, my own wee texts—can be linked
together in a kind of electronic-semantic web. You can access my
"essay" on Mozart, for example, from any number of other texts
on the disc, simply by finding the word "Mozart" in highlighted,
or "hot," text and clicking on it with your mouse. You could be
reading something on eighteenth-century music, say, or Viennese
opera, and—*click*—up pops my terse little bio. But there's more.
Once inside my text, you might click on the words "Don Giovanni," and get yet another text, or perhaps a few seconds of
music from the opera, or a video clip from *Amadeus.* And once
in "Don Giovanni," you might encounter the word "Italy" and

click up a nice little geopolitical summary. And so on. Each multimedia text—and, theoretically, each word in each text—can
serve as an electronic portal to an infinite number of other digital locations. With a series of clicks, you can hop from one object of fascination to any number of others, branching this way
and that along various semantic trails, creating your very own,
custom-built, nonlinear narrative from a vast reservoir of re-
combinant texts.

> Clear waters and abundant marine life make Mafia, an island off the
> coast of Tanzania, one of the best diving spots in the world. Tropical
> temperatures are ideal for many varieties of crustaceans, including
> lobsters. Divers also encounter huge schools of fantastically colored
> fish and can swim with sea turtles, octopuses, large but docile whale
> sharks, and, occasionally, the manatee-like dugong.

Nonlinearity might seem like little more than channel surfing,   5
but its proponents—ranging from wealthy software gurus to
tenured English professors—champion it as an authentic yet functional postmodern form, a critical break from the age-old, rigidly
linear format of the printed page. Nonlinearity, we're told, redis-
tributes narrative power to readers. It undermines the tyranny of
the Author. Its branching "intertextuality" is a much closer match
to the brain's own networks. Indeed, advocates believe that with
nonlinear text, or *hypertext,* literature can at last give full expression to the kinds of unconventional discursive impulses that folks
like Joyce and Barthes were forced to convey via the grotesquely
obsolete linear format. For that matter, nonlinearity provides a
kind of running critique of the linear format, laying open the
myth that "stories" can be told only one way, in only one direction, and toward only one conclusion: toward "closure." With
nonlinearity, as with thought itself, there is no closure, only additional links. Thus nonlinearity, to its proponents, is the beginning
of a new, more honest and complex literature—and, perhaps, the
beginning of the end of an old one. "The printed book . . . seems
destined to move to the margin of our literate culture," writes Jay
David Bolter, a Georgia Tech professor of communications and
one of the more articulate exponents of electronic texts. "Print
will no longer define the organization and presentation of knowledge, as it has for the past five centuries."

*   *   *

Personally, I never achieved the degree of literary transcen- 6
dence that these advocates describe. Down at the level where I
operate, the digital "revolution" is actually something of a bust,
a high-tech revival of the piecemeal sensibility that animated the
pulp magazines and the early broadsheets. But mine, it seems, is
a minority view. Even as you read this, editors and publishers the
world over are practically wetting themselves in the rush to get
their content "on disc" or "online." Meanwhile, my brethren are
flocking in ever greater numbers to digital-writing conferences
with an enthusiasm more typically encountered at Tony Robbins
seminars. Last year, to offer just one example, a Seattle arts organization sponsored a workshop for writers hoping to break
into multimedia—nothing special, just a local CD-ROM producer sharing insights and showing demos. It sold out. Tickets,
at $40 each, were snapped up weeks in advance. The night of the
event, organizers ran out of chairs, and folks who hadn't bothered to preregister actually had to wait on standby, like fans at a
rock concert, praying for no-shows. What a poignant comment
on the digital revolution: an overflow crowd of writers—sensitive, struggling artistic types, by and large—forking over a week's
grocery money to hear not some world-famous poet or author
but a mid-level exec in an industry whose greatest hit is an interactive game called Myst and whose primary unit of literary
meaning is a toneless, unsigned blurb that, for all the cleverness
of its high-tech format, could have been written anytime during
the previous five hundred years:

> Tormons Tablets cure all disorders of the Liver, Stomach, and Bow-
> els, Headache, Dyspepsia, Constipation, Biliousness, Dizziness,
> Clear the Complexion, Increase the Appetite, Tone the System, and
> are a sure Remedy for Depression of Spirits, General Debility, Kid-
> ney Complaints, Nervousness, Sour Stomach, Disturbed Sleep, etc.

I'm making most of these examples up, by necessity. The multi- 7
media industry is hugely paranoid about leaks and we're all required to sign fiercely worded nondisclosure agreements, or NDAs,
before we're even told the topic of our next assignment. Such secrecy usually baffles the newly initiated, particularly after they see
what they'll be writing and how unlikely a target of industrial es-
pionage it is. Still, I can't reveal the names of my client companies
and bosses, or the CD-ROM titles I've worked on. Technically, I'm

not even supposed to disclose the existence of the nondisclosure agreements. It's as if multimedia companies want deniability, as if the transaction between writer and publisher never occurred. In multimedia, as in other instances of corporate creativity, text simply *happens*. It appears on-screen without any evidence of being authored by a single, living individual.

NDAs notwithstanding, it's probably safe to reveal that I am, 8 in fact, a real person, thirty-four, married, with a two-year-old daughter and four-year communications degree. Like many multimedia writers, I got my literary start in newspapers and magazines, settling finally at an alternative newsweekly in Seattle. Also like many multimedia writers, I work mostly at home. My text-production facility is a small second-floor study in my eighty-year-old house, in a wooded, hillside neighborhood seven miles from downtown Seattle. My workspace resembles that of any busy writer: computer, reference books, coffee cups. The giveaway is the floor. It's almost always buried beneath thick strata of mimeographed articles on a range of topics too diverse for a normal journalist: Roman history, Greek philosophy, rain forest ecology, medieval battle tactics, Mayan archaeology, Romantic poets, mountain climbing.

Sadly, multimedia writers are too harried to savor the variety 9 of subject matter. Although a single CD-ROM title might contain several thousand separate text blocks, text budgets are typically small in comparison with budgets for the more time- and memory-consuming video or audio components. Thus, the famously high wages for writers—anywhere from $18 to $30 an hour—are based on the expectation that we will extrude texts with machine-like efficiency. Producers are always encouraging us, dropping such helpful comments as "These really shouldn't take more than thirty minutes apiece" and "I was getting about three of these done an hour." I've no idea where they get these estimates, but the tactic is effective. Before I developed the rhythms and strategies of the seasoned multimedia writer, I kept a stopwatch by my computer, struggling to crank out each blurb in under fifteen minutes. This follows another irony of the information revolution: the texts of the next century are being manufactured much like the products of the last one—on an hourly basis in a vast, decentralized electronic sweatshop.

For a time I was able to take a romantic pleasure in the fren- 10 zied pace of the work. It seemed so classic, so nineteenth-century.

Dostoevsky and Dickens both poured forth prodigious streams of words every week. George Gissing hammered out the 220,000-word novel *New Grub Street,* the portrait of a hack writer, at the rate of about 3,500 words a day—half again as much as my best performance. But my fantasies soon buckled under the load. Those walking word machines wound up with true works of art. All I have at the end of the day is screen after screen of blurbs.

> Invented by Christopher Sholes in 1867, the typewriter transformed both the process and content of written communication. Typewritten letters were initially dismissed as cold and impersonal but quickly came to dominate business writing, while the type writers themselves helped open office work to women. Mechanical typewriters were eventually replaced by electric models, which in turn have been rendered all but obsolete by computer word processors.

Most multimedia writers I know didn't plan their move into electronic publishing. I, for example, was never a computer enthusiast. To the degree that I considered it at all, the entire phenomenon of interactive CD-ROM—which even then was being invented in suburban office parks just a few miles east of my house—seemed like a brush war in another hemisphere: vaguely interesting, mostly irrelevant. But things change. My newspaper's rumor mill warned of impending layoffs, my daughter arrived, and I began to notice that many of my writer-acquaintances were disappearing, one by one, from the freelance ranks. I'd meet them at parties and no sooner had talk turned to jobs than they'd launch into breathless depictions of the *work* they were doing, and the *technology* they were using, and, more to the point, the buckets of money they were earning. No one had ever talked this way about writing. It was like hearing some just-returned settler describing the frontier: wide-open and mine for the taking. 11

My first multimedia assignment, finagled through a friend of a friend, came in the spring of 1994. A man called me at home and asked whether I knew what CD-ROM was and if I had ever written for digital publications. I mumbled an ambiguous reply and found myself the following afternoon in a small beige office in the suburban megalopolis known hereabouts as the Eastside. The voice on the phone turned out to belong to the project producer, a gaunt fellow in his thirties whom I'll call Bob. 12

Bob shook hands hastily. He wore faded blue jeans and an un-
tucked polo shirt. A year before, he'd been editing a magazine
somewhere east of the Rockies. Today, he seemed harassed
and tired and in serious need of cigarettes. Bob asked a few
perfunctory questions about my writing, interrupting my answers with a staccato "uh-huh, uh-huh," then, apparently satisfied, hauled out a nondisclosure agreement. I signed it. Bob
explained that I was now legally barred from telling anyone,
including family and friends, anything about the Project. I laughed.
Bob looked cross. He related a story of several loose-lipped former employees who had been tracked down and prosecuted.
"They're serious about this," said Bob, catching and holding my
gaze.

Later, as I learned more about the industry, the NDAs became   13
more understandable. Title budgets can top $1 million, with no
profits expected for three years. The more excited a company is
about a project under development, the more paranoid its staff
becomes that a single leak might let a rival get to market first
with a similar product. I'm still not sure if these fears are valid or
simply an extension of the militaristic paranoia and manic
team-spiritedness that have long energized the software industry.
In any case, secrecy remains a central component of multimedia's
corporate character, infusing what is essentially an entertainment
business with a gravity both absurd and titillating.

At least, I found it so. Bob, apparently, was well past the   14
philosophizing stage and was also in a hurry. He moved deftly
from the NDA to a terse discussion of production schedules,
software requirements, and, finally, the Assignment, handing
me a list of fifty subjects, somewhat historical in nature, and
a thick stack of reference materials. He wanted seventy-five
words on each by the start of the following week. Nothing fancy.
Simple declarative sentences. High school reading level. Tight.
No one had ever talked to me about writing like this before,
either. I felt disoriented, like Barton Fink after he receives
his first assignment for a "wrestling movie." I scanned Bob's
office, looking for clues as to what I'd gotten myself into. On
the wall, I spied a chalkboard sketch, a series of small circles,
each labeled with an abbreviation ("Intro.," "Vid.," "Aud.")
and all interconnected by spokes. A nonlinear conceptual blue-
print, Bob explained vaguely, waving at it. For the project. For

the first time, he smiled. "But you guys don't need to worry about that."

The truth is that multimedia writers needn't worry about a   15
great many things. We get our assignments, write our texts, and some months later, a shiny disc wrapped in an inordinate amount of packaging hits the shelves at Egghead or Waldenbooks. No one expects us to understand or care what happens to our texts in the interim, because writers are mere cogs in the multimedia machine. We're never asked to generate story ideas and pitch them to editors. We needn't concern ourselves with story structure, or themes, or any of the other, more celebrated elements of traditional writing. All that is handled by the engineers and designers and scriptwriters who lay out the disc's schematic, who decide where and when the digital objects will appear, which object will be linked to which, and why. Questions traditional writers might agonize over for hours or days—lead paragraphs, say, or transitions—have been rendered moot by the peculiarities of the nonlinear narrative.

What remains for CD-ROM writers isn't so much writing as   16
tailoring; tucking specified content into a specified space. Producers send us off with sage, neo-Strunkish advice: avoid complex syntax and vocabulary; suppress "voice" or "attitude"; do not, under any circumstances, exceed the specific word count. It's a strange way to write. Strange, too, to see how easily the brain shifts from the extended symphonic rhythms of a longer article to the staccato jingle of the 100-word blurb. Dismaying, actually. Yet the self-disgust pales, at least initially, against the sensation of relief. Conventional, linear writing can be a gruesome task. Beyond the lame pay and the feast-or-famine job cycle, the pounding of disparate facts and feelings into a tightly structured narrative is like digging a ditch across a concrete parking lot. By contrast, squirting out blurbs is a cakewalk, a lower-order process managed, I'm sure, by the same lobe that handles heart rate and knitting. For the first few months, I felt as if I'd entered a writers' fairy land, where one could earn a good living without anxieties or writer's block, without the corrosive oscillations between depression and ecstasy—just a steady putt-putt-putt of words. I'd fire up the computer at 8:00 A.M., shut it down at supper, and by the time I'd raised the fork to my lips, whatever I had been working on six minutes earlier had evaporated from my head.

The fifty-word caption typically begins with a declarative sentence summarizing the photographed subject. The second sentence puts the first in context with a general topic statement. The third adds interesting, even humorous detail. Beginning multimedia writers are often advised to study magazines famous for their captions, including *National Geographic* and *Life*.

My disillusionment with multimedia grew less out of any 17 principled objection than from a slow accretion of insults and revelations. There was the sheer tedium of blurb writing. There were also the routine demonstrations of text's low rank on the CD-ROM totem pole: whenever software engineers had trouble cramming all the visual components onto a disc, we writers would simply be told to chop our texts in half. As my meager status sunk in, I found it ever harder at parties to wax enthusiastic about my job. My humor darkened. I took to introducing myself as a hack, a blurbmeister, affecting a cynicism that I didn't quite feel but I knew was coming.

*   *   *

From a distance, a multimedia text looks exactly like a para- 18 graph plucked from a standard linear narrative. But closer inspection reveals important differences. In "normal" writing, the writer uses the paragraph as a bridge between specific points. Not so with the multimedia text block. Each blurb must, almost by definition, carry out its minimal literary function in virtual independence from the rest of the story If I'm writing multimedia Text A, for example, I can assume no specific prior knowledge on the part of the reader, because he or she may be arriving at Text A from any of a number of previous texts. Similarly, I can't use Text A to set up Text B, because the reader may be bouncing to any number of Text Bs. For that matter, I can't even infuse Text A with a meaning or sentiment that is essential to the reader's understanding of, or pleasure in, the larger narrative, because the reader, as narrative boss, may skip Text A entirely. The style of the multimedia text, if you want to call it a style, is one of expendability.

I realize that even in a conventional article, I can't make my 19 "linear" readers read what I write in the order that I write it. Linear readers skim. They jump ahead, looking for interesting parts, then refer back for context—behaving, in some respects, like the multimedia user. the nonlinear interactive process undeniably accelerates this haphazardness. The nexus of creativity is shifted from the writer to either the producers, who lay out the text links, or the readers, who make use of those links.

To be fair, if a multimedia writers has the technical expertise and the financial resources to control the entire story-line process, some interesting literary and journalistic forms are possible. Allowing readers to choose their own research paths, or, in the case of nonlinear fiction, to choose among multiple outcomes, probably qualifies as a genuine step forward in literary evolution. The reality, however, is that most multimedia writers are not (and, given the complexity and expense of production. aren't likely to be) in control of the entire process or even a large chunk thereof. Multimedia is the epitome of corporate production, of breaking projects into elements and doling them out. As such, the average writer is effectively, if not intentionally, sealed off from the larger narrative, and quickly learns not even to think about how the texts will be used or where the writing is going because it doesn't matter. One text is pretty much like another, a self-contained literary unit modular, disposable, accessible from any angle, leading both everywhere and nowhere. [20]

> Larger text blocks, though providing more freedom than captions, often prove harder to write. Readers anticipate more information, so more hard data—distances, ages, sizes, dates, etc.—are critical. Larger texts also require some adherence to standard writing "rules," such as varying sentence length, as well as some degree of structural innovation. Themes raised in an opening sentence, for example, may require mention or resolution in the conclusion. Ultimately, however, larger texts can grant only the temporary illusion of conventional writing, such that writers embark in directions that, while interesting, simply cannot be explored within the allotted space.

Nonlinearity advocates often claim that a conventional writer's frustration with this new form stems from the loss of authorial control. We are angry that readers can pick and choose among our ideas or can mix our texts with information from entirely separate sources. Mostly, though, we are threatened by the new kind of mind that such writing requires. "A philosophy of mind for the coming age of writing." Bolter writes. "will have to rec- [21]

ognize the mind as a network . . . spreading out beyond the individual mind to embrace other texts, written in other minds. . . . The most radical solution would dispense altogether with the notion of intentionality; there is no privileged author but simply textual networks that are always open to interpretation. Such a philosophy may be nothing less than the end of the ego, the end of the Cartesian self as the defining quality of humanity."

I admit that the thought of losing narrative control is excruci-   22
ating. But is my frustration so selfish or authoritarian? We hardly expect musicians or sculptors to allow their work to be pulled apart and reassembled with hits and pieces from other artists. We writers are no less invested in our work and cannot be expected to delight in the prospect of merely contributing to a collective, egoless supertext. Nor are we likely to be persuaded that the journalistic imperative—to educate and inform a readership—can come about via a format that is so antithetical to persuasion or extended analysis.

Ultimately, what depresses me most about multimedia writing   23
is its sheer pleasurelessness. Conventional writing, even at its low-paying, psychotic worst, provides me with an intellectual challenge, and lets me attempt a mastery of language and form. Writing allows me to tell stories. Multimedia writing is not about telling a story. It's about telling fragments of stones, fragments that may or may not add up to anything. It's about preparation and research—everything but the actual narrative release. At the end of the project, you're left saturated and unfulfilled, ready to burst. One Saturday night, at a friend's house for dinner, having spent the previous four weeks writing tidbits for a science title, I found myself rambling almost uncontrollably about the project. For a full forty-five minutes, I flouted the nondisclosure agreement marshaling facts and figures prying open 100-word capsules and spreading their contents into a tale I'd been unable to tell for nearly a month.

> The universe is believed to be between 10 billion and 20 billion years old. Composed mainly of empty space, the universe is dotted with countless stars, galaxies, and planets. Some scientists theorize the universe began as a single, ultradense ball of matter, which exploded. This so-called Big Bang Theory may explain why all known objects, including those in our galaxy, are moving away from one another at high speeds.

We are living, according to some high-tech advocates in the   24
"late age of print," and I have to say that the business of writing

is being transformed with amazing speed. Publishers continue to pour out new discs by the cargo-container load. Conferences go on inviting neo-luminati to discuss the shape and substance of the New Literature. Phone and cable and computer companies, meanwhile, are developing fantastic new technologies to bring interactive everything to consumers' fingertips. So while the explosive growth of the CD-ROM industry is waning somewhat, the creative slack is being vacuumed up by online services, whose technical criteria place similar requirements on writing and whose managers seem to be hiring writers with almost as much vigor.

Indeed I can imagine a not-so-distant future when a sizable fraction of professional writers won't ever enter the world of print but will go directly from school to digital publishing. Maybe they'll be constrained at first by the needs of older readers who were raised on print and who have only recently and partially and timidly converted to the nonlinear faith. But in time, this will change, as printing comes to be seen as too expensive and cumbersome, as computers become more powerful and more interlinked and as they show up in every classroom and office, in every living room and den. My twelve-year-old nephew lives in a small, rural eastern Washington town, yet he is as comfortable with on-screen multimedia presentations as with comic books. He represents the mind that writers will write for. Perhaps his generation will perceive language in a different way. Perhaps the understanding and meaning and pleasure they will derive from creating and consuming nonlinear text will be as significant and as beautiful as anything that has come during print's 3,500-year reign. Yet I can't help viewing this future with alarm and sadness not simply because I question the quality of the literature these people will have but because I can already see that I won't be capable of comprehending it. I have participated in, and in some small way precipitated, my own obsolescence. For those raised in the tradition of linear print, this may represent the bleakest irony of the digital revolution—that we so willingly took part in our own extinction.

PERRI KLASS

Learning the Language

Perri Klass graduated from Harvard Medical School in 1986. During her years as a medical student, she published a novel, gave birth to a son, and contributed articles to newspapers and magazines. "Learning the Language" was first published in *The New York Times* in 1984 and was later republished in *A Not Entirely Benign Procedure: Four Years as a Medical Student* (1987).

"Mrs. Tolstoy is your basic LOL in NAD, admitted for a soft   1
rule-out MI," the intern announces. I scribble that on my patient list. In other words, Mrs. Tolstoy is a Little Old Lady in No Apparent Distress who is in the hospital to make sure she hasn't had a heart attack (rule out a Myocardial Infarction). And we think it's unlikely that she has had a heart attack (a *soft* rule-out).

If I learned nothing else during my first three months of work-   2
ing in the hospital as a medical student, I learned endless jargon and abbreviations. I started out in a state of primeval innocence, in which I didn't even know that "s̄ CP, SOB, N/V" meant "without chest pain, shortness of breath, or nausea and vomiting." By the end I took the abbreviations so much for granted that I would complain to my mother the English professor, "And can you believe I had to put down *three* NG tubes last night?"

"You'll have to tell me what an NG tube is if you want me to   3
sympathize properly," my mother said. NG, nasogastric—isn't it obvious?

I picked up not only the specific expressions but also the pat-   4
terns of speech and the grammatical conventions; for example, you never say that a patient's blood pressure fell or that his cardiac enzymes rose. Instead, the patient is always the subject of the verb: "He dropped his pressure." "He bumped his enzymes." This sort of construction probably reflects the profound irritation of the intern when the nurses come in the middle of the night to say that Mr. Dickinson has disturbingly low blood pressure. "Oh, he's gonna hurt me bad tonight," the intern might say, inevitably angry at Mr. Dickinson for dropping his pressure and creating a problem.

When chemotherapy fails to cure Mrs. Bacon's cancer, what 5
we say is, "Mrs. Bacon failed chemotherapy."

Well, we've already had one hit today, and we're up next, but 6
at least we've got mostly stable players on our team." This
means that our team (group of doctors and medical students) has
already gotten one new admission today, and it is our turn again,
so we'll get whoever is admitted next in emergency, but at least
most of the patients we already have are fairly stable, that is, unlikely to drop their pressures or in any other way get suddenly
sicker and hurt us bad. Baseball metaphor is pervasive. A no-
hitter is a night without any new admissions. A player is always
a patient—a nitrate player is a patient on nitrates, a unit player
is a patient in the intensive care unit, and so on, until you reach
the terminal player.

It is interesting to consider what it means to be winning, or 7
doing well, in this perennial baseball game. When the intern
hangs up the phone and announces, "I got a hit," that is not
cause for congratulations. The team is not scoring points; rather,
it is getting hit, being bombarded with new patients. The object
of the game from the point of view of the doctors, considering
the players for whom they are already responsible, is to get as
few new hits as possible.

This special language contributes to a sense of closeness and 8
professional spirit among people who are under a great deal of
stress. As a medical student, I found it exciting to discover that
I'd finally cracked the code, that I could understand what doctors said and wrote, and could use the same formulations myself.
Some people seem to become enamored of the jargon for its own
sake, perhaps because they are so deeply thrilled with the idea of
medicine, with the idea of themselves as doctors.

I knew a medical student who was referred to by the interns 9
on the team as Mr. Eponym because he was so infatuated with
eponymous terminology, the more obscure the better. He never
said "capillary pulsations" if he could say "Quincke's pulses."
He would lovingly tell over the multinamed syndromes—Wolff-
Parkinson-White, Lown-Ganong-Levine, Schönlein-Henoch—
until the temptation to suggest Schleswig-Holstein or Stevenson-
Kefauver or Baskin-Robbins became irresistible to his less reverent colleagues.

And there is the jargon that you don't ever want to hear your-   10
self using. You know that your training is changing you, but there
are certain changes you think would be going a little too far.

The resident was describing a man with devastating terminal   11
pancreatic cancer. "Basically he's CTD," the resident concluded.
I reminded myself that I had resolved not to be shy about asking
when I didn't understand things. "CTD?" I asked timidly.

The resident smirked at me. "Circling The Drain."   12

The images are vivid and terrible. "What happened to Mrs.   13
Melville?"

"Oh, she boxed last night." To box is to die, of course.   14

Then there are the more pompous locutions that can make the   15
beginning medical student nervous about the effects of medical
training. A friend of mine was told by his resident, "A pregnant
woman with sickle-cell represents a failure of genetic counseling."

Mr. Eponym, who tried hard to talk like the doctors, once ex-   16
plained to me, "An infant is basically a brainstem preparation."
The term "brainstem preparation," as used in neurological research, refers to an animal whose higher brain functions have
been destroyed so that only the most primitive reflexes remain,
like the sucking reflex, the startle reflex, and the rooting reflex.

And yet at other times the harshness dissipates into a strangely   17
elusive euphemism. "As you know, this is a not entirely benign
procedure," some doctor will say, and that will be understood to
imply agony, risk of complications, and maybe even a significant
mortality rate.

The more extreme forms aside, one most important function   18
of medical jargon is to help doctors maintain some distance from
their patients. By reformulating a patient's pain and problems
into a language that the patient doesn't even speak, I suppose we
are in some sense taking those pains and problems under our
jurisdiction and also reducing their emotional impact. This linguistic separation between doctors and patients allows conversations to go on at the bedside that are unintelligible to the patient.
"Naturally, we're worried about adeno-CA," the intern can say
to the medical student, and lung cancer need never be mentioned.

I learned a new language this past summer. At times it thrills   19
me to hear myself using it. It enables me to understand my colleagues, to communicate effectively in the hospital. Yet I am un-

comfortably aware that I will never again notice the peculiarities and even atrocities of medical language as keenly as I did this summer. There may be specific expressions I manage to avoid, but even as I remark them, promising myself I will never use them, I find that this language is becoming my professional speech. It no longer sounds strange in my ears—or coming from my mouth. And I am afraid that as with any new language, to use it properly you must absorb not only the vocabulary but also the structure, the logic, the attitudes. At first you may notice these new and alien assumptions every time you put together a sentence, but with time and increased fluency you stop being aware of them at all. And as you lose that awareness, for better or for worse, you move closer and closer to being a doctor instead of just talking like one.

WILLIAM CARLOS WILLIAMS

Jean Beicke

William Carlos Williams spent most of his life as a physician in Rutherford, New Jersey, but achieved national stature as a poet whose direct, colloquial style continues to inspire imitation. He also wrote short stories, most of them based on his medical experience, and several novels. "Jean Beicke" was first published in *Blast: A Magazine of Proletarian Short Stories* in 1933.

During a time like this, they kid a lot among the doctors and   1
nurses on the obstetrical floor because of the rushing business in new babies that's pretty nearly always going on up there. It's the Depression, they say, nobody has any money so they stay home nights. But one bad result of this is that in the children's ward, another floor up, you see a lot of unwanted children.

The parents get them into the place under all sorts of pretexts.   2
For instance, we have two premature brats, Navarro and Cryschka, one a boy and one a girl; the mother died when Cryschka was born, I think. We got them within a few days of each other, one weighing four pounds and one a few ounces more. They dropped

down below four pounds before we got them going but there they are; we had a lot of fun betting on their daily gains in weight but we still have them. They're in pretty good shape though now. Most of the kids that are left that way get along swell. The nurses grow attached to them and get a real thrill when they begin to pick up. It's great to see. And the parents sometimes don't even come to visit them, afraid we'll grab them and make them take the kids out, I suppose.

A funny one is a little Hungarian Gypsy girl that's been up there for the past month. She was about eight weeks old maybe when they brought her in with something on her lower lip that looked like a chancre. Everyone was interested but the Wassermann was negative. It turned out finally to be nothing but a peculiarly situated birthmark. But that kid is still there too. Nobody can find the parents. Maybe they'll turn up some day.

Even when we do get rid of them, they often come back in a week or so—sometimes in terrible condition, full of impetigo, down in weight—everything we'd done for them to do over again. I think it's deliberate neglect in most cases. That's what happened to this little Gypsy. The nurse was funny after the mother had left the second time. I couldn't speak to her, she said. I just couldn't say a word I was so mad. I wanted to slap her.

We had a couple of Irish girls a while back named Cowley. One was a red head with beautiful wavy hair and the other a straight haired blonde. They really were good looking and not infants at all. I should say they must have been two and three years old approximately. I can't imagine how the parents could have abandoned them. But they did. I think they were habitual drunkards and may have had to beat it besides on short notice. No fault of theirs maybe.

But all these are, after all, not the kind of kids I have in mind. The ones I mean are those they bring in stinking dirty, and I mean stinking. The poor brats are almost dead sometimes, just living skeletons, almost, wrapped in rags, their heads caked with dirt, their eyes stuck together with pus and their legs all excoriated from the dirty diapers no one has had the interest to take off them regularly. One poor little tot we have now with a thin purplish skin and big veins standing out all over its head had a big sore place in the fold of its neck under the chin. The nurse told me that when she started to undress it it had on a shirt with a neckband that rubbed right into that place. Just dirt. The mother gave a story of having had it in some sort of home in Paterson. We couldn't get it straight. We never try. What the hell? We take 'em and try to make something out of them.

Sometimes, you'd be surprised, some doctor has given the parents a ride before they bring the child to the clinic. You wouldn't believe it. They clean 'em out, maybe for twenty-five dollars—they maybe had to borrow—and then tell 'em to move on. It happens. Men we all know too. Pretty bad. But what can you do? 7

And sometimes the kids are not only dirty and neglected but sick, ready to die. You ought to see those nurses work. You'd think it was the brat of their best friend. They handle those kids as if they were worth a million dollars. Not that some nurses aren't better than others but in general they break their hearts over those kids, many times, when I, for one, wish they'd never get well. 8

I often kid the girls. Why not? I look at some miserable specimens they've dolled up for me when I make the rounds in the morning and I tell them: Give it an enema, maybe it will get well and grow up into a cheap prostitute or something. The country needs you, brat. I once proposed that we have a mock wedding between a born garbage hustler we'd saved and a little female with a fresh mug on her that would make anybody smile. 9

Poor kids! You really wonder sometimes if medicine isn't all wrong to try to do anything for them at all. You actually want to see them pass out, especially when they're deformed or—they're awful sometimes. Every one has rickets in an advanced form, scurvy too, flat chests, spindly arms and legs. They come in with pneumonia, a temperature of a hundred and six, maybe, and before you can do a thing, they're dead. 10

This little Jean Beicke was like that. She was about the worst you'd expect to find anywhere. Eleven months old. Lying on the examining table with a blanket half way up her body, stripped, lying there, you'd think it a five months baby, just about that long. But when the nurse took the blanket away, her legs kept on going for a good eight inches longer. I couldn't get used to it. I covered her up and asked two of the men to guess how long she was. Both guessed at least half a foot too short. One thing that helped the illusion besides her small face was her arms. They 11 came about to her hips. I don't know what made that. They should come down to her thighs, you know.

She was just skin and bones but her eyes were good and she 12 looked straight at you. Only if you touched her anywhere, she started to whine and then cry with a shrieking, distressing sort of cry that no one wanted to hear. We handled her as gently as we knew how but she had to cry just the same.

She was one of the damnedest looking kids I've ever seen. Her 13 head was all up in front and flat behind, I suppose from lying on the back of her head so long the weight of it and the softness of the bones from the rickets had just flattened it out and pushed it up forward. And her legs and arms seemed loose on her like the arms and legs of some cheap dolls. You could bend her feet up on her shins absolutely flat—but there was no real deformity, just all loosened up. Nobody was with her when I saw her though her mother had brought her in.

It was about ten in the evening, the interne had asked me to 14 see her because she had a stiff neck, and how! and there was some thought of meningitis—perhaps infantile paralysis. Anyhow, they didn't want her to go through the night without at least a lumbar puncture if she needed it. She had a fierce cough and a fairly high fever. I made it out to be a case of bronchopneumonia with meningismus but no true involvement of the central nervous system. Besides she had inflamed ear drums.

I wanted to incise the drums, especially the left, and would 15 have done it only the night superintendent came along just then and made me call the ear man on service. You know. She also looked to see if we had an operative release from the parents. There was. So I went home, the ear man came in a while later and opened the ears—a little bloody serum from both sides and that was that.

Next day we did a lumbar puncture, tapped the spine that is, 16 and found clear fluid with a few lymphocytes in it, nothing diagnostic. The X-ray of the chest clinched the diagnosis of bronchopneumonia, there was an extensive involvement. She was pretty sick. We all expected her to die from exhaustion before she'd gone very far.

I had to laugh every time I looked at the brat after that, she 17 was such a funny looking one but one thing that kept her from being a total loss was that she did eat. Boy! how that kid could eat! As sick as she was she took her grub right on time every three hours, a big eight ounce bottle of whole milk and digested it perfectly. In this depression you got to be such a hungry baby, I heard the nurse say to her once. It's a sign of intelligence, I told her. But anyway, we all got to be crazy about Jean. She'd just lie there and eat and sleep. Or she'd lie and look straight in front of her by the hour. Her eyes were blue, a pale sort of blue. But if you went to touch her, she'd begin to scream. We just didn't, that's all, unless we absolutely had to. And she began to gain in weight. Can you imagine that? I suppose she had been so terribly run down that food, real food, was an entirely new experience to her. Anyway she took her food and gained on it though her temperature continued to run steadily around between a hundred and three and a hundred and four for the first eight or ten days. We were surprised.

When we were expecting her to begin to show improvement, however, she didn't. We did another lumbar puncture and found fewer cells. That was fine and the second X-ray of the chest showed it somewhat improved also. That wasn't so good though, because the temperature still kept up and we had no way to account for it. I looked at the ears again and thought they ought to be opened once more. The ear man disagreed but I kept after him and next day he did it to please me. He didn't get anything but a drop of serum on either side.

Well, Jean didn't get well. We did everything we knew how to do except the right thing. She carried on for another two—no I think it was three—weeks longer. A couple of times her temperature shot up to a hundred and eight. Of course we knew then it was the end. We went over her six or eight times, three or four of us, one after the other, and nobody thought to take an X-ray of the mastoid regions. It was dumb, if you want to say it, but there wasn't a sign of anything but the history of the case to point to it. The ears had been opened early, they had been watched carefully, there was no discharge to speak of at any time and from the external examination, the mastoid processes showed no change from the normal. But that's what she died of, acute purulent mastoiditis of the left side, going on to involvement of the left lateral sinus and finally the meninges. We might, however, have taken a culture of the pus when the ear was first opened and I shall always, after this, in suspicious cases. I have been told since that if you get a virulent bug like the streptococcus mucosus capsulatus it's wise at least to go in behind the ear for drainage if the temperature keeps up. Anyhow she died.

I went in when she was just lying there gasping. Somehow or   20 other, I hated to see that kid go. Everybody felt rotten. She was such a scrawny, misshapen, worthless piece of humanity that I had said many times that somebody ought to chuck her in the garbage chute—but after a month watching her suck up her milk and thrive on it—and to see those alert blue eyes in that face— well, it wasn't pleasant. Her mother was sitting by the bed crying quietly when I came in, the morning of the last day. She was a young woman, didn't look more than a girl, she just sat there looking at the child and crying without a sound.

I expected her to begin to ask me questions with that look on   21 her face all doctors hate—but she didn't. I put my hand on her shoulder and told her we had done everything we knew how to do for Jean but that we really didn't know what, finally, was killing her. The woman didn't make any sign of hearing me. Just sat there looking in between the bars of the crib. So after a moment watching the poor kid beside her, I turned to the infant in the next crib to go on with my rounds. There was an older woman there looking in at that baby also—no better off than Jean, surely. I spoke to her, thinking she was the mother of this one, but she wasn't.

Before I could say anything, she told me she was the older sis   22 ter of Jean's mother and that she knew that Jean was dying and that it was a good thing. That gave me an idea—I hated to talk to Jean's mother herself—so I beckoned the woman to come out into the hall with me.

I'm glad she's going to die, she said. She's got two others   23 home, older, and her husband has run off with another woman. It's better off dead—never was any good anyway. You know her husband came down from Canada about a year and a half ago. She seen him and asked him to come back and live with her and the children. He come back just long enough to get her pregnant with this one then he left her again and went back to the other woman. And I suppose knowing she was pregnant, and suffering, and having no money and nowhere to get it, she was worrying and this one never was formed right. I seen it as soon as it was born. I guess the condition she was in was the cause. She's

got enough to worry about now without this one. The husband's
gone to Canada again and we can't get a thing out of him. I been
keeping them, but we can't do much more. She'd work if she
could find anything but what can you do with three kids in times
like this? She's got a boy nine years old but her mother-in-law
sneaked it away from her and now he's with his father in
Canada. She worries about him too, but that don't do no good.

Listen, I said, I want to ask you something. Do you think   24
she'd let us do an autopsy on Jean if she dies? I hate to speak to
her of such a thing now but to tell you the truth, we've worked
hard on that poor child and we don't exactly know what is the
trouble. We know that she's had pneumonia but that's been getting well. Would you take it up with her for me, if—of course—
she dies.

Oh, she's gonna die all right, said the woman. Sure, I will. If   25
you can learn anything, it's only right. I'll see that you get the
chance. She won't make any kick, I'll tell her.

Thanks, I said.   26

The infant died about five in the afternoon. The pathologist   27
was dog-tired from a lot of extra work he'd had to do due to the
absence of his assistant on her vacation so he put off the autopsy
till next morning. They packed the body in ice in one of the service hoppers. It worked perfectly.

Next morning they did the postmortem. I couldn't get the   28
nurse to go down to it. I may be a sap, she said, but I can't do it,
that's all. I can't. Not when I've taken care of them. I feel as if
they're my own.

I was amazed to see how completely the lungs had cleared up.   29
They were almost normal except for a very small patch of resid-
ual pneumonia here and there which really amounted to nothing. Chest and abdomen were in excellent shape, otherwise,
throughout—not a thing aside from the negligible pneumonia.
Then he opened the head.

It seemed to me the poor kid's convolutions were unusually   30
well developed. I kept thinking it's incredible that that complicated mechanism of the brain has come into being just for this. I
never can quite get used to an autopsy.

The first evidence of the real trouble—for there had been no   31
gross evidence of meningitis—was when the pathologist took the
brain in his hand and made the long steady cut which opened up

the left lateral ventricle. There was just a faint color of pus on the bulb of the choroid plexus there. Then the diagnosis all cleared up quickly. The left lateral sinus was completely thrombosed and on going into the left temporal bone from the inside the mastoid process was all broken down.

I called up the ear man and he came down at once. A clear miss, he said. I think if we'd gone in there earlier, we'd have saved her. 32

For what? said I. Vote the straight Communist ticket. 33

Would it make us any dumber? said the ear man. 34

7

Faith and Practice

Martin Luther King, Jr. at the Lincoln Memorial, August 28, 1963.
© BOB ADELMAN/Magnum Photos.

OVERVIEW

To some the word faith suggests strictly religious belief, but millions of people who say they have no religion will admit that they act on faith every day: parents on faith in their children's potential, investors on faith in the market, patriots on faith in their country, teachers on faith in education, lovers on faith in love. "Faith," a professor of religion once told me, "is anything that makes it possible, in the face of discouraging evidence, to look forward with hope." Albert Schweitzer had a similar thought: "All work that is worth doing is done in faith." One question readers of this unit may ask themselves is how the great religious creeds and practices are related to the kinds of faith that make it possible for "nonbelievers" to hope and to work. Another question is how faith, sacred or secular, actually affects the way people behave. Some other questions worth asking are historical. Clearly, everyone alive today acts on beliefs that can't be arrived at or challenged by logic alone: beliefs about the nature of the world and about the sources of good and evil. Where do these beliefs come from? How do they connect us with traditions of faith that are centuries old? How can an understanding of other traditions of religion or faith help us understand the lives of our neighbors—or the lives of those who live halfway around the world?

Most of the writers in this section deal with organized religious traditions—Christianity, Islam, and Judaism—but we also hear from one writer who is an atheist and another who sees sacred and secular traditions blending until one is hard to distinguish from another.

- E. M. Forster, who does not "believe in Belief," finds that he must formulate "a creed of his own." The result is a classic statement of humanistic values.
- Patricia Nelson Limerick points out that the factual history of the American West is saturated with religious belief and that today "an imagined . . . version of western American history has become, for many believers, a sacred story."
- Huston Smith explains the "five pillars" of Islam and the social practices that grow out of them.

- Robert Kegan, himself half in the faith and half outside it, describes one morning of his life in a community of Hasidic Jews.
- Martin Luther King Jr. explains to his fellow clergymen—and to the world—the beliefs that underlay his political actions in the famous Birmingham protests of 1963.
- Flannery O'Connor gives us a portrait of a woman whose faith, sometimes so reassuring to her, is about to take her in an unexpected direction.

E. M. FORSTER

What I Believe

During the 1930s and 1940s, when totalitarianism and nationalism were gaining ground, the great English novelist E. M. Forster
wrote several essays articulating his belief in the absolute value of
individual humans and their private relationships. "What I Believe," published in 1939, is one of these essays: a liberal humanist's defense of his values in a time when they were being
challenged by the rise of fascism around the world.

I do not believe in Belief. But this is an age of faith, and there   1
are so many militant creeds that, in self-defence, one has to formulate a creed of one's own. Tolerance, good temper and sympathy are no longer enough in a world which is rent by religious
and racial persecution, in a world where ignorance rules, and science, who ought to have ruled, plays the subservient pimp. Tolerance, good temper and sympathy—they are what matter really,
and if the human race is not to collapse they must come to the
front before long. But for the moment they are not enough, their
action is no stronger than a flower, battered beneath a military
jackboot. They want stiffening, even if the process coarsens
them. Faith, to my mind, is a stiffening process, a sort of mental
starch, which ought to be applied as sparingly as possible. I dislike the stuff. I do not believe in it, for its own sake, at all. Herein
I probably differ from most people, who believe in Belief, and
are only sorry they cannot swallow even more than they do. My
law-givers are Erasmus and Montaigne, not Moses and St. Paul.
My temple stands not upon Mount Moriah but in that Elysian
Field where even the immoral are admitted. My motto is: "Lord,
I disbelieve—help thou my unbelief."[1]

I have, however, to live in an Age of Faith—the sort of epoch   2
I used to hear praised when I was a boy. It is extremely unpleasant

1. Erasmus/Montaigne: humanists, not religious figures, as were Moses and
Paul: Mt. Moriah: biblical site where Abraham was to sacrifice his son Isaac:
Elysian Fields: in Greek mythology, Paradise, a happy land; Lord, I disbelieve:
Forster's adaptation of the words of a man witnessing Jesus' performance of a
miracle in healing his son—"Lord, I believe . . ." (Mark 9:24).

really. It is bloody in every sense of the word. And I have to keep my end up in it. Where do I start?

With personal relationships. Here is something comparatively solid in a world full of violence and cruelty. Not absolutely solid, for Psychology has split and shattered the idea of a "Person," and has shown that there is something incalculable in each of us, which may at any moment rise to the surface and destroy our normal balance. We don't know what we are like. We can't know what other people are like. How, then, can we put any trust in personal relationships, or cling to them in the gathering political storm? In theory we cannot. But in practice we can and do. Though A is not unchangeably A or B unchangeably B, there can still be love and loyalty between the two. For the purpose of living one has to assume that the personality is solid, and the "self" is an entity, and to ignore all contrary evidence. And since to ignore evidence is one of the characteristics of faith, I certainly can proclaim that I believe in personal relationships. 3

Starting from them, I get a little order into the contemporary chaos. One must be fond of people and trust them if one is not to make a mess of life, and it is therefore essential that they should not let one down. They often do. The moral of which is that I must, myself, be as reliable as possible, and this I try to be. But reliability is not a matter of contract—that is the main difference between the world of personal relationships and the world of business relationships. It is a matter for the heart, which signs no documents. In other words, reliability is impossible unless there is a natural warmth. Most men possess this warmth, though they often have bad luck and get chilled. Most of them, even when they are politicians, *want* to keep faith. And one can, at all events, show one's own little light here, one's own poor little trembling flame, with the knowledge that it is not the only light that is shining in the darkness, and not the only one which the darkness does not comprehend. Personal relations are despised today. They are regarded as bourgeois luxuries, as products of a time of fair weather which is now past, and we are urged to get rid of them, and to dedicate ourselves to some movement or cause instead. I hate the idea of causes, and if I had to choose between betraying my country and betraying my friend, I hope I should have the guts to betray my country. Such a choice may scandalise the modern reader, and he may stretch out his patriotic hand to the telephone at once and ring up the 4 police. It would not have shocked Dante, though. Dante places Brutus and Cassius in the lowest circle of Hell[2] because they had chosen to betray their friend Julius Caesar rather than their country Rome. Probably one will not be asked to make such an agonising choice. Still, there lies at the back of every creed something terrible and hard for which the worshipper may one day be required to suffer, and there is even a terror and a hardness in this creed of personal relationships, urbane and mild though it sounds. Love and loyalty to an individual can run counter to the claims of the State. When they do—down with the State, say I, which means that the State would down me.

This brings me along to Democracy, "even Love, the Beloved   5 Republic, which feeds upon Freedom and lives." Democracy is not a Beloved Republic really, and never will be. But it is less hateful than other contemporary forms of government, and to that extent it deserves our support. It does start from the assumption that the individual is important, and that all types are needed to make a civilisation. It does not divide its citizens into the bossers and the bossed—as an efficiency-regime tends to do. The people I admire most are those who are sensitive and want to create something or discover something, and do not see life in terms of power, and such people get more of a chance under a democracy than elsewhere. They found religions, great or small, or they produce literature and art, or they do disinterested scientific research, or they may be what is called "ordinary people," who are creative in their private lives, bring up their children decently, for instance, or help their neighbours. All these people need to express themselves; they cannot do so unless society allows them liberty to do so, and the society which allows them most liberty is a democracy.

Democracy has another merit. It allows criticism, and if there   6 is not public criticism there are bound to be hushed-up scandals. That is why I believe in the Press, despite all its lies and vulgarity, and why I believe in Parliament. Parliament is often sneered at because it is a Talking Shop. I believe in it *because* it is a talking shop. I believe in the Private Member who makes himself a nuisance. He gets snubbed and is told that he is cranky or ill-informed, but he does expose abuses which would otherwise

2. In *The Divine Comedy*, masterpiece of Italian poet Dante Alighieri (1265–1321).

never have been mentioned, and very often an abuse gets put right just by being mentioned. Occasionally, too, a well-meaning public official starts losing his head in the cause of efficiency, and thinks himself God Almighty. Such officials are particularly frequent in the Home Office. Well, there will be questions about them in Parliament sooner or later, and then they will have to mind their steps. Whether Parliament is either a representative body or an efficient one is questionable, but I value it because it criticises and talks, and because its chatter gets widely reported.

So Two Cheers for Democracy: one because it admits variety   7
and two because it permits criticism. Two cheers are quite enough: there is no occasion to give three. Only Love the Beloved Republic deserves that.

What about Force, though? While we are trying to be sensi-   8
tive and advanced and affectionate and tolerant, an unpleasant question pops up: does not all society rest upon force? If a government cannot count upon the police and the army, how can it hope to rule? And if an individual gets knocked on the head or sent to a labour camp, of what significance are his opinions?

This dilemma does not worry me as much as it does some. I   9
realise that all society rests upon force. But all the great creative actions, all the decent human relations, occur during the intervals when force has not managed to come to the front. These intervals are what matter. I want them to be as frequent and as lengthy as possible, and I call them "civilisation." Some people idealise force and pull it into the foreground and worship it, instead of keeping it in the background as long as possible. I think they make a mistake, and I think that their opposites, the mystics, err even more when they declare that force does not exist. I believe that it exists, and that one of our jobs is to prevent it from getting out of its box. It gets out sooner or later, and then it destroys us and all the lovely things which we have made. But it is not out all the time, for the fortunate reason that the strong are so stupid. Consider their conduct for a moment in the Niebelung's Ring.[3] The giants there have the guns, or in other words the gold; but they do nothing with it, they do not realise that they are all-powerful, with the result that the catastrophe is

3. *Der Ring des Nibelungen* (first performance 1876): opera in four parts by German composer Richard Wagner, based on medieval Scandinavian legends. Forster, writing on the eve of World War II, sees in the story certain lessons for his contemporaries.

delayed and the castle of Walhalla, insecure but glorious, fronts the storms. Fafnir, coiled round his hoard, grumbles and grunts; we can hear him under Europe today; the leaves of the wood already tremble, and the Bird calls its warnings uselessly. Fafnir will destroy us, but by a blessed dispensation he is stupid and slow, and creation goes on just outside the poisonous blast of his breath. The Nietzschean would hurry the monster up, the mystic would say he did not exist, but Wotan, wiser than either, hastens to create warriors before doom declares itself. The Valkyries are symbols not only of courage but of intelligence; they represent the human spirit snatching its opportunity while the going is good, and one of them even finds time to love. Brünnhilde's last song hymns the recurrence of love, and since it is the privilege of art to exaggerate, she goes even further, and proclaims the love which is eternally triumphant and feeds upon freedom, and lives.

So that is what I feel about force and violence. It is, alas! the ultimate reality on this earth, but it does not always get to the front. Some people call its absences "decadence"; I call them "civilisation" and find in such interludes the chief justification for the human experiment. I look the other way until fate strikes me. Whether this is due to courage or to cowardice in my own case I cannot be sure. But I know that if men had not looked the other way in the past, nothing of any value would survive. The people I respect most behave as if they were immortal and as if society was eternal. Both assumptions are false: both of them must be accepted as true if we are to go on eating and working and loving, and are to keep open a few breathing holes for the human spirit. No millennium seems likely to descend upon humanity; no better and stronger League of Nations will be instituted; no form of Christianity and no alternative to Christianity will bring peace to the world or integrity to the individual; no "change of heart" will occur. And yet we need not despair, indeed, we cannot despair; the evidence of history shows us that men have always insisted on behaving creatively under the shadow of the sword; that they have done their artistic and scientific and domestic stuff for the sake of doing it, and that we had better follow their example under the shadow of the aeroplanes. Others, with more vision or courage than myself, see the salvation of humanity ahead, and will dismiss my conception of civilisation as paltry, a sort of tip-and-run game. Certainly it is presumptuous to say that we *cannot* improve, and that Man, who has only been in power for a few thousand years, will never learn to make use of his power. All I mean is that, if people continue to kill one another as they do, the world cannot get better than it is, and that since there are more people than formerly, and their means for destroying one another superior, the world may well get worse. What is good in people—and consequently in the world—is their insistence on creation, their belief in friendship and loyalty for their own sakes; and though Violence remains and is, indeed, the major partner in this muddled establishment, I believe that creativeness remains too, and will always assume direction when violence sleeps. So, though I am not an optimist, I cannot agree with Sophocles that it were better never to have been born. And although, like Horace, I see no evidence that each batch of births is superior to the last, I leave the field open for the more complacent view. This is such a difficult moment to live in, one cannot help getting gloomy and also a bit rattled, and perhaps short-sighted.

In search of a refuge, we may perhaps turn to hero-worship. 11 But here we shall get no help, in my opinion. Hero-worship is a dangerous vice, and one of the minor merits of a democracy is that it does not encourage it, or produce that unmanageable type of citizen known as the Great Man. It produces instead different kinds of small men—a much finer achievement. But people who cannot get interested in the variety of life, and cannot make up their own minds, get discontented over this, and they long for a hero to bow down before and to follow blindly. It is significant that a hero is an integral part of the authoritarian stock-in-trade today. An efficiency-regime cannot be run without a few heroes stuck about it to carry off the dullness—much as plums have to be put into a bad pudding to make it palatable. One hero at the top and a smaller one each side of him is a favourite arrangement, and the timid and the bored are comforted by the trinity, and, bowing down, feel exalted and strengthened.

No, I distrust Great Men. They produce a desert of uniformity 12 around them and often a pool of blood too, and I always feel a little man's pleasure when they come a cropper. Every now and then one reads in the newspapers some such statement as: "The coup d'état appears to have failed, and Admiral Toma's whereabouts is at present unknown." Admiral Toma had probably every qualification for being a Great Man—an iron will; personal magnetism, dash, flair, sexlessness—but fate was against him, so he retires to unknown whereabouts instead of parading history with his peers. He fails with a completeness which no artist and no lover can experience, because with them the process of creation is itself an achievement, whereas with him the only possible achievement is success.

I believe in aristocracy, though—if that is the right word, and   13
if a democrat may use it. Not an aristocracy of power, based upon rank and influence, but an aristocracy of the sensitive, the considerate and the plucky. Its members are to be found in all nations and classes, and all through the ages, and there is a secret understanding between them when they meet. They represent the true human tradition, the one permanent victory of our queer race over cruelty and chaos. Thousands of them perish in obscurity, a few are great names. They are sensitive for others as well as for themselves, they are considerate without being fussy, their pluck is not swankiness but the power to endure, and they can take a joke. I give no examples—it is risky to do that—but the reader may as well consider whether this is the type of person he would like to meet and to be, and whether (going farther with me) he would prefer that this type should *not* be an ascetic one. I am against asceticism myself. I am with the old Scotsman who wanted less chastity and more delicacy. I do not feel that my aristocrats are a real aristocracy if they thwart their bodies, since bodies are the instruments through which we register and enjoy the world. Still, I do not insist. This is not a major point. It is dearly possible to be sensitive, considerate and plucky and yet be an ascetic too. If anyone possesses the first three qualities, I will let him in! On they go—an invincible army, yet not a victorious one. The aristocrats, the elect, the chosen, the Best People—all the words that describe them are false, and all attempts to organise them fail. Again and again Authority, seeing their value, has tried to net them and to utilise them as the Egyptian Priesthood or the Christian Church or the Chinese Civil Service or the Group Movement, or some other worthy stunt. But they slip through the net and are gone; when the door is shut, they are no longer in the room; their temple, as one of them remarked, is the Holiness of the Heart's Affection,[4] and their kingdom, though they never possess it, is the wide-open world.

4. English poet John Keats (1795–1821) wrote, "I am certain of nothing but the holiness of the Heart's affection and the truth of Imagination."

With this type of person knocking about, and constantly   14
crossing one's path if one has eyes to see or hands to feel, the experiment of earthly life cannot be dismissed as a failure. But it
may well be hailed as a tragedy, the tragedy being that no device
has been found by which these private decencies can be transmitted to public affairs. As soon as people have power they go
crooked and sometimes dotty as well, because the possession of
power lifts them into a region where normal honesty never pays.
For instance, the man who is selling newspapers outside the
Houses of Parliament can safely leave his papers to go for a
drink and his cap beside them: anyone who takes a paper is sure
to drop a copper into the cap. But the men who are inside the
Houses of Parliament—they cannot trust one another like that,
still less can the Government they compose trust other governments. No caps upon the pavement here, but suspicion, treachery and armaments. The more highly public life is organised the
lower does its morality sink; the nations of today behave to each
other worse than they ever did in the past, they cheat, rob, bully
and bluff, make war without notice, and kill as many women
and children as possible; whereas primitive tribes were at all
events restrained by taboos. It is a humiliating outlook—though
the greater the darkness, the brighter shine the little lights, reassuring one another, signalling: "Well, at all events, I'm still here.
I don't like it very much, but how are you?" Unquenchable lights
of my aristocracy! Signals of the invincible army! "Come
along—anyway, let's have a good time while we can." I think
they signal that too.

The Saviour of the future—if ever he comes—will not preach   15
a new Gospel. He will merely utilise my aristocracy, he will make
effective the good will and the good temper which are already
existing. In other words, he will introduce a new technique. In
economics, we are told that if there was a new technique of distribution, there need be no poverty, and people would not starve
in one place while crops were being ploughed under in another.
A similar change is needed in the sphere of morals and politics.
The desire for it is by no means new; it was expressed, for example, in theological terms by Jacopone da Todi over six hundred years ago. "Ordina questo amore, O tu che m'ami," he
said; "O thou who lovest me—set this love in order." His prayer
was not granted, and I do not myself believe that it ever will be,

but here, and not through a change of heart, is our probable route. Not by becoming better, but by ordering and distributing his native goodness, will Man shut up Force into its box, and so gain time to explore the universe and to set his mark upon it worthily. At present he only explores it at odd moments, when Force is looking the other way, and his divine creativeness appears as a trivial byproduct, to be scrapped as soon as the drums beat and the bombers hum.

Such a change, claim the orthodox, can only be made by   16
Christianity, and will be made by it in God's good time: man always has failed and always will fail to organise his own goodness, and it is presumptuous of him to try. This claim—solemn as it is—leaves me cold. I cannot believe that Christianity will ever cope with the present world-wide mess, and I think that such influence as it retains in modern society is due to the money behind it, rather than to its spiritual appeal. It was a spiritual force once, but the indwelling spirit will have to be restated if it is to calm the waters again, and probably restated in a non-Christian form. Naturally a lot of people, and people who are not only good but able and intelligent, will disagree here; they will vehemently deny that Christianity has failed, or they will argue that its failure proceeds from the wickedness of men, and really proves its ultimate success. They have Faith, with a large F. My faith has a very small one, and I only intrude it because these are strenuous and serious days, and one likes to say what one thinks while speech is comparatively free: it may not be free much longer.

The above are the reflections of an individualist and a liberal   17
who has found liberalism crumbling beneath him and at first felt ashamed. Then, looking around, he decided there was no special reason for shame, since other people, whatever they felt, were equally insecure. And as for individualism—there seems no way of getting off this, even if one wanted to. The dictator-hero can grind down his citizens till they are all alike, but he cannot melt them into a single man. That is beyond his power. He can order them to merge, he can incite them to mass-antics, but they are obliged to be born separately, and to die separately, and, owing to these unavoidable termini, will always be running off the totalitarian rails. The memory of birth and the expectation of death always lurk within the human being, making him separate from his fellows and consequently capable of intercourse with

them. Naked I came into the world, naked I shall go out of it! And a very good thing too, for it reminds me that I am naked under my shirt, whatever its colour.

PATRICIA NELSON LIMERICK

Believing in the American West

Patricia Nelson Limerick, a professor of history at the University of Colorado at Boulder, is one of the central figures of what has been called "New Western History," a movement that connects the history of America's frontier to themes that continue to preoccupy us today: climate change, colonialism, and the conflict of cultures and religious faiths. "Believing in the American West" was published as a section of Geoffrey C. Ward's *The West: An Illustrated History* (1996).

My father and I are not Mormons. This fact is true of many   1
other people in the American West, but it is particularly true of us. My father was raised Mormon in Brigham City, Utah. Although it is common for fallen-away members of the Church of Jesus Christ of Latter-day Saints to become fervent believers in other churches, my father took a different path. When he cut his ties to the Mormon Church and moved to California, he turned away from all organized religion.

My sisters and I thus grew up with a particular opportunity to   2
drive our father batty. Here was our distinctive and very gratifying channel of rebellion: we could insist on our First Amendment right to freedom of religion, get dressed up for church, and demand that Father drive us there. The peak of this soul-satisfying mutiny came in asking him for money to put in the collection plate. And, since Mother was (and is) a non-church-attending Congregationalist and thus nearly as vulnerable as Father to the abrasive powers of our piety, there was also considerable pleasure to be gained from coming home from church, sitting down to Sunday dinner, and delivering an earnest prayer on behalf of our parents' redemption.

Such rebellion, however, came at a cost. For me, the cost was   3
repeated exposure to the misery of the unbaptized heathen.
Churched or not, our parents had installed into our thinking a
great devotion to justice and fairness. And so the dilemma of the
poor souls in Africa and Asia, living and dying and heading off
to hell without the opportunity to hear the Christian gospel,
weighed heavily on me. If God really had decided to let salvation
hinge on the basis of the arbitrary facts of place of birth (a fact
that He, in His omnipotence, had determined), then God seemed
to be following rather questionable values Himself, showing a
pretty tenuous understanding of the concept of fairness.

The pleasures of bugging my father were, therefore, already   4
wearing thin on a memorable day in 1962 at the First Baptist
Church in Banning, the day on which my rebellion ended. The
membership of the First Baptist Church was entirely white. On
this Sunday, a black woman, new in town, came to church. I
happened to be behind her in the line, waiting to shake hands
with the minister. We had spent some time, in Sunday school,
singing about Jesus' transcendence of racial prejudice:

> Red and yellow, black and white,
> They're all sacred in His sight.
> Jesus loves the little children of the world.

This little song was not easy to reconcile with the dilemma of the
unbaptized heathen, and our minister had, himself, not gotten
very far in reconciling Jesus' sentiments with his own. When the
black woman shook hands with him, the minister told her that
her church was on the other side of town.

Since that Sunday, I have learned more about the ways in   5
which race relations in the American West came to bear an unhappy resemblance to race relations in the rest of the country. In
religious terms, it was not simply a matter of segregation in
western churches, it was often a matter of the active use of the
church as a social institution to maintain racial separation and
inequality. The minister of the First Baptist Church not only gave
me a memorable introduction to this topic, he also persuaded me
that my rebellion against my father had gone far enough. Since
then I have taken the path leading away from organized religion
and toward what I will call disorganized religion. My father and
I remain post-Mormon and unchurched, but nonetheless driven
by convictions about right and wrong.

For decades, I thought that Father and I had placed ourselves 6
on the margins of conventional religious behavior. But, like so
many other westerners who treasured a picture of themselves as
odd birds, we have turned out to be birds positioned right at the
center of the flock. "[P]oor church attendance is characteristic of
westerners generally," the historian Michael Quinn has written.
This is the West's principal claim to distinctiveness in religious
terms: it is the region with the lowest rates of church participation, in both the nineteenth and the twentieth centuries. In the nation as a whole, "the West as a region has the lowest attendance
(36 percent) in church or synagogue." The West thus holds the
status of the nation's "Unchurched Belt." In this region, participants in disorganized religion have held and hold a considerable
numerical advantage over participants in organized religion.

My father and I turn out to be not rebels and eccentrics, but 7
representative westerners. Still, without official papers of membership, we and our many disaffiliated comrades are not likely to
register in the records of western religious history. Contemplat-
ing the prospect of one's invisibility, one finds good reason to
question how much the fact of church membership reveals about
a matter as subjective and private as religious belief. Churches
are, of course, the places where *records* of official religious performance accumulate. Historians of religion, oriented to written
documents, have had good reason to place churches and their
members at the center of their inquiry, in the manner of labor
historians who, for a time, hinged their history of the working
class on the much more narrow topic of membership in unions.

"In comparison with Whites in the United States today," the 8
anthropologist Harold Driver once wrote, "the Indians [of the
past] were at least ten times as religious." Of all the improbable
proclamations of academics made over the last forty years, this
one is my personal favorite, an example of confident, social-
scientific thinking at its goofiest. And yet, whatever Harold Driver meant by this memorable assertion, one suspects that he did
not mean that Indians were ten times as religious because they
were ten times more likely to join formally chartered and organized churches. On the contrary, Driver thought (and he shared
this conviction with many others) that Indian people were more
religious because they unmistakably and consistently demonstrated their faith, observing little separation between the secular

and the spiritual. They did not need to join churches and attend formal services, because they lived virtually every moment in a religious way. By contrast, in Driver's equally widely shared but considerably more questionable assumption, modern white American people have been a very secular group, driven primarily by economic motives. For a group of people holding their souls on such a tight leash, religious conviction could only appear in official membership in an institutional church, with even that level of religious commitment often confined to attendance at Sunday services, cresting at Easter and Christmas.

Consider, by contrast, the state of affairs in mid-nineteenth-century rural Oregon. True to the western pattern, church membership there was very limited. But a low percentage of church attendance, historian Dean May has argued, "does not imply . . . an absence of religious sentiment and feelings." The settlers' religious activity was, emphatically, local, often practiced within households, "involving them rarely, if at all, in any broader community." They had Bibles in their homes, and recorded significant family events in those Bibles. "Blessings on food, prayers, prayer meetings, hymn singing, and exhortation were held in home and schoolhouse for gatherings of families and close neighbors." Preachers sent by home missionary societies found Oregon's "seeming incoherence of religious organization" both puzzling and frustrating. In a curious convergence of opinion, historians would come to share the judgment of the preachers: "religion in any setting other than an established congregation was to them hardly religion at all."

Few of the people of the Oregon settlements were joining churches, but they gave many other signs of religiousness. The pattern of Oregon may well be the pattern of the western United States. "[E]xcept in Mormon territory, the majority of far westerners have cared little about traditional religious institutions and practices," the historian Eldon G. Ernst put it. "They form the most secular society in the United States if gauged by church membership statistics, yet when questioned they claim to be religiously concerned and find religion to be important in their personal lives."

We return to the common difficulty faced by anyone exploring this topic: in its subjectivity and privacy, religious belief is very hard to track. A few groups—Indians, missionaries, and Mormons—have made the task easier: for all their differences, these groups were believers who consistently and visibly demonstrated their faith in frequent public rituals, steering by religious principles in everyday activities. Whether the ritual was a dance, a hymn, or a ward-house meeting, whether the consecrated activity was hunting, teaching, or irrigated farming, Indians, missionaries, and Mormons placed their faith front and center, where no one could miss it. Thus, western historians fell into a perfectly logical habit of confining the explicit discussion of religion to topics where it simply could not be avoided. For all the other westerners—for the sizable numbers who were *not* Indians, *not* missionaries, and *not* Mormons—the most resolutely secular history is all they seemed to deserve, and generally all they got.

The fact that American westward expansion was so strongly 12 governed by economic motives reinforced the apparent wisdom of this strategy of reserving religious history for the few, and leaving secular history for the majority. The daily experience of overland travel during the gold rush had many of the qualities of a sacred pilgrimage, testing determination and persistence in a thousand ways. But a journey undertaken as a tribute to Mammon surrendered its credentials as pilgrimage. Fervent participation in mineral rushes and land rushes, in timber booms and cattle speculation deepened the impression that the determination of white Americans to develop the West's natural resources left very little room for the development of their souls. Often invoked in support of these expanding commercial enterprises, God's name looked as if it had become little more than another product endorsement.

Consider, as a striking example of this linkage of religion with 13 commerce, the memorable song "The Cowboy's Prayer":

Lord, please help me, lend me Thine ear,
The prayer of a troubled cowman to hear.
No doubt my prayer to you may seem strange,
But I want you to bless my cattle range. . . .

As you O Lord my fine herds behold,
They represent a sack of pure gold.
I think that at least five cents on the pound
Would be a good price for beef the year round.

When God was asked to intervene on behalf of rising cattle prices, the theological seemed to have made a full surrender to the secular. But then again, when whites asked God to bless their economic undertakings, was this *entirely* different from an Indian hunter's hope that the right gestures of respect would recruit the spirits as the sponsors of a successful hunt? Didn't both practices serve as examples of a people's refusal to draw a hard line between the spiritual and the worldly? If God wanted the best for His Chosen People, wouldn't He *want* them to prosper in the cattle market?

In 1973, my husband and I were driving west, crossing the country on yet another secular pilgrimage. Through the journey, we had invested a great deal in the services of auto mechanics, purchasing, among other things, an entire replacement engine for our VW Bug. We were not entirely sure that we had enough money left to get to California. On a Sunday morning, we turned on the radio and found an evangelist in the middle of a prayer that spoke directly to our dilemma: "Lord," the evangelist asked, "heal our families; heal our hearts; and heal our finances." When my father wired us money in Laramie, we felt that prayer had been heard.

Westward the Course of Chaos Takes Its Way

The year after I parted with the First Baptist Church, a remarkable event occurred in the demography of Banning, California. A bunch of kids appeared out of nowhere. Banning was a town of eight or nine thousand people, and I thought I knew most of them; I certainly knew the ones around my own age. But when we left the sixth grade at Central Elementary School and moved on to the seventh grade at Susan B. Coombs Junior High School, some fifteen or twenty strangers joined us. Had a large caravan of families all moved to town over the summer? On the contrary, and very mysteriously, the strangers claimed that they had lived in Banning most, in some cases all, of their lives. But where had they been? How had they stayed hidden all those years?

The strangers were, it turned out, Catholics. They had been hidden in parochial school, but parochial school—whatever that was—ended in sixth grade, and so now they were out of hiding. The term "Mormon" I understood, but "Catholic"? Or, even more puzzling, "Jew"? In the First Baptist Sunday School, our education on that particular topic had been *very* brief. One of the children had said to the Sunday school teacher, "We keep seeing the word 'Jew' in the Bible, but we don't know what it means." The teacher looked unhappy, and then seized on her way out. "You all know Jeff," she said, pointing to one member of the class. "Jeff used to be a Jew, but now he's a Baptist."

The extent of my Sunday school teacher's—and my—ignorance in these matters was at a cosmic scale, and quite surprising, given the West's great history of religious diversity. This diversity represented the realization of the worst fears of many Protestants in the nineteenth-century West. Protestant clergymen in the West con: fronted a region in which every moment in daily life told them that they were working against a great disadvantage. White American Protestants in the nineteenth-century West knew that they were outnumbered. They knew that they had before them a long struggle to find a permanent place in a society in which neither Episcopalians nor Baptists, Presbyterians nor Congregationalists could dominate. In many western areas, Catholics and Mormons had gotten the jump in timing, as well as in membership, on Protestants of any denomination. Jews were early arrivals in many western settlements. At the same time, American Indian religions and the Buddhism, Taoism, and Confucianism of Asian immigrants stretched the categories of faith along an extraordinarily wide continuum. In the nineteenth-century West, as historian Ferenc Szasz has written, the mainline Protestant groups "confronted the greatest challenge of their day: dealing with religious diversity." Several decades before their counterparts in the eastern United States would come to face a comparable challenge, western Protestant ministers "dealt with pluralism on a daily basis." In religious terms, the West was the American future. 17

For many of those getting an advance look at this future, religious pluralism proved to be fruitful soil for discomfort and doubt. Where we might see an extraordinary and fascinating mosaic of religious practice, the Protestant ministers were more inclined to see chaos, and dangerous chaos at that. Take the concerns and worries recorded by the Reverend Josiah Strong. After two years' service as a Congregationalist minister in Cheyenne, Wyoming, the reverend came down with a pronounced case of western Protestant anxiety. The West, he wrote in his book *Our Country* (1886), was "peculiarly exposed" to the principal "dangers" of the times: "Mam- 18 monism, materialism, luxuriousness, and the centralization of wealth." The region was particularly burdened, as well, with the threats posed by socialism, the saloon, Mormonism, Catholicism, and foreign immigration. Not only were the dangers greatest in the West, the Protestant churches were at their weakest, ill-equipped to respond to any of these challenges.

If this was a region in which all its enemies ganged up on   19
Protestant Christianity, might the good news be that the region's sparse population rendered its religious condition irrelevant to the nation's well-being? On the contrary: in Rev. Josiah Strong's judgment, the West determined the national future. With its vast resources, ready to support an equally sizable population, the West "is to dominate the East"; in the near future, "the West will direct the policy of the Government, and by virtue of her preponderating population and influence will determine our national character and, therefore, destiny."

If Protestant Christianity could not save the West, then noth-   20
ing could save the nation. And the stakes went considerably beyond the national. In the reverend's vision, the settling of the American West would be only one test of the Anglo-Saxon's "instinct or genius for colonizing," a genius that would finally work its way around the entire planet in *the final competition of races, for which the Anglo-Saxon is being schooled* [his emphasis]." Through the religious challenge posed by the American West, "God was training the Anglo-Saxon race for an hour sure to come in the world's future."

Full of distrust for European immigrants, for Mormons, and   21
for New Mexican Hispanics, Rev. Josiah Strong nonetheless reserved his greatest distrust for the actions and beliefs of his fellow Anglo-Saxons, those "church-members who seem to have left their religion behind when they crossed the Missouri." Of course, the reverend would worry about all those "others," but it is, at first, a surprise to see how doubtful he was about the religious reliability of his fellow whites. Given the continued status of the West as the nation's unchurched region, he was right to be worried. My father and I, and our many disaffiliated fellow westerners, are the reverend's worst nightmare come true.

In the intervening century, few writers have been able to   22
produce texts that can match *Our Country* in its remarkable mixture of confidence and doubt. In the space of a few pages, Rev. Josiah Strong could shift from a cosmic confidence in

Anglo-Saxon destiny to rule the world and to install God's kingdom in the process to a dark vision of a West soon to collapse before the pressures of evil and disorder. How could he be at once so confident and so anxious? The paradox here was a great one. On the ground level the American West had the greatest religious diversity of any part of the nation, and the heightened anxiety of the nineteenth-century Protestant clergy testified to the challenge posed by that diversity. And yet, in the broader sweep of history, expansion into the American West seemed to have shown white American religious belief at its most homogeneous, combining a Christian sense of mission with patriotism to form a virtual state religion. Faith in the United States' Manifest Destiny had long ago melted the division between the sacred and the secular. And yet, by a considerable irony, when Protestant fervor merged into national policy, it ended up producing the region in which Protestant denominations had their weakest hold.

Whites had an indisputable claim on the West, Senator   23
Thomas Hart Benton had said, because they used the land "according to the intentions of the CREATOR." As historian Albert Weinberg observed, "[T]heological literature was scarcely more abundant in reference to Providence than was the literature of expansionism." To one typical expansionist during the Mexican-American War, war was "the religious execution of our country's glorious mission, under the direction of Divine Providence, to civilize and christianize, and raise up from anarchy and degradation a most ignorant, indolent, wicked and unhappy people." And yet one outcome of this enterprise was not the redemption of the Mexican people, but the slide into religious "anarchy and degradation" of many of the Americans who were supposed to be the agents of the West's redemption. As William Jennings Bryan put it after the start of the Philippine insurrection, "'Destiny' is not as manifest as it was" a while ago.

The *Kiva* in My Soul

In New Mexico, it was never possible to draw a firm border   24
between the secular and the sacred. For centuries, Indian religious belief erased any line between faith and worldly activity. In the Spanish colonization of the sixteenth and seventeenth cen-

turies, missionaries played a role in conquest as important as, if not more important than, the role of soldiers. For the Spanish, religious motives came interwoven with economic and political motives; even when governors fought with friars for the control of colonies, those struggles dramatized the central role that religion played in the whole undertaking. In the nineteenth century, when white Americans entered the scene, Protestant disapproval of Catholicism added to the contest over land and labor and to the frictions of nationality and race. In the history unrolling in New Mexico, religious belief had been everywhere, shaping and being shaped by even the most secular elements of human thought and behavior.

In the summer of 1992, Santa Fe—the town called "Holy   25
Faith"—permitted me a memorable visit to the blurred border between the secular and the sacred. I was meeting with a group of international scholars studying American regionalism. From Senegal to Thailand, from Belgium to the Philippines, all of my companions had grown up watching western movies, and watching them with feelings that bordered on reverence. No conventionally religious mission society, one could learn from the testimony of these visitors, has ever come close to matching the achievements of the Hollywood western in global proselytizing and conversion.

On our last day of class, the participants were having a com-   26
petition to see who had been the most influenced or tainted by the Wild West myth. We had heard a number of eloquent statements from men whose childhoods had included frequent visits to "Old West" tourist towns in Germany and Austria, where they had cheerfully fired away at the Indian targets in shooting galleries. Then a woman from Poland suddenly and urgently announced her candidacy as the most mythically influenced. "The first thing I can remember," she told us, "is my father reading to me from Karl May's western novels. As soon as I could read, I read them for myself. I loved old Shatterhand, and even after I saw a movie with a fat Frenchman playing his part, my love for him did not change. You may tell me they are factually wrong, but Karl May's novels are . . ." Here she paused and searched for the right word, seizing on a term she had learned the day before during a tour of a pueblo. "Karl May's novels," she ended, with the right word firmly grasped, "are the *kiva* in my soul."

Here was yet another piece of testimony from Santa Fe, re-   27
minding me of the hopelessness of trying to separate faith from
worldly fact in western America. Once again, Santa Fe offered a
reminder that of all the places on the planet where the sacred and
the secular meet, the American West is one of the hot spots. One
could argue (as indeed one had, and at length) that the vision of
the West as a romantic place, where strong and good men went
down to Main Street or out to the wilderness to take their courageous stands, held little connection to historical fact. And yet, if
Karl May's western fantasies had provided a spiritual and emotional sanctuary for a young woman growing up in Poland in
tough times, then we were clearly talking about a realm of belief
out of reach of historical fact checking.

Trained in movie theaters in Senegal or Thailand, New York   28
City or Denver, the human spirit has developed the conditioned
response of soaring when it confronts certain images: horses gal-
loping across open spaces; wagon trains moving through a landscape of mesas and mountains; cruel enemies and agents of
disorder defeated by handsome white men with nerves of steel
and tremendous—and justified—self-esteem. And when the human spirit undertakes to soar, it is not necessarily the obligation
of the historian to act as air traffic controller and force the spirit
down for a landing. Improbable as it may seem to the prosaic
historian, an imagined and factually unsubstantiated version of
western American history has become, for many believers, a sacred story. For those believers, a challenge to that story can
count as sacrilege.

In American life today, lots of groups have made a heavy emo-   29
tional investment in the proposition that history is a sacred, not
a secular, tale. The best and clearest example of this comes from
the Mormons. In the last few years, historians who are Mormon
believers but who try to write searchingly and critically about
Mormon history have had a rough time. Some of them have been
excommunicated for their failure to write what the church's
General Authorities call faith-affirming history. But the pattern
seen among the Mormons appears everywhere. Consider, for instance, how similar the Mormon call for faith-affirming history
is to the Afro-centric call for a history of African-American
people that consistently praises their accomplishments and affirms their self-esteem. Or consider the desire, on the part of

some American Indian people, for a writing of Indian history that enshrines Indian people as ecological and environmental saints and traces an unbroken line of nobility and solidarity among tribal people. When white politicians condemn "revisionist" or "multicultural" history and call for a narrative of the past that affirms the achievements and virtues of white Americans, those politicians show a striking kinship to the Afro-centric intellectuals and to the General Authorities of the Mormon Church. *Everyone* wants faith-affirming history; the disagreement is just a question of which faith any particular individual wants to see affirmed. Each group wants history to provide guidance, legitimacy, justification, and direction for its particular chosen people.

These contests over history, often focused on the West, resemble and echo more familiar contests over religious faith. Different versions of history have become creation stories or origin stories for the people who treasure them, and, with so much feeling at stake, the clash between these sacred tales grows increasingly bitter. And yet, while these separate and contesting claims on history proliferate, more and more evidence emerges from the historical record to counter these assertions of exclusivity. Explorations of western American history reveal many examples of unexpected kinship, mixed heritage, cultural trading, syncretism, and borrowing. It is not simply a matter of the blending of the West's people through intermarriage, though this is certainly an enormous part of the region's story. It is also a matter of reciprocal influence and mutual assimilation. The various peoples of the American West have been bumping into each other for an awfully long time, and it cannot be a surprise to discover that their habits and beliefs have rubbed off on each other. 30

Indian religious movements—from the ghost dance to the Native American Church with its use of peyote—show many Christian elements. Perhaps the best example of this complexity in religious identity is the Lakota religious leader Black Elk. Thanks to the writer John G. Neihardt's telling of his life story in *Black Elk Speaks,* Black Elk came to stand for the most traditional practice of Indian religion, a practice brought to a tragic end by conquest. But his daughter, Lucy Black Elk Looks Twice, hoped to correct and deepen the standing image of her father, and, working with the anthropologist Michael Steltencamp, 31

Lucy told the post-conquest story of Nicholas Black Elk, who became a leading Catholic convert and cathechist on his reservation. This was not a matter of Black Elk "selling out" or betraying his traditional beliefs; this was a matter of sincere religious conviction responding to new beliefs in new times.

In the nineteenth-century West, white Americans had denounced the religions of the "others," labeling other systems of belief as paganism, heathenism, superstition, barbarism, or savagery, and struggling to convert American Indians and Asian immigrants to Protestant Christianity. In the late-twentieth-century West, the tide seems to be reversing, as a number of white Americans have developed an enthusiasm for tribal religions, as well as for the varieties of Asian Buddhism. Particularly well represented in the West, "New Age" religion has appropriated pieces and parts of American Indian religions, with both Indian and white claimants to enlightenment, in the familiar area of overlap between commerce and religion, cashing in on the opportunities so presented. Rev. Josiah Strong and his colleagues were presumably tossing in their graves, but all over the West, the lines dividing the vision quest from communion, the *kiva* from the church, were shifting and wavering.

DREAM OTHER DREAMS, AND BETTER

To many white Americans in our times, belief in the mythic Old West has come to resemble belief in more conventional religious doctrines. For these believers, the Old Frontier is the nation's creation story, the place where the virtues and values of the nation were formed. And yet, for all the faith now invested in it, the mythic version of the Old West had little room for ministers and pastors, congregations and parishes. In a story full of cowboys, sheriffs, saloon girls, outlaws, gunfighters, prospectors, and stagecoach drivers, the church was, at best, the place where the frightened townspeople gathered to sing hymns and await rescue by the all-too-worldly hero. The church, after all, was aligned with the forces of respectability, the forces that would eventually tame the Wild West and end all the fun and adventure of the glory days. If one went in search of the classic heroes in the mythic turf of the Old West, one would not bother to look among the clergy.

In the quest for western heroes, there is good reason now to   34
look in unexpected, less explored places. The old heroes are a
pretty battered and discredited lot, with their character flaws on
permanent display. The examples they provide often affirm the
wrong faith entirely—the faith in guns and violence—or serve
solely as individual examples of courage and determination, attached to no particular principle. Driven by the values of conquest and domination, or purely by the goal of personal
fortune-seeking, the old heroes are looking pretty tired—de-
pleted, exhausted, and ready for retirement. In truth, they deserve a rest.

And yet, when the critics of academic historians say that we   35
have discredited the old heroes and failed to replace them with
any new ones, they are right. But this is not because we lack the
resources. We have all the material we need to put forward a better team, people whose examples affirm a faith of considerably
greater promise. It is time for a different kind of western hero:
the sustainable hero who can replace the old, exhausted, and de-
pleted western heroes. As Wallace Stegner said of the old western
myths, "Dream other dreams, and better."

Sustainability in a hero means, very concretely, providing   36
inspiration that sustains the spirit and the soul. While inconsis-
tency can disqualify a conventional hero, a degree of inconsis-
tency is one of the essential qualifications of a sustainable hero.
Models of sustainable heroism are drawn from the record of
people doing the right thing *some of the time*—people practicing
heroism at a level that we can actually aspire to match. The fact
that these people fell, periodically, off the high ground of heroism but then determinedly climbed back, even if only in order to
fall again, is exactly what makes their heroism sustainable. Because it is uneven and broken, this kind of heroism is resilient,
credible, possible, reachable. Sustainable heroism comes only in
moments and glimpses, but they are moments and glimpses in
which the universe lights up.

Assigned in 1867 to preside over the vast district of Montana,   37
Idaho, and Utah, Bishop Daniel Tuttle "traveled more than forty
thousand miles" by stagecoach. "Most times I enjoyed that
mode of traveling," he remembered, "many times I grimly endured it, a few times I was rendered miserable by it." Think
about what it meant to ride with strangers for hours and hours,
jammed into an inflexible, jostling container, and the fact that

Bishop Tuttle kept his temper and most of the time enjoyed the ride is its own measure of sustainable heroism.

While misery most often derived from the rough road condi-   38
tions or the inadequacy of stagecoach shock-protection, fellow passengers could sometimes match the bumps in the road in their power to annoy. In one case, a fellow passenger "by manner and act was insulting to a colored woman in the coach." Bishop Tuttle firmly "reproved him." When words proved insufficient and the passenger "repeated the offense," Tuttle reported, "I shook him soundly." If this demonstration of muscular Christianity failed to produce a conversion, it still made for a happier ride. "At the next station," the offender "got out and slunk entirely away from our sight."

Bishop Tuttle was a complicated man, full of self-righteous   39
disapproval in his appraisal of Mormon belief and earnestly committed to the growth of his denomination. But when Bishop Tuttle took his stand on behalf of the right of African-American women to travel with dignity, he offered a memorable demonstration of sustainable heroism, an episode in faith-affirming history for those trying to hold on to a belief in an American commitment to justice and fairness.

And then there is the remarkable example of heroism set by   40
Rev. Howard Thurman. An African-American who was the chaplain at Howard University, he headed west to team up with a white man as co-pastor of a new and courageous church. As a young child, he had attended his father's funeral and listened to a preacher condemn his father as an example of an unredeemed, unchurched sinner. Ever since then, Thurman had been on a campaign against exclusivity in Christian practice, fighting the exclusivity of the smugly saved as persistently as he fought the exclusivity of race. When he learned of an effort to form a church in San Francisco uniting people of all races and backgrounds, he felt called. The year was 1943, more than ten years before the Montgomery, Alabama, bus boycott.

The location and the timing were both crucial. "Segregation   41
of the races," Thurman wrote, "was a part of the mores, and of the social behavior of the country." "San Francisco with its varied nationalities, its rich intercultural heritages, and its face resolutely fixed toward the Orient" was the ideal place to undertake a trial run toward a better future in American race re-

lations. War work had brought a much increased black population to San Francisco and heightened the prospects of community friction. Responding to these challenges, an interracial
group had decided to form the Church for the Fellowship of All
Peoples, and Thurman joined them, following his quest to find
out "whether or not it is true that experiences of spiritual unity
and fellowship are more compelling than the fears and dogmas
and prejudices that separate men." There was considerable risk,
financial and otherwise, in the "mission" that brought him and
his family "three thousand miles across the continent." And
there were constant tests of the spirit, as the Fellowship Church
and its founder faced the prospects of sponsoring interracial
marriages and other challenges to the social order. Simply visiting a member of the congregation in the hospital could prove to
be a test of Thurman's spirit; hospital staffs repeatedly stumbled
over and resisted the notion that a white believer could be in the
care of a black pastor.

Fellowship Church under Rev. Howard Thurman's leadership   42
proved to be a great success, navigating its way through the difficult divisions between denominations as well as those between
races. In God's presence, Thurman always insisted, "the wor-
shiper is neither male nor female, black nor white, Protestant nor
Catholic nor Buddhist nor Hindu, but a human spirit laid bare."
"Religious experience," he believed—and he had lived this
gospel—"must unite rather than divide men."

The examples set by heroes like Bishop Tuttle and Reverend   43
Thurman encourage me to believe in the real American West, a
place—in the past and in the present—of dazzling human and
natural possibility. Believing in the other West, the mythic and
imagined West, has never been much of an option for me. Instead, the very notion of investing any faith in a simple, romantic, glorified West always brought to mind the verse that I
learned from my father when I was very young:

> With this bright, believing band,
> I have no claim to be.
> What seems so true to them,
> Seems fantasy to me.

This verse has kept me on course in the company of those who
have fallen head over heels in love with a western illusion; and

yet, in the presence of more traditional religious believers, it gives me much less comfort. The company of people secure in their faith, whether that faith is a tribal religion, Catholicism, Judaism, Mormonism, or a Protestant denomination, can make me melt with envy. But then the verse—"With this bright, believing band, I have no claim to be"—comes to mind and interrupts the melting. I remain a member of a battered, disorganized, but still pretty bright, believing band of my own, churched and unchurched, composed of all races and backgrounds—people who hold on to a faith that fairness and justice might someday prevail in this region and in this nation. That faith, the faith of my father and my mother, of Bishop Tuttle and Reverend Thurman, is the *kiva* in my soul.

HUSTON SMITH

The Straight Path of Islam

Huston Smith is probably the best-known scholar of world religion in the United States. In addition to scholarly publications, he has produced a number of award-winning films, a popular television series, and a book that has sold well over a million copies: *The Religions of Man* (republished in 1990 as *The World's Religions*), from which this selection is taken. Smith's own beliefs are mystical—"The world," he says, "stands to God's total reality as a postcard of Everest stands to Everest"— but a remarkable quality of his work is his ability to articulate accurately and empathically the views of mainline practitioners of all the faiths he has studied.

If a Muslim were asked to summarize the way Islam counsels   1
people to live, the answer might be: It teaches them to walk the straight path. The phrase comes from the opening *surah* of the Koran, which is repeated many times in the Muslim's five daily prayers.

In the Name of Allah the Merciful, the Compassionate:
Praise be to Allah, Creator of the worlds,
The Merciful, the Compassionate,
Ruler of the day of Judgment.

Thee do we worship, and Thee do we ask for aid.
Guide us in the straight path,
The path of those on whom Thou hast poured forth Thy grace.
Not the path of those who have incurred Thy wrath and gone astray.

This *surah* has been called the heartbeat of the Muslim's re- 2
sponse to God. At the moment, though, the question is why "the
straight path"? One meaning is obvious; a straight path is one
that is not crooked or corrupt. The phrase contains another
meaning, however, which addresses something that in Islam is
distinctive. The straight path is one that is straightforward; it is
direct and explicit. Compared with other religions, Islam spells
out the way of life it proposes; it pinpoints it, nailing it down
through clear injunctions. Every major type of action is classified
on a sliding scale from the "forbidden," through the "indifferent," to the "obligatory." This gives the religion a flavor of defi-
niteness that is quite its own. Muslims know where they stand.

They claim this as one of their religion's strengths. God's rev- 3
elation to humankind, they say, has proceeded through four
great stages. First, God revealed the truth of monotheism, God's
oneness, through Abraham. Second, God revealed the Ten Com-
mandments through Moses. Third, God revealed the Golden
Rule—that we are to do unto others as we would have them do
unto us—through Jesus. All three of these prophets were authentic messengers; each introduced important features of the
God-directed life. One question yet remained, however: *How*
should we love our neighbor? Once life became complicated, instructions were needed to answer that question, and the Koran
provides them. "The glory of Islam consists in having embodied
the beautiful sentiments of Jesus in definite laws."[1]

What, then, is the content of this straight path that spells out 4
human duties? We shall divide our presentation into two parts.
In this section we shall consider the Five Pillars of Islam, the
principles that regulate the private life of Muslims in their dealings with God. In the next section we shall consider the Koran's
social teachings.

The first of the Five Pillars is Islam's creed, or confession of 5
faith known as the *Shahadah*. Every religion contains professions that orient its adherents' lives. Islam's wastes no words.

1. Ameer Ali, *The Spirit of Islam*, 1902, rev. ed. (London: Christophers, 1923),
170.

Brief, simple, and explicit, it consists of a single sentence: "There is no god but God, and Muhammad is His Prophet." The first half of the proclamation announces the cardinal principle of monotheism. "There is no god but Allah." There is no god but *the* God. More directly still, there is no God but *God,* for the word is not a common noun embracing a class of objects; it is a proper name designating a unique being and him only. The second affirmation—that "Muhammad is God's prophet"—registers the Muslim's faith in the authenticity of Muhammad and in the validity of the book he transmitted.

At least once during his or her lifetime a Muslim must say the   6
Shahadah correctly, slowly, thoughtfully, aloud, with full understanding and with heartfelt conviction. In actuality Muslims pronounce it often, especially its first half, *La ilaha illa 'llah.* In every crisis and at every moment when the world threatens to overwhelm them, not excepting the approach of death, "There is no god but God" will spring to their lips. "A pious man, seized by rage, will appear suddenly to have been stopped in his tracks as he remembers the *Shahadah* and, as it were, withdraws, putting a great distance between himself and his turbulent emotions. A woman crying out in childbirth will as suddenly fall silent, remembering; and a student, bowed anxiously over his desk in an examination hall, will raise his head and speak these words, and a barely audible sigh of relief passes through the whole assembly. This is the ultimate answer to all questions."[2]

The second pillar of Islam is the canonical prayer, in which the   7
Koran adjures the faithful to "be constant" (29:45).

Muslims are admonished to be constant in prayer to keep   8
their lives in perspective. The Koran considers this the most difficult lesson people must learn. Though they are obviously creatures, having created neither themselves nor their worlds, they can't seem to get this straight and keep placing themselves at the center of things, living as if they were laws unto themselves. This produces havoc. When we ask, then, why Muslims pray, a partial answer is: in response to life's natural impulse to give thanks for its existence. The deeper answer, however, is the one with which this paragraph opened: to keep life in perspective—to see

2. Charles Le Gai Eaton, *Islam and the Destiny of Man* (Albany: State University of New York Press, 1985), 55. [author's note]

it objectively, which involves acknowledging human creature-
liness before its Creator. In practice this comes down to submit-
ting one's will to God's (*islam*) as its rightful sovereign.

How often should Muslims pray? There is an account in the   9
Koran that speaks to this point.

One of the crucial events in Muhammad's life, we are told,   10
was his renowned Night Journey to Heaven. On a certain night
in the month of Ramadan, he was spirited on a wondrous white
steed with wings to Jerusalem and upward from there through
the seven heavens to the presence of God, who instructed him
that Muslims were to pray fifty times each day. On his way back
to earth, he stopped in the sixth heaven, where he reported the
instruction to Moses, who was incredulous. "Fifty times a day!"
he said in effect. "You've got to be kidding. That will never
work. Go back and negotiate." Muhammad did so and returned
with the number reduced to forty, but Moses was not satisfied. "I
know those people," he said. "Go back." This routine was repeated four more times, with the number reduced successively to
thirty, twenty, ten, and then five. Even this last figure struck
Moses as excessive. "Your people are not capable of observing
five daily prayers," he said. "I have tested men before your time
and have labored most earnestly to prevail over the [sons of] Is-
ra'il, so go back to your Lord and ask Him to make things lighter
for your people." This time, however, Muhammad refused. "I
have asked my Lord till I am ashamed, but now I am satisfied
and I submit." The number remained fixed at five.[3]

The times of the five prayers are likewise stipulated: on aris-   11
ing, when the sun reaches its zenith, its mid-decline, sunset, and
before retiring. The schedule is not absolutely binding. The Koran says explicitly, for example, that "When you journey about
the earth it is no crime that you come short in prayer if you fear
that those who disbelieve will attack you." Under normal conditions, however, the fivefold pattern should be maintained. While
in Islam no day of the week is as sharply set apart from the others as is the Sabbath for the Jews or Sunday for the Christians,
Friday most nearly approximates a weekly holy day. Congrega-
tional worship is not stressed as much in Islam as it is in Judaism

3. A *hadith* of the Prophet, reported in *Mishkat al-Masabih*, James Robson,
trans. (Lahore: Sh. Muhammad Ashraf, 1965), 1264–67.

and Christianity; even so, Muslims are expected to pray in mosques when they can, and the Friday noon prayer is emphasized in this respect. Visitors to Muslim lands testify that one of the most impressive religious sights in the world comes to view when, in a dimly lighted mosque, hundreds of Muslims stand shoulder to shoulder, then repeatedly kneel and prostrate themselves toward Mecca.

Although Muslims first prayed in the direction of Jerusalem, a koranic revelation later instructed them to pray in the direction of Mecca; and the realization that Muslims throughout the world do this creates a sense of participating in a worldwide fellowship, even when one prays in solitude. Beyond this matter of direction the Koran says almost nothing, but Muhammad's teachings and practices moved in to structure the void. Washing, to purify the body and symbolically the soul, precedes the prayer, which begins in dignified, upright posture but climaxes when the supplicant has sunk to his or her knees with forehead touching the floor. This is the prayer's holiest moment, for it carries a twofold symbolism. On the one hand, the body is in a fetal position, ready to be reborn. At the same time it is crouched in the smallest possible space, signifying human nothingness in the face of the divine.   12

As for prayer's content, its standard themes are praise, gratitude, and supplication. There is a Muslim saying that every time a bird drinks a drop of water it lifts its eyes in gratitude toward heaven. At least five times each day, Muslims do likewise.   13

The third pillar of Islam is charity. Material things are important in life, but some people have more than others. Why? Islam is not concerned with this theoretical question. Instead, it turns to the practical issue of what should be done about the disparity. Its answer is simple. Those who have much should help lift the burden of those who are less fortunate. It is a principle that twentieth-century democracies have embraced in secular mode in their concept of the welfare state. The Koran introduced its basic principle in the seventh century by prescribing a graduated tax on the haves to relieve the circumstances of the have-nots.   14

Details aside, the figure the Koran set for this tax was 2½ percent. Alongside the tithe of Judaism and Christianity (which, being directed more to the maintenance of religious institutions than to the direct relief of human need, is not strictly comparable), this looks modest until we discover that it refers not just to   15 income but to holdings. Poorer people owe nothing, but those in the middle and upper income brackets should annually distribute among the poor one-fortieth of the value of all they possess.

And to whom among the poor should this money be given? [16] This too is prescribed: to those in immediate need; to slaves in the process of buying their freedom; to debtors unable to meet their obligations; to strangers and wayfarers; and to those who collect and distribute the alms.

The fourth pillar of Islam is the observance of Ramadan. Ramadan is a month in the Islamic calendar—Islam's holy month, [17] because during it Muhammad received his initial revelation and (ten years later) made his historic *Hijrah* (migration) from Mecca to Medina. To commemorate these two great occasions, able-bodied Muslims (who are not ill or involved in crises like war or unavoidable journeys) fast during Ramadan. From the first moment of dawn to the setting of the sun, neither food nor drink nor smoke passes their lips; after sundown they may partake in moderation. As the Muslim calendar is lunar, Ramadan rotates around the year. When it falls in the winter its demands are not excessive. When, on the other hand, it falls during the scorching heat of the summer, to remain active during the long days without so much as a drop of water is an ordeal.

Why, then, does the Koran require it? For one thing, fasting [18] makes one think, as every Jew who has observed the fast of Yom Kippur will attest. For another thing, fasting teaches self-discipline; one who can endure its demands will have less difficulty controlling the demands of appetites at other times. Fasting underscores the creature's dependence on God. Human beings, it is said, are as frail as rose petals; nevertheless, they assume airs and pretensions. Fasting calls one back to one's frailty and dependence. Finally, fasting sensitizes compassion. Only those who have been hungry can know what hunger means. People who have fasted for twenty-nine days within the year will be apt to listen more carefully when next approached by someone who is hungry.

Islam's fifth pillar is pilgrimage. Once during his or her life- [19] time every Muslim who is physically and economically in a position to do so is expected to journey to Mecca, where God's climactic revelation was first disclosed. The basic purpose of the pilgrimage is to heighten the pilgrim's devotion to God and his revealed will, but the practice has fringe benefits as well. It is, for example, a reminder of human equality. Upon reaching Mecca, pilgrims remove their normal attire, which carries marks of social status, and don two simple sheet-like garments. Thus everyone, on approaching Islam's earthly focus, wears the same thing. Distinctions of rank and hierarchy are removed, and prince and pauper stand before God in their undivided humanity. Pilgrimage also provides a useful service in international relations. It brings together people from various countries, demonstrating thereby that they share a loyalty that transcends loyalty to their nations and ethnic groupings. Pilgrims pick up information about other lands and peoples, and return to their homes with better understanding of one another.

The Five Pillars of Islam consist of things Muslims do to keep   20
the house of Islam erect. There are also things they should not do. Gambling, thieving, lying, eating pork, drinking intoxicants, and being sexually promiscuous are some of these. Even Muslims who transgress these rulings acknowledge their acts as transgressions.

With the exception of charity, the precepts we have consid-   21
ered in this section pertain to the Muslim's personal life. We turn now to the social teachings of Islam.

SOCIAL TEACHINGS

"O men! listen to my words and take them to heart! Know ye   22
that every Muslim is a brother to every other Muslim, and that you are now one brotherhood." These notable words, spoken by the Prophet during his "farewell pilgrimage" to Mecca shortly before his death, epitomize one of Islam's loftiest ideals and strongest emphases. The intrusion of nationalism in the last two centuries has played havoc with this ideal on the political level, but on the communal level it has remained discernibly intact. "There is something in the religious culture of Islam which inspired, in even the humblest peasant or peddler, a dignity and a courtesy toward others never exceeded and rarely equalled in other civilizations," a leading Islamicist has written.[4]

Looking at the difference between pre- and post-Islamic Ara-   23
bia, we are forced to ask whether history has ever witnessed a comparable moral advance among so many people in so short a

---

4. Bernard Lewis, *The Atlantic Monthly* (September 1990): 59.

time. Before Muhammad there was virtually no restraint on intertribal violence. Glaring inequities in wealth and possession were accepted as the natural order of things. Women were regarded more as possessions than as human beings. Rather than say that a man could marry an unlimited number of wives, it would be more accurate to say that his relations with women were so casual that beyond the first wife or two they scarcely approximated marriage at all. Infanticide was common, especially of girls. Drunkenness and large-scale gambling have already been remarked upon. Within a half-century there was effected a remarkable change in the moral climate on all of these counts.

Something that helped it to accomplish this near-miracle is a feature of Islam that we have already alluded to, namely its explicitness. Its basic objective in interpersonal relations, Muslims will say, is precisely that of Jesus and the other prophets: brotherly and sisterly love. The distinctive thing about Islam is not its ideal but the detailed prescriptions it sets forth for achieving it. We have already encountered its theory on this point. If Jesus had had a longer career, or if the Jews had not been so socially powerless at the time, Jesus might have systematized his teachings more. As it was, his work "was left unfinished. It was reserved for another Teacher to systematize the laws of morality."[5] The Koran is this later teacher. In addition to being a spiritual guide, it is a legal compendium. When its innumerable prescriptions are supplemented by the only slightly less authoritative *hadith*—traditions based on what Muhammad did or said on his own initiative—we are not surprised to find Islam the most socially explicit of the Semitic religions. Westerners who define religion in terms of personal experience would never be understood by Muslims, whose religion calls them to establish a specific kind of social order. Islam joins faith to politics, religion to society, inseparably.

Islamic law is of enormous scope. It will be enough for our purposes if we summarize its provisions in four areas of collective life.

1. Economics.   Islam is acutely aware of the physical foundations of life. Until bodily needs are met, higher concerns cannot flower. When one of Muhammad's followers ran up to him

24

25

26

5. Ali, *Spirit of Islam*, 173. [author's note]

crying, "My Mother is dead; what is the best alms I can give away for the good of her soul?" the Prophet, thinking of the heat of the desert, answered instantly, "Water! Dig a well for her, and give water to the thirsty."

Just as the health of an organism requires that nourishment be   27
fed to its every segment, so too a society's health requires that material goods be widely and appropriately distributed. These are the basic principles of Islamic economics, and nowhere do Islam's democratic impulses speak with greater force and clarity. The Koran, supplemented by *hadith,* propounded measures that broke the barriers of economic caste and enormously reduced the injustices of special interest groups.

The model that animates Muslim economics is the body's cir-   28
culatory system. Health requires that blood flow freely and vigorously; sluggishness can bring on illness, blood clots occasion death. It is not different with the body politic, in which wealth takes the place of blood as the life-giving substance. As long as this analogy is honored and laws are in place to insure that wealth is in vigorous circulation, Islam does not object to the profit motive, economic competition, or entrepreneurial ventures—the more imaginative the latter, the better. So freely are these allowed that some have gone so far as to characterize the Koran as "a businessman's book." It does not discourage people from working harder than their neighbors, nor object to such people being rewarded with larger returns. It simply insists that acquisitiveness and competition be balanced by the fair play that "keeps arteries open," and by compassion that is strong enough to pump life-giving blood—material resources—into the circulatory system's smallest capillaries. These "capillaries" are fed by the Poor Due, which (as has been noted) stipulates that annually a portion of one's holdings be distributed to the poor.

As for the way to prevent "clotting," the Koran went after   29
the severest economic curse of the day—primogeniture—and flatly outlawed it. By restricting inheritance to the oldest son, this institution had concentrated wealth in a limited number of enormous estates. In banning the practice, the Koran sees to it that inheritance is shared by all heirs, daughters as well as sons. F. S. C. Northrop describes the settlement of a Muslim's estate that he chanced to witness. The application of Islamic law that afternoon resulted in the division of some $53,000 among no less than seventy heirs.

One verse in the Koran prohibits the taking of interest. At the   30
time this was not only humane but eminently just, for loans were
used then to tide the unfortunate over in times of disaster. With
the rise of capitalism, however, money has taken on a new meaning. It now functions importantly as venture capital, and in this
setting borrowed money multiplies. This benefits the borrower,
and it is patently unjust to exclude the lender from his or her
gain. The way Muslims have accommodated to this change is by
making lenders in some way partners in the venture for which
their monies are used. When capitalism is approached in this
manner, Muslims find no incompatibility between its central feature, venture capital, and Islam. Capitalism's excesses—which
Muslims consider to be glaringly exhibited in the secular West—
are another matter. The equalizing provisos of the Koran would,
if duly applied, offset them.

2. The Status of Women.   Chiefly because it permits a plu-   31
rality of wives, the West has accused Islam of degrading women.

If we approach the question historically, comparing the status   32
of Arabian women before and after Muhammad, the charge is
patently false. In the pre-Islamic "days of ignorance," marriage
arrangements were so loose as to be scarcely recognizable.
Women were regarded as little more than chattel, to be done
with as fathers or husbands pleased. Daughters had no inheritance rights and were often buried alive in their infancy.

Addressing conditions in which the very birth of a daughter   33
was regarded as a calamity, the koranic reforms improved
woman's status incalculably. They forbade infanticide. They required that daughters be included in inheritance—not equally, it
is true, but to half the proportion of sons, which seems just, in
view of the fact that unlike sons, daughters would not assume financial responsibility for their households. In her rights as citizen—education, suffrage, and vocation—the Koran leaves open
the possibility of woman's full equality with man, an equality
that is being approximated as the customs of Muslim nations become modernized.[6] If in another century women under Islam do
not attain the social position of their Western sisters, a position

6. As of this writing the Prime Minister of Pakistan and the leader of the opposition party in Bangladesh are both women. Muslim women could hold property
in their own names from the start, whereas married women in the United States
did not win that right until the twentieth century. [author's note]

to which the latter have been brought by industrialism and democracy rather than religion, it will then be time, Muslims say, to hold Islam accountable.

It was in the institution of marriage, however, that Islam made   34
its greatest contribution to women. It sanctified marriage, first, by making it the sole lawful locus of the sexual act.[7]

To the adherents of a religion in which the punishment for   35
adultery is death by stoning and social dancing is proscribed, Western indictments of Islam as a lascivious religion sound ill-directed. Second, the Koran requires that a woman give her free consent before she may be wed; not even a sultan may marry without his bride's express approval. Third, Islam tightened the wedding bond enormously. Though Muhammad did not forbid divorce, he countenanced it only as a last resort. Asserting repeatedly that nothing displeased God more than the disruption of marital vows, he instituted legal provisions to keep marriages intact. At the time of marriage husbands are required to provide the wife with a sum on which both agree and which she retains in its entirety should a divorce ensue. Divorce proceedings call for three distinct and separate periods, in each of which arbiters drawn from both families try to reconcile the two parties. Though such devices are intended to keep divorces to a minimum, wives no less than husbands are permitted to instigate them.

There remains, however, the issue of polygamy, or more precisely polygyny. It is true that the Koran permits a man to have   36
up to four wives simultaneously, but there is a growing consensus that a careful reading of its regulations on the matter point toward monogamy as the ideal. Supporting this view is the Koran's statement that "if you cannot deal equitably and justly with [more than one wife], you shall marry only one." Other passages make it clear that "equality" here refers not only to material perquisites but to love and esteem. In physical arrangements each wife must have private quarters, and this in itself is a limiting factor. It is the second proviso, though—equality of love and esteem—that leads jurists to argue that the Koran virtually en-

7. Outside slavery, we must add—a subject that, due to the variety of its local and historical forms, is too complex to consider here. See Bernard Lewis, *Race and Slavery in the Middle East* (New York: Oxford University Press, 1990). [author's note]

joins monogamy, for it is almost impossible to distribute affection and regard with exact equality. This interpretation has been
in the Muslim picture since the third century of the *Hijrah*, and
it is gaining increasing acceptance. To avoid any possible misunderstanding, many Muslims now insert in the marriage deed a
clause by which the husband formally renounces his supposed
right to a second concurrent spouse, and in point of fact—with
the exception of African tribes where polygyny is customary—
multiple wives are seldom found in Islam today.

Nevertheless, the fact remains that the Koran does permit   37
polygyny: "You may marry two, three, or four wives, but not
more." And what are we to make of Muhammad's own multiple
marriages? Muslims take both items as instances of Islam's ver-
satility in addressing diverse circumstances.

There are circumstances in the imperfect condition we know   38
as human existence when polygyny is morally preferable to its
alternative. Individually, such a condition might arise if, early in
marriage, the wife were to contract paralysis or another disability that would prevent sexual union. Collectively, a war that decimated the male population could provide an example, forcing
(as this would) the option between polygyny and depriving a
large proportion of women of motherhood and a nuclear family
of any sort. Idealists may call for the exercise of heroic conti-
nence in such circumstances, but heroism is never a mass option.
The actual choice is between a legalized polygyny in which sex is
tightly joined to responsibility, and alternatively monogamy,
which, being unrealistic, fosters prostitution, where men disclaim responsibility for their sexual partners and their progeny.
Pressing their case, Muslims point out that multiple marriages
are at least as common in the West; the difference is that they are
successive. Is "serial polygyny," the Western version, self-evidently
superior to its coeval form, when women have the right to opt
out of the arrangement (through divorce) if they want to? Finally, Muslims, though they have spoken frankly from the first of
female sexual fulfillment as a marital right, do not skirt the
volatile question of whether the male sexual drive is stronger
than the female's. "Hoggledy higamous, men are polygamous; /
Higgledy hogamous, women monogamous," Dorothy Parker
wrote flippantly. If there is biological truth in her limerick,
"rather than allowing this sensuality in the male to run riot,

obeying nothing but its own impulses, the Law of Islam sets down a polygynous framework that provides a modicum of control. [It] confers a conscious mold on the formless instinct of man in order to keep him within the structures of religion."[8]

As for the veiling of women and their seclusion generally, the koranic injunction is restrained. It says only to "Tell your wives and your daughters and the women of the believers to draw their cloaks closely round them (when they go abroad). That will be better, so that they may be recognised and not annoyed" (33:59). Extremes that have evolved from this ruling are matters of local custom and are not religiously binding. [39]

Somewhere in this section on social issues the subject of penalties should be mentioned, for the impression is widespread that Islamic law imposes ones that are excessively harsh. This is a reasonable place to address this issue, for one of the most frequently cited examples is the punishment for adultery, which repeats the Jewish law of death by stoning—two others that are typically mentioned are severance of the thief's hand, and flogging for a number of offenses. These stipulations are indeed severe, but (as Muslims see matters) this is to make the point that the injuries that occasion these penalties are likewise severe and will not be tolerated. Once this juridical point is in place, mercy moves in to temper the decrees. "Avert penalties by doubt," Muhammad told his people, and Islamic jurisprudence legitimizes any stratagem that averts the penalty without outright impugning the Law. Stoning for adultery is made almost impossible by the proviso that four unimpeachable witnesses must have observed the act in detail. "Flogging" can be technically fulfilled by using a light sandal or even the hem of a garment, and thieves may retain their hands if the theft was from genuine need. [40]

3. Race Relations.   Islam stresses racial equality and "has achieved a remarkable degree of interracial coexistence."[9] The ultimate test in this area is willingness to intermarry, and Muslims see Abraham as modeling this willingness in marrying Hagar, a black woman whom they regard as his second wife rather [41]

8. Victor Danner, *The Islamic Tradition* (Amity, NY: Amity House, 1988), 131. [author's note]
9. Kenneth Cragg, *The House of Islam* (Belmont, CA: Wadsworth, 1975), 122. [author's note]

than a concubine. Under Elijah Muhammad the Black Muslim movement in America—it has had various names—was militant toward the whites; but when Malcolm X made his 1964 pilgrimage to Mecca, he discovered that racism had no precedent in Islam and could not be accommodated to it.[10] Muslims like to recall that the first *muezzin*, Bilal, was an Ethiopian who prayed regularly for the conversion of the Koreish—"whites" who were persecuting the early believers, many of whom were black. The advances that Islam continues to make in Africa is not unrelated to this religion's principled record on this issue.

4. The Use of Force.   Muslims report that the standard West- 42 ern stereotype that they encounter is that of a man marching with sword outstretched, followed by a long train of wives. Not surprisingly, inasmuch as from the beginning (a historian reports) Christians have believed that "the two most important aspects of Muhammad's life . . . are his sexual licence and his use of force to establish religion."[11] Muslims feel that both Muhammad and the Koran have been maligned on these counts. License was discussed above. Here we turn to force.

Admit, they say, that the Koran does not counsel turning the 43 other cheek, or pacifism. It teaches forgiveness and the return of good for evil when the circumstances warrant—"turn away evil with that which is better" (42:37)— but this is different from not resisting evil. Far from requiring the Muslim to turn himself into a doormat for the ruthless, the Koran allows punishment of wanton wrongdoers to the full extent of the injury they impart (22:39–40). Justice requires this, they believe; abrogate reciprocity, which the principle of fair play requires, and morality descends to impractical idealism if not sheer sentimentality. Extend this principle of justice to collective life and we have as one instance *jihad,* the Muslim concept of a holy war, in which the martyrs who die are assured of heaven. All this the Muslim will affirm as integral to Islam, but we are still a far cry from the familiar charge that Islam spread primarily by the sword and was upheld by the sword.

10. See Malcolm X, *The Autobiography of Malcolm X* (New York: Grove Press, 1964), 338–47.
11. Norman Daniel, *Islam and the West: The Making of an Image,* 1960, rev. ed. (Edinburgh: Edinburgh University Press, 1966), 274. [author's note]

As an outstanding general, Muhammad left many traditions   44
regarding the decent conduct of war. Agreements are to be honored and treachery avoided; the wounded are not to be muti-
lated, nor the dead disfigured. Women, children, and the old are
to be spared, as are orchards, crops, and sacred objects. These,
however, are not the point. The important question is the definition of a righteous war. According to prevailing interpretations
of the Koran, a righteous war must either be defensive or to right
a wrong. "Defend yourself against your enemies, but do not attack them first: God hates the aggressor" (2:190). The aggressive
and unrelenting hostility of the idolaters forced Muhammad to
seize the sword in self-defense, or, together with his entire community and his God-entrusted faith, be wiped from the face of
the earth. That other teachers succumbed under force and became martyrs was to Muhammad no reason that he should do
the same. Having seized the sword in self-defense he held onto it
to the end. This much Muslims acknowledge; but they insist that
while Islam has at times spread by the sword, it has mostly
spread by persuasion and example.

The crucial verses in the Koran bearing on conversion read as   45
follows:

Let there be no compulsion in religion (2:257).

*To every one have We given a law and a way. . . . And if God had
pleased, he would have made [all humankind] one people [people of
one religion]. But he hath done otherwise, that He might try you in
that which He hath severally given unto you: wherefore press forward in good works. Unto God shall ye return, and He will tell you
that concerning which ye disagree (5:48).*

Muslims point out that Muhammad incorporated into his   46
charter for Medina the principle of religious toleration that these
verses announce. They regard that document as the first charter
of freedom of conscience in human history and the authoritative
model for those of every subsequent Muslim state. It decreed
that "the Jews who attach themselves to our commonwealth
[similar rights were later mentioned for Christians, these two being the only non-Muslim religions on the scene] shall be protected from all insults and vexations; they shall have an equal
right with our own people to our assistance and good offices: the
Jews . . . and all others domiciled in Yathrib, shall . . . practice

their religion as freely as the Muslims." Even conquered nations were permitted freedom of worship contingent only on the payment of a special tax in lieu of the Poor Due, from which they were exempt; thereafter every interference with their liberty of conscience was regarded as a direct contravention of Islamic law. If clearer indication than this of Islam's stand on religious tolerance be asked, we have the direct words of Muhammad: "Will you then force men to believe when belief can come only from God?"[12] Once, when a deputy of Christians visited him, Muhammad invited them to conduct their service in his mosque, adding, "It is a place consecrated to God."

This much for theory and Muhammad's personal example. How well Muslims have lived up to his principles of toleration is a question of history that is far too complex to admit of a simple, objective, and definitive answer. On the positive side Muslims point to the long centuries during which, in India, Spain, and the Near East. Christians, Jews, and Hindus lived quietly and in freedom under Muslim rule. Even under the worst rulers Christians and Jews held positions of influence and in general retained their religious freedom. It was Christians, not Muslims, we are reminded, who in the fifteenth century expelled the Jews from Spain where, under Islamic rule, they had enjoyed one of their golden ages. To press this example, Spain and Anatolia changed hands at about the same time—Christians expelled the Moors from Spain, while Muslims conquered what is now Turkey. Every Muslim was driven from Spain, put to the sword, or forced to convert, whereas the seat of the Eastern Orthodox church remains in Istanbul to this day. Indeed, if comparisons are what we want, Muslims consider Christianity's record as the darker of the two. Who was it, they ask, who preached the Crusades in the name of the Prince of Peace? Who instituted the Inquisition, invented the rack and the stake as instruments of religion, and plunged Europe into its devastating wars of religion? Objective historians are of one mind in their verdict that, to put the matter minimally, Islam's record on the use of force is no darker than that of Christianity.

Laying aside comparisons, Muslims admit that their own record respecting force is not exemplary. Every religion at some stages in its career has been used by its professed adherents to

12. Quoted by Ali, *Spirit of Islam*, 212. [author's note]

mask aggression, and Islam is no exception. Time and again it has provided designing chieftains, caliphs, and now heads of state with pretexts for gratifying their ambitions. What Muslims deny can be summarized in three points.

First, they deny that Islam's record of intolerance and aggres- 49 sion is greater than that of the other major religions. (Buddhism may be an exception here.)

Second, they deny that Western histories are fair to Islam in 50 their accounts of its use of force.[13] *Jihad,* they say, is a case in point. To Westerners it conjures scenes of screaming fanatics being egged into war by promises that they will be instantly transported to heaven if they are slain. In actuality: (a) *jihad* literally means exertion, though because war requires exertion in exceptional degree the word is often, by extension, attached thereto. (b) The definition of a holy war in Islam is virtually identical with that of a just war in Christianity, where too it is sometimes called a holy war. (c) Christianity, too, considers those who die in such wars to be martyrs, and promises them salvation. (d) A *hadith* (canonical saying) of Muhammad ranks the battle against evil within one's own heart above battles against external enemies. "We have returned from the lesser *jihad,*" the Prophet observed, following an encounter with the Meccans, "to face the greater *jihad,*" the battle with the enemy within oneself.

Third, Muslims deny that the blots in their record should be 51 charged against their religion whose presiding ideal they affirm in their standard greeting, *as-salamu 'alaykum* ("Peace be upon you").

ROBERT KEGAN

The *Mitzvah* of *Kaporis*

Robert Kegan, now a well-known developmental psychologist affiliated with Harvard, has a long-standing interest in Hasidism, a mystical movement within orthodox Judaism. Early in his career this interest led him to live for several months in the Lubavitcher

13. Norman Daniel's *Islam and the West* supports them on this point. [author's note]

Hasidic Community of Crown Heights, Brooklyn, studying with the rabbis and participating in the rituals. The following excerpt from *The Sweeter Welcome* (1976) gives a snapshot of the life Kegan experienced in the Lubavitcher community and the way it affected his consciousness of the world.

As we were about to separate I told Reuven I didn't think I could get myself up at four in the morning, especially to kill chickens. "Roosters," he said. "The women will kill chickens." 1

Reuven was my *chaver,* literally *friend.* We studied, as was the tradition, in pairs. One finds a *chaver* to be one's teacher and student of Talmud and Tanya (the mystical book of Lubavitcher Hasidism), after the rabbi's lessons. Mine taught me many other things besides: that the little Ⓤ and K on food packages were *kashruth* signs, standing for "Union of Orthodox Rabbis" and "Kosher," respectively; but that ⒶⒸ stood for the American Can Company. On this day, only a few days from Yom Kippur, the Day of Atonement, he was telling me about the *mitzvah* of *kaporis* to be performed some minutes before sunrise tomorrow. 2

It can't be time when, later, Reuven rings the bell; I'm sure I've just fallen asleep. And it's dark out. And if I pretend I don't hear him then my wife will be awakened by the ringing. And certainly she won't go to the door, since her hair isn't covered and she knows Reuven will not enter a house with another man's wife if it is not established that the husband is both present and awake. And he's not. And it's still ringing. 3

"How do I get there?" this, from me, in the car, as I try the starter. 4

"I don't know exactly. They said to follow the cars." 5

It is a little after four in the morning and all the cars look as if they have been followed as far as one can. I say something to this effect and Reuven laughs. But he has been doing that since I opened the door. I had expected this early morning cheer to annoy me but it doesn't. Maybe because the cheer is so quiet. 6

"Why don't you go to the *shul* and we'll pick someone up," he says. 7

Five blocks later there is, sure enough, human activity, dozens of men dressed in long black coats, black hats, white muslin shirts, beards of various size and color. This is a standard procedure standing in front of the *shul* ("school," synagogue) if you need a ride. For each of them the walk from home to *shul* is the 8 closest, most familiar walk in the world. Aside from work, anything farther away, it seemed, would be an extension of the *shul*, and getting there only meant getting to the *shul*. Those with cars would be by to find those without.

The two that joined us didn't know exactly where we wanted 9
to go either, but they knew the general direction and were similarly unconcerned. "We'll run into them."

This was true again. After a time on deserted Brooklyn streets 10
there suddenly appeared a swarm of activity, cars parked in no order, blocking each other, left in the street. We were at a poultry butcher shop.

Inside there was a flurry of chicken feathers and black-suited 11
men, Hasidic women wrestling down poultry cages or standing in pairs. We had come late, someone said to us, running past us, as if we had missed the better part of some bargain sale. It was not late enough for me. Almost from the moment I entered I felt I had found the experience that could only be experience; I was weak in my knees and nauseous in my stomach. I had had no breakfast and the smell was incredibly dense.

After the moment in which I thought I might faint had passed, 12
Reuven and I went to find our roosters. It was a self-service affair. Grabbing one by its legs and neck I could do no better at containing the bird than the old Hasids who looked slightly frightened and disgusted all around me. In this we were completely alike: urban through and through.

Although I had learned the prayer—an especially difficult one, 13
I found—it had not occurred to me how different holding a rooster while reading from a prayer book might be from, say, holding a cup of wine or a loaf of bread. I stumbled through it, but I think the message came across. Roughly translated: I had many times failed myself during the year now ending; I had taken such poor care of my life I could not be sure I deserved to keep on living; but I could change, I am made of promise; this rooster is now for the moment me; it will die that I can go on living.

After the prayer I stood in a line feeling grateful to the old 14
bird, waiting to have the butcher, before my eyes, cut its neck. To stand in a line with a group of dignified, elaborately dressed men and women, each holding a large, squirming bird, and trying, for some reason, to look as if they were only waiting together for a bus—that is why I was given breath today, I thought, putting it in terms the Hasids used.

There were not many people behind us in line. We had come   15
late. When an old Hasid came in through the door a dawn light
came through with him. He was in a very great hurry, turning
over crates in search of an unblessed bird. He found one and
thrust it before a butcher's assistant. "A *zucher?*" he said wildly,
asking if it were a male. It was not. "Oy" said the old man,
throwing it in the air, searching for another, checking the light
outside. "A *zucher?* A *zucher?*" I heard him say a second time.
He was panicked that the sun would rise before he had traded
places with a bird.

I came home and went to sleep. When I awoke there were   16
three pieces of mail in the mailbox.

A card from a fellow student at the *yeshivah:* "A man who did   17
t'chuvah ["returned"] and closed his store on Saturdays is losing
customers. It is our responsibility to help. Rosen's Laundry and
Dry Cleaning. 342 Union Street."

A flyer from a Manhattan chapter of Esalen: "You are invited   18
to a meeting which will be led by Dr. Jack Revere guiding some
experiences involving the sharing of secrets among strangers."

A card from Norfolk and Dedham Mutual Fire Insurance   19
Company: "In conjunction with your application for insurance,
a routine inspection will be made developing information on
your general reputation, character and mode of living."

MARTIN LUTHER KING JR.

Letter from Birmingham Jail

Martin Luther King Jr. was the dominant leader of the American
civil rights movement from the late 1950s until his assassination
in 1968. After taking his Ph.D. in theology from Boston University in 1955, King became pastor of a church in Montgomery, Alabama, where he led a famous bus boycott that initiated a decade
of civil rights protests. Soon he organized the Southern Christian
Leadership Conference, a network of civil rights workers. King
wrote "Letter from Birmingham Jail" after being arrested during
desegregation demonstrations in Birmingham, Alabama, in 1963.
His letter received national attention when it was published in

The Christian Century and *The Atlantic Monthly.* The following version is from King's *Why We Can't Wait* (1964).

April 16, 1963[1]

MY DEAR FELLOW CLERGYMEN:

While confined here in the Birmingham city jail, I came across   1
your recent statement calling my present activities "unwise and untimely." Seldom do I pause to answer criticism of my work and ideas. If I sought to answer all the criticisms that cross my desk, my secretaries would have little time for anything other than such correspondence in the course of the day, and I would have no time for constructive work. But since I feel that you are men of genuine good will and that your criticisms are sincerely set forth, I want to try to answer your statement in what I hope will be patient and reasonable terms.

I think I should indicate why I am here in Birmingham, since you   2
have been influenced by the view which argues against "outsiders coming in." I have the honor of serving as president of the Southern Christian Leadership Conference, an organization operating in every southern state, with headquarters in Atlanta, Georgia. We have some eighty-five affiliated organizations across the South, and one of them is the Alabama Christian Movement for Human Rights. Frequently we share staff, educational, and financial resources with our affiliates. Several months ago the affiliate here in Birmingham asked us to be on call to engage in a nonviolent direct-action program if such were deemed necessary. We readily consented, and when the hour came we lived up to our promise. So I, along with several members of my staff, am here because I was invited here. I am here because I have organizational ties here.

But more basically, I am in Birmingham because injustice is   3
here. Just as the prophets of the eighth century B.C. left their vil-

1. This response to a published statement by eight fellow clergymen from Alabama (Bishop C. C. J. Carpenter. Bishop Joseph A. Durick, Rabbi Hilton L. Grafman, Bishop Paul Hardin, Bishop Holan B. Harmon, the Reverend George M. Murray, the Reverend Edward V. Ramage and the Reverend Earl Stallings) was composed under somewhat constricting circumstances. Begun on the margins of the newspaper in which the statement appeared while I was in jail, the letter was continued on scraps of writing paper supplied by a friendly Negro trusty, and concluded on a pad my attorneys were eventually permitted to leave me. Although the text remains in substance unaltered, I have indulged in the author's prerogative of polishing it for publication. [author's note]

lages and carried their "thus saith the Lord" far beyond the boundaries of their home towns, and just as the Apostle Paul left his village of Tarsus and carried the gospel of Jesus Christ to the far corners of the Greco-Roman world, so am I compelled to carry the gospel of freedom beyond my own home town. Like Paul, I must constantly respond to the Macedonian call for aid.

Moreover, I am cognizant of the interrelatedness of all com-   4
munities and states. I cannot sit idly by in Atlanta and not be concerned about what happens in Birmingham. Injustice anywhere is a threat to justice everywhere. We are caught in an inescapable network of mutuality, tied in a single garment of destiny. Whatever affects one directly, affects all indirectly. Never again can we afford to live with the narrow, provincial "outside agitator" idea. Anyone who lives inside the United States can never be considered an outsider anywhere within its bounds.

You deplore the demonstrations taking place in Birmingham.   5
But your statement, I am sorry to say, fails to express a similar concern for the conditions that brought about the demonstrations. I am sure that none of you would want to rest content with the superficial kind of social analysis that deals merely with effects and does not grapple with underlying causes. It is unfortunate that demonstrations are taking place in Birmingham, but it is even more unfortunate that the city's white power structure left the Negro community with no alternative.

In any nonviolent campaign there are four basic steps: collec-   6
tion of the facts to determine whether injustices exist; negotiation; self-purification; and direct action. We have gone through all these steps in Birmingham. There can be no gainsaying the fact that racial injustice engulfs this community. Birmingham is probably the most thoroughly segregated city in the United States. Its ugly record of brutality is widely known. Negroes have experienced grossly unjust treatment in the courts. There have been more unsolved bombings of Negro homes and churches in Birmingham than in any other city in the nation. These are the hard, brutal facts of the case. On the basis of these conditions, Negro leaders sought to negotiate with the city fathers. But the latter consistently refused to engage in good-faith negotiation.

Then, last September, came the opportunity to talk with lead-   7
ers of Birmingham's economic community. In the course of the negotiations, certain promises were made by the merchants—for

example, to remove the stores' humiliating racial signs. On the basis of these promises, the Reverend Fred Shuttlesworth and the leaders of the Alabama Christian Movement for Human Rights agreed to a moratorium on all demonstrations. As the weeks and months went by, we realized that we were the victims of a broken promise. A few signs, briefly removed, returned; the others remained.

As in so many past experiences, our hopes had been blasted, 8 and the shadow of deep disappointment settled upon us. We had no alternative except to prepare for direct action, whereby we would present our very bodies as a means of laying our case before the conscience of the local and the national community. Mindful of the difficulties involved, we decided to undertake a process of self-purification. We began a series of workshops on nonviolence, and we repeatedly asked ourselves: "Are you able to accept blows without retaliating?" "Are you able to endure the ordeal of jail?" We decided to schedule our direct-action program for the Easter season, realizing that except for Christmas, this is the main shopping period of the year. Knowing that a strong economic withdrawal program would be the by-product of direct action, we felt that this would be the best time to bring pressure to bear on the merchants for the needed change.

Then it occurred to us that Birmingham's mayoral election 9 was coming up in March, and we speedily decided to postpone action until after election day. When we discovered that the Commissioner of Public Safety, Eugene "Bull" Connor, had piled up enough votes to be in the runoff, we decided again to postpone action until the day after the run-off so that the demonstrations could not be used to cloud the issues. Like many others, we waited to see Mr. Connor defeated, and to this end we endured postponement after postponement. Having aided in this community need, we felt that our direct-action program could be delayed no longer.

You may well ask: "Why direct action? Why sit-ins, marches, 10 and so forth? Isn't negotiation a better path?" You are quite right in calling for negotiation. Indeed, this is the very purpose of direct action. Nonviolent direct action seeks to create such a crisis and foster such a tension that a community which has constantly refused to negotiate is forced to confront the issue. It seeks so to dramatize the issue that it can no longer be ignored. My citing the creation of tension as part of the work of the nonviolent-resister may sound rather shocking. But I must confess that I am not afraid of the word "tension." I have earnestly opposed violent tension, but there is a type of constructive, nonviolent tension which is necessary for growth. Just as Socrates felt that it was necessary to create a tension in the mind so that individuals could rise from the bondage of myths and half-truths to the unfettered realm of creative analysis and objective appraisal, so must we see the need for nonviolent gadflies to create the kind of tension in society that will help men rise from the dark depths of prejudice and racism to the majestic heights of understanding and brotherhood.

The purpose of our direct-action program is to create a situation so crisis-packed that it will inevitably open the door to negotiation. I therefore concur with you in your call for negotiation. Too long has our beloved Southland been bogged down in a tragic effort to live in monologue rather than dialogue. 11

One of the basic points in your statement is that the action that I and my associates have taken in Birmingham is untimely. Some have asked: "Why didn't you give the new city administration time to act?" The only answer that I can give to this query is that the new Birmingham administration must be prodded about as much as the outgoing one, before it will act. We are sadly mistaken if we feel that the election of Albert Boutwell as mayor will bring the millennium to Birmingham. While Mr. Boutwell is a much more gentle person than Mr. Connor, they are both segregationists, dedicated to maintenance of the status quo. I have hope that Mr. Boutwell will be reasonable enough to see the futility of massive resistance to desegregation. But he will not see this without pressure from devotees of civil rights. My friends, I must say to you that we have not made a single gain in civil rights without determined legal and nonviolent pressure. Lamentably, it is an historical fact that privileged groups seldom give up their privileges voluntarily. Individuals may see the moral light and voluntarily give up their unjust posture; but, as Reinhold Niebuhr has reminded us, groups tend to be more immoral than individuals. 12

We know through painful experience that freedom is never voluntarily given by the oppressor; it must be demanded by the oppressed. Frankly, I have yet to engage in a direct-action campaign that was "well timed" in the view of those who have not 13 suffered unduly from the disease of segregation. For years now I have heard the word "Wait!" It rings in the ear of every Negro with piercing familiarity. This "Wait" has almost always meant "Never." We must come to see, with one of our distinguished jurists, that "justice too long delayed is justice denied."

We have waited for more than 340 years for our constitutional   14
and God-given rights. The nations of Asia and Africa are moving with jetlike speed toward gaining political independence, but we still creep at horse-and-buggy pace toward gaining a cup of coffee at a lunch counter. Perhaps it is easy for those who have never felt the stinging darts of segregation to say, "Wait." But when you have seen vicious mobs lynch your mothers and fathers at will and drown your sisters and brothers at whim; when you have seen hate-filled policemen curse, kick, and even kill your black brothers and sisters; when you see the vast majority of your twenty million Negro brothers smothering in an airtight cage of poverty in the midst of an affluent society; when you suddenly find your tongue twisted and your speech stammering as you seek to explain to your six-year-old daughter why she can't go to the public amusement park that has just been advertised on television, and see tears welling up in her eyes when she is told that Funtown is closed to colored children, and see ominous clouds of inferiority beginning to form in her little mental sky, and see her beginning to distort her personality by developing an unconscious bitterness toward white people; when you have to concoct an answer for a five-year-old son who is asking: "Daddy, why do white people treat colored people so mean?"; when you take a cross-country drive and find it necessary to sleep night after night in the uncomfortable corners of your automobile because no motel will accept you; when you are humiliated day in and day out by nagging signs reading "white" and "colored"; when your first name becomes "nigger," your middle name becomes "boy" (however old you are) and your last name becomes "John," and your wife and mother are never given the respected title "Mrs."; when you are harried by day and haunted by night by the fact that you are a Negro, living constantly at tiptoe stance, never quite knowing what to expect next, and are plagued with inner fears and outer resentments; when you are forever fighting a degenerating sense of "nobodiness"—then you will understand why we find it difficult to wait. There comes a time

when the cup of endurance runs over, and men are no longer willing to be plunged into the abyss of despair. I hope, sirs, you can understand our legitimate and unavoidable impatience.

You express a great deal of anxiety over our willingness to break laws. This is certainly a legitimate concern. Since we so diligently urge people to obey the Supreme Court's decision of 1954 outlawing segregation in the public schools, at first glance it may seem rather paradoxical for us consciously to break laws. One may well ask: "How can you advocate breaking some laws and obeying others?" The answer lies in the fact that there are two types of laws: just and unjust. I would be the first to advocate obeying just laws. One has not only a legal but a moral responsibility to obey just laws. Conversely, one has a moral responsibility to disobey unjust laws. I would agree with St. Augustine that "an unjust law is no law at all." 15

Now, what is the difference between the two? How does one determine whether a law is just or unjust? A just law is a man-made code that squares with the moral law or the law of God. An unjust law is a code that is out of harmony with the moral law. To put it in the terms of St. Thomas Aquinas: An unjust law is a human law that is not rooted in eternal law and natural law. Any law that uplifts human personality is just. Any law that degrades human personality is unjust. All segregation statutes are unjust because segregation distorts the soul and damages the personality. It gives the segregator a false sense of superiority and the segregated a false sense of inferiority. Segregation, to use the terminology of the Jewish philosopher Martin Buber, substitutes an "I-it" relationship for an "I-thou" relationship and ends up relegating persons to the status of things. Hence segregation is not only politically, economically, and sociologically unsound, it is morally wrong and sinful. Paul Tillich has said that sin is separation. Is not segregation an existential expression of man's tragic separation, his awful estrangement, his terrible sinfulness? Thus it is that I can urge men to obey the 1954 decision of the Supreme Court, for it is morally right; and I can urge them to disobey segregation ordinances, for they are morally wrong. 16

Let us consider a more concrete example of just and unjust laws. An unjust law is a code that a numerical or power majority group compels a minority group to obey but does not make 17

binding on itself. This is *difference* made legal. By the same token, a just law is a code that a majority compels a minority to
follow and that it is willing to follow itself. This is *sameness*
made legal.

Let me give another explanation. A law is unjust if it is in-   18
flicted on a minority that, as a result of being denied the right to
vote, had no part in enacting or devising the law. Who can say
that the legislature of Alabama which set up that state's segregation laws was democratically elected? Throughout Alabama all
sorts of devious methods are used to prevent Negroes from becoming registered voters, and there are some counties in which,
even though Negroes constitute a majority of the population,
not a single Negro is registered. Can any law enacted under such
circumstances be considered democratically structured?

Sometimes a law is just on its face and unjust in its applica-   19
tion. For instance, I have been arrested on a charge of parading
without a permit. Now, there is nothing wrong in having an or-
dinance which requires a permit for a parade. But such an ordi-
nance becomes unjust when it is used to maintain segregation
and to deny citizens the First-Amendment privilege of peaceful
assembly and protest.

I hope you are able to see the distinction I am trying to point   20
out. In no sense do I advocate evading or defying the law, as
would the rabid segregationist. That would lead to anarchy. One
who breaks an unjust law must do so openly, lovingly, and with
a willingness to accept the penalty. I submit that an individual
who breaks a law that conscience tells him is unjust, and who
willingly accepts the penalty of imprisonment in order to arouse
the conscience of the community over its injustice, is in reality
expressing the highest respect for law.

Of course, there is nothing new about this kind of civil dis-   21
obedience. It was evidenced sublimely in the refusal of Shadrach,
Meshach, and Abednego to obey the laws of Nebuchadnezzar,[2]
on the ground that a higher moral law was at stake. It was practiced superbly by the early Christians, who were willing to face
hungry lions and the excruciating pain of chopping blocks rather
than submit to certain unjust laws of the Roman Empire. To a
degree, academic freedom is a reality today because Socrates

2. King refers to the biblical story recorded in Dan. 3.

practiced civil disobedience. In our own nation, the Boston Tea Party represented a massive act of civil disobedience.

We should never forget that everything Adolf Hitler did in   22
Germany was "legal" and everything the Hungarian freedom fighters did in Hungary was "illegal." It was "illegal" to aid and comfort a Jew in Hitler's Germany. Even so, I am sure that, had I lived in Germany at the time, I would have aided and comforted my Jewish brothers. If today I lived in a Communist country where certain principles dear to the Christian faith are suppressed, I would openly advocate disobeying that country's antireligious laws.

I must make two honest confessions to you, my Christian and   23
Jewish brothers. First, I must confess that over the past few years I have been gravely disappointed with the white moderate. I have almost reached the regrettable conclusion that the Negro's great stumbling block in his stride toward freedom is not the White Citizen's Counciler or the Ku Klux Klanner, but the white moderate, who is more devoted to "order" than to justice; who prefers a negative peace which is the absence of tension to a positive peace which is the presence of justice; who constantly says: "I agree with you in the goal you seek, but I cannot agree with your methods of direct action"; who paternalistically believes he can set the timetable for another man's freedom; who lives by a mythical concept of time and who constantly advises the Negro to wait for a "more convenient season." Shallow understanding from people of good will is more frustrating than absolute misunderstanding from people of ill will. Lukewarm acceptance is much more bewildering than outright rejection.

I had hoped that the white moderate would understand that   24
law and order exist for the purpose of establishing justice and that when they fail in this purpose they become the dangerously structured dams that block the flow of social progress. I had hoped that the white moderate would understand that the present tension in the South is a necessary phase of the transition from an obnoxious negative peace, in which the Negro passively accepted his unjust plight, to a substantive and positive peace, in which all men will respect the dignity and worth of human personality. Actually, we who engage in nonviolent direct action are not the creators of tension. We merely bring to the surface the hidden tension that is already alive. We bring it out in the open,

where it can be seen and dealt with. Like a boil that can never be cured so long as it is covered up but must be opened with all its ugliness to the natural medicines of air and light, injustice must be exposed, with all the tension its exposure creates, to the light of human conscience and the air of national opinion before it can be cured.

In your statement you assert that our actions, even though peaceful, must be condemned because they precipitate violence. But is this a logical assertion? Isn't this like condemning a robbed man because his possession of money precipitated the evil act of robbery? Isn't this like condemning Socrates because his unswerving commitment to truth and his philosophical inquiries precipitated the act by the misguided populace in which they made him drink hemlock? Isn't this like condemning Jesus because his unique God-consciousness and never-ceasing devotion to God's will precipitated the evil act of crucifixion? We must come to see that, as the federal courts have consistently affirmed, it is wrong to urge an individual to cease his efforts to gain his basic constitutional rights because the quest may precipitate violence. Society must protect the robbed and punish the robber. 25

I had also hoped that the white moderate would reject the myth concerning time in relation to the struggle for freedom. I have just received a letter from a white brother in Texas. He writes: "All Christians know that the colored people will receive equal rights eventually, but it is possible that you are in too great a religious hurry It has taken Christianity almost two thousand years to accomplish what it has. The teachings of Christ take time to come to earth." Such an attitude stems from a tragic misconception of time, from the strangely irrational notion that there is something in the very flow of time that will inevitably cure all ills. Actually, time itself is neutral; it can be used either destructively or constructively. More and more I feel that the people of ill will have used time much more effectively than have the people of good will. We will have to repent in this generation not merely for the hateful words and actions of the bad people but for the appalling silence of the good people. Human progress never rolls in on wheels of inevitability; it comes through the tireless efforts of men willing to be co-workers with God, and without this hard work, time itself becomes an ally of the forces of social stagnation. We must use time creatively, in the knowl- 26 edge that the time is always ripe to do right. Now is the time to make real the promise of democracy and transform our pending national elegy into a creative psalm of brotherhood. Now is the time to lift our national policy from the quicksand of racial injustice to the solid rock of human dignity.

You speak of our activity in Birmingham as extreme. At first I was rather disappointed that fellow clergymen would see my nonviolent efforts as those of an extremist. I began thinking about the fact that I stand in the middle of two opposing forces in the Negro community. One is a force of complacency, made up in part of Negroes who, as a result of long years of oppression, are so drained of self-respect and a sense of "somebodiness" that they have adjusted to segregation; and in part of a few middle-class Negroes who, because of a degree of academic and economic security and because in some ways they profit by segregation, have become insensitive to the problems of the masses. The other force is one of bitterness and hatred, and it comes perilously close to advocating violence. It is expressed in the various black nationalist groups that are springing up across the nation, the largest and best-known being Elijah Muhammad's Muslim movement. Nourished by the Negro's frustration over the continued existence of racial discrimination, this movement is made up of people who have lost faith in America, who have absolutely repudiated Christianity, and who have concluded that the white man is an incorrigible "devil."

I have tried to stand between these two forces, saying that we need emulate neither the "do-nothingism" of the complacent nor the hatred and despair of the black nationalist. For there is the more excellent way of love and nonviolent protest. I am grateful to God that, through the influence of the Negro church, the way of nonviolence became an integral part of our struggle.

If this philosophy had not emerged, by now many streets of the South would, I am convinced, be flowing with blood. And I am further convinced that if our white brothers dismiss as "rabble-rousers" and "outside agitators" those of us who employ nonviolent direct action, and if they refuse to support our nonviolent efforts, millions of Negroes will, out of frustration and despair, seek solace and security in black-nationalist ideologies—a development that would inevitably lead to a frightening racial nightmare.

Oppressed people cannot remain oppressed forever. The   30
yearning for freedom eventually manifests itself, and that is what
has happened to the American Negro. Something within has reminded him of his birthright of freedom, and something without
has reminded him that it can be gained. Consciously or unconsciously, he has been caught up by the *Zeitgeist*,[3] and with his
black brothers of Africa and his brown and yellow brothers of
Asia, South America and the Caribbean, the United States Negro
is moving with a sense of great urgency toward the promised
land of racial justice. If one recognizes this vital urge that has engulfed the Negro community, one should readily understand
why public demonstrations are taking place. The Negro has
many pent-up resentments and latent frustrations, and he must
release them. So let him march; let him make prayer pilgrimages
to the city hall; let him go on freedom rides—and try to understand why he must do so. If his repressed emotions are not released in nonviolent ways, they will seek expression through
violence; this is not a threat but a fact of history. So I have not
said to my people: "Get rid of your discontent." Rather, I have
tried to say that this normal and healthy discontent can be chan-
neled into the creative outlet of nonviolent direct action. And
now this approach is being termed extremist.

But though I was initially disappointed at being categorized as   31
an extremist, as I continued to think about the matter I gradually
gained a measure of satisfaction from the label. Was not Jesus an
extremist for love: "Love your enemies, bless them that curse
you, do good to them that hate you, and pray for them which de-
spitefully use you, and persecute you." Was not Amos an extremist for justice: "Let justice roll down like waters and
righteousness like an ever-flowing stream." Was not Paul an extremist for the Christian gospel: "I bear in my body the marks of
the Lord Jesus." Was not Martin Luther an extremist: "Here I
stand; I cannot do otherwise, so help me God." And John Bun-
yan: "I will stay in jail to the end of my days before I make a
butchery of my conscience." And Abraham Lincoln: "This nation cannot survive half slave and half free." And Thomas Jefferson: "We hold these truths to be self-evident, that all men are
created equal. . . ." So the question is not whether we will be extremists, but what kind of extremists we will be. Will we be ex-

3. *Zeitgeist:* spirit of the age (German).

tremists for hate or for love? Will we be extremists for the preservation of injustice or for the extension of justice? In that dramatic scene on Calvary's hill three men were crucified. We must never forget that all three were crucified for the same crime—the crime of extremism. Two were extremists for immorality, and thus fell below their environment. The other, Jesus Christ, was an extremist for love, truth, and goodness, and thereby rose above his environment. Perhaps the South, the nation, and the world are in dire need of creative extremists.

I had hoped that the white moderate would see this need. Perhaps I was too optimistic; perhaps I expected too much. I suppose I should have realized that few members of the oppressor race can understand the deep groans and passionate yearnings of the oppressed race, and still fewer have the vision to see that injustice must be rooted out by strong, persistent, and determined action. I am thankful, however, that some of our white brothers in the South have grasped the meaning of this social revolution and committed themselves to it. They are still all too few in quantity, but they are big in quality. Some—such as Ralph McGill, Lillian Smith, Harry Golden, James McBride Dabbs, Ann Braden, and Sarah Patton Boyle—have written about our struggle in eloquent and prophetic terms. Others have marched with us down nameless streets to the South. They have languished in filthy, roach-infested jails, suffering the abuse and brutality of policemen who view them as "dirty nigger-lovers." Unlike so many of their moderate brothers and sisters, they have recognized the urgency of the moment and sensed the need for powerful "action" antidotes to combat the disease of segregation. 32

Let me take note of my other major disappointment. I have been so greatly disappointed with the white church and its leadership. Of course, there are some notable exceptions. I am not unmindful of the fact that each of you has taken some significant stands on this issue. I commend you, Reverend Stallings, for your Christian stand on this past Sunday, in welcoming Negroes to your worship service on a nonsegregated basis. I commend the Catholic leaders of this state for integrating Spring Hill College several years ago. 33

But despite these notable exceptions, I must honestly reiterate that I have been disappointed with the church. I do not say this as one of those negative critics who can always find something 34 wrong with the church. I say this as a minister of the gospel, who loves the church; who was nurtured in its bosom; who has been sustained by its spiritual blessings and who will remain true to it as long as the cord of life shall lengthen.

When I was suddenly catapulted into the leadership of the bus protest in Montgomery, Alabama, a few years ago, I felt we would be supported by the white church. I felt that the white ministers, priests, and rabbis of the South would be among our strongest allies. Instead, some have been outright opponents, refusing to understand the freedom movement and misrepresenting its leaders; all too many others have been more cautious than courageous and have remained silent behind the anesthetizing security of stained-glass windows. [35]

In spite of my shattered dreams, I came to Birmingham with the hope that the white religious leadership of this community would see the justice of our cause and, with deep moral concern, would serve as the channel through which our just grievances could reach the power structure. I had hoped that each of you would understand. But again I have been disappointed. [36]

I have heard numerous southern religious leaders admonish their worshipers to comply with a desegregation decision because it is the law, but I have longed to hear white ministers declare: "Follow this decree because integration is morally right and because the Negro is your brother." In the midst of blatant injustices inflicted upon the Negro, I have watched white churchmen stand on the sideline and mouth pious irrelevancies and sanctimonious trivialities. In the midst of a mighty struggle to rid our nation of racial and economic injustice, I have heard many ministers say: "Those are social issues, with which the gospel has no real concern." And I have watched many churches commit themselves to a completely otherworldly religion which makes a strange, un-Biblical distinction between body and soul, between the sacred and the secular. [37]

I have traveled the length and breadth of Alabama, Mississippi, and all the other southern states. On sweltering summer days and crisp autumn mornings I have looked at the South's beautiful churches with their lofty spires pointing heavenward. I have beheld the impressive outlines of her massive religious-education buildings. Over and over I have found myself asking: "What kind of people worship here? Who is their God? Where [38] were their voices when the lips of Governor Barnett[4] dripped with words of interposition and nullification? Where were they when Governor Wallace[5] gave a clarion call for defiance and hatred? Where were their voices of support when bruised and weary Negro men and women decided to rise from the dark dungeons of complacency to the bright hills of creative protest?"

Yes, these questions are still in my mind. In deep disappointment I have wept over the laxity of the church. But be assured that my tears have been tears of love. There can be no deep disappointment where there is not deep love. Yes, I love the church. How could I do otherwise? I am in the rather unique position of being the son, the grandson and the great-grandson of preachers. Yes, I see the church as the body of Christ. But, oh! How we have blemished and scarred that body through social neglect and through fear of being nonconformists. 39

There was a time when the church was very powerful—in the time when the early Christians rejoiced at being deemed worthy to suffer for what they believed. In those days the church was not merely a thermometer that recorded the ideas and principles of popular opinion; it was a thermostat that transformed the mores of society. Whenever the early Christians entered a town, the people in power became disturbed and immediately sought to convict the Christians for being "disturbers of the peace" and "outside agitators." But the Christians pressed on, in the conviction that they were "a colony of heaven," called to obey God rather than man. Small in number, they were big in commitment. They were too God-intoxicated to be "astronomically intimidated." By their effort and example they brought an end to such ancient evils as infanticide and gladiatorial contests. 40

Things are different now. So often the contemporary church is a weak, ineffectual voice with an uncertain sound. So often it is an archdefender of the status quo. Far from being disturbed by the presence of the church, the power structure of the average community is consoled by the church's silent—and often even vocal—sanction of things as they are. 41

4. Ross Barnett, governor of Mississippi, in 1962 ordered resistance to the registration of a black student, James Meredith, at the University of Mississippi.
5. George Wallace, governor of Alabama, stood in a doorway of the University of Alabama in a symbolic effort to block the registration of two black students in 1963.

But the judgment of God is upon the church as never before.   42
If today's church does not recapture the sacrificial spirit of the
early church, it will lose its authenticity, forfeit the loyalty of millions, and be dismissed as an irrelevant social club with no meaning for the twentieth century. Every day I meet young people
whose disappointment with the church has turned into outright
disgust.

Perhaps I have once again been too optimistic. Is organized re-   43
ligion too inextricably bound to the status quo to save our nation and the world? Perhaps I must turn my faith to the inner
spiritual church, the church within the church, as the true *ekklesia*[6] and the hope of the world. But again I am thankful to God
that some noble souls from the ranks of organized religion have
broken loose from the paralyzing chains of conformity and
joined us as active partners in the struggle for freedom. They
have left their secure congregations and walked the streets of Albany, Georgia, with us. They have gone down the highways of
the South on tortuous rides for freedom. Yes, they have gone to
jail with us. Some have been dismissed from their churches, have
lost the support of their bishops and fellow ministers. But they
have acted in the faith that right defeated is stronger than evil triumphant. Their witness has been the spiritual salt that has preserved the true meaning of the gospel in these troubled times.
They have carved a tunnel of hope through the dark mountain of
disappointment.

I hope the church as a whole will meet the challenge of this de-   44
cisive hour. But even if the church does not come to the aid of
justice, I have no despair about the future. I have no fear about
the outcome of our struggle in Birmingham, even if our motives
are at present misunderstood. We will reach the goal of freedom
in Birmingham and all over the nation, because the goal of
America is freedom. Abused and scorned though we may be, our
destiny is tied up with America's destiny. Before the pilgrims
landed at Plymouth, we were here. Before the pen of Jefferson
etched the majestic words of the Declaration of Independence
across the pages of history, we were here. For more than two
centuries our forebears labored in this country without wages;
they made cotton king; they built the homes of their masters
while suffering gross injustice and shameful humiliation—and

6. *ekklesia:* literally, "assembly of the people" (Greek).

yet out of a bottomless vitality they continued to thrive and develop. If the inexpressible cruelties of slavery could not stop us, the opposition we now face will surely fail. We will win our freedom because the sacred heritage of our nation and the eternal will of God are embodied in our echoing demands.

Before closing I feel impelled to mention one other point in   45
your statement that has troubled me profoundly. You warmly commended the Birmingham police force for keeping "order" and "preventing violence." I doubt that you would have so warmly commended the police force if you had seen its dogs sinking their teeth into unarmed, nonviolent Negroes. I doubt that you would so quickly commend the policemen if you were to observe their ugly and inhumane treatment of Negroes here in the city jail; if you were to watch them push and curse old Negro women and young Negro girls; if you were to see them slap and kick old Negro men and young boys; if you were to observe them, as they did on two occasions, refuse to give us food because we wanted to sing our grace together. I cannot join you in your praise of the Birmingham police department.

It is true that the police have exercised a degree of discipline   46
in handling the demonstrators. In this sense they have conducted them selves rather "nonviolently" in public. But for what purpose? To preserve the evil system of segregation. Over the past few years I have consistently preached that nonviolence demands that the means we use must be as pure as the ends we seek. I have tried to make clear that it is wrong to use immoral means to attain moral ends. But now I must affirm that it is just as wrong, or perhaps even more so, to use moral means to preserve immoral ends. Perhaps Mr. Connor and his policemen have been rather nonviolent in public, as was Chief Pritchett in Albany, Georgia, but they have used the moral means of nonviolence to maintain the immoral end of racial injustice. As T. S. Eliot has said: "The last temptation is the greatest treason: To do the right deed for the wrong reason."

I wish you had commended the Negro sit-inners and demon-   47
strators of Birmingham for their sublime courage, their willingness to suffer, and their amazing discipline in the midst of great provocation. One day the South will recognize its real heroes. They will be the James Merediths, with the noble sense of purpose that enables them to face jeering and hostile mobs, and with the agonizing loneliness that characterizes the life of the pioneer.

They will be old, oppressed, battered Negro women, symbolized in a seventy-two-year-old woman in Montgomery, Alabama, who rose up with a sense of dignity and with her people decided not to ride segregated buses, and who responded with ungrammatical profundity to one who inquired about her weariness: "My feets is tired, but my soul is at rest." They will be the young high school and college students, the young ministers of the gospel and a host of their elders, courageously and nonviolently sitting in at lunch counters and willingly going to jail for conscience' sake. One day the South will know that when these disinherited children of God sat down at lunch counters, they were in reality standing up for what is best in the American dream and for the most sacred values in our Judaeo-Christian heritage, thereby bringing our nation back to those great wells of democracy which were dug deep by the founding fathers in their formulation of the Constitution and the Declaration of Independence.

Never before have I written so long a letter. I'm afraid it is   48
much too long to take your precious time. I can assure you that it would have been much shorter if I had been writing from a comfortable desk, but what else can one do when he is alone in a narrow jail cell, other than write long letters, think long thoughts, and pray long prayers?

If I have said anything in this letter that overstates the truth   49
and indicates an unreasonable impatience, I beg you to forgive me. If I have said anything that understates the truth and indicates my having a patience that allows me to settle for anything less than brotherhood, I beg God to forgive me.

I hope this letter finds you strong in the faith. I also hope that   50
circumstances will soon make it possible for me to meet each of you, not as an integrationist or a civil-rights leader but as a fellow clergyman and a Christian brother. Let us all hope that the dark clouds of racial prejudice will soon pass away and the deep fog of misunderstanding will be lifted from our fear-drenched communities, and in some not too distant tomorrow the radiant stars of love and brotherhood will shine over our great nation with all their scintillating beauty.

Yours for the cause of Peace and Brotherhood,
MARTIN LUTHER KING JR.

FLANNERY O'CONNOR

Revelation

Flannery O'Connor was one of the leading southern writers of the twentieth century. A devout Catholic who grew up in rural Georgia in the Protestant "Bible Belt," she wrote stories that combined religious themes, grotesque humor, and the realism of someone who has studied her neighbors carefully. Her subject, she once said, was "the action of grace in a territory controlled largely by the devil." "Revelation" was first published in *The Sewanee Review* in 1964.

The doctor's waiting room, which was very small, was almost full when the Turpins entered and Mrs. Turpin, who was very large, made it look even smaller by her presence. She stood looming at the head of the magazine table set in the center of it, a living demonstration that the room was inadequate and ridiculous. Her little bright black eyes took in all the patients as she sized up the seating situation. There was one vacant chair and a place on the sofa occupied by a blond child in a dirty blue romper who should have been told to move over and make room for the lady. He was five or six, but Mrs. Turpin saw at once that no one was going to tell him to move over. He was slumped down in the seat, his arms idle at his sides and his eyes idle in his head; his nose ran unchecked.

Mrs. Turpin put a firm hand on Claud's shoulder and said in a voice that included everyone that wanted to listen, "Claud, you sit in that chair there," and gave him a push down into the vacant one. Claud was florid and bald and sturdy, somewhat shorter than Mrs. Turpin, but he sat down as if he were accustomed to doing what she told him to.

Mrs. Turpin remained standing. The only man in the room besides Claud was a lean stringy old fellow with a rusty hand spread out on each knee, whose eyes were closed as if he were asleep or dead or pretending to be so as not to get up and offer her his seat. Her gaze settled agreeably on a well-dressed grey-haired lady whose eyes met hers and whose expression said: if that child belonged to me, he would have some manners and move over—there's plenty of room there for you and him too.

Claud looked up with a sigh and made as if to rise.   4

"Sit down," Mrs. Turpin said. "You know you're not sup-   5
posed to stand on that leg. He has an ulcer on his leg," she explained.

Claud lifted his foot onto the magazine table and rolled his   6
trouser leg up to reveal a purple swelling on a plump
marble-white calf.

"My!" the pleasant lady said. "How did you do that?"   7

"A cow kicked him," Mrs. Turpin said.   8

"Goodness!" said the lady.   9

Claud rolled his trouser leg down.   10

"Maybe the little boy would move over," the lady suggested,   11
but the child did not stir.

"Somebody will be leaving in a minute," Mrs. Turpin said. She   12
could not understand why a doctor—with as much money as they
made charging five dollars a day just to stick their head in the hospital door and look at you—couldn't afford a decent-sized waiting room. This one was hardly bigger than a garage. The table
was cluttered with limp-looking magazines and at one end of it
there was a big green glass ash tray full of cigaret butts and cotton wads with little blood spots on them. If she had had anything
to do with the running of the place, that would have been emptied every so often. There were no chairs against the wall at the
head of the room. It had a rectangular-shaped panel in it that permitted a view of the office where the nurse came and went and the
secretary listened to the radio. A plastic fern in a gold pot sat in
the opening and trailed its fronds down almost to the floor. The
radio was softly playing gospel music.

Just then the inner door opened and a nurse with the highest   13
stack of yellow hair Mrs. Turpin had ever seen put her face in the
crack and called for the next patient. The woman sitting beside
Claud grasped the two arms of her chair and hoisted herself up;
she pulled her dress free from her legs and lumbered through the
door where the nurse had disappeared.

Mrs. Turpin eased into the vacant chair, which held her tight   14
as a corset. "I wish I could reduce," she said, and rolled her eyes
and gave a comic sigh.

"Oh, *you* aren't fat," the stylish lady said.   15

"Ooooo I am too," Mrs. Turpin said. "Claud he eats all he   16
wants to and never weighs over one hundred and seventy-five

pounds, but me I just look at something good to eat and I gain some weight," and her stomach and shoulders shook with laughter. "You can eat all you want to, can't you, Claud?" she asked turning to him.

Claud only grinned. 17

"Well, as long as you have such a good disposition," the stylish lady said, "I don't think it makes a bit of difference what size you are. You just can't beat a good disposition." 18

Next to her was a fat girl of eighteen or nineteen, scowling into a thick blue book which Mrs. Turpin saw was entitled *Human Development*. The girl raised her head and directed her scowl at Mrs. Turpin as if she did not like her looks. She appeared annoyed that anyone should speak while she tried to read. The poor girl's face was blue with acne and Mrs. Turpin thought how pitiful it was to have a face like that at that age. She gave the girl a friendly smile but the girl only scowled the harder. Mrs. Turpin herself was fat but she had always had good skin, and, though she was forty-seven years old, there was not a wrinkle in her face except around her eyes from laughing too much. 19

Next to the ugly girl was the child, still in exactly the same position, and next to him was a thin leathery old woman in a cotton print dress. She and Claud had three sacks of chicken feed in their pump house that was in the same print. She had seen from the first that the child belonged with the old woman. She could tell by the way they sat—kind of vacant and white-trashy, as if they would sit there until Doomsday if nobody called and told them to get up. And at right angles but next to the well-dressed pleasant lady was a lank-faced woman who was certainly the child's mother. She had on a yellow sweat shirt and wine-colored slacks, both gritty-looking, and the rims of her lips were stained with snuff. Her dirty yellow hair was tied behind with a piece of red paper ribbon. Worse than niggers any day, Mrs. Turpin thought. 20

The gospel hymn playing was, "When I looked up and He looked down," and Mrs. Turpin, who knew it, supplied the last line mentally, "And wona these days I know I'll we-eara crown." 21

Without appearing to, Mrs. Turpin always noticed people's feet. The well-dressed lady had on red and grey suede shoes to match her dress. Mrs. Turpin had on her good black patent leather pumps. The ugly girl had on Girl Scout shoes and heavy socks. The old woman had on tennis shoes and the white-trashy 22 mother had on what appeared to be bedroom slippers, black straw with gold braid threaded through them—exactly what you would have expected her to have on.

Sometimes at night when she couldn't go to sleep, Mrs. 23 Turpin would occupy herself with the question of who she would have chosen to be if she couldn't have been herself. If Jesus had said to her before he made her, "There's only two places available for you. You can either be a nigger or white-trash," what would she have said? "Please, Jesus, please," she would have said, "just let me wait until there's another place available," and he would have said, "No, you have to go right now and I have only those two places so make up your mind." She would have wiggled and squirmed and begged and pleaded but it would have been no use and finally she would have said, "All right, make me a nigger then—but that don't mean a trashy one." And he would have made her a neat clean respectable Negro woman, herself but black.

Next to the child's mother was a red-headed youngish 24 woman, reading one of the magazines and working a piece of chewing gum, hell for leather, as Claud would say. Mrs. Turpin could not see the woman's feet. She was not white-trash, just common. Sometimes Mrs. Turpin occupied herself at night naming the classes of people. On the bottom of the heap were most colored people, not the kind she would have been if she had been one, but most of them; then next to them—not above, just away from—were the white-trash; then above them were the home-owners, and above them the home-and-land owners, to which she and Claud belonged. Above she and Claud were people with a lot of money and much bigger houses and much more land. But here the complexity of it would begin to bear in on her, for some of the people with a lot of money were common and ought to be below she and Claud and some of the people who had good blood had lost their money and had to rent and then there were colored people who owned their homes and land as well. There was a colored dentist in town who had two red Lincolns and a swimming pool and a farm with registered white-face cattle on it. Usually by the time she had fallen asleep all the classes of people were moiling and roiling around in her head, and she would dream they were all crammed in together in a box car, being ridden off to be put in a gas oven.

"That's a beautiful clock," she said and nodded to her right.   25
It was a big wall clock, the face encased in a brass sunburst.

"Yes, it's very pretty," the stylish lady said agreeably. "And   26
right on the dot too," she added, glancing at her watch.

The ugly girl beside her cast an eye upward at the clock,   27
smirked, then looked directly at Mrs. Turpin and smirked again.
Then she returned her eyes to her book. She was obviously the
lady's daughter because, although they didn't look anything
alike as to disposition, they both had the same shape of face and
same blue eyes. On the lady they sparkled pleasantly but in the
girl's seared face they appeared alternately to smolder and to
blaze.

What if Jesus had said, "All right, you can be white-trash or a   28
nigger or ugly!"

Mrs. Turpin felt an awful pity for the girl, though she thought   29
it was one thing to be ugly and another to act ugly.

The woman with the snuff-stained lips turned around in her   30
chair and looked up at the clock. Then she turned back and appeared to look a little to the side of Mrs. Turpin. There was a
cast in one of her eyes. "You want to know wher you can get one
of themther clocks?" she asked in a loud voice.

"No, I already have a nice clock," Mrs. Turpin said. Once   31
somebody like her got a leg in the conversation, she would be all
over it.

"You can get you one with green stamps," the woman said.   32
"That's most likely wher he got hisn. Save you up enough, you
can get you most anythang. I got me some joo'ry."

Ought to have got you a wash rag and some soap, Mrs.   33
Turpin thought.

"I get contour sheets with mine," the pleasant lady said.   34

The daughter slammed her book shut. She looked straight   35
in front of her, directly through Mrs. Turpin and on through
the yellow curtain and the plate glass window which made
the wall behind her. The girl's eyes seemed lit all of a sudden with
a peculiar light, an unnatural light like night road signs give.
Mrs. Turpin turned her head to see if there was anything going
on outside that she should see, but she could not see anything.
Figures passing cast only a pale shadow through the curtain.
There was no reason the girl should single her out for her ugly
looks.

"Miss Finley," the nurse said, cracking the door. The gum-   36
chewing woman got up and passed in front of her and Claud and
went into the office. She had on red high-heeled shoes.

Directly across the table, the ugly girl's eyes were fixed on   37
Mrs. Turpin as if she had some very special reason for disliking
her.

"This is wonderful weather, isn't it?" the girl's mother said.   38

"It's good weather for cotton if you can get the niggers to pick   39
it," Mrs. Turpin said, "but niggers don't want to pick cotton any
more. You can't get the white folks to pick it and now you can't
get the niggers—because they got to be right up there with the
white folks."

"They gonna *try* anyways," the white-trash woman said,   40
leaning forward.

"Do you have one of those cotton-picking machines?" the   41
pleasant lady asked.

"No," Mrs. Turpin said, "they leave half the cotton in the   42
field. We don't have much cotton anyway. If you want to make it
farming now, you have to have a little of everything. We got a
couple of acres of cotton and a few hogs and chickens and just
enough white-face that Claud can look after them himself."

"One thang I don't want," the white-trash woman said, wip-   43
ing her mouth with the back of her hand. "Hogs. Nasty stinking
things, a-gruntin and a-rootin all over the place."

Mrs. Turpin gave her the merest edge of her attention: "Our   44
hogs are not dirty and they don't stink," she said. "They're
cleaner than some children I've seen. Their feet never touch the
ground. We have a pig-parlor—that's where you raise them on
concrete," she explained to the pleasant lady, "and Claud scoots
them down with the hose every afternoon and washes off the
floor." Cleaner by far than that child right there, she thought.
Poor nasty little thing. He had not moved except to put the
thumb of his dirty hand into his mouth.

The woman turned her face away from Mrs. Turpin. "I know   45
I wouldn't scoot down no hog with no hose," she said to the
wall.

You wouldn't have no hog to scoot down, Mrs. Turpin said to   46
herself.

"A-gruntin and a-rootin and a-groanin," the woman mut-   47
tered.

"We got a little of everything," Mrs. Turpin said to the pleas- 48
ant lady. "It's no use in having more than you can handle yourself with help like it is. We found enough niggers to pick our
cotton this year but Claud he has to go after them and take them
home again in the evening. They can't walk that half a mile. No
they can't. I tell you," she said and laughed merrily, "I sure am
tired of buttering up niggers, but you got to love em if you want
em to work for you. When they come in the morning, I run out
and I say, 'Hi yawl this morning?' and when Claud drives them
off to the field I just wave to beat the band and they just wave
back." And she waved her hand rapidly to illustrate.

"Like you read out of the same book," the lady said, showing 49
she understood perfectly.

"Child, yes," Mrs. Turpin said. "And when they come in from 50
the field, I run out with a bucket of icewater. That's the way it's
going to be from now on," she said. "You may as well face it."

"One thang I know," the white-trash woman said. "Two 51
thangs I ain't going to do: love no niggers or scoot down no hog
with no hose." And she let out a bark of contempt.

The look that Mrs. Turpin and the pleasant lady exchanged 52
indicated they both understood that you had to *have* certain
things before you could *know* certain things. But every time Mrs.
Turpin exchanged a look with the lady, she was aware that the
ugly girl's peculiar eyes were still on her, and she had trouble
bringing her attention back to the conversation.

"When you got something," she said, "you got to look after 53
it." And when you ain't got a thing but breath and britches, she
added to herself, you can afford to come to town every morning
and just sit on the Court House coping and spit.

A grotesque revolving shadow passed across the curtain be- 54
hind her and was thrown palely on the opposite wall. Then a bicycle clattered down against the outside of the building. The
door opened and a colored boy glided in with a tray from the
drug store. It had two large red and white paper cups on it with
tops on them. He was a tall, very black boy in discolored white
pants and a green nylon shirt. He was chewing gum slowly, as if
to music. He set the tray down in the office opening next to the
fern and stuck his head through to look for the secretary. She
was not in there. He rested his arms on the ledge and waited, his
narrow bottom stuck out, swaying slowly to the left and right.

He raised a hand over his head and scratched the base of his skull.

"You see that button there, boy?" Mrs. Turpin said. "You can punch that and she'll come. She's probably in the back somewhere."

"Is thas right?" the boy said agreeably, as if he had never seen the button before. He leaned to the right and put his finger on it. "She sometime out," he said and twisted around to face his audience, his elbows behind him on the counter. The nurse appeared and he twisted back again. She handed him a dollar and he rooted in his pocket and made the change and counted it out to her. She gave him fifteen cents for a tip and he went out with the empty tray. The heavy door swung to slowly and closed at length with the sound of suction. For a moment no one spoke.

"They ought to send all them niggers back to Africa," the white-trash woman said. "That's wher they come from in the first place."

"Oh, I couldn't do without my good colored friends," the pleasant lady said.

"There's a heap of things worse than a nigger," Mrs. Turpin agreed. "It's all kinds of them just like it's all kinds of us."

"Yes, and it takes all kinds to make the world go round," the lady said in her musical voice.

As she said it, the raw-complexioned girl snapped her teeth together. Her lower lip turned downwards and inside out, revealing the pale pink inside her mouth. After a second it rolled back up. It was the ugliest face Mrs. Turpin had ever seen anyone make and for a moment she was certain that the girl had made it at her. She was looking at her as if she had known and disliked her all her life—all of Mrs. Turpin's life, it seemed too, not just all the girl's life. Why, girl, I don't even know you, Mrs. Turpin said silently.

She forced her attention back to the discussion. "It wouldn't be practical to send them back to Africa," she said. "They wouldn't want to go. They got it too good here."

"Wouldn't be what they wanted—if I had anythang to do with it," the woman said.

"It wouldn't be a way in the world you could get all the niggers back over there," Mrs. Turpin said. "They'd be hiding out and lying down and turning sick on you and wailing and holler-

ing and raring and pitching. It wouldn't be a way in the world to
get them over there."

"They got over here," the trashy woman said. "Get back like   65
they got over."

"It wasn't so many of them then," Mrs. Turpin explained.   66

The woman looked at Mrs. Turpin as if here was an idiot in-   67
deed but Mrs. Turpin was not bothered by the look, considering
where it came from.

"Nooo," she said, "they're going to stay here where they can   68
go to New York and marry white folks and improve their color.
That's what they all want to do, every one of them, improve their
color."

"You know what comes of that, don't you?" Claud asked.   69

"No, Claud, what?" Mrs. Turpin said.   70

Claud's eyes twinkled. "White-faced niggers," he said with   71
never a smile.

Everybody in the office laughed except the white-trash and   72
the ugly girl. The girl gripped the book in her lap with white fingers. The trashy woman looked around her from face to face as
if she thought they were all idiots. The old woman in the feed
sack dress continued to gaze expressionless across the floor at
the high-top shoes of the man opposite her, the one who had
been pretending to be asleep when the Turpins came in. He was
laughing heartily, his hands still spread out on his knees. The
child had fallen to the side and was lying now almost face down
in the old woman's lap.

While they recovered from their laughter, the nasal chorus on   73
the radio kept the room from silence.

> *You go to blank blank*
> *And I'll go to mine*
> *But we'll all blank along*
> *To-geth-ther,*
> *And all along the blank*
> *We'll hep eachother out*
> *Smile-ling in any kind of*
> *Weath-ther!*

Mrs. Turpin didn't catch every word but she caught enough to
agree with the spirit of the song and it turned her thoughts sober.
To help anybody out that needed it was her philosophy of life.

She never spared herself when she found somebody in need, whether they were white or black, trash or decent. And of all she had to be thankful for, she was most thankful that this was so. If Jesus had said, "You can be high society and have all the money you want and be thin and svelte-like, but you can't be a good woman with it," she would have had to say, "Well don't make me that then. Make me a good woman and it don't matter what else, how fat or how ugly or how poor!" Her heart rose. He had not made her a nigger or white-trash or ugly! He had made her herself and given her a little of everything. Jesus, thank you! she said. Thank you thank you thank you! Whenever she counted her blessings she felt as buoyant as if she weighed one hundred and twenty-five pounds instead of one hundred and eighty.

"What's wrong with your little boy?" the pleasant lady asked   74
the white-trashy woman.

"He has a ulcer," the woman said proudly. "He ain't give me   75
a minute's peace since he was born. Him and her are just alike," she said, nodding at the old woman, who was running her leathery fingers through the child's pale hair. "Look like I can't get nothing down them two but Co' Cola and candy."

That's all you try to get down em, Mrs. Turpin said to herself.   76
Too lazy to light the fire. There was nothing you could tell her about people like them that she didn't know already. And it was not just that they didn't have anything. Because if you gave them everything, in two weeks it would all be broken or filthy or they would have chopped it up for lightwood. She knew all this from her own experience. Help them you must, but help them you couldn't.

All at once the ugly girl turned her lips inside out again. Her   77
eyes were fixed like two drills on Mrs. Turpin. This time there was no mistaking that there was something urgent behind them.

Girl, Mrs. Turpin exclaimed silently, I haven't done a thing to   78
you! The girl might be confusing her with somebody else. There was no need to sit by and let herself be intimidated. "You must be in college," she said boldly, looking directly at the girl. "I see you reading a book there."

The girl continued to stare and pointedly did not answer.   79

Her mother blushed at this rudeness. "The lady asked you a   80
question, Mary Grace," she said under her breath.

"I have ears," Mary Grace said.   81

The poor mother blushed again. "Mary Grace goes to Welles-   82
ley College," she explained. She twisted one of the buttons on
her dress. "In Massachusetts," she added with a grimace. "And
in the summer she just keeps right on studying. Just reads all the
time, a real book worm. She's done real well at Wellesley; she's
taking English and Math and History and Psychology and Social
Studies," she rattled on, "and I think it's too much. I think she
ought to get out and have fun."

The girl looked as if she would like to hurl them all through   83
the plate glass window.

"Way up north," Mrs. Turpin murmured and thought, well, it   84
hasn't done much for her manners.

"I'd almost rather to have him sick," the white-trash woman   85
said, wrenching the attention back to herself. "He's so mean
when he ain't. Look like some children just take natural to meanness. It's some gets bad when they get sick but he was the opposite. Took sick and turned good. He don't give me no trouble
now. It's me waitin to see the doctor," she said.

If I was going to send anybody back to Africa, Mrs. Turpin   86
thought, it would be your kind, woman. "Yes, indeed," she said
aloud, but looking up at the ceiling, "it's a heap of things worse
than a nigger." And dirtier than a hog, she added to herself.

"I think people with bad dispositions are more to be pitied   87
than anyone on earth," the pleasant lady said in a voice that was
decidedly thin.

"I thank the Lord he has blessed me with a good one," Mrs.   88
Turpin said. "The day has never dawned that I couldn't find
something to laugh at."

"Not since she married me anyways," Claud said with a com-   89
ical straight face.

Everybody laughed except the girl and the white-trash.   90

Mrs. Turpin's stomach shook. "He's such a caution," she said,   91
"that I can't help but laugh at him."

The girl made a loud ugly noise through her teeth.   92

Her mother's mouth grew thin and tight. "I think the worst   93
thing in the world," she said, "is an ungrateful person. To have
everything and not appreciate it. I know a girl," she said, "who
has parents who would give her anything, a little brother who
loves her dearly, who is getting a good education, who wears the

best clothes, but who can never say a kind word to anyone, who never smiles, who just criticizes and complains all day long."

"Is she too old to paddle?" Claud asked.   94

The girl's face was almost purple.   95

"Yes," the lady said, "I'm afraid there's nothing to do but leave her to her folly. Some day she'll wake up and it'll be too late."   96

"It never hurt anyone to smile," Mrs. Turpin said. "It just makes you feel better all over."   97

"Of course," the lady said sadly, "but there are just some people you can't tell anything to. They can't take criticism."   98

"If it's one thing I am," Mrs. Turpin said with feeling, "it's grateful. When I think who all I could have been besides myself and what all I got, a little of everything, and a good disposition besides, I just feel like shouting, 'Thank you, Jesus, for making everything the way it is!' It could have been different!" For one thing, somebody else could have got Claud. At the thought of this, she was flooded with gratitude and a terrible pang of joy ran through her. "Oh thank you, Jesus, Jesus, thank you!" she cried aloud.   99

The book struck her directly over her left eye. It struck almost at the same instant that she realized the girl was about to hurl it. Before she could utter a sound, the raw face came crashing across the table toward her, howling. The girl's fingers sank like clamps into the soft flesh of her neck. She heard the mother cry out and Claud shout, "Whoa!" There was an instant when she was certain that she was about to be in an earthquake.   100

All at once her vision narrowed and she saw everything as if it were happening in a small room far away, or as if she were looking at it through the wrong end of a telescope. Claud's face crumpled and fell out of sight. The nurse ran in, then out, then in again. Then the gangling figure of the doctor rushed out of the inner door. Magazines flew this way and that as the table turned over. The girl fell with a thud and Mrs. Turpin's vision suddenly reversed itself and she saw everything large instead of small. The eyes of the white-trashy woman were staring hugely at the floor. There the girl, held down on one side by the nurse and on the other by her mother, was wrenching and turning in their grasp. The doctor was kneeling astride her, trying to hold her arm down. He managed after a second to sink a long needle into it.   101

Mrs. Turpin felt entirely hollow except for her heart which   102
swung from side to side as if it were agitated in a great empty
drum of flesh.

"Somebody that's not busy call for the ambulance," the doc-   103
tor said in the off-hand voice young doctors adopt for terrible
occasions.

Mrs. Turpin could not have moved a finger. The old man who   104
had been sitting next to her skipped nimbly into the office and
made the call, for the secretary still seemed to be gone.

"Claud!" Mrs. Turpin called.   105

He was not in his chair. She knew she must jump up and find   106
him but she felt like some one trying to catch a train in a dream,
when everything moves in slow motion and the faster you try to
run the slower you go.

"Here I am," a suffocated voice, very unlike Claud's, said.   107

He was doubled up in the corner on the floor, pale as paper,   108
holding his leg. She wanted to get up and go to him but she could
not move. Instead, her gaze was drawn slowly downward to the
churning face on the floor, which she could see over the doctor's
shoulder.

The girl's eyes stopped rolling and focused on her. They   109
seemed a much lighter blue than before, as if a door that had
been tightly closed behind them was now open to admit light
and air.

Mrs. Turpin's head cleared and her power of motion returned.   110
She leaned forward until she was looking directly into the fierce
brilliant eyes. There was no doubt in her mind that the girl did
know her, knew her in some intense and personal way, beyond
time and place and condition. "What you got to say to me?" she
asked hoarsely and held her breath, waiting, as for a revelation.

The girl raised her head. Her gaze locked with Mrs. Turpin's.   111
"Go back to hell where you came from, you old wart hog," she
whispered. Her voice was low but clear. Her eyes burned for a
moment as if she saw with pleasure that her message had struck
its target.

Mrs. Turpin sank back in her chair.   112

After a moment the girl's eyes closed and she turned her head   113
wearily to the side.

The doctor rose and handed the nurse the empty syringe. He   114
leaned over and put both hands for a moment on the mother's

shoulders, which were shaking. She was sitting on the floor, her lips pressed together, holding Mary Grace's hand in her lap. The girl's fingers were gripped like a baby's around her thumb. "Go on to the hospital," he said. "I'll call and make the arrangements."

"Now let's see that neck," he said in a jovial voice to Mrs.   115
Turpin. He began to inspect her neck with his two fingers. Two little moon-shaped lines like pink fish bones were indented over her windpipe. There was the beginning of an angry red swelling above her eye. His fingers passed over this also.

"Let me be," she said thickly and shook him off. "See about   116
Claud. She kicked him."

"I'll see about him in a minute," he said and felt her pulse. He   117
was a thin grey-haired man, given to pleasantries. "Go home and have yourself a vacation the rest of the day," he said and patted her on the shoulder.

Quit your pattin me, Mrs. Turpin growled to herself.   118

"And put an ice pack over that eye," he said. Then he went   119
and squatted down beside Claud and looked at his leg. After a moment he pulled him up and Claud limped after him into the office.

Until the ambulance came, the only sounds in the room were   120
the tremulous moans of the girl's mother, who continued to sit on the floor. The white-trash woman did not take her eyes off the girl. Mrs. Turpin looked straight ahead at nothing. Presently the ambulance drew up, a long dark shadow, behind the curtain. The attendants came in and set the stretcher down beside the girl and lifted her expertly onto it and carried her out. The nurse helped the mother gather up her things. The shadow of the ambulance moved silently away and the nurse came back in the office.

"That ther girl is going to be a lunatic, ain't she?" the   121
white-trash woman asked the nurse, but the nurse kept on to the back and never answered her.

"Yes, she's going to be a lunatic," the white-trash woman said   122
to the rest of them.

"Po' critter," the old woman murmured. The child's face was   123
still in her lap. His eyes looked idly out over her knees. He had not moved during the disturbance except to draw one leg up under him.

"I thank Gawd," the white-trash woman said fervently, "I 124
ain't a lunatic."

Claud came limping out and the Turpins went home. 125

As their pick-up truck turned into their own dirt road and 126
made the crest of the hill, Mrs. Turpin gripped the window ledge
and looked out suspiciously. The land sloped gracefully down
through a field dotted with lavender weeds and at the start of the
rise their small yellow frame house, with its little flower beds
spread out around it like a fancy apron, sat primly in its accustomed place between two giant hickory trees. She would not
have been startled to see a burnt wound between two blackened
chimneys.

Neither of them felt like eating so they put on their house 127
clothes and lowered the shade in the bedroom and lay down,
Claud with his leg on a pillow and herself with a damp washcloth over her eye. The instant she was flat on her back, the image of a razor-backed hog with warts on its face and horns
coming out behind its ears snorted into her head. She moaned, a
low quiet moan.

"I am not," she said tearfully, "a wart hog. From hell." But 128
the denial had no force. The girl's eyes and her words, even the
tone of her voice, low but clear, directed only to her, brooked no
repudiation. She had been singled out for the message, though
there was trash in the room to whom it might justly have been
applied. The full force of this fact struck her only now. There
was a woman there who was neglecting her own child but she
had been overlooked. The message had been given to Ruby
Turpin, a respectable, hard-working, church-going woman. The
tears dried. Her eyes began to burn instead with wrath.

She rose on her elbow and the washcloth fell into her hand. 129
Claud was lying on his back, snoring. She wanted to tell him
what the girl had said. At the same time, she did not wish to put
the image of herself as a wart hog from hell into his mind.

"Hey, Claud," she muttered and pushed his shoulder. 130

Claud opened one pale baby blue eye. 131

She looked into it warily. He did not think about anything. He 132
just went his way.

"Wha, whasit?" he said and closed the eye again. 133

"Nothing," she said. "Does your leg pain you?" 134

"Hurts like hell," Claud said. 135

"It'll quit terreckly," she said and lay back down. In a moment   136
Claud was snoring again. For the rest of the afternoon they lay
there. Claud slept. She scowled at the ceiling. Occasionally she
raised her fist and made a small stabbing motion over her chest as
if she was defending her innocence to invisible guests who were
like the comforters of Job, reasonable-seeming but wrong.

About five-thirty Claud stirred. "Got to go after those nig-   137
gers," he sighed, not moving.

She was looking straight up as if there were unintelligible   138
handwriting on the ceiling. The protuberance over her eye had
fumed a greenish-blue. "Listen here," she said.

"What?"   139

"Kiss me."   140

Claud leaned over and kissed her loudly on the mouth. He   141
pinched her side and their hands interlocked. Her expression of
ferocious concentration did not change. Claud got up, groaning
and growling, and limped off. She continued to study the ceiling.

She did not get up until she heard the pick-up truck coming   142
back with the Negroes. Then she rose and thrust her feet in her
brown oxfords, which she did not bother to lace, and stumped
out onto the back porch and got her red plastic bucket. She emptied a tray of ice cubes into it and filled it half full of water and
went out into the back yard. Every afternoon after Claud
brought the hands in, one of the boys helped him put out hay
and the rest waited in the back of the truck until he was ready to
take them home. The truck was parked in the shade under one of
the hickory trees.

"Hi yawl this evening?" Mrs. Turpin asked grimly, appearing   143
with the bucket and the dipper. There were three women and a
boy in the truck.

"Us doin nicely," the oldest woman said. "Hi you doin?" and   144
her gaze struck immediately on the dark lump on Mrs. Turpin's
forehead. "You done fell down, ain't you?" she asked in a solic-
itous voice. The old woman was dark and almost toothless. She
had on an old felt hat of Claud's set back on her head. The other
two women were younger and lighter and they both had new
bright green sun hats. One of them had hers on her head; the
other had taken hers off and the boy was grinning beneath it.

Mrs. Turpin set the bucket down on the floor of the truck.   145
"Yawl hep yourselves," she said. She looked around to make

sure Claud had gone. "No. I didn't fall down," she said, folding her arms. "It was something worse than that."

"Ain't nothing bad happen to you!" the old woman said. She said it as if they all knew that Mrs. Turpin was protected in some special way by Divine Providence. "You just had you a little fall."   146

"We were in town at the doctor's office for where the cow kicked Mr. Turpin," Mrs. Turpin said in a flat tone that indicated they could leave off their foolishness. "And there was this girl there. A big fat girl with her face all broke out. I could look at that girl and tell she was peculiar but I couldn't tell how. And me and her mama were just talking and going along and all of a sudden WHAM! She throws this big book she was reading at me and . . ."   147

"Naw!" the old woman cried out.   148

"And then she jumps over the table and commences to choke me."   149

"Naw!" they all exclaimed, "naw!"   150

"Hi come she do that?" the old woman asked. "What ail her?"   151

Mrs. Turpin only glared in front of her.   152

"Somethin ail her," the old woman said.   153

"They carried her off in an ambulance," Mrs. Turpin continued, "but before she went she was rolling on the floor and they were trying to hold her down to give her a shot and she said something to me." She paused. "You know what she said to me?"   154

"What she say?" they asked.   155

"She said," Mrs. Turpin began, and stopped, her face very dark and heavy. The sun was getting whiter and whiter, blanching the sky overhead so that the leaves of the hickory tree were black in the face of it. She could not bring forth the words. "Something real ugly," she muttered.   156

"She sho shouldn't said nothin ugly to you," the old woman said. "You so sweet. You the sweetest lady I know."   157

"She pretty too," the one with the hat on said.   158

"And stout," the other one said. "I never knowed no sweeter white lady."   159

"That's the truth befo' Jesus," the old woman said. "Amen! You jes as sweet and pretty as you can be."   160

Mrs. Turpin knew just exactly how much Negro flattery was 161
worth and it added to her rage. "She said," she began again and
finished this time with a fierce rush of breath, "that I was an old
wart hog from hell."

There was an astounded silence. 162

"Where she at?" the youngest woman cried in a piercing 163
voice.

"Lemme see her. I'll kill her!" 164

"I'll kill her with you!" the other one cried. 165

"She b'long in the sylum," the old woman said emphatically. 166
"You the sweetest white lady I know."

"She pretty too," the other two said. "Stout as she can be and 167
sweet. Jesus satisfied with her!"

"Deed he is," the old woman declared. 168

Idiots! Mrs. Turpin growled to herself. You could never say 169
anything intelligent to a nigger. You could talk at them but not
with them. "Yawl ain't drunk your water," she said shortly.
"Leave the bucket in the truck when you're finished with it. I got
more to do than just stand around and pass the time of day," and
she moved off and into the house.

She stood for a moment in the middle of the kitchen. The dark 170
protuberance over her eye looked like a miniature tornado cloud
which might any moment sweep across the horizon of her brow.
Her lower lip protruded dangerously. She squared her massive
shoulders. Then she marched into the front of the house and out
the side door and started down the road to the pig parlor. She
had the look of a woman going single-handed, weaponless, into
battle.

The sun was a deep yellow now like a harvest moon and was 171
rising westward very fast over the far tree line as if it meant to
reach the hogs before she did. The road was rutted and she kicked
several good-sized stones out of her path as she strode along. The
pig parlor was on a little knoll at the end of a lane that ran off
from the side of the barn. It was a square of concrete as large as a
small room, with a board fence about four feet high around it.
The concrete floor sloped slightly so that the hog wash could
drain off into a trench where it was carried to the field for fertilizer. Claud was standing on the outside, on the edge of the concrete, hanging onto the top board, hosing down the floor inside.
The hose was connected to the faucet of a water trough nearby.

Mrs. Turpin climbed up beside him and glowered down at the   172
hogs inside. There were seven long-spouted bristly shoats in it—
tan with liver-colored spots—and an old sow a few weeks off
from farrowing. She was lying on her side grunting. The shoats
were running about shaking themselves like idiot children, their
little slit pig eyes searching the floor for anything left. She had
read that pigs were the most intelligent animal. She doubted it.
They were supposed to be smarter than dogs. There had even
been a pig astronaut. He had performed his assignment perfectly
but died of a heart attack afterwards because they left him in his
electric suit, sitting upright throughout his examination when
naturally a hog should be on all fours.

A-gruntin and a-rootin and a-groanin.   173

"Gimme that hose," she said, yanking it away from Claud.   174
"Go on and carry them niggers home and then get off that leg."

"You look like you might have swallowed a mad dog," Claud   175
observed, but he got down and limped off. He paid no attention
to her humors.

Until he was out of earshot, Mrs. Turpin stood on the side   176
of the pen, holding the hose and pointing the stream of water
at the hind quarters of any shoat that looked as if it might try
to lie down. When he had had time to get over the hill, she
fumed her head slightly and her wrathful eyes scanned the
path. He was nowhere in sight. She fumed back again and
seemed to gather herself up. Her shoulders rose and she drew in
her breath.

"What do you send me a message like that for?" she said in a   177
low fierce voice, barely above a whisper but with the force of a
shout in its concentrated fury. "How am I a hog and me both?
How am I saved and from hell too?" Her free fist was knotted
and with the other she gripped the hose, blindly pointing the
stream of water in and out of the eye of the old sow whose outraged squeal she did not hear.

The pig parlor commanded a view of the back pasture where   178
their twenty beef cows were gathered around the hay-bales
Claud and the boy had put out. The freshly cut pasture sloped
down to the highway. Across it was their cotton field and beyond
that a dark green dusty wood which they owned as well. The sun
was behind the wood, very red, looking over the paling of trees
like a farmer inspecting his own hogs.

"Why me?" she rumbled. "It's no trash around here, black or   179
white, that I haven't given to. And break my back to the bone
every day working. And do for the church."

She appeared to be the right size woman to command the   180
arena before her. "How am I a hog?" she demanded. "Exactly
how am I like them?" and she jabbed the stream of water at the
shoals. "There was plenty of trash there. It didn't have to be me."

"If you like trash better, go get yourself some trash then," she   181
railed. "You could have made me trash. Or a nigger. If trash is
what you wanted why didn't you make me trash?" She shook
her fist with the hose in it and a watery snake appeared momen-
tarily in the air. "I could quit working and take it easy and be
filthy," she growled. "Lounge about the sidewalks all day drinking root beer. Dip snuff and spit in every puddle and have it all
over my face. I could be nasty.

"Or you could have made me a nigger. It's too late for me to   182
be a nigger," she said with deep sarcasm, "but I could act like
one. Lay down in the middle of the road and stop traffic. Roll on
the ground."

In the deepening light everything was taking on a mysterious   183
hue. The pasture was growing a peculiar glassy green and the
streak of highway had turned lavender. She braced herself for a
final assault and this time her voice rolled out over the pasture.
"Go on," she yelled, "call me a hog! Call me a hog again. From
hell. Call me a wart hog from hell. Put that bottom rail on top.
There'll still be a top and bottom!"

A garbled echo resumed to her.   184

A final surge of fury shook her and she roared, "Who do you   185
think you are?"

The color of everything, field and crimson sky, burned for a   186
moment with a transparent intensity. The question carried over
the pasture and across the highway and the cotton field and resumed to her clearly like an answer from beyond the wood.

She opened her mouth but no sound came out of it.   187

A tiny truck, Claud's, appeared on the highway, heading rap-   188
idly out of sight. Its gears scraped thinly. It looked like a child's
toy. At any moment a bigger truck might smash into it and scat-
ter Claud's and the niggers' brains all over the road.

Mrs. Turpin stood there, her gaze fixed on the highway, all her   189
muscles rigid, until in five or six minutes the truck reappeared,

returning. She waited until it had had time to turn into their own road. Then like a monumental statue coming to life, she bent her head slowly and gazed, as if through the very heart of mystery, down into the pig parlor at the hogs. They had settled all in one comer around the old sow who was grunting softly. A red glow suffused them. They appeared to pant with a secret life.

Until the sun slipped finally behind the tree line, Mrs. Turpin   190
remained there with her gaze bent to them as if she were absorbing some abysmal life-giving knowledge. At last she lifted her head. There was only a purple streak in the sky, cutting through a field of crimson and leading, like an extension of the highway, into the descending dusk. She raised her hands from the side of the pen in a gesture hieratic and profound. A visionary light settled in her eyes. She saw the streak as a vast swinging bridge extending upward from the earth through a field of living fire. Upon it a vast horde of souls were rumbling toward heaven. There were whole companies of white-trash, clean for the first time in their lives, and bands of black niggers in white robes, and battalions of freaks and lunatics shouting and clapping and leaping like frogs. And bringing up the end of the procession was a tribe of people whom she recognized at once as those who, like herself and Claud, had always had a little of everything and the God-given wit to use it right. She leaned forward to observe them closer. They were marching behind the others with great dignity, accountable as they had always been for good order and common sense and respectable behavior. They alone were on key. Yet she could see by their shocked and altered faces that even their virtues were being burned away. She lowered her hands and gripped the rail of the hog pen, her eyes small but fixed unblinkingly on what lay ahead. In a moment the vision faded but she remained where she was, immobile.

At length she got down and turned off the faucet and made   191
her slow way on the darkening path to the house. In the woods around her the invisible cricket choruses had struck up, but what she heard were the voices of the souls climbing upward into the starry field and shouting hallelujah.

8

PROGRESS
AND ITS PRICE

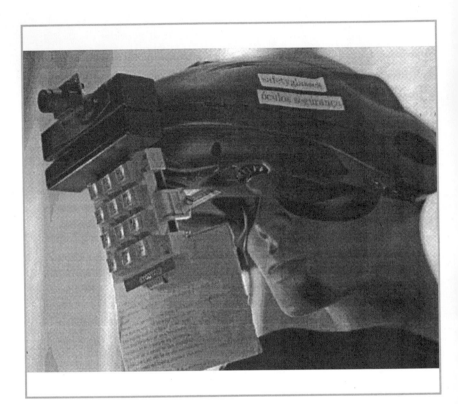

Wearcam created by Professor Steve Mann, http://wearcam.org/cyborg.htm. Photo reprinted by permission from *Cyborg: Digital Destiny and Human Possibility in the Age of the Wearable Computer,* by STEVE MANN, published by Random House.

OVERVIEW

In the days before houseflies were controlled by chemicals or sealed out of air-conditioned houses, the fly bottle was a common household implement. In its simplest form it consisted of a clear soda bottle standing upright with a paper funnel in its mouth. In the bottom of the bottle was a spoonful of honey ("You catch more flies with honey than vinegar," we still say). Flies attracted by the scent would enter the funnel at the large end, pass through a tiny hole at the small end, and eat their fill. Then they would attempt to fly away, but would find themselves blocked by glass in every direction. Without a scent to guide them, they would be unable to find their way through the small end of the funnel to freedom.

That we no longer rely on fly bottles is a small example of the way that technological progress has made our lives more comfortable, sanitary, and healthy. And yet it would be simple-minded to believe that advanced technology has been a pure gain. The chemicals that control insects and the air-conditioners that control the indoor climate cost us something, economically, ecologically, and even socially. We live our lives increasingly indoors, in spaces that isolate us not only from uninvited insects, but also from much of our contact with the natural world and some of the face-to-face interaction we might have had with our neighbors. Some might say that the fly bottle, a glass house with food mysteriously provided, is a good metaphor for the economic and technological trap we are in danger of falling into.

To what extent the technologies that have flourished in the last hundred years serve us and to what extent they reduce our actual freedom and happiness are questions addressed in every essay and story in this unit.

- Daniel Boorstin surveys the effects of "our fantastic success in industry and technology and in invention" and points out four consequences that were surely not intended.
- Alice Bloom contrasts the imagined life of a woman from a more "developed" culture with that of a woman from a less "developed" culture and hesitates, at least, to decide who is better off.

- C. S. Lewis explains why he believes that "man's power over Nature turns out to be a power exercised by some men over other men with Nature as its instrument."
- Barbara Ehrenreich, distressed that America is becoming a nation of couch potatoes, discovers what we are looking for when we turn on the television.
- Randall Jarrell complains that "the Medium," a great network of marketing and packaged entertainment, is choking out all values that don't translate into cash.
- E. M. Forster's story, written nearly a century ago, foresees a world in which dependence on "the Machine" has become almost complete.

Daniel J. Boorstin

Technology and Democracy

Daniel J. Boorstin, a lawyer by training, has become one of America's best-known historians, largely because of his interest in topics that historians with more formal training have tended to ignore. In most of his works there is an optimism about the effects of technology and prosperity that some critics have labeled "boosterism." Therefore, when Boorstin talks about the disadvantages of technological progress, as he did in this 1972 lecture delivered at the University of Michigan and later collected in *Democracy and Its Discontents* (1974), he deserves special attention because he is examining the limitations of his own pet thesis.

One of the most interesting and characteristic features of   1
democracy is, of course, the difficulty of defining it. And this difficulty has been compounded in the United States, where we have been giving new meanings to almost everything. It is, therefore, especially easy for anyone to say that democracy in America has failed.

"Democracy," according to political scientists, usually de-   2
scribes a form of government by the people, either directly or through their elected representatives. But I prefer to describe a democratic society as one which is governed by a spirit of equality and dominated by the desire to equalize, to give everything to everybody. In the United States the characteristic wealth and skills and know-how and optimism of our country have dominated this quest.

My first and overshadowing proposition is that our problems   3
arise not so much from our failures as from our successes. Of course no success is complete; only death is final. But we have probably come closer to attaining our professed objectives than any other society of comparable size and extent, and it is from this that our peculiarly American problems arise.

The use of technology to democratize our daily life has given   4
a quite new shape to our hopes. In this final chapter I will explore some of the consequences of democracy, not for government but for experience. What are the consequences for everybody every

day of this effort to democratize life in America? And especially the consequences of our fantastic success in industry and technology and in invention?

There have been at least four of these consequences. I begin   5
with what I call *attenuation,* which means the thinning out or the flattening of experience. We might call this the democratizing of experience. It might otherwise be described as the decline of poignancy. One of the consequences of our success in technology, of our wealth, of our energy and our imagination, has been the removal of distinctions, not just between people but between everything and everything else, between every place and every other place, between every time and every other time. For example, television removes the distinction between being here and being there. And the same kind of process, of thinning out, of removing distinctions, has appeared in one area after another of our lives.

For instance, in the seasons. One of the great unheralded   6
achievements of American civilization was the rise of transportation and refrigeration, the development of techniques of canning and preserving meat, vegetables, and fruits in such a way that it became possible to enjoy strawberries in winter, to enjoy fresh meat at seasons when the meat was not slaughtered, to thin out the difference between the diet of winter and the diet of summer. There are many unsung heroic stories in this effort.

One of them, for example, was the saga of Gustavus Swift in   7
Chicago. In order to make fresh meat available at a relatively low price to people all over the country, it was necessary to be able to transport it from the West, where the cattle were raised, to the Eastern markets and the cities where population was concentrated. Gustavus Swift found the railroad companies unwilling to manufacture refrigerator cars. They were afraid that, if refrigeration was developed, the cattle would be butchered in the West and then transported in a more concentrated form than when the cattle had to be carried live. The obvious consequence, they believed, would be to reduce the amount of freight. So they refused to develop the refrigerator car. Gustavus Swift went ahead and developed it, only to find that he had more cars than he had use for. The price of fresh meat went down in the Eastern cities, and Gustavus Swift had refrigerator cars on his hands. He then sent agents to the South and to other parts of the country,

and tried to encourage people to raise produce which had to be carried in refrigerator cars. One of the consequences of this was the development of certain strains of fruit and vegetables, especially of fruit, which would travel well. And Georgia became famous for the peaches which were grown partly as a result of Swift's efforts to encourage people to raise something that he could carry in his refrigerator cars.

There were other elements in this story which we may easily forget—for example, how central heating and air conditioning have affected our attitude toward the seasons, toward one time of year or another. Nowadays visitors from abroad note that wherever they are in our country, it is not unusual to find that in winter it is often too warm indoors, and in summer, often too cool. 8

But the development of central heating during the latter part of the nineteenth century had other, less obvious consequences. For example, as people built high-rise apartments in the cities they found it impossible to have a fireplace in every room. You could not construct a high building with hundreds of apartments and have enough room for all the chimneys. So central heating was developed and this became a characteristic of city life. As central heating was developed it was necessary to have a place to put the machinery, and the machinery went in the cellar. But formerly people, even in the cities, had used their cellars to store fruit and vegetables over the winter. When the basement was heated by a furnace, of course it was no longer possible to store potatoes or other vegetables or fruit there. This increased the market for fresh fruits and vegetables that were brought in from truck farms just outside the cities or by refrigerator cars from greater distances. And this was another way of accelerating the tendency toward equalizing the seasons and equalizing the diet of people all over the country. 9

Also important in attenuating experience was the development of what I would call homogenized space, especially the development of vertical space as a place to live in. There is a great deal less difference between living on the thirty-fifth floor and living on the fortieth floor of an apartment building than there is between living in a house in the middle of a block and living on the corner. The view is pretty much the same as you go up in the air. Vertical space is much more homogenized, and as we live in 10 vertical space more and more, we live in places where "where we are" makes much less difference than it used to.

An important element in this which has been a product of 11 American technology is, of course, glass. We forget that the innovations in the production of glass resulting in large sheets which you could look through was an achievement largely of American technology in the nineteenth century. Of course, one by-product was the development of the technology of bottling, which is related to some of the levelings-out of the seasons which I mentioned before in relation to food. But we forget that when we admire those old leaded-glass windows which we see in medieval or early modern buildings, what we are admiring is the inability of people to produce plate glass.

When a large plate of glass became technologically possible, 12 this affected daily life in the United States. It affected merchandising, for example, because the "show window" became possible in which you could, with a relatively unobstructed view, display garments and other large objects in a way to make them appealing to people who passed by. But glass was also important in producing one of the main characteristics of modern American architecture—an architecture in which there is relatively less difference between the indoors and the outdoors than elsewhere. And that is one of the great functions of glass in modern architecture.

Along with the attenuation of places and time comes the at- 13 tenuation of occasions and events. One of the more neglected aspects of modern technology is what I have called the rise of "repeatable experience." It used to be thought that one of the characteristics of life, one of the things that distinguished being alive from being dead, was the uniqueness of the individual moment. Something happened which could never happen again. If you missed it then, you were out of luck. But the growth of popular photography, which we can trace from about 1888 when Kodak #1 went on the market, began to allow everybody to make his own experience repeatable. If you had not seen this baby when he was so cute, you could still see him that way right now if you were so unlucky as to be in the living room with the parents who wanted to show you. Kodak #1 was a great achievement and was the beginning of our taking for granted that there was such a thing as a repeatable experience.

The phonograph, of course, beginning about 1877, created 14 new opportunities to repeat audible experience. If you want to hear the voice of Franklin Delano Roosevelt now, you can hear him on a record. At the opening of the Woodrow Wilson Center for International Scholars at the Smithsonian Institution in 1971, part of the dedicating ceremony was the playing of a record with the voice of Woodrow Wilson. It was not a very warm voice, but it was identifiable and distinctive. The growth of the phonograph, then, has accustomed us to the fact that experience is not a onetime thing.

When we watch the Winter Olympics in our living room and   15 see the ski jumper in the seventy-meter jump who makes a mistake or who performs very well, we can see the same performance just a minute later with all the failures and successes pointed out. Is instant replay the last stage in the technology of repeatable experience?

In the attenuating of events there is another element which I   16 call the "pseudo-event." As more and more of the events which have public notice are planned in advance, as the accounts of them are made available before they happen, then it becomes the responsibility of the event to live up to its reputation. In this way the spontaneity of experience, the unpredictableness of experience, dissolves and disappears. The difference between the present and the future becomes less and less.

Another aspect of this is what I have called the "neutralization   17 of risks," a result of the rise of insurance. For insurance, too, is a way of reducing the difference between the future and the present. You reduce risks by assuring yourself that if your house burns down, at least you will have the money so you can rebuild it. In this sense, insurance, and especially casualty insurance, provides a way of thinning out the difference between present and future, removing the suspense and the risk of experience.

What have been the everyday consequences of the democra-   18 tizing of property for our experience of property? In his classic defense of property in his essay *On Civil Government* (1690), John Locke argued that because property is the product of the mixing of a person's labor with an object, no government has the right to take it without his consent. This simplistic conception of property has dominated a great deal of political and economic thinking. It was prominent in the thinking of the authors of the Declaration of Independence and of the Founding Fathers of the Constitution. It was based on a simpler society where there was something poignant and characteristic about the experience of ownership. Owning meant the right to exclude people. You had the pleasure of possession.

But what has happened to property in our society? Of course,   19 the most important new form of property in modern American life is corporate property: shares of stock in a corporation. And the diffusion of the ownership of shares is one of the most prominent features of American life. There are companies like AT&T, for example, which have as many as a million stockholders. What does it mean to be a stockholder? You are a lucky person. You own property and you have some shares. So what? One doesn't need to be rich or even middle-class in this country to own shares of stock. But very few of my friends who own shares of stock know precisely what it means or what their legal powers are as stockholders. They are solicited to send in their proxies—by somebody who has a special interest in getting them to vote for something or other. They feel very little pleasure of control; they don't have the sense of wreaking themselves on any object. Yet this—a share of stock—is the characteristic and most important form of property in modern times. This property, too, is attenuated.

Other developments in American life concerning property   20 have had a similar effect. For example, installment and credit buying. This phenomenon first grew in connection with the wide marketing of the sewing machine and then in relation to the cash register, but its efflorescence has come with the automobile. When it became necessary to sell millions of automobiles—and necessary in order to keep the machinery of our society going to sell them to people who could not afford to lay out the full cost of an automobile—it was necessary to find ways of financing their purchases. Installment and credit buying was developed. One of the results was that people became increasingly puzzled over whether they did or did not (and if so in what sense) own their automobile. Of course, it is not uncommon for people to divest themselves of their physical control of an object like an automobile or a color television set before they have really acquired full ownership—and then to enter on another ambiguous venture of part ownership.

Another aspect of this is the rise of franchising: the develop-   21 ment of what I would call the "semi- independent businessman." In the United States today, between 35 percent and 50 percent of all retail merchandising is done through franchised outlets. Well, of course, we all know what a franchised outlet is; a typical example would be a McDonald's hamburger stand or any other outlet in which the person who is in control of the shop has been authorized to use a nationally advertised name like Midas Mufflers or Colonel Sanders' Kentucky Fried Chicken. He is then instructed in the conduct of his business. He must meet certain standards in order to be allowed to continue to advertise as a Holiday Inn or Howard Johnson or whatever. And he is in business "for himself." Now, what does that mean? If you go into a franchised outlet and you find the hamburger unsatisfactory, what can you do? Whom would you complain to? The man who runs the shop has received his instructions and his materials from the people who have franchised him. It is not his fault. And, of course, it's not the fault of the people at the center who franchised him, because the shop is probably badly run by the franchisee.

This phenomenon grew out of the needs of the automobile be-   22
cause in order to sell Fords or any other makes, it was necessary to have an outlet which would take continuous responsibility for stocking parts. Then the purchaser could replace that part at the outlet where he had purchased the car. After automobile franchising came the franchising of filling stations. People wanted some assurance about the quality of the fuel they put in their cars; they were given this by the identification of what they purchased with some nationally advertised brand in which they had confidence.

Now, perhaps the most important example of attenuation, of   23
the decline of poignancy in our experience in relation to property, is so obvious and so universal that it has hardly been discussed. That is packaging. Until relatively recently if you went into a store to buy coffee, you would have to bring a container to the grocery store, and the grocer would ladle out the coffee to you.

Packaging began to develop in this country after the Civil   24
War. In a sense it was a by-product of the Civil War because the necessities of the war (especially the need to package flour) produced certain innovations which were important. And later there were decisive, although what seem to us rather trivial, innovations. For example, the invention of the folding box was important. Until there was a way to make boxes which could be transported and stored compactly, it was impossible or impractical to use them for industrial purposes. The folding box and certain improvements in the paper bag, such as the paper bag that had a square bottom so that it could stand up, and on the side of

which you could print an advertisement—these were American inventions.

If we will risk seeming pompous or pedantic, we can say that   25
the most important consequences of packaging have been epistemological. They have had to do with the nature of knowledge
and they have especially had the effect of confusing us about
what knowledge is, and what's real, about what's form and what's
substance. When you think about a Winston cigarette, you don't
think about the tobacco inside the cigarette. You think about the
package. And in one area after another of American life, the
form and the content become confused, and the form becomes
that which dominates our consciousness. One area perhaps in
which this has ceased to be true, happily or otherwise, is the area
which I have always thought of as an aspect of packaging—
namely, clothing. In the United States we have developed ready-
made clothing, too, in such a way as to obscure the differences of
social class and even of sex.

All around us we see attenuation—as our technology has   26
succeeded, as we have tried to make everything available to
everybody. The very techniques we use in preparing our food, in
transporting our food, in controlling the climate and temperature of the rooms we live in, the shapes of the buildings in which
we do business and reside, the ways we look at past experience—
in all these ways our experience becomes attenuated. As we democratize experience, the poignancy of the moment, of the season,
of the control of the object, of the spontaneous event, declines.

Now to a second consequence of the success of our technol-   27
ogy for our daily experience. This is what I would call the *decline
of congregation.* Or it might be called a new segregation. This is
the consequence of increasingly organized and centralized sources
of anything and everything. Example: Rebecca at the well.[1] When
I wrote an article for the issue of *Life* magazine which was intended to celebrate the twenty-fifth anniversary of the introduction of television in this country, I entitled the article at first
"Rebecca at the TV Set." But my friends at *Life* said, "Rebecca
who?" Deferring to their greater, wider knowledge of American
life and of the literariness of the American people, instead we
called it simply "The New Segregation."

1. In the Bible, the wife of Isaac and mother of Jacob and Esau, Gen. 24.

When Rebecca lived in her village and needed to get water for   28
the household, she went to the well. At the well she met the other
women of the village; she heard the gossip; she met her fiancé
there, as a matter of fact. And then what happened? With the
progress of democracy and technology, running water was introduced; and Rebecca stayed in the kitchenette of her eighth-floor
apartment. She turned the faucet on and got the water out of the
faucet; she didn't have to go to the well any more. She had only
the telephone to help her collect gossip and she would have to
find other ways to meet her fiancé. This is a parable of the problem of centralizing sources of everything.

The growth of centralized plumbing was itself, of course, a   29
necessary by-product of the development of the skyscraper and
the concentration of population in high buildings. You had to
have effective sanitary facilities. But we forget other features of
this development. Even those of us who have never made much
use of the old "privy" know that the privy characteristically
had more than one hole in it. Why was this? The plural facility
was not peculiar simply to the privy; it was also found in the sanitary arrangements of many older buildings, including some of
the grandest remaining medieval structures. The development of
centralized plumbing led to privatizing; "privy" was the wrong
word for the old facility. The privatizing of the bodily functions
made them less sociable. People engaged in them in private.

The most dramatic example today of the privatizing of expe-   30
rience by centralizing a facility is, of course, television. We could
start with the newspaper, for that matter. The town crier communicated the news to people in their presence. If you wanted to
hear it you had to be there, or talk to somebody else who was
there when he brought the news. But as the newspaper developed, with inexpensive printing, the messages were brought to
you and you could look at them privately as you sat by yourself
at breakfast. Television is perhaps one of the most extreme examples of the decline of congregation. Until the development of
television, if you wanted to see a play you had to go out to a theater; if you wanted to hear a concert you had to go to a concert
hall. These performances were relatively rare. They were special
events. But with the coming of television, everybody acquired his
private theater. Rebecca had her theater in her kitchen. She no
longer needed to go out for entertainment.

The centralized source, the centralizing of the source, then,   31
led to the isolating of the consumer. Of course, much was gained
by this. But one of the prices paid was the decline of congregation—congregation being the drawing together of people where
they could enjoy and react to and respond to the reactions and
feelings of their fellows.

There is a third consequence of our technological success in   32
democratic America, which I would call the new determinism, or
the rising sense of momentum. Technology has had a deep and
pervasive effect on our attitude toward history, and especially on
the citizen's attitude toward his control over the future. In the
seventeenth century the Puritans spoke about Providence; that
was their characteristic way of describing the kind of control
that God exercised over futurity. In the nineteenth century, when
people became more scientifically minded, they still retained
some notion of divine foresight in the form of the concept of destiny or mission or purpose. But in our time in this country we
have developed a different kind of approach toward futurity;
and this is what I would call the sense of momentum.

Momentum in physics is the product of a body's mass and its   33
linear velocity. Increasing scale and speed of operation increase
the momentum. One of the characteristics of our technology and
especially of our most spectacular successes has been to increase
this sense of momentum. I will mention three obvious examples.
It happens that each of these developments came, too, as a result
of overwhelming international pressure. When such pressures
added to the forces at work inside the nation, in each case they
produced a phenomenon of great mass and velocity which became very difficult to stop.

The first example is, of course, atomic research. The large-   34
scale concerted efforts in this country to build an atomic bomb
began and were accelerated at the time of World War II because
of rumors that the Nazis were about to succeed in nuclear fis-
sion. When this information became available, national resources
were massed and organized in an unprecedented fashion; futurity was scheduled and groups were set to work in all parts of the
continent exploring different possible ways of finding the right
form of uranium or of some other element. And the search for
the first atomic chain reaction, which was accomplished at my
University of Chicago, went on.

One of the more touching human aspects of this story is the account, now well chronicled by several historians, of the frantic efforts of the atomic scientists, the people who had been most instrumental in getting this process started (Albert Einstein, Leo Szilard, and James Franck, among others), when they saw that the atomic bomb was about to become possible, to persuade the President of the United States either not to use the bomb or to use it only in a demonstration in the uninhabited mid-Pacific. Such a use, they urged, would so impress the enemy with the horrors of the bomb that he would surrender, eliminating the need for us to use the bomb against a live target. They pursued this purpose—trying to put the brakes on military use of the bomb—with a desperation that even exceeded the energy they had shown in developing the bomb. But, of course, they had no success.

They could develop the bomb, but they couldn't stop it. Why? There were many reasons, including President Truman's reasonable belief that use of the bomb could in the long run save the hundreds of thousands of Japanese and American lives that would have been lost in an invasion, and also would shorten the war. But surely one reason was that there had already been too much investment in the bomb. Billions of dollars had gone into the making of it. People were organized all over the country in various ways. It was impossible to stop.

Another example of this kind of momentum is the phenomenon of space exploration. I happen to be an enthusiast for space exploration, so by describing this momentum I do not mean to suggest that I think the space enterprise itself has not been a good thing. Nevertheless, as a historian I am increasingly impressed by the pervasive phenomenon of momentum in our time. Billions of dollars have been spent in developing the machinery for going off to the moon or going then to Mars or elsewhere. The mass of the operation has been enormous. The velocity of it is enormous, and it becomes virtually impossible to stop. The recent problem with the SST is a good example. For when any enterprise in our society has reached a certain scale, the consequences in unemployment and in dislocation of the economy are such that it becomes every year more difficult to cease doing what we are already doing.

A third example, more in the area of institutions, is foreign aid: the international pressures to give foreign aid to one country

35

36

37

38

or another. We have an enormous mass of wealth being invested, a great velocity with lots of people going off all over the world and performing this operation of giving aid, and it becomes almost impossible to stop it. The other countries resent the decline of aid and consider it a hostile act, even though they might not have felt that way if we hadn't started the aid in the first place. Foreign aid is, I think, the most characteristic innovation in foreign policy in this century.

Each of these three enterprises illustrates the attitude of the   39
American citizen in the later twentieth century toward his control over experience. Increasingly, the citizen comes to feel that events are moving, and moving so fast with such velocity and in such mass that he has very little control. The sense of momentum itself becomes possible only because of our success in achieving these large purposes which no other democratic society, no other society before us, had even imagined.

Now, what does this bring us to? Before I come to my fourth   40
and concluding point on the ways in which the successes of democracy have affected our experience, I would like briefly to recall some of the remedies that have been suggested for the ills of democracy and the problems of democracy in the past. Al Smith once said, "All the ills of democracy can be cured by more democracy." I must confess, though I admire Al Smith for some of his enterprises, the Empire State Building for example, I think he was on the wrong track here. In fact, I would take an almost contrary position. Even at the risk of seeming flip, I might sum up the democratic paradoxes that I have been describing: "Getting there is *all* the fun."

Is there a law of democratic impoverishment? Is it possible   41
that while *democratizing* enriches experience, *democracy* dilutes experience?

Example: photography. Before the invention of photography,   42
it was a remarkable experience to see an exact likeness of the Sphinx or of Notre Dame or of some exotic animal or to see a portrait of an ancestor. Then, as photography was publicized in the 1880's and thoroughly popularized in this century, it opened up a fantastic new range of experience for everybody. Suddenly people were able to see things they had never been able to see before. And then what happened? Everyone had a camera, or two or three cameras; and everywhere he went he took pictures and

when he came home he had to find a victim, somebody to show the pictures to. And this became more and more difficult.

While photography was being introduced, it was life-enriching   43
and vista-opening; but once it was achieved, once everybody had a camera, the people were looking in their cameras instead of looking at the sight they had gone to see. It had an attenuating effect. A picture came to mean less and less, simply because people saw pictures everywhere. And the experience of being there also somehow meant less because the main thing people saw everywhere was the inside of their viewfinders, and their concern over their lens cap and finding the proper exposure made it hard for them to notice what was going on around them at the moment.

Another example is, of course, the phonograph. Has the   44
phonograph—in its universal late-twentieth-century uses—necessarily made people more appreciative of music? In the 1920's when I was raised in Tulsa, Oklahoma, I had never heard an opera, nor had I really heard any classical music properly performed by an orchestra. But in our living room we had a wind-up Victrola, and I heard Galli-Curci singing arias from *Rigoletto*, and I heard Caruso, and I heard some symphonies, and it was fantastic. And then hi-fi came and everybody had a phonograph, a hi-fi machine or a little transistor radio which you could carry with you and hear music any time.

Today when I walk into the elevator in an office building, it is   45
not impossible that I will hear Beethoven or Verdi. Sitting in the airplane I hear Mozart coming out of the public-address system. Wherever we go we hear music whether we want to hear it or not, whether we are in the mood for it or not. It becomes an everywhere, all-the-time thing. The experience is attenuated.

And one of the most serious consequences of all this, finally, is   46
the attenuation of community itself. What holds people together? What has held people together in the past? For the most part it has been their sense of humanity, their pleasure in the presence of one another, their feeling for another person's expression, the sound of a voice, the look on his or her face. But the kind of community I describe increasingly becomes attenuated. People are trying to enjoy the community all by themselves.

We are led to certain desperate quests in American life. These,   47
the by-products of our success, are clues to the vitality and energy of our country, to the quest for novelty to keep life interesting and vistas open, to the quest for community and the quest for

autonomy. Can we inoculate ourselves against these perils of our technological success? Samuel Butler once said, "If I die prematurely, at any rate I shall be saved from being bored by my own success." Our problem, too, is partly that.

And now a fourth characteristic of the relation of technology to democracy in our time: *the belief in solutions*. One of the most dangerous popular fallacies—nourished by American history and by some of our most eloquent and voluble patriots—is the notion that democracy is attainable. There is a subtle difference between American democratic society and many earlier societies in the extent to which their ideals could be attained. The objectives of other societies have for the most part been definable and attainable. Aristocracy and monarchy do present attainable ideals. Even totalitarianism presents objectives which can be attained in the sense in which the objectives of democracy never can be.

This nation has been a place of renewal, of new beginnings for nations and for man. Vagueness has been a national resource: the vagueness of the continent, the mystery of our resources, the vagueness of our social classes, the misty miasma of our hopes.

Our society has been most distinctively a way of reaching for rather than of finding. American democracy, properly speaking, has been a process and not a product, a quest and not a discovery. But a great danger which has been nourished by our success in technology has been the belief in solutions. For technological problems there *are* solutions. It is possible to set yourself the task of developing an economic and workable internal-combustion engine, a prefabricated house, or a way of reaching the moon. Technological problems are capable of solutions.

We are inclined, then, using the technological problem as our prototype, to believe that somehow democracy itself is a solution, a dissolving of the human condition. But we should have learned, and even the history of technology—especially the history of technology in our democratic society—should have taught us otherwise.

In human history in the long run there are no solutions, only problems. This is what I have suggested in my description of "self-liquidating" ideals. And the examples are all around us— in our effort to create a pluralistic society by assimilating and Americanizing people, in our effort to give everybody an uncrowded wilderness vacation, in our effort to find an exciting new model each year.

Every seeming solution is a new problem. When you demo- 53
cratize the speedy automobile and give everybody an automobile, the result is a traffic jam; and this is the sense in which the
"solution" of technological problems presents us with obstacles
to the fulfillment of what is human in our society. When we think
about American democratic society, then, we must learn not to
think about a condition, but about a process; not about democracy, but about the quest for democracy, which we might call
"democratizing."

The most distinctive feature of our system is not a system, but 54
a quest, not a neat arrangement of men and institutions, but a
flux. What other society has ever committed itself to so tantaliz-
ing, so fulfilling, so frustrating a community enterprise?

To prepare ourselves for this view of American democracy there 55
are two sides to our personal need. One is on the side of prudence
and wisdom; the other on the side of poetry and imagination.

On the side of prudence, there is a need for a sense of history. 56
Only by realizing the boundaries that we have been given can we
discover how to reach beyond them. Only so can we have the
wisdom not to mistake passing fads for great movements, not to
mistake the fanaticisms of a few for the deep beliefs of the many,
not to mistake fashion for revolution. This wisdom is necessary
if we are to secure sensibly the benefits of a free society for those
who have for whatever reason been deprived of its benefits. We
were not born yesterday, nor was the nation. And between the
day before yesterday and yesterday, crucial events have happened. We can discover these and come to terms with them only
through history. As Pascal[2] said, "It is only by knowing our condition that we can transcend it." Our technology brings us the
omnipresent present. It dulls our sense of history, and if we are
not careful it can destroy it.

We in the U.S.A. are always living in an age of transition. Yet 57
we have tended to believe that our present is always the climax
of history, even though American history shows that the climax
is always in the future. By keeping suspense alive, we can prepare
ourselves for the shocks of change.

And finally, on the side of poetry and imagination, how do we 58
keep alive the spirit of adventure, what I would call the explor-

2. Blaise Pascal: French philosopher and mathematician (1623–1662).

ing spirit? This should be the easiest because it is the most traditional of our achievements and efforts. We must remember that
we live in a new world. We must keep alive the exploring spirit.
We must not sacrifice the infinite promise of the unknown, of
man's unfulfilled possibilities in the universe's untouched mysteries, for the cozy satisfactions of predictable, statistical benefits.
Space exploration is a symbol.

Recently I had the pleasure of talking with Thor Heyerdahl,   59
the *Kon Tiki* man, whose latest venture was the Ra expedition,
in which he explored the possibilities of men having come from
Egypt or elsewhere in the Mediterranean to this continent long
ago in boats made of reeds. He and his crew, to test their hypothesis, actually crossed the Atlantic in a reed boat. And as I
talked to Thor Heyerdahl about the Ra expedition, I said that it
must have been a terrible feeling of risk when you suddenly left
the sight of land and got out into the open sea. It seemed to me
that the fear and perils of the open sea would be the greatest.
Thor Heyerdahl said not at all: the great dangers, the dangers of
shoals and rocks, existed along the shore. The wonderful sense
of relief, he observed, came when he went out on the ocean
where there was openness all around, although also high waves
and strong currents. The promise of American democracy, I suggest, depends on our ability to stay at sea, to work together in
community while we all reach to the open horizon.

ALICE BLOOM

On a Greek Holiday

After living much of her adult life in Midwestern suburbs, Alice
Bloom moved to rural Maine, where she learned how to fish for
smelt and make maple syrup. "On a Greek Holiday," excerpted
from a 1983 article in *The Hudson Review,* reflects her interest in
returning to ways of life some might call "less advanced." The excerpt begins after she has set the scene, an isolated strip of bare
sand to which tourists are ferried so that they can take off as
many of their clothes as they dare and lie exposed to a burning

sun. Most of the women are bare-breasted. The men "lie on their beach mats, clothed in their tiny suits," reading the latest best-sellers or "adjusting the knobs on multiwave radios."

. . . Two women are walking toward us, at noon, across the 1 nearly deserted rocks. Most of the other swimmers and sun-bathers are up in the cafe, eating lunch under the fig trees, the grapevine. These two women are not together, they walk several feet apart, and they do not look at each other. One is tall and blond, dressed in a flowered bikini and clogs, a tourist, English or American or Scandinavian or German. The other woman, a Greek, is carrying a basket, walking quickly, and gives the im-pression of being on a neighborhood errand. She is probably from one of the small old farms—sheep, olive trees, hens, gar-dens, goats—that border this stretch of sea and climb a little way into the pine arid cypress woods.

Both are smoking and both walk upright. Beyond that, there 2 is so little similarity they could belong to different planets, eras, species, sexes. The tourist looks young, the Greek looks old; ac-tually, she looks as old as a village well and the blonde looks like a drawn-out infant, but there could be as little as five or ten years difference between them.

The Greek woman is short and heavy, waistless, and is wear- 3 ing a black dress, a black scarf pulled low around her eyes, a black sweater, thick black stockings, black shoes. She is stupen-dously there, black but for the walnut of her face, in the white sun, against the white space. She looks, at once, as if she could do everything she's ever done, anything needed, and also at once, she gives off an emanation of humor, powers, secrets, determinations, acts. She is moving straight ahead, like a moving church, a black peaked roof, a hot black hat, a dark tent, like a doom, a govern-ment, a force for good and evil, an ultimatum, a determined ani-mal. She probably can't read, or write; she may never in her life have left this island; but she is beautiful, she could crush you, love you, mend you, deliver you of child or calf or lamb or illusion, bleed a pig, spear a fish, wring a supper's neck, till a field, coax an egg into life. Her sex is like a votive lamp flickering in a black, air-less room. As she comes closer, she begins to crochet—that's what's in her basket, balls of cotton string and thick white lace coming off the hook and her brown fingers.

The blond tourist, struggling along the hot pebbles in her   4
clogs, is coming back to her beach mat and friends. She looks as
though she couldn't dress a doll without having a fit of sulks and
throwing it down in a tantrum. It may not be the case, of course.
She is on holiday, on this Greek island, which fact means both
money and time. She is no doubt capable, well meaning, and by
the standards and expectations of most of the world's people, well
educated and very rich and very comfortable. She can undoubtedly read and write, most blond people can, and has, wherever
she comes from, a vote, a voice, a degree of some kind, a job, a
career perhaps, money certainly, opinions, friends, health, talents, habits, central heating, living relatives, personalized checks,
a return ticket, a summer wardrobe, the usual bits and clamor
we all, tourists, have. But presence, she has not. Nor authority,
nor immediacy, nor joy for the eye, nor a look of adding to the
world, not of strength nor humor nor excitement. Nearly naked,
pretty, without discernible blemish, blond, tall, tan, firm, the
product of red meat and whole milk, vitamins, orange juice,
women's suffrage, freedom of religion, child labor laws, compul-
sory education, the anxious, dancing, lifelong attendance of un-
counted numbers of furrow-browed adults, parents, teachers,
pediatricians, orthodontists, counselors, hairdressers, diet and health
and career and exercise and fashion consultants, still, she is not
much to look at. She looks wonderful, but your eye, your heart,
all in you that wants to look out on the substance of the people
of the day, doesn't care, isn't interested long, is, in fact, diminished a little.

She could be anything—a professor of Romance languages at   5
a major university, a clerk in a Jermyn Street shop, a flight attendant, a Stockholm lawyer, but nothing shows of that life or luck
or work or history, not world, not pain or freedom or sufficiency.
What you think of, what her person walking toward you in the
fierce noon light forces you to think of, after the momentary, automatic envy of her perfections, is that she looks as though she's
never had enough—goods or rights or attention or half-decent
days. Whether she is or not, she looks unutterably dissatisfied and
peevish. And yet, in order to be here on this blue-white beach on
this July day, unless you are chasing your own stray goat across
the rocks, requires a position of luxury, mobility, and privilege
common to us but beyond any imagining of the Greek woman
who walks here too with a basket of string and her hot, rusty

clothes but who, however, and not at all paradoxically, exudes a deep, sustained bass note of slumbering, solid contentment.

Insofar as ignorance always makes a space, romance rushes in 6 to people it. With so little fact at hand about either of these lives, fact that might make things plain and profound as only fact can do, there is little but romance, theories, guesswork, and yet, it seems, this accidental conjunction of women in the sun, considered, says it is not a matter of the one, the blonde, being discontent in spite of much and the other, the farm woman in black, being smugly, perhaps ignorantly content with little. That theory is too much the stuff of individual virtue, and of fairy tales: grateful peasant, happy with scraps and rags, and querulous, bitchy princess, untried, suffering every pea, pursued by frogs, awaiting a magic deliverance. Because in literal, daily fact, the Greek woman has more than the tourist, and the tourist, wherever she comes from and despite her list of equipment and privileges, is also, in literal daily fact, deprived. To see this as a possible deciphering of this scene means to stop thinking of the good life strictly in terms of goods, services, and various rights, and think instead, insofar as we can, of other, almost muted because so nearly lost to us, needs of life.

Beyond seeing that she has two arms, two good legs, a tanned 7 skin, blond hair, and friends, I know nothing about this particular tourist. Beyond knowing that she has two arms, two good legs, a face that could stop or move an army, a black dress, and can crochet lace, I know nothing about this particular peasant woman. I don't even know, it's only a clumsy guess, that "peasant" should be the qualifying adjective. I can only talk about these women as they appeared, almost a mirage in the shimmer of beach heat, almost icons, for a moment and walked past; and as they are on an island where I, too, have spent a notch of time. Whatever the Greek woman, and her kind, have enjoyed or missed, have suffered or lost in war, under dictatorship, under occupation, from men, in poverty or plenty, I don't know. The other woman, I won't further describe, won't guess at, for she is familiar to us; she is us.

I don't know in what order of importance, should that order 8 exist or be articulable, the Greek woman would place what occurs on the visible street of her life. For that is all I do see, all that we can see, and it wrings the heart, that visible street. For one thing, in most places, the street is not yet given over to the demands of the motor. The Greek is still a citizen and a large part of this day is given to whatever life goes on in public, and that life takes place on the street. Much of what we do in private, in isolation, in small personally chosen groups—eating, drinking, talking, staring into space—is, in Greece, done on the impersonal, random street. This habit of daily gathering, which is done for no particular reason, that is, there is no special occasion, lends to every day and night the feel of mild, but lively festival.

Second, among the other visible things that "underdeveloped" means, it means that—due either to a generous wisdom that has survived or else to funding that is not yet available—there is not enough money for the fit to invent shelters for the unfit. For whatever reasons, the Greek woman still lives in a culture where this has not yet happened. That is, not only are the streets used by and for people, but all sorts of people are on them, still privileged to their piece of the sun, the common bread, the work, the gossip, the ongoing parade. Our children are pitying and amazed. After several days on these streets they assume that in Greece there are more fat and slow and old, more crippled and maimed, more feeble of mind and body, more blind and begging, more, in general, outcast folks than we, Americans, have. They are especially amazed at how *old* people get to be in Greece. Being young and American, and not living in New York, the only city we have that approximates the fullness and variety of a village, they assume this is evidence of extreme longevity on the one hand, and evidence of extreme bad health on the other. It was as hard to explain about American nursing homes and other asylums and institutions as it was to explain about public nudity, how archeologists find hidden ruins, and other questions that came up on the trip.

A "developed" country is seldom mysterious but always mystifying. Where do things come from and where do they go? Life can be looked at, but not often comprehended in any of its ordinary particulars: food, shelter, work, money, producing and buying and selling. The Greek woman on the beach, again for many reasons, does still live in a world that, in those particulars—food, shelter, work, product, etc.—is comprehensible. Outside the few urban, industrial areas in Greece, it is still possible to build and conduct life without the benefit of technicians, specialists, explainers, bureaucrats, middlemen, and other modern experts. This means that there is possible an understanding of, a connection with, and a lack of technological mystification to many of the elements, objects, and products commonly lived with in any day. A typical Greek house is so simple and cunning that it could be built, or destroyed, by almost anyone. This may mean less convenience, but it also means more comprehension. For the ordinary person, there is relatively little of the multiform, continual, hardly-much-thought-about incomprehensibility of daily things—where does this lamb chop come from? where does this wash water go?—that most people in developed countries live with, or manage to ignore, every day. Therefore, for this Greek woman on the beach and her kind, there is another mind possible, one that sees, and understands, and in most instances can control many details; and a mind in which, therefore, many mysteries can grow a deeper root.

Food, to take another example, is eaten in season and most of it is locally grown, harvested or butchered, processed, sold, and consumed. There is no particular moral virtue in this fact, but this fact does signify the possibility of a sharper, more acute (it sees, it has to see and comprehend more details), and more satisfied intelligence. Having money means being able to buy the end product; therefore, money replaces the need for intricate knowledge of processes; therefore, money replaces knowledge. The understanding of a glass of water or wine, a melon, an onion, or a fried fish, from inception to end, does mean living with a different kind of mind than the one that results from having merely bought and consumed the wine or fish or onion at the end. In that sense, therefore, it is possible that the unhappy peevishness and dissatisfaction on the face of the pretty tourist comes in part from a life of being left out of knowledge of the intricate details of the complete cycle of any single thing she is able to consume. 11

Including the country of Greece. 12

There is a new world everywhere now that money will buy. It 13 is a world without a nation, though it exists as an overlay of life, something on the order of the computer, in almost any country of the globe. It is an international accommodation, and wherever it exists—whether in Madrid, London, Istanbul, Athens, Cleveland—it resembles a large airport lounge. In this way, the new world specially constructed everywhere for tourists is something like the thousands of Greek churches, as alike as eggs, and no matter what their size all modeled on the single great discovered design of Constantine's Hagia Sophia.

Inside this international accommodation is allowed only so   14
much of any specific country as lends itself as background, decor, and trinkets. In this sense, the travel posters are an accurate portrayal of exactly how little can happen on a well-engineered trip: scenery and "gifts." Because most of the world is still what would be termed "poor," the more money you can spend, nearly anyplace, the more you are removed from the rich, complex life of that place. It is possible to buy everything that puts an average American life—taps that mix hot and cold, flush toilets, heating and cooling systems, menus in English—on top of any other existing world. It is possible to pay for every familiar security and comfort and, as the posters show, still have been *there* having it. At the end of the trip, you can say that you were there.

However, the extent to which one buys familiarity, in most of   15
the world today, is also the extent to which one will not see, smell, taste, feel, or in any way be subjected to, enlightened by, or entered by that piece of the world and its people. The world's people are not blind to this fear of the unfamiliar and uncomfortable, nor insensitive to the dollars that will be paid to ward it off. In the winter months, when life returns to normal, the friendly Greek "waiters" resume their lives as masons, carpenters, builders, mechanics, schoolteachers, and so forth, a fact unknown to or overlooked by many tourists who assume, for example, that many unfinished buildings, seen languishing in the summer season, are due to neglect, laziness, disinterest, or what have you.

We all assume, and usually safely, that the more money you   16
have the more you can buy. In travel, however, the opposite is true. The less money you spend, the less money you have to spend, perhaps, the more your chances of getting a whiff, now and then, of what another place is like. There are the ideals: walking a country, living there, learning its language. Short of that, those conditions which most of us cannot meet, one can try spending as little as possible: class-D hotels, public transportation, street meals. And then one must try to be as brave and patient and good-humored and healthy as possible because, without a doubt, the less money you spend the closer you come to partaking of very annoying, confusing, exhausting, foreign, debilitating, sometimes outrageous discomfort.

For instance, the two things one would most want to avoid in   17
Greece in the summer are the intense heat and the unworldly,
unimaginable, unforeseeable amount of din. Pandemonium is, after all, a Greek idea, but in actual life, it is hardly confined to the
hour of noon. Silence is a vacuum into which, like proverbial nature, a single Greek will rush with a pure love of noise. Two
Greeks together produce more noise than 200 of any other Western nation. Greeks love above all else the human voice, raised in
any emotion; next to that they love their actions with objects.
One Greek with any object—a string of beads, a two-cylinder engine, preferably one on the eternal blink, a rug to beat, a single
child to mind, a chair to be moved—will fill all time and space
with his operation; it will be the Platonic scrape of metal chair leg
on stone street; it will be the one explanation to last for all eternity why the child should not torture the cat in the garden. A generalization: Greeks love horns, bells, animal cries, arguments,
dented fenders, lengthy explanations, soccer games, small motors,
pots and pans, cases of empty bottles, vehicles without mufflers,
cups against saucers, fireworks, political songs, metal awnings,
loudspeakers, musical instruments, grandmothers, the Orthodox
liturgy, traffic jams, the sound of breaking glass, and Mercedes
taxicabs that tootle "Mary Had a Little Lamb."

A further generalization: the above generalization is one that   18
only *not* spending money will buy. That is, you have to be in a
class-F room, in a hotel on the harbor, one flight above a taverna
frequented by fishermen, 120 degrees in the room, no screens,
mosquito coils burning in the unmoving air through the night,
and through the night—a donkey in heat tethered in the walled
garden below your shuttered, only shuttered, window. In other
words, it's quiet and cool, at the Hilton; and there are, God and
international capitalism be thanked, no donkeys.

C. S. LEWIS

The Abolition of Man

C. S. Lewis, a Cambridge professor of medieval literature, was
also a novelist, a popular speaker on moral and religious issues,
and a writer of children's books *(The Lion, the Witch, and the*

Wardrobe). "The Abolition of Man" was the last of a series of three lectures delivered at the University of Durham (England) and later published as *The Abolition of Man* (1947).

"Man's conquest of Nature" is an expression often used to de-   1
scribe the progress of applied science. "Man has Nature whacked" said someone to a friend of mine not long ago. In their context the words had a certain tragic beauty, for the speaker was dying of tuberculosis. "No matter," he said, "I know I'm one of the casualties. Of course there are casualties on the winning as well as on the losing side. But that doesn't alter the fact that it is winning." I have chosen this story as my point of departure in order to make it clear that I do not wish to disparage all that is really beneficial in the process described as "Man's conquest," much less all the real devotion and self-sacrifice that has gone to make it possible. But having done so I must proceed to analyse this conception a little more closely. In what sense is Man the possessor of increasing power over Nature?

Let us consider three typical examples: the aeroplane, the wire-   2
less, and the contraceptive. In a civilized community, in peacetime, anyone who can pay for them may use these things. But it cannot strictly be said that when he does so he is exercising his own proper or individual power over Nature. If I pay you to carry me, I am not therefore myself a strong man. Any or all of the three things I have mentioned can be withheld from some men by other men—by those who sell, or those who allow the sale, or those who own the sources of production, or those who make the goods. What we call Man's power is, in reality, a power possessed by some men which they may, or may not, allow other men to profit by. Again, as regards the powers manifested in the aeroplane or the wireless, Man is as much the patient or subject as the possessor, since he is the target both for bombs and for propaganda. And as regards contraceptives, there is a paradoxical, negative sense in which all possible future generations are the patients or subjects of a power wielded by those already alive. By contraception simply, they are denied existence; by contraception used as a means of selective breeding, they are, without their concurring voice, made to be what one generation, for its own reasons, may choose to prefer. From this point of view, what we call Man's power over Nature turns out to be a power exercised by some men over other men with Nature as its instrument.

It is, of course, a commonplace to complain that men have 3
hitherto used badly, and against their fellows, the powers that
science has given them. But that is not the point I am trying to
make. I am not speaking of particular corruptions and abuses
which an increase of moral virtue would cure: I am considering
what the thing called "Man's power over Nature" must always
and essentially be. No doubt, the picture could be modified by
public ownership of raw materials and factories and public control of scientific research. But unless we have a world state this
will still mean the power of one nation over others. And even
within the world state or the nation it will mean (in principle) the
power of majorities over minorities, and (in the concrete) of a
government over the people. And all long-term exercises of power,
especially in breeding, must mean the power of earlier generations over later ones.

The latter point is not always sufficiently emphasized, because 4
those who write on social matters have not yet learned to imitate
the physicists by always including Time among the dimensions.
In order to understand fully what Man's power over Nature, and
therefore the power of some men over other men, really means,
we must picture the race extended in time from the date of its
emergence to that of its extinction. Each generation exercises
power over its successors: and each, in so far as it modifies the
environment bequeathed to it and rebels against tradition, resists
and limits the power of its predecessors. This modifies the picture which is sometimes painted of a progressive emancipation
from tradition and a progressive control of natural processes resulting in a continual increase of human power. In reality, of
course, if any one age really attains, by eugenics and scientific education, the power to make its descendants what it pleases, all
men who live after it are the patients of that power. They are
weaker, not stronger: for though we may have put wonderful
machines in their hands we have pre-ordained how they are to
use them. And if, as is almost certain, the age which had thus attained maximum power over posterity were also the age most
emancipated from tradition, it would be engaged in reducing the
power of its predecessors almost as drastically as that of its successors. And we must also remember that, quite apart from this,
the later a generation comes—the nearer it lives to that date at
which the species becomes extinct—the less power it will have in
the forward direction, because its subjects will be so few. There

is therefore no question of a power vested in the race as a whole steadily growing as long as the race survives. The last men, far from being the heirs of power, will be of all men most subject to the dead hand of the great planners and conditioners and will themselves exercise least power upon the future. The real picture is that of one dominant age—let us suppose the hundredth century A.D.—which resists all previous ages most successfully and dominates all subsequent ages most irresistibly, and thus is the real master of the human species. But even within this master generation (itself an infinitesimal minority of the species) the power will be exercised by a minority smaller still. Man's conquest of Nature, if the dreams of some scientific planners are realized, means the rule of a few hundreds of men over billions upon billions of men. There neither is nor can be any simple increase of power on Man's side. Each new power won *by* man is a power *over* man as well. Each advance leaves him weaker as well as stronger. In every victory, besides being the general who triumphs, he is also the prisoner who follows the triumphal car.

I am not yet considering whether the total result of such ambivalent victories is a good thing or a bad. I am only making clear what Man's conquest of Nature really means and especially that final stage in the conquest, which, perhaps, is not far off. The final stage is come when Man by eugenics, by pre-natal conditioning, and by an education and propaganda based on a perfect applied psychology, has obtained full control over himself. *Human* nature will be the last part of Nature to surrender to Man. The battle will then be won. We shall have "taken the thread of life out of the hand of Clotho"[1] and be henceforth free to make our species whatever we wish it to be. The battle will indeed be won. But who, precisely, will have won it?

For the power of Man to make himself what he pleases means, as we have seen, the power of some men to make other men what *they* please. In all ages, no doubt, nurture and instruction have, in some sense, attempted to exercise this power. But the situation to which we must look forward will be novel in two respects. In the first place, the power will be enormously increased. Hitherto the plans of educationalists have achieved very little of

1. In Greek mythology Clotho was one of the Fates—female deities who supervised the destiny of humans and gods. Clotho spun the thread of destiny, Lachesis drew it, and Atropos cut it.

what they attempted and indeed, when we read them—how Plato would have every infant "a bastard nursed in a bureau," and Elyot would have the boy see no men before the age of seven and, after that, no women,[2] and how Locke wants children to have leaky shoes and no turn for poetry[3]—we may well thank the beneficent obstinacy of real mothers, real nurses, and (above all) real children for preserving the human race in such sanity as it still possesses. But the man-moulders of the new age will be armed with the powers of an omnicompetent state and an irresistible scientific technique: we shall get at last a race of conditioners who really can cut out all posterity in what shape they please. The second difference is even more important. In the older systems both the kind of man the teachers wished to produce and their motives for producing him were prescribed by the Tao[4]—a norm to which the teachers themselves were subject and from which they claimed no liberty to depart. They did not cut men to some pattern they had chosen. They handed on what they had received: they initiated the young neophyte into the mystery of humanity which overarched him and them alike. It was but old birds teaching young birds to fly. This will be changed. Values are now mere natural phenomena. Judgements of value are to be produced in the pupil as part of the conditioning. Whatever Tao there is will be the product, not the motive, of education. The conditioners have been emancipated from all that. It is one more part of Nature which they have conquered. The ultimate springs of human action are no longer, for them, something given. They have surrendered—like electricity: it is the

2. *The Boke Named the Governour*, I. iv: "Al men except physitions only shulde be excluded and kepte out of the norisery." I. vi: "After that a childe is come to seuen yeres of age . . . the most sure counsaile is to withdrawe him from all company of women." [author's note]

3. *Some Thoughts concerning Education*, §7: "I will also advise his *Feet to be wash'd* every Day in cold Water, and to have his Shoes so thin that they might leak and *let in Water,* whenever he comes near it." §174: "If he have a poetick vein, 'tis to me the strangest thing in the World that the Father should desire or suffer it to be cherished or improved. Methinks the Parents should labour to have it stifled and suppressed as much as may be." Yet Locke is one of our most sensible writers on education. [author's note]

4. Lewis uses this Chinese term, which means "the Way," to encompass the whole body of traditional wisdom that assumes ethical, moral, and aesthetic values to be "objective." He points out in an earlier chapter that these values are remarkably similar the world over.

function of the Conditioners to control, not to obey them. They know how to *produce* conscience and decide what kind of conscience they will produce. They themselves are outside, above. For we are assuming the last stage of Man's struggle with Nature. The final victory has been won. Human nature has been conquered—and, of course, has conquered, in whatever sense those words may now bear.

The Conditioners, then, are to choose what kind of artificial   7
Tao they will, for their own good reasons, produce in the Human race. They are the motivators, the creators of motives. But how are they going to be motivated themselves? For a time, perhaps, by survivals, within their own minds, of the old "natural" *Tao.* Thus at first they may look upon themselves as servants and guardians of humanity and conceive that they have a "duty" to do it "good." But it is only by confusion that they can remain in this state. They recognize the concept of duty as the result of certain processes which they can now control. Their victory has consisted precisely in emerging from the state in which they were acted upon by those processes to the state in which they use them as tools. One of the things they now have to decide is whether they will, or will not, so condition the rest of us that we can go on having the old idea of duty and the old reactions to it. How can duty help them to decide that? Duty itself is up for trial: it cannot also be the judge. And "good" fares no better. They know quite well how to produce a dozen different conceptions of good in us. The question is which, if any, they should produce. No conception of good can help them to decide. It is absurd to fix on one of the things they are comparing and make it the standard of comparison.

To some it will appear that I am inventing a factitious diffi-   8
culty for my Conditioners. Other, more simple-minded, critics may ask "Why should you suppose they will be such bad men?" But I am not supposing them to be bad men. They are, rather, not men (in the old sense) at all. They are, if you like, men who have sacrificed their own share in traditional humanity in order to devote themselves to the task of deciding what "Humanity" shall henceforth mean. "Good" and "bad," applied to them, are words without content: for it is from them that the content of these words is henceforward to be derived. Nor is their difficulty factitious. We might suppose that it was possible to say "After

all, most of us want more or less the same things—food and drink and sexual intercourse, amusement, art, science, and the longest possible life for individuals and for the species. Let them simply say, This is what we happen to like, and go on to condition men in the way most likely to produce it. Where's the trouble?" But this will not answer. In the first place, it is false that we all really like the same things. But even if we did, what motive is to impel the Conditioners to scorn delights and live laborious days in order that we, and posterity, may have what we like? Their duty? But that is only the *Tao*, which they may decide to impose on us, but which cannot be valid for them. If they accept it, then they are no longer the makers of conscience but still its subjects, and their final conquest over Nature has not really happened. The preservation of the species? But why should the species be preserved? One of the questions before them is whether this feeling for posterity (they know well how it is produced) shall be continued or not. However far they go back, or down, they can find no ground to stand on. Every motive they try to act on becomes at once a *petitio*.[5] It is not that they are bad men. They are not men at all. Stepping outside the *Tao*, they have stepped into the void. Nor are their subjects necessarily unhappy men. They are not men at all: they are artefacts. Man's final conquest has proved to be the abolition of Man.

Yet the Conditioners will act. When I said just now that all   9
motives fail them, I should have said all motives except one. All motives that claim any validity other than that of their felt emotional weight at a given moment have failed them. Everything except the *sic volo, sic jubeo*[6] has been explained away. But what never claimed objectivity cannot be destroyed by subjectivism. The impulse to scratch when I itch or to pull to pieces when I am inquisitive is immune from the solvent which is fatal to my justice, or honour, or care for posterity. When all that says "it is good" has been debunked, what says "I want" remains. It cannot be exploded or "seen through" because it never had any pretensions. The Conditioners, therefore, must come to be motivated simply by their own pleasure. I am not here speaking of the corrupting influence of power nor expressing the fear that under

5. *petitio principii*: begging the question; circular argument.
6. *sic volo, sic jubeo*: "This I want, this I command."

it our Conditioners will degenerate. The very words *corrupt* and *degenerate* imply a doctrine of value and are therefore meaningless in this context. My point is that those who stand outside all judgements of value cannot have any ground for preferring one of their own impulses to another except the emotional strength of that impulse. We may legitimately hope that among the impulses which arise in minds thus emptied of all "rational" or "spiritual" motives, some will be benevolent. I am very doubtful myself whether the benevolent impulses, stripped of that preference and encouragement which the *Tao* teaches us to give them and left to their merely natural strength and frequency as psychological events, will have much influence. I am very doubtful whether history shows us one example of a man who, having stepped outside traditional morality and attained power, has used that power benevolently. I am inclined to think that the Conditioners will hate the conditioned. Though regarding as an illusion the artificial conscience which they produce in us their subjects, they will yet perceive that it creates in us an illusion of meaning for our lives which compares favourably with the futility of their own: and they will envy us as eunuchs envy men. But I do not insist on this, for it is mere conjecture. What is not conjecture is that our hope even of a "conditioned" happiness rests on what is ordinarily called "chance"—the chance that benevolent impulses may on the whole predominate in our Conditioners. For without the judgement "Benevolence is good"—that is, without re-entering the *Tao*—they can have no ground for promoting or stabilizing their benevolent impulses rather than any others. By the logic of their position they must just take their impulses as they come, from chance. And Chance here means Nature. It is from heredity, digestion, the weather, and the association of ideas, that the motives of the Conditioners will spring. Their extreme rationalism, by "seeing through" all "rational" motives, leaves them creatures of wholly irrational behaviour. If you will not obey the *Tao*, or else commit suicide, obedience to impulse (and therefore, in the long run, to mere "nature") is the only course left open.

At the moment, then, of Man's victory over Nature, we find   10
the whole human race subjected to some individual men, and those individuals subjected to that in themselves which is purely "natural"—to their irrational impulses. Nature, untrammelled

by values, rules the Conditioners and, through them, all humanity. Man's conquest of Nature turns out, in the moment of its consummation, to be Nature's conquest of Man. Every victory we seemed to win has led us, step by step, to this conclusion. All Nature's apparent reverses have been but tactical withdrawals. We thought we were beating her back when she was luring us on. What looked to us like hands held up in surrender was really the opening of arms to enfold us for ever. If the fully planned and conditioned world (with its *Tao* a mere product of the planning) comes into existence, Nature will be troubled no more by the restive species that rose in revolt against her so many millions of years ago, will be vexed no longer by its chatter of truth and mercy and beauty and happiness. *Ferum victorem cepit:*[7] and if the eugenics are efficient enough there will be no second revolt, but all snug beneath the Conditioners, and the Conditioners beneath her, till the moon falls or the sun grows cold.

My point may be clearer to some if it is put in a different   11
form. Nature is a word of varying meanings, which can best be understood if we consider its various opposites. The Natural is the opposite of the Artificial, the Civil, the Human, the Spiritual, and the Supernatural. The Artificial does not now concern us. If we take the rest of the list of opposites, however, I think we can get a rough idea of what men have meant by Nature and what it is they oppose to her. Nature seems to be the spatial and temporal, as distinct from what is less fully so or not so at all. She seems to be the world of quantity, as against the world of quality: of objects as against consciousness: of the bound, as against the wholly or partially autonomous: of that which knows no values as against that which both has and perceives value: of efficient causes (or, in some modern systems, of no causality at all) as against final causes. Now I take it that when we understand a thing analytically and then dominate and use it for our own convenience we reduce it to the level of "Nature" in the sense that we suspend our judgements of value about it, ignore its final cause (if any), and treat it in terms of quantity. This repression of elements in what would otherwise be our total reaction to it is sometimes very noticeable and even painful: something has to be overcome before we can cut up a dead man or a live animal in a

---

7. *ferum victorem cepit:* "Nature captures the victor."

dissecting room. These objects *resist* the movement of the mind whereby we thrust them into the world of mere Nature. But in other instances too, a similar price is exacted for our analytical knowledge and manipulative power, even if we have ceased to count it. We do not look at trees either as Dryads or as beautiful objects while we cut them into beams: the first man who did so may have felt the price keenly, and the bleeding trees in Virgil and Spenser may be far-off echoes of that primeval sense of impiety. The stars lost their divinity as astronomy developed, and the Dying God has no place in chemical agriculture. To many, no doubt, this process is simply the gradual discovery that the real world is different from what we expected, and the old opposition to Galileo or to "bodysnatchers" is simply obscurantism. But that is not the whole story. It is not the greatest of modern scientists who feel most sure that the object, stripped of its qualitative properties and reduced to mere quantity, is wholly real. Little scientists, and little unscientific followers of science, may think so. The great minds know very well that the object, so treated, is an artificial abstraction, that something of its reality has been lost.

From this point of view the conquest of Nature appears in a   12
new light. We reduce things to mere Nature *in order that* we may "conquer" them. We are always conquering Nature, because "Nature" is the name for what we have, to some extent, conquered. The price of conquest is to treat a thing as mere Nature. Every conquest over Nature increases her domain. The stars do not become Nature till we can weigh and measure them: the soul does not become Nature till we can psycho-analyse her. The wresting of powers *from* Nature is also the surrendering of things *to* Nature. As long as this process stops short of the final stage we may well hold that the gain outweighs the loss. But as soon as we take the final step of reducing our own species to the level of mere Nature, the whole process is stultified, for this time the being who stood to gain and the being who has been sacrificed are one and the same. This is one of the many instances where to carry a principle to what seems its logical conclusion produces absurdity. It is like the famous Irishman who found that a certain kind of stove reduced his fuel bill by half and thence concluded that two stoves of the same kind would enable him to warm his house with no fuel at all. It is the magician's bargain: give up our soul, get power in return. But once our

souls, that is, our selves, have been given up, the power thus conferred will not belong to us. We shall in fact be the slaves and puppets of that to which we have given our souls. It is in Man's power to treat himself as a mere "natural object" and his own judgements of value as raw material for scientific manipulation to alter at will. The objection to his doing so does not lie in the fact that his point of view (like one's first day in a dissecting room) is painful and shocking till we grow used to it. The pain and the shock are at most a warning and a symptom. The real objection is that if man chooses to treat himself as raw material, raw material he will be: not raw material to be manipulated, as he fondly imagined, by himself, but by mere appetite, that is, mere Nature, in the person of his dehumanized Conditioners.

We have been trying, like Lear,[8] to have it both ways: to lay   13
down our human prerogative and yet at the same time to retain it. It is impossible. Either we are rational spirit obliged for ever to obey the absolute values of the *Tao,* or else we are mere nature to be kneaded and cut into new shapes for the pleasures of masters who must, by hypothesis, have no motive but their own "natural" impulses. Only the *Tao* provides a common human law of action which can overarch rulers and ruled alike. A dogmatic belief in objective value is necessary to the very idea of a rule which is not tyranny or an obedience which is not slavery.

I am not here thinking solely, perhaps not even chiefly, of   14
those who are our public enemies at the moment. The process which, if not checked, will abolish Man, goes on apace among Communists and Democrats no less than among Fascists. The methods may (at first) differ in brutality. But many a mild-eyed scientist in pince-nez, many a popular dramatist, many an amateur philosopher in our midst, means in the long run just the same as the Nazi rulers of Germany. Traditional values are to be "debunked" and mankind to be cut out into some fresh shape at the will (which must, by hypothesis, be an arbitrary will) of some few lucky people in one lucky generation which has learned how to do it. The belief that we can invent "ideologies" at pleasure, and the consequent treatment of mankind as mere ὕλη, specimens, preparations, begins to affect our very language. Once we killed bad men: now we liquidate unsocial elements. Virtue has

---

8. Shakespeare's King Lear surrenders his authority and then is dismayed to find that others rule him.

become *integration* and diligence *dynamism,* and boys likely to be worthy of a commission are "potential officer material." Most wonderful of all, the virtues of thrift and temperance, and even of ordinary intelligence, are *sales-resistance.*

The true significance of what is going on has been concealed   15 by the use of the abstraction Man. Not that the word Man is necessarily a pure abstraction. In the *Tao* itself, as long as we remain within it, we find the concrete reality in which to participate is to be truly human: the real common will and common reason of humanity, alive, and growing like a tree, and branching out, as the situation varies, into ever new beauties and dignities of application. While we speak from within the *Tao* we can speak of Man having power over himself in a sense truly analogous to an individual's self-control. But the moment we step outside and regard the *Tao* as a mere subjective product, this possibility has disappeared. What is now common to all men is a mere abstract universal, an H.C.F.,[9] and Man's conquest of himself means simply the rule of the Conditioners over the conditioned human material, the world of post-humanity which, some knowingly and some unknowingly, nearly all men in all nations are at present labouring to produce.

Nothing I can say will prevent some people from describing   16 this lecture as an attack on science. I deny the charge, of course: and real Natural Philosophers (there are some now alive) will perceive that in defending value I defend *inter alia*[10] the value of knowledge, which must die like every other when its roots in the *Tao* are cut. But I can go further than that. I even suggest that from Science herself the cure might come. I have described as a "magician's bargain" that process whereby man surrenders object after object, and finally himself, to Nature in return for power. And I meant what I said. The fact that the scientist has succeeded where the magician failed has put such a wide contrast between them in popular thought that the real story of the birth of Science is misunderstood. You will even find people who write about the sixteenth century as if Magic were a medieval survival and Science the new thing that came to sweep it away. Those who have studied the period know better. There was very little magic in the Middle Ages: the sixteenth and seventeenth

---

9. H.C.F.: highest common factor.
10. *inter alia:* "among other things."

centuries are the high noon of magic. The serious magical endeavour and the serious scientific endeavour are twins: one was sickly and died, the other strong and throve. But they were twins. They were born of the same impulse. I allow that some (certainly not all) of the early scientists were actuated by a pure love of knowledge. But if we consider the temper of that age as a whole we can discern the impulse of which I speak. There is something which unites magic and applied science while separating both from the "wisdom" of earlier ages. For the wise men of old the cardinal problem had been how to conform the soul to reality, and the solution had been knowledge, self-discipline, and virtue. For magic and applied science alike the problem is how to subdue reality to the wishes of men: the solution is a technique; and both, in the practice of this technique, are ready to do things hitherto regarded as disgusting and impious—such as digging up and mutilating the dead. If we compare the chief trumpeter of the new era (Bacon) with Marlowe's Faustus,[11] the similarity is striking. You will read in some critics that Faustus has a thirst for knowledge. In reality, he hardly mentions it. It is not truth he wants from his devils, but gold and guns and girls. "All things that move between the quiet poles shall be at his command" and "a sound magician is a mighty god." In the same spirit Bacon condemns those who value knowledge as an end in itself: this, for him, is to use as a mistress for pleasure what ought to be a spouse for fruit. The true object is to extend Man's power to the performance of all things possible. He rejects magic because it does not work, but his goal is that of the magician. In Paracelsus[12] the characters of magician and scientist are combined. No doubt those who really founded modern science were usually those whose love of truth exceeded their love of power; in every mixed movement the efficacy comes from the good elements not from the bad. But the presence of the bad elements is not irrelevant to the direction the efficacy takes. It might be going too far to say that the modern scientific movement was tainted from its

11. Francis Bacon (1561–1626) advocated methodical scientific study. Faustus, protagonist of Christopher Marlowe's 1606 play, was a magician who gained his power over nature, according to legend, by selling his soul to the devil.
12. Phillipus Aureolus Paracelsus (1493–1541), the German-Swiss sixteenth-century father of pharmaceutical medicine, as well as an alchemist, contended that, "Magic is a great hidden wisdom—Reason is a great open folly."

birth: but I think it would be true to say that it was born in an unhealthy neighbourhood and at an inauspicious hour. Its triumphs may have been too rapid and purchased at too high a price: reconsideration, and something like repentance, may be required.

Is it, then, possible to imagine a new Natural Philosophy, continually conscious that the "natural object" produced by analysis and abstraction is not reality but only a view, and always correcting the abstraction? I hardly know what I am asking for. I hear rumours that Goethe's approach to nature deserves fuller consideration—that even Dr. Steiner[13] may have seen something that orthodox researchers have missed. The regenerate science which I have in mind would not do even to minerals and vegetables what modern science threatens to do to man himself. When it explained it would not explain away. When it spoke of the parts it would remember the whole. While studying the *It* it would not lose what Martin Buber calls the *Thou*-situation. The analogy between the *Tao* of Man and the instincts of an animal species would mean for it new light cast on the unknown thing, Instinct, by the only known reality of conscience and not a reduction of conscience to the category of Instinct. Its followers would not be free with the words *only* and *merely*. In a word, it would conquer Nature without being at the same time conquered by her and buy knowledge at a lower cost than that of life.

Perhaps I am asking impossibilities. Perhaps, in the nature of things, analytical understanding must always be a basilisk which kills what it sees and only sees by killing. But if the scientists themselves cannot arrest this process before it reaches the common Reason and kills that too, then someone else must arrest it. What I most fear is the reply that I am "only one more" obscurantist, that this barrier, like all previous barriers set up against the advance of science, can be safely passed. Such a reply springs from the fatal serialism of the modern imagination—the image of infinite unilinear progression which so haunts our minds. Be-

13. Both Johann Wolfgang von Goethe (German poet and dramatist, 1749–1832) and his admirer Rudolf Steiner (Austrian social philosopher, 1861–1925) thought the analytic nature of science too restrictive. They emphasized the importance of knowledge that synthesizes human intellect and spirit with the supposedly objective world.

cause we have to use numbers so much we tend to think of every process as if it must be like the numeral series, where every step, to all eternity, is the same kind of step as the one before. I implore you to remember the Irishman and his two stoves. There are progressions in which the last step is *sui generis*—incommensurable with the others—and in which to go the whole way is to undo all the labour of your previous journey. To reduce the *Tao* to a mere natural product is a step of that kind. Up to that point, the kind of explanation which explains things away may give us something, though at a heavy cost. But you cannot go on "explaining away" for ever: you will find that you have explained explanation itself away. You cannot go on "seeing through" things for ever. The whole point of seeing through something is to see something through it. It is good that the window should be transparent, because the street or garden beyond it is opaque. How if you saw through the garden too? It is no use trying to "see through" first principles. If you see through everything, then everything is transparent. But a wholly transparent world is an invisible world. To "see through" all things is the same as not to see.

Barbara Ehrenreich

Spudding Out

Barbara Ehrenreich earned a Ph.D. in biology and taught health sciences at the university level before she became a full-time writer. Her first books, written with her husband or with collaborator Deirdre English, focus on the politics of health care, particularly on male domination of the field of women's health. Later Ehrenreich acquired a reputation as a leftist firebrand and as a writer who could mix her political convictions with her remarkable sense of humor: One of her collections of essays is wryly and somewhat accurately titled *The Snarling Citizen* (1995). "Spudding Out" is from *The Worst Years of Our Lives* (1990).

Someone has to speak for them, because they have, to a person, lost the power to speak for themselves. I am referring to that   1 great mass of Americans who were once known as the "salt of the earth," then as "the silent majority," more recently as "the viewing public," and now, alas, as "couch potatoes." What drives them—or rather, leaves them sapped and spineless on their reclining chairs? What are they seeking—beyond such obvious goals as a tastefully colorized version of *The Maltese Falcon?*

My husband was the first in the family to "spud out," as the   2
expression now goes. Soon everyone wanted one of those zip-up "Couch Potato Bags," to keep warm in during David Letterman. The youngest, and most thoroughly immobilized, member of the family relies on a remote that controls his TV, stereo, and VCR, and can also shut down the neighbor's pacemaker at fifteen yards.

But we never see the neighbors anymore, nor they us. This   3
saddens me, because Americans used to be a great and restless people, fond of the outdoors in all of its manifestations, from Disney World to miniature golf. Some experts say there are virtues in mass agoraphobia, that it strengthens the family and reduces highway deaths. But I would point out that there are still a few things that cannot be done in the den, especially by someone zipped into a body bag. These include racquetball, voting, and meeting strange people in bars.

Most psychologists interpret the couch potato trend as a neg-   4
ative reaction to the outside world. Indeed, the list of reasons to stay safely tucked indoors lengthens yearly. First there was crime, then AIDS, then side-stream smoke. To this list should be added "fear of the infrastructure," for we all know someone who rashly stepped outside only to be buried in a pothole, hurled from a collapsing bridge, or struck by a falling airplane.

But it is not just the outside world that has let us down. Let's   5
face it, despite a decade-long campaign by the "profamily" movement, the family has been a disappointment. The reason lies in an odd circular dynamic: we watch television to escape from our families because television shows us how dull our families really are.

Compare your own family to, for example, the Huxtables, the   6
Keatons, or the peppy young people on *thirtysomething*. In those families, even the three-year-olds are stand-up comics, and the most insipid remark is hailed with heartening outbursts of canned laughter. When television families aren't gathered around the kitchen table exchanging wisecracks, they are experiencing brief but moving dilemmas, which are handily solved by the youngest

child or by some cute extraterrestrial house-guest. Emerging from *Family Ties* or *My Two Dads*, we are forced to acknowledge that our own families are made up of slow-witted, emotionally crippled people who would be lucky to qualify for seats in the studio audience of *Jeopardy!*

But gradually I have come to see that there is something besides fear of the outside and disgust with our families that drives us to spudhood—some positive attraction, some deep cathexis to television itself. For a long time it eluded me. When I watched television, mainly as a way of getting to know my husband and children, I found that my mind wandered to more interesting things, like whether to get up and make ice cubes.

Only after many months of viewing did I begin to understand the force that has transformed the American people into root vegetables. If you watch TV for a very long time, day in, day out, you will begin to notice something eerie and unnatural about the world portrayed therein. I don't mean that it is two-dimensional or lacks a well-developed critique of the capitalist consumer culture or something superficial like that. I mean something so deeply obvious that it's almost scary: when you watch television, you will see people doing many things—chasing fast cars, drinking lite beer, shooting each other at close range, etc. But you will never see people *watching television*. Well, maybe for a second, before the phone rings or a brand-new, multiracial adopted child walks into the house. But never *really watching*, hour after hour, the way *real* people do.

Way back in the beginning of the television era, this was not so strange, because real people actually did many of the things people do on TV, even if it was only bickering with their mothers-in-law about which toilet paper to buy. But modern people, i.e., couch potatoes, do nothing that is ever shown on television (because it is either dangerous or would involve getting up from the couch). And what they do do—watch television—is far too boring to be televised for more than a fraction of a second, not even by Andy Warhol, bless his boredom-proof little heart.[1]

1. Artist and filmmaker Andy Warhol (1928–1987) became well known for his use of popular culture in art. Warhol's intentional repetition of images and deliberately boring recordings of mundane activities—such as *Empire*, which filmed the Empire State Building for 24 hours from a position across the street—led one critic to announce that "not one ounce of sentiment disturbs the numb silence of these images."

So why do we keep on watching? The answer, by now, should   10
be perfectly obvious: we love television because television brings
us a world in which television does not exist. In fact, deep in
their hearts, this is what the spuds crave most: a rich, new, par-
ticipatory life, in which family members look each other in the
eye, in which people walk outside and banter with the neighbors,
where there is adventure, possibility, danger, feeling, all in natural color, stereophonic sound, and three dimensions, without
commercial interruptions, and starring . . . us.

"You mean some new kind of computerized interactive   11
medium?" the children asked hopefully, pert as the progeny on a
Tuesday night sitcom. But before I could expand on this concept—known to our ancestors as "real life"—they were back at
the box, which may be, after all, the only place left to find it.

RANDALL JARRELL

A Sad Heart at the Supermarket

Randall Jarrell is primarily known as a poet and a critic of poetry.
His best-known early work reflected his experience in the U.S.
Army Air Corps during World War II. In the years following the
war he witnessed with alarm the social changes created by America's rising prosperity and rising commercialism. The nation that
triumphed over fascism seemed to him to be surrendering to a set
of values that were soulless and superficial. "A Sad Heart at the
Supermarket," from which the selection here is excerpted, was
first published in *Daedalus* in 1960.

Advertising men, businessmen speak continually of *media* or   1
the media or *the mass media*. One of their trade journals is
named, simply, *Media*. It is an impressive word: one imagines
Mephistopheles offering Faust[1] *media that no man has ever
known;* one feels, while the word is in one's ear, that abstract,

1. According to legend, Mephistopheles (the personification of the devil) offered
the learned Doctor Faust youth, knowledge, and magic—in exchange for his
soul. In the German dramatist Goethe's (1749–1832) *Faust*, Mephistopheles tells
Faust, "I am giving you things that no man has ever known."

overmastering powers, of a scale and intensity unimagined yesterday, are being offered one by the technicians who discovered and control them—offered, and at a price. The word has the clear fatal ring of that new world whose space we occupy so luxuriously and precariously; the world that produces mink stoles, rockabilly records, and tactical nuclear weapons by the million; the world that Attila, Galileo, Hansel and Gretel never knew.

And yet, it's only the plural of *medium.* "*Medium,*" says the 2
dictionary, "that which lies in the middle; hence, middle condition or degree . . . A substance through which a force acts or an effect is transmitted . . . That through or by which anything is accomplished; as, an advertising *medium* . . . *Biol.* A nutritive mixture or substance, as broth, gelatin, agar, for cultivating bacteria, fungi, etc."

Let us name *our* trade journal *The Medium.* For all these 3
media—television, radio, movies, newspapers, magazines, and the rest—are a single medium, in whose depths we are all being cultivated. This Medium is of middle condition or degree, mediocre; it lies in the middle of everything, between a man and his neighbor, his wife, his child, his self; it, more than anything else, is the substance through which the forces of our society act upon us, and make us into what our society needs.

And what does it need? For us to need. 4

Oh, it needs for us to do or be many things: workers, techni- 5
cians, executives, soldiers, housewives. But first of all, last of all, it needs for us to be buyers; consumers; beings who want much and will want more—who want consistently and insatiably. Find some spell to make us turn away from the stoles, the records, and the weapons, and our world will change into something to us unimaginable. Find some spell to make us see that the product or service that yesterday was an unthinkable luxury today is an inexorable necessity, and, our world will go on. It is the Medium which casts this spell—which is this spell. As we look at the television set, listen to the radio, read the magazines, the frontier of necessity is always being pushed forward. The Medium shows us what our new needs are—how often, without it, we should not have known!—and it shows us how they can be satisfied by buying something. The act of buying something is at the root of our world; if anyone wishes to paint the genesis of things in our society, he will paint a picture of God holding out to Adam a check-book or credit card or Charge-A-Plate.

But how quickly our poor naked Adam is turned into a con- 6
sumer, is linked to others by the great chain of buying!

> No outcast he, bewildered and depressed:
> Along his infant veins are interfused
> The gravitation and the filial bond
> Of nature that connect him with the world.²

Children of three or four can ask for a brand of cereal, sing some
soap's commercial; by the time that they are twelve or thirteen they
are not children but teen-age consumers, interviewed, graphed,
analyzed. They are well on their way to becoming that ideal figure of our culture, the knowledgeable consumer. Let me define
him: the knowledgeable consumer is someone who, when he comes
to Weimar,³ knows how to buy a Weimaraner.

Daisy's voice sounded like money;⁴ everything about the knowl- 7
edgeable consumer looks like or sounds like or feels like money,
and informed money at that. To live is to consume, to understand
life is to know what to consume: he has learned to understand
this, so that his life is a series of choices—correct ones—among
the products and services of the world. He is able to choose to
consume something, of course, only because sometime, somewhere, he or someone else produced something—but just when
or where or what no longer seems to us of as much interest. We
may still go to Methodist or Baptist or Presbyterian churches on
Sunday, but the Protestant ethic of frugal industry, of production
for its own sake, is gone.

Production has come to seem to our society not much more 8
than a condition prior to consumption. "The challenge of today," an advertising agency writes, "is to make the consumer
raise his level of demand." This challenge has been met: the
Medium has found it easy to make its people feel the continually
increasing lacks, the many specialized dissatisfactions (merging
into one great dissatisfaction, temporarily assuaged by new purchases) that it needs for them to feel. When in some magazine we
see the Medium at its most nearly perfect, we hardly know
which half is entertaining and distracting us, which half making

2. William Wordsworth, *The Prelude*, 2: 241–244.
3. Weimar is a German city rich with cultural and historical associations; a
Weimaraner is a breed of dog.
4. Daisy Buchanan, in F. Scott Fitzgerald's *The Great Gatsby*.

us buy: some advertisement may be more ingeniously entertaining than the text beside it, but it is the text which has made us long for a product more passionately. When one finishes *Holiday* or *Harper's Bazaar* or *House and Garden* or *The New Yorker* or *High Fidelity* or *Road and Track* or—but make your own list—buying something, going somewhere seems a necessary completion to the act of reading the magazine.

Reader, isn't buying or fantasy-buying an important part of your and my emotional life? (If you reply, *No*, I'll think of you with bitter envy as more than merely human; as deeply un-American.) It is a standard joke that when a woman is bored or sad she buys something, to cheer herself up; but in this respect we are all women together, and can hear complacently the reminder of how feminine this consumerworld of ours has become. One imagines as a characteristic dialogue of our time an interview in which someone is asking of a vague gracious figure, a kind of Mrs. America: "But while you waited for the intercontinental ballistic missiles what did you *do?*" She answers: "I bought things."

She reminds one of the sentinel at Pompeii[5]—a space among ashes, now, but at his post: she too did what she was supposed to do. Our society has delivered us—most of us—from the bonds of necessity, so that we no longer struggle to find food to keep from starving, clothing and shelter to keep from freezing; yet if the ends for which we work and of which we dream are only clothes and restaurants and houses, possessions, consumption, how have we escaped?—we have exchanged man's old bondage for a new voluntary one. It is more than a figure of speech to say that the consumer is trained for his job of consuming as the factory-worker is trained for his job of producing; and the first can be a longer, more complicated training, since it is easier to teach a man to handle a tool, to read a dial, than it is to teach him to ask, always, for a name-brand aspirin—to want, someday, a stand-by generator.

What is that? You don't know? I used not to know, but the readers of *House Beautiful* all know, so that now I know. It is the electrical generator that stands in the basement of the suburban

9

10

11

---

5. The ancient Italian city of Pompeii was buried by an eruption of Mount Vesuvius in A.D. 79; the cinders and ashes remarkably preserved the city's ruins, including the remains of human beings who died on the spot.

houseowner, shining, silent, till at last one night the lights go out, the furnace stops, the freezer's food begins to—

Ah, but it's frozen for good, the lights are on forever; the   12 owner has switched on the stand-by generator.

But you don't see that he really needs the generator, you'd   13 rather have seen him buy a second car? He has two. A second bathroom? He has four. When the People of the Medium doubled everything, he doubled everything; and now that he's gone twice round he will have to wait three years, or four, till both are obsolescent—but while he waits there are so many new needs that he can satisfy, so many things a man can buy. "Man wants but little here below / Nor wants that little long," said the poet;[6] what a lie! Man wants almost unlimited quantities of almost everything, and he wants it till the day he dies.

Sometimes in *Life* or *Look* we see a double-page photograph of   14 some family standing on the lawn among its possessions: station-wagon, swimming-pool, power-cruiser, sports-car, tape-recorder, television sets, radios, cameras, power lawn-mower, garden tractor, lathe, barbecue-set, sporting equipment, domestic appliances—all the gleaming, grotesquely imaginative paraphernalia of its existence. It was hard to get everything on two pages, soon it will need four. It is like a dream, a child's dream before Christmas; yet if the members of the family doubt that they are awake, they have only to reach out and pinch something. The family seems pale and small, a negligible appendage, beside its possessions; only a human being would need to ask: "Which owns which?" We are fond of saying that something is not just something but "a way of life"; this too is a way of life—our way, the way.

Emerson, in his spare stony New England, a few miles from   15 Walden, could write: "Things are in the saddle / And ride mankind."[7] He could say more now: that they are in the theater and studio, and entertain mankind; are in the pulpit and preach to mankind. The values of business, in a business society like our own, are reflected in every sphere: values which agree with them are reinforced, values which disagree are cancelled out or have lip service paid to them. In business what sells is good, and that's the end of it—that is what *good* means; if the world doesn't beat

6. British poet Oliver Goldsmith (1728–1774).
7. American poet and philosopher Ralph Waldo Emerson (1803–1882).

a path to your door, your mouse-trap wasn't better. The values of the Medium—which is both a popular business itself and the cause of popularity in other businesses—are business values: money, success, celebrity. If we are representative members of our society, the Medium's values are ours; and even if we are unrepresentative, non-conforming, our hands are—too often— subdued to the element they work in, and our unconscious expectations are all that we consciously reject. Darwin said that he always immediately wrote down evidence against a theory because otherwise, he'd noticed, he would forget it; in the same way, we keep forgetting the existence of those poor and unknown failures whom we might rebelliously love and admire.

If you're so smart why aren't you rich? is the ground-bass of our society, a grumbling and quite unanswerable criticism, since the society's non-monetary values *are* directly convertible into money. Celebrity turns into testimonials, lectures, directorships, presidencies, the capital gains of an autobiography *Told To* some professional ghost who photographs the man's life as Bachrach[8] photographs his body. I read in the newspapers a lyric and perhaps exaggerated instance of this direct conversion of celebrity into money: his son accompanied Adlai Stevenson[9] on a trip to Russia, took snapshots of his father, and sold them (to accompany his father's account of the trip) *to Look* for $20,000. When Liberace said that his critics' unfavorable reviews hurt him so much that he cried all the way to the bank, one had to admire the correctness and penetration of his press-agent's wit—in another age, what might not such a man have become!

16

E. M. FORSTER

The Machine Stops

E. M. Forster was born in London but spent most of his childhood in the Hertfordshire countryside. He took degrees in classics and history from Cambridge University in 1901, and then for two decades he lived alternately in England and abroad—in Greece, Italy, India, and Egypt—developing in the process a world view

8. well-known American photography studio.
9. Adlai Stevenson (1900–1965): American statesman.

antithetical to that of the safe, conventional British middle class. By the time he settled permanently in England in 1925, he had published four novels, including his masterpiece, *A Passage to India* (1924). "The Machine Stops" was first published in the *Oxford and Cambridge Review* in 1909.

I. THE AIR SHIP

Imagine, if you can, a small room, hexagonal in shape, like   1
the cell of a bee. It is lighted neither by window nor by lamp, yet it is filled with a soft radiance. There are no apertures for ventilation, yet the air is fresh. There are no musical instruments, and yet, at the moment that my meditation opens, this room is throbbing with melodious sounds. An arm-chair is in the centre, by its side a reading-desk—that is all the furniture. And in the arm-chair there sits a swaddled lump of flesh—a woman, about five feet high, with a face as white as a fungus. It is to her that the little room belongs.

An electric bell rang.   2

The woman touched a switch and the music was silent.   3

"I suppose I must see who it is," she thought, and set her chair   4
in motion. The chair, like the music, was worked by machinery, and it rolled her to the other side of the room, where the bell still rang importunately.

"Who is it?" she called. Her voice was irritable, for she had   5
been interrupted often since the music began. She knew several thousand people; in certain directions human intercourse had advanced enormously.

But when she listened into the receiver, her white face wrin-   6
kled into smiles, and she said:

"Very well. Let us talk, I will isolate myself. I do not expect   7
anything important will happen for the next five minutes—for I can give you fully five minutes, Kuno. Then I must deliver my lecture on 'Music during the Australian Period.'"

She touched the isolation knob, so that no one else could   8
speak to her. Then she touched the lighting apparatus, and the little room was plunged into darkness.

"Be quick!" she called, her irritation returning. "Be quick,   9
Kuno; here I am in the dark wasting my time."

But it was fully fifteen seconds before the round plate that she   10
held in her hands began to glow. A faint blue light shot across it,

darkening to purple, and presently she could see the image of her son, who lived on the other side of the earth, and he could see her.

"Kuno, how slow you are."

He smiled gravely.

"I really believe you enjoy dawdling."

"I have called you before, mother, but you were always busy or isolated. I have something particular to say."

"What is it, dearest boy? Be quick. Why could you not send it by pneumatic post?"

"Because I prefer saying such a thing. I want———"

"Well?"

"I want you to come and see me."

Vashti watched his face in the blue plate.

"But I can see you!" she exclaimed. "What more do you want?"

"I want to see you not through the Machine," said Kuno. "I want to speak to you not through the wearisome Machine."

"Oh, hush!" said his mother, vaguely shocked. "You mustn't say anything against the Machine."

"Why not?"

"One mustn't."

"You talk as if a god had made the Machine," cried the other. "I believe that you pray to it when you are unhappy. Men made it, do not forget that. Great men, but men. The Machine is much, but it is not everything. I see something like you in this plate, but I do not see you. I hear something like you through this telephone, but I do not hear you. That is why I want you to come. Come and stop with me. Pay me a visit, so that we can meet face to face, and talk about the hopes that are in my mind."

She replied that she could scarcely spare the time for a visit.

"The air-ship barely takes two days to fly between me and you."

"I dislike air-ships."

"Why?"

"I dislike seeing the horrible brown earth, and the sea, and the stars when it is dark. I get no ideas in an air-ship."

"I do not get them anywhere else."

"What kind of ideas can the air give you?"

He paused for an instant.

"Do you not know four big stars that form an oblong, and three stars close together in the middle of the oblong, and hanging from these stars, three other stars?"

"No, I do not. I dislike the stars. But did they give you an   35
idea? How interesting; tell me."

"I had an idea that they were like a man."   36

"I do not understand."   37

"The four big stars are the man's shoulders and his knees. The   38
three stars in the middle are like the belts that men wore once,
and the three stars hanging are like a sword."

"A sword?"   39

"Men carried swords about with them, to kill animals and   40
other men."

"It does not strike me as a very good idea, but it is certainly   41
original. When did it come to you first?"

"In the air-ship————" He broke off and she fancied that he   42
looked sad. She could not be sure, for the Machine did not trans-
mit *nuances* of expression. It only gave a general idea of people—
an idea that was good enough for all practical purposes, Vashti
thought. The imponderable bloom, declared by a discredited philosophy to be the actual essence of intercourse, was rightly ignored by the Machine, just as the imponderable bloom of the
grape was ignored by the manufacturers of artificial fruit. Something "good enough" had long since been accepted by our race.

"The truth is," he continued, "that I want to see these stars   43
again. They are curious stars. I want to see them not from the
air-ship, but from the surface of the earth, as our ancestors did,
thousands of years ago. I want to visit the surface of the earth."

She was shocked again.   44

"Mother, you must come, if only to explain to me what is the   45
harm of visiting the surface of the earth."

"No harm," she replied, controlling herself. "But no advan-   46
tage. The surface of the earth is only dust and mud, no life remains on it, and you would need a respirator, or the cold of the
outer air would kill you. One dies immediately in the outer air."

"I know; of course I shall take all precautions."   47

"And besides————"   48

"Well?"   49

She considered, and chose her words with care. Her son had a   50
queer temper, and she wished to dissuade him from the expedition.

"It is contrary to the spirit of the age," she asserted.   51

"Do you mean by that, contrary to the Machine?"   52

"In a sense, but————"   53

His image in the blue plate faded.   54

"Kuno!"   55

He had isolated himself.   56

For a moment Vashti felt lonely.   57

Then she generated the light, and the sight of her room, flooded   58
with radiance and studded with electric buttons, revived her. There
were buttons and switches everywhere—buttons to call for food,
for music, for clothing. There was the hot-bath button, by pressure of which a basin of (imitation) marble rose out of the floor,
filled to the brim with a warm deodorized liquid. There was the
cold-bath button. There was the button that produced literature.
And there were of course the buttons by which she communicated
with her friends. The room, though it contained nothing, was in
touch with all that she cared for in the world.

Vashti's next move was to turn off the isolation-switch, and   59
all the accumulations of the last three minutes burst upon her.
The room was filled with the noise of bells, and speaking-tubes.
What was the new food like? Could she recommend it? Had she
had any ideas lately? Might one tell her one's own ideas? Would
she make an engagement to visit the public nurseries at an early
date?—say this day month.

To most of these questions she replied with irritation—a grow-   60
ing quality in that accelerated age. She said that the new food was
horrible. That she could not visit the public nurseries through
press of engagements. That she had no ideas of her own but had
just been told one—that four stars and three in the middle were
like a man: she doubted there was much in it. Then she switched
off her correspondents, for it was time to deliver her lecture on
Australian music.

The clumsy system of public gatherings had been long since   61
abandoned; neither Vashti nor her audience stirred from their
rooms. Seated in her arm-chair she spoke, while they in their
arm-chairs heard her, fairly well, and saw her, fairly well. She
opened with a humorous account of music in the pre-Mongolian
epoch, and went on to describe the great outburst of song that
followed the Chinese conquest. Remote and primeval as were
the methods of I-San-So and the Brisbane school, she yet felt (she
said) that study of them might repay the musician of today: they
had freshness; they had, above all, ideas.

Her lecture, which lasted ten minutes, was well received, and   62
at its conclusion she and many of her audience listened to a lecture on the sea; there were ideas to be got from the sea; the

speaker had donned a respirator and visited it lately. Then she
fed, talked to many friends, had a bath, talked again, and summoned her bed.

The bed was not to her liking. It was too large, and she had a   63
feeling for a small bed. Complaint was useless, for beds were of
the same dimension all over the world, and to have had an alternative size would have involved vast alterations in the Machine.
Vashti isolated herself—it was necessary, for neither day nor
night existed under the ground—and reviewed all that had happened since she had summoned the bed last. Ideas? Scarcely any.
Events—was Kuno's invitation an event?

By her side, on the little reading-desk, was a survival from the   64
ages of litter—one book. This was the Book of the Machine. In
it were instructions against every possible contingency. If she was
hot or cold or dyspeptic or at loss for a word, she went to the
book, and it told her which button to press. The Central Committee published it. In accordance with a growing habit, it was
richly bound.

Sitting up in the bed, she took it reverently in her hands. She   65
glanced round the glowing room as if some one might be watching her. Then, half ashamed, half joyful, she murmured "O Machine! O Machine!" and raised the volume to her lips. Thrice she
kissed it, thrice inclined her head, thrice she felt the delirium of
acquiescence. Her ritual performed, she turned to page 1367,
which gave the times of the departure of the air-ships from the island in the southern hemisphere, under whose soil she lived, to
the island in the northern hemisphere, whereunder lived her son.

She thought, "I have not the time."   66

She made the room dark and slept; she awoke and made the   67
room light; she ate and exchanged ideas with her friends, and listened to music and attended lectures; she made the room dark
and slept. Above her, beneath her, and around her, the Machine
hummed eternally; she did not notice the noise, for she had been
born with it in her ears. The earth, carrying her, hummed as it
sped through silence, turning her now to the invisible sun, now
to the invisible stars. She awoke and made the room light.

"Kuno!"   68

"I will not talk to you," he answered, "until you come."   69

"Have you been on the surface of the earth since we spoke   70
last?"

His image faded.   71

Again she consulted the book. She became very nervous and   72
lay back in her chair palpitating. Think of her as without teeth or
hair. Presently she directed the chair to the wall, and pressed an
unfamiliar button. The wall swung apart slowly. Through the
opening she saw a tunnel that curved slightly, so that its goal was
not visible. Should she go to see her son, here was the beginning
of the journey.

Of course she knew all about the communication-system. There   73
was nothing mysterious in it. She would summon a car and it
would fly with her down the tunnel until it reached the lift that
communicated with the air-ship station: the system had been in
use for many, many years, long before the universal establishment
of the Machine. And of course she had studied the civilization
that had immediately preceded her own—the civilization that had
mistaken the functions of the system, and had used it for bringing
people to things, instead of for bringing things to people. Those
funny old days, when men went for change of air instead of
changing the air in their rooms! And yet—she was frightened of
the tunnel: she had not seen it since her last child was born. It
curved—but not quite as she remembered; it was brilliant—but
not quite as brilliant as a lecturer had suggested. Vashti was seized
with the terrors of direct experience. She shrank back into the
room, and the wall closed up again.

"Kuno," she said, "I cannot come to see you. I am not well."   74

Immediately an enormous apparatus fell on to her out of the   75
ceiling, a thermometer was automatically inserted between her
lips, a stethoscope was automatically laid upon her heart. She lay
powerless. Cool pads soothed her forehead. Kuno had telegraphed to her doctor.

So the human passions still blundered up and down in the   76
Machine. Vashti drank the medicine that the doctor projected
into her mouth, and the machinery retired into the ceiling. The
voice of Kuno was heard asking how she felt.

"Better." Then with irritation: "But why do you not come to   77
me instead?"

"Because I cannot leave this place."   78

"Why?"   79

"Because, any moment, something tremendous may happen."   80

"Have you been on the surface of the earth yet?"   81

"Not yet."   82

"Then what is it?"   83

"I will not tell you through the Machine."   84

She resumed her life.   85

But she thought of Kuno as a baby, his birth, his removal to the   86
public nurseries, her one visit to him there, his visits to her—visits
which stopped when the Machine had assigned him a room on the
other side of the earth. "Parents, duties of," said the book of the
Machine, "cease at the moment of birth. P. 422327483." True,
but there was something special about Kuno—indeed there had
been something special about all her children—and, after all, she
must brave the journey if he desired it. And "something tremendous might happen." What did that mean? The nonsense of a
youthful man, no doubt, but she must go. Again she pressed the
unfamiliar button, again the wall swung back, and she saw the
tunnel that curved out of sight. Clasping the Book, she rose, tottered on to the platform, and summoned the car. Her room closed
behind her: the journey to the northern hemisphere had begun.

Of course it was perfectly easy. The car approached and in it   87
she found arm-chairs exactly like her own. When she signalled,
it stopped, and she tottered into the lift. One other passenger
was in the lift, the first fellow creature she had seen face to face
for months. Few travelled in these days, for, thanks to the advance of science, the earth was exactly alike all over. Rapid intercourse, from which the previous civilization had hoped so
much, had ended by defeating itself. What was the good of going
to Pekin when it was just like Shrewsbury? Why return to
Shrewsbury when it would be just like Pekin? Men seldom
moved their bodies; all unrest was concentrated in the soul.

The air-ship service was a relic from the former age. It was   88
kept up, because it was easier to keep it up than to stop it or to
diminish it, but it now far exceeded the wants of the population.
Vessel after vessel would rise from the vomitories of Rye or of
Christchurch (I use the antique names), would sail into the
crowded sky, and would draw up the wharves of the south—
empty. So nicely adjusted was the system, so independent of me-
teorology, that the sky, whether calm or cloudy, resembled a vast
kaleidoscope whereon the same patterns periodically recurred.
The ship on which Vashti sailed started now at sunset, now at
dawn. But always, as it passed above Rheims, it would neigh-

bour the ship that served between Helsingfors and the Brazils, and, every third time it surmounted the Alps, the fleet of Palermo would cross its track behind. Night and day, wind and storm, tide and earthquake, impeded man no longer. He had harnessed Leviathan. All the old literature, with its praise of Nature, and its fear of Nature, rang false as the prattle of a child.

Yet as Vashti saw the vast flank of the ship, stained with exposure to the outer air, her horror of direct experience returned. It was not quite like the air-ship in the cinematophote. For one thing it smelt—not strongly or unpleasantly, but it did smell, and with her eyes shut she should have known that a new thing was close to her. Then she had to walk to it from the lift, had to submit to glances from the other passengers. The man in front dropped his Book—no great matter, but it disquieted them all. In the rooms, if the Book was dropped, the floor raised it mechanically, but the gangway to the air-ship was not so prepared, and the sacred volume lay motionless. They stopped—the thing was unforeseen—and the man, instead of picking up his property, felt the muscles of his arm to see how they had failed him. Then some one actually said with direct utterance: "We shall be late"—and they trooped on board, Vashti treading on the pages as she did so.   89

Inside, her anxiety increased. The arrangements were old-fashioned and rough. There was even a female attendant, to whom she would have to announce her wants during the voyage. Of course a revolving platform ran the length of the boat, but she was expected to walk from it to her cabin. Some cabins were better than others, and she did not get the best. She thought the attendant had been unfair, and spasms of rage shook her. The glass valves had closed, she could not go back. She saw, at the end of the vestibule, the lift in which she had ascended going quietly up and down, empty. Beneath those corridors of shining tiles were rooms, tier below tier, reaching far into the earth, and in each room there sat a human being, eating, or sleeping, or producing ideas. And buried deep in the hive was her own room. Vashti was afraid.   90

"O Machine! O Machine!" she murmured, and caressed her Book, and was comforted.   91

Then the sides of the vestibule seemed to melt together, as do the passages that we see in dreams, the lift vanished, the Book   92 that had been dropped slid to the left and vanished, polished tiles rushed by like a stream of water, there was a slight jar, and the air-ship, issuing from its tunnel, soared above the waters of a tropical ocean.

It was night. For a moment she saw the coast of Sumatra 93 edged by the phosphorescence of waves, and crowned by light-houses, still sending forth their disregarded beams. These also vanished, and only the stars distracted her. They were not motionless, but swayed to and fro above her head, thronging out of one skylight into another, as if the universe and not the air-ship was careening. And, as often happens on clear nights, they seemed now to be in perspective, now on a plane; now piled tier beyond tier into the infinite heavens, now concealing infinity, a roof limiting for ever the visions of men. In either case they seemed intolerable. "Are we to travel in the dark?" called the passengers angrily, and the attendant, who had been careless, generated the light, and pulled down the blinds of pliable metal. When the air-ships had been built, the desire to look direct at things still lingered in the world. Hence the extraordinary number of skylights and windows, and the proportionate discomfort to those who were civilised and refined. Even in Vashti's cabin one star peeped through a flaw in the blind, and after a few hours' uneasy slumber, she was disturbed by an unfamiliar glow, which was the dawn.

Quick as the ship had sped westwards, the earth had rolled 94 eastwards quicker still, and had dragged back Vashti and her companions towards the sun. Science could prolong the night, but only for a little, and those high hopes of neutralizing the earth's diurnal revolution had passed, together with hopes that were possibly higher. To "keep pace with the sun," or even to outstrip it, had been the aim of the civilisation preceding this. Racing aeroplanes had been built for the purpose, capable of enormous speed, and steered by the greatest intellects of the epoch. Round the globe they went, round and round, westward, westward, round and round, amidst humanity's applause. In vain. The globe went eastward quicker still, horrible accidents occurred, and the Committee of the Machine, at the time rising into prominence, declared the pursuit illegal, unmechanical, and punishable by Homelessness.

Of Homelessness more will be said later. 95

Doubtless the Committee was right. Yet the attempt to "defeat the sun" aroused the last common interest that our race experienced about the heavenly bodies, or indeed about anything. It was the last time that men were compacted by thinking of a power outside the world. The sun had conquered, yet it was the end of his spiritual dominion. Dawn, midday, twilight, the zodiacal path, touched neither men's lives nor their hearts, and science retreated into the ground, to concentrate herself upon problems that she was certain of solving. 96

So when Vashti found her cabin invaded by a rosy finger of light, she was annoyed, and tried to adjust the blind. But the blind flew up altogether, and she saw through the skylight small pink clouds, swaying against a background of blue, and as the sun crept higher, its radiance entered direct, brimming down the wall, like a golden sea. It rose and fell with the air-ship's motion, just as waves rise and fall, but it advanced steadily, as a tide advances. Unless she was careful, it would strike her face. A spasm of horror shook her and she rang for the attendant. The attendant too was horrified, but she could do nothing; it was not her place to mend the blind. She could only suggest that the lady should change her cabin, which she accordingly prepared to do. 97

People were almost exactly alike all over the world, but the attendant of the air-ship, perhaps owing to her exceptional duties, had grown a little out of the common. She had often to address passengers with direct speech, and this had given her a certain roughness and originality of manner. When Vashti swerved away from the sunbeams with a cry, she behaved barbarically—she put out her hand to steady her. 98

"How dare you!" exclaimed the passenger. "You forget yourself!" 99

The woman was confused, and apologized for not having let her fall. People never touched one another. The custom had become obsolete, owing to the Machine. 100

"Where are we now?" asked Vashti haughtily. 101

"We are over Asia," said the attendant, anxious to be polite. 102

"Asia?" 103

"You must excuse my common way of speaking. I have got into the habit of calling places over which I pass by their unmechanical names." 104

"Oh, I remember Asia. The Mongols came from it." 105

"Beneath us, in the open air, stood a city that was once called 106
Simla."

"Have you ever heard of the Mongols and of the Brisbane 107
school?"

"No." 108

"Brisbane also stood in the open air." 109

"Those mountains to the right—let me show you them." She 110
pushed back a metal blind. The main chain of the Himalayas
was revealed. "They were once called the Roof of the World,
those mountains."

"What a foolish name!" 111

"You must remember that, before the dawn of civilization, 112
they seemed to be an impenetrable wall that touched the stars. It
was supposed that no one but the gods could exist above their
summits. How we have advanced, thanks to the Machine!"

"How we have advanced, thanks to the Machine!" said 113
Vashti.

"How we have advanced, thanks to the Machine!" echoed the 114
passenger who had dropped his Book the night before, and who
was standing in the passage.

"And that white stuff in the cracks?—what is it?" 115

"I have forgotten its name." 116

"Cover the window, please. These mountains give me no ideas." 117

The northern aspect of the Himalayas was in deep shadow: on 118
the Indian slope the sun had just prevailed. The forests had been
destroyed during the literature epoch for the purpose of making
newspaper-pulp, but the snows were awakening to their morning glory, and clouds still hung on the breasts of Kinchinjunga. In
the plain were seen the ruins of cities, with diminished rivers
creeping by their walls, and by the sides of these were sometimes
the signs of vomitories, marking the cities of today. Over the
whole prospect air-ships rushed, crossing and intercrossing with
incredible *aplomb,* and rising nonchalantly when they desired to
escape the perturbations of the lower atmosphere and to traverse
the Roof of the World.

"We have indeed advanced, thanks to the Machine," repeated 119
the attendant, and hid the Himalayas behind a metal blind.

The day dragged wearily forward. The passengers sat each in 120
his cabin, avoiding one another with an almost physical repul-
sion and longing to be once more under the surface of the earth.

There were eight or ten of them, mostly young males, sent out from the public nurseries to inhabit the rooms of those who had died in various parts of the earth. The man who had dropped his Book was on the homeward journey. He had been sent to Sumatra for the purpose of propagating the race. Vashti alone was travelling by her private will.

At midday she took a second glance at the earth. The air-ship was crossing another range of mountains, but she could see little, owing to clouds. Masses of black rock hovered below her, and merged indistinctly into gray. Their shapes were fantastic; one of them resembled a prostrate man. 121

"No ideas here," murmured Vashti, and hid the Caucasus behind a metal blind. 122

In the evening she looked again. They were crossing a golden sea, in which lay many small islands and one peninsula. 123

She repeated, "No ideas here," and hid Greece behind a metal blind. 124

II. The Mending Apparatus

By a vestibule, by a lift, by a tubular railway, by a platform, by a sliding door—by reversing all the steps of her departure did Vashti arrive at her son's room, which exactly resembled her own. She might well declare that the visit was superfluous. The buttons, the knobs, the reading-desk with the Book, the temperature, the atmosphere, the illumination—all were exactly the same. And if Kuno himself, flesh of her flesh, stood close beside her at last, what profit was there in that? She was too well-bred to shake him by the hand. 125

Averting her eyes, she spoke as follows: 126

"Here I am. I have had the most terrible journey and greatly retarded the development of my soul. It is not worth it, Kuno, it is not worth it. My time is too precious. The sunlight almost touched me, and I have met with the rudest people. I can only stop a few minutes. Say what you want to say, and then I must return." 127

"I have been threatened with Homelessness," said Kuno. 128

She looked at him now. 129

"I have been threatened with Homelessness, and I could not tell you such a thing through the Machine." 130

Homelessness means death. The victim is exposed to the air,   131
which kills him.

"I have been outside since I spoke to you last. The tremendous   132
thing has happened, and they have discovered me."

"But why shouldn't you go outside!" she exclaimed. "It is   133
perfectly legal, perfectly mechanical, to visit the surface of the
earth. I have lately been to a lecture on the sea; there is no objection to that; one simply summons a respirator and gets an
Egression-permit. It is not the kind of thing that spiritually-
minded people do, and I begged you not to do it, but there is no
legal objection to it."

"I did not get an Egression-permit."   134

"Then how did you get out?"   135

"I found out a way of my own."   136

The phrase conveyed no meaning to her, and he had to re-   137
peat it.

"A way of your own?" she whispered. "But that would be   138
wrong."

"Why?"   139

The question shocked her beyond measure.   140

"You are beginning to worship the Machine," he said coldly.   141
"You think it irreligious of me to have found out a way of my
own. It was just what the Committee thought, when they threatened me with Homelessness."

At this she grew angry. "I worship nothing!" she cried. "I am   142
most advanced. I don't think you irreligious, for there is no such
thing as religion left. All the fear and the superstition that existed
once have been destroyed by the Machine. I only meant that to
find out a way of your own was—— Besides, there is no new
way out."

"So it is always supposed."   143

"Except through the vomitories, for which one must have an   144
Egression-permit, it is impossible to get out. The Book says so."

"Well, the Book's wrong, for I have been out on my feet."   145

For Kuno was possessed of a certain physical strength.   146

By these days it was a demerit to be muscular. Each infant was   147
examined at birth, and all who promised undue strength were
destroyed. Humanitarians may protest, but it would have been
no true kindness to let an athlete live; he would never have been
happy in that state of life to which the Machine had called him;
he would have yearned for trees to climb, rivers to bathe in,

meadows and hills against which he might measure his body. Man must be adapted to his surroundings, must he not? In the dawn of the world our weakly must be exposed on Mount Taygetus, in its twilight our strong will suffer euthanasia, that the Machine may progress, that the Machine may progress, that the Machine may progress eternally.

"You know that we have lost the sense of space. We say 'space is annihilated,' but we have annihilated not space, but the sense thereof. We have lost a part of ourselves. I determined to recover it, and I began by walking up and down the platform of the railway outside my room. Up and down, until I was tired, and so did recapture the meaning of 'Near' and 'Far.' 'Near' is a place to which I can get quickly *on my fees,* not a place to which the train or the air-ship will take me quickly. 'Far' is a place to which I cannot get quickly on my feet; the vomitory is 'far,' though I could be there in thirty-eight seconds by summoning the train. Man is the measure. That was my first lesson. Man's feet are the measure for distance, his hands are the measure for ownership, his body is the measure for all that is lovable and desirable and strong. Then I went further: it was then that I called to you for the first time, and you would not come. 148

"This city, as you know, is built deep beneath the surface of the earth, with only the vomitories protruding. Having paced the platform outside my own room, I took the lift to the next platform and paced that also, and so with each in turn, until I came to the topmost, above which begins the earth. All the platforms were exactly alike, and all that I gained by visiting them was to develop my sense of space and my muscles. I think I should have been content with this—it is not a little thing—but as I walked and brooded, it occurred to me that our cities had been built in the days when men still breathed the outer air, and that there had been ventilation shafts for the workmen. I could think of nothing but these ventilation shafts. Had they been destroyed by all the food-tubes and medicine-tubes and music-tubes that the Machine has evolved lately? Or did traces of them remain? One thing was certain. If I came upon them anywhere, it would be in the railway-tunnels of the topmost story. Everywhere else, all space was accounted for. 149

"I am telling my story quickly, but don't think that I was not a coward or that your answers never depressed me. It is not the proper thing, it is not mechanical, it is not decent to walk along 150 a railway-tunnel. I did not fear that I might tread upon a live rail and be killed. I feared something far more intangible—doing what was not contemplated by the Machine. Then I said to myself, 'Man is the measure,' and I went, and after many visits I found an opening.

"The tunnels, of course, were lighted. Everything is light, ar-   151
tificial light; darkness is the exception. So when I saw a black gap in the tiles, I knew that it was an exception, and rejoiced. I put in my arm—I could put in no more at first—and waved it round and round in ecstasy. I loosened another tile, and put in my head, and shouted into the darkness: 'I am coming, I shall do it yet,' and my voice reverberated down endless passages. I seemed to hear the spirits of those dead workmen who had returned each evening to the starlight and to their wives, and all the generations who had lived in the open air called back to me, 'You will do it yet, you are coming.' "

He paused, and, absurd as he was, his last words moved her.   152
For Kuno had lately asked to be a father, and his request had been refused by the Committee. His was not a type that the Machine desired to hand on.

"Then a train passed. It brushed by me, but I thrust my head   153
and arms into the hole. I had done enough for one day, so I crawled back to the platform, went down in the lift, and summoned my bed. Ah, what dreams! And again I called you, and again you refused."

She shook her head and said: 154

"Don't. Don't talk of these terrible things. You make me mis-   155
erable. You are throwing civilization away."

"But I had got back the sense of space and a man cannot rest   156
then. I determined to get in at the hole and climb the shaft. And so I exercised my arms. Day after day I went through ridiculous movements, until my flesh ached, and I could hang by my hands and hold the pillow of my bed outstretched for many minutes. Then I summoned a respirator, and started.

"It was easy at first. The mortar had somehow rotted, and I   157
soon pushed some more tiles in, and clambered after them into the darkness, and the spirits of the dead comforted me. I don't know what I mean by that. I just say what I felt. I felt, for the first time, that a protest had been lodged against corruption, and that even as the dead were comforting me, so I was comforting the

unborn. I felt that humanity existed, and that it existed without clothes. How can I possibly explain this? It was naked, humanity seemed naked, and all these tubes and buttons and machineries neither came into the world with us, nor will they follow us out, nor do they matter supremely while we are here. Had I been strong, I would have torn off every garment I had, and gone out into the outer air unswaddled. But this is not for me, nor perhaps for my generation. I climbed with my respirator and my hygienic clothes and my dietetic tabloids! Better thus than not at all.

"There was a ladder, made of some primeval metal. The light from the railway fell upon its lowest rungs, and I saw that it led straight upwards out of the rubble at the bottom of the shaft. Perhaps our ancestors ran up and down it a dozen times daily, in their building. As I climbed, the rough edges cut through my gloves so that my hands bled. The light helped me for a little, and then came darkness and, worse still, silence which pierced my ears like a sword. The Machine hums! Did you know that? Its hum penetrates our blood, and may even guide our thoughts. Who knows! I was getting beyond its power. Then I thought: 'This silence means that I am doing wrong.' But I heard voices in the silence, and again they strengthened me." He laughed. "I had need of them. The next moment I cracked my head against something." 158

She sighed. 159

"I had reached one of those pneumatic stoppers that defend us from the outer air. You may have noticed them on the air-ship. Pitch dark, my feet on the rungs of an invisible ladder, my hands cut; I cannot explain how I lived through this part, but the voices still comforted me, and I felt for fastenings. The stopper, I suppose, was about eight feet across. I passed my hand over it as far as I could reach. It was perfectly smooth. I felt it almost to the centre. Not quite to the centre, for my arm was too short. Then the voice said: 'Jump. It is worth it. There may be a handle in the centre, and you may catch hold of it and so come to us your own way. And if there is no handle, so that you may fall and are dashed to pieces—it is still worth it: you will still come to us your own way.' So I jumped. There was a handle, and———" 160

He paused. Tears gathered in his mother's eyes. She knew that he was fated. If he did not die to-day he would die to-morrow. There was no room for such a person in the world. And with her pity disgust mingled. She was ashamed of having borne such a 161 son, she who had always been so respectable and so full of ideas. Was he really the little boy to whom she had taught the use of his stops and buttons, and to whom she had given his first lesson in the Book? The very hair that disfigured his lip showed that he was reverting to some savage type. On atavism the Machine can have no mercy.

"There was a handle, and I did catch it. I hung tranced over   162
the darkness and heard the hum of these workings as the last whisper in a dying dream. All the things I had cared about and all the people I had spoken to through tubes appeared infinitely little. Meanwhile the handle revolved. My weight had set something in motion and I span slowly, and then————

"I cannot describe it. I was lying with my face to the sunshine.   163
Blood poured from my nose and ears and I heard a tremendous roaring. The stopper, with me clinging to it, had simply been blown out of the earth, and the air that we make down here was escaping through the vent into the air above. It burst up like a fountain. I crawled back to it—for the upper air hurts—and, as it were, I took great sips from the edge. My respirator had flown goodness knows where, my clothes were torn. I just lay with my lips close to the hole, and I sipped until the bleeding stopped. You can imagine nothing so curious. This hollow in the grass—I will speak of it in a minute,—the sun shining into it, not brilliantly but through marbled clouds,—the peace, the nonchalance, the sense of space, and, brushing my cheek, the roaring fountain of our artificial air! Soon I spied my respirator, bobbing up and down in the current high above my head, and higher still were many air-ships. But no one ever looks out of air-ships, and in my case they could not have picked me up. There I was, stranded. The sun shone a little way down the shaft, and revealed the topmost rung of the ladder, but it was hope less trying to reach it. I should either have been tossed up again by the escape, or else have fallen in, and died. I could only lie on the grass, sipping and sipping, and from time to time glancing around me.

"I knew that I was in Wessex, for I had taken care to go to a   164
lecture on the subject before starting. Wessex lies above the room in which we are talking now. It was once an important state. Its kings held all the southern coast from the Andredswald to Cornwall, while the Wansdyke protected them on the north, running over the high ground. The lecturer was only concerned with the

rise of Wessex, so I do not know how long it remained an international power, nor would the knowledge have assisted me. To tell the truth I could do nothing but laugh, during this part. There was I, with a pneumatic stopper by my side and a respirator bobbing over my head, imprisoned, all three of us, in a grass-grown hollow that was edged with fern."

Then he grew grave again.

"Lucky for me that it was a hollow. For the air began to fall back into it and to fill it as water fills a bowl. I could crawl about. Presently I stood. I breathed a mixture, in which the air that hurts predominated whenever I tried to climb the sides. This was not so bad. I had not lost my tabloids and remained ridiculously cheerful, and as for the Machine, I forgot about it altogether. My one aim now was to get to the top, where the ferns were, and to view whatever objects lay beyond.

"I rushed the slope. The new air was still too bitter for me and I came rolling back, after a momentary vision of something gray. The sun grew very feeble, and I remembered that he was in Scorpio—I had been to a lecture on that too. If the sun is in Scorpio and you are in Wessex, it means that you must be as quick as you can, or it will get too dark. (This is the first bit of useful information I have ever got from a lecture, and I expect it will be the last.) It made me try frantically to breathe the new air, and to advance as far as I dared out of my pond. The hollow filled so slowly. At times I thought that the fountain played with less vigour. My respirator seemed to dance nearer the earth; the roar was decreasing."

He broke off.

"I don't think this is interesting you. The rest will interest you even less. There are no ideas in it, and I wish that I had not troubled you to come. We are too different, mother."

She told him to continue.

"It was evening before I climbed the bank. The sun had very nearly slipped out of the sky by this time, and I could not get a good view. You, who have just crossed the Roof of the World, will not want to hear an account of the little hills that I saw—low colourless hills. But to me they were living and the turf that covered them was a skin, under which their muscles rippled, and I felt that those hills had called with incalculable force to men in the past, and that men had loved them. Now they sleep—perhaps for ever. They commune with humanity in dreams. Happy the man, happy the woman, who awakes the hills of Wessex. For though they sleep, they will never die."

His voice rose passionately.   172

"Cannot you see, cannot all your lecturers see, that it is we   173
who are dying, and that down here the only thing that really lives is the Machine? We created the Machine, to do our will, but we cannot make it do our will now. It has robbed us of the sense of space and of the sense of touch, it has blurred every human relation and narrowed down love to a carnal act, it has paralyzed our bodies and our wills, and now it compels us to worship it. The Machine develops—but not on our lines. The Machine proceeds—but not to our goal. We only exist as the blood corpuscles that course through its arteries, and if it could work without us, it would let us die. Oh, I have no remedy—or, at least, only one—to tell men again and again that I have seen the hills of Wessex as Ælfrid[1] saw them when he overthrew the Danes.

"So the sun set. I forgot to mention that a belt of mist lay be-   174
tween my hill and other hills, and that it was the colour of pearl."

He broke off for a second time.   175

"Go on," said his mother wearily.   176

He shook his head.   177

"Go on. Nothing that you say can distress me now. I am hard-   178
ened."

"I had meant to tell you the rest, but I cannot: I know that I   179
cannot: good-bye."

Vashti stood irresolute. All her nerves were tingling with his   180
blasphemies. But she was also inquisitive.

"This is unfair," she complained. "You have called me across   181
the world to hear your story, and hear it I will. Tell me—as briefly as possible, for this is a disastrous waste of time—tell me how you returned to civilization."

"Oh—that!" he said, starting. "You would like to hear about   182
civilization. Certainly. Had I got to where my respirator fell down?"

"No—but I understand everything now. You put on your res-   183
pirator, and managed to walk along the surface of the earth to a vomitory, and there your conduct was reported to the Central Committee."

---

1. Alfred the Great: Saxon king in southwestern England from 871 to 879.

"By no means."   184

He passed his hand over his forehead, as if dispelling some   185
strong impression. Then, resuming his narrative, he warmed to it
again.

"My respirator fell about sunset. I had mentioned that the   186
fountain seemed feebler, had I not?"

"Yes."   187

"About sunset, it let the respirator fall. As I said, I had entirely   188
forgotten about the Machine, and I paid no great attention at the
time, being occupied with other things. I had my pool of air, into
which I could dip when the outer keenness became intolerable,
and which would possibly remain for days, provided that no
wind sprang up to disperse it. Not until it was too late, did I realize what the stoppage of the escape implied. You see—the gap
in the tunnel had been mended; the Mending Apparatus; the
Mending Apparatus, was after me.

"One other warning I had, but I neglected it. The sky at night   189
was clearer than it had been in the day, and the moon, which was
about half the sky behind the sun, shone into the dell at moments
quite brightly. I was in my usual place—on the boundary between the two atmospheres—when I thought I saw something
dark move across the bottom of the dell, and vanish into the
shaft. In my folly, I ran down. I bent over and listened, and I
thought I heard a faint scraping noise in the depths.

"At this—but it was too late—I took alarm. I determined to   190
put on my respirator and to walk right out of the dell. But my
respirator had gone. I knew exactly where it had fallen—between
the stopper and the aperture—and I could even feel the mark
that it had made in the turf. It had gone, and I realized that
something evil was at work, and I had better escape to the other
air, and, if I must die, die running towards the cloud that had
been the colour of a pearl. I never started. Out of the shaft—it is
too horrible. A worm, a long white worm, had crawled out of
the shaft and was gliding over the moonlit grass.

"I screamed. I did everything that I should not have done, I   191
stamped upon the creature instead of flying from it, and it at
once curled round the ankle. Then we fought. The worm let me
run all over the dell, but edged up my leg as I ran. 'Help!' I cried.
(That part is too awful. It belongs to the part that you will never
know.) 'Help!' I cried. (Why cannot we suffer in silence?) 'Help!'

I cried. Then my feet were wound together, I fell, I was dragged away from the dear ferns and the living hills, and past the great metal stopper (I can tell you this part), and I thought it might save me again if I caught hold of the handle. It also was enwrapped, it also. Oh, the whole dell was full of the things. They were searching it in all directions, they were denuding it, and the white snouts of others peeped out of the hole, ready if needed. Everything that could be moved they brought—brushwood, bundles of fern, everything, and down we all went intertwined into hell. The last things that I saw, ere the stopper closed after us, were certain stars, and I felt that a man of my sort lived in the sky. For I did fight, I fought till the very end, and it was only my head hitting against the ladder that quieted me. I woke up in this room. The worms had vanished. I was surrounded by artificial air, artificial light, artificial peace, and my friends were calling to me down speaking-tubes to know whether I had come across any new ideas lately."

Here his story ended. Discussion of it was impossible, and Vashti turned to go. 192

"It will end in Homelessness," she said quietly. 193

"I wish it would," retorted Kuno. 194

"The Machine has been most merciful." 195

"I prefer the mercy of God." 196

"By that superstitious phrase, do you mean that you could live in the outer air?" 197

"Yes." 198

"Have you ever seen, round the vomitories, the bones of those who were extruded after the Great Rebellion?" 199

"Yes." 200

"They were left where they perished for our edification. A few crawled away, but they perished, too—who can doubt it? And so with the Homeless of our own day. The surface of the earth supports life no longer." 201

"Indeed." 202

"Ferns and a little grass may survive, but all higher forms have perished. Has any air-ship detected them?" 203

"No." 204

"Has any lecturer dealt with them?" 205

"No." 206

"Then why this obstinacy?" 207

"Because I have seen them," he exploded.   208

"Seen *what?*"   209

"Because I have seen her in the twilight—because she came to   210
my help when I called—because she, too, was entangled by the
worms, and, luckier than I, was killed by one of them piercing
her throat."

He was mad. Vashti departed, nor, in the troubles that fol-   211
lowed, did she ever see his face again.

III. THE HOMELESS

During the years that followed Kuno's escapade, two impor-   212
tant developments took place in the Machine. On the surface
they were revolutionary, but in either case men's minds had been
prepared beforehand, and they did but express tendencies that
were latent already.

The first of these was the abolition of respirators.   213

Advanced thinkers, like Vashti, had always held it foolish to   214
visit the surface of the earth. Air-ships might be necessary, but
what was the good of going out for mere curiosity and crawling
along for a mile or two in a terrestrial motor? The habit was vulgar and perhaps faintly improper: it was unproductive of ideas,
and had no connection with the habits that really mattered. So
respirators were abolished, and with them, of course, the terrestrial motors, and except for a few lecturers, who complained
that they were debarred access to their subject-matter, the development was accepted quietly. Those who still wanted to know
what the earth was like had after all only to listen to some
gramophone, or to look into some cinematophote. And even the
lecturers acquiesced when they found that a lecture on the sea
was none the less stimulating when compiled out of other lectures that had already been delivered on the same subject. "Be-
ware of first-hand ideas!" exclaimed one of the most advanced
of them. "First-hand ideas do not really exist. They are but the
physical impressions produced by love and fear, and on this
gross foundation who could erect a philosophy? Let your ideas
be second-hand, and if possible tenth-hand, for then they will
be far removed from the disturbing element—direct observation.
Do not learn anything about this subject of mine—the French

Revolution. Learn instead what I think that Enicharmon thought Urizen thought Gutch thought Ho-Yung thought Chi-Bo-Sing thought Lafcadio Hearn thought Carlyle thought Mirabeau said about the French Revolution. Through the medium of these eight great minds, the blood that was shed at Paris and the windows that were broken at Versailles will be clarified to an idea which you may employ most profitably in your daily lives. But be sure that the intermediates are many and varied, for in history one authority exists to counteract another. Urizen must counteract the scepticism of Ho-Yong and Enicharmon, I must myself counteract the impetuosity of Gutch. You who listen to me are in a better position to judge about the French Revolution than I am. Your descendants will be even in a better position than you, for they will learn what you think I think, and yet another intermediate will be added to the chain. And in time"—his voice rose—"there will come a generation that has got beyond facts, beyond impressions, a generation absolutely colourless, a generation.

seraphically free
From taint of personality,

which will see the French Revolution not as it happened, nor as they would like it to have happened, but as it would have happened, had it taken place in the days of the Machine."

Tremendous applause greeted this lecture, which did but voice a feeling already latent in the minds of men—a feeling that terrestrial facts must be ignored, and that the abolition of respirators was a positive gain. It was even suggested that air-ships should be abolished too. This was not done, because air-ships had somehow worked themselves into the Machine's system. But year by year they were used less, and mentioned less by thoughtful men. 215

The second great development was the re-establishment of religion. 216

This, too, had been voiced in the celebrated lecture. No one could mistake the reverent tone in which the peroration had concluded, and it awakened a responsive echo in the heart of each. Those who had long worshipped silently, now began to talk. They described the strange feeling of peace that came over them when they handled the Book of the Machine, the pleasure that it 217 was to repeat certain numerals out of it, however little meaning those numerals conveyed to the outward ear, the ecstasy of touching a button, however unimportant, or or ringing an electric bell, however superfluously.

"The Machine," they exclaimed, "feeds us and clothes us and 218 houses us; through it we speak to one another, through it we see one another, in it we have our being. The Machine is the friend of ideas and the enemy of superstition: the Machine is omnipotent, eternal; blessed is the Machine." And before long this allocution was printed on the first page of the Book, and in subsequent editions the ritual swelled into a complicated system of praise and prayer. The word "religion" was sedulously avoided, and in theory the Machine was still the creation and the implement of man. But in practice all, save a few retrogrades, worshipped it as divine. Nor was it worshipped in unity. One believer would be chiefly impressed by the blue optic plates, through which he saw other believers; another by the mending apparatus, which sinful Kuno had compared to worms; another by the lifts, another by the Book. And each would pray to this or to that, and ask it to intercede for him with the Machine as a whole. Persecution— that also was present. It did not break out, for reasons that will be set forward shortly. But it was latent, and all who did not accept the minimum known as "undenominational Mechanism" lived in danger of Homelessness, which means death, as we know.

To attribute these two great developments to the Central 219 Committee, is to take a very narrow view of civilization. The Central Committee announced the developments, it is true, but they were no more the cause of them than were the kings of the imperialistic period the cause of war. Rather did they yield to some invincible pressure, which came no one knew whither, and which, when gratified, was succeeded by some new pressure equally invincible. To such a state of affairs it is convenient to give the name of progress. No one confessed the Machine was out of hand. Year by year it was served with increased efficiency and decreased intelligence. The better a man knew his own duties upon it, the less he understood the duties of his neighbour, and in all the world there was not one who understood the monster as a whole. Those master brains had perished. They had left full directions, it is true, and their successors had each of them

mastered a portion of those directions. But Humanity, in its desire for comfort, had overreached itself. It had exploited the
riches of nature too far. Quietly and complacently, it was sinking
into decadence, and progress had come to mean the progress of
the Machine.

As for Vashti, her life went peacefully forward until the final   220
disaster She made her room dark and slept; she awoke and made
the room light. She lectured and attended lectures. She exchanged
ideas with her innumerable friends and believed she was growing
more spiritual. At times a friend was granted Euthanasia, and
left his or her room for the homelessness that is beyond all human conception. Vashti did not much mind. After an unsuccessful lecture, she would sometimes ask for Euthanasia herself. But
the death-rate was not permitted to exceed the birth-rate, and
the Machine had hitherto refused it to her.

The troubles began quietly, long before she was conscious of   221
them.

One day she was astonished at receiving a message from her   222
son. They never communicated, having nothing in common, and
she had only heard indirectly that he was still alive, and had been
transferred from the northern hemisphere, where he had behaved so mischievously, to the southern—indeed, to a room not
far from her own.

"Does he want me to visit him?" she thought. "Never again,   223
never. And I have not the time."

No, it was madness of another kind.   224

He refused to visualize his face upon the blue plate, and   225
speaking out of the darkness with solemnity said:

"The Machine stops."   226

"What do you say?"   227

"The Machine is stopping, I know it. I know the signs."   228

She burst into a peal of laughter. He heard her and was angry,   229
and they spoke no more.

"Can you imagine anything more absurd?" she cried to a   230
friend. "A man who was my son believes that the Machine is
stopping. It would be impious if it was not mad."

"The Machine is stopping?" her friend replied. "What does   231
that mean? The phrase conveys nothing to me."

"Nor to me."   232

"He does not refer, I suppose, to the trouble there has been   233
lately with the music?"

"Oh no, of course not. Let us talk about music."   234

"Have you complained to the authorities?"   235

"Yes, and they say it wants mending, and referred me to the   236
Committee of the Mending Apparatus. I complained of those curious gasping sighs that disfigure the symphonies of the Brisbane
school. They sound like some one in pain. The Committee of the
Mending Apparatus say that it shall be remedied shortly."

Obscurely worried, she resumed her life. For one thing, the   237
defect in the music irritated her. For another thing, she could not
forget Kuno's speech. If he had known that the music was out of
repair—he could not know it, for he detested music—if he had
known that it was wrong, "the Machine stops" was exactly the
venomous sort of remark he would have made. Of course he had
made it at a venture, but the coincidence annoyed her, and she
spoke with some petulance to the Committee of the Mending
Apparatus.

They replied, as before, that the defect would be set right   238
shortly.

"Shortly! At once!" she retorted. "Why should I be worried   239
by imperfect music? Things are always put right at once. If you
do not mend it at once, I shall complain to the Central Committee."

"No personal complaints are received by the Central Com-   240
mittee," the Committee of the Mending Apparatus replied.

"Through whom am I to make my complaint, then?"   241

"Through us."   242

"I complain then."   243

"Your complaint shall be forwarded in its turn.   244

"Have others complained?"   245

This question was unmechanical, and the Committee of the   246
Mending Apparatus refused to answer it.

"It is too bad!" she exclaimed to another of her friends.   247
"There never was such an unfortunate woman as myself. I can
never be sure of my music now. It gets worse and worse each
time I summon it."

"I too have my troubles," the friend replied. "Sometimes my   248
ideas are interrupted by a slight jarring noise."

"What is it?"   249

"I do not know whether it is inside my head, or inside the   250
wall."

"Complain, in either case."   251

"I have complained, and my complaint will be forwarded in   252
its turn to the Central Committee."

Time passed, and they resented the defects no longer. The de-   253
fects had not been remedied, but the human tissues in that latter
day had become so subservient, that they readily adapted themselves to every caprice of the Machine. The sigh at the crisis of
the Brisbane symphony no longer irritated Vashti; she accepted it
as part of the melody. The jarring noise, whether in the head or
in the wall, was no longer resented by her friend. And so with the
mouldy artificial fruit, so with the bath water that began to
stink, so with the defective rhymes that the poetry machine had
taken to emit, All were bitterly complained of at first, and then
acquiesced in and forgotten. Things went from bad to worse unchallenged.

It was otherwise with the failure of the sleeping apparatus.   254
That was a more serious stoppage. There came a day when over
the whole world—in Sumatra, in Wessex, in the innumerable
cities of Courland and Brazil—the beds, when summoned by
their tired owners, failed to appear. It may seem a ludicrous matter, but from it we may date the collapse of humanity. The Committee responsible for the failure was assailed by complainants,
whom it referred, as usual, to the Committee of the Mending
Apparatus, who in its turn assured them that their complaints
would be forwarded to the Central Committee. But the discontent grew, for mankind was not yet sufficiently adaptable to do
without sleeping.

"Some one is meddling with the Machine——" they began.   255
"Some one is trying to make himself king, to re-introduce the   256
personal element."

"Punish that man with Homelessness."   257
"To the rescue! Avenge the Machine! Avenge the Machine!"   258
"War! Kill the man!"   259

But the Committee of the Mending Apparatus now came for-   260
ward, and allayed the panic with well-chosen words. It confessed
that the Mending Apparatus was itself in need of repair.

The effect of this frank confession was admirable.   261

"Of course," said a famous lecturer—he of the French Revo-   262
lution, who gilded each new decay with splendour—"of course
we shall not press our complaints now. The Mending Apparatus
has treated us so well in the past that we all sympathize with it,
and will wait patiently for its recovery. In its own good time it

will resume its duties. Meanwhile let us do without our beds, our tabloids, our other little wants. Such, I feel sure, would be the wish of the Machine."

Thousands of miles away his audience applauded. The Machine still linked them. Under the seas, beneath the roots of the mountains, ran the wires through which they saw and heard, the enormous eyes and ears that were their heritage, and the hum of many workings clothed their thoughts in one garment of subserviency. Only the old and the sick remained ungrateful, for it was rumoured that Euthanasia, too, was out of order, and that pain had reappeared among men. 263

It became difficult to read. A blight entered the atmosphere and dulled its luminosity. At times Vashti could scarcely see across her room. The air, too, was foul. Loud were the complaints, impotent the remedies, heroic the tone of the lecturer as he cried: "Courage, courage! What matter so long as the Machine goes on? To it the darkness and the light are one." And though things improved again after a time, the old brilliancy was never recaptured, and humanity never recovered from its entrance into twilight. There was an hysterical talk of "measures," of "provisional dictatorship," and the inhabitants of Sumatra were asked to familiarize themselves with the workings of the central power station, the said power station being situated in France. But for the most part panic reigned, and men spent their strength praying to their Books, tangible proofs of the Machine's omnipotence. There were gradations of terror—at times came rumours of hope—the Mending Apparatus was almost mended—the enemies of the Machine had been got under—new "nerve-centres" were evolving which would do the work even more magnificently than before. But there came a day when, without the slightest warning, without any previous hint of feebleness, the entire communication-system broke down, all over the world, and the world, as they understood it, ended. 264

Vashti was lecturing at the time and her earlier remarks had been punctuated with applause. As she proceeded the audience became silent, and at the conclusion there was no sound. Somewhat displeased, she called to a friend who was a specialist in sympathy. No sound: doubtless the friend was sleeping. And so with the next friend whom she tried to summon, and so with the next, until she remembered Kuno's cryptic remark, "The Machine stops." 265

The phrase still conveyed nothing. If Eternity was stopping it   266
would of course be set going shortly.

For example, there was still a little light and air—the atmo-   267
sphere had improved a few hours previously. There was still the
Book, and while there was the Book there was security.

Then she broke down, for with the cessation of activity came   268
an unexpected terror—silence.

She had never known silence, and the coming of it nearly   269
killed her—it did kill many thousands of people outright. Ever
since her birth she had been surrounded by the steady hum. It
was to the ear what artificial air was to the lungs, and agonizing
pains shot across her head. And scarcely knowing what she did,
she stumbled forward and pressed the unfamiliar button, the one
that opened the door of her cell.

Now the door of the cell worked on a simple hinge of its own.   270
It was not connected with the central power station, dying far
away in France. It opened, rousing immoderate hopes in Vashti,
for she thought that the Machine had been mended. It opened,
and she saw the dim tunnel that curved far away towards freedom. One look, and then she shrank back. For the tunnel was full
of people—she was almost the last in the city to have taken alarm.

People at any time repelled her, and these were nightmares   271
from her worst dreams. People were crawling about; people
were screaming, whimpering, gasping for breath, touching each
other, vanishing in the dark, and ever and anon being pushed off
the platform on to the live rail. Some were fighting round the
electric bells, trying to summon trains which could not be summoned. Others were yelling for Euthanasia or for respirators, or
blaspheming the Machine. Others stood at the doors of their
cells fearing, like herself, either to stop in them or to leave them.
And behind all the uproar was silence—the silence which is the
voice of the earth and of the generations who have gone.

No—it was worse than solitude. She closed the door again and   272
sat down to wait for the end. The disintegration went on, accompanied by horrible cracks and rumbling. The valves that restrained
the Medical Apparatus must have been weakened, for it ruptured
and hung hideously from the ceiling. The floor heaved and fell and
flung her from her chair. A tube oozed towards her serpent fashion. And at last the final horror approached—light began to ebb,
and she knew that civilization's long day was closing.

She whirled round, praying to be saved from this, at any rate,   273
kissing the Book, pressing button after button. The uproar outside was increasing, and even penetrated the wall. Slowly the
brilliancy of her cell was dimmed, the reflections faded from her
metal switches. Now she could not see the reading-stand, now
not the Book, though she held it in her hand. Light followed the
flight of sound, air was following light, and the original void returned to the cavern from which it had been so long excluded.
Vashti continued to whirl, like the devotees of an earlier religion,
screaming, praying, striking at the buttons with bleeding hands.

It was thus that she opened her prison and escaped—escaped   274
in the spirit: at least so it seems to me, ere my meditation closes.
That she escapes in the body—I cannot perceive that. She struck,
by chance, the switch that released the door, and the rush of foul
air on her skin, the loud throbbing whispers in her ears, told
her that she was facing the tunnel again, and that tremendous
platform on which she had seen men fighting. They were not
fighting now. Only the whispers remained, and the little whimpering groans. They were dying by hundreds out in the dark.

She burst into tears.   275

Tears answered her.   276

They wept for humanity, those two, not for themselves. They   277
could not bear that this should be the end. Ere silence was completed their hearts were opened, and they knew what had been important on the earth. Man, the flower of all flesh, the noblest of all
creatures visible, man who had once made god in his image, and
had mirrored his strength on the constellations, beautiful naked
man was dying, strangled in the garments that he had woven. Century after century had he toiled, and here was his reward. Truly the
garment had seemed heavenly at first, shot with the colours of culture, sewn with the threads of self-denial. And heavenly it had
been so long as it was a garment and no more, so long as man
could shed it at will and live by the essence that is his soul, and the
essence, equally divine, that is his body. The sin against the body—
it was for that they wept in chief; the centuries of wrong against
the muscles and the nerves, and those five portals by which we can
alone apprehend—glozing it over with talk of evolution, until the
body was white pap, the home of ideas as colourless, last sloshy
stirrings of a spirit that had grasped the stars.

"Where are you?" she sobbed.   278

His voice in the darkness said, "Here."   279

"Is there any hope, Kuno?"   280

"None for us."   281

"Where are you?"   282

She crawled towards him over the bodies of the dead. His   283
blood spurted over her hands.

"Quicker," he gasped, "I am dying—but we touch, we talk,   284
not through the Machine."

He kissed her.   285

"We have come back to our own. We die, but we have recap-   286
tured life, as it was in Wessex, when Ælfrid overthrew the
Danes. We know what they know outside, they who dwelt in the
cloud that is the colour of a pearl."

"But, Kuno, is it true? Are there still men on the surface of the   287
earth? Is this—this tunnel, this poisoned darkness—really not
the end?"

He replied: 288

"I have seen them, spoken to them, loved them. They are hid-   289
ing in the mist and the ferns until our civilization stops. To-day
they are the Homeless—to-morrow————"

"Oh, to-morrow—some fool will start the Machine again,   290
to-morrow."

"Never," said Kuno, "never. Humanity has learnt its lesson."   291

As he spoke, the whole city was broken like a honeycomb. An   292
air-ship had sailed in through the vomitory into a ruined wharf.
It crashed downwards, exploding as it went, rending gallery after gallery with its wings of steel. For a moment they saw the nations of the dead, and, before they joined them, scraps of the
untainted sky.

9

Their Lives and Times

Wayne Jones in his mother's apartment, 2000. © MARY ELLEN MARK.

OVERVIEW

The four selections in this final unit are *bigger* works than those that precede them, bigger not only in number of pages, but also in the amount of effort they required of the writers and the number of themes that become intertwined in the writing. Each essay involves a subject that was, in a sense, "foreign" to the writer, something that couldn't be understood by intuition or introspection, but that had to be investigated—by extensive reading in letters and historical documents or by interviews or by firsthand study of the scene. Each involves an attempt to understand people in the context of a particular time and place. Viewing people in their context requires the writers to deal with the questions that underlie the other units of *The Dolphin Reader*: How can anyone get at the truth here? How does this subject fit with my aims as a writer? How does the community support or fail to support the people I am writing about? How important are conceptions of masculinity and femininity to the story I have to tell? What relations exist between the prosperous and the poor? How do the people I am writing about view their work? How are they affected by the technology of their times? What beliefs sustain them?

Varied as they are in style, the four works collected here are impressive examples of a type of writing somewhat clumsily called "nonfiction." Like fiction, nonfiction focuses on characters more than on statistics, on particular experiences more than on generalizations. Like fiction, it attempts to give the reader a sense of what a life means as viewed from the inside rather than as analyzed from the outside. Unlike the novelist or the short story writer, however, the serious practitioner of nonfiction must achieve his or her effects without altering any objective fact. Our four authors practice this severe discipline on four very different subjects:

- Lytton Strachey reconsiders a revered figure from the Victorian period: Florence Nightingale, founder of modern nursing, the "angel of mercy," the "lady with the lamp." Without denying her a kind of greatness, he shows us that she was tougher and more complex than everyone had imagined.

- Writing in 1967, when a generation of Americans seemed poised to reject all traditional values, Joan Didion reports on life at the epicenter of the youth revolution: the Haight-Ashbury district of San Francisco.
- During the major league player's strike of 1981, sports writer Roger Angell travels to northern Vermont to sit in the bleachers with a community college teacher and watch the Burlington A's play the Walpole Bluejays.
- Katherine Boo captures one face of America at the beginning of the twenty-first century as she describes the life of a single mother struggling, against great odds, to raise healthy, happy children in a tough neighborhood in Washington, D.C.

LYTTON STRACHEY

Florence Nightingale

Lytton Strachey, a prominent figure on the London literary scene early in the twentieth century, revolutionized the writing of biography. His goal—"a brevity which excludes everything that is redundant and nothing that is significant"—made the biographer less a cataloguer of facts and more an artist striving to create a coherent portrait. "Florence Nightingale" is from *Eminent Victorians* (1918).

I

Everyone knows the popular conception of Florence Nightingale. The saintly, self-sacrificing woman, the delicate maiden of high degree who threw aside the pleasures of a life of ease to succour the afflicted, the Lady with the Lamp, gliding through the horrors of the hospital at Scutari, and consecrating with the radiance of her goodness the dying soldier's couch—the vision is familiar to all. But the truth was different. The Miss Nightingale of fact was not as facile fancy painted her. She worked in another fashion, and towards another end; she moved under the stress of an impetus which finds no place in the popular imagination. A Demon possessed her. Now demons, whatever else they may be, are full of interest. And so it happens that in the real Miss Nightingale there was more that was interesting than in the legendary one; there was also less that was agreeable.

Her family was extremely well-to-do, and connected by marriage with a spreading circle of other well-to-do families. There was a large country house in Derbyshire; there was another in the New Forest; there were Mayfair rooms for the London season and all its finest parties; there were tours on the Continent with even more than the usual number of Italian operas and of glimpses at the celebrities of Paris. Brought up among such advantages, it was only natural to suppose that Florence would show a proper appreciation of them by doing her duty in that state of life unto which it had pleased God to call her—in other words, by marrying, after a fitting number of dances and dinner-parties, an eligible gentleman, and living happily ever afterwards.

Her sister, her cousins, all the young ladies of her acquaintance, were either getting ready to do this or had already done it. It was inconceivable that Florence should dream of anything else; yet dream she did. Ah! To do her duty in that state of life unto which it had pleased God to call her! Assuredly she would not be behindhand in doing her duty; but unto what state of life *had* it pleased God to call her? That was the question. God's calls are many, and they are strange. Unto what state of life had it pleased Him to call Charlotte Corday, or Elizabeth of Hungary[1]? What was that secret voice in her ear, if it was not a call? Why had she felt, from her earliest years, those mysterious promptings towards . . . she hardly knew what but certainly towards something very different from anything around her? Why, as a child in the nursery, when her sister had shown a healthy pleasure in tearing her dolls to pieces, had *she* shown an almost morbid one in sewing them up again? Why was she driven now to minister to the poor in their cottages, to watch by sick-beds, to put her dog's wounded paw into elaborate splints as if it was a human being? Why was her head filled with queer imaginations of the country house at Embley turned, by some enchantment, into a hospital, with herself as matron moving about among the beds? Why was even her vision of heaven itself filled with suffering patients to whom she was being useful? So she dreamed and wondered, and, taking out her diary, she poured into it the agitations of her soul. And then the bell rang, and it was time to go and dress for dinner.

As the years passed, a restlessness began to grow upon her. She was unhappy, and at last she knew it. Mrs. Nightingale, too, began to notice that there was something wrong. It was very odd; what could be the matter with dear Flo? Mr. Nightingale suggested that a husband might be advisable; but the curious thing was that she seemed to take no interest in husbands. And with her attractions, and her accomplishments, too! There was nothing in the world to prevent her making a really brilliant match. But no! She would think of nothing but how to satisfy that singular craving of hers to be *doing* something. As if there

1. Charlotte Corday (1768–1793), a moderate during the French Revolution, assassinated the radical Jean-Paul Marat. Elizabeth (1837–1898), queen of Hungary and empress consort of Austria, known for her beauty and compassion, was the victim of an assassin.

was not plenty to do in any case, in the ordinary way, at home. There was the china to look after, and there was her father to be read to after dinner. Mrs. Nightingale could not understand it; and then one day her perplexity was changed to consternation and alarm. Florence announced an extreme desire to go to Salisbury Hospital for several months as a nurse; and she confessed to some visionary plan of eventually setting up in a house of her own in a neighbouring village, and there founding "something like a Protestant Sisterhood, without vows, for women of educated feelings." The whole scheme was summarily brushed aside as preposterous; and Mrs. Nightingale, after the first shock of terror, was able to settle down again more or less comfortably to her embroidery. But Florence, who was now twenty-five and felt that the dream of her life had been shattered, came near to desperation.

And, indeed, the difficulties in her path were great. For not only was it an almost unimaginable thing in those days for a woman of means to make her own way in the world and to live in independence, but the particular profession for which Florence was clearly marked out both by her instincts and her capacities was at that time a peculiarly disreputable one. A "nurse" meant then a coarse old woman, always ignorant, usually dirty, often brutal, a Mrs. Gamp,[2] in bunched-up sordid garments, tippling at the brandy-bottle or indulging in worse irregularities. The nurses in the hospitals were especially notorious for immoral conduct; sobriety almost unknown among them; and they could hardly be trusted to carry out the simplest medical duties. Certainly, things have changed since those days; and that they *have* changed is due, far more than to any other human being, to Miss Nightingale herself. It is not to be wondered at that her parents should have shuddered at the notion of their daughter devoting her life to such an occupation. "It was as if," she herself said afterwards, "I had wanted to be a kitchen-maid." Yet the want, absurd, impracticable as it was, not only remained fixed immovably in her heart, but grew in intensity day by day. Her wretchedness deepened into a morbid melancholy. Everything about her was vile, and she herself, it was clear, to have deserved

4

---

2. Mrs. Gamp, a character in Charles Dickens's *Martin Chuzzlewit*, is a midwife who nerves herself with "a little sip of liquor" before undertaking various medical tasks.

such misery, was even viler than her surroundings. Yes, she had sinned—"standing before God's judgment seat." "No one," she declared, "has so grieved the Holy Spirit"; of that she was quite certain. It was in vain that she prayed to be delivered from vanity and hypocrisy, and she could not bear to smile or to be gay, "because she hated God to hear her laugh, as if she had not repented of her sin."

A weaker spirit would have been overwhelmed by the load of such distresses—would have yielded or snapped. But this extraordinary young woman held firm, and fought her way to victory. With an amazing persistency, during the eight years that followed her rebuff over Salisbury Hospital, she struggled and worked and planned. While superficially she was carrying on the life of a brilliant girl in high society, while internally she was a prey to the tortures of regret and of remorse, she yet possessed the energy to collect the knowledge and to undergo the experience which alone could enable her to do what she had determined she would do in the end. In secret she devoured the reports of medical commissions, the pamphlets of sanitary authorities, the histories of hospitals and homes. She spent the intervals of the London season in ragged schools and workhouses. When she went abroad with her family, she used her spare time so well that there was hardly a great hospital in Europe with which she was not acquainted, hardly a great city whose slums she had not passed through. She managed to spend some days in a convent school in Rome, and some weeks as a " Sœur de Charité" in Paris. Then, while her mother and sister were taking the waters at Carlsbad, she succeeded in slipping off to a nursing institution at Kaiserswerth, where she remained for more than three months. This was the critical event of her life. The experience which she gained as a nurse at Kaiserswerth formed the foundation of all her future action and finally fixed her in her career.

But one other trial awaited her. The allurements of the world she had brushed aside with disdain and loathing; she had resisted the subtler temptation which, in her weariness, had sometimes come upon her, of devoting her baffled energies to art or literature; the last ordeal appeared in the shape of a desirable young man. Hitherto, her lovers had been nothing to her but an added burden and a mockery; but now—. For a moment, she wavered. A new feeling swept over her—a feeling which she had never known before, which she was never to know again. The most powerful and the profoundest of all the instincts of humanity laid claim upon her. But it rose before her, that instinct, arrayed—how could it be otherwise?—in the inevitable habiliments of a Victorian marriage; and she had the strength to stamp it underfoot.

> I have an intellectual nature which requires satisfaction [she noted], and that would find it in him. I have a passional nature which requires satisfaction, and that would find it in him. I have a moral, an active nature which requires satisfaction, and that would not find it in his life. Sometimes I think that I will satisfy my passional nature at all events. . . .

But no, she knew in her heart that it could not be. "To be nailed to a continuation and exaggeration of my present life . . . to put it out of my power ever to be able to seize the chance of forming for myself a true and rich life"—that would be a suicide. She made her choice, and refused what was at least a certain happiness for a visionary good which might never come to her at all. And so she returned to her old life of waiting and bitterness.

> The thoughts and feelings that I have now [she wrote] I can remember since I was six years old. A profession, a trade, a necessary occupation, something to fill and employ all my faculties, I have always felt essential to me, I have always longed for. The first thought I can remember, and the last, was nursing work; and in the absence of this, education work, but more the education of the bad than of the young. . . . Everything has been tried, foreign travel, kind friends, everything. My God! What is to become of me?

A desirable young man? Dust and ashes! What was there desirable in such a thing as that? "In my thirty-first year," she noted in her diary, "I see nothing desirable but death."

Three more years passed, and then at last the pressure of time told; her family seemed to realise that she was old enough and strong enough to have her way; and she became the superintendent of a charitable nursing home in Harley Street. She had gained her independence, though it was in a meagre sphere enough; and her mother was still not quite resigned: surely Florence might at least spend the summer in the country. At times, indeed, among her intimates, Mrs. Nightingale almost wept. "We are ducks," she said with tears in her eyes, "who have hatched a wild swan." But the poor lady was wrong; it was not a swan that they had hatched; it was an eagle.

II

Miss Nightingale had been a year in her nursing-home in   8
Harley Street, when Fate knocked at the door. The Crimean War
broke out; the battle of the Alma was fought; and the terrible
condition of our military hospitals at Scutari began to be known
in England. It sometimes happens that the plans of Providence are
a little difficult to follow, but on this occasion all was plain; there
was a perfect co-ordination of events. For years Miss Nightingale
had been getting ready; at last she was prepared—experienced,
free, mature, yet still young—she was thirty-four—desirous to
serve, accustomed to command: at that precise moment the desperate need of a great nation came, and she was there to satisfy it.
If the war had fallen a few years earlier, she would have lacked the
knowledge, perhaps even the power, for such a work; a few years
later and she would, no doubt, have been fixed in the routine of
some absorbing task, and moreover, she would have been growing old. Nor was it only the coincidence of Time that was remarkable. It so fell out that Sidney Herbert was at the War Office
and in the Cabinet; and Sidney Herbert was an intimate friend of
Miss Nightingale's, convinced, from personal experience in charitable work, of her supreme capacity. After such premises, it
seems hardly more than a matter of course that her letter, in
which she offered her services for the East, and Sidney Herbert's
letter, in which he asked for them, should actually have crossed in
the post. Thus it all happened, without a hitch. The appointment
was made, and even Mrs. Nightingale, overawed by the magnitude of the venture, could only approve. A pair of faithful friends
offered themselves as personal attendants; thirty-eight nurses
were collected; and within a week of the crossing of the letters
Miss Nightingale, amid a great burst of popular enthusiasm, left
for Constantinople.

Among the numerous letters which she received on her depar-   9
ture was one from Dr. Manning, who at that time was working in
comparative obscurity as a Catholic priest in Bayswater. "God will
keep you," he wrote, "and my prayer for you will be that your one
object of Worship, Pattern of Imitation, and source of consolation
and strength may be the Sacred Heart of our Divine Lord."

To what extent Dr. Manning's prayer was answered must re-   10
main a matter of doubt; but this much is certain, that, if ever a

prayer was needed, it was needed then for Florence Nightingale. For dark as had been the picture of the state of affairs at Scutari, revealed to the English public in the despatches of the *Times* correspondent and in a multitude of private letters, yet the reality turned out to be darker still. What had occurred was, in brief, the complete break-down of our medical arrangements at the seat of war. The origins of this awful failure were complex and manifold; they stretched back through long years of peace and carelessness in England; they could be traced through endless ramifications of administrative incapacity—from the inherent faults of confused systems to the petty bunglings of minor officials, from the inevitable ignorance of Cabinet Ministers to the fatal exactitudes of narrow routine. In the inquiries which followed it was clearly shown that the evil was in reality that worst of all evils—one which has been caused by nothing in particular and for which no one in particular is to blame. The whole organisation of the war machine was incompetent and out of date. The old Duke[3] had sat for a generation at the Horse Guards repressing innovations with an iron hand. There was an extraordinary overlapping of authorities, an almost incredible shifting of responsibilities to and fro. As for such a notion as the creation and the maintenance of a really adequate medical service for the army—in that atmosphere of aged chaos, how could it have entered anybody's head? Before the war, the easy-going officials at Westminster were naturally persuaded that all was well—or at least as well as could be expected; when someone, for instance, actually had the temerity to suggest the formation of a corps of army nurses, he was at once laughed out of court. When the war had begun, the gallant British officers in control of affairs had other things to think about than the petty details of medical organisation. Who had bothered with such trifles in the Peninsula? And surely, on that occasion, we had done pretty well. Thus the most obvious precautions were neglected, the most necessary preparations put off from day to day. The principal medical officer of the army, Dr. Hall, was summoned from India at a moment's notice, and was unable to visit England before taking up his duties at the front. And it was not until after the battle of the

3. Arthur Wellesley (1769–1852), Duke of Wellington, who defeated Napoleon at Waterloo and was a leading conservative politician.

Alma, when we had been at war for many months, that we acquired hospital accommodation at Scutari for more than a thousand men. Errors, follies, and vices on the part of individuals
there doubtless were; but, in the general reckoning, they were of
small account—insignificant symptoms of the deep disease of the
body politic—the enormous calamity of administrative collapse.

Miss Nightingale arrived at Scutari—a suburb of Constan-   11
tinople, on the Asiatic side of the Bosphorus—on November 4th,
1854; it was ten days after the battle of Balaclava, and the day
before the battle of Inkerman. The organisation of the hospitals,
which had already given way under the stress of the battle of the
Alma, was now to be subjected to the further pressure which
these two desperate and bloody engagements implied. Great de-
tachments of wounded were already beginning to pour in. The
men, after receiving such summary treatment as could be given
them at the smaller hospitals in the Crimea itself, were forthwith
shipped in batches of two hundred across the Black Sea to Scutari. This voyage was in normal times one of four days and a
half; but the times were no longer normal, and now the transit
often lasted for a fortnight or three weeks. It received, not without reason, the name of "the middle passage.[4]" Between, and
sometimes on the decks, the wounded, the sick, and the dying
were crowded—men who had just undergone the amputation of
limbs, men in the clutches of fever or of frostbite, men in the last
stages of dysentery and cholera—without beds, sometimes without blankets, often hardly clothed. The one or two surgeons on
board did what they could; but medical stores were lacking, and
the only form of nursing available was that provided by a handful of invalid soldiers, who were usually themselves prostrate by
the end of the voyage. There was no other food beside the ordinary salt rations of ship diet; and even the water was sometimes
so stored that it was out of reach of the weak. For many months,
the average of deaths during these voyages was seventy-four in
the thousand; the corpses were shot out into the waters; and who
shall say that they were the most unfortunate? At Scutari, the
landing-stage, constructed with all the perverseness of Oriental
ingenuity, could only be approached with great difficulty, and, in
rough weather, not at all. When it was reached, what remained

---

4. The Middle Passage was the horrifying journey from Africa to America
aboard overcrowded slave ships.

of the men in the ships had first to be disembarked, and then conveyed up a steep slope of a quarter of a mile to the nearest of the hospitals. The most serious cases might be put upon stretchers—for there were far too few for all; the rest were carried or dragged up the hill by such convalescent soldiers as could be got together, who were not too obviously infirm for the work. At last the journey was accomplished; slowly, one by one, living or dying, the wounded were carried up into the hospital. And in the hospital what did they find?

Lasciate ogni speranza, voi ch'entrate[5]: the delusive doors   12
bore no such inscription; and yet behind them Hell yawned. Want, neglect, confusion, misery—in every shape and in every degree of intensity—filled the endless corridors and the vast apartments of the gigantic barrack-house, which, without forethought or preparation, had been hurriedly set aside as the chief shelter for the victims of the war. The very building itself was radically defective. Huge sewers underlay it, and cess-pools loaded with filth wafted their poison into the upper rooms. The floors were in so rotten a condition that many of them could not be scrubbed; the walls were thick with dirt; incredible multitudes of vermin swarmed everywhere. And, enormous as the building was, it was yet too small. It contained four miles of beds, crushed together so close that there was but just room to pass between them. Under such conditions, the most elaborate system of ventilation might well have been at fault; but here there was no ventilation. The stench was indescribable. "I have been well acquainted," said Miss Nightingale, "with the dwellings of the worst parts of most of the great cities in Europe, but have never been in any atmosphere which I could compare with that of the Barrack Hospital at night." The structural defects were equalled by the deficiencies in the commonest objects of hospital use. There were not enough bedsteads; the sheets were of canvas, and so coarse that the wounded men recoiled from them, begging to be left in their blankets; there was no bedroom furniture of any kind, and empty beer-bottles were used for candlesticks. There were no basins, no towels, no soap, no brooms, no mops, no trays, no plates; there were neither slippers nor scissors, neither shoebrushes nor blacking; there were no knives or forks or

---

5. *Lasciate ogni speranza, voi ch'entrate:* "Abandon hope, all ye who enter here." The inscription on the gate to Hell in Dante's *Inferno*.

spoons. The supply of fuel was constantly deficient. The cooking arrangements were preposterously inadequate, and the laundry was a farce. As for purely medical materials, the tale was no better. Stretchers, splints, bandages—all were lacking; and so were the most ordinary drugs.

To replace such wants, to struggle against such difficulties, 13 there was a handful of men overburdened by the strain of ceaseless work, bound down by the traditions of official routine, and enfeebled either by old age or inexperience or sheer incompetence. They had proved utterly unequal to their task. The principal doctor was lost in the imbecilities of a senile optimism. The wretched official whose business it was to provide for the wants of the hospital was tied fast hand and foot by red tape. A few of the younger doctors struggled valiantly, but what could they do? Unprepared, disorganised, with such help only as they could find among the miserable band of convalescent soldiers drafted off to tend their sick comrades, they were faced with disease, mutilation, and death in all their most appalling forms, crowded multitudinously about them in an ever increasing mass. They were like men in a shipwreck, fighting, not for safety, but for the next moment's bare existence—to gain, by yet another frenzied effort, some brief respite from the waters of destruction.

In these surroundings, those who had been long inured to 14 scenes of human suffering—surgeons with a world-wide knowledge of agonies, soldiers familiar with fields of carnage, missionaries with remembrances of famine and of plague—yet found a depth of horror which they had never known before. There were moments, there were places, in the Barrack Hospital at Scutari, where the strongest hand was struck with trembling, and the boldest eye would turn away its gaze.

Miss Nightingale came, and she, at any rate, in that Inferno, 15 did not abandon hope. For one thing, she brought material succour. Before she left London she had consulted Dr. Andrew Smith, the head of the Army Medical Board, as to whether it would be useful to take out stores of any kind to Scutari; and Dr. Andrew Smith had told her that "nothing was needed." Even Sidney Herbert had given her similar assurances; possibly, owing to an oversight, there might have been some delay in the delivery of the medical stores, which, he said, had been sent out from England "in profusion," but "four days would have remedied this." She preferred to trust her own instincts, and at Marseilles purchased a large quantity of miscellaneous provisions, which were of the utmost use at Scutari. She came, too, amply provided with money—in all, during her stay in the East, about £7000 reached her from private sources; and, in addition, she was able to avail herself of another valuable means of help. At the same time as herself, Mr. Macdonald, of the *Times,* had arrived at Scutari, charged with the duty of administering the large sums of money collected through the agency of that newspaper in aid of the sick and wounded; and Mr. Macdonald had the sense to see that the best use he could make of the *Times* Fund was to put it at the disposal of Miss Nightingale.

> I cannot conceive [wrote an eye-witness], as I now calmly look back on the first three weeks after the arrival of the wounded from Inkerman, how it could have been possible to have avoided a state of things too disastrous to contemplate, had not Miss Nightingale been there, with the means placed at her disposal by Mr. Macdonald.

But the official view was different. What! Was the public service to admit, by accepting outside charity, that it was unable to discharge its own duties without the assistance of private and irregular benevolence? Never! And accordingly when Lord Stratford de Redcliffe, our Ambassador at Constantinople, was asked by Mr. Macdonald to indicate how the *Times* Fund could best be employed, he answered that there was indeed one object to which it might very well be devoted—the building of an English Protestant Church at Pera.

Mr. Macdonald did not waste further time with Lord Stratford, and immediately joined forces with Miss Nightingale. But, with such a frame of mind in the highest quarters, it is easy to imagine the kind of disgust and alarm with which the sudden intrusion of a band of amateurs and females must have filled the minds of the ordinary officer and the ordinary military surgeon. They could not understand it; what had women to do with war? Honest Colonels relieved their spleen by the cracking of heavy jokes about "the Bird"; while poor Dr. Hall, a rough terrier of a man, who had worried his way to the top of his profession, was struck speechless with astonishment, and at last observed that Miss Nightingale's appointment was extremely droll.

Her position was, indeed, an official one, but it was hardly the easier for that. In the hospitals it was her duty to provide the services of herself and her nurses when they were asked for by the doctors, and not until then. At first some of the surgeons would have nothing to say to her, and, though she was welcomed by others, the majority were hostile and suspicious. But gradually she gained ground. Her good will could not be denied, and her capacity could not be disregarded. With consummate tact, with all the gentleness of supreme strength, she managed at last to impose her personality upon the susceptible, overwrought, discouraged, and helpless group of men in authority who surrounded her. She stood firm; she was a rock in the angry ocean; with her alone was safety, comfort, life. And so it was that hope dawned at Scutari. The reign of chaos and old night began to dwindle; order came upon the scene, and common sense, and forethought, and decision, radiating out from the little room off the great gallery in the Barrack Hospital where day and night, the Lady Superintendent was at her task. Progress might be slow, but it was sure. The first sign of a great change came with the appearance of some of those necessary objects with which the hospitals had been unprovided for months. The sick men began to enjoy the use of towels and soap, knives and forks, combs and tooth-brushes. Dr. Hall might snort when he heard of it, asking, with a growl, what a soldier wanted with a tooth-brush; but the good work went on. Eventually the whole business of purveying to the hospitals was, in effect, carried out by Miss Nightingale. She alone, it seemed, whatever the contingency, knew where to lay her hands on what was wanted; she alone could dispense her stores with readiness; above all she alone possessed the art of circumventing the pernicious influences of official etiquette. This was her greatest enemy, and sometimes even she was baffled by it. On one occasion 27,000 shirts sent out at her instance by the Home Government, arrived, were landed, and were only waiting to be unpacked. But the official "Purveyor" intervened; "he could not unpack them," he said, "without a Board." Miss Nightingale pleaded in vain; the sick and wounded lay half-naked shivering for want of clothing; and three weeks elapsed before the Board released the shirts. A little later, however, on a similar occasion, Miss Nightingale felt that she could assert her own authority. She ordered a Government consignment to be forcibly opened, while the miserable "Purveyor" stood by, wringing his hands in departmental agony.

Vast quantities of valuable stores sent from England lay, she   18 found, engulfed in the bottomless abyss of the Turkish Customs House. Other ship-loads, buried beneath munitions of war destined for Balaclava, passed Scutari without a sign, and thus hospital materials were sometimes carried to and fro three times over the Black Sea, before they reached their destination. The whole system was clearly at fault, and Miss Nightingale suggested to the home authorities that a Government Store House should be instituted at Scutari for the reception and distribution of the consignments. Six months after her arrival this was done.

In the meantime she had reorganised the kitchens and the laundries in the hospitals. The ill-cooked hunks of meat, vilely served at irregular intervals, which had hitherto been the only diet for the sick men were replaced by punctual meals, well-prepared and appetising, while strengthening extra foods—soups and wines, and jellies ("preposterous luxuries," snarled Dr. Hall)—were distributed to those who needed them. One thing, however, she could not effect. The separation of the bones from the meat was no part of official cookery: the rule was that the food must be divided into equal portions, and if some of the portions were all bone—well, every man must take his chance. The rule, perhaps, was not a very good one; but there it was. "It would require a new Regulation of the Service," she was told, "to bone the meat." As for the washing arrangements, they were revolutionised. Up to the time of Miss Nightingale's arrival the number of shirts which the authorities had succeeded in washing was seven. The hospital bedding, she found, was "washed" in cold water. She took a Turkish house, had boilers installed, and employed soldiers' wives to do the laundry work. The expenses were defrayed from her own funds and that of the *Times;* and henceforward the sick and wounded had the comfort of clean linen.

Then she turned her attention to their clothing. Owing to military exigencies the greater number of the men had abandoned their kit; their knapsacks were lost for ever; they possessed nothing but what was on their persons, and that was usually only fit for speedy destruction. The "Purveyor," of course, pointed out that, according to the regulations, all soldiers should bring with them into hospital an adequate supply of clothing, and he declared that it was no business of his to make good their deficiencies. Apparently, it was the business of Miss Nightingale. She procured socks, boots, and shirts in enormous quantities; she had trousers

19

20

made, she rigged up dressing-gowns. "The fact is," she told Sidney Herbert, "I am now clothing the British Army."

All at once, word came from the Crimea that a great new contingent of sick and wounded might shortly be expected. Where were they to go? Every available inch in the wards was occupied; the affair was serious and pressing, and the authorities stood aghast. There were some dilapidated rooms in the Barrack Hospital, unfit for human habitation, but Miss Nightingale believed that if measures were promptly taken they might be made capable of accommodating several hundred beds. One of the doctors agreed with her; the rest of the officials were irresolute: it would be a very expensive job, they said; it would involve building; and who could take the responsibility? The proper course was that a representation should be made to the Director-General of the Army Medical Department in London; then the Director-General would apply to the Horse Guards, the Horse Guards would move the Ordnance, the Ordnance would lay the matter before the Treasury, and, if the Treasury gave its consent, the work might be correctly carried through, several months after the necessity for it had disappeared. Miss Nightingale, however, had made up her mind, and she persuaded Lord Stratford—or thought she had persuaded him—to give his sanction to the required expenditure. A hundred and twenty-five workmen were immediately engaged, and the work was begun. The workmen struck; whereupon Lord Stratford washed his hands of the whole business. Miss Nightingale engaged two hundred other workmen on her own authority, and paid the bill out of her own resources. The wards were ready by the required date; five hundred sick men were received in them; and all the utensils, including knives, forks, spoons, cans and towels, were supplied by Miss Nightingale.

This remarkable woman was in truth performing the function of an administrative chief. How had this come about? Was she not in reality merely a nurse? Was it not her duty simply to tend to the sick? And indeed, was it not as a ministering angel, a gentle "lady with a lamp" that she actually impressed the minds of her contemporaries? No doubt that was so; and yet it is no less certain that, as she herself said, the specific business of nursing was "the least important of the functions into which she had been forced." It was clear that in the state of disorganisation into which the hospitals at Scutari had fallen the most pressing, the really vital, need was for something more than nursing; it was for the necessary elements of civilised life—the commonest material objects, the most ordinary cleanliness, the rudimentary habits of order and authority. "Oh, dear Miss Nightingale," said one of her party as they were approaching Constantinople, "when we land, let there be no delays, let us get straight to nursing the poor fellows!" "The strongest will be wanted at the wash-tub," was Miss Nightingale's answer. And it was upon the wash-tub, and all that the wash-tub stood for, that she expended her greatest energies. Yet to say that is perhaps to say too much. For to those who watched her at work among the sick, moving day and night from bed to bed, with that unflinching courage, with that indefatigable vigilance, it seemed as if the concentrated force of an undivided and unparalleled devotion could hardly suffice for that portion of her task alone. Wherever, in those vast wards, suffering was at its worst and the need for help was greatest; there, as if by magic, was Miss Nightingale. Her superhuman equanimity would, at the moment of some ghastly operation, nerve the victim to endure and almost to hope. Her sympathy would assuage the pangs of dying and bring back to those still living something of the forgotten charm of life. Over and over again her untiring efforts rescued those whom the surgeons had abandoned as beyond the possibility of cure. Her mere presence brought with it a strange influence. A passionate idolatry spread among the men: they kissed her shadow as it passed. They did more. "Before she came," said a soldier, "there was cussin' and swearin', but after that it was as 'oly as a church." The most cherished privilege of the fighting man was abandoned for the sake of Miss Nightingale. In those "lowest sinks of human misery," as she herself put it, she never heard the use of one expression "which could distress a gentlewoman."

She was heroic; and these were the humble tributes paid by those of grosser mould to that high quality. Certainly, she was heroic. Yet her heroism was not of that simple sort so dear to the readers of novels and the compilers of hagiologies—the romantic sentimental heroism with which mankind loves to invest its chosen darlings: it was made of sterner stuff. To the wounded soldier on his couch of agony she might well appear in the guise of a gracious angel of mercy; but the military surgeons, and the orderlies, and her own nurses, and the "Purveyor," and Dr. Hall, and even Lord Stratford himself could tell a different story. It was not by gentle sweetness and womanly self-abnegation that she had brought order out of chaos in the Scutari Hospitals, that, from her own resources, she had clothed the British Army, that she had spread her dominion over the serried and reluctant powers of the official world; it was by strict method, by stern discipline, by rigid attention to detail, by ceaseless labour, by the fixed determination of an indomitable will. Beneath her cool and calm demeanour lurked fierce and passionate fires. As she passed through the wards in her plain dress, so quiet, so unassuming, she struck the casual observer simply as the pattern of a perfect lady; but the keener eye perceived something more than that— the serenity of high deliberation in the scope of the capacious brow, the sign of power in the dominating curve of the thin nose, and the traces of a harsh and dangerous temper—something peevish, something mocking, and yet something precise—in the small and delicate mouth. There was humour in the face; but the curious watcher might wonder whether it was humour of a very pleasant kind; might ask himself, even as he heard the laughter and marked the jokes with which she cheered the spirits of her patients, what sort of sardonic merriment this same lady might not give vent to, in the privacy of her chamber. As for her voice, it was true of it, even more than of her countenance, that it "had that in it one must fain call master." Those clear tones were in no need of emphasis: "I never heard her raise her voice," said one of her companions. Only, when she had spoken, it seemed as if nothing could follow but obedience. Once, when she had given some direction, a doctor ventured to remark that the thing could not be done. "But it must be done," said Miss Nightingale. A chance bystander, who heard the words, never forgot through all his life the irresistible authority of them. And they were spoken quietly—very quietly indeed.

Late at night, when the long miles of beds lay wrapped in darkness, Miss Nightingale would sit at work in her little room, over her correspondence. It was one of the most formidable of all her duties. There were hundreds of letters to be written to the friends and relations of soldiers; there was the enormous mass of official documents to be dealt with; there were her own private letters to be answered; and, most important of all, there was the composition of her long and confidential reports to Sidney Herbert. These were by no means official communications. Her soul, pent up all day in the restraint and reserve of a vast responsibility, now at last poured itself out in these letters with all its natural vehemence, like a swollen torrent through an open sluice. Here, at least, she did not mince matters. Here she painted in her darkest colours the hideous scenes which surrounded her; here she tore away remorselessly the last veils still shrouding the abominable truth. Then she would fill pages with recommendations and suggestions, with criticisms of the minutest details of organisation, with elaborate calculations of contingencies, with exhaustive analyses and statistical statements piled up in breathless eagerness one on the top of the other. And then her pen, in the virulence of its volubility, would rush on to the discussion of individuals, to the denunciation of an incompetent surgeon or the ridicule of a self-sufficient nurse. Her sarcasm searched the ranks of the officials with the deadly and unsparing precision of a machine-gun. Her nicknames were terrible. She respected no one: Lord Stratford, Lord Raglan, Lady Stratford, Dr. Andrew Smith, Dr. Hall, the Commissary-General, the Purveyor—she fulminated against them all. The intolerable futility of mankind obsessed her like a nightmare, and she gnashed her teeth against it. "I do well to be angry," was the burden of her cry. How many just men were there at Scutari? How many who cared at all for the sick, or had done anything for their relief? Were there ten? Were there five? Was there even one? She could not be sure.

At one time, during several weeks, her vituperations descended   25
upon the head of Sidney Herbert himself. He had misinterpreted her wishes, he had traversed her positive instructions, and it was not until he had admitted his error and apologised in abject terms that he was allowed again into favour. While this misunderstanding was at its height an aristocratic young gentleman arrived at Scutari with a recommendation from the Minister. He had come out from England filled with a romantic desire to render homage to the angelic heroine of his dreams. He had, he said, cast aside his life of ease and luxury; he would devote his days and nights to the service of that gentle lady; he would perform the most menial offices, he would "fag" for her, he would be her footman—and feel requited by a single smile. A single smile, indeed, he had, but it was of an unexpected kind. Miss Nightingale at first refused to see him, and then, when she consented, believing that he was an emissary sent by Sidney Herbert to put her in the wrong over their dispute, she took notes of her conversation with him, and insisted on his signing them at the end of it. The young gentleman returned to England by the next ship.

This quarrel with Sidney Herbert was, however, an excep-   26
tional incident. Alike by him, and by Lord Panmure, his successor at the War Office, she was firmly supported; and the fact that
during the whole of her stay at Scutari she had the Home Government at her back, was her trump card in her dealings with the
hospital authorities. Nor was it only the Government that was
behind her: public opinion in England early recognised the high
importance of her mission, and its enthusiastic appreciation of
her work soon reached an extraordinary height. The Queen herself was deeply moved. She made repeated inquiries as to the
welfare of Miss Nightingale; she asked to see her accounts of the
wounded, and made her the intermediary between the throne
and the troops.

> Let Mrs. Herbert know [she wrote to the War Minister] that I wish
> Miss Nightingale and the ladies would tell these poor noble, wounded,
> and sick men that *no one* takes a warmer interest or feels *more* for
> their sufferings or admires their courage and heroism *more* than their
> Queen. Day and night she thinks of her beloved troops. So does the
> Prince. Beg Mrs. Herbert to communicate these my words to those
> ladies, as I know that *our* sympathy is much valued by these noble
> fellows.

The letter was read aloud in the wards by the Chaplain. "It is a
very feeling letter," said the men.

And so the months passed, and that fell winter which had be-   27
gun with Inkerman and had dragged itself out through the long
agony of the investment of Sebastopol, at last was over. In May,
1855, after six months of labour, Miss Nightingale could look
with something like satisfaction at the condition of the Scutari
hospitals. Had they done nothing more than survive the terrible
strain which had been put upon them, it would have been a matter for congratulation; but they had done much more than that;
they had marvellously improved. The confusion and the pressure
in the wards had come to an end; order reigned in them, and
cleanliness; the supplies were bountiful and prompt; important
sanitary works had been carried out. One simple comparison of
figures was enough to reveal the extraordinary change: the rate
of mortality among the cases treated had fallen from 42 per cent.
to 22 per thousand. But still the indefatigable lady was not satisfied. The main problem had been solved—the physical needs of
the men had been provided for; their mental and spiritual needs

remained. She set up and furnished reading-rooms and recreation-rooms. She started classes and lectures. Officers were amazed to see her treating their men as if they were human beings, and assured her that she would only end by "spoiling the brutes." But that was not Miss Nightingale's opinion, and she was justified. The private soldier began to drink less, and even—though that seemed impossible—to save his pay. Miss Nightingale became a banker for the army, receiving and sending home large sums of money every month. At last, reluctantly, the Government followed suit, and established machinery of its own for the remission of money. Lord Panmure, however, remained sceptical; "it will do no good," he pronounced; "the British soldier is not a re-mitting animal." But, in fact, during the next six months, £71,000 was sent home.

Amid all these activities, Miss Nightingale took up the further task of inspecting the hospitals in the Crimea itself. The labour was extreme, and the conditions of life were almost intolerable. She spent whole days in the saddle, or was driven over those bleak and rocky heights in a baggage cart. Sometimes she stood for hours in the heavily falling snow, and would only reach her hut at dead of night after walking for miles through perilous ravines. Her powers of resistance seemed incredible, but at last they were exhausted. She was attacked by fever, and for a moment came very near to death. Yet she worked on; if she could not move, she could at least write; and write she did until her mind had left her; and after it had left her, in what seemed the delirious trance of death itself, she still wrote. When, after many weeks, she was strong enough to travel, she was to return to England, but she utterly refused. She would not go back, she said, before the last of the soldiers had left Scutari.

This happy moment had almost arrived, when suddenly the smouldering hostilities of the medical authorities burst out into a flame. Dr. Hall's labours had been rewarded by a K.C.B.—letters which, as Miss Nightingale told Sidney Herbert, she could only suppose to mean "Knight of the Crimean Burial-grounds"—and the honour had turned his head. He was Sir John, and he would be thwarted no longer. Disputes had lately arisen between Miss Nightingale and some of the nurses in the Crimean hospitals. The situation had been embittered by rumours of religious dissensions, for, while the Crimean nurses were Roman Catholics, many of those at Scutari were suspected of a regrettable propensity towards the tenets of Dr. Pusey.[6] Miss Nightingale was by no means disturbed by these sectarian differences, but any suggestion that her supreme authority over all the nurses with the Army was in doubt was enough to rouse her to fury; and it appeared that Mrs. Bridgeman, the Reverend Mother in the Crimea, had ventured to call that authority in question. Sir John Hall thought that his opportunity had come, and strongly supported Mrs. Bridgeman—or, as Miss Nightingale preferred to call her, the "Reverend Brickbat." There was a violent struggle; Miss Nightingale's rage was terrible. Dr. Hall, she declared, was doing his best to "root her out of the Crimea." She would bear it no longer; the War Office was playing her false; there was only one thing to be done—Sidney Herbert must move for the production of papers in the House of Commons, so that the public might be able to judge between her and her enemies. Sidney Herbert with great difficulty calmed her down. Orders were immediately dispatched putting her supremacy beyond doubt, and the Reverend Brickbat withdrew from the scene. Sir John, however, was more tenacious. A few weeks later, Miss Nightingale and her nurses visited the Crimea for the last time, and the brilliant idea occurred to him that he could crush her by a very simple expedient—he would starve her into submission; and he actually ordered that no rations of any kind should be supplied to her. He had already tried this plan with great effect upon an unfortunate medical man whose presence in the Crimea he had considered an intrusion; but he was now to learn that such tricks were thrown away upon Miss Nightingale. With extraordinary foresight, she had brought with her a great supply of food; she succeeded in obtaining more at her own expense and by her own exertions; and thus for ten days, in that inhospitable country, she was able to feed herself and twenty-four nurses. Eventually the military authorities intervened in her favour, and Sir John had to confess that he was beaten.

It was not until July, 1856—four months after the Declaration of Peace—that Miss Nightingale left Scutari for England. Her reputation was now enormous, and the enthusiasm of the public   30

6. Edward Boverie Pusey (1800–1882) was a leader of the Oxford Movement, which attempted to reestablish in the Anglican church some High Church ideals and doctrines abandoned in the eighteenth century.

was unbounded. The Royal approbation was expressed by the gift of a brooch, accompanied by a private letter.

> You are, I know, well aware [wrote Her Majesty] of the high sense I entertain of the Christian devotion which you have displayed during this great and bloody war, and I need hardly repeat to you how warm my admiration is for your services, which are fully equal to those of my dear and brave soldiers, whose sufferings you have had the *privilege* of alleviating in so merciful a manner. I am, however, anxious of marking my feelings in a manner which I trust will be agreeable to you, and therefore send you with this letter a brooch, the form and emblems of which commemorate your great and blessed work, and which I hope you will wear as a mark of the high approbation of your Sovereign!

"It will be a very great satisfaction to me," Her Majesty 31 added, "to make the acquaintance of one who has set so bright an example to our sex."

The brooch, which was designed by the Prince Consort, bore 32 a St. George's cross in red enamel, and the Royal cypher surmounted by diamonds. The whole was encircled by the inscription, "Blessed are the Merciful."

III

The name of Florence Nightingale lives in the memory of the 33 world by virtue of the lurid and heroic adventure of the Crimea. Had she died—as she nearly did—upon her return to England, her reputation would hardly have been different; her legend would have come down to us almost as we know it to-day—that gentle vision of female virtue which first took shape before the adoring eyes of the sick soldiers at Scutari. Yet, as a matter of fact, she lived for more than half a century after the Crimean War; and during the greater part of that long period all the energy and all the devotion of her extraordinary nature were working at their highest pitch. What she accomplished in those years of unknown labour could, indeed, hardly have been more glorious than her Crimean triumphs; but it was certainly more important. The true history was far stranger even than the myth. In Miss Nightingale's own eyes the adventure of the Crimea was a mere incident—scarcely more than a useful stepping-stone in her career. It was the fulcrum with which she hoped to move the world; but it was only the fulcrum. For more than a generation she was to sit in secret, working her lever: and her real life began at the very moment when, in the popular imagination, it had ended.

She arrived in England in a shattered state of health. The hardships and the ceaseless effort of the last two years had undermined her nervous system; her heart was pronounced to be affected; she suffered constantly from fainting-fits and terrible attacks of utter physical prostration. The doctors declared that one thing alone would save her—a complete and prolonged rest. But that was also the one thing with which she would have nothing to do. She had never been in the habit of resting; why should she begin now? Now, when her opportunity had come at last; now, when the iron was hot, and it was time to strike? No; she had work to do; and, come what might, she would do it. The doctors protested in vain; in vain her family lamented and entreated, in vain her friends pointed out to her the madness of such a course. Madness? Mad—possessed—perhaps she was. A demoniac frenzy had seized upon her. As she lay upon her sofa, gasping, she devoured blue-books, dictated letters, and, in the intervals of her palpitations, cracked her febrile jokes. For months at a stretch she never left her bed. For years she was in daily expectation of Death. But she would not rest. At this rate, the doctors assured her, even if she did not die, she would become an invalid for life. She could not help that; there was the work to be done; and, as for rest, very likely she might rest . . . when she had done it.

Wherever she went, in London or in the country, in the hills of Derbyshire, or among the rhododendrons at Embley, she was haunted by a ghost. It was the spectre of Scutari—the hideous vision of the organisation of a military hospital. She would lay that phantom, or she would perish. The whole system of the Army Medical Department, the education of the Medical Officer, the regulations of hospital procedure . . . *rest?* How could she rest while these things were as they were, while, if the like necessity were to arise again, the like results would follow? And, even in peace and at home, what was the sanitary condition of the Army? The mortality in the barracks was, she found, nearly double the mortality in civil life. "You might as well take 1100 men every year out upon Salisbury Plain and shoot them," she said. After inspecting the hospitals at Chatham, she smiled grimly.

"Yes, this is one more symptom of the system which, in the Crimea, put to death 16,000 men." Scutari had given her knowledge; and it had given her power too: her enormous reputation was at her back—an incalculable force. Other work, other duties, might lie before her; but the most urgent, the most obvious of all was to look to the health of the Army.

One of her very first steps was to take advantage of the invitation which Queen Victoria had sent her to the Crimea, together with the commemorative brooch. Within a few weeks of her return, she visited Balmoral, and had several interviews both with the Queen and the Prince Consort. "She put before us," wrote the Prince in his diary, "all the defects of our present military hospital system and the reforms that are needed." She related the whole story of her experiences in the East; and, in addition, she managed to have some long and confidential talks with His Royal Highness on metaphysics and religion. The impression which she created was excellent. "Sie gefällt uns sehr,[7]" noted the Prince, "ist sehr bescheiden." Her Majesty's comment was different—"Such a *head!* I wish we had her at the War Office."

But Miss Nightingale was not at the War Office, and for a very simple reason: she was a woman. Lord Panmure, however, *was* (though indeed the reason for that was not quite so simple); and it was upon Lord Panmure that the issue of Miss Nightingale's efforts for reform must primarily depend. That burly Scottish nobleman had not, in spite of his most earnest endeavours, had a very easy time of it as Secretary of State for War. He had come into office in the middle of the Sebastopol campaign, and had felt himself very well fitted for the position, since he had acquired in former days an inside knowledge of the Army—as a Captain of Hussars. It was this inside knowledge which had enabled him to inform Miss Nightingale with such authority that "the British soldier is not a remitting animal." And perhaps it was this same consciousness of a command of his subject which had impelled him to write a dispatch to Lord Raglan, blandly informing the Commander-in-Chief in the Field just how he was neglecting his duties, and pointing out to him that if he would only try he really might do a little better next time. Lord Raglan's reply, calculated as it was to make its recipient sink into the

7. *Sie gefällt uns sehr . . . ist sehr bescheiden:* She pleases us very much; is very modest.

earth, did not quite have that effect upon Lord Panmure, who, whatever might have been his faults, had never been accused of being supersensitive. However, he allowed the matter to drop; and a little later Lord Raglan died—worn out, some people said, by work and anxiety. He was succeeded by an excellent red-nosed old gentleman, General Simpson, whom nobody has ever heard of, and who took Sebastopol. But Lord Panmure's relations with him were hardly more satisfactory than his relations with Lord Raglan; for, while Lord Raglan had been too independent, poor General Simpson erred in the opposite direction, perpetually asked advice, suffered from lumbago, doubted, his nose growing daily redder and redder, whether he was fit for his post, and, by alternate mails, sent in and withdrew his resignation. Then, too, both the General and the Minister suffered acutely from that distressingly useful new invention, the electric telegraph. On one occasion General Simpson felt obliged actually to expostulate.

> I think, my Lord [he wrote], that some telegraphic messages reach us that cannot be sent under due authority, and are perhaps unknown to you, although under the protection of your Lordship's name. For instance, I was called up last night, a dragoon having come express with a telegraphic message in these words, "Lord Panmure to General Simpson—Captain Jarvis has been bitten by a centipede. How is he now?"

General Simpson might have put up with this, though to be sure it did seem "rather too trifling an affair to call for a dragoon to ride a couple of miles in the dark that he may knock up the Commander of the Army out of the very small allowance of sleep permitted him"; but what was really more than he could bear was to find "upon sending in the morning another mounted dragoon to inquire after Captain Jarvis, four miles off, that he never has been bitten at all, but has had a boil, from which he is fast recovering." But Lord Panmure had troubles of his own. His favourite nephew, Captain Dowbiggin, was at the front, and to one of his telegrams to the Commander-in-Chief the Minister had taken occasion to append the following carefully qualified sentence—"I recommend Dowbiggin to your notice, should you have a vacancy, and if he is fit." Unfortunately, in those early days, it was left to the discretion of the telegraphist to compress the messages which passed through his hands; so that the result was that Lord Panmure's delicate appeal reached its destination in the laconic form of "Look after Dowb." The Headquarters Staff were at first extremely puzzled; they were at last extremely amused. The story spread; and "Look after Dowb" remained for many years the familiar formula for describing official hints in favour of deserving nephews.

And now that all this was over, now that Sebastopol had been,   38 somehow or another, taken, now that peace was, somehow or another, made, now that the troubles of office might surely be expected to be at an end at last—here was Miss Nightingale breaking in upon the scene, with her talk about the state of the hospitals and the necessity for sanitary reform. It was most irksome; and Lord Panmure almost began to wish that he was engaged upon some more congenial occupation—discussing, perhaps, the constitution of the Free Church of Scotland—a question in which he was profoundly interested. But no; duty was paramount; and he set himself, with a sigh of resignation, to the task of doing as little of it as he possibly could.

"The Bison" his friends called him; and the name fitted both   39 his physical demeanour and his habit of mind. That large low head seemed to have been created for butting rather than for anything else. There he stood, four-square and menacing, in the door way of reform; and it remained to be seen whether the bulky mass, upon whose solid hide even the barbed arrows of Lord Raglan's scorn had made no mark, would prove amenable to the pressure of Miss Nightingale. Nor was he alone in the doorway. There loomed behind him the whole phalanx of professional conservatism, the stubborn supporters of the out-of-date, the worshippers and the victims of War Office routine. Among these it was only natural that Dr. Andrew Smith, the head of the Army Medical Department, should have been pre-eminent—Dr. Andrew Smith, who had assured Miss Nightingale before she left England that "nothing was wanted at Scutari." Such were her opponents; but she too was not without allies. She had gained the ear of Royalty—which was something; at any moment that she pleased she could gain the ear of the public—which was a great deal. She had a host of admirers and friends; and—to say nothing of her personal qualities—her knowledge, her tenacity, her tact—she possessed, too, one advantage which then, far more even than now, carried an immense weight—she belonged to the highest circle of society. She moved naturally among Peers and Cabinet Ministers—she was one of their own set; and in those days their set was a very narrow one. What kind of attention would such persons have paid to some middle-class woman with whom they were not acquainted, who possessed great experience of army nursing and had decided views upon hospital reform? They would have politely ignored her; but it was impossible to ignore Flo Nightingale. When she spoke, they were obliged to listen; and, when they had once begun to do that—what might not follow? She knew her power, and she used it. She supported her weightiest minutes with familiar witty little notes. The Bison began to look grave. It might be difficult—it might be damned difficult—to put down one's head against the white hand of a lady.

Of Miss Nightingale's friends, the most important was Sidney   40
Herbert. He was a man upon whom the good fairies seemed to have showered, as he lay in his cradle, all their most enviable gifts. Well born, handsome, rich, the master of Wilton—one of those great country-houses, clothed with the glamour of a historic past, which are the peculiar glory of England—he possessed, besides all these advantages, so charming, so lively, so gentle a disposition that no one who had once come near him could ever be his enemy. He was, in fact, a man of whom it was difficult not to say that he was a perfect English gentleman. For his virtues were equal even to his good fortune. He was religious—deeply religious: "I am more and more convinced every day," he wrote, when he had been for some years a Cabinet Minister, "that in politics, as in everything else, nothing can be right which is not in accordance with the spirit of the Gospel." No one was more unselfish; he was charitable and benevolent to a remarkable degree; and he devoted the whole of his life with an unwavering conscientiousness to the public service. With such a character, with such opportunities, what high hopes must have danced before him, what radiant visions of accomplished duties, of ever-increasing usefulness, of beneficent power, of the consciousness of disinterested success! Some of those hopes and visions were, indeed, realised; but, in the end, the career of Sidney Herbert seemed to show that, with all their generosity, there was some gift or other—what was it?—some essential gift—which the good fairies had withheld, and that even the qualities of a perfect English gentleman may be no safeguard against anguish, humiliation, and defeat.

That career would certainly have been very different if he had   41
never known Miss Nightingale. The alliance between them, which
had begun with her appointment to Scutari, which had grown
closer and closer while the war lasted, developed, after her return,
into one of the most extraordinary of friendships. It was the
friendship of a man and a woman intimately bound together by
their devotion to a public cause; mutual affection, of course,
played a part in it, but it was an incidental part; the whole soul of
the relationship was a community of work. Perhaps out of England such an intimacy could hardly have existed—an intimacy so
utterly untinctured not only by passion itself but by the suspicion
of it. For years Sidney Herbert saw Miss Nightingale almost daily,
for long hours together, corresponding with her incessantly when
they were apart; and the tongue of scandal was silent; and one of
the most devoted of her admirers was his wife. But what made the
connection still more remarkable was the way in which the parts
that were played in it were divided between the two. The man who
acts, decides, and achieves; the woman who encourages, applauds,
and—from a distance—inspires:—the combination is common
enough; but Miss Nightingale was neither an Aspasia nor an Egeria.[8] In her case it is almost true to say that the rôles were reversed;
the qualities of pliancy and sympathy fell to the man, those of
command and initiative to the woman. There was one thing only
which Miss Nightingale lacked in her equipment for public life;
she had not—she never could have—the public power and authority which belong to the successful politician. That power and
authority Sidney Herbert possessed; the fact was obvious, and the
conclusion no less so: it was through the man that the woman
must work her will. She took hold of him, taught him, shaped him,
absorbed him, dominated him through and through. He did not
resist—he did not wish to resist; his natural inclination lay along
the same path as hers; only that terrific personality swept him forward at her own fierce pace and with her own relentless stride.
Swept him—where to? Ah! Why had he ever known Miss Nightingale? If Lord Panmure was a bison, Sidney Herbert, no doubt, was
a stag—a comely, gallant creature springing through the forest;
but the forest is a dangerous place. One has the image of those
wide eyes fascinated suddenly by something feline, something

8. Aspasia, a famous courtesan of ancient Athens, mistress and adviser of Pericles; Egeria, a water spirit, said to have been the mistress and advisor of the legendary Roman king Numa Pompilius.

strong; there is a pause; and then the tigress has her claws in the quivering haunches; and then————!

Besides Sidney Herbert, she had other friends who, in a more   42 restricted sphere, were hardly less essential to her. If, in her condition of bodily collapse, she were to accomplish what she was determined that she should accomplish, the attentions and the services of others would be absolutely indispensable. Helpers and servers she must have; and accordingly there was soon formed about her a little group of devoted disciples upon whose affections and energies she could implicitly rely. Devoted, indeed, these disciples were, in no ordinary sense of the term; for certainly she was no light task-mistress, and he who set out to be of use to Miss Nightingale was apt to find, before he had gone very far, that he was in truth being made use of in good earnest— to the very limit of his endurance and his capacity. Perhaps, even beyond those limits; why not? Was she asking of others more than she was giving herself? Let them look at her lying there pale and breathless on the couch; could it be said that she spared herself? Why, then, should she spare others? And it was not for her own sake that she made these claims. For her own sake, indeed! No! They all knew it! it was for the sake of the work. And so the little band, bound body and soul in that strange servitude, laboured on ungrudgingly. Among the most faithful was her "Aunt Mai," her father's sister, who from the earliest days had stood beside her, who had helped her to escape from the thraldom of family life, who had been with her at Scutari, and who now acted almost the part of a mother to her, watching over her with infinite care in all the movements and uncertainties which her state of health involved. Another constant attendant was her brother-in-law, Sir Harry Verney, whom she found particularly valuable in parliamentary affairs. Arthur Clough, the poet, also a connection by marriage, she used in other ways. Ever since he had lost his faith at the time of the Oxford Movement, Clough had passed his life in a condition of considerable uneasiness, which was increased rather than diminished by the practice of poetry. Unable to decide upon the purpose of an existence whose savour had fled together with his belief in the Resurrection, his spirits lowered still further by ill-health, and his income not all that it should be, he had determined to seek the solution of his difficulties in the United States of America. But, even there, the solution was not forthcoming; and when, a little later, he was offered a post in a government department at home, he accepted it, came to live in London, and immediately fell under the influence of Miss Nightingale. Though the purpose of existence might be still uncertain and its nature still unsavoury, here, at any rate, under the eye of this inspired woman, was something real, something earnest: his only doubt was—could he be of any use? Certainly he could. There were a great number of miscellaneous little jobs which there was nobody handy to do. For instance, when Miss Nightingale was travelling, there were the railway-tickets to be taken; and there were proof-sheets to be corrected; and then there were parcels to be done up in brown paper, and carried to the post. Certainly he could be useful. And so, upon such occupations as these, Arthur Clough was set to work. "This that I see, is not all," he comforted himself by reflecting, "and this that I do is but little; nevertheless it is good, though there is better than it."

As time went on, her "Cabinet," as she called it, grew larger. 43 Officials with whom her work brought her into touch and who sympathised with her objects, were pressed into her service; and old friends of the Crimean days gathered round her when they returned to England. Among these the most indefatigable was Dr. Sutherland, a sanitary expert, who for more than thirty years acted as her confidential private secretary, and surrendered to her purposes literally the whole of his life. Thus sustained and assisted, thus slaved for and adored, she prepared to beard the Bison.

Two facts soon emerged, and all that followed turned upon 44 them. It became clear, in the first place, that that imposing mass was not immovable, and, in the second, that its movement, when it did move, would be exceeding slow. The Bison was no match for the Lady. It was in vain that he put down his head and planted his feet in the earth; he could not withstand her; the white hand forced him back. But the process was an extraordinarily gradual one. Dr. Andrew Smith and all his War Office phalanx stood behind, blocking the way; the poor Bison groaned inwardly, and cast a wistful eye towards the happy pastures of the Free Church of Scotland; then slowly, with infinite reluctance, step by step, he retreated, disputing every inch of the ground.

The first great measure, which, supported as it was by the 45 Queen, the Cabinet, and the united opinion of the country, it was impossible to resist, was the appointment of a Royal Commission to report upon the health of the Army. The question of the composition of the Commission then immediately arose; and it was over this matter that the first hand-to-hand encounter between Lord Panmure and Miss Nightingale took place. They met, and Miss Nightingale was victorious; Sidney Herbert was appointed Chairman; and, in the end the only member of the commission opposed to her views was Dr. Andrew Smith. During the interview, Miss Nightingale made an important discovery: she found that "the Bison was bullyable"—the hide was the hide of a Mexican buffalo, but the spirit was the spirit of an Alderney calf. And there was one thing above all others which the huge creature dreaded—an appeal to public opinion. The faintest hint of such a terrible eventuality made his heart dissolve within him; he would agree to anything—he would cut short his grouse-shooting—he would make a speech in the House of Lords—he would even overrule Dr. Andrew Smith—rather than that. Miss Nightingale held the fearful threat in reserve—she would speak out what she knew; she would publish the truth to the whole world, and let the whole world judge between them. With supreme skill, she kept this sword of Damocles poised above the Bison's head, and more than once she was actually on the point of really dropping it. For his recalcitrancy grew and grew. The *personnel* of the Commission once determined upon, there was a struggle, which lasted for six months, over the nature of its powers. Was it to be an efficient body, armed with the right of full inquiry and wide examination, or was it to be a polite official contrivance for exonerating Dr. Andrew Smith? The War Office phalanx closed its ranks, and fought tooth and nail; but it was defeated: the Bison was bullyable.

> Three months from this day [Miss Nightingale had written at last] I publish my experience of the Crimean Campaign, and my suggestions for improvement, unless there has been a fair and tangible pledge by that time for reform.

Who could face that?

And, if the need came, she meant to be as good as her word. 46 For she had now determined, whatever might be the fate of the Commission, to draw up her own report upon the questions at issue. The labour involved was enormous; her health was almost desperate; but she did not flinch, and after six months of incredible industry she had put together and written with her own hand her "Notes affecting the Health, Efficiency, and Hospital Administration of the British Army." This extraordinary composition, filling more than eight hundred closely printed pages, laying down vast principles of far-reaching reform, discussing the minutest details of a multitude of controversial subjects, containing an enormous mass of information of the most varied kinds—military, statistical, sanitary, architectural—was never given to the public, for the need never came; but it formed the basis of the Report of the Royal Commission; and it remains to this day the leading authority on the medical administration of armies.

Before it had been completed the struggle over the powers of the Commission had been brought to a victorious close. Lord Panmure had given way once more; he had immediately hurried to the Queen to obtain her consent; and only then, when her Majesty's initials had been irrevocably affixed to the fatal document, did he dare to tell Dr. Andrew Smith what he had done. The Commission met, and another immense load fell upon Miss Nightingale's shoulders. To-day she would, of course, have been one of the Commission herself; but at that time the idea of a woman appearing in such a capacity was unheard of; and no one even suggested the possibility of Miss Nightingale's doing so. The result was that she was obliged to remain behind the scenes throughout, to coach Sidney Herbert in private at every important juncture, and to convey to him and to her other friends upon the Commission the vast funds of her expert knowledge—so essential in the examination of witnesses—by means of innumerable consultations, letters, and memoranda. It was even doubtful whether the proprieties would admit of her giving evidence; and at last, as a compromise, her modesty only allowed her to do so in the form of written answers to written questions. At length the grand affair was finished. The Commission's Report, embodying almost word for word the suggestions of Miss Nightingale, was drawn up by Sidney Herbert. Only one question remained to be answered—would anything, after all, be done? Or would the Royal Commission, like so many other Royal Commissions before and since, turn out to have achieved nothing but the concoction of a very fat blue-book on a very high shelf?

And so the last and the deadliest struggle with the Bison began. Six months had been spent in coercing him into granting the Commission effective powers; six more months were occupied by the work of the Commission; and now yet another six were to pass in extorting from him the means whereby the recommendations

47

48

of the Commission might be actually carried out. But, in the end, the thing was done. Miss Nightingale seemed indeed, during these months, to be upon the very brink of death. Accompanied by the faithful Aunt Mai, she moved from place to place—to Hampstead, to Highgate, to Derbyshire, to Malvern—in what appeared to be a last desperate effort to find health somewhere; but she carried that with her which made health impossible. Her desire for work could now scarcely be distinguished from mania. At one moment she was writing a "last letter" to Sidney Herbert; at the next she was offering to go out to India to nurse the sufferers in the Mutiny.[9] When Dr. Sutherland wrote, imploring her to take a holiday, she raved. Rest!—

> I am lying without my head, without my claws, and you all peck at me. It is *de rigueur, d'obligation,* like the saying something to one's hat, when one goes into church, to say to me all that has been said to me 110 times a day during the last three months. It is the *obbligato* on the violin, and the twelve violins all practise it together, like the clocks striking 12 o'clock at night all over London, till I say like Xavier de Maistre, *Assez, je le sais, je ne le sais que trop.*[10] I am not a penitent; but you are like the R. C. confessor, who says what is *de rigueur....*

Her wits began to turn, and there was no holding her. She worked like a slave in a mine. She began to believe, as she had begun to believe at Scutari, that none of her fellow-workers had their hearts in the business; if they had, why did they not work as she did? She could only see slackness and stupidity around her. Dr. Sutherland, of course, was grotesquely muddle-headed; and Arthur Clough incurably lazy. Even Sidney Herbert . . . oh yes, he had simplicity and candour and quickness of perception, no doubt; but he was an eclectic; and what could one hope for from a man who went away to fish in Ireland just when the Bison most needed bullying? As for the Bison himself he had fled to Scotland, where he remained buried for many months. The fate of the vital recommendation in the Commission's Report—the appointment of four Sub-Commissions charged with the duty of determining upon the details of the proposed reforms and of put-

9. The Indian (or Sepoy) Mutiny of 1857–1858.
10. *Assez, je le sais, je ne le sais que trop:* "Enough, I know it, I know it only too well."

ting them into execution—still hung in the balance. The Bison consented to everything; and then, on a flying visit to London, withdrew his consent and hastily returned to Scotland. Then for many weeks all business was suspended; he had gout—gout in the hands, so that he could not write. "His gout was always handy," remarked Miss Nightingale. But eventually it was clear even to the Bison that the game was up, and the inevitable surrender came.

There was, however, one point in which he triumphed over 49 Miss Nightingale. The building of Netley Hospital had been begun, under his orders, before her return to England. Soon after her arrival she examined the plans, and found that they reproduced all the worst faults of an out-of-date and mischievous system of hospital construction. She therefore urged that the matter should be reconsidered, and in the meantime building stopped. But the Bison was obdurate; it would be very expensive, and in any case it was too late. Unable to make any impression on him, and convinced of the extreme importance of the question, she determined to appeal to a higher authority. Lord Palmerston was Prime Minister, she had known him from her childhood; he was a near neighbour of her father's in the New Forest. She went down to the New Forest, armed with the plans of the proposed hospital and all the relevant information, stayed the night at Lord Palmerston's house, and convinced him of the necessity of rebuilding Netley.

> It seems to me [Lord Palmerston wrote to Lord Panmure] that at Netley all consideration of what would best tend to the comfort and recovery of the patients has been sacrificed to the vanity of the architect, whose sole object has been to make a building which should cut a dash when looked at from the Southampton river. . . . Pray, therefore, stop all further progress in the work until the matter can be duly considered.

But the Bison was not to be moved by one peremptory letter, even if it was from the Prime Minister. He put forth all his powers of procrastination, Lord Palmerston lost interest in the subject, and so the chief military hospital in England was triumphantly completed on unsanitary principles, with unventilated rooms, and with all the patients' windows facing northeast.

But now the time had come when the Bison was to trouble 50 and to be troubled no more. A vote in the House of Commons brought about the fall of Lord Palmerston's Government, and Lord Panmure found himself at liberty to devote the rest of his life to the Free Church of Scotland. After a brief interval, Sidney Herbert became Secretary of State for War. Great was the jubilation in the Nightingale Cabinet; the day of achievement had dawned at last. The next two and a half years (1859–61) saw the introduction of the whole system of reforms for which Miss Nightingale had been struggling so fiercely—reforms which make Sidney Herbert's tenure of power at the War Office an important epoch in the history of the British Army. The four Sub-Commissions, firmly established under the immediate control of the Minister, and urged forward by the relentless perseverance of Miss Nightingale, set to work with a will. The barracks and the hospitals were remodelled; they were properly ventilated and warmed and lighted for the first time; they were given a water supply which actually supplied water, and kitchens where, strange to say, it was possible to cook. Then the great question of the Purveyor—that portentous functionary whose powers and whose lack of powers had weighed like a nightmare upon Scutari—was taken in hand, and new regulations were laid down, accurately defining his responsibilities and his duties. One Sub-Commission reorganised the medical statistics of the Army. Another established—in spite of the last convulsive efforts of the Department—an Army Medical School. Finally the Army Medical Department itself was completely reorganised; an administrative code was drawn up; and the great and novel principle was established that it was as much a part of the duty of the authorities to look after the soldier's health as to look after his sickness. Besides this, it was at last officially admitted that he had a moral and intellectual side. Coffee-rooms and reading-rooms, gymnasiums and workshops were instituted. A new era did in truth appear to have begun. Already by 1861 the mortality in the Army had decreased by one half since the days of the Crimea. It was no wonder that even vaster possibilities began now to open out before Miss Nightingale. One thing was still needed to complete and to assure her triumphs. The Army Medical Department was indeed reorganised; but the great central machine was still untouched. The War Office itself—!—If she could remould *that* nearer to her heart's desire—there indeed would be a victory! And until that final act was accomplished, how could she be certain that all the rest of her achievements might not, by some capricious turn of Fortune's wheel—a change of Ministry, perhaps, replacing Sidney Herbert by some puppet of the permanent official gang—be swept to limbo in a moment?

Meanwhile, still ravenous for more and yet more work, her activities had branched out into new directions. The army in India claimed her attention. A Sanitary Commission, appointed at her suggestion, and working under her auspices, did for our troops there what the four Sub-Commissions were doing for those at home. At the same time, these very years which saw her laying the foundations of the whole modern system of medical work in the army, saw her also beginning to bring her knowledge, her influence, and her activity into the service of the country at large. Her *Notes on Hospitals* (1859) revolutionised the theory of hospital construction and hospital management. She was immediately recognised as the leading expert upon all the questions involved; her advice flowed unceasingly and in all directions, so that there is no great hospital today which does not bear upon it the impress of her mind. Nor was this all. With the opening of the Nightingale Training School for Nurses at St. Thomas's Hospital (1860), she became the founder of modern nursing. 51

But a terrible crisis was now fast approaching. Sidney Herbert had consented to undertake the root and branch reform of the War Office. He had sallied forth into that tropical jungle of festooned obstructiveness, of intertwisted irresponsibilities, of crouching prejudices, of abuses grown stiff and rigid with antiquity, which for so many years to come was destined to lure reforming ministers to their doom. 52

> The War Office [said Miss Nightingale] is a very slow office, an enormously expensive office, and one in which the Minister's intentions can be entirely negatived by all his sub-departments, and those of each of the sub-departments by every other.

It was true; and, of course, at the first rumour of a change, the old phalanx of reaction was bristling with its accustomed spears. At its head stood no longer Dr. Andrew Smith, who, some time since, had followed the Bison into outer darkness, but a yet more formidable figure, the permanent Under-Secretary himself, Sir Benjamin Hawes—Ben Hawes the Nightingale Cabinet irreverently dubbed him—a man remarkable even among civil servants for adroitness in baffling inconvenient inquiries, resource in raising false issues, and, in short, a consummate command of all the arts of officially sticking in the mud. "Our scheme will probably result in Ben Hawes's resignation," Miss Nightingale said; "and that is another of its advantages." Ben Hawes himself, however, did not quite see it in that light. He set himself to resist the wishes of the Minister by every means in his power. The struggle was long and desperate; and, as it proceeded, it gradually became evident to Miss Nightingale that something was the matter with Sidney Herbert. What was it? His health, never very strong, was, he said, in danger of collapsing under the strain of his work. But, after all, what is illness, when there is a War Office to be reorganised? Then he began to talk of retiring altogether from public life. The doctors were consulted, and declared that, above all things, what was necessary was rest. Rest! She grew seriously alarmed. Was it possible that, at the last moment, the crowning wreath of victory was to be snatched from her grasp? She was not to be put aside by doctors; they were talking nonsense; the necessary thing was not rest but the reform of the War Office; and, besides, she knew very well from her own case what one could do even when one was on the point of death. She expostulated vehemently, passionately: the goal was so near, so very near; he could not turn back now! At any rate, he could not resist Miss Nightingale. A compromise was arranged. Very reluctantly, he exchanged the turmoil of the House of Commons for the dignity of the House of Lords, and he remained at the War Office. She was delighted. "One fight more, the best and the last," she said.

For several more months the fight did indeed go on. But the 53
strain upon him was greater even than she perhaps could realise. Besides the intestine war in his office, he had to face a constant battle in the Cabinet with Mr. Gladstone—a more redoubtable antagonist even than Ben Hawes—over the estimates. His health grew worse and worse. He was attacked by fainting-fits; and there were some days when he could only just keep himself going by gulps of brandy. Miss Nightingale spurred him forward with her encouragements and her admonitions, her zeal and her example. But at last his spirit began to sink as well as his body. He could no longer hope; he could no longer desire; it was useless, all useless; it was utterly impossible. He had failed. The

dreadful moment came when the truth was forced upon him: he would never be able to reform the War Office. But a yet more dreadful moment lay behind; he must go to Miss Nightingale and tell her that he was a failure, a beaten man.

Blessed are the merciful! What strange ironic prescience had led Prince Albert, in the simplicity of his heart, to choose that motto for the Crimean brooch? The words hold a double lesson; and, alas! when she brought herself to realise at length what was indeed the fact and what there was no helping, it was not in mercy that she turned upon her old friend.

> Beaten! [she exclaimed]. Can't you see that you've simply thrown away the game? And with all the winning cards in your hands! And so noble a game! Sidney Herbert beaten! And beaten by Ben Hawes! It is a worse disgrace . . . [her full rage burst out at last] . . . a worse disgrace than the hospitals at Scutari.

He dragged himself away from her, dragged himself to Spa, hoping vainly for a return of health, and then, despairing, back again to England, to Wilton, to the majestic house standing there resplendent in the summer sunshine, among the great cedars which had lent their shade to Sir Philip Sidney, and all those familiar, darling haunts of beauty which he loved, each one of them, "as if they were persons"; and at Wilton he died. After having received the Eucharist he had become perfectly calm; then, almost unconscious, his lips were seen to be moving. Those about him bent down. "Poor Florence! Poor Florence!" they just caught. ". . . Our joint work . . . unfinished . . . tried to do . . ." and they could hear no more.

When the onward rush of a powerful spirit sweeps a weaker one to its destruction, the commonplaces of the moral judgment are better left unmade. If Miss Nightingale had been less ruthless, Sidney Herbert would not have perished; but then, she would not have been Miss Nightingale. The force that created was the force that destroyed. It was her Demon that was responsible. When the fatal news reached her, she was overcome by agony. In the revulsion of her feelings, she made a worship of the dead man's memory; and the facile instrument which had broken in her hand she spoke of for ever after as her "Master." Then, almost at the same moment, another blow fell upon her. Arthur Clough, worn out by labours very different from those of Sidney

Herbert, died too: never more would he tie up her parcels. And yet a third disaster followed. The faithful Aunt Mai did not, to be sure, die; no, she did something almost worse: she left Miss Nightingale. She was growing old, and she felt that she had closer and more imperative duties with her own family. Her niece could hardly forgive her. She poured out, in one of her enormous letters, a passionate diatribe upon the faithlessness, the lack of sympathy, the stupidity, the ineptitude of women. Her doctrines had taken no hold among them; she had never known one who had *appris à apprendre*[11]; she could not even get a woman secretary; "they don't know the names of the Cabinet Ministers—they don't know which of the Churches has Bishops and which not." As for the spirit of self-sacrifice, well—Sidney Herbert and Arthur Clough were men, and they indeed had shown their devotion; but women—! She would mount three widow's caps "for a sign." The first two would be for Clough and for her Master; but the third, "the biggest widow's cap of all"—would be for Aunt Mai. She did well to be angry; she was deserted in her hour of need; and, after all, could she be sure that even the male sex was so impeccable? There was Dr. Sutherland, bungling as usual. Perhaps even he intended to go off, one of these days, too? She gave him a look, and he shivered in his shoes. No!—she grinned sardonically; she would always have Dr. Sutherland. And then she reflected that there was one thing more that she would always have—her work.

IV

Sidney Herbert's death finally put an end to Miss Nightingale's dream of a reformed War Office. For a moment, indeed, in the first agony of her disappointment, she had wildly clutched at a straw; she had written to Mr. Gladstone to beg him to take up the burden of Sidney Herbert's work. And Mr. Gladstone had replied with a sympathetic account of the funeral.   57

Succeeding Secretaries of State managed between them to undo a good deal of what had been accomplished, but they could not undo it all; and for ten years more (1862–72) Miss Nightingale remained a potent influence at the War Office. After that, her   58

11. *appris à apprendre:* "learned to learn."

direct connection with the army came to an end, and her energies began to turn more and more completely towards more general objects. Her work upon hospital reform assumed enormous proportions; she was able to improve the conditions in infirmaries and workhouses; and one of her most remarkable papers forestalls the recommendations of the Poor Law Commission of 1909. Her training school for nurses, with all that it involved in initiative, control, responsibility, and combat, would have been enough in itself to have absorbed the whole efforts of at least two lives of ordinary vigour. And at the same time her work in connection with India, which had begun with the Sanitary Commission on the Indian Army, spread and ramified in a multitude of directions. Her tentacles reached the India Office and succeeded in establishing a hold even upon those slippery high places. For many years it was *de rigueur* for the newly appointed Viceroy, before he left England, to pay a visit to Miss Nightingale.

After much hesitation, she had settled down in a small house 59 in South Street, where she remained for the rest of her life. That life was a very long one; the dying woman reached her ninety-first year. Her ill-health gradually diminished; the crises of extreme danger became less frequent, and at last, altogether ceased; she remained an invalid, but an invalid of a curious character—an invalid who was too weak to walk downstairs and who worked far harder than most Cabinet Ministers. Her illness, whatever it may have been, was certainly not inconvenient. It involved seclusion; and an extraordinary, an unparalleled seclusion was, it might almost have been said, the main spring of Miss Nightingale's life. Lying on her sofa in the little upper room in South Street, she combined the intense vitality of a dominating woman of the world with the mysterious and romantic quality of a myth. She was a legend in her lifetime, and she knew it. She tasted the joys of power, like those Eastern Emperors whose autocratic rule was based upon invisibility, with the mingled satisfactions of obscurity and fame. And she found the machinery of illness hardly less effective as a barrier against the eyes of men than the ceremonial of a palace. Great statesmen and renowned generals were obliged to beg for audiences; admiring princesses from foreign countries found that they must see her at her own time, or not at all; and the ordinary mortal had no hope of ever getting beyond the downstairs sitting-room and Dr. Sutherland.

For that indefatigable disciple did, indeed, never desert her. He might be impatient, he might be restless, but he remained. His "incurable looseness of thought," for so she termed it, continued at her service to the end. Once, it is true, he had actually ventured to take a holiday; but he was recalled, and he did not repeat the experiment. He was wanted downstairs. There he sat, transacting business, answering correspondence, interviewing callers, and exchanging innumerable notes with the unseen power above. Sometimes word came down that Miss Nightingale was just well enough to see one of her visitors. The fortunate man was led up, was ushered, trembling, into the shaded chamber, and, of course, could never afterwards forget the interview. Very rarely, indeed, once or twice a year, perhaps, but nobody could be quite certain, in deadly secrecy, Miss Nightingale went out for a drive in the Park. Unrecognised, the living legend flitted for a moment before the common gaze. And the precaution was necessary; for there were times when, at some public function, the rumour of her presence was spread abroad; and ladies, mistaken by the crowd for Miss Nightingale, were followed, pressed upon, and vehemently supplicated—"Let me touch your shawl,"—"Let me stroke your arm"; such was the strange adoration in the hearts of the people. That vast reserve of force lay there behind her; she could use it, if she would. But she preferred never to use it. On occasions, she might hint or threaten; she might balance the sword of Damocles over the head of the Bison; she might, by a word, by a glance, remind some refractory minister, some unpersuadable viceroy, sitting in audience with her in the little upper room, that she was something more than a mere sick woman, that she had only, so to speak, to go to the window and wave her handkerchief, for . . . dreadful things to follow. But that was enough; they understood; the myth was there—obvious, portentous, impalpable; and so it remained to the last.

With statesmen and governors at her beck and call, with her hands on a hundred strings, with mighty provinces at her feet, with foreign governments agog for her counsel, building hospitals, training nurses—she still felt that she had not enough to do. She sighed for more worlds to conquer—more, and yet more. She looked about her—what was there left? Of course! Philosophy! After the world of action, the world of thought. Having set   60 right the health of the British Army, she would now do the same good service for the religious convictions of mankind. She had long noticed—with regret—the growing tendency towards free-thinking among artisans. With regret, but not altogether with surprise: the current teaching of Christianity was sadly to seek; nay, Christianity itself was not without its defects. She would rectify these errors. She would correct the mistakes of the Churches; she would point out just where Christianity was wrong; and she would explain to the artisans what the facts of the case really were. Before her departure for the Crimea, she had begun this work; and now, in the intervals of her other labours, she completed it. Her "Suggestions for Thought to the Searchers after Truth among the Artisans of England" (1860), unravels, in the course of three portly volumes, the difficulties— hitherto, curiously enough, unsolved—connected with such matters as Belief in God, the Plan of Creation, the Origin of Evil, the Future Life, Necessity and Free Will, Law, and the Nature of Morality. The Origin of Evil, in particular, held no perplexities for Miss Nightingale. "We cannot conceive," she remarks, "that Omnipotent Righteousness would find satisfaction in *solitary existence.*" This being so, the only question remaining to be asked is, "What beings should we then conceive that God would create?" Now, He cannot create perfect beings, "since, essentially, perfection is one"; if He did so, He would only be adding to Himself. Thus the conclusion is obvious: He *must* create *imperfect* ones. Omnipotent Righteousness, faced by the intolerable *impasse* of a solitary existence, finds itself bound, by the very nature of the case, to create the hospitals at Scutari. Whether this argument would have satisfied the artisans, was never discovered, for only a very few copies of the book were printed for private circulation. One copy was sent to Mr. Mill,[12] who acknowledged it in an extremely polite letter. He felt himself obliged, however, to confess that he had not been altogether convinced by Miss Nightingale's proof of the existence of God. Miss Nightingale was surprised and mortified; she had thought better of Mr. Mill; for surely her proof of the existence of God could hardly be improved upon. "A law," she had pointed out, "implies a lawgiver." Now the Universe is full of laws—the law of

12. John Stuart Mill: prominent philosopher and political theorist (1806–1873).

gravitation, the law of the excluded middle, and many others; hence it follows that the Universe has a lawgiver—and what would Mr. Mill be satisfied with, if he was not satisfied with that?

Perhaps Mr. Mill might have asked why the argument had not   61
been pushed to its logical conclusion. Clearly, if we are to trust the analogy of human institutions, we must remember that laws are, as a matter of fact, not dispensed by lawgivers, but passed by Act of Parliament. Miss Nightingale, however, with all her experience of public life, never stopped to consider the question whether God might not be a Limited Monarchy.

Yet her conception of God was certainly not orthodox. She   62
felt towards Him as she might have felt towards a glorified sanitary engineer; and in some of her speculations she seems hardly to distinguish between the Deity and the Drains. As one turns over these singular pages, one has the impression that Miss Nightingale has got the Almighty too into her clutches, and that, if He is not careful, she will kill Him with overwork.

Then, suddenly, in the very midst of the ramifying generalities   63
of her metaphysical disquisitions there is an unexpected turn, and the reader is plunged all at once into something particular, something personal, something impregnated with intense experience—a virulent invective upon the position of women in the upper ranks of society. Forgetful alike of her high argument and of the artisans, the bitter creature rails through a hundred pages of close print at the falsities of family life, the ineptitudes of marriage, the emptinesses of convention, in the spirit of an Ibsen or a Samuel Butler. Her fierce pen, shaking with intimate anger, depicts in biting sentences the fearful fate of an unmarried girl in a wealthy household. It is a *cri du cœur;* and then, as suddenly, she returns once more to instruct the artisans upon the nature of Omnipotent Righteousness.

Her mind was, indeed, better qualified to dissect the concrete   64
and distasteful fruits of actual life than to construct a coherent system of abstract philosophy. In spite of her respect for Law, she was never at home with a generalisation. Thus, though the great achievement of her life lay in the immense impetus which she gave to the scientific treatment of sickness, a true comprehension of the scientific method itself was alien to her spirit. Like most great men of action—perhaps like all—she was simply an em-

piricist. She believed in what she saw, and she acted accordingly; beyond that she would not go. She had found in Scutari that fresh air and light played an effective part in the prevention of the maladies with which she had to deal; and that was enough for her; she would not inquire further; what were the general principles underlying that fact—or even whether there were any—she refused to consider. Years after the discoveries of Pasteur and Lister,[13] she laughed at what she called the "germ-fetish." There was no such thing as "infection"; she had never seen it, therefore it did not exist. But she *had* seen the good effects of fresh air; therefore there could be no doubt about them; and therefore it was essential that the bedrooms of patients should be well ventilated. Such was her doctrine; and in those days of hermetically sealed windows it was a very valuable one. But it was a purely empirical doctrine, and thus it led to some unfortunate results. When, for instance, her influence in India was at its height, she issued orders that all hospital windows should be invariably kept open. The authorities, who knew what an open window in the hot weather meant, protested, but in vain; Miss Nightingale was incredulous. She knew nothing of the hot weather, but she did know the value of fresh air—from personal experience; the authorities were talking nonsense and the windows must be kept open all the year round. There was a great outcry from all the doctors in India, but she was firm; and for a moment it seemed possible that her terrible commands would have to be put into execution. Lord Lawrence, however, was Viceroy, and he was able to intimate to Miss Nightingale, with sufficient authority, that he himself had decided upon the question, and that his decision must stand, even against her own. Upon that, she gave way, but reluctantly and quite unconvinced; she was only puzzled by the unexpected weakness of Lord Lawrence. No doubt, if she had lived to-day, and if her experience had lain, not among cholera cases at Scutari but among yellow-fever cases in Panama, she would have declared fresh air a fetish, and would have maintained to her dying day that the only really effective way of dealing with disease was by the destruction of mosquitoes.

13. Louis Pasteur (1822–1895) proved that germs cause disease; Joseph Lister (1827–1912) introduced antiseptics into surgery.

Yet her mind, so positive, so realistic, so ultra-practical, had its   65
singular revulsions, its mysterious moods of mysticism and of
doubt. At times, lying sleepless in the early hours, she fell into
long strange agonised meditations, and then, seizing a pencil,
she would commit to paper the confessions of her soul. The morbid longings of her pre-Crimean days came over her once more;
she filled page after page with self-examination, self-criticism,
self-surrender. "O Father," she wrote, "I submit, I resign myself, I
accept with all my heart this stretching out of Thy hand to save
me. . . . O how vain it is, the vanity of vanities, to live in men's
thoughts instead of God's!" She was lonely, she was miserable.
"Thou knowest that through all these horrible twenty years, I have
been supported by the belief that I was working with Thee who
wert bringing everyone, even our poor nurses, to perfection,"—
and yet, after all, what was the result? Had not even she been an
unprofitable servant? One night, waking suddenly, she saw, in the
dim light of the night-lamp, tenebrous shapes upon the wall. The
past rushed back upon her. "Am I she who once stood on that
Crimean height?" she wildly asked— "'The Lady with a lamp
shall stand. . . .' The lamp shows me only my utter shipwreck."
      She sought consolation in the writings of the Mystics and in a   66
correspondence with Mr. Jowett.[14] For many years the Master of
Balliol acted as her spiritual adviser. He discussed with her in a
series of enormous letters the problems of religion and philosophy; he criticised her writings on those subjects with the tactful
sympathy of a cleric who was also a man of the world; and he
even ventured to attempt at times to instil into her rebellious nature some of his own peculiar suavity. "I sometimes think," he
told her, "that you ought seriously to consider how your work
may be carried on, not with less energy, but in a calmer spirit. I
am not blaming the past. . . . But I want the peace of God to settle on the future." He recommended her to spend her time no
longer in "conflicts with Government offices," and to take up
some literary work. He urged her to "work out her notion of Divine Perfection," in a series of essays for *Frazer's Magazine*. She
did so; and the result was submitted to Mr. Froude, who pronounced the second essay to be "even more pregnant than the

14. Benjamin Jowett (1817–1893), a distinguished classical scholar, a great
teacher, and an Anglican priest was elected Master of Balliol College, Oxford
University, in 1870.

first. I cannot tell," he said, "how sanitary, with disordered intellects, the effects of such papers will be." Mr. Carlyle, indeed, used different language, and some remarks of his about a lost lamb bleating on the mountains having been unfortunately repeated to Miss Nightingale, all Mr. Jowett's suavity was required to keep the peace. In a letter of fourteen sheets, he turned her attention from this painful topic towards a discussion of Quietism. "I don't see why," said the Master of Balliol, "active life might not become a sort of passive life too." And then, he added, "I sometimes fancy there are possibilities of human character much greater than have been realised." She found such sentiments helpful, underlining them in blue pencil; and, in return, she assisted her friend with a long series of elaborate comments upon the Dialogues of Plato, most of which he embodied in the second edition of his translation. Gradually her interest became more personal; she told him never to work again after midnight, and he obeyed her. Then she helped him to draw up a special form of daily service for the College Chapel, with selections from the Psalms, under the heads of "God the Lord, God the Judge, God the Father, and God the Friend,"—though, indeed, this project was never realised; for the Bishop of Oxford disallowed the alterations, exercising his legal powers, on the advice of Sir Travers Twiss.

Their relations became intimate. "The spirit of the twenty-third psalm and the spirit of the nineteenth psalm should be united in our lives," Mr. Jowett said. Eventually, she asked him to do her a singular favour. Would he, knowing what he did of her religious views, come to London and administer to her the Holy Sacrament? He did not hesitate, and afterwards declared that he would always regard the occasion as a solemn event in his life. He was devoted to her; though the precise nature of his feelings towards her never quite transpired. Her feelings towards him were more mixed. At first, he was "that great and good man,"—"that true saint, Mr. Jowett"; but, as time went on, some gall was mingled with the balm; the acrimony of her nature asserted itself. She felt that she gave more sympathy than she received; she was exhausted, she was annoyed, by his conversation. Her tongue, one day, could not refrain from shooting out at him. "He comes to me, and he talks to me," she said, "as if I were someone else."

V

At one time she had almost decided to end her life in retirement,   68
as a patient at St. Thomas's Hospital. But partly owing to the per-
suasions of Mr. Jowett, she changed her mind; for forty-five years
she remained in South Street; and in South Street she died. As old
age approached, though her influence with the official world gradually diminished, her activities seemed to remain as intense and
widespread as before. When hospitals were to be built, when
schemes of sanitary reform were in agitation, when wars broke
out, she was still the adviser of all Europe. Still, with a characteristic self-assurance, she watched from her Mayfair bedroom over
the welfare of India. Still, with an indefatigable enthusiasm, she
pushed forward the work, which, perhaps, was nearer to her
heart, more completely her own, than all the rest—the training of
nurses. In her moments of deepest depression, when her greatest
achievements seemed to lose their lustre, she thought of her nurses,
and was comforted. The ways of God, she found, were strange indeed. "How inefficient I was in the Crimea," she noted. "Yet He
has raised up from it trained nursing."

At other times she was better satisfied. Looking back, she was   69
amazed by the enormous change which, since her early days, had
come over the whole treatment of illness, the whole conception
of public and domestic health—a change in which, she knew, she
had played her part. One of her Indian admirers, the Aga Khan,
came to visit her. She expatiated on the marvellous advances she
had lived to see in the management of hospitals, in drainage, in
ventilation, in sanitary work of every kind. There was a pause;
and then, "Do you think you are improving?" asked the Aga
Khan. She was a little taken aback, and said, "What do you
mean by 'improving'?" He replied, "Believing more in God."
She saw that he had a view of God which was different from
hers. "A most interesting man," she noted after the interview;
"but you could never teach him sanitation."

When old age actually came, something curious happened.   70
Destiny, having waited very patiently, played a queer trick on
Miss Nightingale. The benevolence and public spirit of that long
life had only been equalled by its acerbity. Her virtue had dwelt
in hardness, and she had poured forth her unstinted usefulness
with a bitter smile upon her lips. And now the sarcastic years
brought the proud woman her punishment. She was not to die as

she had lived. The sting was to be taken out of her: she was to be made soft; she was to be reduced to compliance and complacency. The change came gradually, but at last it was unmistakable. The terrible commander who had driven Sidney Herbert to his death, to whom Mr. Jowett had applied the words of Homer, ἄμοτον μεμαὖια—raging insatiably—now accepted small compliments with gratitude, and indulged in sentimental friendships with young girls. The author of *Notes on Nursing*—that classical compendium of the besetting sins of the sisterhood, drawn up with the detailed acrimony, the vindictive relish, of a Swift—now spent long hours in composing sympathetic Addresses to Probationers, whom she petted and wept over in turn. And, at the same time there appeared a corresponding alteration in her physical mould. The thin, angular woman, with her haughty eye and her acrid mouth had vanished; and in her place was the rounded bulky form of a fat old lady, smiling all day long. Then something else became visible. The brain which had been steeled at Scutari was indeed, literally, growing soft. Senility—an ever more and more amiable senility—descended. Towards the end, consciousness itself grew lost in a roseate haze, and melted into nothingness. It was just then, three years before her death, when she was eighty-seven years old (1907), that those in authority bethought them that the opportune moment had come for bestowing a public honour on Florence Nightingale. She was offered the Order of Merit. That Order, whose roll contains, among other distinguished names, those of Sir Laurence Alma Tadema and Sir Edward Elgar, is remarkable chiefly for the fact that, as its title indicates, it is bestowed because its recipient deserves it, and for no other reason. Miss Nightingale's representatives accepted the honour, and her name, after a lapse of many years, once more appeared in the Press. Congratulations from all sides came pouring in. There was a universal burst of enthusiasm—a final revivification of the ancient myth. Among her other admirers, the German Emperor took this opportunity of expressing his feelings towards her. "His Majesty," wrote the German Ambassador, "having just brought to a close a most enjoyable stay in the beautiful neighbourhood of your old home near Romsey, has commanded me to present you with some flowers as a token of his esteem."

Then, by Royal command, the Order of Merit was brought to South Street, and there was a little ceremony of presentation. Sir

Douglas Dawson, after a short speech, stepped forward, and handed the insignia of the Order to Miss Nightingale. Propped up by pillows, she dimly recognised that some compliment was being paid her. "Too kind—too kind," she murmured; and she was not ironical.

Bibliography
Sir E. Cook. *Life of Florence Nightingale.*
A. W. Kinglake. *The Invasion of the Crimea.*
Lord Sidney Godolphin Obsorne. *Scutari and Its Hospitals.*
S. M. Mitra. *Life of Sir John Hall.*
Lord Stanmore. *Sidney Herbert.*
Sir G. Douglas. *The Panmure Papers.*
Sir H. Maxwell. *Life and Letters of the Fourth Earl of Clarendon.*
E. Abbot and L. Campbell. *Life and Letters of Benjamin Jowett.*
A. H. Clough. *Poems and Memoir.*

JOAN DIDION

Slouching Toward Bethlehem

By the mid-1960s, when San Francisco became a mecca for hippies, Joan Didion had established a reputation as a writer who understood California's mixture of traditional and alternative cultures. "Slouching Toward Bethlehem," her report of what she witnessed in "the cold late spring of 1967," was published in *The Saturday Evening Post* only four months later, on September 23.

.   .   .   .

Things fall apart; the centre cannot hold;
Mere anarchy is loosed upon the world
.   .   .   .

Surely some revelation is at hand;
Surely the Second Coming is at hand.
.   .   .   .

And what rough beast, its hour come round at last,
Slouches towards Bethlehem to be born?
                    W. B. YEATS, "THE SECOND COMING" (1921)

The center was not holding. It was a country of bankruptcy   1
notices and public-auction announcements and commonplace
reports of casual killings and misplaced children and abandoned
homes and vandals who misspelled even the four-letter words
they scrawled. It was a country in which families routinely disappeared, trailing bad checks and repossession papers. Adolescents drifted from city to torn city, sloughing off both the past
and the future as snakes shed their skins, children who were
never taught and would never now learn the games that had held
the society together. People were missing. Children were missing.
Parents were missing. Those left behind filed desultory missing-
persons reports, then moved on themselves.

It was not a country in open revolution. It was not a country   2
under enemy siege. It was the United States of America in the
cold late spring of 1967, and the market was steady and the
G.N.P. high and a great many articulate people seemed to have a
sense of high social purpose and it might have been a spring of
brave hopes and national promise, but it was not, and more and
more people had the uneasy apprehension that it was not. All
that seemed clear was that at some point we had aborted ourselves and butchered the job, and because nothing else seemed so
relevant I decided to go to San Francisco. San Francisco was
where the social hemorrhaging was showing up. San Francisco
was where the missing children were gathering and calling themselves "hippies." When I first went to San Francisco in that
cold late spring of 1967 I did not even know what I wanted to
find out, and so I just stayed around awhile, and made a few
friends.

A sign on Haight Street, San Francisco: 3

Last Easter Day
My Christopher Robin wandered away.
He called April 10th
But he hasn't called since
He said he was coming home
But he hasn't shown.

If you see him on Haight
Please tell him not to wait
I need him now

I don't care how
If he needs the bread
I'll send it ahead.

If there's hope
Please write me a note
If he's still there
Tell him how much I care
Where he's at I need to know
For I really love him so!

                    Deeply,
                    Marla

Marla Pence
12702 NE. Multnomah
Portland, Ore. 97230
503/252-2720.

I am looking for somebody called Deadeye and I hear he is on   4
the Street this afternoon doing a little business, so I keep an eye
out for him and pretend to read the signs in the Psychedelic Shop
on Haight Street when a kid, sixteen, seventeen, comes in and
sits on the floor beside me.

"What are you looking for," he says.   5

I say nothing much.   6

"I been out of my mind for three days," he says. He tells me   7
he's been shooting crystal, which I already pretty much know because he does not bother to keep his sleeves rolled down over the
needle tracks. He came up from Los Angeles some number of
weeks ago, he doesn't remember what number, and now he'll
take off for New York, if he can find a ride. I show him a sign offering a ride to Chicago. He wonders where Chicago is. I ask
where he comes from. "Here," he says. I mean before here. "San
Jose, Chula Vista, I dunno. My mother's in Chula Vista."

A few days later I run into him in Golden Gate Park when the   8
Grateful Dead are playing. I ask if he found a ride to New York.
"I hear New York's a bummer," he says.

Deadeye never showed up that day on the Street, and some-   9
body says maybe I can find him at his place. It is three o'clock
and Deadeye is in bed. Somebody else is asleep on the

living-room couch, and a girl is sleeping on the floor beneath a poster of Allen Ginsberg, and there are a couple of girls in paja-mas making instant coffee. One of the girls introduces me to the friend on the couch, who extends one arm but does not get up because he is naked. Deadeye and I have a mutual acquaintance, but he does not mention his name in front of the others. "The man you talked to," he says, or "that man I was referring to ear-lier." The man is a cop.

The room is overheated and the girl on the floor is sick. Dead-eye says she has been sleeping for twenty-four hours now. "Lemma ask you something," he says. "You want some grass?" I say I have to be moving on. "You want it," Deadeye says, "it's yours." Deadeye used to be an Angel around Los Angeles but that was a few years ago. "Right now," he says, "I'm trying to set up this groovy religious group—'Teenage Evangelism.'"

10

Don and Max want to go out to dinner but Don is only eating macrobiotic so we end up in Japantown again. Max is telling me how he lives free of all the old middle-class Freudian hang-ups. "I've had this old lady for a couple of months now, maybe she makes something special for my dinner and I come in three days late and tell her I've been balling some other chick, well, maybe she shouts a little but then I say 'That's me, baby,' and she laughs and says 'That's you, Max.'" Max says it works both ways. "I mean if she comes in and tells me she wants to ball Don, maybe, I say 'O.K., baby, it's your trip.'"

11

Max sees his life as a triumph over "don'ts." Among the don'ts he had done before he was twenty-one were peyote, alco-hol, mescaline, and Methedrine. He was on a Meth trip for three years in New York and Tangier before he found acid. He first tried peyote when he was in an Arkansas boys' school and got down to the Gulf and met "an Indian kid who was doing a don't. Then every weekend I could get loose I'd hitchhike seven hundred miles to Brownsville, Texas, so I could cop peyote. Pey-ote went for thirty cents a button down in Brownsville on the street." Max dropped in and out of most of the schools and fash-ionable clinics in the eastern half of America, his standard tech-nique for dealing with boredom being to leave. Example: Max was in a hospital in New York and "the night nurse was a groovy spade, and in the afternoon for therapy there was a chick from

12

Israel who was interesting, but there was nothing much to do in the morning, so I left."

We drink some more green tea and talk about going up to   13 Malakoff Diggings in Nevada County because some people are starting a commune there and Max thinks it would be a groove to take acid in the diggings. He says maybe we could go next week, or the week after, or anyway sometime before his case comes up. Almost everybody I meet in San Francisco has to go to court at some point in the middle future. I never ask why.

I am still interested in how Max got rid of his middle-class   14 Freudian hang-ups and I ask if he is now completely free.

"Nah," he says. "I got acid."   15

Max drops a 250- or 350-microgram tab every six or seven   16 days.

Max and Don share a joint in the car and we go over to North   17 Beach to find out if Otto, who has a temporary job there, wants to go to Malakoff Diggings. Otto is pitching some electronics engineers. The engineers view our arrival with some interest, maybe, I think, because Max is wearing bells and an Indian headband. Max has a low tolerance for straight engineers and their Freudian hang-ups. "Look at 'em," he says. "They're always yelling 'queer' and then they come sneaking down to the Haight-Ashbury trying to get the hippie chick because she fucks."

We do not get around to asking Otto about Malakoff Dig-   18 gings because he wants to tell me about a fourteen-year-old he knows who got busted in the Park the other day. She was just walking through the Park, he says, minding her own, carrying her schoolbooks, when the cops took her in and booked her and gave her a pelvic. *Fourteen years old,* " Otto says. "A *pelvic.*"

"Coming down from acid," he adds, "that could be a real bad   19 trip."

I call Otto the next afternoon to see if he can reach the   20 fourteen-year-old. It turns out she is tied up with rehearsals for her junior-high-school play, *The Wizard of Oz.* "Yellow-brick-road time," Otto says. Otto was sick all day. He thinks it was some cocaine-and-wheat somebody gave him.

There are always little girls around rock groups—the same lit-   21 tle girls who used to hang around saxophone players, girls who live on the celebrity and power and sex a band projects when it plays—and there are three of them out here this afternoon in Sausalito where the Grateful Dead rehearse. They are all pretty and two of them still have baby fat and one of them dances by herself with her eyes closed.

I ask a couple of the girls what they do. 22

"I just kind of come out here a lot," one of them says. 23

"I just sort of know the Dead," the other says. 24

The one who just sort of knows the Dead starts cutting up a loaf of French bread on the piano bench. The boys take a break and one of them talks about playing the Los Angeles Cheetah, which is in the old Aragon Ballroom. "We were up there drinking beer where Lawrence Welk used to sit," Jerry Garcia says. 25

The little girl who was dancing by herself giggles. "Too much," she says softly. Her eyes are still closed. 26

Somebody said that if I was going to meet some runaways I better pick up a few hamburgers and Cokes on the way, so I did, and we are eating them in the Park together, me, Debbie who is fifteen, and Jeff who is sixteen. Debbie and Jeff ran away twelve days ago, walked out of school one morning with $100 between them. Because a missing-juvenile is out on Debbie—she was already on probation because her mother had once taken her down to the police station and declared her incorrigible—this is only the second time they have been out of a friend's apartment since they got to San Francisco. The first time they went over to the Fairmont Hotel and rode the outside elevator, three times up and three times down. "Wow," Jeff says, and that is all he can think to say, about that. 27

I ask why they ran away. 28

"My parents said I had to go to church," Debbie says. "And they wouldn't let me dress the way I wanted. In the seventh grade my skirts were longer than anybody's—it got better in the eighth grade, but still." 29

"Your mother was kind of a bummer," Jeff agrees. 30

"They didn't like Jeff. They didn't like my girlfriends. My father thought I was cheap and he told me so. I had a C average and he told me I couldn't date until I raised it, and that bugged me too." 31

"My mother was just a genuine all-American bitch," Jeff says. "She was really troublesome about hair. Also she didn't like boots. It was really weird." 32

"Tell about the chores," Debbie says.   33

"For example I had chores. If I didn't finish ironing my shirts   34
for the week I couldn't go out for the weekend. It was weird.
Wow."

Debbie giggles and shakes her head. "This year's gonna be   35
wild."

"We're just gonna let it all happen," Jeff says. "Everything's   36
in the future, you can't pre-plan it. First we get jobs, then a place
to live. Then, I dunno."

Jeff finishes off the French fries and gives some thought to   37
what kind of job he could get. "I always kinda dug metal shop,
welding, stuff like that." Maybe he could work on cars, I say.
"I'm not too mechanically minded," he says. "Anyway you can't
pre-plan."

"I could get a job baby-sitting," Debbie says. "Or in a dime   38
store."

"You're always talking about getting a job in a dime store,"   39
Jeff says.

"That's because I worked in a dime store already."   40

Debbie is buffing her fingernails with the belt to her suède   41
jacket. She is annoyed because she chipped a nail and because I
do not have any polish remover in the car. I promise to get her to
a friend's apartment so that she can redo her manicure, but
something has been bothering me and as I fiddle with the igni-
tion I finally ask it. I ask them to think back to when they were
children, to tell me what they had wanted to be when they were
grown up, how they had seen the future then.

Jeff throws a Coca-Cola bottle out the car window. "I can't   42
remember I ever thought about it," he says.

"I remember I wanted to be a veterinarian once," Debbie   43
says. "But now I'm more or less working in the vein of being an
artist or a model or a cosmetologist. Or something."

I hear quite a bit about one cop, Officer Arthur Gerrans,   44
whose name has become a synonym for zealotry on the Street.
"He's our Officer Krupke,[1]" Max once told me. Max is not personally wild about Officer Gerrans because Officer Gerrans took
Max in after the Human Be-In last winter, that's the big Human

1. Officer Krupke: a stereotype of the unimaginative policeman in the Broadway
musical *West Side Story* (1957; film, 1961).

Be-In in Golden Gate Park where 20,000 people got turned on free, or 10,000 did, or some number did, but then Officer Gerrans has busted almost everyone in the District at one time or another. Presumably to forestall a cult of personality, Officer Gerrans was transferred out of the District not long ago, and when I see him it is not at the Park Station but at the Central Station on Greenwich Avenue.

We are in an interrogation room, and I am interrogating Officer Gerrans. He is young and blond and wary and I go in slow. I wonder what he thinks "the major problems" in the Haight are.

Officer Gerrans thinks it over. "I would say the major problems there," he says finally, "the major problems are narcotics and juveniles. Juveniles and narcotics, those are your major problems."

I write that down.

"Just one moment," Officer Gerrans says, and leaves the room. When he comes back he tells me that I cannot talk to him without permission from Chief Thomas Cahill.

"In the meantime," Officer Gerrans adds, pointing at the notebook in which I have written *major problems: juveniles, narcotics,* "I'll take those notes."

The next day I apply for permission to talk to Officer Gerrans and also to Chief Cahill. A few days later a sergeant returns my call.

"We have finally received clearance from the Chief per your request," the sergeant says, "and that is taboo."

I wonder why it is taboo to talk to Officer Gerrans.

Officer Gerrans is involved in court cases coming to trial.

I wonder why it is taboo to talk to Chief Cahill.

The Chief has pressing police business.

I wonder if I can talk to anyone at all in the Police Department.

"No," the sergeant says, "not at the particular moment."

Which was my last official contact with the San Francisco Police Department.

Norris and I are standing around the Panhandle and Norris is telling me how it is all set up for a friend to take me to Big Sur. I say what I really want to do is spend a few days with Norris and his wife and the rest of the people in their house. Norris says it

would be a lot easier if I'd take some acid. I say I'm unstable.
Norris says all right, anyway, *grass,* and he squeezes my hand.

One day Norris asks how old I am. I tell him I am thirty-two.   60
It takes a few minutes, but Norris rises to it. "Don't worry," he
says at last. "There's old hippies too."

It is a pretty nice evening and nothing much happening and   61
Max brings his old lady, Sharon, over to the Warehouse. The
Warehouse, which is where Don and a floating number of other
people live, is not actually a warehouse but the garage of a condemned hotel. The Warehouse was conceived as total theater, a
continual happening, and I always feel good there. What happened ten minutes ago or what is going to happen a half hour
from now tends to fade from mind in the Warehouse. Somebody
is usually doing something interesting, like working on a light
show, and there are a lot of interesting things around, like an old
Chevrolet touring car which is used as a bed and a vast American flag fluttering up in the shadows and an overstuffed chair
suspended like a swing from the rafters, the point of that being
that it gives you a sensory-deprivation high.

One reason I particularly like the Warehouse is that a child   62
named Michael is staying there now. Michael's mother, Sue Ann,
is a sweet wan girl who is always in the kitchen cooking seaweed
or baking macrobiotic bread while Michael amuses himself with
joss sticks or an old tambourine or a rocking horse with the
paint worn off. The first time I ever saw Michael was on that
rocking horse, a very blond and pale and dirty child on a rocking horse with no paint. A blue theatrical spotlight was the only
light in the Warehouse that afternoon, and there was Michael in
it, crooning softly to the wooden horse. Michael is three years
old. He is a bright child but does not yet talk.

This particular night Michael is trying to light his joss sticks   63
and there are the usual number of people floating through and
they all drift into Don's room and sit on the bed and pass joints.
Sharon is very excited when she arrives. *"Don,"* she cries,
breathless. "We got some STP today." At this time STP is a
pretty big deal, remember; nobody yet knew what it was and it
was relatively, although just relatively, hard to come by. Sharon
is blond and scrubbed and probably seventeen, but Max is a little vague about that since his court case comes up in a month or

so and he doesn't need statutory rape on top of it. Sharon's parents were living apart when last she saw them. She does not miss school or anything much about her past, except her younger brother. "I want to turn him on," she confided one day. "He's fourteen now, that's the perfect age. I know where he goes to high school and someday I'll just go get him."

Time passes and I lose the thread and when I pick it up again Max seems to be talking about what a beautiful thing it is the way Sharon washes dishes.   64

"Well it *is* beautiful," Sharon says. "*Every*thing is. I mean you watch that blue detergent blob run on the plate, watch the grease cut—well, it can be a real trip."   65

Pretty soon now, maybe next month, maybe later, Max and Sharon plan to leave for Africa and India, where they can live off the land. "I got this little trust fund, see," Max says, "which is useful in that it tells cops and border patrols I'm O.K., but living off the land is the thing. You can get your high and get your dope in the city, O.K., but we gotta get out somewhere and live organically."   66

"Roots and things," Sharon says, lighting another joss stick for Michael. Michael's mother is still in the kitchen cooking seaweed. "You can eat them."   67

Maybe eleven o'clock, we move from the Warehouse to the place where Max and Sharon live with a couple named Tom and Barbara. Sharon is pleased to get home ("I hope you got some hash joints fixed in the kitchen," she says to Barbara by way of greeting) and everybody is pleased to show off the apartment, which has a lot of flowers and candles and paisleys. Max and Sharon and Tom and Barbara get pretty high on hash, and everyone dances a little and we do some liquid projections and set up a strobe and take turns getting a high on that. Quite late, somebody called Steve comes in with a pretty, dark girl. They have been to a meeting of people who practice a Western yoga, but they do not seem to want to talk about that. They lie on the floor awhile, and then Steve stands up.   68

"Max," he says, "I want to say one thing."   69

"It's your trip." Max is edgy.   70

"I found love on acid. But I lost it. And now I'm finding it again. With nothing but grass."   71

Max mutters that heaven and hell are both in one's karma.   72

"That's what bugs me about psychedelic art," Steve says. 73

"What about psychedelic art," Max says. "I haven't seen 74 much psychedelic art."

Max is lying on a bed with Sharon, and Steve leans down to 75 him. "Groove, baby," he says. "You're a groove."

Steve sits down then and tells me about one summer when he 76 was at a school of design in Rhode Island and took thirty trips, the last ones all bad. I ask why they were bad. "I could tell you it was my neuroses," he says, "but fuck that."

A few days later I drop by to see Steve in his apartment. He 77 paces nervously around the room he uses as a studio and shows me some paintings. We do not seem to be getting to the point.

"Maybe you noticed something going on at Max's," he says 78 abruptly.

It seems that the girl he brought, the dark pretty one, had once 79 been Max's girl. She had followed him to Tangier and now to San Francisco. But Max has Sharon. "So she's kind of staying around here," Steve says.

Steve is troubled by a lot of things. He is twenty-three, was 80 raised in Virginia, and has the idea that California is the beginning of the end. "I feel it's insane," he says, and his voice drops. "This chick tells me there's no meaning to life but it doesn't matter, we'll just flow right out. There've been times I felt like packing up and taking off for the East Coast again, at least there I had a *target*. At least there you expect that it's going to *happen*." He lights a cigarette for me and his hands shake. "Here you know it's not going to."

I ask what it is that is supposed to happen. 81

"I don't know," he says. "Something. Anything." 82

Arthur Lisch is on the telephone in his kitchen, trying to sell 83 VISTA a program for the District. "We already *got* an emergency," he says into the telephone, meanwhile trying to disentangle his daughter, age one and a half, from the cord. "We don't get help here, nobody can guarantee what's going to happen. We've got people sleeping in the streets here. We've got people starving to death." He pauses. "All right," he says then, and his voice rises. "So they're doing it by choice. So what."

By the time he hangs up he has limned what strikes me as 84 a pretty Dickensian picture of life on the edge of Golden Gate Park, but then this is my first exposure to Arthur Lisch's "riot-on-the-Street-unless" pitch. Arthur Lisch is a kind of leader of the Diggers, who, in the official District mythology, are supposed to be a group of anonymous good guys with no thought in their collective head but to lend a helping hand. The official District mythology also has it that the Diggers have no "leaders," but nonetheless Arthur Lisch is one. Arthur Lisch is also a paid worker for the American Friends' Service Committee and he lives with his wife, Jane, and their two small children in a railroad flat, which on this particular day lacks organization. For one thing the telephone keeps ringing. Arthur promises to attend a hearing at city hall. Arthur promises to "send Edward, he's O.K." Arthur promises to get a good group, maybe the Loading Zone, to play free for a Jewish benefit. For a second thing the baby is crying, and she does not stop until Jane Lisch appears with a jar of Gerber's Junior Chicken Noodle Dinner. Another confusing element is somebody named Bob, who just sits in the living room and looks at his toes. First he looks at the toes on one foot, then at the toes on the other. I make several attempts to include Bob in the conversation before I realize he is on a bad trip. Moreover, there are two people hacking up what looks like a side of beef on the kitchen floor, the idea being that when it gets hacked up, Jane Lisch can cook it for the daily Digger feed in the Park.

Arthur Lisch does not seem to notice any of this. He just keeps talking about cybernated societies and the guaranteed annual wage and riot on the Street, unless. [85]

I call the Lisches a day or so later and ask for Arthur. Jane Lisch says he's next door taking a shower because somebody is coming down from a bad trip in their bathroom. Besides the freak-out in the bathroom they are expecting a psychiatrist in to look at Bob. Also a doctor for Edward, who is not O.K. at all but has the flu. Jane says maybe I should talk to Chester Anderson. She will not give me his number. [86]

Chester Anderson is a legacy of the Beat Generation, a man in his middle thirties whose peculiar hold on the District derives from his possession of a mimeograph machine, on which he prints communiqués signed "the communication company." It is another tenet of the official District mythology that the communication company will print anything anybody has to say, but in fact Chester Anderson prints only what he writes himself, agrees [87] with, or considers harmless or dead matter. His statements, which are left in piles and pasted on windows around Haight Street, are regarded with some apprehension in the District and with considerable interest by outsiders, who study them, like China watchers, for subtle shifts in obscure ideologies. An Anderson communiqué might be doing something as specific as fingering someone who is said to have set up a marijuana bust, or it might be working in a more general vein:

> Pretty little 16-year-old middle-class chick comes to the Haight to see what it's all about & gets picked up by a 17-year-old street dealer who spends all day shooting her full of speed again & again, then feeds her 3,000 mikes & raffles off her temporarily unemployed body for the biggest Haight Street gangbang since the night before last. The politics and ethics of ecstasy. Rape is as common as bullshit on Haight Street. Kids are starving on the Street. Minds and bodies are being maimed as we watch, a scale model of Vietnam.

Somebody other than Jane Lisch gave me an address for 88 Chester Anderson, 443 Arguello, but 443 Arguello does not exist. I telephone the wife of the man who gave me 443 Arguello and she says it's 742 Arguello.

"But don't go up there," she says.   89

I say I'll telephone.   90

"There's no number," she says. "I can't give it to you."   91

"742 Arguello," I say.   92

"No," she says. "I don't know. And don't go there. And don't   93 use either my name or my husband's name if you do."

She is the wife of a full professor of English at San Francisco   94 State College. I decide to lie low on the question of Chester Anderson for awhile.

Paranoia strikes deep—
Into your life it will creep—
        is a song the Buffalo
        Springfield sing.

The appeal of Malakoff Diggings has kind of faded out but   95 Max says why don't I come to his place, just be there, the next time he takes acid. Tom will take it too, probably Sharon, maybe Barbara. We can't do it for six or seven days because Max and Tom are in STP space now. They are not crazy about STP but it has advantages. "You've still got your forebrain," Tom says. "I could write behind STP, but not behind acid." This is the first time I have heard of anything you can't do behind acid, also the first time I have heard that Tom writes.

Otto is feeling better because he discovered it wasn't the cocaine-and-wheat that made him sick. It was the chicken pox, which he caught baby-sitting for Big Brother and the Holding Company one night when they were playing. I go over to see him and meet Vicki, who sings now and then with a group called the Jook Savages and lives at Otto's place. Vicki dropped out of Laguna High "because I had mono," followed the Grateful Dead up to San Francisco one time and has been here "for a while." Her mother and father are divorced, and she does not see her father, who works for a network in New York. A few months ago he came out to do a documentary on the District and tried to find her, but couldn't. Later he wrote her a letter in care of her mother urging her to go back to school. Vicki guesses maybe she will sometime but she doesn't see much point in it right now.

We are eating a little tempura in Japantown, Chet Helms and I, and he is sharing some of his insights with me. Until a couple of years ago Chet Helms never did much besides hitchhiking, but now he runs the Avalon Ballroom and flies over the Pole to check out the London scene and says things like "Just for the sake of clarity I'd like to categorize the aspects of primitive religion as I see it." Right now he is talking about Marshall McLuhan and how the printed word is finished, out, over. "The *East Village Other* is one of the few papers in America whose books are in the black," he says. "I know that from reading *Barron's*."

A new group is supposed to play in the Panhandle today but they are having trouble with the amplifier and I sit in the sun listening to a couple of little girls, maybe seventeen years old. One of them has a lot of makeup and the other wears Levi's and cowboy boots. The boots do not look like an affectation, they look like she came up off a ranch about two weeks ago. I wonder what she is doing here in the Panhandle trying to make friends with a city girl who is snubbing her but I do not wonder long, because she is homely and awkward and I think of her going all the way through the consolidated union high school out there where she comes from and nobody ever asking her to go into Reno on

Saturday night for a drive-in movie and a beer on the riverbank, so she runs. "I know a thing about dollar bills," she is saying now. "You get one that says '1111' in one corner and '1111' in another, you take it down to Dallas, Texas, they'll give you $15 for it."

"Who will?" the city girl asks.   99

"I don't know."   100

"There are only three significant pieces of data in the world   101
today," is another thing Chet Helms told me one night. We were at the Avalon and the big strobe was going and the colored lights and the Day-Glo painting and the place was full of high-school kids trying to look turned on. The Avalon sound system projects 126 decibels at 100 feet but to Chet Helms the sound is just there, like the air, and he talks through it. "The first is," he said, "God died last year and was obited by the press. The second is, fifty percent of the population is or will be under twenty-five." A boy shook a tambourine toward us and Chet smiled benevolently at him. "The third," he said, "is that they got twenty billion irresponsible dollars to spend."

Thursday comes, some Thursday, and Max and Tom and   102
Sharon and maybe Barbara are going to take some acid. They want to drop it about three o'clock. Barbara has baked fresh bread, Max has gone to the Park for fresh flowers, and Sharon is making a sign for the door which reads "DO NOT DISTURB, RING, KNOCK, OR IN ANY OTHER WAY DISTURB. LOVE." This is not how I would put it to either the health inspector, who is due this week, or any of the several score narcotics agents in the neighborhood, but I figure the sign is Sharon's trip.

Once the sign is finished Sharon gets restless. "Can I at least   103
play the new record?" she asks Max.

"Tom and Barbara want to save it for when we're high."   104

"I'm getting bored, just sitting around here."   105

Max watches her jump up and walk out. "That's what you   106
call pre-acid uptight jitters," he says.

Barbara is not in evidence. Tom keeps walking in and out.   107
"All these innumerable last-minute things you have to do," he mutters.

"It's a tricky thing, acid," Max says after a while. He is turning   108
the stereo on and off. "When a chick takes acid, it's all right if she's

alone, but when she's living with somebody this edginess comes out. And if the hour-and-a-half process before you take the acid doesn't go smooth . . ." He picks up a roach and studies it, then adds, "They're having a little thing back there with Barbara."

Sharon and Tom walk in. 109

"You pissed off too?" Max asks Sharon. 110

Sharon does not answer. 111

Max turns to Tom. "Is she all right?" 112

"Yeh." 113

"Can we take acid?" Max is on edge. 114

"I don't know what she's going to do." 115

"What do you want to do?" 116

"What I want to do depends on what she wants to do." Tom 117 is rolling some joints, first rubbing the papers with a marijuana resin he makes himself. He takes the joints back to the bedroom, and Sharon goes with him.

"Something like this happens every time people take acid," 118 Max says. After a while he brightens and develops a theory around it. "Some people don't like to go out of themselves, that's the trouble. You probably wouldn't. You'd probably like only a quarter of a tab. There's still an ego on a quarter tab, and it wants things. Now if that thing is balling—and your old lady or your old man is off somewhere flashing and doesn't want to be touched—well, you get put down on acid, you can be on a bummer for months."

Sharon drifts in, smiling. "Barbara might take some acid, 119 we're all feeling better, we smoked a joint."

At three-thirty that afternoon Max, Tom, and Sharon placed 120 tabs under their tongues and sat down together in the living room to wait for the flash. Barbara stayed in the bedroom, smoking hash. During the next four hours a window banged once in Barbara's room, and about five-thirty some children had a fight on the street. A curtain billowed in the afternoon wind. A cat scratched a beagle in Sharon's lap. Except for the sitar music on the stereo there was no other sound or movement until seven-thirty, when Max said "Wow."

I spot Deadeye on Haight Street, and he gets in the car. Until 121 we get off the Street he sits very low and inconspicuous. Deadeye wants me to meet his old lady, but first he wants to talk to me about how he got hip to helping people.

"Here I was, just a tough kid on a motorcycle," he says, "and   122
suddenly I see that young people don't have to walk alone."
Deadeye has a clear evangelistic gaze and the reasonable rhetoric
of a car salesman. He is society's model product. I try to meet his
gaze directly because he once told me he could read character in
people's eyes, particularly if he has just dropped acid, which he
did, about nine o'clock this morning. "They just have to remember one thing," he says. "The Lord's Prayer. And that can help
them in more ways than one."

He takes a much-folded letter from his wallet. The letter is   123
from a little girl he helped. "My loving brother," it begins. "I
thought I'd write you a letter since I'm a part of you. Remember
that: When you feel happiness, I do, when you feel . . ."

"What I want to do now," Deadeye says, "is set up a house   124
where a person of any age can come, spend a few days, talk over
his problems. *Any age.* People your age, they've got problems too."

I say a house will take money.   125

"I've found a way to make money," Deadeye says. He hesi-   126
tates only a few seconds. "I could've made eighty-five dollars on
the Street just then. See, in my pocket I had a hundred tabs of
acid. I had to come up with twenty dollars by tonight or we're
out of the house we're in, so I knew somebody who had acid,
and I knew somebody who wanted it, so I made the connection."

> Since the Mafia moved into the LSD racket, the quantity is up and
> the quality is down . . . Historian Arnold Toynbee celebrated his
> 78th birthday Friday night by snapping his fingers and tapping his
> toes to the Quicksilver Messenger Service . . . are a couple of items
> from Herb Caen's column one morning as the West declined in the
> spring of 1967.

When I was in San Francisco a tab, or a cap, of LSD-25 sold   127
for three to five dollars, depending upon the seller and the district. LSD was slightly cheaper in the Haight-Ashbury than in the
Fillmore, where it was used rarely, mainly as a sexual ploy, and
sold by pushers of hard drugs, *e.g.,* heroin, or "smack." A great
deal of acid was being cut with Methedrine, which is the trade
name for an amphetamine, because Methedrine can simulate the
flash that low-quality acid lacks. Nobody knows how much
LSD is actually in a tab, but the standard trip is supposed to be
250 micrograms. Grass was running ten dollars a lid, five dollars

a matchbox. Hash was considered "a luxury item." All the amphetamines, or "speed"—Benzedrine, Dexedrine, and particularly Methedrine—were in far more common use in the late spring than they had been in the early spring. Some attributed this to the presence of the Syndicate; others to a general deterioration of the scene, to the incursions of gangs and younger part-time, or "plastic," hippies, who like the amphetamines and the illusions of action and power they give. Where Methedrine is in wide use, heroin tends to be available, because, I was told, "You can get awful damn high shooting crystal, and smack can be used to bring you down."

Deadeye's old lady, Gerry, meets us at the door of their place.   128
She is a big, hearty girl who has always counseled at Girl Scout camps during summer vacations and was "in social welfare" at the University of Washington when she decided that she "just hadn't done enough living" and came to San Francisco. "Actually the heat was bad in Seattle," she adds.

"The first night I got down here," she says, "I stayed with a   129
gal I met over at the Blue Unicorn. I looked like I'd just arrived, had a knapsack and stuff." After that, Gerry stayed at a house the Diggers were running, where she met Deadeye. "Then it took time to get my bearings, so I haven't done much work yet."

I ask Gerry what work she does. "Basically I'm a poet," she   130
says, "but I had my guitar stolen right after I arrived, and that kind of hung up my thing."

"Get your books," Deadeye orders. "Show her your books."   131

Gerry demurs, then goes into the bedroom and comes back   132
with several theme books full of verse. I leaf through them but Deadeye is still talking about helping people. "Any kid that's on speed," he says, "I'll try to get him off it. The only advantage to it from the kids' point of view is that you don't have to worry about sleeping or eating."

"Or sex," Gerry adds.   133

"That's right. When you're strung out on crystal you don't   134
need *nothing.*"

"It can lead to the hard stuff," Gerry says. "Take your aver-   135
age Meth freak, once he's started putting the needle in his arm, it's not too hard to say, well, let's shoot a little smack."

All the while I am looking at Gerry's poems. They are a very   136 young girl's poems, each written out in a neat hand and finished off with a curlicue. Dawns are roseate, skies silver-tinted. When Gerry writes "crystal" in her books, she does not mean Meth.

"You gotta get back to your writing," Deadeye says fondly, but Gerry ignores this. She is telling about somebody who propositioned her yesterday. "He just walked up to me on the Street, offered me six hundred dollars to go to Reno and do the thing." 137

"You're not the only one he approached," Deadeye says. 138

"If some chick wants to go with him, fine," Gerry says. "Just don't bum my trip." She empties the tuna-fish can we are using for an ashtray and goes over to look at a girl who is asleep on the floor. It is the same girl who was sleeping on the floor the first day I came to Deadeye's place. She has been sick a week now, ten days. "Usually when somebody comes up to me on the Street like that," Gerry adds, "I hit him for some change." 139

When I saw Gerry in the Park the next day I asked her about the sick girl, and Gerry said cheerfully that she was in the hospital, with pneumonia. 140

Max tells me about how he and Sharon got together. "When I saw her the first time on Haight Street, I flashed. I mean flashed. So I started some conversation with her about her beads, see, but I didn't care about her beads." Sharon lived in a house where a friend of Max's lived, and the next time he saw her was when he took the friend some bananas. "It was during the great banana bubble. You had to kind of force your personality and the banana peels down their throats. Sharon and I were like kids—we just smoked bananas and looked at each other and smoked more bananas and looked at each other." 141

But Max hesitated. For one thing he thought Sharon was his friend's girl. "For another I didn't know if I wanted to get hung up with an old lady." But the next time he visited the house, Sharon was on acid. 142

"So everybody yelled 'Here comes the banana man,'" Sharon interrupts, "and I got all excited." 143

"She was living in this crazy house," Max continues. "There was this one kid, all he did was scream. His whole trip was to practice screams. It was too much." Max still hung back from Sharon. "But then she offered me a tab, and I knew." 144

Max walked to the kitchen and back with the tab, wondering   145
whether to take it. "And then I decided to flow with it, and that
was that. Because once you drop acid with somebody you flash
on, you see the whole world melt in her eyes."

"It's stronger than anything in the world," Sharon says.   146

"Nothing can break it up," Max says. "As long as it lasts."   147

No milk today—
My love has gone away . . .
The end of my hopes—
The end of all my dreams—
is a song I heard every morning in the
cold late spring of 1967 on KFRC, the
Flower Power Station, San Francisco.

Deadeye and Gerry tell me they plan to be married. An Epis-   148
copal priest in the District has promised to perform the wedding
in Golden Gate Park, and they will have a few rock groups there,
"a real community thing." Gerry's brother is also getting married, in Seattle. "Kind of interesting," Gerry muses, "because,
you know, his is the traditional straight wedding, and then you
have the contrast with ours."

"I'll have to wear a tie to his," Deadeye says.   149

"Right," Gerry says.   150

"Her parents came down to meet me, but they weren't ready   151
for me," Deadeye notes philosophically.

"They finally gave it their blessing," Gerry says. "In a way."   152

"They came to me and her father said, 'Take care of her,'"   153
Deadeye reminisces. "And her mother said, 'Don't let her go to
jail.'"

Barbara baked a macrobiotic apple pie and she and Tom and   154
Max and Sharon and I are eating it. Barbara tells me how she
learned to find happiness in "the woman's thing." She and Tom
had gone somewhere to live with the Indians, and although she
first found it hard to be shunted off with the women and never
to enter into any of the men's talk, she soon got the point. "That
was where the *trip* was," she says.

Barbara is on what is called the woman's trip to the exclusion   155
of almost everything else. When she and Tom and Max and
Sharon need money, Barbara will take a part-time job, modeling

or teaching kindergarten, but she dislikes earning more than ten or twenty dollars a week. Most of the time she keeps house and bakes. "Doing something that shows your love that way," she says, "is just about the most beautiful thing I know." Whenever I hear about the woman's trip, which is often, I think a lot about nothin'-says-lovin'-like-something-from-the-oven and the Feminine Mystique and how it is possible for people to be the unconscious instruments of values they would strenuously reject on a conscious level, but I do not mention this to Barbara.

It is a pretty nice day and I am just driving down the Street and I see Barbara at a light. 156

What am I doing, she wants to know. 157

I am just driving around. 158

"Groovy," she says. 159

It's a beautiful day, I say. 160

"Groovy," she agrees. 161

She wants to know if I will come over. Sometime soon, I say. 162

"Groovy," she says. 163

I ask if she wants to drive in the Park but she is too busy. She is out to buy wool for her loom. 164

Arthur Lisch gets pretty nervous whenever he sees me now because the Digger line this week is that they aren't talking to "media poisoners," which is me. So I still don't have a tap on Chester Anderson, but one day in the Panhandle I run into a kid who says he is Chester's "associate." He has on a black cape, black slouch hat, mauve Job's Daughters sweatshirt and dark glasses, and he says his name is Claude Hayward, but never mind that because I think of him just as The Connection. The Connection offers to "check me out." 165

I take off my dark glasses so he can see my eyes. He leaves his on. 166

"How much you get paid for doing this kind of media poisoning?" he says for openers. 167

I put my dark glasses back on. 168

"There's only one way to find out where it's at," The Connection says, and jerks his thumb at the photographer I'm with. "Dump him and get out on the Street. Don't take money. You won't need money." He reaches into his cape and pulls out a 169

Mimeographed sheet announcing a series of classes at the Digger Free Store on How to Avoid Getting Busted, Gangbangs, VD, Rape, Pregnancy, Beatings, and Starvation. "You oughta come," The Connection says. "You'll need it."

I say maybe, but meanwhile I would like to talk to Chester   170
Anderson.

"If we decide to get in touch with you at all," The Connection   171
says, "we'll get in touch with you real quick." He kept an eye on me in the Park after that but never called the number I gave him.

It is twilight and cold and too early to find Deadeye at the   172
Blue Unicorn so I ring Max's bell. Barbara comes to the door.

"Max and Tom are seeing somebody on a kind of business   173
thing," she says. "Can you come back a little later?"

I am hard put to think what Max and Tom might be seeing   174
somebody about in the way of business, but a few days later in the Park I find out.

"Hey," Max calls. "Sorry you couldn't come up the other day,   175
but *business* was being done." This time I get the point. "We got some great stuff," he says, and begins to elaborate. Every third person in the Park this afternoon looks like a narcotics agent and I try to change the subject. Later I suggest to Max that he be more wary in public. "Listen, I'm very cautious," he says. "You can't be too careful."

By now I have an unofficial taboo contact with the San Fran-   176
cisco Police Department. What happens is that this cop and I meet in various late-movie ways, like I happen to be sitting in the bleachers at a baseball game and he happens to sit down next to me, and we exchange guarded generalities. No information actually passes between us, but after a while we get to kind of like each other.

"The kids aren't too bright," he is telling me on this particu-   177
lar day. "They'll tell you they can always spot an undercover, they'll tell you about 'the kind of car he drives.' They aren't talking about undercovers, they're talking about plainclothesmen who just happen to drive unmarked cars, like I do. They can't tell an undercover. An undercover doesn't drive some black Ford with a two-way radio."

He tells me about an undercover who was taken out of the   178

District because he was believed to be overexposed, too familiar. He was transferred to the narcotics squad, and by error was sent immediately back into the District as a narcotics undercover.

The cop plays with his keys. "You want to know how smart   179 these kids are?" he says finally. "The first week, this guy makes forty-three cases."

The Jook Savages are supposed to be having a May Day party   180 in Larkspur and I go by the Warehouse and Don and Sue Ann think it would be nice to drive over there because Sue Ann's three-year-old, Michael, hasn't been out lately. The air is soft and there is a sunset haze around the Golden Gate and Don asks Sue Ann how many flavors she can detect in a single grain of rice and Sue Ann tells Don maybe she better learn to cook *yang,* maybe they are all too *yin* at the Warehouse, and I try to teach Michael "Frère Jacques." We each have our own trip and it is a nice drive. Which is just as well because there is nobody at all at the Jook Savages' place, not even the Jook Savages. When we get back Sue Ann decides to cook up a lot of apples they have around the Warehouse and Don starts working with his light show and I go down to see Max for a minute. "Out of sight," Max says about the Larkspur caper. "Somebody thinks it would be groovy to turn on five hundred people the first day in May, and it would be, but then they turn on the last day in April instead, so it doesn't happen. If it happens, it happens. If it doesn't, it doesn't. Who cares. Nobody cares."

Some kid with braces on his teeth is playing his guitar and   181 boasting that he got the last of the STP from Mr. O. himself and somebody else is talking about how five grams of acid will be liberated within the next month and you can see that nothing much is happening this afternoon around the *San Francisco Oracle* office. A boy sits at a drawing board drawing the infinitesimal figures that people do on speed, and the kid with the braces watches him. *"I'm gonna shoot my wo–man,"* he sings softly. *"She been with a–noth–er man."* Someone works out the numerology of my name and the name of the photographer I'm with. The photographer's is all white and the sea ("If I were to make you some beads, see, I'd do it mainly in white," he is told), but mine has a double death symbol. The afternoon does not seem to be getting anywhere, so it is suggested that we go over to Japantown and find somebody named Sandy who will take us to the Zen temple.

Four boys and one middle-aged man are sitting on a grass mat [182] at Sandy's place, sipping anise tea and watching Sandy read Laura Huxley's *You Are Not the Target.*

We sit down and have some anise tea. "Meditation turns us [183] on," Sandy says. He has a shaved head and the kind of cherubic face usually seen in newspaper photographs of mass murderers. The middle-aged man, whose name is George, is making me uneasy because he is in a trance next to me and stares at me without seeing me.

I feel that my mind is going—George is *dead,* or we *all* are— [184] when the telephone rings.

"It's for George," Sandy says. [185]

"George, *tele*phone." [186]

"*George.*" [187]

Somebody waves his hand in front of George and George fi- [188] nally gets up, bows, and moves toward the door on the balls of his feet.

"I think I'll take George's tea," somebody says. "George—are [189] you coming back?"

George stops at the door and stares at each of us in turn. "In [190] a *mo*ment," he snaps.

Do you know who is the first eternal spaceman
  of this universe?
The first to send his wild wild vibrations
To all those cosmic superstations?
For the song he always shouts
Sends the planets flipping out . . .
But I'll tell you before you think me loony
That I'm talking about Narada Muni . . .
Singing
HARE KRISHNA   HARE KRISHNA
KRISHNA KRISHNA HARE HARE
HARE RAMA   HARE RAMA
RAMA RAMA   HARE HARE
is a Krishna song. Words by
Howard Wheeler and music by
Michael Grant.

Maybe the trip is not in Zen but in Krishna, so I pay a visit to   191
Michael Grant, the Swami A. C. Bhaktivedanta's leading disciple
in San Francisco. Michael Grant is at home with his brother-in-
law and his wife, a pretty girl wearing a cashmere pullover, a
jumper, and a red caste mark on her forehead.

"I've been associated with the Swami since about last July,"   192
Michael says. "See, the Swami came here from India and he was
at this ashram in upstate New York and he just kept to himself
and chanted a lot. For a couple of months. Pretty soon I helped
him get his storefront in New York. Now it's an international
movement, which we spread by teaching this chant." Michael is
fingering his red wooden beads and I notice that I am the only
person in the room with shoes on. "It's catching on like wildfire."

"If everybody chanted," the brother-in-law says, "there   193
wouldn't be any problem with the police or anybody."

"Ginsberg[2] calls the chant ecstasy, but the Swami says that's   194
not exactly it." Michael walks across the room and straightens a
picture of Krishna as a baby. "Too bad you can't meet the
Swami," he adds. "The Swami's in New York now."

"Ecstasy's not the right word at all," says the brother-in-law,   195
who has been thinking about it. "It makes you think of some . . .
mun*dane* ecstasy."

The next day I drop by Max and Sharon's, and find them in   196
bed smoking a little morning hash. Sharon once advised me that
half a joint even of grass would make getting up in the morning
a beautiful thing. I ask Max how Krishna strikes him.

"You can get a high on a mantra," he says. "But I'm holy on   197
acid."

Max passes the joint to Sharon and leans back. "Too bad   198
you couldn't meet the Swami," he says. "The Swami was the
turn-on."

> *Anybody who thinks this is all about drugs has his head in a bag. It's*
> *a social movement, quintessentially romantic, the kind that recurs in*
> *times of real social crisis. The themes are always the same. A return*
> *to innocence. The invocation of an earlier authority and control. The*
> *mysteries of the blood. An itch for the transcendental, for purifica-*
> *tion. Right there you've got the ways that romanticism historically*
> *ends up in trouble, lends itself to authoritarianism. When the direc-*

---

2. Allen Ginsberg: Beat poet and student of Buddhism (b. 1926).

tion appears. How long do you think it'll take for that to happen? is
a question a San Francisco psychiatrist asked me.

At the time I was in San Francisco the political potential of   199
what was then called the movement was just becoming clear. It
had always been clear to the revolutionary core of the Diggers,
whose every guerrilla talent was now bent toward open con-
frontations and the creation of a summer emergency, and it was
clear to many of the straight doctors and priests and sociologists
who had occasion to work in the District, and it could rapidly
become clear to any outsider who bothered to decode Chester
Anderson's call-to-action communiqués or to watch who was
there first at the street skirmishes which now set the tone for life
in the District. One did not have to be a political analyst to see
it; the boys in the rock groups saw it, because they were often
where it was happening. "In the Park there are always twenty or
thirty people below the stand," one of the Dead complained to
me. "Ready to take the crowd on some militant trip."

But the peculiar beauty of this political potential, as far as the   200
activists were concerned, was that it remained not clear at all to
most of the inhabitants of the District, perhaps because the few
seventeen-year-olds who are political realists tend not to adopt
romantic idealism as a life style. Nor was it clear to the press,
which at varying levels of competence continued to report "the
hippie phenomenon" as an extended panty raid; an artistic
avant-garde led by such comfortable YMHA[3] regulars as Allen
Ginsberg; or a thoughtful protest, not unlike joining the Peace
Corps, against the culture which had produced Saran-Wrap and
the Vietnam War. This last, or they're-trying-to-tell-us-something
approach, reached its apogee in a *Time* cover story which revealed that hippies "scorn money—they call it 'bread'" and remains the most remarkable, if unwitting, extant evidence that
the signals between the generations are irrevocably jammed.

Because the signals the press was getting were immaculate of   201
political possibilities, the tensions of the District went unremarked upon, even during the period when there were so many
observers on Haight Street from *Life* and *Look* and CBS that
they were largely observing one another. The observers believed
roughly what the children told them: that they were a generation

3. YMHA: Young Men's Hebrew Association.

dropped out of political action, beyond power games, that the New Left was just another ego trip. *Ergo*, there really were no activists in the Haight-Ashbury, and those things which happened every Sunday were spontaneous demonstrations because, just as the Diggers say, the police are brutal and juveniles have no rights and runaways are deprived of their right to self-determination and people are starving to death on Haight Street, a scale model of Vietnam.

Of course the activists—not those whose thinking had become rigid, but those whose approach to revolution was imaginatively anarchic—had long ago grasped the reality which still eluded the press: we were seeing something important. We were seeing the desperate attempt of a handful of pathetically unequipped children to create a community in a social vacuum. Once we had seen these children, we could no longer overlook the vacuum, no longer pretend that the society's atomization could be reversed. This was not a traditional generational rebellion. At some point between 1945 and 1967 we had somehow neglected to tell these children the rules of the game we happened to be playing. Maybe we had stopped believing in the rules ourselves, maybe we were having a failure of nerve about the game. Maybe there were just too few people around to do the telling. These were children who grew up cut loose from the web of cousins and great-aunts and family doctors and lifelong neighbors who had traditionally suggested and enforced the society's values. They are children who have moved around a lot, *San Jose, Chula Vista, here.* They are less in rebellion against the society than ignorant of it, able only to feed back certain of its most publicized self-doubts, *Vietnam, Saran-Wrap, diet pills, the Bomb.*

They feed back exactly what is given them. Because they do not believe in words—words are for "typeheads," Chester Anderson tells them, and a thought which needs words is just one more of those ego trips—their only proficient vocabulary is in the society's platitudes. As it happens I am still committed to the idea that the ability to think for one's self depends upon one's mastery of the language, and I am not optimistic about children who will settle for saying, to indicate that their mother and father do not live together, that they come from "a broken home." They are sixteen, fifteen, fourteen years old, younger all the time, an army of children waiting to be given the words.

Peter Berg knows a lot of words. 204
"Is Peter Berg around?" I ask. 205
"Maybe." 206
"Are you Peter Berg?" 207
"Yeh."

The reason Peter Berg does not bother sharing too many words 208
with me is because two of the words he knows are "media poisoning." Peter Berg wears a gold earring and is perhaps the only
person in the District on whom a gold earring looks obscurely
ominous. He belongs to the San Francisco Mime Troupe, some
of whose members started the Artist's Liberation Front for "those
who seek to combine their creative urge with socio-political involvement." It was out of the Mime Troupe that the Diggers grew,
during the 1966 Hunter's Point riots, when it seemed a good idea
to give away food and do puppet shows in the streets making fun
of the National Guard. Along with Arthur Lisch, Peter Berg is part
of the shadow leadership of the Diggers, and it was he who more or
less invented and first introduced to the press the notion that there
would be an influx into San Francisco during the summer of 1967
of 200,000 indigent adolescents. The only conversation I ever have
with Peter Berg is about how he holds me personally responsible
for the way *Life* captioned Henri Cartier-Bresson's pictures out
of Cuba, but I like to watch him at work in the Park.

Janis Joplin is singing with Big Brother in the Panhandle and 209
almost everybody is high and it is a pretty nice Sunday afternoon
between three and six o'clock, which the activists say are the
three hours of the week when something is most likely to happen
in the Haight-Ashbury, and who turns up but Peter Berg. He is
with his wife and six or seven other people, along with Chester
Anderson's associate The Connection, and the first peculiar thing
is, they're in blackface.

I mention to Max and Sharon that some members of the 210
Mime Troupe seem to be in blackface.

"It's street theater," Sharon assures me. "It's supposed to be 211
really groovy."

The Mime Troupers get a little closer, and there are some 212
other peculiar things about them. For one thing they are tapping
people on the head with dime-store plastic nightsticks, and for
another they are wearing signs on their backs. "HOW MANY
TIMES YOU BEEN RAPED, YOU LOVE FREAKS?" and "WHO STOLE

CHUCK BERRY'S MUSIC?," things like that. Then they are distributing communication company fliers which say:

> & this summer thousands of un-white un-suburban boppers are going to want to know why you've given up what they can't get & how you get away with it & how come you not a faggot with hair so long & they want haight street one way or the other. IF YOU DON'T KNOW, BY AUGUST HAIGHT STREET WILL BE A CEMETERY.

Max reads the flier and stands up. "I'm getting bad vibes," he   213
says, and he and Sharon leave.

I have to stay around because I'm looking for Otto so I walk   214
over to where the Mime Troupers have formed a circle around a
Negro. Peter Berg is saying if anybody asks that this is street theater, and I figure the curtain is up because what they are doing
right now is jabbing the Negro with the nightsticks. They jab,
and they bare their teeth, and they rock on the balls of their feet
and they wait.

"I'm beginning to get annoyed here," the Negro says. "I'm   215
gonna get mad."

By now there are several Negroes around, reading the signs   216
and watching.

"Just beginning to get annoyed, are you?" one of the Mime   217
Troupers says. "Don't you think it's about time?"

"Nobody *stole* Chuck Berry's music, man," says another Ne-   218
gro who has been studying the signs. "Chuck Berry's music belongs to *every*body."

"Yeh?" a girl in blackface says. "Everybody *who?*"   219

"Why," he says, confused. "Everybody. In America."   220

"In *America*," the blackface girl shrieks. "Listen to him talk   221
about *America*."

"Listen," he says helplessly. "Listen here."   222

"What'd *America* ever do for you?" the girl in blackface jeers.   223
"White kids here, they can sit in the Park all summer long, listening to the music they stole, because their bigshot parents keep
sending them money. Who ever sends you money?"

"Listen," the Negro says, his voice rising. "You're gonna start   224
something here, this isn't right—"

"You tell us what's right, black boy," the girl says.   225

The youngest member of the blackface group, an earnest tall   226
kid about nineteen, twenty, is hanging back at the edge of the
scene. I offer him an apple and ask what is going on. "Well," he

says, "I'm new at this, I'm just beginning to study it, but you see the capitalists are taking over the District, and that's what Peter—well, ask Peter."

I did not ask Peter. It went on for a while. But on that particular Sunday between three and six o'clock everyone was too high and the weather was too good and the Hunter's Point gangs who usually come in between three and six on Sunday afternoon had come in on Saturday instead, and nothing started. While I waited for Otto I asked a little girl I knew slightly what she had thought of it. "It's something groovy they call street theater," she said. I said I had wondered if it might not have political overtones. She was seventeen years old and she worked it around in her mind awhile and finally she remembered a couple of words from somewhere. "Maybe it's some John Birch thing," she said.

When I finally find Otto he says "I got something at my place that'll blow your mind," and when we get there I see a child on the living-room floor, wearing a reefer coat, reading a comic book. She keeps licking her lips in concentration and the only off thing about her is that she's wearing white lipstick.

"Five years old," Otto says. "On acid."

The five-year-old's name is Susan, and she tells me she is in High Kindergarten. She lives with her mother and some other people, just got over the measles, wants a bicycle for Christmas, and particularly likes Coca-Cola, ice cream, Marty in the Jefferson Airplane, Bob in the Grateful Dead, and the beach. She remembers going to the beach once a long time ago, and wishes she had taken a bucket. For a year now her mother has given her both acid and peyote. Susan describes it as getting stoned.

I start to ask if any of the other children in High Kindergarten get stoned, but I falter at the key words.

"She means do the other kids in your class turn on, *get stoned*," says the friend of her mother's who brought her to Otto's.

"Only Sally and Anne," Susan says.

"What about Lia?" her mother's friend prompts.

"Lia," Susan says, "is not in High Kindergarten."

Sue Ann's three-year-old Michael started a fire this morning before anyone was up, but Don got it out before much damage was done. Michael burned his arm though, which is probably why Sue Ann was so jumpy when she happened to see him chewing on an electric cord. "You'll fry like rice," she screamed. The only people around were Don and one of Sue Ann's macrobiotic friends and somebody who was on his way to a commune in the Santa Lucias, and they didn't notice Sue Ann screaming at Michael because they were in the kitchen trying to retrieve some very good Moroccan hash which had dropped down through a floorboard damaged in the fire.

ROGER ANGELL

In the Country

Roger Angell lives in New York City and has been a frequent contributor to *The New Yorker* since 1957. Most of his writing has been about baseball, but he can hardly be called a sports reporter in the usual sense. His *New Yorker* essays, which show a deep interest in the lives of people who find their way to the ballpark, have won him a following among readers who rarely go there themselves. Critic George Robinson says that Angell's reputation among baseball writers is "like the 1927 Yankees—the greatest ever, an untouchable." "In the Country" appeared in *The New Yorker* on August 17, 1981.

Baseball is a family for those who care about it, and members   1
of close families like to exchange letters. Three years ago, I received a letter from a woman named Linda Kittell, who was living in Clinton, Montana.

"I was born in 1952," she wrote. "I remember listening to the   2
Yankees—with Mel Allen, it must have been—on a little yellow transistor radio on an island in Lake Champlain, where we spent our summers. Not listening but sort of doing the everyday things of an eight- or ten-year-old—drinking chocolate milk and eating animal crackers—while my sister, two years older, flirted with her boyfriend, who *listened* to the Yankee games on the yellow radio. I only paid attention when I heard Mickey Mantle's name or Roger Maris's name. And I was in love with Whitey Ford. Maris was hitting home runs as often as we went uptown that summer—every day. . . .

"I forgot about baseball later, except in September, when I   3
paid attention if the Yankees were close to getting into the Series.
I went to college, and then to graduate school in Montana. One
night in a bar in Missoula, I met a man who just about fell flat
when I complained about the games on the TV set there because
they didn't put on the Yankees enough. He looked at me as if
he'd been struck. You're a *Yankee* fan? I told him I had a perfect
right, because I was from upstate New York and because I'd
been in love with Whitey Ford all my life, practically. Ron was a
Mantle fan (his name is Ron Goble; he's a lanky six foot five),
and I tended more toward Maris, but we both loved Whitey
Ford. We talked and drank beer. He'd played Legion ball for five
years in his home town of Boise, Idaho, and he'd won a baseball
scholarship to Linfield College, in Oregon. He'd been scouted
in school by the Yankees, the Angels, and the Pirates. He's a
left-handed pitcher. His fastball was clocked at more than ninety
m.p.h., and he told me he'd held back on it, at that, because he
was afraid of hurting his arm. He said how he'd recognized the
scouts in the stands because they were all tan in May and June in
southern Idaho. He talked about how he'd come to think a college education was more important than athletics, and how the
student riots in the late nineteen-sixties had turned him against
sports, so he'd stopped playing. He talked about Vietnam and
drugs and what it was like then, and what a waste it had been for
him to forget about ball.

"We started living together about three years ago. Christ-   4
mases, birthdays, surprises from me—all those special days had
to do with baseball. A baseball book, a baseball picture, a pack
of new baseball cards—anything. Then last year Seattle got the
Mariners. Our vacation from Montana was a twelve-hour train
ride and three days' worth of games—*Yankee* games: the Yankees at the Kingdome. I cried when I saw them out there. Ron
said I was being silly. But, God, there was Mickey Rivers. I mean,
Mickey Rivers! . . .

"The third day, I found a sympathetic usher who let me stand   5
down close to the field with about ten little kids trying to get autographs. I lied through my teeth and said one of them was my
little brother. Sparky Lyle and Catfish and Chambliss were playing pepper, and then a player out beyond them called, 'Hey, you
girl!' I looked up. 'Yeah, you,' and he threw me a ball. Paul Blair
threw me a baseball. All the little boys waist-high around me

looked disgusted. 'Why'd he throw *her* a ball?' . . . 'Mom, Dad, that one threw that *girl* a ball.' It was an Official American League ball. I read it over and rushed up to my seat, where Ron was waiting for the game to start. 'It's a real ball,' I told him. '*Look* at it.' There I was, a perfectly sensible, sensitive twenty-four-year-old woman getting goose bumps over a baseball. I asked Ron if I should go down for more autographs, but something had changed. He rubbed the ball and kept looking at it. He was years away, and sad about it. . . . I went back down, and the autograph I got in the end was Elston Howard's. Memory and imagination make you think about anything you want. I'd picked Ellie Howard—and not Mickey Rivers or Catfish Hunter or Thurman Munson—because I thought it would make him happy, and because his name reminded me of my little yellow radio back in Vermont on August afternoons. Because I'm sentimental.

"We drove back to Montana with a friend, and Ron and I sat   6
in the back seat. 'Can I see the ball again?' he said. I handed it to him and watched Ron hold it for a fastball, a slider, a curve. He looked far-off still. . . .

"This spring, there was an article in *The Sporting News* about   7
a Class A team being formed in Boise, called the Buckskins. Tryouts were in June, and you needed three thousand dollars from a sponsor if you made the team. Something different, all right, but it was a chance to play ball. They'd signed the Sundown Kid—Danny Thomas—and a twenty-seven-year-old catcher from southern Idaho. I wanted Ron to go down and try out. He said he wasn't in shape. He said he was happy playing on the Clinton Clowns, our town's fast-pitch softball team. It was obvious that he *wasn't* happy playing softball, and especially obvious in the fall, when he'd pitch by himself—pitch baseball by throwing rotten apples from our tree against a telephone pole, and call balls and strikes, hits and outs. . . ."

Linda persuaded Ron to try out for the Buckskins, but he   8
didn't get around to it until a few days before their season was about to begin. A letter from the Buckskin manager, Gerry Craft, said they were looking for a left-handed pitcher, and that did the trick.

"Our truck broke down," Linda's letter went on. "Planes   9
were on strike. Finally, Ron's brother George drove him down.

Ron was signed on the first day he threw—a good rotation on his curveball, they said. I didn't even know what Ron meant by that when he told me about it by long-distance. Gerry Craft had said he could go far in baseball, but what Gerry didn't know was that Ron had thrown his arm out—just about ruined it, it turned out—with the second curve he'd thrown. So Ron waited, in ice packs. Three days later, he came home with a swollen arm and a professional baseball player's contract. Five hundred dollars a month. We started packing up his stuff and spent long hours looking for a sponsor. We ended up putting up our own money. Three thousand dollars may not sound like much to some people, but it was everything we had. I served Ron a steak dinner and kissed him goodbye.

"I don't think it really sank in until I made the trip down to   10
Boise to see the Buckskins play in their first home stand. Ron was standing there in his tan-and-black uniform, with a satin warmup jacket and real cleats, and I was just as excited about that as I'd been when I saw Mickey Rivers on the field in Seattle. I was goofy. . . .

"Now, anyone will tell you that this Buckskins team is dif-   11
ferent. The general manager, Lanny Moss [Lanny Moss is a woman], is very religious, and so is Gerry Craft. In right field at their park there's a huge billboard with 'JESUS' written on it in twelve-foot letters. In left field there's a strange picture of Christ Himself. Craft says he had a vision that told him to look around Spokane for a cabin in the woods, and that's where he found Danny Thomas, the Sundown Kid. Danny left major-league ball [Thomas, an out-fielder, had played for two seasons with the Brewers] because his religion required him to read the Bible from sundown Friday to sundown Saturday, which meant he mostly couldn't play on those days. And Craft has game strategy confirmed to him by the Bible, and stuff. Some of his ballplayers have been baptized on their road trips—I picture a clean white sink at the Salem Inn as the font, with the neat sample Ivory soap tablets resting at the side. But these ballplayers are the nicest people I've ever met.

"I'm not the typical wife/girlfriend of a baseball player—those   12
women you see on TV with their hair done up and their Rose Bowl Parade wave to the crowds. I like to watch baseball. I love the game, and I'm one of the loudest fans in the stands. And

when Ron's pitching I find myself almost praying for a win. But the Buckskins don't win many games. The newspapers around the league have put too much stress on the religious aspect of the team. The players aren't all Jesus people. Most of them drink beer and swear. Gerry Craft rhubarbs with the umps with his hands in his jacket pockets. Danny Thomas hits a grand-slammer half an hour before sunset and trots around the bases on his way to his Bible. It's all wonderful. The beer, the hot dogs with everything on them, and seeing old Ron Goble out on the mound working on his curveball and about to turn twenty-seven. What a good way to turn twenty-seven—finally doing something you've tried to ignore for eight years. I love it. It's a hit in the bottom of the ninth, with the score tied and the ball sailing over the right-field wall."

I answered this letter, needless to say, and in time Linda wrote back. We became baseball correspondents and baseball friends. She wrote in October that year and told me about the rest of the Buckskins' season. The team had gone bad, at one point losing eleven straight games. Money was short, and the team's religious fervor made for difficulties. After the Buckskins suffered a 25–3 loss to the Salem Senators, Gerry Craft released the losing pitcher, saying that God had made it clear to him that He didn't want that pitcher on the team. In Eugene, Oregon, Craft announced that God had told him they were going to lose a game to the Emeralds, and, sure enough, they did, blowing a 6–4 lead in the ninth. Some of the benchwarmers on the club began to wonder if they were being kept on the roster because of their three-thousand-dollar sponsor deposits—an inevitable development, perhaps. The Buckskins finished last in the Northwest League, fourteen games behind their divisional winner, Eugene, and twenty-five games worse than the eventual champions, the Gray's Harbor (Washington) Loggers. Danny Thomas led the league with a .359 batting average, but the Buckskins had the worst pitching in the league—a club earned-run average of 6.42. Ron Goble wound up with a 2–3 record and an earned-run average of 8.18—his lifetime figures in professional baseball.

There were some good moments, even in a season like that.

"I went down to Boise in August," Linda wrote in that next letter. "Ron met me at the airport, and we went straight to the

field. There was talk that Charlie Finley had sent for the Sun-
downer, to help his Oakland A's, and talk that two new pitchers
were coming from Milwaukee. It was hot—a hundred degrees,
easy. I sat in the only shade in the ballpark and watched batting
practice. Danny Thomas was running around with a coonskin
cap on, and Bo McConnaughy, one of my favorites on the team,
came out in a bright-yellow hard hat. Bo was the Buckskins'
shortstop—a ballplayers' ballplayer. He had been in the minor
leagues for years, in the Orioles organization—the wrong place
at the wrong time, because the Orioles had a shortstop named
Mark Belanger. Then Bo had gotten too old to be of any interest
to them. Bo loves baseball, and you don't notice his gray hair until he's back in street clothes.

"Raymie Odermott started the game against Bend that night, 16
and went six and two-thirds innings, until Gerry brought in Ron
with the score 4–3, Boise. Two outs, men on first and second.
Ron went in, and this left-hand batter was waiting for him and
got a hit that tied the score. Boise scored two runs in the seventh
and one in the eighth, and Ron held Bend scoreless the rest of the
game, striking out their last two batters. Just fine.

"He was off in the ozone the rest of the night. He sat over a 17
beer with friends, quietly reviewing the game. His curveball had
been right for the first time since the June tryout. We both
thought—or hoped, I suppose—that the days of Tenderyl and
the threat of cortisone were over. It's hard to explain how happy
he was that night. It's as if he believed for a moment that he
wasn't eight years too late. . . .

"Still, there were rumblings on the team. Pitchers went to 18
Gerry and complained that they didn't get to pitch. Mark Garland was one, and he got to start. He got blown away. The next
night, it was Dennis Love, who'd also complained. He looked
real bad, too, and Gerry brought in Ron. Ron let up a home
run—to the first batter. It was a bad time. The next day, at batting practice, Dennis Love said he'd been released, along with
Mark Garland. Ron went in to talk to Gerry about *his* future,
and I drove down to the Circle K to get some pop. Mark Garland
was crying beside a bridge over an irrigation canal. And I hoped
I wouldn't end up comforting Ron some day, squeezing his hand
and talking softly to him, the way Mark's wife stood comforting
him.

"The last two weeks of the season, the team played without
pay, until Lanny Moss could borrow the money to pay their
checks. Danny Thomas left, saying he wasn't going to play ball
for free. There was no money for hotels or food. Once, the bus
broke down, and the team had to sleep on the floor of a church.
They left on a last road trip to Victoria and Bellingham. I went
up to visit friends in Seattle and to catch some of the Bellingham
games. The Kingdome didn't wow me so much this time. The
Yankees were there again, but I knew more about people on the
field than I used to. I got Ron Guidry's autograph, and I still
loved Mickey Rivers, but it was different. People, not heroes. In
Bellingham, I spent a rainy evening watching 'Monday Night
Baseball' with Ron and Bo. Then I danced with all the team, at
Bellingham's imitation disco.

"Season's over. Ron's been back a month. Two weeks ago, he
went grouse hunting with the dogs and a friend, and came home
tipsy drunk. He'd remembered his doctor's appointment the next
day, and had spent his time trying to forget about it. He made a
mock pitch for me, and his elbow *clicked* at the end of the motion.
He said, 'At least, Gerry Craft told me I could have been in
the bigs. I know that much. It's enough.'

"A shot of cortisone and rest. Ron doesn't lie to the scouts
about his age, you know. He and Bo are honest about that. We
have tons of fallen apples, if Ron's arm starts to come around.
Bo's in Boise, studying to be a mechanic. Gerry's been released.
Everybody's waiting through the winter."

There were more letters back and forth. It meant a lot to me
to hear from someone—from two people, really—who could tell
me what baseball was like far from the crowds and the noise and
the fame and the big money that I had been writing about for
many summers. And by this time, of course, I cared about Ron
and Linda, and worried about what would happen to them.
Linda wrote me that Ron and his brother George and a friend
named Ray were spending a great deal of their time that winter
playing an extremely complicated baseball-by-dice game called
Extra Innings. From time to time, Ron would get out his mitt
and persuade someone to catch him, but when he threw, in gingerly
fashion, he found that his elbow was still horribly painful.
He couldn't get over how foolish he had been to throw that hard

19

20

21

22

curve during his Buckskins tryout. He read a book by Jim Bouton, in which Bouton said that his sore arm felt as if it had been bitten by alligators; Ron's felt exactly the same way. The Buckskins, in any case, had folded. The Phillies had expressed some interest in picking them up as a farm team, but the city of Boise would not refurbish its ancient ballpark, so the Phillies went elsewhere. Then the Northwest League adopted a rule favoring younger players and making it harder for older players to find a place on its team rosters—the last blow for Ron. That winter, he sent letters to all the major-league clubs asking for some kind of employment in their organizations, but the answers were a long time coming back. He told Linda he had really been collecting major-league letterheads. Linda described an evening of theirs on the town, and its ending: "We walked through the streets of Missoula in the 4 A.M. drizzle, Ron in his Buckskin jacket and me feeling very maudlin, remembering the walk from the field to the Buckskins' dressing room. What fun it was being a Baseball Annie, arm in arm with some semblance of a professional ballplayer, rain drizzling on my arm and on the satin warm-up jacket. How romantic and far away it seems now."

At about this time, I wrote an article about the difficulties that 23 women sports reporters had experienced in gaining access to the clubhouses of major-league ball teams on their beat, and Linda commented on that, too: "Oh, as to women in the clubhouse, I think they're a necessity. Why, this summer when the Buckskins got locked out of their locker room, I was the only one who could fit through the window and over the top row of the lockers, to unlock the door. And for that one quiet moment between lockers and door I imagined myself in uniform, imagined the feel of oiled leather and dust, the long trip from this town to the next."

There was a long trip just ahead for Ron and Linda—from 24 Montana to northwestern Vermont, where they moved into a farmhouse about forty miles from Burlington: "It took us six days to drive across the country in a calico Chevy truck, with the two dogs in back and a U-Haul in back of that. I think the only thing that got Ron across the plains was the radio reception. We kept tuning in game after game, from all the big-league cities along the way, including a French-Canadian station, near the end, with the Expos on it. French baseball cracked me up. We're close to Montreal here, and we went to an Expos-Cardinals doubleheader last weekend. Saw Cash's grand slam and drank Canadian beer. Ron was frustrated by the French and English announcements—a whole bunch of French with 'Ellis Valentine' in the middle of it. Whenever the Expos did anything, the French-Canadians sitting around us would slap each other on the back and pull on their pints of vodka."

Linda had come East to be closer to her family for a while. (She was born in Troy, New York, and Burlington is on Lake Champlain, where she passed those early summers listening to the Yankees.) She went to work as a feature writer and sports editor for a Vermont newspaper, the *Lamoille County Weekly*. The main object, she wrote me, was to get as many players' names as possible into her stories, so that their mothers would buy the paper. "I have a funny press pass that the publisher made up," she added. "It's an attempt to make me seem very professional, but the publisher, who's an old friend of mine, can't spell very well. 'This card,' it says, 'entitles the barer . . .' It didn't get me into the press room in Montreal." *25*

Ron was working as a carpenter and a substitute high-school teacher, and he and Linda were excited by the discovery that Burlington had a team (more than one team, it turned out) in a local semi-pro league. Ron hoped to play there—hoped to pitch, in fact, if he got any help from a local orthopedist who was said to specialize in sports medicine. "We'll see," Linda concluded. "I'd rather see Ron pitching and playing than substituting Great Civilization." She urged me to come and visit them, and watch Ron pitch. *26*

I put it in my mind to keep that date—it would be the coming summer, the summer of 1980—but the next letter changed my plans. Ron had cancer. They had found a lump in his abdomen, which was removed by surgery. Subsequently, he underwent another operation and lost one testicle. It was seminoma—a highly curable form of the disease, the doctors said. Ron was going into the Burlington hospital every day for radiation treatments. "I can't stand to see him hooked up to all those tubes in the hospital, and worried about how he's going to look in the locker room," Linda wrote. "I'm not sure I understand why it is that good people and athletes can be struck this way. It's pretty weird, *27* is all. But Ron is unflappable. He's out pitching snowballs at trees and making plans to play on the Burlington team somehow. But I have a feeling it's going to take a lot to get the boy in shape this spring. Street & Smith's are out [the early-season baseball yearbook]. Ron and his buddies are ranking the teams and giving them their finishing places this year. Winner gets a six-pack from each loser."

Ron Goble had a good summer, though—much better than he or anyone else had expected. In May and June, he coached a team of thirteen-to-fifteen-year-olds in the local Babe Ruth League, and at the same time he tried out for the Burlington A's, in the semi-pro Northern League, and made the club. For a time, he was so weak from the effects of his illness and the radiation that he could pitch no more than two or three innings at a stretch, but he learned how to conserve his energy by warming up only briefly and by trying to throw ground-ball outs. By the end of the brief season, he was able to pitch a full game, and he wound up with a respectable 4–1 record. He never told anyone on the club, last year or this year, that he had had cancer. Last winter, he worked as a teacher's aide at the Bellows Free Academy, in St. Albans, Vermont, and as a custodian at the local rink, but most of his energy went into an attempt to organize a new Northern League club in St. Albans. It fell through—not enough local money, not enough local commercial enthusiasm—but by springtime Ron had been signed on as a regional commission scout by the Milwaukee Brewers (Gerry Craft, his old manager, was a Brewers district scout, and had recommended Ron), and he was umpiring high-school games. He would pitch again for the A's this summer. Linda was teaching humanities courses at the local community college. Things were looking good; they wanted me to drive up and see them.

The bad news, Linda wrote, had come earlier and from far away: Danny Thomas had hanged himself in a jail cell in Alabama, where he had been facing trial on a rape charge. "It came as a real shock," Linda wrote. "What bothers me is that baseball has been a savior for Ron. Last spring, it brought back his confidence in himself and in his body. And here's someone like Danny Thomas who saw baseball as his pain. Danny had a strange look in his eyes when he talked about religion, and reporters were always after him to talk about his beliefs. Everyone knew he was slightly wacko, but the man had principles. His wife, Judy, was really afraid he'd take Charlie Finley up on that offer to come back to major-league ball. She said she couldn't stand that stuff again. Ron says Danny could hit a baseball farther than anyone he's ever seen. I saw him hit a home run out of every ballpark where I saw the Buckskins play. The last day I saw him play was in Bellingham. It was raining, and Danny's little daughter, Renee, was sitting up in the bleachers with Gerry Craft's daughter, Maizee, and singing 'Take me out to the ballgame, take me out to the ballgame,' slapping their hands on their thighs. The girls didn't know any of the other words, so they sang that over and over again."

On a cool, windy-bright Saturday at the end of last June, I drove straight north through Connecticut, through Massachusetts, and into Vermont, crossing and recrossing the narrowing Connecticut River along the way, and at last, over the river one more time, I found the Burlington A's at play against the Walpole (New Hampshire) Blue Jays on the Walpole home field—a neat little American Legion diamond just beneath a steep, thickly wooded hillside, hard by the Hubbard Farms fertilizer plant. At play and then *not* at play, since the A's had knocked off the Jays, 4–1, at the moment of my arrival, in the first game of a doubleheader. I met Linda Kittell at the field—a dark-haired young woman in faded bluejeans, with pale eyes, an open, alert expression, and an enormous smile. Then I shook hands with the A's manager, Paul Farrar; with Paul's wife, Sue; and, at last, with Ron Goble—a pitcher, all right: long arms, long hands, long body, very long legs, a sun-burnished nose, a surprising blondish Fu Manchu mustache, a shy smile, and one bulging cheek (not tobacco, it turned out, but sunflower seeds). Ron and Paul said what a shame it was I'd missed the opener, and then quickly ducked back out onto the field and into their little concrete dugout to get ready for the next one—Ron to chart pitches and keep score (he would pitch the next day, down in Brattleboro), and his skipper, of course, to worry. Linda and I sat down in an upper row of a tiny rack of bleachers in short right field. We had no trouble finding seats. My quick count of the house, after the nightcap had begun, came to thirty-three, including babies in strollers. Several young women—players' wives or players' girlfriends, probably—were lying on blankets spread out behind the backstop, where they took turns slathering each other's backs with suntan goop. Near the Walpole dugout, a ten- or twelve-year-old girl on an aluminum camp chair watched the game in company with a big chocolate-brown Labrador, holding him out of the action (and breaking his heart) with a yellow leash. Whenever a foul ball flew past us, someone in the audience would get up and amble after it, while we in the bleachers called out directions ("More right, more right—*now* another step!") until it had been tracked down in the thick meadow weeds around the field. There was a lot of clapping and cries of encouragement ("Good eye, batter! Good eye!") from the little crowd, and between batters and innings you could hear the cool, gusty northwest wind working through the green treetop canopies of ash and oak and maple on the hillside out beyond right field.

In the first inning, the Walpole batters whacked some long ³¹ drives against the visitors' starting pitcher, and some short ones, too, and pretty soon Burlington's designated hitter, Darcy Spear, came out of the dugout and began warming up with a catcher— not a good turn of events, Linda told me, because the team had been able to scrape up only four pitchers for its two-day, four-game weekend road trip here to the southern end of the league. The players had driven down in their own cars and pick-ups, but the team, she said, would pay for their motel accommodations in Brattleboro that night. There were no programs, and I was lucky to have Linda there to identify some of the A's whose style afield or at the plate I was beginning to pick up—a diminutive second baseman, Greg Wells, who had a nice way of looking the ball into his glove on grounders; a strong-armed shortstop named Rob DelBianco; and Tinker Jarvis, at third, who had driven in a pair of runs in the top of the first inning with a line-drive double and then singled sharply in the third. The A's wore the same combination of garish buttercup-yellow shirts, white pants, and white shoes first made famous by the Oakland A's, while the Walpole nine sported a variation of Toronto Blue Jays home whites, but there was no connection between these local teams and their big-league namesakes, Linda explained; rather, the manufacturer supplying the Northern League had offered bargain rates on these pre-styled uniforms—sort of like a Seventh Avenue dress house knocking off mass copies of Diors and Balmains. A distinguishing feature of this particular summer line was the names of various hometown commercial sponsors that the players wore on their backs, and before long I realized that I had begun to identify the different A's players by these billboards rather than by the names that Linda had murmured to me. Thus Darcy Spear became Uncle Sam's Dairy Bar, and it was Coca-Cola, the left-handed first baseman, who kept up a patter of encouraging talk to Red Barn on the mound (Red Barn had settled down after that first inning), while Slayton's Roofing (Manager Farrar) paced up and down in front of his dugout and waited for a chance to send the large and menacing-looking Cake World up to pinch-hit and get something started out there. Linda said it was all right for me to think of the players this way, because they often called each other by the sponsors' names anyway, for fun—except for Ron (Community Bingo), who was called Pigeon, because of his sunflower seeds. The A's players had been expected to hunt up their own sponsors at the beginning of the season, but not all of them, I noticed, had been successful. Each sponsor had put up a hundred dollars for his walking (or running and throwing, and sometimes popping-up-in-the-clutch) advertisement, and each sponsored player had sewn on his own commercial or had prevailed upon someone else—his mother, perhaps—to sew it on for him.

The Northern League, which encompasses six teams—the Burlington A's, the Burlington Expos, the South Burlington Queen City Royals, the Walpole Blue Jays, the Brattleboro Maples, and the Saxtons River Pirates—and also plays against the Glens Falls (New York) Glensox, is a semi-professional circuit, with the stronger emphasis, I had begun to understand, falling on the "semi." In the distant past, semi-pro ball teams were often composed of skilled local amateurs plus a handful of ringers—a couple of hard-hitting rookie outfielders just starting on their professional careers, perhaps, or a wily, shopworn pro pitcher at the very end of his—who played for modest salaries, or even for a flat per-game fee. This system fell into difficulties when increasing numbers of young athletes began to go off to college, where they found that they were not permitted to play varsity ball, because their semi-pro experience had compromised their status as amateurs. An earlier, extremely popular Northern League, with teams at Burlington, Montpelier, Rutland, St. Johnsbury, and other northwestern New England towns, came apart in 1952, partly because its Big Ten college stars were withdrawn by their schools to prevent the loss of their amateur status, and thus never appeared in games with professionals of the likes of Johnny Antonelli, Robin Roberts, Ray Scarborough, Snuffy Stirnweiss, Johnny Podres, and Boo Ferriss, who had all played on its diamonds at one time or another before moving on up through the minors and then to fame and success as major-leaguers. Nowadays, many semi-pro teams simply find summer jobs for their players—a lumber company, let's say, putting a college fastball pitcher to work in the drying sheds by day so that he may advertise the concern out on the mound at the town field by night or on weekend afternoons—but only the Burlington Expos, who are looked upon as the Yankees of the Northern League, had managed to arrange this kind of tie-in this summer, and then only for a few of their players.

The Northern League is an independent body, with its own commissioner, its own set of rules (the d.h., aluminum bats for those who want to use them), and its own ways (including a ritual handshake between the players on rival clubs at the conclusion of every game—a pleasing custom probably lifted from the National Hockey League, whose teams line up and shake hands at the conclusion of each Stanley Cup elimination series). The six clubs play an official two-month schedule, from late May to late July, with playoffs and a championship series thereafter—about twenty-five or twenty-seven games each, with a good number of additional, informal, outside-the-standings games thrown in whenever they can be arranged. A minimum team budget, I learned, runs about three thousand dollars, and, beyond the obvious expenditures for equipment, goes for umpires (two umps, at twenty-five dollars each, for every game), a league fee of two hundred dollars (to keep statistics, handle publicity, and stage the league's All-Star Game), a modest insurance policy covering minor player injuries, and so forth. Income, beyond sponsorships, comes from ticket sales—a dollar for adults, fifty cents for children, babies and dogs free. The Burlington A's' entire season's operation probably costs less than a major-league team's bill for adhesive tape and foul balls during a week's play, but the Northern League, now in its third year, is doing well and expects to add at least two more clubs next summer.

All semi-pro leagues, it should be understood, are self-sustaining, and have no farm affiliation or other connection with the twenty-six major-league clubs, or with the seventeen leagues and hundred and fifty-two teams (ranging from Rookie League at the lowest level, to Class A and Summer Class A, up to the AAA designation at the highest) that make up the National Association—the minors, that is. There is no central body of semi-pro teams, and semi-pro players are not included among the six hundred and fifty major-leaguers, the twenty-five hundred-odd minor-leaguers, plus all the managers, coaches, presidents, commissioners, front-office people, and scouts, who, taken together, constitute the great tent called organized ball. (A much diminished tent, at that; back in 1949, the minors included fifty-nine leagues, about four hundred and forty-eight teams, and perhaps ten thousand players.) Also outside the tent, but perhaps within its shade, are five college leagues, ranging across the country from Cape Cod to Alaska, where the most promising freshman, sophomore, and junior-college ballplayers may compete against each other in the summertime without losing their amateur status; the leagues are administered by the National Collegiate Athletic Association and receive indirect support— bats, balls, uniforms, and the like—from the major leagues, whose scouts keep a careful eye on their young stars. If the college leagues are semi-pro, the accent there probably should fall on the second word, for a considerable number of their best batters and pitchers are snapped up in the major-league amateur draft toward the end of their college careers. Scouts cover the Northern League as well—two pitchers with the Burlington Expos were signed to professional contracts this June, and they moved along at once to join their assigned minor-league clubs— but the level of play is not up to that of the college leagues. Most of the A's players, I learned in time, are undergraduates or recent graduates of local or eastern colleges (five of them from the University of Vermont, one from the University of New Hampshire, one from Amherst, one from the University of New Haven, and so on) who play for the fun of the game and the heat of the competition, and perhaps with half an eye turned toward the stands between pitches, in search of a major-league scout sitting there one afternoon who might just possibly be writing notes about this one good-looking outfielder or batter out there, whom he had somehow passed over the first time around. Ron Goble, at twenty-nine, was the oldest regular with the Burlington A's, and one of the few players in the league with any experience in professional ball.

How well did the A's play baseball? I found the question a dif- 35
ficult one at first, for the over-all quality of play in any one game
tends to blur one's baseball judgment, but it did seem plain that
most of the young players here on the Walpole ball field were far
too slow afoot to merit comparison with professionals. Some
threw well, as I have said, and others attacked the ball at the
plate with consistency and power, but these two gifts did not
seem to coexist in any one player. Most of all, the A's seemed
young. They were all extremely cheerful, and, as I now found
out, they loved to win. Down a run in their last at-bats (the seventh inning, in this doubleheader), the A's put their lead-off man
aboard on a walk and instantly moved him up with a dazzling
bunt by second baseman Greg Wells, who also knocked the
catcher's peg out of the first baseman's mitt as he crossed the bag,
and was safe. A moment later, with the bases loaded, Uncle
Sam's Dairy Bar (Darcy Spear) whacked a single, good for two
runs, and then the commercially anonymous catcher (Bob Boucher)
tripled to deep center. Walpole, whose handful of wives and parents had gone speechless with dismay, changed pitchers, but
Churchill's (Tinker Jarvis) singled, too, and before it was over
the visiting A's had scored six runs and won the game, 9–4,
sweeping the doubleheader. Ron Goble, ambling over to join us,
hugged Linda and grinned at me and asked if I couldn't take the
rest of the summer off to watch the A's and thus bring them
through the rest of their season undefeated.

Steve Gallacher pitched the opener against the Brattleboro 36
Maples the next afternoon—a strong twenty-two-year-old right-
hander with a good, live fastball. The A's took up their hitting
where they had left off the previous evening and moved smartly
to a three-run lead in the top of the first. Linda and I sat in the
last row of the grandstand, behind the decaying foul screen; it
was a high-school field, a bit seedy but with a nice view to the
south of some distant farms and silos and long fields of young
corn sloping down toward the Connecticut River.

Linda told me that Steve Gallacher was said to have been the 37
last man cut at a Pirates' tryout camp a year or two ago, and
later had a Dodger scout on his trail, although nothing had come
of it. I asked her how many people in the league still hoped to
make a career in professional ball someday.

"If you have a chance, you have to see it through," she said at   38
once. "It doesn't mean anything if you don't do something about
it—really find out. So many of these players are unrealistic to
think they could ever play minor-league ball. They go out and
buy these expensive A's warmup jackets, which they can't really
afford. I can see them all seventy-five years from now, saying,
'Well, I used to play semi-pro ball.' And Ron will probably be
saying, 'I pitched this one great game for the Boise Buckskins.'
I'd like to see something better than that for him in the end. Ron
is always looking backward, and I think I like to look ahead.
When he goes out scouting for the Brewers, he watches pitchers
a lot, and maybe left-handed pitchers most of all. I think he still
thinks he's better than most of the young pitchers he scouts."

She had been talking in an edged, hard tone I had not heard   39
before, but now she stopped and shook her head and then
laughed at herself a little—a habit of hers, I had begun to notice.
"I guess Ron is even more of a hero to me than Whitey Ford
was," she said more softly. "I like heroes. I have a lot of trouble
with reality, too. I hate it when he plays softball, because all the
other players on his team take it so seriously. Softball is—well,
it's like badminton, or something. It's nothing, compared to
baseball. I've told Ron he'll have to give up baseball when he
looks better in his street clothes than he does in his uniform."
She laughed again—almost a giggle. "He's still a long way from
that!" she said.

We watched the game for a while, but Linda seemed tense and   40
distracted, and it came to me at last that she was worrying about
how well Ron would pitch in the second game. Suddenly she
said, "With all the people I've known in baseball, I can't think of
one happy ending. Danny Thomas, Gerry Craft, Ron—none of it
came out happily. You know, it isn't like Chris Chambliss coming up in the ninth inning of that playoff game and unbuttoning
the top button of his shirt and then hitting that home run. You
just don't see that happen. Ron hurt his arm before he got
started. Gerry Craft got up as far as Lodi, in the Orioles system,
and he was on his way—a good outfielder. Then he got hurt and
it was all finished, overnight. Danny Thomas is dead. What's the
reality? I ask myself that all the time."

The Brattleboro hitters kept after Steve Gallacher, and then   41
caught up with him and went ahead by 5–4 in the bottom of the

fifth, with three solid blows. They were looking for his fastball by this time, and I wondered what would happen if he could show them a breaking pitch now and then in a tough spot. Young pitchers love the heater, but so do good young hitters. The A's put their lead-off man aboard in the top of the seventh, but the Maples' pitcher, a young redhead named Parmenter, threw some impressive-looking sliders and shut off the rally. It was a quick, well-played game, and the local fans—a much better turnout today—gave their boys a good hand at the end.

Ron Goble started the second game, and I found that I was a 42 bit nervous, too. I needn't have worried. He set down the side in order in the first, and even though the Maples touched him up for a pair of runs in the second, on a walk and a couple of singles, he looked unstressed and in control out there, never attempting to force a delivery or to work beyond his capacities. He ended up the inning by fanning the side—a good sign. He is a graceful-looking pitcher. My game notes about him read:

> Tall, v. long legs. Minimal rock & motion. Drops glove behind leg-crook (southpaw). Long upper-bod. and uses good upper-bod. with fastball. Fastball just fair. Good curve. Goes sidearm at times for strikeout. About ¾ otherwise. Good pitcher's build. Control fair. Long stride but doesn't drop down. Curve/slider break down. Changes speed w/o effort. Sense of flow. Pitches patterned. Intell. Knows how to pitch.

On this particular day, Ron also had the A's hitters going for 43 him, for they came up with six runs in the third and six more in the sixth, the latter outburst including two singles, a nifty squeeze bunt, a double, a pinch-hit triple by Cake World, and a home run by Coca-Cola. The last batter of the inning was Manager Paul Farrar, who sent himself up as a pinch-hitter now that matters were in hand. He is a friendly, medium-sized man with curly hair and metal-rimmed glasses—he is also a backup catcher for the club—and his players razzed him happily when he stepped up to the plate, calling him Satch and asking if he didn't want the Maples' pitcher to throw from farther back out there. He fanned, to raucous cheers. The A's won it by 16–4—a laugher, but Ron had pitched well, surrendering only four hits. Near the end, Linda began to relax a little in her seat. At one point, she saw me watching her, and she laughed and shrugged.

"Ron's mother used to tell me what to do when he was pitching," she said. "She always said, 'Watch the ball, not the pitcher. Never look at the pitcher.' I wish I could remember that."

Ron and Linda live in a worn brown farmhouse next to a collapsing gray shingle barn, at the very end of a twisting, climbing two-mile-long dirt road. On a map, they are in the upper northwest corner of the state. St. Albans, the nearest real town, is fifteen miles to the west, on the shore of Lake Champlain, and the Canadian border is about the same distance due north. The house, which they rent, is on the side of a hill (*everything* in Vermont is on the side of a hill) and is set about with maples, an elderly lilac bush, and a high stand of burdock. Ron's vegetable garden is up the hill, behind the house. There is a small unpainted front porch with missing steps, which makes it look a little like the front stoop of a sharecropper's place. No matter: the view from here is across many miles of hazy-green rolling farmland toward some distant blue mountains. There isn't much furniture inside—a few castoff schoolroom chairs, with iron pedestal bases, that stand around the dining table, and one overflowing easy chair. The most prominent object is a modern cast-iron heating stove, right in the middle of the room, with a long outlet pipe snaking up through the ceiling. Upstairs, the bathroom has been recently panelled and fitted out with a shower. The best room in the house is a sun-filled upstairs bedroom, five windows wide. A cluster of sports pennants is pinned to one wall there, with their points all streaming to starboard, as if in a stiff breeze: the Mariners, the Yankees, Idaho U., the Clinton Clowns (Ron's old softball team), and one banner with a misshapen felt baseball and the words "I'm a Backer" (a Buckskin backer, that is) on it. On the opposite wall, there is a framed Idaho potato bag depicting (as best one can depict on burlap) a full-rigged ship and inscribed "Tradewind Brand." Linda's desk and Selectric are under one window, next to an overflowing bookshelf: contemporary poets (she writes poetry), classics, English Lit. textbooks—everything. On one windowsill, a philodendron is growing in a small white pot in the shape of a baseball shoe; on another rests a narrow cardboard box containing the complete 1981 Topps bubble-gum baseball-card collection. At the other end of the room, another bookcase offers a considerable paperback collection of contemporary Latin-American fiction, in translation: Borges, García Márquez, Jorge Amado, Machado de Assis, and others. These, I learned, are Ron's. "When I finished my season with the Buckskins, I was told my arm might heal if I could rest it long enough," he told me, "and I began to fantasize that it *would* heal. It was an excuse not to work, so I just sat and read. I was reading García Márquez's 'Leaf Storm' just then, and when I finished that I read 'One Hundred Years of Solitude' and then 'The Autumn of the Patriarch.' I drank a lot of Colombian coffee while I read, and it was like I'd gone off to another country."

When Ron Goble graduated from Capital High School in   45
Boise in the spring of 1969, he accepted a fifteen-hundred-dollar baseball scholarship at Linfield, a small (one thousand students) college in McMinnville, Oregon. He had been an outstanding player in his local American Legion baseball program for several summers (young ballplayers who start in the Little Leagues at the age of eight may graduate to the Babe Ruth League at the age of thirteen and then move along to American Legion teams at sixteen), and he had been named to the all-state team in his senior year at school, as a first baseman. His pitching arm began to mature at about the same time, and when his fastball was clocked at better than ninety miles an hour the scouts began to take notice of him. When he went to Linfield, his real hope was not just to pitch for the varsity team there but to find a more relaxed and varied social and political atmosphere. At Capital High, sports and unquestioning patriotism had seemed to go hand in hand. Capital's teams were known as the Eagles, and varsity athletes were told to keep their hair cut in the "Eagle-pride" style—so short that it couldn't be parted—and there was constant pressure on the larger and quicker boys to make their major school commitment to the football team. Ron played tight end and safety and sometimes quarterback for the Eagles, but he didn't much like football; he was also made uncomfortable by the fact that his own sport, baseball, was considered effete—"sort of a pansy game," as he put it. But things weren't much different at Linfield, he discovered. The jocks there were expected to keep their hair cut short, too, and to think more about winning seasons than about Vietnam and Cambodia and the other political and social crises that were convulsing the

nation at the time. Ron was not an activist, but his parents—his father is a state fire-insurance inspector—had always encouraged their three sons to think for themselves. Ron's older brother, Dale, had been an undergraduate at Columbia during the student riots there in 1968, and had brought home tapes he had recorded of the impassioned speeches and the crowd roars during those tumultuous days, and Ron had played these over many times. He was an athlete but he was also a reader and a student, and he felt isolated at Linfield. Early in May of his freshman year, he heard the news of the appalling events at Kent State University, and he and five or six friends went to the Linfield student-union building and lowered the flags there, in honor of the demonstrating students who had been shot by National Guardsmen in Ohio. Only two or three people of the hundreds who walked by stopped to ask what the lowered flags meant, and the next day one of Ron's coaches told him that he had "the wrong orientation" about politics. The next fall, Ron transferred to the University of Idaho and gave up varsity sports.

Ron told me all this in a quiet, almost apologetic manner. His   46
voice is modulated and unforced, and somehow suggests his pitching motion. Like some other young men and women of his generation, or quarter-generation, he takes pains never to sound assured, never to strike an attitude. "I wasn't a real political dissident, you understand," he said. "I cared—I still care—but I didn't know what I was doing. At Idaho, I went down to the R.O.T.C. Building one night and stole Richard Nixon's picture out of its frame there. Big piddly-assed deal."

He laughed, and Linda joined in the laughter. We were sitting   47
out on their porch, drinking beer, and their two English setters, Boone and Hannah, were running and sniffing through an overgrown meadow before us, with their feathery white tails marking their progress through the long grass. Once, Boone got on the trail of something and took off downhill, but Ron turned him with a piercing, two-fingered whistle.

"Tell about the time you decided to go back and play ball,"   48
Linda said.

"Oh, geezum," Ron said, smiling. "Well, after a while there at   49
Moscow"—Moscow, Idaho, is the university seat—"I began to reconcile sports and politics a little, and I saw that I wasn't quite the great political radical I'd thought I was. For a while, I'd even

stopped collecting baseball cards, but I sure missed playing ball, especially in the spring, and so one day I went down to see the baseball coach. I was going to offer to come out, if he wanted me, but when I got there his office was closed, and I took that as a sign. I decided it wasn't my karma to play ball yet."

"It wasn't your *karma!*" Linda said, doubled over with laugh- 50 ter. "Can you *believe* that now!" They cracked up, thinking about it.

In his last two years at Idaho, Ron lived with two friends on a 51 farm twenty-six miles away from the campus, where they raised chickens and helped the farmer with his planting and other chores. Ron was a pre-law student, majoring in political science, and he had looked forward to going to law school, but now something had changed for him, and he found himself more interested in the farm and in outdoor life. "I just got tired of school," he said. He had let his hair grow long, and he realized that most of his classmates probably thought of him as a hippie. After he graduated, he moved to Missoula because he loved its setting—the high country and the cold streams of the Bitterroot Range and the Garnet Mountains—and found work as a janitor at the University of Montana.

"I just wanted something to do so I could keep on fishing and 52 backpacking," he said. "There were a lot of people with the same idea there at that time. It was what was happening. That's great country, out along the Clark Fork and the Big Blackfoot, if you like fishing. You could walk across the Milwaukee Road railroad tracks behind our house and cross the floodplain and you'd be fishing in just five minutes."

Our house: He had met Linda, and they had moved into a log 53 cabin in Clinton, which is twenty miles southeast of Missoula. She was in graduate school at Montana, majoring in creative writing. She also tutored undergraduates in English and Greek, and after she had picked up her master's degree she worked in a Poetry in the Schools program in the state school system and then became poet-in-residence and a teacher at a private school in Missoula. She and Ron talked baseball and followed the Yankees from a distance, as she wrote me in her first letter, but softball was the only game in town.

Ron said, "Every spring, I'd think, Geezum, I've made it 54 through the winter again—and they were long, long winters there, you know—and I'd get that little urge. I'd go off fishing, and when I got my arm working back and forth with the fishing pole [he said "pole," not "rod"] it was sort of like throwing a curveball. I was spring-strong, and I'd get to wondering what I could have done if I'd gone on in baseball. Each spring was like that. Then when I read that notice in *The Sporting News* about the Buckskins' tryout camp, I realized that it had been eight years since I'd pitched in a ballgame. I couldn't believe it."

This must have sounded self-pitying to Ron when he said it to   55
me, there on the porch, and he corrected himself at once. "It was my own fault," he said. "There was fear, I guess, and then I began to rationalize it all and remind myself that I'd have to go to a tryout camp if I wanted to come back, and maybe I'd fail. What I'd had was a marginal talent—a pretty good high-school fastball—and if I was ever going to do something with it, I would have had to pay the price. I didn't want to have to work at it, I think, or else I just didn't want to work that hard. So I let it go by."

Late one afternoon that week, I watched another team of   56
country ballplayers wearing sponsors' names on the backs of their uniform shirts—Waterville Garage, Tobin Construction, Gerald W. Tatro—in a game played on still another hillside diamond. The field was unfenced, and the woods and brush along the rightfield foul line crowded in so close that there wouldn't have been room for bleachers or any other kind of seats there. It was a *field*: the shaggy grass around second base was white with clover blossoms. We were in Belvidere, Vermont—a Green Mountain village a bit to the north and east of Mt. Mansfield— and the game pitted the home team of Belvidere-Waterville against the visiting Morrisville nine. These were Babe Ruth League teams, whose players range in age from thirteen to fifteen years, but the Belvidere-Watervilles seemed to be outweighed by a couple of dozen pounds and outsized by a couple of inches at almost every position. Outmanned, too: only eight home-team players had turned up for the game, and their coach, Curt Koonz, was filling in at shortstop. The disparity was most noticeable on the mound, for the Belvidere-Waterville pitcher, Earl Domina, was so short that the white pants of his uniform were within an inch or two of swallowing his shoes. He worked hard out there, toeing the rubber in good style and hiding the ball behind his hip while he stared in at his catcher for the sign, but he

wasn't big enough to get much stuff on his pitches, and it sometimes looked as if he were throwing uphill against the tall, half-
grinning Morrisville boys. Earl was being hit hard—the bases
were repeatedly loaded and then unloaded against him in the
two or three innings I saw him play—and he also had to put up
with a few throwing-uphill jokes from his own teammates, but
he kept his concentration and his seriousness, jutting his jaw on
the mound and staring the base runners into place before each
pitch, and in time the smiles and the jokes died away. He was
a battler.

I had heard a good deal about the problems and triumphs of
the Belvidere-Waterville Babe Ruth League team from its previous coach, Ron Goble, who had been greeted with hand slaps
and jokes and cheerful body blocks by his former troops when
we turned up at the game that afternoon. (He and Linda lived in
Waterville when they first came to Vermont, but their present
house is some thirty miles to the northwest—too far for him to
keep up with his Babe Ruth League coaching while he also continues to pitch for the A's.) Now he pointed out some of his stal-
warts from the previous year's squad—Peanut Coburn, the
team's best shortstop, best outfielder, best first baseman, best
everything, who had graduated to assistant coach; the Eldred
brothers, Keith and Mike; some others. He said that a few of his
players last year had come up through a Little League program,
but others had never played an inning of baseball before their
season got under way. There weren't many players in either category, to tell the truth, so everybody got a chance to play, including Kim Wescom and Angie Tourangeau, who are girls. Kim,
a second baseperson, always wore blue eyeshadow with her
game uniform—a complicated announcement, Linda thought.
All the teams that Belvidere-Waterville faced were larger and
more experienced than they were, and the enemy players razzed
them unmercifully for playing girls and for looking like hicks.

"Well, we *were* hicks," Ron said to me. "We were a country
team, and most of our players came from poor families, so after
a while we took that as our team name. We became the Hicks."
The razzing never got entirely out of hand, in any case, because
after a couple of innings of it, Frank Machia, the Belvidere-
Waterville first baseman, would take a few steps over toward the
other team bench and invite the critics there to step forward.
Frank was fifteen, but he has a Boog Powell-style chest and belly,

topped off by a full beard, and so things usually quieted down in a hurry. The continuing trouble—the real trouble—was that the team wasn't good enough to win. One very bad day came at Stowe, a wealthy ski-resort town at the foot of Mt. Mansfield (its Babe Ruth League team even has different uniforms for home and away games), where the game was called, by mutual consent, when Belvidere-Waterville had fallen behind by 35–3, or 36–5, or something like that.

Ron told me that one of the team's handicaps had been the lack of a decent home field to practice and play on, and after the Stowe disaster he and Linda and a few other devout team backers—Larry and Shirley Brown, Olive McClain, and Emmett Eldred—went over to the abandoned Smithville diamond, in Belvidere, which had long ago turned into a meadow, and attacked it with hand mowers. After three long, hot days' work—a horrendous job, everyone agreed—the hay was cut and raked, and a new backstop had been erected, just in time for the return game against Stowe, which turned up with a considerable entourage to watch the continuation of the slaughter.

"Well, we didn't beat them," Ron said. "It was 9–6, Stowe, in the end, but we *almost* beat them, and they sure knew they'd been in a game. We showed them we could play, and that made the whole season worthwhile."

I asked how the team had fared after that.

"The truth is, we lost all fourteen games on our schedule," he said. "No, that's not right—we took one on a forfeit, when the other team didn't turn up. But it meant a lot to these kids, learning how to play ball, learning to enjoy it. By the end of the season, they were backing up plays and sometimes hitting the cutoff man on their throws, even though that was mostly because they couldn't throw the ball all the way home anyway. They're all good kids. There isn't much else to do around here in the summers, you know, and that kept them at it."

The game we had been watching ended at 11–4, Morrisville, and the young players began to drift away, some in their parents' cars and pickups, some on bikes, and some on foot. The Belvidere-Waterville bats and batting helmets were stuffed into a gunnysack and toted away. It was evening, or almost evening, by now, but the field was at once repopulated by softball players—a pickup, slow-pitch game, arranged by telephone earlier that day. Ron played and so did Earl Domina—a long pitcher and a very short one, both playing in the same outfield now—and more cars pulled up by the field as the news of the game got around, and soon there were twelve or thirteen players on a side out there in the warm, mosquitoey half-light. Linda didn't play, and I sat it out, too, keeping her company. We were at a worn, teetery old picnic table, where we gnawed on some cold roast chicken she had brought along, and in time we were joined there by Larry Brown, a shy, slightly built, soft-spoken man, who often looks at the ground when he speaks. Larry Brown is the Branch Rickey of Belvidere baseball. He is an asbestos miner—a laborer—with a modest seasonal sideline in maple syrup made from his own hillside sugar bush. Still in his forties, he has six children and two grandchildren.

He told me that he had been a catcher for the Belvidere town team when he was a younger man. "It was all town teams around here then," he said. "I'd like to see those days come back again. Maybe they will. Back when I was a boy, all I had was a bat and one old taped-up ball. It wasn't all organized, the way it is now. Now I don't think there's a single town team in Lamoille County, but there are eight hundred boys playing Little League and Babe Ruth ball." 64

His doing—in part, at least. Larry Brown got the Belvidere Little League started, about five years ago. (In fact, a Little League game had been in progress off at the other end of the same field that the Babe Ruth teams were using that afternoon, and I had been struck by the fact that all the players on both teams had full uniforms. Seeing so many players in action at the same time almost reminded me of spring training.) Larry Brown found sponsors, got the parents involved, raised the money for uniforms and bats and balls. Last year, when Ron and Linda turned up in Waterville, he sought out Ron and persuaded him to take on the town's very first Babe Ruth team. Larry didn't know that Ron was still recovering from his cancer surgery and from the debilitating radiation treatments that had ensued, but Larry had been wonderfully persuasive, and the job, Ron must have realized almost at once, was a perfect one for him at that moment: cheerful and funny and full of hope. When the season ended, with most of those hopes still unrewarded, Larry Brown and his wife threw a big potluck dinner for the team. Ron gave a speech, summarizing the summer's high points—the time Mike Eldred lost both sneakers while trying to steal second base (and 65 turned back at once to get them), Angie Tourangeau's single that didn't count because the ump said he wasn't ready, the two games against Stowe. . . . Everyone had such a good time at the dinner that they all decided to chip in and arrange a team trip up to Montreal for an Expos game. Later in the summer, they did it again. Baseball has caught on in Belvidere.

I asked Larry Brown if anyone from Lamoille County had   66
ever made it to the big leagues.

"No, I don't think so," he said, still smiling and still looking   67
at the ground. "Though there was so many that played ball and watched ball around here in the old days you'd think it'd happen, wouldn't you? Why, I can remember going over to St. Albans when they had a team in the old Northern League here—the Giants, they were—and they'd have a thousand people there at Coote Field. A thousand, easy. But we had some mighty good players around here. Don McCuin played for our team—the Belvidere team, I mean—right after the war. He was a left-handed pitcher. He was signed by the Cardinals organization, but when he got down there he found he couldn't play ball in the heat, there in the South. And there was another good left-hander, named Sonny Davis, just about that time. Funny you'd have two so good, who was both the same kind. He played for Stowe. He signed up with the Braves, back in the nineteen-forties. Sonny told me once that he'd played in a game with young Henry Aaron, who was just a beginner, too, at the time, and when Sonny saw Aaron hit some drives in batting practice he suddenly understood that he was never going to make it in major-league baseball."

All three of us laughed. It was almost dark now, and when-   68
ever somebody on the ball field made contact (with that heavy, smacking sound that a softball makes against the bat), the arching ball looked like some strange gray night bird suddenly rising out of the treetops.

"Leonard McCuin was as good as Don was, from all I hear,"   69
Larry went on. "He was Don's father. Leonard once played on a team over to Saranac Lake, where Christy Mathewson was his coach. Mathewson was there because he had tuberculosis, you know. I guess he was about dead of it by then. Funny, I always thought Don McCuin had the head for major-league baseball. It was his arm that was at fault. But I liked the way he pitched. I always compared Don to Warren Spahn—a classic left-hander

with that high kick. I don't think there was ever a smarter pitcher than Spahn. But I'm not one of those who goes around always saying that the old players were the best. I've been up to Montreal for some games, now that the teams are so close—I almost went *broke* the first summer the Expos was playing!—and I think there's been no better players than some we've seen in our time. You only have to go back a few years to when Aaron and Mays and Clemente were still playing, you know, and you just couldn't come up with a better outfield than that. They say Roberto Clemente was the least appreciated ballplayer of his time. Well, *I* appreciated him."

It was dark now, and the softball game had ended at last. Ron joined us at the picnic table, and some of his friends sat down with us, too, drinking beer and swatting mosquitoes. Little Earl Domina had gone home, waving shyly to us as he walked away into the shadows, and I told Larry how much I'd admired him in the Babe Ruth League game we'd seen.

"He's about half size for his age, but he always puts out," Larry said. "There are others I wished cared as much about it as he does. Size don't have much to do with it in this game."

Roberto Clemente and Leonard McCuin, Don McCuin and Warren Spahn, Sonny Davis and Hank Aaron, Christy Mathewson and Earl Domina—they were all together in baseball for Larry Brown. For him, the game had no fences.

I was pleased but in fact not much surprised to find someone like Larry Brown here in a corner of Vermont, for I had already met other friends of Ron's and Linda's who seemed sustained and nourished by a similar passion for baseball. One of them was Paul Farrar, the A's' manager, who normally gives six or seven hours of his day to the team during the season, beginning at four in the afternoon on weekdays, when he gets off work at the I.B.M. plant in Burlington. If there is a home game (there are also practices on some off days) at the University of Vermont's Centennial Field, where the A's play, Farrar is usually the first man to arrive. He carries in the field rakes from his car and then unlocks the concession stand and carries out the dusty bases that have been stored there since the last game. The players begin to drift onto the field while he is raking the base paths or carefully laying down the foul lines and the batter's boxes with a lime cart, and he kids them cheerfully and asks about their bruises. Long before this, while he paused at home to put on his uniform, he has picked up the day's team telephone messages from his wife, Sue. Tinker Jarvis will have to work until past seven tonight, she told him, which means not only that he won't be there in time to play but that his girlfriend, Helen Rigby, probably won't be around to work in the hotdog stand. Southpaw Joe Gay's arm is coming along, his father called to say, but the doctor still thinks it'll be another week before he'll be ready to pitch. One of the troubles is that Joe has this summer job as a housepainter, which makes it hard for him to give his arm the kind of rest it should have. (Why can't Joe paint *right*-handed for a while, Paul wonders for an instant.) The other team tonight will be perfectly willing to play nine innings, instead of seven, if the A's want to, but which of them will pay the seventy-five bucks that U.V.M. wants as a fee for using the lights? Then, there are the automobile arrangements to be made for the weekend doubleheader over at Saxtons River. . . . Paul thinks about some of this while he pitches batting practice, but then he tries to put it all out of his head when he makes out his lineup in the dugout and begins to concentrate on the game at hand. Who's got to play if we're going to win? Who ought to play because he hasn't got into enough games lately? . . .

Paul grew up in the Bronx and, of course, dreamed of playing in Yankee Stadium someday, as a big-leaguer. Then his family moved to South Burlington, and in time Paul went off to Rensselaer Polytechnic, in Troy, New York, where he played catcher for four years on the varsity team. Then he coached at R.P.I. for two years, as an assistant with the varsity, while he got his graduate degree. He is a senior associate engineer with I.B.M. He is twenty-six years old.

"Ron and I and Tinker Jarvis are the old men on the team," he said to me, "but I think it may be more fun for us than for the others. And managing is—well, it's *involving*. These games don't mean anything, but I play them again in my mind when they're over. The bunt signal we missed. The pitcher I maybe took out one batter too late. I lie in bed and play baseball in my head in the middle of the night."

Herbie Pearo lives in East Alburg, Vermont, on a peninsula jutting into Lake Champlain. He is the manager of the East Al-

burg Beavers, an amateur slow-pitch softball team that Ron
plays for whenever the A's' schedule permits it. Upstairs in his
house there, one walks into a narrow room and a narrow loft
above it—a baseball museum—stuffed to bursting with baseball
uniforms, autographed baseball bats, autographed baseballs,
caps, pairs of spikes, old baseball photographs, albums of baseball tickets, baseball programs, bubble-gum baseball cards,
everything. Some of the uniform shirts are framed, showing
names and numbers on their backs, and these include the shirts
of many present and recently past Expos—Andre Dawson, Ellis
Valentine, Steve Rogers, Rusty Staub, Warren Cromartie—for
Herbie is a terrific Expos fan. He is also a former terrific Mets
fan. The centerpiece of his present collection is Tom Seaver's
1967 Mets uniform (1967 was Seaver's first year in the majors),
which Herbie values at one thousand dollars. "Not that I'd automatically sell it," he adds. Selling items like these is Herbie
Pearo's business—a baseball-souvenir-and-tradables line known
as Centerfield Eight Sales. The business is advertised in most
standard baseball publications, and the turnover is brisk. Brisk
but often painful, because Herbie, one senses quickly, would
much rather hold on to his best stuff. He is still writhing over the
recent loss of a genuine Rogers Hornsby St. Louis Browns uniform. "I *had* to do it," he says apologetically. "The man made
me an offer I couldn't refuse—seven guaranteed All-Stars' uniforms, plus a lot of other things, but still . . ." His voice trails off,
and in his face you can almost see the Hornsby uniform still
hanging in its old place on the long wall.

Centerfield Eight is one of the hardest stores to walk out of I
have ever walked into. I was there for an hour or more, and each
time I edged closer to the staircase my eye would fasten on some
new wonder or Herbie would draw me back to look at something else. He wasn't trying to sell me anything; he simply
wanted to share it all. He was a great curator, and we were at the
Louvre. . . . Here is a ball signed by Sadaharu Oh, and a bat
signed by the Babe. Here is Pete Rose's very first Reds' shirt—
with a rookie's number, 33, on the back. Here is a Reggie Jack-
son Oakland A's shirt; here is a Roberto Clemente shirt (in the
old, sleeveless Pirates' style); and over here is an orange Charlie
Finley baseball (Finley once lobbied to have the major leagues
shift to orange baseballs); and—oh, yes—upstairs, there in the
corner, is a player's battered old locker from Connie Mack Sta-

dium, now long gone, alas. And look *here* (here in a desk drawer): A pair of genuine Phillies World Series tickets from 1962—the year the Phillies folded so horribly and didn't make the Series after all. Here is a genuine scout's contract, signed by Connie Mack himself. This is a photograph of the 1908 Portland Mohawks ("Maine's Premier Amateur Baseball Team"), and here are some 1975 White Sox World Series ducats (another blasted hope), and that's an usher's cap from Anaheim Stadium—a bargain at twenty-five bucks. But oh, *wait!* And he holds up a pair of snowy, still pressed Washington Senator home-uniform shirts on wire hangers, with a "1" on one of them and a "2" on the other—commemorative shirts made for presentation to President Nixon and Vice-President Agnew at the Senators' opening game in 1970. I stare at these particular relics in slow surprise, astounded by the possibility that I have at last come upon an object—*two* objects—in this world that may truly be said to have no meaning whatsoever.

Stunned with memorabilia, I descend the stairs at last (the balusters are bats, each with its own history), and Herbie Pearo's voice follows me down. "I wish you'd seen my Carl Furillo shirt, from the 1957 season," he says. "The real thing. I wish I hadn't sold that. I've been *kicking* myself ever since . . ."

As I have explained, my trip to visit Linda Kittell and Ron Goble was something I had looked forward to for years. It came while the midsummer major-league baseball strike was about two weeks along, but there was no connection between the two events. I was not visiting a semi-pro player because I would have preferred to call on a big-leaguer. I was not out to prove some connection or lack of connection between the expensive upper flowerings of the game and its humble underbrush. Everyone in Vermont talked about the strike, but not for long; we wanted it over, because we missed the games and the standings and the news of the sport, but I heard no bitter talk about money and free agency, "spoiled" ballplayers or selfish owners. At the same time, it occurred to me again and again while I was there (it would have been impossible to ignore the comparison or not to think about its ironies) to wonder how many big-league owners and famous players and baseball businessmen (the league presidents, and so forth, and perhaps even some of the writers) had an involvement in the game—a connection that was simply part of life itself—like Ron Goble's and Larry Brown's and Linda Kittell's. Not many, I would think, and yet at the same time it seemed quite likely to me—almost a certainty, in fact—that if I had stopped and visited friends in almost any other county or state corner in the United States I would have found their counterparts there, their friends in baseball.

Late one afternoon, Linda and Ron and I drove into Burlington for an A's game against the Queen City Royals. We were in their wheezy, ancient red Vega, and Ron kept cocking his head and listening to the engine in a nervous sort of way; a couple of weeks earlier, the car had conked out altogether on the same trip, and he had missed the game and his turn on the mound. He was in uniform tonight, but he wasn't going to play; his next start would be the following night, against the hated Burlington Expos. We were all eating ice-cream cones.

I asked Ron if he could tell me a little more about his summer with the Boise Buckskins, when he had pitched in organized ball for the first time, and everything had gone so badly for him and his teammates.

"In some ways, it wasn't exactly what you'd call a rewarding experience," he said after a moment or two. "Our pitching was downright terrible. We won on opening day, and that was sort of the highlight. Gerry Craft said opening day was God's greatest blessing but the rest of it was our trial. We had those ugly uniforms, and the fans got on us because of the religion thing, and we were always jumping off buses and going right into some park to play. It was good we had a few things going for us, like Danny Thomas. The real battle for me was not to let any of that bother me too much. I was there to prove myself. That summer answered a lot of questions for me that I would have gone on asking myself all my life. I got that albatross off my neck at last. What I discovered was that I'd had a talent at one time for throwing the ball—maybe not a major-league talent, at that. But I found out that although I couldn't throw by then—not really— I was at least a pitcher." He paused and then added his little disclaimer: "Although that may be too much of a complimentary term."

What was it about Danny Thomas, I asked. What had made him so special to them and to the whole team?

"Well, he was tall and he had those good long muscles," Ron   84
said. "You know—he looked like a ballplayer."

"And that fantastic smile," Linda said from the back seat.   85

"Yes, there was never a better-looking ballplayer, anywhere,"   86
Ron said. "And his hitting! I remember once when we were playing against the Emeralds on a road trip, and the whole park was
down on us for some reason—everyone yelling and booing and
laughing. Because we'd been looking so bad, I guess. And then
he hit one. I mean, he *hit* it—it went out over the lights and out
of the ballpark, and even before he got to first base there was this
absolute hush in the place. It was beautiful. He'd shut them up."

"Plus he wore No. 7," Linda said.   87

"That's right," Ron said at once. "The same number."   88

It was a minute before I understood. Mickey Mantle's old   89
number had been 7.

At this moment, the Vega gave a couple of despairing wheezes   90
and slowly glided to halt. We came to rest at meadowside on a
singularly unpopulated and unpromising stretch of macadam.

"Damn *carburetor*," Ron said. He popped the hood. "Ham-   91
mer," he said, swinging his long legs out, and Linda, reaching
down between her feet, found a hammer and wordlessly handed
it to him, exactly like a good instrument nurse working with
a surgeon. This operation entailed some thunderous banging
noises from up forward—not a promising prognosis at all, I
thought—but when Ron reappeared, red-faced, and restarted
the engine, it spluttered and groaned but then caught. A miracle.
"Remind me to park facing downhill when we get there," he
muttered as we resumed our course.

And so I asked him about his pitching now—pitching for the   92
Burlington A's.

"Well, it's still enjoyable," he said. "The thing about pitching   93
is—it's that it requires your concentration. It requires your entire
thought. There aren't many things in life that can bring that to
you. And every situation, every day and every inning, is different. You have to work on so many little details. Finding the flu-
idity of your body. Adjusting for different mounds. Bringing the
leg up higher, bringing it over more. You kind of expect standards of yourself, and when they're not there you have to find
out what's going wrong, and why. Maybe you're not opening up
quickly enough. Maybe you're not following through enough, or
maybe you're throwing too much across your body. Some days,

you're not snapping your wrist so much. Some days, the seams on the ball aren't so nice. It's always different."

He shook his head, and laughed at himself again. "Actually," 94 he went on, "at some level I'm always pitching in the hope that the curveball—the real old curveball—might come back some- day. Geezum, wouldn't that be nice, I think to myself. It doesn't happen, though. It's gone. Now it's different, being a pitcher, and sometimes I think it's almost more fun, because you can't just throw it by them now. You've got to trick 'em, because you've got nothing much to get them out with. So you try to set them up—get them looking away and then throw them inside. Get them backing off, and go down and away. I don't play often enough to have that happen too much—just to be able to think about location like that—but that's what it's all about."

He was right: this is what pitching is all about. I have heard a 95 good many big-league pitchers talk about their craft—hundreds of them, I suppose, including a few of the best of our time— and when they got into it, really got talking pitching, they all sounded almost exactly like Ron Goble. He probably would have denied it if I'd said it, but he was one of them, too—a pitcher.

"I know baseball is important to me," he said after another 96 moment or two. "Playing now is like getting a present, and you don't expect presents."

In Burlington, Ron swung into a gravelly downhill road lead- 97 ing to Centennial Field, and then stopped the Vega unexpectedly and walked over to a small shed on the left-hand side of the road and took from it a large, triangular wooden sign, hinged at the top like a kitchen stepladder. He and Linda carried it up to East Avenue, which we had just left, and set it up on the sidewalk there. "BASEBALL TODAY," it read. "6:00." We parked facing downhill and went down to the park—an ancient dark-green beauty, with the outfield terminating in a grove of handsome old trees. The roofed stands were steeply tilted, and the cast-iron arm at the end of each row of seats bore a "UVM" stamped into the metal. Swallows dipped in and out of the shadows under the grandstand roof. Linda and Ron pointed out the football sta- dium that rose beyond the left-field fence, and then drew my at- tention to the back of the football press box perched on its topmost rim—a good hundred feet up there, I suppose. This was history: history made about two weeks earlier, when Darcy Spear had whacked a home run against the Expos that cleared the top of the press box—a Kingman shot, an all-timer.

Ron went off to batting practice, and Linda told me she would be selling tickets up at the main automobile gate. It was still a good hour before the game with the Queen City Royals would begin, and I went along. Linda was carrying a big roll of blue tickets and a small envelope of loose change. "Shall we abscond?" I said. She looked into the envelope. "Better wait until a few customers turn up," she said. We leaned on the chain-link fence beside the open gate, listening to the distant crack of bats from the field below, and passed a bottle of warmish beer back and forth. It was a heavy, quiet summer evening.

Linda said she had hardly ever heard Ron talk about his pitching the way he had talked in the car that night. "Basically, I realize I know absolutely nothing about baseball compared to Ron," she said. "But I get tired of the other women around players, who say 'Don't you get tired of him talking about nothing but baseball?' *I hate* that. I think I like the part of Ron that I don't understand. I feel I could get all the knowledge of baseball that he has, and still not understand, because I never played baseball. It's a mystery between us, and I like that. If you know everything about a person, it's sort of a letdown. I just have no idea what he goes through out there on the mound. I get glimpses sometimes, but that's all.

"Ron is truly modest about his talent—you've seen that. I believe all the things about him that he doesn't think or say himself. I believe he could have been a major-league pitcher. I wanted everyone to know about it when he was pitching and was still sick, but he wouldn't let me tell anyone. He didn't want to bother them with it. I think that's sort of heroic. He still doesn't have his fastball back, you know."

The first two or three cars rolled up and stopped for their tickets. "Looks like a nice evening," one man said.

"Yes, it does," Linda said. "Have a nice time, now."

She came back and leaned against the fence again. "I get scared about the day when he can't play ball anymore," she said. "I get teary thinking about it sometimes. He couldn't have planned his life any differently, but sometimes I wish he wouldn't give up on himself so much. There are a lot of other things he could have done. But if he'd planned his life differently I wouldn't be around. There's no one here he can ask, but I get the idea that he knows as much about the technical side of pitching as anyone else. He just learned it himself, I think."

I said I had exactly the same impression.   104

"Sometimes he asks me to watch a particular thing when   105
he's pitching—whether he's opening his hips, say. But if he asks me about something else afterward—where his foot is coming down, or something like that—then I've totally missed it. I keep wishing his brother George was here, so he could talk baseball with him. There's so much *to* it. To me, baseball is like learning a foreign language. You never learn all the vocabulary, all the endings and idioms. It's what I love about languages."

It came back to me—it was stupid of me not to have remem-   106
bered it, all this time—that Linda had gone to college right here. The main college buildings were just behind us, over the top of the hill. This was her campus. I asked her what languages she had taken, here at U.V.M.

"The Classics Department got upset with me, because I al-   107
ways wanted to take up more languages, all at the same time," she said, smiling. "I was studying classical Greek, modern Greek, Latin, Russian, and Japanese. I switched majors over and over. I'd do more than anyone expected of me in one thing—like creative writing—and let everything else slide. If I had to do a Milton paper, or something, I'd do it in twenty minutes and hand it in—I didn't care. But if I was studying something like rondo alliteration or chiastic alliteration, I'd get so excited I'd forget everything else." She shook her head. "Not *organized.*"

I asked about her own poetry. She had declined to show me   108
her poems.

"I'll never catch up in baseball, but I have my own world,"   109
she said. "Ron can read something I've written and he'll say 'That has a nice sound,' or something, but he doesn't see that for once I've got a good slant rhyme in there. And he'll never see things I suddenly notice when I'm reading—that 'chrysanthemum' is such a perfect iambic word, for instance—that so excite me. When we went out to some friends who were having Hayden Carruth for dinner—Ron has read maybe one poem of Carruth's, I'd say—I said to him, 'Remember, you're having dinner with Mickey Mantle.' But maybe I should have said Catfish

Hunter, because Ron respects Catfish Hunter in such a special way." She giggled.

More cars were coming in now. A man in one car said, "I'm one of the umpires." and Linda waved him in. He waved back and drove in. His license plate said "UMP." 110

"I feel a little disappointed in my own career," Linda went on during the next pause. "But it isn't as if you're ever too old to write a good poem. But I don't know many ninety-year-old pitchers—do you? Maybe Ron and I are both wrong to make baseball so important to us. But what the hell, writing a poem isn't so important, either." 111

I asked what would happen to Ron in the next couple of years. 112

"If he isn't going to go on playing ball—and he can't for much longer—and if he can't find something that will take up as much of his attention as baseball, I don't know what's going to happen to him," she said. "Maybe he'll get into teaching, or some kind of coaching. He's supposed to teach in a kids' baseball camp later this summer, and then maybe . . ." She shrugged. "He lets things happen. He's that kind of a person. At least he found out he's a professional-level pitcher, but I think he'd feel better if it had got him to the major leagues. And he'll never feel he knows everything about baseball. Sometimes I'll watch him in the store when we're shopping together, and he'll have a cantaloupe in his hands and he'll be practicing his motion, right there in the store. It's true! And sometimes I'll see him sitting at home in the evening and shaking his head, and I'll ask him why, and he'll say, 'I can't *believe* I threw that pitch.' " 113

Some cars were rolling up to the gate, and Linda went over to meet them. "I know one thing," she said. "You can't rewrite a pitch." 114

The A's had another easy time of it that night. Charlie Corbally pitched and went the distance, and Darcy Spear had three hits and four runs batted in, and the team rolled to a 12–3 win over the Royals. I'd had a hard time finding out the A's place in the standings, because Ron said he couldn't always remember which games counted in the league and which were the informal ones, but he asked Paul, who said the club was now four and four in the league, and something like eight and five for the sea- 115 son over all. None of it mattered much. The next night was what mattered—the game against the Expos.

A lot of people turned out for that one—more than three hundred fans, including Larry Brown, who had brought his wife, Shirley, and one of his daughters, Laureen, and one of his sons, Stephen, and Earl Domina. We all sat together, behind first base. Even before the game began, I could see that the Expos—they wore the same parti-colored red-and-blue-and-white caps that the Montreal players do—were quicker and much more confident than most of the other Northern League players I had seen. They all looked like ballplayers. It was a wonderful game, it turned out, stuffed with close plays and heads-up, opportunistic baseball, and the A's won it, 3–2. Darcy Spear got the big hit once again—a two-run, two-out single in the third. Ron Goble started, but Paul Farrar had said beforehand he wouldn't let him pitch more than four innings; then he would bring in Steve Gallacher to mop up. Both pitchers were tired, and the staff was a little thin just now. Ron retired the first two Expos batters in the first and then gave up a bunt single. He walked the next man. He was falling behind on the count, and I noticed that he didn't seem to have his full, free motion out there. The next batter hit a sure third-out grounder to Greg Wells, but the ball took a bad hop at the last instant and jumped over Wells' glove for a single and an Expos run. Ron walked the next batter, and Paul came out to the mound to settle him down. Ron fell behind on the following batter, too, and eventually walked him, forcing in another run. Linda stared out at the field without expression. The next Expo rammed a hard shot toward third, but Tinker Jarvis made a good play on the ball and threw to second for the force, ending the inning.

In the next inning, Ron gave up two trifling singles through the middle. With two out, the Expos tried a fancy delayed double steal, with the base runner heading toward second intentionally getting himself hung up in the hope that his man from third could score before the out, but Greg Wells made the play perfectly, stopping and wheeling and firing to the plate in time to nail the runner there. Ron also got through the third unscathed, although he surrendered a single and hit a batter with one of his pitches. From time to time, Ron came off the mound between pitches and stared at the ground, his hands on his hips. In the top of the fourth, now defending a 3–2 lead, he walked the lead-off Expos hitter. The next Expos batter, a right-handed hitter, stood in and Ron hit him on the knee with his first pitch, and Paul Farrar came onto the field slowly and took him out of the game. It hadn't been a disastrous outing—with a couple of small breaks, Ron probably could have gone his four innings without giving up a run—but his struggles on the mound in search of his control had been painful to watch, especially for those of us who remembered his easy, elegant dominance over the batters in his previous game, down in Brattleboro. This kind of turnabout is a frightful commonplace for pitchers, as Ron had said himself, the day before in the car: It's always different.

Steve Gallacher came in and got the next Expos man to rap into an instant double play, and then retired the next man on a fly-ball, ending the threat. Then Gallacher set down the remaining nine men in succession, fanning four of them—an outstanding pitching performance that nailed down the win. He got a terrific hand when he came off the field, and he deserved it.

After the game, Ron spotted Larry Brown's car just as it was about to leave the parking lot and ran over to say hello. He squatted down beside the driver's side of the car for a good five minutes, talking to Larry about the game. All around the parking lot, you could see the young Expo and A's players standing in their uniforms beside their cars, tossing their spikes and gloves into the back seats, lifting a beer here and there, and laughing with little groups of friends and with their young wives or girlfriends. I was sorry to be leaving. I was staying in Burlington that night, at a motel, so that I could make an early start back to New York the next morning.

Ron and Linda and I went to a bar-restaurant she knew, up a flight of stairs in Burlington. Linda and I ordered drinks and sandwiches. Ron asked for three large glasses of water, and drank them off, one after the other. Then he had a gin rickey and a sandwich, too. He was still in uniform.

"I learned how to drink in here, I think," Linda said, looking around. "A long time ago."

Ron said, "The last time I pitched, I started from the middle of the plate and began to work it out toward the corners. Tonight, it was the other way around. I started on the outside and I never did get it together." He shook his head. "I can't think how long it's been since I hit two batters."

"Well, at least we won," Linda said.   123
"Yes, at least we won," I said. "You guys ought to keep me   124
around some more."
Ron had stopped listening. He was staring across the room,   125
with a quiet, faraway look on his face. Linda put her hand on his
crossed left leg, just above the white part of his cutouts, and
watched him with an expression of immense care and affection.
He was still in the game.

KATHERINE BOO

After Welfare

Katherine Boo, Pulitzer Prize–winning reporter for the *Washington Post*, is known for her meticulous research. She sometimes spends months researching a story, and she refuses to re-create a scene that she didn't witness herself. Interviews, direct observation, and fact-checking allow her to write about the lives of others with the kind of detail one might expect from a good novelist, but, as she says, "good writing doesn't have to preclude tough thinking about important things—taxes, health care, welfare policy, abortion." "After Welfare" was published in *The New Yorker* in 2001.

When children on the easternmost tip of the District of Co-   1
lumbia try to explain where they live, they often say "by the
Shrimp Boat," a worn seafood carryout whose small, barred
windows look east to the city's hardest ghetto and west to the
United States Capitol. That the Shrimp Boat has come to stand
for a neighborhood of ten thousand people speaks less to the
quality of its crab legs than to the featurelessness of the surrounding landscape. Among large housing projects and old brick
homes, there is no other landmark. At the start of the twentieth
century, this patch of the District was known for the industry of
its inhabitants, black craftsmen who bivouacked in shanties
while constructing the monuments of the federal city. At the end
of the century, the supposed indolence of communities like the
Shrimp Boat helped inspire in the federal city the most celebrated

social-policy initiative in a generation—the Personal Responsibility and Work Opportunity Act of 1996.

Last August 22nd was the fourth anniversary of the passage   2
of the welfare-reform bill. Five miles from the capitol, at a stand
outside the Shrimp Boat, extra-large T-shirts flapped in the
breeze like a country's colors at the border. Their inscriptions testified to a culture's changing aspirations. The wrestling hulks and
marijuana leaves of previous years had been supplanted by ex-
hortations in the red, black, and green of African independence.
"Educate 2 Elevate," the shirts read. "Each 1, Teach 1." Such
sun-drenched sentiments moved me more than I cared to admit,
for I had come to the Shrimp Boat to see three children whose el-
evation I particularly root for.

Dernard, Drenika, and Wayne were ten, eleven, and thirteen,   3
respectively, last August. I have known them, first as a newspaper reporter and then as a friend, since 1996, when they were living in public housing with their mother, Elizabeth Jones, who
was then twenty-six and had been on welfare for nine years.
Worried that the world would mistake her good kids for ghetto
thugs, Elizabeth decided that welfare reform could be her family's rescue. She got a secondhand suit from a charitable organization and reached up for the socioeconomic ladder's lowest
rung.

Since the law's passage, Miss Cookie, as Shrimp Boat kids call   4
Elizabeth, has done everything that reformers could reasonably
ask of the daughter of a single mother and a father she never met
who, by the age of twenty-one, had a high-school diploma, a history of victimization by rape and domestic abuse, and three babies by three hit-and-run men. After a volunteer clerkship and a
course in WordPerfect, she got, at twenty-seven, the first real job
of her life, as a receptionist, with a salary of twenty-two thousand dollars a year. Not long after, she saw, on the side of a bus,
a recruitment poster for the Metropolitan Police Department. In
September of 1998, she graduated from the police academy and
became an officer on the night shift in Southeast D.C., the city's
most violent quadrant—her own.

Cookie is funny and smart and tells the truth even when it   5
makes her look bad. She dislikes melodrama and is, in her own
estimation, a mediocre cop. ("For real, I'd rather go to school for
mortuary science," she says. "Dead people, you just pump them

up and they don't talk back.") She is also, at age thirty-one, a Shrimp Boat phenomenon, subject to high fives when she takes her boys to Campbell's barbershop for a shapeup. She is among the most successful former welfare recipients in the District's inner city.

One premise of welfare reform, which transfers federal power to local government, is that the public and private institutions closest to the poor can best see their needs. But the inverse is also true: the closer you get to families like Elizabeth's, the more clearly you see the flaws in the infrastructure that serves the children of the post-welfare world.

On the August day last year when I arrived at Elizabeth's house, it was lunchtime, and, as usual, she wasn't there. Her police shift runs all night, and after it ended, just before dawn, she went downtown to work as a security guard—a part-time job she has taken in order to meet her car payments. Her children had been home alone since seven the night before. In the living room, a pillow-lipped slacker on MTV's "Real World Miami" wore a T-shirt that said "F**k work." In the kitchen, eleven-year-old Drenika lit the stove and dropped a clump of ramen into a pot of water. Drenika's heart-shaped face has a perpetual squint, as if a private sun were blasting into her eyes. That day, she wanted to run the streets with Rico, a thirteen-year-old who had begun showing an interest after she started refusing to wear her eyeglasses. But ever since Drenika was seven, when a day-care subsidy stopped because of a municipal error, she has been taking care of her younger brother, Dernard, who is bright and anxious, and her older brother, Wayne, who is learning-disabled. The day before, Drenika had packed a plastic bag in anticipation of an overnight stay with her father, who didn't materialize. The bag was still on a chair by the door.

"Dernard, you want one boiled egg with your noodles or two?" Drenika asked. Her fingernails were bitten to the quick. "And which one of you was so trifling as to leave your gum stuck on the floor?"

Dernard licked powdered chicken seasoning from his palm as he waited for his egg. He was worried, he told his sister, about his imminent entrance into fifth grade, where it might become clear to the meaner of his classmates that he is not a club-level thug—"that all I am is a nerd without glasses," he told Drenika, mournfully. Drenika, putting out plates, agreed with her younger brother's assessment: "You'd be beat every day at my school." She recommended silence in class until he grew taller.

Then thirteen-year-old Wayne, still in his pajamas, emerged   10
from the basement, where he had spent the morning in a world of his own devising. Elizabeth cannot afford private tutoring or therapy for her son, who is six feet two and whose eyes tilt slightly toward the ceiling. To help Wayne make a neighborhood friend, she had recently registered him for a local peewee-football team. But his mother is gentle with him, as the world at large sometimes is not, and in her absence Wayne prefers the companionship he has created in his mother's old toy chest. With deft craftsmanship and small thefts from school and dollar stores, he has been perfecting, over half his life, a private shrine to middle-class comfort. In Wayne's wooden box—do not call it a doll house—pipe-cleaner curtains swag just so. The sister has a parrot to talk to when she's lonely, which is not often, thanks to the businessman father and the live-in grandmother. In the bedroom, the windows are not taped over with cardboard. There is, instead, a classic boyhood enchantment: a tall ship that has somehow slipped into a narrow-necked bottle.

At lunchtime, working security at a chemists' convention,   11
Elizabeth stole a minute to make a laminated name badge for each of her children: "Hello, My Name Is . . . Wayne. Architect. Washington, D.C." Meanwhile, in a frame house in the Shrimp Boat, Drenika tried to enforce the standards that she'd learned from her mother the striver. "Don't be ghetto, Wayne, eating all standing up." And the three children sat and ate their ramen and egg in silence.

Elizabeth Jones earns around thirty-nine thousand dollars a   12
year from her two jobs. Compared with the average income of those who leave the welfare rolls in the District (seventeen thousand dollars, an Urban Institute study says), this is an astronomical sum. Compared with what is required to meet the basic needs of a family of four in Washington (fifty-two thousand dollars, says another study), it is not. Elizabeth's rent and car payments consume twelve hundred and twenty dollars of her sixteen-hundred-dollar monthly take-home from the police department. Her other bills include a two-hundred-and-eighty-two-dollar monthly payment on a student loan she took out

years ago for a fly-by-night trade school, so a second job is essential. The material rewards of the two jobs are real: a car, a Suzuki Esteem, with the names of her children stenciled on the rear window, like a university affiliation, and a rented frame house four crucial blocks from East Capitol Dwellings, a notorious public-housing project where she used to live. In the small dining room, there is a computer, on which the kids can play Frogger, which they do frequently, because their mother, whose work keeps her abreast of the perils of the neighborhood, forbids them to play outside when she's not there. The children no longer have to wear shoes with the size stamped conspicuously on the sole (stigmata of Payless), and, until Elizabeth decides that she can't afford it, they enjoy a legitimate cable-television hookup, instead of the bootleg connections known around here as "fable." But when Dernard hears gunshots outside the house at midnight and shakes with terror, he can't cry out for his mother. He has to page her.

Elizabeth, who as a rule does not belabor the obvious, rarely 13 talks of fatigue. She does speak of missing her kids: "Like, I'm at work chasing after some crazy person and I am thinking, Have my kids taken a bath, did they do their homework, did they turn out the lights—the electricity bill is breaking me—did they eat dinner, did they go outside like they're not supposed to, did they watch something terrible on TV? One of her happiest weeks of last year was the time she got bronchitis and had to stay home with her children.

Welfare reform has been chronicled by journalists, academics, 14 and policymakers who are thriving in America's culture of opportunity, and the assumptions of the new law tend to ratify those of the professional class: work leads inexorably to moral (and, by extension, civic) improvement, and the economic good of a mother—a self-sufficient working mother—leads inexorably to the good of a child. If these newly working mothers are weaned of their dependence on public assistance, they will become, to put it bluntly, more like us: less violent, less isolated, less likely to use drugs and alcohol, and better parents. Indeed, the women of the Shrimp Boat—part of a group described not long ago as a permanent underclass—are steadily becoming more like the American middle class.

Washington is divided into four unequal sections, radiating 15 out from the United States Capitol. The Shrimp Boat sits toward the end of East Capitol Street, one of the dividing lines. In 1996, only three per cent of householders in the projects surrounding the carryout earned the majority of their income; most of the rest collected public assistance. Today, one-third work for the greater part of their income, an improvement at least partially attributable to a good economy. As Shrimp Boat parents spend more time at work, their daily dilemmas increasingly mirror those of the middle class, which long ago discovered that the interests of career-conscious parents and demanding children sometimes clash. In the Shrimp Boat, though, these imperatives collide with particular velocity. These families have one parent. Child-care options do not include live-in sitters or after-school piano lessons. The sixth-grade school day in the ghetto begins with a metal detector and a mandatory frisk. "A baby's first words are supposed to be the ABCs," Drenika once observed in frustration. "But where we live their first word be 'bitch.'"

The physical privations of inner-city children are often over-stated, and their parents' resourcefulness undersold. A more logical worry, it seems to me, is whether a cycle of opportunity really is replacing the cycle of pathology, even for the luckiest children of reform. Ghetto children are told regularly to "be positive," and, until faced with overwhelming evidence to the contrary, they usually are. But the exodus of mothers into the workplace has created something new and not wholly positive in the Shrimp Boat: a world of free-range children at the mercy of unreformed institutions that, in the absence of parents, are all they have.   16

On a sweltering evening later that August week, I happened to be in a row house near Elizabeth's where a mother had returned from the first full-time job she'd held in fifteen years and found her fourteen-year-old daughter beating her nineteen-year-old son with an ironing board. The boy had stolen the girl's cheese-burger—the remainder of a two-for-one special she'd bought at McDonald's and squirrelled under a bed for dinner. "I'm not going to lose another job for this Tom-and-Jerry business I have to come home to!" the mother yelled. After dialling 911, she raised a cane to "knock this temper out of you-all's head." As the grievances of mother, sister, and brother intensified and enlarged, I noticed for the first time a seven-year-old girl watching from a doorway, cheeks distended. Her name was Starletta. She was literally holding her breath.   17

I left the house with a perceptive beat cop named Brad Wag-   18
ner, whom the kids call Officer Superman, or Officer Supe-
Doggy-Dogg. We drove past skeletons of tents from a long-gone
gospel revival and into the Shrimp Boat's busiest crack market,
where in the previous year two events had altered the landscape:
a fifty-six-year-old grandmother had been murdered while shoo-
ing toddlers out of the path of bullets, and the authorities had
undertaken some improvements. To hinder the drive-through
drug trade, the city barricaded the block with metal fencing and
erected, in the newly created cul-de-sac, a set of monkey bars.
The old heads observe that these improvements prevent police
cars from pursuing armed drug dealers while, at the same time,
luring toddlers into the crosshairs. But on that August midnight,
like most others, the children of the Shrimp Boat cheerfully assumed the risk. To surf the jungle gym's top tier is not merely to
rise above the addicts bargaining at curbside. It is to secure a private glimpse, over the viscous Anacostia River, of the white-lit
federal city. A boy, naked but for a diaper, hung like a bat from
the bars. A girl who looked about eight waved hello. "We don't
have to go to bed tonight," she called, and seemed surprised
when we walked over. Afterward, Officer Superman said that
sometimes he felt that his service to the children of the community had little to do with public safety; it was, rather, being a
nearby adult. "What these kids want more than anything," he
said, "is just evidence that they exist."

In September, during recess one day in the second week of   19
seventh grade, Drenika and her best friend, Erica, sat self-
consciously by the basketball court of Ronald H. Brown Middle
School. The school sits on drained swampland, and over the
summer nature had reclaimed a bit of the court. It was tufted
now, which skewed the bounce, but Drenika and Erica were only
marginally interested in watching the game. They were hoping to
be watched themselves. On their dark skin, under the oxford
button-downs and green plaid skirts that public-school officials mandated last year in the name of educational focus, they
had customized themselves in glistening white ink. "Sexy," Erica's biceps read. Drenika's said, "Baddest Chick/53rd Street
Mob." On her bony wrist were the words "Love Rico." The two
eleven-year-olds spoke coolly of a classmate—his mother had
a scrub job—who couldn't afford a gel body-write pen. He

had committed the social felony of decorating himself with Wite-Out.

Over the years, Elizabeth has called me periodically with un- 20 settling bulletins: that she has found the bullet-ridden body of a teen-ager she'd been close to since he was a youngster; that she is standing in the middle of her ransacked living room, intruder's whereabouts known, and the police, whom she's called eight times, have not responded. I have never heard her more undone than when Drenika, then barely nine, got her period. Elizabeth, born to a mother who got pregnant at sixteen, became pregnant herself at sixteen. She has impressed on her daughter the importance of breaking that chain. But Drenika, who is expected to act grown up when she is home—who has cooked a perfect sausage link since she was seven—is increasingly adult when she goes outside it. It's as if the ghetto pose that Elizabeth has herself worked so hard to shed had rematerialized on her daughter's slender frame. Elizabeth worries when she learns about a girl in Drenika's school who is pregnant, the one for whom the school guards have been collecting baby clothes. She sees a note written by the nine-year-old daughter of one of her girlfriends, inviting a fellow fifth grader to have sex with her again, and worries more. She sees her own pretty daughter in a throng of boys and feels sick. Drenika is a restive pre-teen target—one whose single mother works the late shift.

Elizabeth, trying to start a conversation with her daughter 21 lately, sometimes feels as if she were interrogating a perp. But one day, as the school year began, Drenika painstakingly informed her notebook of everything that hadn't happened over the latest summer of covering for her mother at home: "I wanted to go to Orlando Florida to Disney World and go shopping. I also so wanted to go away for camp my friend did for a week." She wanted to play with kids her own age, sleep late, go to Senegal and New Jersey and North Carolina and Ocean City, Maryland. What she usually got was house lockdown with two brothers who rely on her to interpret the world. One day, I came upon her in her bedroom, where, feeling grown, she had recently packed eleven years' worth of dolls into a trash bag. Squinting into the mirror, she knotted her T-shirt and pulled a skullcap over her eyes. As Lil' Kim sang on a tiny radio, Drenika danced. The room fairly shook with her impatience.

When Elizabeth was on welfare, she sometimes watched "All   22
My Children." She also volunteered regularly at her children's
schools, keeping an eye on their teachers and friends. This year,
her schedule does not permit such luxuries. When her police shift
ends, at 4 A.M., she sleeps for two hours, wakes her children for
three different schools, sees one to the bus and drives the two
others, along with four neighborhood kids who depend on her,
to their schools. Then she heads downtown to her part-time job
as a private security guard. When she finishes, at 5 P.M., she
fetches her children and the four others from their schools, drops
them all at their doors, and goes to the police station to start her
shift. On days off, she sleeps.

Because she cannot personally watch over Drenika, she signs   23
her up for supervised distractions: track; after-school tutoring;
cheerleading for the Bison, the football team for which she also
registered Wayne and Dernard. Elizabeth is blunt when she talks
to her daughter about her own sexual activity, which began in
junior high school and led to five pregnancies, three children,
and nine years on welfare. ("But you made it with three kids,"
Drenika counters.) Elizabeth doesn't allow her own longtime
boyfriend, a maintenance worker, to stay overnight. She puts a
call block on the telephone to stop Rico from phoning Drenika,
and spies on her, with Dernard in the role of informer.

Still, Elizabeth knows that the best way to protect Drenika,   24
who had straight A's at the beginning of elementary school and
mostly C's at the end, is to keep her interested in school. So Elizabeth petitioned school authorities to get her daughter reas-
signed from the infamous Shrimp Boat middle school, Evans, to
a place where Drenika had a better chance of getting an education. A public middle school on Capitol Hill had encouraging
test scores, but it had seven times as many names on the waiting
list as it had places for children who live outside Capitol Hill.
Elizabeth settled on Ronald H. Brown Middle School, which is
five stops from home on the Washington Metro. There, another
legend of the District ghetto, a no-nonsense principal in a Grace
Jones flattop and a turtleneck, had for years been converting
hard cases into readers. By the time Drenika enrolled, however,
the principal had taken a job in a public school in Maryland.

Students at Ron Brown do far better on standardized tests   25
than students at Evans. But better does not mean good. Last year

at Ron Brown—a year in which one-fifth of the students were judged by tests to be illiterate—a physical-education teacher pleaded guilty to having sex with two fourteen-year-old girls. One was a learning-disabled student he attacked in a bathroom and attempted to silence with a twenty-dollar bill. She later gave birth to his child.

By September, a new physical-education teacher had already been suspended; and after recess Drenika and Erica had ample time to speculate on the reason, because two of their six classes weren't held that day—their teachers weren't there. Drenika and her classmates were put in an unused classroom, where they passed the time talking to each other. Later in the day, the new principal, a warm, earnest woman in her forties, asked what I thought of the school. I remarked that Drenika and the others had spent one-third of their school day doing nothing. She told me that substitutes were in short supply in the system and admonished me to be positive.

Drenika's last class of that day was geography. At its start, the teacher wrote the daily "objective" on the blackboard. Objectives, like uniforms, are part of the new urban catechism of disciplined, outcome-oriented education. This day's objective: Students would review last week's work. Hands shot up. "Miss Carney, we reviewed last week's work yesterday." Miss Carney moved to Objective B: Students would write their reflections about the class. "Write about things you enjoyed, like when we went outside for class," she told them. "It's important that I know what you think, so I can do something you like more." Miss Carney turned on a boom box and soft jazz filled the room. Drenika sucked her pen and then, chin resting on her desk, set to work:

> September 15. The first day of class I thought Mrs. Carney was going to talk a hole in my head but she did not. We played a game called Guess Who we played that for a little while she gave use some Bazooka gum but I gave my to Erica because I did not have a taste for sweets. Something I like about her is that she relate to you she don't give me a hard time. Her homework is easy if you try to do it.

Drenika then pulled out some Crayola pencils and drew sky-blue clouds around her heading, "A Reflection." She really likes her seventh-grade teachers, she told me later. "This year they stoop to our level."

The bell sounded, and students turned in their books. For   29
complex reasons involving a lack of lockers, they were not allowed to take books home. Careering past engraved oak signs
that adorn the school's foyer—celebrating the Philosophy Club,
the Math Club, and other extracurriculars that do not in fact exist at Ron Brown—four hundred and seventy children poured
into the streets. Now Drenika was supposed to go to one ex-
tracurricular that Ron Brown does offer—track. Instead, she declared she had "growing pains," and she, Erica, and her other
best friends headed for the subway station, hot on the trail of
Rico, who had been banned from after-school athletics because
of low grades.

And there he was, sheepish and handsome on the elevated   30
platform on Minnesota Avenue, whispering in the ear of another
seventh-grade girl.

"I heard he was out with a dirty girl. . . ." Drenika's friends,   31
loyally, started to sing.

"I don't want him no more," Drenika told them gloomily as   32
the train glided home.

But wait, her friends told her. Look: Rico was in the next car.   33
He was getting off at her stop. And for the next few hours, as
Elizabeth pictured her daughter running wind sprints, Drenika
was alone with the boy whose name rated prime real estate on
the inside of her wrist.

The new anodyne for bad urban schools is "choice." Here,   34
though, giving parents a wealth of educational options sometimes presents a familiar inner-city conundrum: What if all your
choices are bad ones? Elizabeth had to obtain special permission
to win for Drenika the poor education she's getting now—an education that may well be an improvement over the middle school
closer to home. To judge by test scores, it may also be an improvement over most of the twelve publicly funded charter
schools that have sprouted up around the Shrimp Boat.

Last spring, I occasionally accompanied Elizabeth to one   35
of these schools. Construction-paper flowers bloomed in its
front windows. In the principal's office, there were handsome
brochures from the Massachusetts company that runs it. Elizabeth was particularly moved by the school's namesake: a D.C.
police officer who'd grown up in the Shrimp Boat and was murdered here.

It was to this promising place—the Robert Louis Johnson, Jr.,   36
Arts and Technology Academy—that Elizabeth entrusted her
fourth grader, Dernard, who the year before had tested at a
seventh-grade reading level and had beaten the daylights out of a
boy who had teased him one day in the bathroom. As usual, she
joined the PTA, where for most of the year she constituted
one-third of the regular attendance.

The Shrimp Boat ten-year-old who gets off track at school   37
greatly increases his odds of not reaching the age of twenty. Elizabeth understands this viscerally. A year earlier, a teen-ager had
come pounding on her door. "Miss Cookie! Tank down!" Tank,
the seventeen-year-old son of Elizabeth's closest friend in the
neighborhood, a kid I'd always found dull and decent, was dying
of gunshot wounds behind Elizabeth's house. He had stolen
fifty dollars from a female crackhead whose male friend had a
street-sweeping Mac 12. Paramedics reported difficulty extracting from Tank's hand his own rinky-dink .38. Younger children
on the block expressed dismay at the capture of the killer, who in
addition to being a popular neighborhood drug dealer drove an
ice-cream truck

Perhaps Elizabeth should have reconsidered her choice of   38
schools when, shortly after the academic year began, the widow
of the dead officer demanded the removal of her husband's name
from the enterprise, because she believed the school was mishan-
dling some of its grant money. Or when Elizabeth heard about
the rats in the hallways. Or when Dernard's new teacher—the
third of the year—started telling the ten-year-olds unsettling
tales from his previous job as a corrections officer at the D.C.
jail. But at the public elementary school in her neighborhood,
Shadd, sixty-one per cent of students were unable to read—the
worst test scores in the city. So it wasn't until the academic year
was almost over that Elizabeth gave up, deciding that staying at
home for the few remaining days of class was better for Dernard
than going to the charter school she had carefully chosen for
him.

I went with Elizabeth to pick up his books. In his classroom,   39
ten boys in khakis and maroon polo shirts sat quietly at empty
desks. No books, no paper, not even an objective on the blackboard. They stared into space as the teacher sat at his desk doing
the same. Elizabeth grabbed Dernard's books, jumped in her

Suzuki, and drove maniacally, the air thick with her undetonated anger. "It's like people think that in this part of town we settle for anything," she said.

"I learned," Dernard said later, trying to make her feel better. 40 "I just learned what I learned already."

Elizabeth did not feel better. She hated the thought of return- 41 ing Dernard to the public school she had traded in for the charter, and where, she feared, he had been labelled a troublemaker after his fight. "Like, you know, this other child was having problems in math?" she told me. "An administrator was, like, 'Why? All little black boys know how to count money.' I mean, she already got the boy selling drugs. And, you know, for real I think some of them teachers already got the boy six feet in the ground."

Elizabeth tore through the Shrimp Boat until her fury was 42 contained. Then she pulled to a curb, inhaled, and opened a spelling book that her brainy son had been using that year. Holding it out as if it had landed on her from a great distance, she began to read the words aloud: "'Look.' 'Took.' 'Good.' 'Stood.'" Dernard. Her reader.

A few feet from where we sat, teenage boys strolled past, 43 wearing the coolie hats that were that moment's high fashion. Shortly after, smoke rose around younger children playing double Dutch on the sidewalk. Someone had set the project's parched hedges on fire. A hook-and-ladder came, along with three police cruisers. Someone spoke of the burning bush and Moses. Elizabeth remained fixed on the paperback speller: "Look, "Took"—evidence of a quieter crime.

In the Shrimp Boat, it is possible to see welfare reform as a 44 Ponzi scheme whose currency is children. You put your children in day care so that you can work, but the only work you may be qualified for, after years of being a full-time mother, is in a day-care center. There you take care of the children of other poor women, many of whom now spend their days working at other day-care centers. This child-swapping has a levelling effect. The children of incompetent parents may receive the nurturing of more conscientious parents, while the children of parents like Elizabeth can expect to be tended by less competent parents. This phenomenon, familiar to the middle class, is particularly

unsettling in the Shrimp Boat, where you notice that the operator of a neighborhood crack house, whose own five children
were removed by child-protection services, has, thanks to welfare reform, become a caregiver at a Benning Road recreation
center. Despite a doubling of federal day-care subsidies, many
mothers here make the calculation that Elizabeth made when her
children were six, seven, and nine, and her day-care reimburse-
ments stopped. They note the mentholated-cigarette smoke in
the infant room and the felonry who are monitoring the playground, and decide that the best way to protect their children is
to keep them home, teach them how to make grilled-cheese sandwiches, dial 911, and operate the dead bolts on the door.

Therefore Elizabeth was particularly relieved when she found   45
someone trustworthy in the community to look after her children: a slight, goateed mailman who coaches the after-school
football team. For five months a year, at a quarter to six nightly,
Dernard and a hundred and eighty-four other boys with pad-
broadened shoulders spilled forth from Benning Terrace, East
Capitol Dwellings, Arthur Capper, and neighborhoods across the
Maryland line, and converged on a football field at an abandoned school which became, for two hours an evening, perhaps
the District's safest hundred yards. Their volunteer coach, Andre
(Jay) Ford, grew up in the Shrimp Boat and has delivered mail
for seventeen of his thirty-four years. After walking his five-mile
postal round, he comes to the field and coaches kids aged eight
to fourteen.

In fact, Andre prefers chess—he can riff for hours on the   46
nineteenth-century master Paul Morphy, whose moves seemed
mathematically impossible until he easily defeated his opponents.
But, as Andre knows from his Shrimp Boat childhood, football
offers a more credible cover for kids who want to grow up to
be something other than hardheads. Andre sees the game as a
means, not an end, and that is why the least athletic kids on the
team get playing time and the stars who skip mandatory tutoring
sessions don't. It is also why his coaching points frequently address such athletic imperatives as whether a boy can go blind
from masturbating.

A favorite word of Elizabeth's kids is "fake." Some of the fak-   47
ery that the Shrimp Boat kids see around them is funny, such as
how the kids of crackheads wear "I Love Jesus" bowrettes in

their hair. Some of it isn't funny, such as how, at a local nonprofit organization, funds meant for computer training financed the living-room furniture of the executive director. (Another of the kids' favored words is "nonchalant": when you get screwed, make like you don't care.) Andre Ford, Elizabeth's kids concur, is not fake, and when they are with him they drop their protective attitude of indifference. Last fall, the city sometimes forgot to mow the field the boys play on. Their fathers sometimes forgot to come to games. But six days a week, as armed drug dealers worked the dark slopes north of the field, occasionally descending to headhunt, the letter carrier materialized on the sidelines to yell "Knees up!" to hundreds of backward-running boys. For much of the season, the high beams of cars served as field lights, and some evenings they made a living palimpsest: the boys' shadows eclipsing and then revealing the foul graffiti on the vacant school's façade.

Andre calls his players the Bison, for the once endangered   48
species that has been nurtured back to health. He grew up with Dernard's father, a smart kid who was an addict by the age of twenty. Dernard, whom Andre calls the Philosopher, was so joyful that he could barely speak the day he realized that the coach knew his name.

"One-fourth of one person in this program will even have a   49
chance at an N.F.L. tryout," Andre tells his kids, "though five might get a scholarship to college." Still, the average Bison believes he will get out of the ghetto by going pro. This belief is fomented by a few of the assistant coaches—recovering addicts and blue-collar jobbers who were once youth-league superstars themselves. But when Elizabeth observed Andre's effect on Dernard she saw possibilities unrelated to athletic achievement. She saw a chance to engage her remote older son.

For as long as I have known Wayne, his bright brother and   50
sister have spoken on his behalf, reflexively translating his needs. For as long as I've known Elizabeth, she has been battling someone or another over Wayne's intellectual and emotional potential. When he was younger and smaller, she had to guess his feelings from his posture, because he didn't smile and seldom spoke. As soon as he was old enough to hold a pencil, he created art—from toy-box assemblages to intricate drawings, which he

would throw away as soon as they were finished. He drew, in perfect perspective, terraced cityscapes with steel-and-glass schools and filigreed steeples. He drew vast extended families headed by calm-faced fathers. "He always makes stuff that is," Dernard explains. "Only, he makes it better than it is."

Wayne never had a proper art teacher, but Elizabeth, even at her poorest, kept him in sketch pads. "It's like toilet paper—you just have to have it in the house," she once explained. "He's not himself when he runs out of paper." 51

Wayne's first teachers said he was fine. Elizabeth remembers the day she stopped believing that. She had been volunteering in his second-grade class and looked over his shoulder during a spelling quiz. "He had numbered his paper," she said, "and all the numbers were backward. His name, what he could write of it, was backward, too. And I just started to cry." 52

When school officials delayed testing him for special education, Elizabeth worked the Shrimp Boat grapevine; eventually, a Metrobus driver directed her to a nonprofit agency that would assess Wayne for free. He was diagnosed as dyslexic, and spent the next three years in the Shrimp Boat elementary school's lone special-ed classroom, where he was regularly punished for stealing small objects for use in his toy box. "They treated him like a germ," Elizabeth said. "I felt if I couldn't get him out of there he would end up in a group home." But it wasn't until fifth grade that she got an attorney who, pro bono, pushed the school system to review Wayne's case. Psychologists concluded that he had pervasive developmental disorders and probably Asperger's syndrome, which is marked by an inability to make social and emotional connections, and that the District of Columbia's special-ed programs weren't meeting his needs. He was first placed in a "non-degree" special-education academy—a school for children with no capacity to fulfill the requirements for high-school graduation. Elizabeth pushed again, harder. Now, every weekday morning, Wayne takes a bus to a small private high school for disabled children in a Maryland suburb, where his tuition is covered by the D.C. school system, the classes have only six students, and his art work hangs in the hallway. 53

Wayne began the year by raiding a teacher's handbag, then improved his reading to the third- grade level. "Perceives himself as rejected by others," his current psychological assessment says. 54

"Harbors strong feelings of inadequacy." I read the assessment in a classroom one day while Wayne and an overweight white girl teased each other gently in the hall. He has learned to speak with less fear among his learning-disabled classmates, who are fascinated by the intense, artistic boy from the ghetto. He has never had a friend in the Shrimp Boat, and that is why Elizabeth turned to Andre.

Andre told Elizabeth that Wayne, who weighs a hundred and fifty-two pounds, would have to scrimmage in the top weight class, with the biggest, roughest kids. Both Wayne and Elizabeth worried that those kids would hurt him. The boys themselves worried that Wayne, whom they considered a "retard," would slow them down. Some of them had been playing for Andre since they were eight, and after so many years together they were ready to get good, let fly. Wayne, as far as anyone knew, had never touched a football. But as Andre enforced rules of civility to safeguard Wayne, and as Drenika the cheerleader levelled transgressors with a highly articulate stare, Wayne mastered the playbook and learned to track the ball down the field.

When Wayne is talking to a patient listener, he is increasingly able to keep up his end of a conversation—a conversation that will tend to be more interesting than those one typically has with thirteen-year-olds in the Shrimp Boat. These talks will be filled with questions that Wayne has suppressed for years. ("What are the schools with the furniture outside on Saturday?" he asked one day, trying to solve the riddle of an urban flea market.) But, in a neighborhood with a shortage of such listeners, Wayne's shame about his differences has increased along with his abilities. At football practice, trying to identify the algorithms of ordinary teen-age life (for instance, how to convey interest in the cheerleader who also plays the violin without being ridiculed by his peers), he was finding that he would rather be mocked outright than be patronized by praise he knew he hadn't earned. Once, in Wayne's presence, Dernard gamely asserted that Wayne was now one of the best Bison players. Wayne yelped as if he'd been kicked, "Don't say that! It isn't true." It wasn't. But Elizabeth's son had willed his way from team joke to second-string lineman who was the first to arrive at practice.

As the season progressed, one of Andre's former players, a young man named SeQuan, was murdered on a Shrimp Boat corner—ten shots and nine bystanders who managed to see nothing. A wide receiver's mother was nearly strangled by her boyfriend on the practice field. A thirteen-year-old defensive tackle whose mother was missing and whose father is dead was found to be raising himself, his guardian grandpa having grown senile. And the Bison won game after game.

In the third quarter of a late-season game against Woodland 58 Terrace, with the Bison up by six, the quarterback called a play and Wayne double-checked with his teammates the jersey number of the player he was going to block. The other Bison fell silent, then started to clap. It was the first time they had heard him speak.

Dernard earned an A-plus at his new public school for a 59 writing assignment on his favorite things: "Jordans, Garnetts, Pippens, Paytons, Flights, Timberlands, and Flight Posites." Emboldened, he bore down one November afternoon on "The Mouse and the Motorcycle," by Beverly Cleary. It's a book about a boy who befriends a mouse while living in a luxury hotel, and Dernard was somehow able to wrap his imagination around room service and croquet mallets and antimacassars on overstuffed armchairs. What he couldn't get was why anyone would want a mouse in his room. "Like it was infested?" Then he considered his own lack of companionship. If a boy was sufficiently lonely, he concluded, a mouse would be acceptable to talk to.

Later that rainy night, Elizabeth, sufficiently lonely, called me: 60 "Michael and me, it's over." She was thirty-one and a mother of three, and Michael was the only man she had ever been on a date with—"to the movies, a walk in the park, you know." For five years, he had been her on-and-off boyfriend and her all-time hope for marriage, a permanent means of easing her children's loneliness, as opposed to the short-term Coach Andre solution. "I don't have time in the day to start all over," she said, sighing.

The men who fathered Wayne, Dernard, and Drenika live 61 close to the Shrimp Boat and claim vast regions of the children's psychic maps. But they are all, practically speaking, absentee, with the intervals between their visits often measured in years. Welfare reform has spawned tough new laws to help mothers extract child support from such fathers, and with renewed hope Elizabeth has appeared in court ten times over the past eight months to try to secure from the three men the combined total of a hundred and ninety dollars a month they've been ordered to pay. So far, she has collected nothing, which is basically what she has collected for the last thirteen years. Only thirteen percent of the city's female-headed households receive alimony or child support, according to D.C. government figures.

Wayne's father was an older guy who picked Elizabeth up after junior high had let out for the day. Drenika's father, a crack user, faded from the picture soon after the New Year's Eve on which the baby was conceived. Elizabeth was twenty-one when she left Dernard's father, who had stayed in her life just long enough after her son was born to earn a conviction for assaulting her. Bruised and battered, she looked at her three babies in diapers and found a doctor willing to tie the tubes of a twenty-one-year-old. She gave up on men for five years. "I felt so deep in this hole I didn't want to be in," she said. She took self-esteem classes, then two courses in parenting skills; she focussed on life beyond her living-room couch. And then she met Michael, who seemed compatibly committed to self-improvement. At that time, she was trying to get work experience by volunteering at a community-development agency. He passed her desk daily on his way to Narcotics Anonymous. He was two years clean, went to church, worked maintenance. Unlike most of the men she met, he had never been to jail. One day, he appeared at her desk with a Hershey bar. "That was when I decided to recognize him," she said.

In the five years that Elizabeth had been seeing Michael, he had never given her his home-telephone number. "Still," Elizabeth said, "it was a step up from before." Indeed, if Michael hadn't helped with her children when she had to live for a month at the police academy, she probably wouldn't have made it through the course. Then again, he didn't show up for her academy graduation. When she wondered whether she could afford the house outside the projects, he said he'd help with the rent. He agreed to her idea that they attend a six-week marriage-prep course at the Free Gospel Church. But he never asked her to marry him.

"You know how you remember little things?" Elizabeth said. "I keep thinking about that day when I see at the Marlo Heights theatre there's a dollar movie, 'Air Bud 2'—it's about a dog—and kids get in free. I said, 'Hey, let's take the kids.' And he was just,

62

63

64

'I don't want to.' I mean, I didn't want to, either—nobody grown wants to see 'Air Bud 2.' But it's not for us—it's for the kids. That's being a family. You just go.'"

Michael had also resumed his crack habit. One autumn night,   65 as Elizabeth returned home from the funeral of a murdered law-enforcement colleague, Michael, who for weeks had been ignoring her attempts to page him, called to ask if he could come over. She said no. And there he was, banging on her doors and windows, and, as much as she hated the thought of putting her private life in play at work, she called the police. Now, in November, Michael wanted to reclaim the stuff he had contributed over the years to her household: the shelves that hold her kids' school trophies; the framed print in the living room of an interlocking African man, woman, and child.

The idea of marriage is relatively new in the Shrimp Boat,   66 where for decades even love was something a woman lied about to caseworkers and talkative children. The old welfare system targeted assistance to single parents, so a woman who married, or even cohabited, usually lost her benefits. The 1996 reform law aimed to encourage two-parent families by removing such economic disincentives, but there is little evidence thus far that it has had an effect, which does not surprise in the Shrimp Boat. Lately, the playlist at WKYS, "the people's station," is thick with odes to the newly self-sufficient woman. "All the honeys making moneys, / Throw your hands up at me," goes a Destiny's Child song that Elizabeth favors. To which the Cash Money Millionaires offer an emphatic male counterpose: "Give me a project chick. / Give me a hoodrat bitch, / One that don't give a fuck."

Elizabeth said, "I know how a typical family is supposed to   67 be—man, woman, children, the man first. But I've been raising kids by myself for thirteen years. It's hard to take off the incharge hat and put on the submissive-woman hat. There were things I should have done different—" She stopped herself. Heartbreak is a luxury. Last year about this time, her partner at work, a guy who believed in her potential and taught her most of what she knows about being a cop, killed himself over love trouble. Elizabeth sank into depression. "I can't go there," she said now. "I can't hover over it and say, 'Oh, I'm so sad.'"

One afternoon, between a security gig at a McDonald's and a   68 trip to the football field to watch her children practice before she headed to roll call at the station, Elizabeth went online and was instant-messaged by a police officer in Texas. He had read her profile on A.O.L. and was "quite interested in getting to know you."

She had to laugh. Her kids want a father, yesterday. Michael had placed himself in rehab, but her bride-of-Michael fantasies were finished. With her schedule, where but in cyberspace could she unearth a husband?   69

"Whazzup with U?" she tapped back. Ghetto giveaway. From the other end, silence.   70

A cold front was coming to the Shrimp Boat. A bullet hit the window of a seventy-five-year-old neighbor of Cookie's as she was sitting down to Thanksgiving dinner; outside, a twenty-year-old was dead and three others have been shot in a drive-by. Three health inspectors testing a creek at the project's edge explained to a fifteen-year-old the aquatic ecology of the inner city, after which the boy robbed two of them at gunpoint and raped the other. Cops grumbled about a new annoyance on the streets: teen-agers who choose not to participate in that rite of passage known as getting a driver's license until they're pulled over and sent to chill in the Benning Road lockup. I met a loquacious six-year-old, Anthony, standing sentry over his father's van, which someone had broken into, leaving behind the bladeless shaft of a knife. "That's where they raped the girl and then they took an eraser and erased all the blood," he explained. We talked at length about his aims for his first-grade year, which hadn't begun because his mother had forgotten to enroll him, but when I happened upon him again, an hour later, he was stunned that I recalled our previous encounter. Elizabeth's kids, I was reminded, are the lucky ones.   71

Coach Andre, watching those lucky kids, was growing worried about Drenika. "It's tough for boys out here, but it's tougher for girls, and this girl is on fire," he said one day. "Here's a child, not even a teen-ager, who looks older than she is, who needs her mother to be there. And here's a mother who needs to work. And nowhere is the father. When you grow up in a house where your dad is buying you stuff and telling you he loves you, you don't fall for the okeydoke that comes from other guys. But when you don't get attention from males at home, some guy'll say, 'Damn,   72 you got a nice one,' and that'll sound so good. You begin to peel a little more off, wear the booty shorts, get a little more attention. And sad as it is, and try as Cookie does, Drenika is getting out there. She's being fattened up for the kill."

One night at eight, not long after Drenika's twelfth birthday, Elizabeth called from work to learn that her daughter hadn't come home from school. Elizabeth fled the station, panicked, recalling her own sexual initiation at age thirteen: the walk home from school, the two men on PCP, the fist to the mouth, the chill of the laundry-room floor. Elizabeth pounded on the doors of Drenika's friends—Stevie Wonders, all. She drove up and down the Shrimp Boat's streets. As eleven o'clock approached, she turned onto B Street and found her daughter leaning up against a wall with Rico.

Elizabeth put Drenika on total after-school lockdown: "You get enough air to breathe, but the rest belongs to me." Then she marched to Rico's house, where she encountered a boy far less tough than she expected—a kid whose own mother worked, a kid somewhat disoriented by the raft of girls at his disposal. "It's like I just don't know how to say no," he told her. She felt a frisson of sympathy, and then she scared him within an inch of his life. "You go on and be a player, but you make sure it's not gonna be with Drenika," she told him. "Or when you next see me walking toward you, you had better raise up and run."

She persuaded her superiors to give her the 11:30 P.M.-to-6:30 A.M. shift, which is already overpeopled with single mothers trading sleep and safety for evenings with their children. After a brief reprieve, though, she was returned to 7:30 P.M.-to-4 A.M. duty. She got her first gray hair and didn't pluck it—"This one's yours," she told Drenika. And she went to bed many mornings second-guessing her choices. If she keeps working, will she look back on these years and find she made a minimal living by mortgaging the future of her daughter?

And what about Wayne, whose mind is on fire—whose presumptive slowness now seems more like Edwardian reserve? He wants to learn about the Kennedy Center, the Capitol. He wants a mentor to "teach me the stuff about being a man." He does not want to hear that there are waiting lists for mentors at the programs Elizabeth has called. He has been waiting too long already. And then there's Dernard, smart Dernard, who the coaches say is so starved for attention he's been picking fights at practice, and who sometimes climbs into Cookie's bed on her days off, as he did when he was four. "Is there a pill to stay little?" he asked one day. "'Cause if there was, I'd eat the whole pack."

One morning, it occurred to Cookie that she had ten years of   77
raising teen-agers ahead of her.

The standard reward for academic achievement in the ghetto   78
is a chrome-plated trophy. It is athletic achievement—even pee-wee athletic achievement—that reaps the windfall, and in November the Bison won the D.C. midget-football championship. Then they went to Baltimore, where they just managed a victory in the tri-state, and where the defeated team's fans slashed their tires. On to Pennsylvania, where they beat an East Brunswick, New Jersey, powerhouse in the regionals. Thereupon a fantasy about which Shrimp Boat kids speechify at Junior Toastmasters and confide in their journals suddenly became real: the Bison had earned a December trip to Orlando, Florida—the place where, as Dernard put it, the oranges grow up—to compete in the national youth-football championships at Disney World.

This was, from a parental perspective, problematic, as the   79
Bison had no money to get to Orlando. But Cookie and the coaches put the screws on the Shrimp Boat, and a retired cop, a government-worker uncle, a shoe store, and a community-development organization came through with enough for a bus ride: thirty-six kids, fourteen hours, four cans of Arm & Hammer air freshener. On the first half of the journey, cheerleader Drenika rued the loss of Rico, who, after meeting Cookie, had decided to focus his charms on another seventh-grade girl. On the second half, she began a romance with another boy named Rico, a six-foot-tall guard. Dernard, the water boy, absorbed the information slipping past his window on the first overnight trip of his life. "I never been nowhere but maybe to Virginia once," he said, "so I gotta see everything there is." Elizabeth, team chaperon, was so happy for Wayne that she forgot to fret that the loss of income from her part-time job would mean a lean Christmas. And Wayne himself studied a line drawing materializing in his sketchbook: a minutely realized modern high school encircled by a low boxwood hedge.

Upon arrival in Orlando, Drenika got sunglasses that were   80 dappled like the 102nd Dalmatian. She pushed them up on her forehead and squinted: Christmas lights snaking up the trunks of palm trees, topiary shaped like mouse ears. "We ain't playing now," she said. "This be Disney World for real."

On the Disney playing fields, the Bison promptly provided a return on the Shrimp Boat's investment, crushing a North Carolina team in the quarter-finals, 33–6. In the semifinals, they beat a suburban Illinois squad whose tradition has been celebrated by Wheaties. That put them in the Pop Warner Super Bowl, the ne plus ultra of peewee football. There Andre Ford's team would meet a Miami juggernaut that was undefeated for the last two seasons and had a Web site unofficially sponsored by a law firm.

After sessions on the practice field, the Bison slept four to six to a motel room while Andre lay awake in his room, mentally totting up receipts. Other teams carbo-loaded at Western Sizzlin; the Bison woke up to Fruity Pebbles that Elizabeth bought in bulk at the Orlando Wal-Mart. But even the hardest-faced Bison found themselves grinning. Prep-school and college scouts had gathered; ESPN was filming. The Shrimp Boat kids had come to Disney, where bubble gum has been outlawed for its crimes against clean sidewalks, to have their existence widely acknowledged. Don't say *if* we win, they told me. Say *when* we win.

The night before the Super Bowl, the league held a pregame party for the country's best junior football players and cheerleaders. On the way to the event, the Bison visited a gift shop, where, when they entered, every other customer exited and every clerk and manager closed in. It was unclear whether this reaction was a response to their size, their do-rags, the rubber boa constrictors around their necks, or just their jerseys, which, in the absence of laundry funds, were ripe from the playoff games.

The Bison walked into the party acutely aware of their own smell. At the sight of them, their counterparts from the rest of America started to shriek with unbridled approval. "Follow them Bison boys!" they cheered. "D.C. knows how to party!" It was a momentary astonishment to the Bison that the kids of Tucson and Honolulu and Toms River covet their hard-core culture, or fetishize the store-bought version, anyway. Shrimp Boat music—Jay-Z, OutKast—blasted from the soundstage.

"It's like everybody want to be us," a Bison wide receiver named Joe said as a Louisville girl snapped his picture. But full contemplation of this phenomenon was deferred by an undulating mass of cheerleader tweens. Assessing the situation, Wayne asked me for an Altoid.

"Every time you wobble wobble it gets me horny / So I can ride that ass from the night until in the morning. . . ." As Cookie and I danced on a trembling picnic table, we could look down through the manufactured smoke on Shrimp Boat kids getting loved up by girls in spaghetti straps, orthodontics, and glitter-smeared cheeks. Jealous athletes from other teams raised voices and fists. At home, the Bison would not have let such disrespect go unaddressed. But at Disney they kept dancing.   86

The smoke made everyone look younger, and nothing that happened that night seemed to suggest that the game was rigged against the ghetto kids' future. I thought about what Ralph Ellison called the unexpectedness of the American experience—great achievements that emerge from conditions of profound implausibility. One of the dancing Bison, a thirteen-year-old named Michael Howard, had earlier that evening told me a secret. He'd read a story called "The Tell-Tale Heart." It made no sense, but he couldn't shake all that pounding under the floorboards. So he read it again, and this time broke through the clots of language. Clear as day: the pounding was the guy's own conscience. Michael had felt his mind at work, and liked it.   87

Observing the mingled limbs and sympathies of the youth cultures of Shrimp Boat and suburbia, I imagined that all these children were, in the end, more alike than not—that violence and parental absence and low expectations do only superficial damage; that Shrimp Boat kids might prove competitive in the post-welfare meritocracy by dint of sheer desire. By the time the dj. veered into "Y.M.C.A.," I was deep in the pudding of Shrimp Boat/football-coach/Disney-ad affirmation. Not *if* we win, *when* we win. What you believe you can achieve.   88

Andre reined in the Bison early for a good night's sleep before the game. As Dernard walked out of the theme park, his face tightened and he grabbed my hand. A small red pool was spreading across the sidewalk. Melted Popsicle, I offered. He crouched, dipped a finger, resumed breathing.   89

The next morning, after the N.F.L. film crew miked up the Bison center, Wayne marched proudly onto the playing field in a column of chanting, grunting boys. Four-foot-ten Dernard shouldered an equipment bag as large as he was. Drenika and the other cheerleaders, wearing T-shirts under their sleeveless   90 uniforms in the name of modesty, sang at the top of their lungs, "So good to be a Biiii-son . . ."

The Shrimp Boat kids knelt, held hands, and dedicated the game to God. Then they went out and got obliterated. At the half it was 40–6. Wayne, his arm bloodied, hopelessly chased a Miami back with world-class speed and Division I coaches already plotting his future. The Bison's best back, a boy named Speedy, who wore the T-shirt of his murdered cousin beneath his jersey, sobbed until he hyperventilated. Elizabeth, on the sidelines, struggled not to follow suit. "We ain't got this far for nothing," pleaded tackle Curtis Lynch, trying to rally his teammates as eye black streamed down his own cheeks. "We got here. It must mean something." The assertion came out as a question. In the third quarter, Pop Warner mercy rules kicked in, and the referees ran out the clock. 91

The Bison had thought positive, tried their best, but were not good enough. Afterward, Andre told them so. "You know what champions do?" he said. "Champions get better." The boys, stripped shirtless, seemed smaller now, and the saddest among them mourned more than the loss of one game. Most had played under Andre for the last time. Today, the children aged out into a harsher world. They packed their dirty gear into garbage bags. They loaded the bus and left the Magic Kingdom for the Shrimp Boat, bits of girl glitter still shimmering on their skin. 92

Sometimes Cookie thinks about what her life would be like if she hadn't left welfare. This speculation requires a tolerance for ambiguity. She wouldn't have had the clarity and confidence she has now about what she wants for her children—to finish high school without having children and to go to college—but she might have had more time to help them reach those goals. She would have been a better day-to-day mom but a lousier role model, particularly for Drenika. "Still," she said one day, "it's too hard not to think sometimes about a life where I could have real time with Wayne, to read and really help him with things. You can't just schedule him in for half an hour in between jobs, the way I have to do now—he just doesn't work that way. There'd be time to help them all with homework, answer Dernard's million and two questions, do family things—like make a meal together, me and Drenika, instead of calling her in 93 for a catch-up conversation when I'm taking a shower. I could take them to church more—we totally just don't go anymore, with my schedule, but that's no excuse, not really. We could communicate. We could be a family. I mean, I'm not saying we're not one now, but it could be like in a book."

Drenika was listening from the other end of the dining-room   94
table. "A family like in a fairy tale?" she asked. For a moment, she sounded very young.

In January, during the Inauguration of George W. Bush, Offi-   95
cer Elizabeth Jones worked crowd control over demonstrators for twenty-four hours straight, most of those hours in icy rain. She spent the next four days in the hospital with a hundred-and-four-degree fever and chest pains, after which she resumed her two jobs and started a remedial-math class, in order to better help her kids with their homework.

Drenika, who failed geography in the first half of seventh   96
grade, was, at the start of the second half, thrown to the floor at school by a boy who had previously run over the assistant principal with a stolen car. She kept it to herself so as not to worry her mother, for whom she continued to run an efficient household.

Dernard, at home, discovered Harry Potter and invented an   97
imaginary companion named DreSean. At school one day, shortly after failing art because a teacher misplaced the tepee he had built out of twigs, he was assigned to hide an old computer under a table as a teacher sprayed Lysol around the classroom. "They said the First Lady was going to pay a visit, and I guess the school didn't look so well," Dernard explained. The First Lady didn't come. Three weeks later, the school was scrubbed again. This time, President Bush himself arrived. As network-news crews filmed, he read the children a story about a poor black boy who loved learning and grew up to be a great leader.

"I'd say he was nice, almost like a regular man," Dernard   98
said. "But why doesn't our school have to look right on all days and not just some days?"

Wayne continued to progress markedly in reading at his   99
school, where his therapists are coming to believe that his gravest disability was being ostracized by his peers. The child once considered retarded is in fact bright, they say—a real striver—and will soon be ready for full-scale mainstreaming.

This astonishing achievement will end Wayne's special-education funding and send him back to the public schools of the Shrimp Boat. At home, he started a diet, hoping to grow smaller and reclaim a position on Andre's team. He began as well to disassemble his toy box, in an effort to force himself further into the realer world outside his door. Then he realized he wasn't ready, not just yet.

Author/Title Index

ACKNOWLEDGMENTS

ROGER ANGELL: "In the Country." Reprinted by permission; © 1981 Roger Angell. Originally published in *The New Yorker*. All rights reserved.

JAMES BALDWIN: "Fifth Avenue, Uptown: A Letter from Harlem." Reprinted from *Nobody Knows My Name* by James Baldwin. "Fifth Avenue Uptown" © 1960 by Esquire, Inc. Copyright renewed 1988 by Gloria Baldwin Karefa-Smith. Used by arrangement with the James Baldwin Estate.

ALICE BLOOM: "On a Greek Holiday." Reprinted by permission from *The Hudson Review*, Vol. XXXVI, No. 3 (Autumn 1983). Copyright © 1983 by Hudson Review, Inc.

CAROL BLY: "Getting Tired." From *Letters from the Country* by Carol Bly. Reprinted with permission from the author's agent, Lukeman Literary Management, Ltd.

CAROL BLY: "Growing Up Expressive." From *Letters from the Country*, pp. 175–184. Reprinted with permission from the author's agent, Lukeman Literary Management, Ltd.

KATHERINE BOO: "After Welfare." © 2001, *The Washington Post*. Reprinted with permission.

DANIEL J. BOORSTIN: "Technology and Democracy." Copyright 1974 by Daniel J. Boorstin. From *Democracy and Its Discontents* (Random House, New York, 1974).

DAVID BRADLEY: "The Faith." Reprinted with permission from the Wendy Weil Agency, Inc.

JACOB BRONOWSKI: "The Creative Mind." Reprinted with the permission of Simon & Schuster, Inc., from *Science and Human Values* by Jacob Bronowski. Copyright © 1956, 1965 by Jacob Bronowski; copyright renewed 1984, 1993 by Rita Bronowski.

SUSAN BROWNMILLER: "Femininity." Reprinted with the permission of Simon & Schuster from *Femininity* by Susan Brownmiller. Copyright © 1983 by Susan Brownmiller.

VINCENT G. DETHIER: "Extracting Information from a Fly." From *To Know a Fly* by Vincent Dethier, pp. 18–27. Copyright © 1962 by McGraw-Hill. Reprinted with permission from The McGraw-Hill Companies.

JOAN DIDION: "Slouching Toward Bethlehem." From *Slouching Toward Bethlehem* by Joan Didion. Copyright © 1966, 1968, renewed 1998 by Joan Didion. Reprinted by permission of Farrar, Straus and Giroux, LLC.

JOAN DIDION: "Why I Write." Copyright © 1976 by Joan Didion. Originally published in the *New York Times Book Review*. Reprinted by permission of the author.

ANNIE DILLARD: "Samson in Chains." Pages 110–117 from *An American Childhood* by Annie Dillard. Copyright © 1987 by Annie Dillard. Reprinted by permission of HarperCollins Publishers Inc.

BARBARA EHRENREICH: "Spudding Out." From *The Worst Years of Our Lives* by Barbara Ehrenreich. Copyright © 1990 by Barbara Ehrenreich. Reprinted with permission from the author and International Creative Management.

LARS EIGHNER: "On Dumpster Diving." Copyright © 1993 by Lars Eighner. From *Travels with Lizbeth* by Lars Eighner. Reprinted by permission of St. Martin's Press, LLC.

E. M. FORSTER: "The Machine Stops." First published in 1909.

E. M. FORSTER: "My Wood." From *Abinger Harvest,* copyright 1936 and renewed 1964 by Edward M. Forster, reprinted by permission of Harcourt, Inc.

E. M. FORSTER: "What I Believe." From *Two Cheers for Democracy,* copyright 1939 and renewed 1967 by Edward M. Forster, reprinted by permission of Harcourt, Inc.

JOHN KENNETH GALBRAITH: "How to Get the Poor Off Our Conscience." This article originally appeared in *Harper's Magazine,* November 1985. Reprinted with permission from John Kenneth Galbraith.

SUSAN GLASPELL: "Trifles." Copyright 1916 by Frank Shay; copyright 1920 by Dodd, Mead & Company, Inc. Copyright renewed 1948 by Susan Glaspell. Text revised, prompt book added and new material, copyright 1951 by Walter H. Baker Company. For production rights contact Baker's Plays, Boston, MA 02111.

LINDA HOGAN: "Hearing Voices." Reprinted by permission of her agent, Sanford J. Greenburger Associates Inc.

SUE HUBBELL: "Beekeeper." From *A Country Year: Living the Questions* by Sue Hubbell. © 1983, 1984, 1985, 1986 by Sue Hubbell. Reprinted with permission from Darhansoff, Verrill, Feldman Literary Agents.

JANE JACOBS: "The Uses of Sidewalks." From *The Death and Life of Great American Cities* by Jane Jacobs, copyright © 1961 by Jane Jacobs. Used by permission of Random House, Inc.

RANDALL JARRELL: "A Sad Heart at the Supermarket." Reprinted by permission of Mary von S. Jarrell, Executrix

ROBERT KEGAN: "The Mitzvah of Kaporis." "The Mitzvah of Kaporis" by Robert Kegan appears by permission of the author and was first published in R. Kegan, *The Sweeter Welcome,* Humanities Press, 1976.

MARTIN LUTHER KING JR.: "Letter from Birmingham Jail." Reprinted by arrangement with the Estate of Martin Luther King Jr., c/o Writers House as agent for the proprietor New York, NY. Copyright 1963 Dr. Martin Luther King Jr., copyright renewed 1991 Coretta Scott King.

H. D. F. KITTO: "The Polis." From *The Greeks,* pp. 64–79. Copyright © 1957 by Pelican Books. Reproduced by permission of Penguin Books Ltd.

PERRI KLASS: "Learning the Language." From *A Not Entirely Benign Procedure* by Perri Klass, copyright © 1987 by Perri Klass. Used by permission of G.P. Putnam's Sons, a division of Penguin Putnam Inc.

PATRICIA NELSON LIMERICK: "Believing in the American West." From *The West* by Geoffrey Ward. Copyright © 1996 by The West Book Project, Inc. By permission of Little, Brown and Company (Inc.)

JAN MORRIS: "To Everest." From *Conundrum* by Jan Morris. © 1974 Jan Morris. First published by Harcourt Brace Jovanovich, Inc.

CHARLES MURRAY: "What's So Bad About Being Poor?" Reprinted by permission of International Creative Management, Inc. Copyright © 1988 by Cox and Murray, Inc.

FLANNERY O'CONNOR: "Revelation." From *The Complete Stories* by Flannery O'Connor. Copyright © 1971 by the Estate of Mary Flannery O'Connor.

GEORGE ORWELL: "Politics and the English Language." Copyright 1946 by Sonia Brownell Orwell and renewed 1974 by Sonia Orwell, reprinted from his volume *Shooting an Elephant and Other Essays* by permission of Harcourt, Inc.

GEORGE ORWELL: "Why I Write." From *Such, Such Were The Joys* by George Orwell, copyright 1953 by Sonia Brownell Orwell and renewed 1981 by Mrs. George K. Perutz, Mrs. Miriam Gross, and Dr. Michael Dickson, Executors of the Estate of Sonia Brownell Orwell. Reprinted by permission of Harcourt, Inc.

NOEL PERRIN: "The Androgynous Man." Copyright © 1984 by The New York Times Co. Reprinted by permission. All rights reserved.

WILLIAM G. PERRY JR.: "Examsmanship and the Liberal Arts." *Examining in Harvard College.* Reprinted by permission of Harvard University Press.

KATHA POLLITT: "The Smurfette Principle." Copyright © 1991 by The New York Times Co. Reprinted by permission. All rights reserved.

KATHA POLLITT: "For Whom the Ball Rolls." This article originally appeared in *The Nation,* April 15, 1996. Reprinted with permission from Katha Pollitt.

ROBERT PUTNAM: "Bowling Alone: America's Declining Social Capital." "Bowling Alone: America's Declining Social Capital" by Robert D. Putnam appeared in the *Journal of Democracy,* Volume 6, Number 1, January 1995. Reprinted with permission from the author's agent, Raphael Sagalyn, Inc.

ADRIENNE RICH: "Claiming an Education." From *On Lies, Secrets, and Silence: Selected Prose 1966–1978* by Adrienne Rich. Copyright © 1979 by W. W. Norton & Company, Inc. Used by permission of W. W. Norton & Company, Inc.

ADRIENNE RICH: "When We Dead Awaken: Writing as Re-Vision." From *Arts of the Possible: Essays and Conversations* by Adrienne Rich. Copyright © 2001 by Adrienne Rich. Used by permission of W. W. Norton & Company, Inc.

ADRIENNE RICH: "Aunt Jennifer's Tigers," copyright © 1993, 1951 by Adrienne Rich. "The Loser," copyright © 1993, 1967, 1963 by Adrienne Rich. Lines from "Snapshots of a Daughter-in-Law," copyright © 1993, 1967, 1963 by Adrienne Rich. "Orion," © 1993 by Adrienne Rich. Copyright © 1969 by W. W. Norton & Company, Inc. "Planetarium," copyright © 1993 by Adrienne Rich. Copyright © 1971 by W. W. Norton & Company, Inc., from *Collected Early Poems: 1950–1970* by Adrienne Rich. Used by permission of W. W. Norton & Company, Inc.

PAUL ROBERTS: "Virtual Grub Street." Copyright © 1996 by *Harper's Magazine.* All rights reserved. Reproduced from the June issue by special permission.

WILLIAM L. RODMAN: "When Questions Are Answers." Reproduced by permission of the American Anthropological Association from *American Anthropologist* 93 (2). Not for sale or for further reproduction.

RICHARD RODRIGUEZ: "Mr. Secrets." From *Hunger of Memory* by Richard Rodriguez. Reprinted by permission of David R. Godine, Publisher, Inc. Copyright © 1982 by Richard Rodriguez.

SCOTT RUSSELL SANDERS: "The Common Life." Copyright © 1994 by Scott Russell Sanders; first appeared in *The Georgia Review;* collected in the author's

Writing from the Center (Indiana U.P., 1995); reprinted by permission of the author.

DOROTHY L. SAYERS: "Living to Work." Reprinted by permission of the Estate of Dorothy L. Sayers and the Watkins/Loomis Agency.

HUSTON SMITH: "The Straight Path of Islam." Pages 243–257 from *The World's Religions* by Huston Smith. Copyright © 1991 by Huston Smith. Reprinted by permission of HarperCollins Publishers Inc.

GARY SOTO: "Black Hair." From *Living Up the Street* (Dell, 1992). © 1985 by Gary Soto. Used by permission of the author.

JOHN STEINBECK: "The Chrysanthemums." Copyright 1937, renewed © 1965 by John Steinbeck, from *The Long Valley* by John Steinbeck. Used by permission of Viking Penguin, a division of Penguin Putnam Inc.

GLORIA STEINEM: "Sex, Lies, and Advertising." *Ms.* July/August 1990, pp. 18–28. Reprinted by permission of the author.

LYTTON STRACHEY: "Florence Nightingale." From *Eminent Victorians*, © 1918.

STUDS TERKEL: "Two Prefaces from *Working*." Reprinted by permission of Donadio & Olson, Inc. Copyright 1974 by Studs Terkel.

SALLIE TISDALE: "Good Soldiers." *The New Republic*, 1/3/94, pp. 22–27. Reprinted by permission of *The New Republic* © 1996, The New Republic, Inc., and the author.

ALICE WALKER: "Everyday Use." From *In Love & Trouble: Stories of Black Women*, copyright © 1973 by Alice Walker, reprinted by permission of Harcourt, Inc.

E. B. WHITE: Drafts of "Notes and Comment" by E. B. White (final draft appearing in *The New Yorker*, July 26, 1969) are reprinted by permission of the Estate of E. B. White.

WILLIAM CARLOS WILLIAMS: "Jean Beicke." From *Doctor Stories*, copyright © 1938 by William Carlos Williams. Reprinted by permission of New Directions Publishing Corp.

TOM WOLFE: "The Right Stuff." Excerpt from *The Right Stuff* by Tom Wolfe. Copyright © 1979 by Tom Wolfe.

JOANN WYPIJEWSKI: "A Boy's Life." Copyright © 1999 by *Harper's Magazine*. All rights reserved. Reproduced from the September issue by special permission.